POLICY GUIDEBOOK FOR SME DEVELOPMENT IN ASIA AND THE PACIFIC

Policy Guidebook for SME Development in Asia and the Pacific

United Nations publication
Sales No. E.12.II.F.2
Copyright © United Nations 2012
All rights reserved
Manufactured in Thailand
ISBN: 978-92-1-120636-4
e-ISBN: 978-92-1-055274-5
ST/ESCAP/2621

For further information on this publication, please contact:

Mr. Ravi Ratnayake
Director
Trade and Investment Division
ESCAP
Rajadamnern Nok Avenue
Bangkok 10200, Thailand
Tel: (66-2) 288-1902
Fax: (66-2) 288-1027, 288-3066
E-mail: escap-tid@un.org

The material in this publication may be freely quoted or reprinted, but acknowledgement is required, and a copy of the publication containing the quotation or reprint should be sent to the ESCAP Publications Office.

The use of this publication for any commercial purpose, including resale, is prohibited unless permission is first obtained from ESCAP. Requests for permission should state the purpose and the extent of reproduction.

Foreword

Small and medium-sized enterprises (SMEs), including start-ups and microenterprises, have emerged as an engine of growth for most of the countries in Asia and the Pacific. Their contributions are well-known; they increase production and exports, generate employment and facilitate income growth amongst the population. SMEs serve as a seedbed for enterprise development. Each country has evolved its own policies, institutional framework and support mechanisms for SMEs according to its needs, stage of economic development and culture. The experience of each one of them is unique.

Developing a policy guidebook for SME development in the developing countries of the Asia-Pacific region has been a daunting task, when the variety of experiences and the varied policies and programmes of each country are taken into consideration. This book documents specific policy guidelines based on various countries' strategies, their best practices and their applicability in the context of development of SMEs in Asia and the Pacific in addition to the vast experience and expertise of the contributors, researchers and authors of the publication.

Many countries as well as various multilateral and bilateral development agencies have implemented a variety of interventions in Asia and the Pacific in line with their SME development strategies, typically in the following key areas:

(a) Business environment, including policy and regulatory framework and infrastructure development;
(b) Entrepreneurship;
(c) Financing;
(d) Business development services;
(e) Innovation and technology; and
(f) Market access.

Their interventions typically use several modalities to address the key issues, including policy advocacy, institutional capacity-building, human resource development and direct support to enterprises.

This comprehensive review of the SME policies and programmes in Asia and the Pacific demonstrates that the nations of the region appreciate the importance of SME development. The SME sector in many countries in the region suffers from numerous threats and challenges that necessitate a proactive approach from policymakers. National governments and various stakeholders in charge of policy planning would do well to recognize not only the threats and challenges, but also the changing needs of SMEs. In this regard, the following useful guidelines are identified for effective policymaking:

(a) The reduction of entry barriers (and thus costs) for new businesses;
(b) The importance of cash flow to SMEs – the major reason most new and small businesses fail is not a lack of profits but a lack of cash;
(c) The strengthening of entrepreneurship through training and education; and
(d) The strengthening of networking and information dissemination, given the fact that a lack of networks and information hinders effective deployment of technology and business development services as well as collaboration with other firms.

This publication should provide the basis for deliberations on policy formulation for SME development in Asia and the Pacific, developing and refining the institutional framework based on intercountry experiences. Implementation of policy options and their appropriate selection, based on key factors, is highlighted. The book may also serve as a training manual for entrepreneurs, educators and business associations, such as chambers of commerce and industry, for building up the capacity of SMEs.

Ravi Ratnayake
Director
Trade and Investment Division

Acknowledgements

The Policy Guidebook for SME Development in Asia and the Pacific was prepared by Masato Abe under the substantive direction and guidance of Ravi Ratnayake, Director, Trade and Investment Division of the Economic and Social Commission for Asia and the Pacific, as well as Marc Proksch, Chief, Private Sector and Development Section, Trade and Investment Division. The team of authors comprised Masato Abe, Michael Troilo, J.S. Juneja and Sailendra Narain.

Inputs and comments provided by Gloria Adapon, Madhurjya Kumar Dutta, Hideaki Fujimoto, Gloria Garcia, Kausalya Gopal, Pham Thi Thu Hang, Takao Hayashi, Baek Hoon, Sheikh Morshed Jahan, Niny Khor, Yoong Yoong Lee, Penchan Manawanitkul, Naylin Oo, Syed Zafar Ali Shah, Shin Seong Shik, Jim Tanburn and Muhammad Hashim Tareen are gratefully acknowledged. Krishnamurthy Ramanathan also provided a number of useful comments, particularly for chapter VII. The technical editors were Michael Troilo and Masato Abe. The ASEAN SME Working Group and the Small and Medium Enterprise Corporation Malaysia also provided comments and inputs to the guidebook which were greatly appreciated. The guidebook particularly benefited from comments and encouragements received from Mahdi Mohd Ariffin. The final editing of the guidebook was undertaken by Robert Oliver.

S.P. Dhupar and Kulwant Singh as well as The Global Projects and Services (P) Ltd. provided research assistance in New Delhi. Paradai Adisayathepkul and Diana Dai led a research assistance team in Bangkok, which comprised Linghe Ye, Fabian Suwanprateep, Pawat Burapakusolsri, Pradeep Kumar Angadi, Wenru Xie, Julia Huepfl, Qi Zhou and Viknesh Sivalinghan. Diana Dai managed the production of the guidebook. Napidchaya Pichedtanavanich developed the book design. The guidebook website was prepared by Wichien Chaleowkraijit. Natthika Charoenphon, Napidchaya Pichedtanavanich and Pranee Suriyan provided secretariat services.

The publication of the guidebook was supported by the Government of Japan.

Authors

Masato Abe is Economic Affairs Officer in the Private Sector and Development Section, Trade and Investment Division, United Nations Economic and Social Commission for Asia and the Pacific (ESCAP). He has extensive experience in enterprise development with special emphasis on the SME sector and supply chain management. Prior to joining the secretariat of the United Nations, he worked in the global automotive, electronics and high-technology industries. He holds degrees in marketing, business administration and economics, and is a research fellow at Thammasat University, Bangkok.

Michael Troilo is an assistant professor of international business and a member of the School of Finance, Operations and International Business at the Collins College of Business, University of Tulsa. He has 20 years of experience in business and academe, and conducts research on institutional arrangements and entrepreneurial activities across countries, particularly in Asia. In addition to working at various SMEs, Mr. Troilo has advised a number of start-up companies. He holds a BBA in accounting from the College of William & Mary, an MBA and an MA in East Asian Studies from the University of Virginia, and a PhD in business economics and international business from the University of Michigan.

J.S. Juneja has more than three decades of experience in both the public and private sectors. He is the Chairman of the Global Projects & Services (P) Ltd., SME Task Force of All India Management Association (AIMA) and the Africa Committee of PhD Chamber of Commerce and Industry. In addition, he is an Independent Director on the Boards of Elder Pharmaceuticals Ltd., Elder Health Care Ltd. and the former Chairman and CEO of India's apex SME Development Organization – National Small Industries Corporation Ltd. He has served on the Boards and Governing Councils of 20 National Institutions and public and private sector companies. He has provided management consultancy services to various Governments in Africa and the Middle East as well as UNDP, UNIDO, ESCAP and Commonwealth Secretariat. He has been the Visiting Professor to the University of Rhode Island, USA and Indian Institute of Technology, New Delhi. He has an MBA from the University of Oregon and PhD in applied economics from the University of Bombay.

Sailendra Narain is an experienced banker and has held many top executive and advisory positions. He is the former Chairman of India's Apex Financial Institution for SMEs, SIDBI. In addition, he has worked with several international organizations such as the World Bank, UNDP, UNIDO, UNCTAD, ESCAP, GIZ in Germany and Swiss Agency for Development and Cooperation (SDC). With strong experience in policymaking, he has served as an international consultant in development banking for the micro, small and medium-sized enterprise sector in India, sub-Saharan Africa and the Greater Mekong Subregion.

Contents

	Page
Explanatory notes	xiii
Acronyms and abbreviations	xv
Executive summary	1

Chapter

		Page
I.	**Introduction**	5
	A. Objectives	5
	B. SME development prospects	5
	C. Policy development and implementation: Stakeholders and strategies	10
	D. Methodology	11
	E. Outline of the guidebook	12
II.	**Contributions, challenges and prospects of SMEs**	13
	A. What does SME development mean?	13
	B. Definition of SMEs	13
	C. Typology of SMEs	16
	D. Common characteristics of SMEs	20
	E. Contribution by SMEs	20
	F. Start-up, growth, maturity and exit	22
	G. Microenterprises	25
	H. SME productivity	27
	I. Determinants of SME competitiveness	28
	J. SME clusters	30
	K. Gender issues related to SME development	31
	L. Summary	35
III.	**Business enabling environment**	37
	A. How does BEE matter?	37
	B. Components of BEE	38
	C. BEE surveys	42
	D. BEE reforms	46
	E. Role of government and policymakers in BEE reforms	48
	F. Toolkits for BEE reforms	50
	G. Lessons learnt from BEE reforms	53
	H. Summary	53
	Annex III.1. Cambodian enabling environment toolkit for SMEs	54
	Annex III.2. SME taxation	59
IV.	**Entrepreneurship development**	65
	A. Entrepreneurship and entrepreneurs: Definitions and concepts	65
	B. Role of entrepreneurship in different phases of economic development	67
	C. Key factors for success of entrepreneurs	68
	D. Entry barriers to entrepreneurship	69
	E. Cultural aspects and their impacts on entrepreneurship	69
	F. Creation of entrepreneurship awareness	72
	G. Education and training for entrepreneurship development	73
	H. Main players in entrepreneurship development	73
	I. Women entrepreneurs	75
	J. Rural entrepreneurship	75
	K. Social entrepreneurship and social enterprises	76
	L. General recommendations	77
	M. Summary	79
	Annex IV.1. Business plan development	80
	Annex IV.2. Modules of entrepreneurship training	85

Contents (continued)

		Page
V.	**Financing a business**	87
	A. Raising capital	87
	B. Business life cycle and the need for cash	88
	C. Overview of SME financing	89
	D. Forms of finance	90
	E. Sources of funds	100
	F. Financial institutions for SMEs and their challenges	102
	G. Credit rating scheme	104
	H. Financial support during economic downturns	105
	I. SMEs' view of major constraints	107
	J. Potential market distortion by public interventions in SME financing	108
	K. Major issues for policy interventions	109
	L. Summary	115
	Annex V.1. Typology of collateral	117
VI.	**Business development services**	119
	A. Design and objectives	119
	B. Channels for delivering BDS: Traditional versus market-oriented	120
	C. BDS actors and their roles	122
	D. Levels of BDS interventions	125
	E. Business and technology incubation	127
	F. Summary	129
VII.	**Innovation and technology**	131
	A. Innovation status at the regional level	131
	B. Why is innovation important for SMEs?	132
	C. Capacity of SMEs to innovate	133
	D. Policy priorities to enhance innovation	134
	E. Key strategies for the development of SME innovation	135
	F. Obstacles to SMEs' innovation through their development or adaptation of technology	147
	G. Highlights of national initiatives	148
	H. Policy recommendations for SME innovation	151
	I. Summary	152
VIII.	**Market access**	153
	A. Market orientation and internationalization of firms	153
	B. SMEs' capabilities and challenges for market access	155
	C. Trade environment for facilitating market access by SMEs	156
	D. Trade promotion tools for SMEs	161
	E. Key players in trade promotion	163
	F. Applications of ICT to facilitate market access	165
	G. Trade finance	167
	H. Special economic zones	171
	I. Foreign direct investment and SMEs' increased market access	172
	J. Participation of SMEs in global supply chains	173
	K. Suggested policies for enhancing SME market access	177
	L. Summary	177
	Annex VIII.1. WTO-related agreements and rules	179
IX.	**Suggested policy framework for the development of SMEs**	181
	A. National policy planning: Major constraints and issues	181
	B. Summary of recommendations	183
	C. Conclusion	187
	Annex IX.1. Monitoring and evaluation	189
References		195
Subject index		217

Contents (continued)

Page

List of figures

II.1.	SMEs' net income in Japan	17
II.2.	GDP contribution of the SME and informal sector, based on income levels	17
II.3.	Simplified SME life cycle	18
II.4.	SME typology by market and technology	19
II.5.	Constitution of enterprises by size	21
II.6.	Number of SMEs per 1,000 people, 2001-2006	22
II.7.	Entry and exit rates, by industry, in Japan, 2004-2006	23
II.8.	Comparison of entry and exit rates between Japan and the United States, 1990-2009	24
II.9.	National culture and entrepreneurship, Japan and the United States	24
II.10.	Productivity (value-added per worker) differentials by enterprise size (large enterprises = 100)	27
II.11.	Labour productivity of micro and small enterprises	28
II.12.	Competitiveness framework for SMEs	29
II.13.	Annual growth of female-owned SMEs	32
II.14.	A woman's quest to get a job or start a business	32
III.1.	Business regulatory compliance costs by firm size, Lao People's Democratic Republic	38
III.2.	SME business enabling environment and its components	39
III.3.	Ease of doing business ranking, by subregion, in Asia and the Pacific	42
III.4.	Subregional corruption ratings in Asia and the Pacific	46
III.5.	Monthly enterprise registrations, 2004	49
A.III.1.	Factors responsible for high tax compliance in New Zealand, 2003	60
IV.1.	Institutional context and its relationship to entrepreneurship	66
IV.2.	Key success factors of entrepreneurs	69
IV.3.	Relationships among culture, policy and entrepreneurship	72
IV.4.	Overview of the TVET programme for entrepreneurship in Sri Lanka	74
IV.5.	Social entrepreneurial activity by country	77
A.IV.1.	Simplified business plan	82
V.1.	SME financing gaps in OECD and non-OECD countries	87
V.2.	Collateral requirement in developing and developed countries	87
V.3.	Interest rates and non-performing loans in developing and developed countries	88
V.4.	SME business growth stages and cash flow	88
V.5.	Main reason for SME failure: Time gap between receivables and payables	89
V.6.	Forms of finance for SMEs	91
V.7.	Examples of working capital management	91
V.8.	Trade credit	92
V.9.	Credit Guarantee Corporation's credit guarantee function	94
V.10.	Institutional framework of Japan's credit guarantee schemes	95
V.11.	Sources of start-up funds in Japan	100
V.12.	Institutions used by European Union-based SMEs to obtain capital, 2005	101
V.13.	External financing sources of European Union-based SMEs, 2009-2011	101
V.14.	Present institutional financing structure of SMEs in Sri Lanka	103
V.15.	Effect of financing constraints on growth	107
V.16.	Financial gap in SME financing	109
V.17.	Institutional framework of public-private partnership in Japan	111
V.18.	Four-tier financial system for SMEs	114
VI.1.	Traditional business development services approach	121
VI.2.	Market-oriented business development services approach	121
VI.3.	Business development services actors and their roles	123
VI.4.	Objectives of incubators	127
VII.1.	Overview of innovation	133
VII.2.	Interrelationships among basic research, applied research and experimental development	135
VII.3.	Gross domestic expenditure on research and development in Asia and the Pacific (purchasing power parity dollars per capita)	136
VII.4.	Share of enterprise R&D in total R&D by country/region, 1996 and 2002	136
VII.5.	Process of technology commercialization	140
VII.6.	Actors and linkages in the innovation system	141
VII.7.	Closed innovation model	143
VII.8.	Open innovation model	144
VIII.1.	Share of total sales sold domestically: Small, medium and large enterprises	154
VIII.2.	Stages in the process of export product identification	158

Contents (continued)

		Page
VIII.3.	Incoterms 2010 rules	160
VIII.4.	Import procedures	161
VIII.5.	Various trade promotion tools: Cost and target	161
VIII.6.	Trade cycle and trade finance methods and instruments for SMEs	167
VIII.7.	Letter of credit transaction process	169
VIII.8.	Comparison between terms of payment	169
VIII.9.	A simplified global or regional supply chain	174
VIII.10.	How SMEs fit into global supply chains	175
IX.1.	Thought process map for policy prioritization	182
A.IX.1.	Logical framework	190
A.IX.2.	Results-based impact chain	190
A.IX.3.	Attributable impact	191

List of tables

I.1.	Development approaches for SMEs implemented by selected bilateral and multilateral agencies	7
I.2.	Typical interventions of the six key areas for SME development	8
I.3.	Common framework of actions for SME development	11
II.1.	Indicators used among international, regional and local sources	14
II.2.	Definitions of SMEs in Asia and the Pacific and other areas	14
II.3.	Start-ups by sector in Japan and SMEs by sector in Thailand	16
II.4.	Categories for SME typology	18
II.5.	Contribution of SMEs to exports/enterprises/workforce in selected economies of the world, and Asia and the Pacific, various years during 2001-2009	21
II.6.	Share of microenterprises in selected Asia-Pacific countries, 2010	26
II.7.	Determinants of SME competitiveness	28
II.8.	Subregional rankings of gender empowerment measure	31
III.1.	Subcomponents of a regulatory and administrative framework	40
III.2.	Ease of doing business in Asia and the Pacific, 2012	43
III.3.	Starting a business, by subregion, in Asia and the Pacific	44
III.4.	Facilitating international trade by developing subregions in Asia and the Pacific	44
III.5.	Economic freedom: Rankings for Asia-Pacific economies	45
III.6.	Global Competitiveness Index: Rankings for Asia-Pacific economies	45
III.7.	Functional areas and levels of business environment reform	47
III.8.	Development stages of SMEs	52
III.9.	BEE policy focus by level of economic development	53
A.III.1.	Advantages and disadvantages of tax non-compliance on various entities	59
A.III.2.	Monetary and non-monetary elements of tax compliance costs	60
A.III.3.	SME taxation criteria	61
A.III.4.	Advantages and disadvantages of presumptive tax systems	63
A.III.5.	VAT and presumptive tax threshold comparison for Asia-Pacific countries	63
IV.1.	Entrepreneurial activity in selected Asia-Pacific countries in 2011, by phase of economic development	67
IV.2.	Minimizing the barriers: A suggested framework	70
IV.3.	Five dimensions of national culture	70
IV.4.	Values of Hofstede's cultural dimensions	71
A.IV.1.	Basic components of a business plan	80
V.1.	Ease of getting credit by subregion	88
V.2.	Different SME financing sources	89
V.3.	Issuance costs of corporate bonds	97
V.4.	Financial sources for Malaysian SMEs, 2004	100
V.5.	Financial sources of SMEs in the United States, 1998 and 2003	101
V.6.	Different bank loan features of different-sized enterprise, 2008	102
V.7.	Comparison of commercial banks and development banks	104
V.8.	Issues and suggestions for strengthening bank-SME relationships	113
V.9.	Matrix of policy measures facilitating access to finance by SMEs	115
VI.1.	Three core segments of BDS	119
VI.2.	Types of advisory and advocacy BDS	120
VI.3.	Distinctive features of traditional and market-oriented channels	122
VII.1.	Innovation capabilities by region	131
VII.2.	Asian enterprises that have undertaken innovative activities, by size of firm	133

Contents (continued)

Page

VII.3.	Trend in R&D spending, by country, 2007	136
VII.4.	Important sources of technological innovations	137
VII.5.	Market failures constraining technology acquisition: Implications for government capabilities	138
VII.6.	APEC SME Innovation Centre mid-term to long-term plan	139
VII.7.	Differences between intellectual property and intellectual property rights	145
VII.8.	Examples of country programmes for technology development and transfer	150
VIII.1.	Major challenges, and SMEs' capabilities and limitations	155
VIII.2.	Quality of trade and transport-related infrastructure by subregion	159
VIII.3.	Incoterms 2010 rules	160
VIII.4.	Burden of customs procedure by subregion	161
VIII.5.	Characteristics of three major export promotion events	162
VIII.6.	National programmes for SMEs' market access	164
VIII.7.	Methods of payment for importing and exporting enterprises, by size, in Thailand	169
VIII.8.	Types of special economic zones	172
VIII.9.	Advantages of special economic zones	172
VIII.10.	Recommended policy interventions to enhance SMEs' market access	178
IX.1.	Recommended actions for challenges of SME development	185
A.IX.1.	Six Steps to Heaven: A method for assessing the impact of SME policies	189
A.IX.2.	Programme logics and indicators at various project levels	190
A.IX.3.	Types of data sources for different types of indicators	192
A.IX.4.	Data collection methods, qualitative and quantitative	192
A.IX.5.	Types of evaluations	193

List of boxes

II.1.	SME typology by market orientation and use of technology	19
II.2.	Start-up profiles in Japan	20
II.3.	Contributions by SMEs in Japan	22
II.4.	Assistance to women entrepreneurs in India	33
II.5.	Women entrepreneurship culture in Thailand	33
II.6.	Corporate social responsibility and SMEs	33
II.7.	SME Corp of Malaysia policy framework	34
III.1.	Importance of infrastructure	39
III.2.	Role of information and communications technology in SME development	41
III.3.	Public-private partnership in perspective	41
III.4.	Singapore's proclaimed business environment	44
III.5.	Value chain approach for BEE reform	48
III.6.	Cambodia's reform in enterprise registration	49
III.7.	Streamlining business permits and licensing procedures in Ormoc City, the Philippines	49
III.8.	Reform of public procurement system	50
III.9.	Limited liability partnership in India	52
IV.1.	Think big, start small: The Cathay Pacific story	66
IV.2.	Realities of entrepreneurship	68
IV.3.	Entry barriers to entrepreneurship for youth in the Greater Mekong Subregion	70
IV.4.	Technical and vocational education and training	74
IV.5.	Women entrepreneurs in the food-processing industry	75
A.IV.1.	Checkpoints for start-ups	81
A.IV.2.	Creating business ideas	84
A.IV.3.	Curriculum of the Know about Business package	85
V.1.	Development of an SME financing support system in China	90
V.2.	Japan's SME credit guarantee schemes	94
V.3.	Examples of credit guarantee schemes: India, Pakistan and Turkey	96
V.4.	Pros and cons of equity financing for SMEs	99
V.5.	SME finance in Sri Lanka	103
V.6.	Challenges of development finance institutions	104
V.7.	Japan's comprehensive policy framework to support SMEs during the global economic crisis, 2008 and 2009	105
V.8.	Urgent policy interventions by Japan and Thailand for SME rehabilitation in disaster-hit areas, 2011	106
V.9.	SME financing through public-private partnership in Japan	111
V.10.	Methods and criteria for bank loan appraisal	113

Contents (continued)

		Page
VI.1.	Role of SME development agencies in business development services facilitation	123
VI.2.	Highlights of SME development agencies in Asia and the Pacific	124
VI.3.	Roles of business associations	126
VI.4.	Tianjin women's business incubator	128
VI.5.	Supply chains, SMEs and business development services	128
VII.1.	Opportunities for SMEs through strengthening innovation capabilities: The case of Viet Nam	133
VII.2.	SME policies for building technological capacity in the Republic of Korea	135
VII.3.	Strengthening SMEs through technology transfer capacity-building	138
VII.4.	APEC SME Innovation Centre	139
VII.5.	Technology transfer through global supply chains	139
VII.6.	National innovation system, Republic of Korea	142
VII.7.	Review of Lao People's Democratic Republic national innovation system	143
VII.8.	Science and technology parks	143
VII.9.	Korean Intellectual Property Office initiatives for IPRs targeted at the SME sector in the Republic of Korea	146
VIII.1.	SPRING, Singapore	159
VIII.2.	Trade fairs: Cost and benefit analysis	162
VIII.3.	Internet marketing: Republic of Korea	166
VIII.4.	East-West Economic Corridor business database	166
VIII.5.	Terms of trade payment: Thailand	169
VIII.6.	Thai EXIM bank	171
VIII.7.	Transnational corporations and SMEs	173
VIII.8.	SMEs' foreign market access through trading companies	173
VIII.9.	Vietnamese SMEs in IBM's global supply chain	174
VIII.10.	Subcontracting	174
VIII.11.	Challenges in global supply chains: Three case studies	175
VIII.12.	Four advantages of the global supply chain approach for SMEs	176
VIII.13.	Implications of global supply chains for climate change	177
IX.1.	Prioritizing policies	182

Explanatory notes

Analysis and interpretations in this Guidebook are based on available data and information up to the middle of February 2012.

The term "Asia and the Pacific" in this SME Policy Guidebook refers to the 58 regional members and associate members of the United Nations Economic and Social Commission for Asia and the Pacific (ESCAP). They include the following group of countries and territories: Afghanistan; American Samoa; Armenia; Australia; Azerbaijan; Bangladesh; Bhutan; Brunei Darussalam; Cambodia; China; Cook Islands; Democratic People's Republic of Korea; Fiji; French Polynesia; Georgia; Guam; Hong Kong, China; India; Indonesia; Iran (Islamic Republic of); Japan; Kazakhstan; Kiribati; Kyrgyzstan; Lao People's Democratic Republic; Macao, China; Malaysia; Maldives; Marshall Islands; Micronesia (Federated States of); Mongolia; Myanmar; Nauru; Nepal; New Caledonia; New Zealand; Niue; Northern Mariana Islands; Pakistan; Palau; Papua New Guinea; Philippines; Republic of Korea; Russian Federation; Samoa; Singapore; Solomon Islands; Sri Lanka; Tajikistan; Thailand; Timor-Leste; Tonga; Turkey; Turkmenistan; Tuvalu; Uzbekistan; Vanuatu; and Viet Nam.

A. Countries and territories by geographic subregion

Time series data are presented according to geographical classification, with the exception of developed economies, which are grouped separately. Throughout this Guidebook, countries and territories may be referred to by a shortened version of their official name or, for some of the graphs presented, their International Organization for Standardization (ISO) code. Where the designation "country or area" appears, it covers countries, territories, areas and/or cities.

Developed Economies: Australia, Japan and New Zealand.

East and North-East Asia: China; Democratic People's Republic of Korea; Hong Kong, China; Macao, China; Mongolia; Republic of Korea.

South-East Asia: Brunei Darussalam; Cambodia; Indonesia; Lao People's Democratic Republic; Malaysia; Myanmar; Philippines; Singapore; Thailand; Timor-Leste; Viet Nam.

South and South-West Asia: Afghanistan; Bangladesh; Bhutan; India; Iran (Islamic Republic of); Maldives; Nepal; Pakistan; Sri Lanka; Turkey.

North and Central Asia: Armenia; Azerbaijan; Georgia; Kazakhstan; Kyrgyzstan; Russian Federation; Tajikistan; Turkmenistan; Uzbekistan.

Pacific: American Samoa; Cook Islands; Fiji; French Polynesia; Guam; Kiribati; Marshall Islands; Micronesia (Federated States of); Nauru; New Caledonia; Niue; Northern Mariana Islands; Palau; Papua New Guinea; Samoa; Solomon Islands; Tonga; Tuvalu; Vanuatu.

B. Notes on legal responsibilities

The opinions and estimates set forth in this publication are the responsibility of the authors, and should not necessarily be considered as reflecting the views or carrying the endorsement of the United Nations. Any errors are the responsibility of the authors.

The designations employed and the presentation of the material in this publication do not imply the expression of any opinion whatsoever on the part of the secretariat of the United Nations concerning the legal status of any country, territory, city or area, or of its authorities, or concerning the delimitation of its frontiers or boundaries.

Mention of firm names and commercial products does not imply the endorsement of the United Nations.

Bibliographical and other references have, wherever possible, been verified. The United Nations bears no responsibility for the availability or functioning of URLs.

C. Notes on style

References to dollars ($) are in United States dollars, unless otherwise stated.

A space is used to distinguish thousands and millions.

Use of a hyphen between dates (e.g., 2005-2010) indicates the full period involved, including the beginning and end years.

The following symbols have been used throughout the publication:

A hyphen (-) indicates that the item is not applicable.
A point (.) is used to indicate decimals.
A space is used to distinguish thousands and millions.
Totals may not add precisely because of rounding.

Acronyms and abbreviations

ADB	Asian Development Bank
APCICT	Asian and Pacific Training Centre for Information and Communication Technology for Development
APCTT	Asian and Pacific Centre for Transfer of Technology
APEC	Asia-Pacific Economic Cooperation
APO	Asian Productivity Organization
APTITUDE	Asia-Pacific Technology Information Tracking and Unified Data Extraction
ASEAN	Association of Southeast Asian Nations
B2B	business-to-business
BANSEA	Business Angel Network South-East Asia
BDC	Business Development Bank of Canada
BDS	business development services
BEE	business enabling environment
BICF	Bangladesh Investment Climate Fund
CAD	computer-aided design
CFIs	cooperative financial institutions
CGC	Credit Guarantee Corporation
CGF	credit guarantee fund
CGS	credit guarantee schemes
CPC	China Productivity Centre
CSR	corporate social responsibility
DCED	Donor Committee for Enterprise Development
DFIs	development financial institutions
DFID	Department for International Development (United Kingdom)
ECAs	export credit agencies
EMPRETEC	entrepreneurs and technology programme (Spanish acronym)
ESCAP	Economic and Social Commission for Asia and the Pacific
EWEC	East-West Economic Corridor
EXIM	export-import
FDI	foreign direct investment
FSPL	Financial Sector Programme Loan (ADB)
FTA	free trade agreement
GATS	general agreement on trade in services
GDP	gross domestic product
GEM	Global Entrepreneurship Monitor
GII	Global Innovation Index
GIS	geographic information system
GNI	gross national income
GPA	WTO Agreement on Government Procurement
GSP	Generalized System of Preferences
GSC	global supply chain
GTZ	Deutsche Gesellschaft für Technische Zusammenarbeit GmbH (German Technical Cooperation)
ICT	information and communications technology
IE	international enterprise
IFAD	International Fund for Agricultural Development

IFC	International Finance Corporation	
ILO	International Labour Organization	
IMF	International Monetary Fund	
IP	intellectual property	
IPCC	International Panel on Climate Change	
IPRs	intellectual property rights	
ISO	International Organization for Standardization	
ITC	International Trade Centre	
JETRO	Japan External Trade Organization	
JICA	Japan International Cooperation Agency	
JFC	Japan Finance Corporation	
JSBRI	Japan Small Business Research Institute	
KOTRA	Korea Trade-Investment Promotion Agency	
L/C	letter of credit	
LDCs	least developed countries	
LLP	limited liability partnership	
M&E	monitoring and evaluation	
MEF	Ministry of Economy and Finance of Cambodia	
MFIs	microfinance institutions	
MFN	most-favoured-nation	
MIGA	Multilateral Investment Guarantee Agency	
MNC	multinational corporation	
MPDF	Mekong Project Development Facility	
MSEs	micro and small enterprises	
NBIA	National Business Incubation Association	
NGO	non-governmental organization	
NIS	national innovation system	
NPO	not-for-profit organization	
NSIC	National Small Industries Corporation	
NPL	non-performing loan	
NTB	non-tariff barrier	
OECD	Organisation for Economic Co-operation and Development	
PPP	public-private partnership	
PSB	postal savings banks	
QCD	quality, cost and delivery	
R&D	research and development	
REAP	responsible entrepreneurs achievement programme	
RoO	rules of origin	
S&T	science and technology	
SBA	United States Small Business Administration	
SDC	Swiss Agency for Development and Cooperation	
SEZ	special economic zone	
SIDBI	Small Industries Development Bank of India	
SIS	subnational innovation system	
SMBA	Small and Medium Business Administration, Republic of Korea	
SMEs	small and medium-sized enterprises	
SPRING	Standards, Productivity and Innovation Board of Singapore	

SPS	sanitary and phytosanitary measures
TBT	technical barriers to trade
TEA	early-stage entrepreneurial activity
TFP	total factor productivity
TNCs	transnational corporations
TRIMs	trade-related investment measures
TRIPS	trade-related aspects of intellectual property rights
TVET	technical and vocational education and training
TWBI	Tianjin women's business incubator
UNCTAD	United Nations Conference on Trade and Development
UNDP	United Nations Development Programme
UNIDO	United Nations Industrial Development Organization
USAID	United States Agency for International Development
VAT	value-added tax
WEF	World Economic Forum
WIPO	World Intellectual Property Organization
WTO	World Trade Organization

Executive summary

In the Asia-Pacific region small and medium-sized enterprises (SMEs), and microenterprises, constitute a significant majority of the economy and play a central role in enhancing economic dynamism, innovation and job creation. Development of this sector has been widely acknowledged as a crucial strategy for growth both in developed and in developing economies of the region. This is not an easy feat, as a number of challenges and barriers need to be understood and overcome. It demands comprehensive policies to address a variety of connected issues while also working with, and meeting the needs of, a range of local, national and global stakeholders.

This publication offers comprehensive and practical policy interventions to facilitate SME development in the region. While proposed interventions are designed to be general and adaptable to individual contexts, they are also as specific as possible to maximize practical application. Within this context, throughout the publication four key guidelines are repeatedly emphasized and all policy interventions are based on them. These four factors are far from exhaustive; however, this guidebook deems the guidelines to be the most integral to SME development in the Asia-Pacific region today. They are:

(a) The reduction of entry barriers (and related costs) for new businesses;
(b) The importance of sufficient and smooth cash flow to SMEs;
(c) The need to strengthen entrepreneurship through education and training; and
(d) The strengthening of networking and information dissemination.

Chapter I provides an introduction to the importance of the SME sector in the global economy. A substantial percentage of enterprises in the world are SMEs, and they require a number of supportive structures, provisions and policies to facilitate development. The development prospects of this sector are promising; however, there are a number of key challenges that must be addressed with a comprehensive approach. The six key areas that such an approach should cover are: (a) a business enabling environment; (b) the promotion of an entrepreneurial culture; (c) business financing; (d) business development services; (e) innovation and technology development; and (f) market access. These six key areas are the focus of the main chapters in this publication.

Governments have a key role to play in SME policy development, which also requires cooperation among multiple actors and especially multilateral institutions and the private sector. Policymakers can facilitate the smooth implementation of policies by employing tactics such as establishing a national steering committee. They may also focus on given sectors by providing direct support to firms. The methodology employed by the policy guidebook consists of an analytical review of existing policy measures, studies, documents and other secondary materials. Academics and industry experts were invited to provide insights and comments. Expert group meetings were held, and feedback from stakeholders was incorporated.

Chapter II on Contributions, challenges and prospects of SMEs offers the background context for the key terms, concepts and subjects discussed throughout the guidebook. Defining SMEs is a problematic task, as different criteria are used by individual countries and even between industries within countries. There is no universal definition; however, the most commonly used indicators are number of employees, business turnover and capital investments. SMEs are also divided according to various typological indicators including: (a) registered or unregistered; (b) the stage of economic development; (c) market orientation; (d) pace of innovation; (e) use of technology; and (f) the stage in the corporate life cycle. Despite the varying definitions and typologies, SMEs do share a number of common characteristics. For example, they tend to be born out of individual initiative, possess greater operational flexibility and high aspiration for innovation and suffer from financing and market access shortages. Microenterprises are a subcategory of small enterprises that are sometimes distinguished as a separate category, although the issues that have an impact on SME development also generally apply.

While SMEs have made significant contributions to national economic development in the region, the sector remains underdeveloped in many countries and requires greater support. SME development involves four key stages (start-up, growth, maturity and exit), and each of them has differing needs in terms of policy interventions. The barriers to SME development can be divided into external and internal. External barriers generally comprise those beyond entrepreneurs' control (e.g., policy environment). Internal barriers are those within their control (e.g., managerial experience). SME competitiveness can be enhanced with strategies such as industrial clusters, which offer advantages including proximity to resources and suppliers, shared infrastructure and knowledge exchange. Furthermore, social considerations such as culture and gender issues influence SME development. Women entrepreneurs are an undersupported sector of most Asia-Pacific economies, and targeted policy measures for their inclusive development are strongly recommended. Policy interventions should be aimed at: (a) increasing the number of SME start-ups and survival rate; (b) encouraging formalization; (c) fostering graduation to become larger firms; (d) facilitating smooth exits; and (e) enhancing market access.

Chapter III on Business Enabling Environment explores the issue of the business enabling environment (BEE), the first of the six key areas for SME development. The business environment provides the fundamentals for all private sector development, and favourable conditions form the foundation of SME growth, survival and competitiveness. The basic BEE components include, but are not limited to, economic policies, factor endowment, regulatory framework, infrastructure, entrepreneurship culture and technology. The chapter analyzes the results of four key international BEE surveys to determine the state of business environments in the Asia-Pacific region. The surveys are: (a) World Bank "Ease of Doing Business" rankings; (b) the Fraser Institute's "Economic Freedom of the World" exercise; (c) the World Economic Forum's Global Competitiveness Index; and (d) Transparency International's Corruption Perception Index. These surveys assist in determining what types of BEE reforms are necessary in an economy.

Governments have a central role to play in making BEEs more conducive to SME development; however, governments in many developing countries are challenged by a lack of skills and knowledge to develop and implement effective policies. To assist the reform process, a number of toolkits can be utilized. Chapter III highlights the value of four in particular by the International Finance Corporation (IFC), International Labour Organization (ILO), Japan International Cooperation Agency (JICA) and the Asian Development Bank (ADB). Effective BEE reforms must cater to individual national needs; however, they all benefit from some common considerations. BEE surveys are a valuable source for identifying and prioritizing specific reforms. A strong political will to commit to undertaking changes is needed, coupled with a genuine receptiveness to learning from existing best practices. It is also important to assess the needs of the target sector regularly, e.g., SMEs, in the policy development and implementation process. Finally, BEE reforms and improvements must be conducted in an accountable and transparent manner.

Chapter IV on Entrepreneurship development explores this challenge. SME development is driven by entrepreneurs, and a dynamic entrepreneurial environment is essential for growth. While the understanding of entrepreneurship varies, this publication defines it as an individual or team process of doing something new or different, with calculated risking-taking behaviour for future gains to add value to society. A number of key factors influence the success of entrepreneurs, and these elements can generally be classified under five categories: (a) internal traits of the entrepreneur; (b) adequate resources; (c) a solid business plan; (d) a favourable external environment; and (e) the wider political, social and cultural contexts. Another key consideration is the existence of entry barriers, especially the "fear of failure", which discourages many potential entrepreneurs in Asia-Pacific countries.

To help overcome potential barriers, governments and relevant agencies can promote awareness about the importance and value of entrepreneurship with strategies such as education and training. It is particularly recommended that certain strategies be aimed at undersupported segments of society such as women, youth and rural entrepreneurs. In recent years, an emerging trend is social entrepreneurship involving businesses that are aimed at addressing important social issues or that operate in environmentally sustainable ways. Many social enterprises are SMEs, and policy interventions should pay close attention to this new subsector. The chapter also highlights a number of key policy recommendations. Offering "single window" assistance to support entrepreneurs, especially for new business registration processes, is crucial to increasing efficiency. Formal property rights must be protected as property is a common form of collateral for bank loans to new businesses. Furthermore, with regard to credit, accurate and timely credit information is essential for entrepreneurs and credit providers alike. Investors must also be protected to help companies raise capital, especially in times of financial uncertainty. Taxation must also be easy to understand and follow. Simplifying tax collection procedures is one method of increasing corporations by decreasing the time needed and the costs involved. More resources for education and training are also recommended, not only to increase awareness and knowledge about entrepreneurship but also to foster more positive attitudes in the wider community.

As access to sufficient and sustained finance is essential for all SMEs, this aspect is the focus of chapter V. Different stages of the business life cycle have varying needs for cash with the start-up, growth and transition stages being particularly important. There are a number of different instruments and sources of SME financing, which can be classified into seven general categories: informal, internal, debt, equity, asset-based, leasing and government grants or subsidies. The major instruments within these seven categories are elaborated in this chapter to provide better understanding about how they work and what type of actors offer such instruments. In general, informal financing such as personal savings and loans from family and friends, and internal financing including retained earnings, are particularly important for small businesses. Commercial banking also plays an important role, particularly in the European Union, Japan and the United States of America where the banking sector is highly developed. The multiple financial instruments are administered by a variety of financial institutions, and there are many associated advantages and challenges that need to be understood in order to introduce effective policy interventions. One example of favourable government intervention to strengthen the connection between financial institutions and SMEs is the implementation of credit rating schemes. This facilitates loans by providing accurate and timely credit information about SMEs, which instills more confidence in financial institutions to provide loans. During an economic downturn, SMEs are generally more vulnerable and in greater need of government financial support, both directly and indirectly.

Chapter V on Financing Business offers a number of key policy considerations. Working capital is essential for the functioning of all businesses, and this needs to be maximized to help SMEs survive and flourish. A balance between the development of debt and equity markets would benefit SMEs, as debt markets tend to assist the early stage of SME development. Equity markets are, however, more conducive to entrepreneurial and innovative ventures. Another important policy consideration is the need to provide adequate and timely information both to SMEs and to financial institutions. The public sector also has an important role to play in facilitating connections between SMEs and sources of equity funding. Financial services, while essential, are not the only determinant of SME success, and they should be combined with business development services for more comprehensive support. Policy interventions should also focus on strengthening the relationship between bankers and small business entrepreneurs in order to facilitate greater understanding and trust. Finally, it is strongly recommended that policymakers consider introducing a four-tier financial system for a clear division of labour and improved institutional coordination.

Chapter VI on Business Development Services considers the importance of comprehensive, affordable and high-quality business development services (BDS), which consist of three core segments: operational, advisory and advocacy. The most sophisticated of the three segments is operational services, which assist with the daily functions of a business. Advisory and advocacy services are currently underdeveloped or short-lived, and these areas should be more fully explored. The delivery of BDS has transformed over the years, shifting from the traditional approach where governments and related agencies engaged in direct provision, to a market-oriented approach where private providers are engaged to deliver services. The latter approach is generally preferable, although this is only a viable option once a certain level of economic development has been attained. Prior to this, the public sector is needed to provide direct support. Cooperation is necessary between the different BDS actors, with varying priorities, capabilities and mandates. Coordination of interventions at the micro, meso and macro levels also increases effective BDS delivery to SMEs. One form of BDS, i.e., business and technology incubation, has proven to be a particularly effective strategy and is explored in greater detail in this chapter. Incubators provide valuable assistance to SME start-ups, and the growing number of incubators worldwide attest to their effectiveness. BDS can ultimately help SMEs join regional or global supply chains, which bring new knowledge, skills and networks. The key policy recommendations for BDS development are: (a) enhancing public-private partnerships; (b) raising awareness about the importance of BDS; (c) creating an enabling environment; and (d) encouraging participation by the private sector.

Chapter VII on Innovation and Technology examines how innovation and technology contribute to SME development. There are four key components of innovations – product, process, marketing and organizational – which can be further divided into incremental or radical innovations. While the benefits of innovation are widely known, SMEs in developing Asia-Pacific economies experience difficulty in building their capabilities. Policymakers need to analyze the key innovation strategies that SMEs can adopt in order to gain a better understanding of what interventions are most effective. This chapter discusses some of these strategies and issues. Research and development (R&D) has shown positive movement in the Asia-Pacific region recently, with countries such as Singapore, Japan and the Republic of Korea investing significant amounts of GDP into R&D activities. SMEs, with their limited capabilities and size, are not often associated with strong R&D; however, effective activities can be simple and affordable.

Another popular strategy for innovation is technology acquisition and transfer. Domestic factors such as institutional structures, supportive policies and regulations and financial assistance have a significant impact on technology acquisition and transfer. New products, processes or services need to be introduced into commercial markets, and successful technology commercialization is most efficient when there is strong and diverse collaboration between multiple actors. Policy interventions should facilitate the creation of these linkages with a national innovation system (NIS), and a related subnational innovation system (SIS). The four key pillars of a strong and effective NIS are human capital, infrastructure, innovation culture and funding. Innovation related to NIS and commercialization can be greatly facilitated by adopting an open innovation model. Under such a model, firms are able to commercialize innovations through a variety of means. While this is primarily driven by enterprises, policy interventions can assist enterprises to pursue such strategies with subsidies, favourable regulation or networking opportunities. Another innovation strategy for SMEs is reverse engineering, which can be effective in reducing product development costs, improving the quality and functionality of products and compensating for limited R&D capabilities. It is important that this method be carefully applied and monitored, as this tool could violate intellectual property rights (IPRs) if used for direct duplication. The protection of IPR has become an increasingly visible issue and it is beneficial for SMEs to receive education and guidance on the issue. This is advantageous not just to avoid violating IPR; SMEs can also use these rights to protect their own innovations.

The final strategy discussed in this chapter is the use of tax incentives, particularly for R&D activities, to help stimulate innovation. Tax incentives can take different forms and be delivered in a variety of ways. The specific needs of SMEs and local conditions must be taken into account when formulating tax strategies. The chapter highlights a number of national initiatives undertaken in Asia-Pacific economies. Five central principles were common to the success of all these initiatives. A comprehensive technology development policy within a strong but simplified institutional framework produces an enabling environment for SMEs. Government-subsidized funding for innovation activities helps reduce financial barriers for SMEs and other key players. Development of an NIS (and SIS) to increase connections, linkages and coordination is especially beneficial to SMEs. The provision of support for open-market policy will facilitate a greater degree of technology transfer and outsourcing among SMEs and other stakeholders, such as large enterprises and research institutions. Finally, officials should offer tools such as business and technology incubation and training for technology-focused SME development.

Chapter VIII focuses on the importance of market access, particularly in regional and global markets. SMEs must continually generate new business; however, this can be challenging when the domestic market is either small or large but highly competitive. SMEs generally face difficulties in accessing new markets as they have limited resources, expertise and market information. This chapter identifies four critical factors in enhancing market entry capability. First, knowledge about business opportunities, customers, competitors, distribution procedures, local rules and regulations and taxation is essential. Second, the policy and regulatory framework must be well-organized, and must provide the necessary trade business infrastructure and other facilitation services. Third, trade barriers, both tariff and non-tariff, can hinder SME access, and this issue needs to be addressed at the national, regional and international levels. Fourth, networking and cooperation between SMEs and larger firms provides an important source of information, knowledge and skills.

The trade environment in which SMEs operate influences the ease of market access, and this chapter explores some of the most pertinent issues in this area. Trade policy and trade investment agreements have a significant impact on SMEs. A policy that lowers trade barriers brings benefits to firms seeking access to foreign markets as well as advantages to local firms in the form of cheaper imported inputs. Investment agreements increase security, stability and predictability, and this creates more investment inflows.

A key player in international trade issues is the World Trade Organization (WTO), and some of the most relevant agreements and rules under this body are highlighted in the chapter. Another factor in facilitating SME market access is the improvement of export product identification, pricing and competitiveness. SMEs would benefit from training in how to control costs and effectively use their competitive advantage. SMEs must also be informed about quality standards and certificates, and trained to meet these standards. Furthermore, with regard to trade logistics in business transactions, the transport system is a central factor and policy interventions should focus on improving the relevant infrastructure. Customs procedures are another area in which policy interventions should be aimed at increasing clarity and efficiency for easier trade across borders.

The chapter also discusses the importance of trade promotion tools and highlights trade fairs, buyer-seller meetings and trade missions. These are important strategies which require careful planning and assistance to ensure that follow-up activities are executed to maximize the benefits. The various actors in trade promotion have their own strengths and policymakers need to understand these to enable cooperation. A useful tool for promoting market access is the use of information and communication technology (ICT), particularly through the Internet, and policy should be aimed at raising awareness about the benefits, strengthening literacy and capacity, and helping ICT firms develop. The chapter also explores the important issue of trade finance. It focuses on the main forms of trade finance, various trade finance instruments and the actors who help facilitate trade finance. Special economic zones (SEZs) have proven to be a particularly useful tool for SME development; there are a number of examples in the Asia-Pacific region.

Foreign direct investment (FDI) should also be facilitated as SMEs can either become direct suppliers or they can participate in global supply chains, both of which are beneficial to their development. The multifaceted issue of market access requires a variety of policy interventions; while the chapter offers a comprehensive set of recommended actions, it is important to adapt these to local needs and conditions as appropriate.

Chapter IX presents a Policy Framework that draws together all the preceding recommendations. A summary of the major constraints to SME development is provided. National policy planning must involve a process for selecting and prioritizing the policies that best fit local conditions and address the most pressing problems. In each of the six key areas (i.e., business environment, entrepreneurship, financing, business development services, innovation and market access), the recommended actions at the national and regional levels are recapitulated. These recommendations are designed not only to be comprehensive but also to enable adaptation to local needs. Every country in the diverse Asia-Pacific region must assess the status of their SME sector and consider the local conditions before embarking on policy reform or implementation. This assessment should inform the plan of action, which should also involve consultation with experts, academics, entrepreneurs and other stakeholders. While the policy frameworks might differ between countries, the ultimate objectives for the entire region are uniform: build SME capacity, increase competitiveness, partner for economic development, generate employment and increase the well-being of all the people in the region. The chapter ends with an annex on the concepts and major frameworks of monitoring and evaluation (M&E) exercises. M&E can be used to ensure proper governance, transparency and accountability of SME development programmes.

CHAPTER I
Introduction

Small and medium-sized enterprises (SMEs)[1] continue to make significant contributions globally. SMEs are a key source of economic growth and dynamism in all economies. Adaptability, resilience and the ability to manufacture goods and to provide services with a high degree of flexibility and cost effectiveness are hallmarks of the SME sector. Innovations based on proper marketing have been the unique and biggest strength of SMEs. Small businesses are particularly important for bringing innovative products and/or services to the market. A number of modern products, especially electronics and ICT products, owe their origin to the SME sector.[2]

In fact, SMEs are a "nursery" for nurturing entrepreneurial talent, in addition to creating employment and fostering industrial development in an economy. SMEs are alleviating poverty around the world as well as increasing the social and economic participation of women, youth and minorities. Some SMEs also have the potential to grow into large enterprises and even transnational corporations (TNCs) or multinational corporations over time, and make important contributions to national, regional and global economies. The Asia-Pacific region – where trade and FDI-driven development strategies with rich natural endowment are commonly undertaken – is also enjoying all of the above-mentioned benefits of SMEs.[3]

In most countries of the world, SMEs generally start as proprietorships, become small business enterprises and then grow into medium-sized enterprises.[4] Indian statistics (Ministry of Science and Technology, 2011) reveal that 99.7 per cent of all enterprises in the world are SMEs while large enterprises only account for 0.3 per cent. On average, SMEs provide between 60-70 per cent of the jobs, especially within the Asia-Pacific context (Hall, 2002). In Asia and the Pacific, SMEs typically account for nearly 50 per cent of all value addition within the economy, directly and indirectly, according to the Asian Association of Management Organizations (AAMO) (2007).

The SME sector is highly dispersed and can even sustain itself with minimal transportation, power and communication infrastructures. Experience also shows that without such supporting infrastructure, advanced technology and modern methods of production, SMEs suffer from low quality and productivity (ESCAP, 2009a). SMEs also require basic support for steady growth in terms of adequate capital, market access, technology adaptation and a skilled workforce. In the SME sector, the paramount role of state policy should be that of a "facilitator"; policymakers must resist controlling and micro-managing entrepreneurs. Proper government policies, supporting infrastructure and development services are required to trigger the individual initiative of entrepreneurs and their resources in productive processes.

A. Objectives

This publication aims to provide comprehensive and practical guidelines for policy formulation for SME development in Asia and the Pacific, clearly outlining policy objectives to be undertaken. Special attention is paid to both the selection and the implementation of policy options in the real world. This guidebook offers feasible policies at the operational level. For this purpose, the publication covers six key areas: business environment, entrepreneurship, finance, business development services, innovation and technology, and market access. The guidelines must be general enough so that individual nations can adapt them to their own industries while reflecting the various stages of economic development within the Asia-Pacific region; hence, this guidebook does not cater to only one development stage. In addition, it provides some practical ideas on how to establish necessary institutional frameworks for the smooth implementation of the policy options. While the guidebook is designed for policymakers, it is also useful for entrepreneurs and trainers as well as business associations, such as chambers of commerce and federations of industry.

B. SME development prospects

The strategic importance of SMEs in overall economic development has been widely recognized in the past and has been even more evident in recent decades, both in developed and in developing nations. To foster the growth of SMEs, a number of cultural, behavioural and social factors need to be considered to obtain the desired outputs from development programmes and initiatives. The overall objectives of SME development are to: (a) create jobs and generate income; (b) improve SME performance and competitiveness; and (c) increase their participation in and contribution to the national economy.

---

[1] Having recognized their expected contribution to inclusive and sustainable industrialization in developing countries in Asia and the Pacific, this publication mainly focuses on the development of export-oriented SMEs as well as SMEs in supporting industries. Those SME segments are typically characterized by high technology adaptation and backward linkages, which are key success factors for their effective penetration into foreign markets. Other major SME segments, i.e., domestic market-oriented SMEs and cottage industries, which mainly serve domestic and local markets, are not discussed extensively in this publication (Uchikawa and Keola, 2009) although they may share some of the similar corporate characteristics to export-oriented and support industry SMEs. For a more detailed discussion, see section C, "Typology of SMEs", in chapter II. Note that the statistics of SMEs in this publication are the aggregate data of all SME segments, including micro enterprises.

[2] For example, Taiwan Province of China's economic transformation is often viewed in this context.

[3] The size of the SME sector in an economy does appear to be positively associated with gross domestic product (GDP) per capita growth in many countries. Strong SME sectors do not necessarily drive economic growth, but they are "characteristic of fast-growing economies" (ESCAP, 2009a).

[4] Every SME does not go through this growth path, as the failure rate of new and small businesses is considerably high; such a rate differs by industry and country. See chapter II for more information.

There are a number of obstacles that need to be overcome to achieve these objectives. The following constraints for SME development in the Asia and the Pacific have been identified by AAMO (2007):

(a) Poor business environment (e.g., bureaucracy, taxation and unfavourable property rights enforcement);

(b) Poor infrastructure (e.g., transportation facilities, power plants, industrial estates and telecommunications);

(c) Inadequate access to finance (e.g., obtaining loans, securing collateral and third-party guarantees and a lack of alternative sources);

(d) Low technological capacities (e.g., rapid technological advancement in markets, locating sources of appropriate technology and acquiring technology to develop attractive products;

(e) Too few applications of ICT (e.g., business communications, marketing intelligence and customer development); and

(f) Intensified competition in domestic, regional and global markets (e.g., trade and investment liberalization, less protectionism, freer movement of goods and capital, lower import duties, cuts in subsidies and cost pressures).

The United States Small Business Administration (2008) outlined five major challenges governments face with regard to small businesses: (a) strengthening the overall economy; (b) regulating taxes; (c) overseeing cost and availability of health insurance; (d) attracting and retaining a quality workforce; and (e) managing global competition (Moutray, 2008). In the Asia-Pacific region, the UPS (2007) Asia Business Monitor identified the top three business concerns for SME owners as the quality of products and services, customer loyalty and the retention of a qualified workforce. The DP Information Group, in a 2011 survey of SME development in Singapore, highlighted several SME needs including internationalization for growth, increased productivity, investment in technology and innovation, and greater financial strength to weather economic downturns (DP Information Group, 2011). A survey by the SME Agency of Japan in 2010 suggested that the four biggest problems encountered by SMEs at and after start-up were financing (55 per cent), staffing (37 per cent), finding customers (28 per cent) and finding suppliers (25 per cent) (Japan Small Business Research Institute, 2011).[5]

Some problems are primarily under the SMEs' control. They typically arise from a lack of one or more resources, i.e., capital, management ability, technical ability and market knowledge. The outlook and capabilities of an SME owner/manager tend to drive these issues, since the owner/manager is crucial to the success of smaller organizations such as SMEs. These internal problems, which are often an outcome of faulty managerial strategies and/or practices, can be placed under the following eight categories:

(a) A lack of scientific management skills;
(b) Poor implementation;

(c) A lack of marketing intelligence;
(d) Inadequate access to raw materials and supplies;
(e) A shortfall in working capital;
(f) Inadequate equity;
(g) Labour issues; and
(h) Technical and operational discrepancies.

A troubled SME tends to show signs of financial weakness beginning with cash flow issues. In terms of proactive policy, emphasis should be placed on cash flow. Policy that puts cash in the hands of SME owners quickly is generally the best course of action, i.e., a front-end tax credit is preferable to a deferred tax benefit, with everything else being equal. This idea is revisited throughout this book, particularly in chapter V on financing SMEs.

Various agencies have designed and implemented SME development interventions in Asia and the Pacific, particularly in less developed economies. The strategic approaches of 13 major bilateral and multilateral development and donor agencies were reviewed to discover their areas of focus and modalities.[6] It was found that their specific and detailed interventions to improve value additions in the SME sector, and strengthen their contributions to their respective economies, covered the following six key areas:

(a) Enabling environment, covering appropriate policy and regulatory framework, including effective institutional framework and pro-business fiscal policy, and supporting infrastructure development, such as power, transport, communication, water, etc.;

(b) Entrepreneurship development, including management skills and human resources;

(c) Financing a business;

(d) Fostering business development services;

(e) Technology transfer and adaptation; and

(f) Market access, including trade promotion.

The findings strongly indicate that a comprehensive SME development approach typically covers the interventions for some or all of the above-mentioned key areas. Tables I.1 and I.2 present the strategic approaches of all 13 development agencies and their typical interventions, followed by a brief discussion on each key area.

1. Business enabling environment

To provide a favourable environment for SMEs to flourish, governmental policy interventions and supporting infrastructure play vital roles (World Bank, 2011a). Transparent policies and regulatory frameworks facilitate enterprise establishment, operation, promulgation, access to resources and markets and the exit of failing firms.

---

[5] Because the respondents were able to list multiple obstacles, the total exceeds 100 per cent.

[6] The corporate strategies of 13 bilateral and multilateral development and donor agencies on SME development in Asia and the Pacific were reviewed (ESCAP, 2011a): ADB, 2000; APO, 2007; Department for International Development (DFID), 2008; Deutsche Gesellschaft für Technische Zusammenarbeit GmbH (GTZ), 2010; ILO, 2009b; JICA, 2006; OECD, 2005; Swiss Agency for Development and Cooperation (SDC), 2010; UNCTAD, 2010a; UNDP, 2007; UNIDO, 2010; USAID, 2010; and the World Bank, 2003.

Table I.1. Development approaches for SMEs implemented by selected bilateral and multilateral agencies

	ADB (2000)	APO (2007)	DFID (2008)	GTZ (2010)	ILO (2009b)	JICA (2006)	OECD (2005)	SDC (2010)	UNCTAD (2010)	UNDP (2007)	UNIDO (2010)	USAID (2010)	World Bank (2002)
Business environment	✓	✓	✓	✓	✓	✓	✓	✓	✓	✓	✓	✓	✓
Access to finance	✓	✓	✓	✓	✓	✓	✓	✓	✓		✓	✓	✓
Entrepreneurship and human resource development	✓	✓	✓	✓	✓		✓	✓	✓	✓	✓	✓	
Business development services		✓		✓	✓	✓			✓		✓	✓	✓
Technology transfer and adaptation		✓	✓	✓		✓	✓		✓		✓		
Market access and export promotion		✓		✓			✓	✓	✓	✓	✓	✓	
Others	✓ (Privatization)	✓ (Supply chains and clusters)	✓	✓ (Sectoral development and CSR)			✓ (Trade facilitation)	✓ (Supply chains and clusters)	✓ (Supply chains)	✓ (Supply chains, investment promotion, and CSR)	✓ (Supply chains, clusters, and CSR)	✓ (Supply chains and clusters)	(Privatization)

Sources: Authors' compilation.
Note: CSR – corporate social responsibility.

Table I.2. Typical interventions of the six key areas for SME development

Business enabling environment		
Policy and regulatory framework		(a) Corporate registration
		(b) Corporate governance
		(c) Fiscal incentives (tax exemptions, subsidies and grants)
		(d) Labour laws
		(e) Bankruptcy laws
		(f) Administrative institutionalization
		(g) Anti-corruption
Infrastructure for business		(a) Transportation
		(b) Power and electricity
		(c) Water
		(d) Communications
		(e) Business premises, industrial estates and incubation centres
Promotion of entrepreneurial culture		(a) Entrepreneurship training and education
		(b) New business nurturing (incubation)
		(c) Women and youth entrepreneurial programmes
		(d) Raising public awareness
Financing the business		(a) Microfinance
		(b) Commercial loans
		(c) Public credit guarantees
		(d) Specialized or development financial institutions
		(e) Corporate bond market
		(f) Leasing and factoring
		(g) Venture capital and angel investment
Business development services		(a) Marketing, laws, accounting, taxation, finance, foreign trade and technology
		(b) Business incubation
		(c) Strengthening service providers, such as business associations and training institutes
		(d) Certified professional services
Innovation and technology development and adaptation		(a) Product and service development through marketing
		(b) Research and development
		(c) Technology transfer
		(d) Technology incubation and commercialization
		(e) Higher education reform
		(f) Quality standards and certificates
		(g) Intellectual property rights
		(h) E-commerce
Market access		(a) Information dissemination on trade and investment liberalization
		(b) Market intelligence
		(c) Trade fairs and missions
		(d) Export promotion agency
		(e) Product and quality certifications
		(f) Regional and global supply chains

Source: Authors' compilation.

Sustainability of the policies and regulation – such as enterprise registration, corporate governance, fiscal incentives (tax exemptions, subsidies, and grants), anti-corruption, labour laws and bankruptcy laws – rely heavily upon adequate judicial and efficient administrative frameworks. Policies and regulatory directives with a clear vision and mission as well as adequate implementation of operation modalities build confidence among SME entrepreneurs; such directives strengthen their capacity to improve linkages with other enterprises, both large and small. The availability of specialized and formal institutional resources for SME development is also a pillar for creating a level playing field and facilitating their access to finance, skills and knowledge.

Adequate and quality infrastructure enhances SME competitiveness. Infrastructure for businesses comprise basic physical and organizational structures that are needed for the operation of enterprises that, include, among others, transportation, water supply and sewers, power grids, telecommunications and training and research facilities. Viewed functionally, infrastructure facilitates the production of goods and provision of services by enterprises. For example, roads enable the transportation of raw materials to factories and the distribution of finished products to markets. Power and water supplies are necessary for the operation of machinery and equipment. For entrepreneurs, access to infrastructure such as business incubators and industrial parks helps tremendously in reducing their entry and running costs by providing lower than market rates for rent and shared supporting services. Almost all major bilateral and multilateral donors are supporting the Asia-Pacific developing countries in building such infrastructure; however, specific infrastructure aimed at SMEs is still lacking (AAMO, 2007). The provision of such infrastructure, such as SME parks, will enhance their productivities and improve their competitiveness in the markets.

2. Promotion of entrepreneurial culture

Entrepreneurial culture is defined here as the tendency of a society to promote or motivate its people to be an entrepreneur. This is an aspect that is highly sensitive to government policy. There are basic conditions that a government must furnish to encourage entrepreneurial activity, with a fair expectation of gain and risk. According to Global Entrepreneurship Monitor (GEM) (2007), these conditions consist of macroeconomic stability, a strong regulatory and institutional framework, market openness, formal education, conducive cultural and social norms and technological readiness. The Asian Productivity Organization (APO) (2007) pointed out that government provisions that created a conducive environment for entrepreneurial culture might involve regulatory reform, entrepreneurial skill development, women and youth entrepreneurial programmes, business incubation and raising public awareness. Technical knowledge for potential entrepreneurs should also be an integral part of overall entrepreneurship-building. An extensive programme for entrepreneurial development, with concomitant support through small business consulting services, would result in higher levels of entrepreneurial activities and thus the strengthening of existing SMEs. Increased donor support for enhancing entrepreneurial culture would also pay big dividends.

3. Financing a business

Financing a business involves enhancing the degree to which financial services are available to all, through easy and affordable means. Well-functioning financial systems and markets are particularly important and critical in attracting private sector investment, and thereby fostering SME development. The ability of SMEs to grow and strengthen their competitiveness depends highly on their potential to invest in development, innovation, improvements and diversification over time. All of these investments need short- and long-term capital; therefore, access to finance is a central issue.

Against this background, SMEs consistently cite lack of access to finance as a severe handicap (ESCAP, 2009a). In attempting to gain access to financial services, SMEs continue to face constraints caused by many common factors, such as an ineffective financial sector, high interest rates, lack of information on capital availability, excessive red tape, lack of collateral, poor property right laws, lack of proper financial products, missing credit rating agencies and poor human resources in the financial sector (ESCAP, 2009a). Government officials should address these factors in order to make financial resources accessible to entrepreneurs. Recommended policy interventions that would provide much assistance include microfinance supplies, affordable commercial loans, public credit guarantees, a credit-rating scheme and SME-specialized financial institutions. Donor assistance in the financing of SMEs, particularly through two-step loans, venture capital, business incubation arrangements and targeted financing for priority sectors, particularly in rural areas, would bring tangible results.[7]

4. Innovation and technology development and adaptation

One of the critical factors that influence the competitiveness of enterprises is the development and marketing of innovative products and services through effective marketing and enhanced technological capability (Drucker, 2008). Innovation is an essential process of change in order to maintain the development and growth of an SME. In times of rapid change, innovation has to be a priority ingrained into management for the firm's survival. It should be integrated into the existing enterprise systems and implemented as entrepreneurial strategies outside the SME in the marketplace (Drucker, 2008). SMEs should construct a policy of systematic innovation, analyze changes within and outside organizations at regular intervals, and regularly identify whether there are opportunities for innovation.

Technology development and adaptation play an important role in innovation. Technology comprises both hardware, in terms of the physical assets, and software, in terms of know-how and skills. Technology development and adaptation encompass R&D, the dissemination of information and knowledge, the matching of technology with needs and the creative adaptation of technologies for new uses (ESCAP, 2007a). SMEs in developing countries often produce products and services of moderate quality, commonly due to outdated technologies. This has resulted in the rejection of their products in competitive markets at both the domestic and international levels. In recent years, their situation has worsened because they have had to survive under intensifying competition due to globalization, widening free trade regimes and the phasing out of tariff barriers under WTO mandates. The best use of technology enables SMEs to be more innovative, market new products and services, reduce costs of production, maintain consistency in quality and standardization, improve productivity and enhance their competitiveness.

To boost innovation, government assistance in technology policy and infrastructural build-up is crucial. However, donor assistance in technological capacity-building remains limited. This is particularly the case with regard to SMEs in the developing countries of Asia and the Pacific. The building of technology-related institutions and R&D facilities as well as increased assistance in widening skills development programmes would bring tangible gains in enhancing SMEs' innovation.

---

[7] It is useful to distinguish between microenterprises operating in the informal sector and small enterprises in the formal sector – particularly in the context of their access to finance. Micro-credit programmes often address the collateral-free credit needs of microenterprises in the informal sector, while small enterprises without an adequate collateral base are the ones suffering from limited access to collateral-free credit. Many of the programmes for facilitating access to credit by these small enterprises through commercial banks have been unsuccessful, mainly because of high operating costs. Current literature highlights the need for developing a mechanism for collateral free access to institutional credit (e.g., ADB, 2009; and DFID, 2008).

5. Business development services

Inadequate business development (and support) services or their relatively higher unit cost has hampered SMEs' efforts in improving their competitiveness. A lack of both information and accessibility to existing services by SMEs has also resulted in weak demand for such facilities. Obtaining information about the laws, taxation, customs regulations, market intelligence, business development, training opportunities and financing sources are generally expensive and time consuming, particularly in less developed countries. Thus, as has been pointed out by ADB (2006), most SMEs remain ignorant of the latest developments. Service providers, particularly lawyers, accountants, and marketing and technical consultants, often do not possess cost-effective management solutions that SMEs require most. It is incumbent upon governments to provide such critical SME development services jointly with commercial service providers as well as with business and industry associations, such as chambers of commerce and federations of industries. As noted by the Donor Committee for Enterprise Development (2011a), donors can also assist through financial assistance and the sharing of experiences in successful cases of business service provisions from other countries.

6. Market access

Given the fact that most domestic markets for SMEs in countries of Asia and the Pacific are saturated, there is a need to encourage those SMEs to seek greater access to international markets through international production networks or global supply chains. Orienting SMEs' efforts towards export markets by providing information about international markets and trade systems as well as incentives to promote linkages to global supply chains would prove beneficial. Traditional ways to facilitate local SME penetration of international markets involve various export promotion activities, such as participation in international trade fairs and exhibitions, organization of buyer-seller meetings, dispatching of trade missions and the establishment of national export promotion agencies. Trade promotion, by its nature, is intended to stimulate interest between foreign buyers and local suppliers, specifically to increase their business by exposing each other to new individuals and firms to conduct business with.

C. Policy development and implementation: Stakeholders and strategies

1. Policy development

Although there have been various national initiatives as well as a number of bilateral and multilateral agencies promoting SMEs in the Asia-Pacific developing countries, the need for SME development is urgent. Existing initiatives have not satisfied demand as of yet. Working with the active involvement of all stakeholders, particularly the SME associations and chambers of commerce, governments need to solicit large donor assistance for SMEs. Since different government agencies, such as those related to agriculture, industry, commerce, enterprise development, trade and finance, are involved in SME development, thorough inter-ministerial coordination and well-designed division of labour are essential. Stakeholders in SME development include:

(a) Governmental agencies, including apex SME development agencies;
(b) Financial institutions (both public and private);
(c) Education and training institutions;
(d) Research institutions;
(e) Business associations (e.g., chambers of commerce and federations of industries);
(f) Labour unions;
(g) Providers of BDS;
(h) Bilateral and multilateral development/donor agencies;
(i) Civil society organizations; and
(j) Individual enterprises and SMEs.

It has been observed that although governments and public-sector organizations play a central role in SME development, comprehensive facilitation requires the involvement of multiple actors (Baig, 2007). For example, governments implement policy reforms with the support of multilateral development institutions and in consultation with the private sector. The private sector embraces more productive and sustainable positions with support from governments or multilateral bodies (Baig, 2007). These interactions are captured in a common framework (see table I.3), which presents an overview of general actions that should inform policy development for different actors to facilitate SME development.

2. Policy implementation

Policymakers in Asia and the Pacific have been implementing SME development programmes in several fields, including: (a) policy advocacy (typically together with reforms in administrative framework); (b) infrastructure development; (c) institutional capacity-building both at the public and the private level; (d) human resource development for governments, business associations and enterprises; (e) reform in financial institutions and markets (developing new financial products); and (f) product-based trade and investment promotion.

In this connection, governments and development agencies share some common tactics to enhance the smooth implementation of policy, particularly in selecting the most effective tools and engaging the needed local organizations as the main counterparts for the projects. These tactics include:

(a) Establishment of a national steering committee of the project comprising of individuals from both the government and the private sector;
(b) Identification of a national focal-point office or a primary counterpart, typically among governmental agencies, including the establishment of a national SME development agency;
(c) Organization of multi-stakeholder consultations and dialogue;
(d) Support to and collaboration with business associations;
(e) Support to and collaboration with BDS providers;

Table I.3. Common framework of actions for SME development

Sector	Public	Public-private partnership	Private
Drivers	• Governments, public sector organizations, multilateral development agencies/donors	• Government-local company, Government-academia Local company-donor Government-CCI/association	• Local/multinational companies, academia, industry associations, chambers of commerce and industry, foundations, non-governmental organizations (NGOs)/civil society, financial institutions
Actions	• Reform policies, regulations, and legal framework for SMEs. • Engage the private sector in policy process. • Promote an entrepreneurial society and entrepreneurial culture. • Monitor entrepreneur profile, entrepreneur activity and entrepreneurial business environment.	• Entrepreneurship trainings and knowledge development. • Strategic public-private partnerships for vital services. • Broadening financing options.	• Encouraging entrepreneurship. • Developing linkages and strengthening networks to nurture small businesses. • Fostering technological upgrading and new business opportunities. • Promoting corporate governance and social responsibility.

Source: Baig, 2007.

    (f) Support to and collaboration with international and local NGOs; and

    (g) Direct support to enterprises.

A few issues have been observed in Asia and the Pacific that are common to all SME development programmes:

    (a) A national steering committee without the strong commitment of stakeholders will not work effectively;

    (b) More involvement of the private sector, particularly SMEs and trade associations, makes programmes more effective;

    (c) Established financial institutions, with the backing of government, must provide adequate financial resources to SMEs;

    (d) Government officials must consult with stakeholders regularly, particularly with SMEs and their representatives; and

    (e) Direct support to individual enterprises in priority sectors should be provided.[8]

In general, SMEs are still in a precarious condition in Asia-Pacific developing countries, and governments must take a leading role in supporting and facilitating their development. Their selection of a proper modality of policy development and implementation particularly affects the effectiveness of SME development in a country.

One trend in technical assistance for SME development in the region is the emergence of large-scale, cost-sharing programmes among development agencies, which typically promote an enabling business environment, access to finance and direct support to individual enterprises' business development, e.g., Katalyst and the Bangladesh Investment Climate Fund (BICF).[9] These joint programmes help the governments, producers' associations, and individual enterprises via business development services and finance. Some of them also are adopting sectoral development and value chain approaches. Joint programmes also tend to establish an independent secretariat to manage their activities and funds; while this saves money, it has the disadvantage of isolating SME development projects from national stakeholders.

D. Methodology

This policy guidebook addresses the policy frameworks, institutional arrangements, public-private sector cooperation mechanisms and technical support for SME development in Asia-Pacific countries. Developing such a manuscript is a daunting task when considering the variety of experiences as well as the varied policies and programmes of each country.

For this purpose, the book focuses on an analytical review of existing policy measures, acts, documents, studies and other secondary materials on SME financing mainly in Asia and the

---

[8] Policymakers must recognize the considerable costs involved in providing direct assistance to individual firms. Within this context, the role of business associations could be further promoted as providers of business development services. See chapter VI for further discussion of this issue.

[9] Katalyst, which has been funded by DFID, SDC and the Swedish International Development Cooperation Agency (SIDA), is one of the largest projects working in the field of SME development in Bangladesh. It started in 2002 and was aimed at uplifting the poor through market-led SME development. It has worked with more than 30 manufacturing and agriculture sectors in Bangladesh, providing technical assistance in the areas of institutional capacity-building, business plan development, technology transfer and business development services. It also works with business associations to foster an enabling environment for businesses (Katalyst, 2010). The Bangladesh Investment Climate Fund (BICF) was jointly established by DFID, European Commission and IFC in 2006, aimed at assisting the Government of Bangladesh in promoting opportunities for destitute people to increase income and employment through improving the business environment. BICF has designed and implemented programmes to institute more business-friendly policies, laws and regulations (GTZ and the Embassy of Japan, 2009).

Pacific, in line with *grounded theory,* a qualitative research methodology (Glaser and Strauss, 1967). Relevant materials were also taken from other regions. The grounded theory methodology can generate or build theory and is well suited for studying both objectives and subjective phenomena that can be derived from different experiences (cf. Locke, 2001). Specific policy implications and guidelines are documented, based on various countries' strategies and practices in the context of financing of SMEs in Asia and the Pacific, apart from the experience and expertise of the contributors, researchers and authors of this volume.

The United Nations Secretariat and the Government of Japan established and financially supported a research team. ESCAP has invited academics and industry experts from inside and outside the region to contribute to the development of the guidebook. Following the first draft, two regional expert group meetings were held separately to review the manuscripts and to obtain additional data. The participants included SME development agencies, commercial banks, SME/exim banks, credit guarantee agencies, multilateral and bilateral development agencies, international financial institutions, business associations, industry experts and academics from the region. Their feedback and follow-up communications via phone and e-mail were also incorporated to the maximum extent possible in subsequent drafts.

E. Outline of the guidebook

This publication comprises nine chapters. Following this introductory chapter, chapter II provides the background and elaborates on the competitiveness and contribution of SMEs in the region. It discusses the underlying need for policy objectives and associated interventions together with specific challenges and constraints faced by policymakers. Chapter III highlights factors enabling a conducive business environment for SMEs' steady growth. Chapter IV addresses issues concerning entrepreneurship development, while chapter V covers finance, which is typically seen as one of the most critical issues of SME development. Chapter VI underscores the crucial role of business development services while chapter VII discusses the importance of innovation and technology for SMEs to compete effectively. Chapter VIII emphasizes the need for greater market access. Chapter IX provides a comprehensive summary of policy guidelines, issues and challenges that need to be addressed for ongoing SME development, in addition to the framework of M&E exercises.

CHAPTER II
Contributions, challenges and prospects of SMEs

A. What does SME development mean?

Most people have a broad sense of what constitutes an SME, if only a rather stereotypical image of a young and relatively fragile business. There is a temptation to liken SMEs to the student generation of the corporate community, containing considerable growth potential if only their energy and enthusiasm can be harnessed and channelled in the right direction. Whereas some SMEs will go on to great things in later life, many will probably achieve more modest goals and sadly most will come to a premature end for one reason or another (Shane, 2008).

SMEs constitute the vast majority of company registrations in any economy, and there is the expectation that an elite few will make the leap "from garage to great". There is also a tendency to believe that a vibrant SME sector helps promote competition and a culture of entrepreneurship, which are both conducive to economic growth. SMEs, especially new small enterprises, help create dynamic efficiencies, are often seen as being nimble and agile in nature and more willing to innovate than their larger and more well-established peers (ADB, 2009). While some of this is true, the picture of SMEs needs to be more detailed if effective policies are to be created. Many SMEs, labouring under severe financial and human resources constraints, are less knowledgeable than their larger competitors. They are, in fact, less likely to access markets or to innovate (Shane, 2008). The potential exists for SMEs to enhance competition and to create new technologies, but only if the environment in which they operate nurtures such development. In the best-case scenario, some of the more innovative and dynamic SMEs can serve as catalysts in transforming developing economies in various structural ways, including advances up the value chain.

For developing and transitional economies[10] in particular, SME development holds the added allure of being a key component of wider economic development and poverty alleviation, by providing a safety net to society. In developing countries, SMEs can serve as a useful bridgehead between the informal economy of family enterprise and the formalized corporate sector. Some SMEs may also be a source of foreign exchange earnings if they are able to meet the quality and quantity standards required to export their products or services overseas (ESCAP, 2009a). In the case of transitional economies, SME development is broadly synonymous with private sector development, although many state-owned enterprises can also be SMEs. The SME community is seen as a major and sustainable generator of employment and income for citizens (and therefore tax revenues) working outside of the state sector.

In the field of SME development, policymakers in Asia and the Pacific face the following challenges:

(a) Scattered targets leading to high transaction costs;
(b) Lack of economies of scale;
(c) Limited public resources;
(d) Limited understanding about the targets, i.e., SMEs;
(e) Limited communication channels; and
(f) Limited knowledge and skills.

The objectives of policymaking include:

(a) Increase the number of start-ups;
(b) Increase their survival rate;
(c) Encourage incorporation or formalization;
(d) Foster SME graduates (to be large enterprises);
(e) Facilitate the smooth exit of failed firms, with leniency for bankruptcy;
(f) Enhance access to markets (e.g., increased exports and exporting to wider markets); and
(g) Sustainable and inclusive enterprise development (e.g., environment, gender, youth and minorities).

B. Definition of SMEs

Definitions of what constitutes an SME vary quite widely from country to country and even within single countries, depending on the business sector concerned – e.g., agriculture, natural resources, manufacturing, services and retailing (ESCAP, 2009a). There is no universal determinant of or criterion for an SME. Much depends on the character of the respective host country, and the profile of its own particular corporate sector, from which a relative measure of an SME is then typically made, sometimes on a rather arbitrary basis.

The form of ownership profile, type of legal entity or general provenance of the company is typically deemed irrelevant when creating the definition. While an SME is often imagined as a locally-owned and privately-held business, there is no reason why it cannot be a state-owned or foreign-invested enterprise. Some countries will distinguish between a microenterprise and a small enterprise, while others – by not setting a limit for SME size – effectively include micro-enterprises within their SME umbrella definition. The above notwithstanding, most SME definitions pertain to businesses that are formal in nature and have been registered in some manner, and exclude small-scale, informal family enterprises (ESCAP, 2009b).

According to a World Bank study, more than 60 definitions of SMEs are used in 75 countries (Indian Institute of Foreign Trade, 2011). Some countries have used the number of employees as the sole criteria for determining whether a business is an

---

[10] Those countries typically undertake all or some of development strategies based on: (a) primary sector (e.g., agribusiness); (b) natural endowment; (c) exports and FDI promotion; and (e) process improvement.

SME or not. Other countries use this same criterion, plus an additional one based on either the value of the firm's assets or the size of revenue in local currency. In cases where a currency value is cited (either for assets or revenues) any marked inflation can pose a problem for the SME definition over time. Some countries recognize this issue and occasionally update their criteria for SMEs, but most do not (ESCAP, 2009a). The three main parameters that have been generally applied to define SMEs are: (a) the number of employees; (b) turnover of business; and (c) capital investment.

Table II.1. Indicators used among international, regional and local sources

Indicator	International	Regional	Local
Number of employees	✓✓✓	✓✓✓✓✓✓	✓✓✓✓✓
Annual sales	✓✓		✓✓✓✓
Registered capital		✓	✓
Total assets	✓✓		✓✓
Total credit facilities[11]			✓✓✓✓✓
Qualitative indicators[12]	✓		✓

Source: USAID, 2007.

Table II.1 illustrates the prevalence of indicators according to a United States Agency for International Development (USAID) (2007) booklet on SME definition. While this publication specifically aimed at providing an applicable definition for the Hashemite Kingdom of Jordan, it contains common patterns and lessons that can be extrapolated to other nations and regions. The booklet analyzed the definitions of SMEs according to various sources at the following levels:

(a) International – European Commission, Multi-lateral Investment Guarantee Agency (MIGA)/ International Finance Corporation (IFC) and United Nations Industrial Development Organization (UNIDO);

(b) Regional – based on World Bank data from 118 countries, collected from various local and international organizations, with a specific focus on Jordan's neighbouring nations in order to garner a regional view; and

(c) Local – industrial establishments' definition, BASEL II Agreement, Accredited Entrepreneur Initiative (AE), Business Development Centre, Jordan Enterprise Development Corporation and local commercial banks.

These definitions were then tabulated according to the prevalence of different indicators. The number of employees was by far the most commonly used indicator at all levels. For USAID (2007), the employment threshold is now a mandatory indicator for an enterprise to be defined as an SME, followed by a specific annual sales threshold and a total assets threshold.

Table II.2 summarizes the definitions of SMEs among selected Asia-Pacific and other economies. The number of employees as well as the size of investment is mainly used for such national definitions, while some countries also set separate definitions among different SME segments, such as manufacturing and services. Developing countries in Asia and the Pacific typically define SMEs, including microenterprises, as commercial entities less than 300 employees. Researchers that aim to compare the status of the SME sector across various countries mainly use the number of employees to define SMEs to avoid cumbersome calculations of foreign exchange rates among different currencies (AAMO, 2007).

The definition in each national context facilitates policy interventions, such as the provision of technical assistance, fiscal and financial concessions and other incentives, that target a specific group of enterprises. It also makes the physical identification of SMEs on the micro level possible, encouraging better articulation of the problems and prospects of the sector. It indicates that the more precise the definition is, the more effective will be the crafting of SME policies.[13]

---

[11] Emphasis is placed among local banks on using the "Total Credit Facilities" as an indicator of the size of the enterprise. However, this is not necessarily relevant to size, as a small amount of credit does not necessarily correlate to the size of the enterprise. Furthermore, a medium-sized enterprise could borrow a large amount of funds (USAID, 2007).

[12] For example, managerial experience, specialization level, education of staff, quality of relationship with buyers, form of production etc. (USAID, 2007).

[13] This is a generalization, since definitions of SMEs that are too nuanced will create many small categories and increase the total transaction costs of reaching all of them, thus undermining effective policy.

Table II.2. Definitions of SMEs in Asia and the Pacific and other areas

Country/area	Category of enterprises	Criteria and country's official definition	Measure
Asia and the Pacific			
Australia	Manufacturing	Manufacturing enterprises with fewer than 100 employees	Employment
	Medium	<100 employees	
	Small	<20 employees	
	Services	Non-manufacturing enterprises with fewer than 50 employees	
Brunei Darussalam	SME	<100 employees	Employment

Table II.2. *(continued)*

Country/area	Category of enterprises	Criteria and country's official definition	Measure
China	Manufacturing		Employment and turnover
	Micro	<20 employees and <yuan 3 million	
	Small	20-299 employees and yuan 3-19.99 million	
	Medium	300-1,000 employees and yuan 20-40 million	
	Wholesale		
	Micro	<5 employees and <yuan 10 million	
	Small	5-19 employees and yuan 10-49.9 million	
	Medium	20-200 employees and yuan 50-400 million	
	Retail		
	Micro	<10 and <yuan 4.99 million	
	Small	10-49 employees and yuan 1-4.99 million	
	Medium	50-300 employees and yuan 5-200 million	
Hong Kong, China	SME	<100 employees	Employment
India	Manufacturing		Manufacturing enterprises are defined in terms of investment in plant and machinery
	Micro	≤Rs 2.5 million	
	Small	≤Rs 50 million	
	Medium	≤Rs 100 million	
	Services		Service enterprises are defined in terms of investment in equipment
	Micro	≤Rs 1 million	
	Small	≤Rs 20 million	
	Medium	≤Rs 50 million	
Indonesia	SME	<100 employees	Employment
Japan	Manufacturing	<300 employees or asset capitalization <¥ 100 million	Employment and asset
	Wholesaling	<50 employees or asset capitalization <¥ 30 million	
	Retailing and services	<50 employees or asset capitalization <¥ 10 million yen	
Malaysia	Manufacturing (including agro-based industries and manufacturing related services)		Employment or annual sales turnover
	Micro	<5 employees or <RM 250,000	
	Small	5-50 employees or RM 250,000-RM 10 million	
	Medium	51-150 employees or RM 10-25 million	
	Services (including ICT) and primary agriculture		
	Micro	<5 employees or <RM 200,000	
	Small	5-19 employees or RM 20,000-RM 10 million	
	Medium	20-50 employees or RM 1-RM 5 million	
Republic of Korea	Manufacturing	<300 employees	Employment
	Services	<200 employees	
Singapore	SME	<S$ 100 million annual sales turnover <200 employees	Employment or turnover
Taiwan Province of China	Manufacturing, mining, and construction	Invested capital ≤NT$ 80 million or employees <200	Employment, invested capital, or turnover
	Others	Sales revenue ≤NT$ 120 million or employment <50	
	Micro	Employment <5	
Thailand	Manufacturing and services		Employment and capital
	Small	≤50 employees or capital ≤B 50 million	
	Medium	51-200 employees or capital over B 50 and ≤B 200 million	
	Wholesale		
	Small	≤25 employees or capital ≤B 50 million	
	Medium	26-50 employees or capital over B 50 and ≤B 100 million baht	
	Retail		
	Small	≤15 employees or capital ≤B 30 million	
	Medium	16-30 employees or capital over B 30 and ≤B 60 million	

Table II.2. *(continued)*

Country/area	Category of enterprises	Criteria and country's official definition	Measure
Viet Nam	SME	≤300 employees; capital ≤D 10 billion	Employment and capital
Other states, regions and multilateral agencies			
Asian Development Bank	SME	No definition	None
European Union	Micro	<10 employees; turnover ≤€ 2 million or balance sheet total ≤€ 2 million	Employment and turnover or balance sheet total
	Small	<50 employees; turnover ≤€ 10 million or balance sheet total ≤€ 10 million	
	Medium	<250 employees; turnover ≤€ 50 million or balance sheet total ≤€ 43 million	
United Nations Development Programme (UNDP)	SME	≤200 employees	Employment
United States of America	Micro	<20 employees	Employment
	Small	20-99 employees	
	Medium	100-499 employees	
World Bank	SME	≤300 employees; turnover ≤$ 15 million; assets ≤$ 15 million	Employment, turnover, and asset

Sources: Agency for SME Development, 2011; *China Briefing,* 2011; European Union, 2003; Gibson and van der Vaart, 2008; M&SSE, 2011; Office of SME Promotion. 2011; Small Industries Development Bank of India, 2010; Small and Medium Enterprise Administration, 2011; and the Standards, Productivity and Innovation Board of Singapore (SPRING), 2011a.

C. Typology of SMEs

As reviewed in the above section, the most common typology of SMEs is based on their line of business, such as mining, manufacturing and services as well as wholesale and retail businesses. The SME definitions of some economies reflect this, such as India, Japan, Malaysia and Taiwan Province of China (table II.1). Table II.3 and figure II.1 present snapshots of SMEs in various sectors in Japan and Thailand, in terms of start-up composition, numbers and net incomes. It is noteworthy that SMEs in the service sector, such as retailers, restaurants and health care, are dominant in both countries. Manufacturing-focused SMEs also play a major role in Thailand and show a higher profit margin in Japan than the service sector.

In almost all of the countries in Asia and the Pacific, two distinguishing types of enterprises exist in the SME sector, i.e., registered enterprises and unregistered enterprises. According to IFC (2010), lower levels of economic development correlate with higher levels of informality.[14] Figure II.2 illustrates the shifts in SME and informal sector contributions to GDP as income levels change. A gradual increase in SME contributions and decrease in informality is seen as the income level increases. Therefore, it can be deduced that higher levels of formality relate to greater efficiency and higher rates of economic growth (IFC, 2010).

The unregistered enterprises in the informal sector dominate in most of the less developed economies in Asia and the Pacific. A study by AAMO (2007) found that in Asia and the Pacific, proprietary ownerships or closely-held partnerships comprised approximately 75 per cent of enterprises, while 22 per cent were private limited enterprises and only

Table II.3. Start-ups by sector in Japan and SMEs by sector in Thailand

(Unit: Per cent)

Sector	Start-ups by sector Japan (2009)	SMEs by sector Thailand (2010)
Services	29.3	8.3
Wholesale and retailing	16.5	49.7
Restaurants and hotels	13.9	9.3
Medical services and health care	14.8	0.3
Construction	9.5	3.5
Manufacturing	6.2	17.9
Transport and storage	3.6	3.9
Education	1.3	0.1
Others	5.1	7.1
Total	100.0	100.0

Sources: Japan Finance Corporation, 2009; and Office of SME Promotion, 2011.

---

[14] The informal sector is a particular part of an economy that is typically characterized by small-scale and labour-intensive operations that offer poor working conditions and low wages. Demographic data for the informal sector, such as employers and type of employment, are particularly difficult to acquire in this region, as businesses in the informal sector are not usually registered in any form for legal purposes. As a rare exception, the ILO database shows that 72.1 per cent of the Thai workforce and 55.7 per cent of the Indian workforce were in the informal sector in 2002 and 2000, respectively, indicating the informal sector's significant role in some Asia-Pacific countries (ILO, 2009). There is a need for public incentives to make businesses formal to reduce the informal sector. Such incentives may include enhanced access to finance, grants, training, networking and information through formalization.

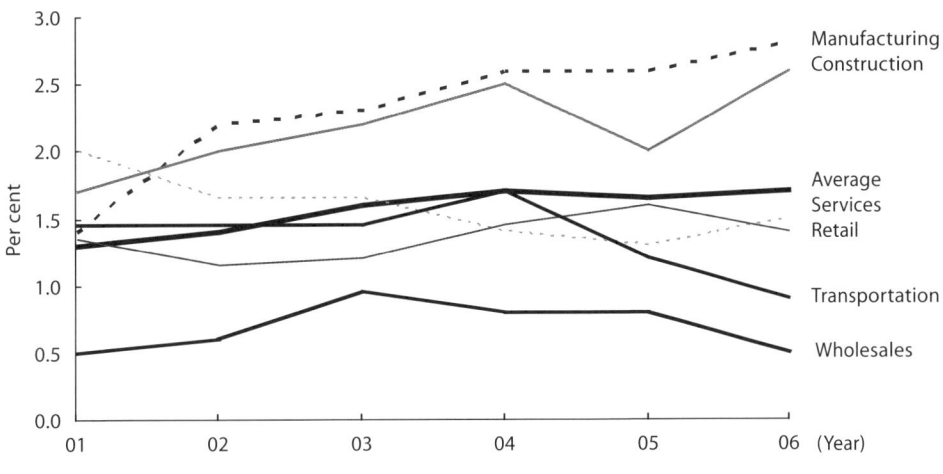

Figure II.1. SMEs' net income in Japan

Source: National Life Finance Corporation (2007).

Figure II.2. GDP contribution of the SME and informal sector, based on income levels*

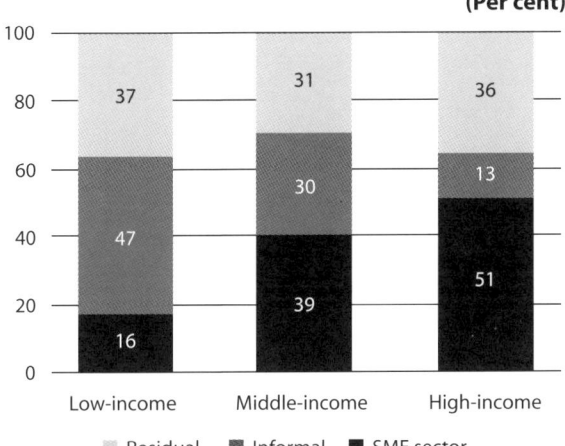

Source: Ayyagari, Beck and Demirgüç-Kunt, 2003.
Note: "Residual" includes large enterprises and public sector.

3 per cent were limited enterprises.[15] Generally, rigid mindsets, lukewarm approaches to change and fear are among the main factors contributing to the continuance of proprietary patterns of ownership, thus hindering the process of their graduation to the formal sector. There has been a perceptible change in this pattern in recent years, as informal enterprises now prefer to be formalized as corporate entities in order to access additional financial sources. This trend of ownership from a proprietorship/partnership to a corporation has been observed in many countries of the Asia-Pacific region (AAMO, 2007).

The activeness of an enterprise or entrepreneur also varies among SMEs; these differences are important as they require different support. According to the Japan Small Business Research Institute (JSBRI) (2011), "passive" entrepreneurs start businesses for negative reasons such as just to make a living whereas "active" entrepreneurs start a business to achieve some personal goals, such as to own an enterprise, increase their income, have flexible working hours or contribute to society. In Japan, survey data indicate that 80 per cent of entrepreneurs can be classified as active and only 20 per cent as passive (JSBRI, 2011). Policy interventions would be different where entrepreneurs feel compelled to establish SMEs.

Enterprises can also be divided into the categories of "lifestyle" and "growth-oriented", each of which has differing demands (ADB, 2006). For example, when it comes to investment, investors will generally exit growth-oriented businesses through third-party purchase of shares, sale of entire company or listing on stock exchanges. In contrast, lifestyle businesses remain as proprietorships or are usually exited through repurchases of shares by the SME or owner/managers. Lifestyle businesses generally try to minimize retained earnings and suppress the value of their equity whereas growth-oriented businesses will aim to increase their share value (ADB, 2006).[16]

Another typology involves the life of an SME. Firms go through stages much like biological organisms – start-up, growth, maturity and exit (Chandler, 1961; and Scott, 1971). At each stage, an SME requires different inputs or different types of the same input. For example, an SME may only need a small loan at inception but may require equity for financing its growth. At the same time, newly-born SMEs usually experience the most vulnerable time at start-up, mainly due to the lack of a business plan and effective marketing that result in weak customer demand, before entering into the growth stages. Policymakers need to understand these nuances if they expect to serve the SME sector well. Making seed capital available for start-ups is a different policy focus

---

[15] An enterprise is a legally-recognized organizational entity that provides goods and services to consumers, and the way it is formed – proprietary owned, private limited or limited – are just different ways that a company chooses to distribute its stocks/shares. Proprietary-owned enterprises are owned and operated by a single individual with no distinction between the owner and the business. Private limited enterprises have at least one shareholder with a limited number of shares, but are usually owned and operated by a number of individuals who share the financial responsibilities; additionally, shares are not offered to the public. Limited enterprises are essentially the same as a private limited enterprise, with the only difference being that the shares may be offered to the public.

[16] Discussions here are very much in line with the concepts of entrepreneurship. For example, GEM uses the designations of "necessity" versus "opportunity" entrepreneurship. Growth orientation is also a key characteristic of entrepreneurship. See further discussion in chapter IV.

from developing equity capital markets; training for business plan development is also different from MBA training for TNC managers. Figure II.3 presents a simplified SME life cycle that explains an SME's growth, maturity and decline over time.

When government officials craft policies, they should remember that SMEs are heterogeneous and therefore have different needs, depending on their stage in the corporate life cycle, the degree of economic development of the country in which they are based etc. While it is impossible to customize policies for each individual SME, policies should be flexible enough to accommodate broad categories of needs. In addition, SME policies require constant updating as market conditions and the country's economy change.

Table II.4 assists in the effort to consider relevant policies for SMEs. It offers various categories influencing SME foundation, survival and growth. It may be useful for policymakers to organize SMEs in other ways, but these categories are the most relevant. The table specifically explains the category-based system where several indicators of business could be considered for SME development policies. This system might be used to assist policymaking for taxation and market orientationa and access (cf., IFC, 2007).[17] Each SME unit should fall in a particular grid based on the categories explained below, which in turn provides policymakers guidance and flexibility while drafting policies. For example, the profitability of an SME can be influenced by policies. Appropriate measures from policymakers may help the company, which is innovative but is domestic market-oriented, to enter into foreign markets.

The income divisions are the World Bank classifications using 2010 per-capita GNI according to the Atlas method (World Bank, undated). Middle income can be divided further into lower-middle income ($ 1,006 to $ 3,975) and upper-middle income ($ 3,976 to $ 12,275). Low income nations typically have a preponderance of the labour force in agriculture and light manufacturing, whereas middle-income nations are in various stages of industrialization. High income economies have a well-developed service sector and knowledge-intensive, high value-added industries. Given these differences, policymakers have to apply local knowledge;

---

[17] Table AIII.2 in annex III.2 presents the list of categories for SME taxation.

Figure II.3. Simplified SME life cycle

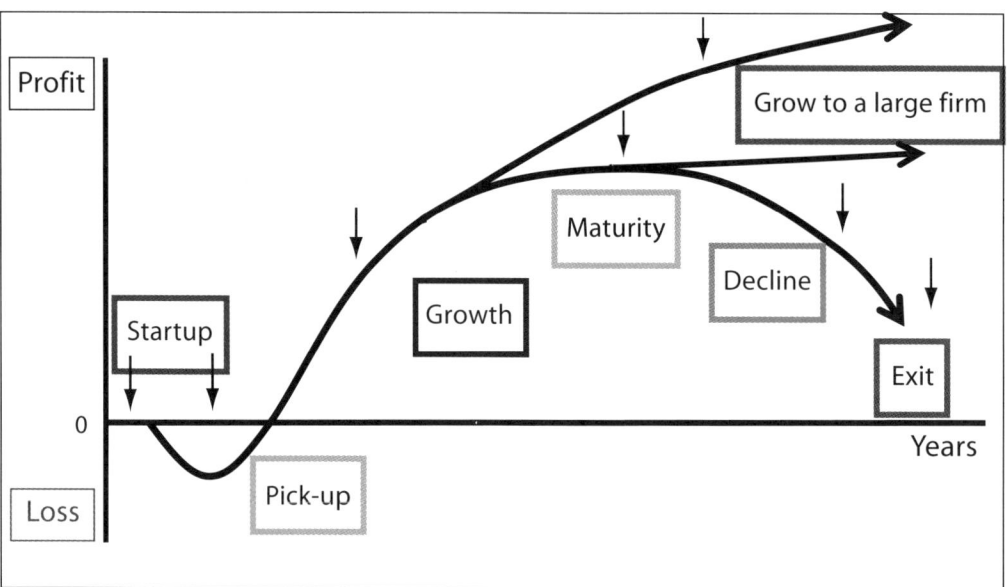

Source: Authors' compilation.
Note: The arrows indicate that different types of support are needed at the different life stages.

Table II.4. Categories for SME typology

Topic	Category 1	Category 2	Category 3 (if applicable)
Stage of economic development[18]	Low income, $ 1,005 or less	Middle income, $ 1,006 to $ 12,275	High income, $ 12,276 or more
Market orientation	Domestic	Gradual global	Born global
Pace of innovation	Incremental	Radical	
Use of technology	Isolated	Connected	
Corporate life stage	Nascent (<2 years)	Young (2-5 years)	Mature (5+ years)

Source: Authors' compilation.

---

[18] Follows the World Bank (undated) country classification based on income per capita.

what may be useful for the Lao People's Democratic Republic may not be for Japan, and vice versa.

Market orientation is another facet of SME typology. Market orientation refers to a firm's assessment of who its customers are and how to meet their needs (Kohl and Jaworski, 1990; and Amario, Ruiz and Amario, 2008). Most SMEs are domestic; they exist only to satisfy their home market. This designation could encompass SMEs focusing on local, provincial or national markets. The "gradual global" SME accesses foreign markets, but typically will only export; however, some may also invest over time as they grow and accumulate knowledge of the foreign market (Johansen and Vahlne, 1977). The "born-global" firm sees the world as its market from inception; it does not internationalize operations incrementally (Oviatt and McDougall, 1994). These SMEs are generally in the high-tech sector and have owners with at least a university education. They use the Internet to satisfy global demand for their product or service. Policymakers should consider the fact that the first type will need the most basic kind of assistance to exploit local markets while the second and third categories require more specialized knowledge, such as navigating customs regulations.

The pace of innovation may also differ among SMEs. Innovations can be considered along a continuum from incremental to radical (Utterback and Abernathy, 1975; and Tushman and Anderson, 1986). The incremental type tend not to disturb markets and involve some minor form of product or service differentiation, e.g., opening a new restaurant. The radical type have disequilibrating effects on markets and perhaps on society (Schumpeter, 1934), e.g., development of the MacIntosh personal computer by Steve Jobs. By their nature, radical innovations tend to be rare and incremental innovations more common. Policies to encourage and support radical innovations are most important, since the SMEs driving them will create more wealth and jobs for the economy. However, policymakers must also serve the great mass of SMEs that only engage in incremental innovation.

Another concept is use of technology (particularly ICT) (see box II.1) such as mobile devices and the Internet. Most SMEs tend to be isolated in the developing countries of the region; they often have limited access to the web and they transact business directly, both with customers and with suppliers. On the other hand, a minority of sophisticated SMEs can handle their affairs remotely and electronically, e.g., receiving orders from customers and placing orders with suppliers on the Internet, managing their finances with wireless banking etc. It encourages policymakers to persuade more SMEs to become connected, as this is essential in a fiercely competitive global economy.

One would expect to find more SMEs engaged in radical innovation in the high-income countries, and that these SMEs are connected and serving global markets.[19] Figure II.4 is a guide to thinking about heterogeneity among SMEs. Policymakers must always apply local knowledge to these rubrics.

Figure II.4. SME typology by market and technology

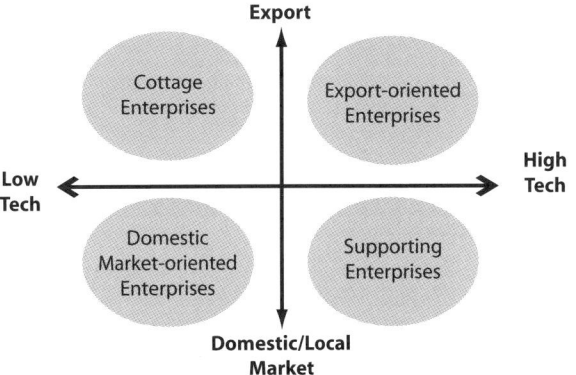

Source: Uchikawa and Keola, 2009.

---

[19] For example, wages and labour productivity of small enterprises in the Republic of Korea are, on average, at least three times higher than those of large enterprises in many other developing Asia-Pacific economies (ADB, 2009).

Box II.1. SME typology by market orientation and use of technology

The typology of SMEs can also be described in terms of both their market orientation (domestic or export; see chapter VIII for a more detailed discussion on this aspect) and the use of technologies they use (also see chapter VII). Based on two criteria, SMEs could be categorized into four groups: (a) supporting industry (see note 1); (b) export-oriented enterprises; (c) domestic market-oriented enterprises; and (d) cottage enterprises (see note 2).

Figure II.4 illustrates these four SME categories. In many developing countries in Asia and the Pacific, SMEs typically use low levels of technology and are categorized as domestic market-oriented SMEs and cottage enterprises that dominate the private sector. Some of the smaller enterprises, however, do play an important role in exporting in some economies and industries (ADB, 2009). For example, there is generally a large technological gap between domestic market-oriented SMEs and SMEs in the supporting industry that are required to supply parts and components with consistent quality and on schedule to industrial buyers. Domestic market-oriented SMEs often do not have adequate quality control and production capability to meet industrial buyers' stringent requirements.

Although it is not easy for domestic market-oriented SMEs to graduate to the supporting industry group, due to required levels of technology and management skills, some have accomplished such a shift. SME development policies could promote such transformations through capacity-building (Uchikawa and Keola, 2009).

Source: Modified from Uchikawa and Keola, 2009.
Notes:
1. Supporting industry is defined as a group of SMEs having domestic forward linkages with the manufacturing sector, including small and medium-sized transport and storage firms and wholesalers.
2. Although a number of cottage enterprises are active in exporting, the majority of them are not export-oriented due to their low supply capacity.

> **Box II.2. Start-up profiles in Japan**
>
> The National Life Finance Corporation of Japan (2008) conducted a survey of 918 enterprises to which it had provided loans between April and September 2006; all the enterprises were in their first or second year of operation. The following results were obtained:
>
> Entrepreneurs:
> - (a) Average age was 41.4 years old;
> - (b) A total of 84.5 per cent were men and 15.5 per cent were women; and
> - (c) A total of 33.1 per cent held a college degree or higher.
>
> Enterprises:
> - (a) An average of 3.9 employees;
> - (b) Start-up funds, $ 100,000
>   - (i) Own capital – 35 per cent;
>   - (ii) Support from family, relatives and friends – 15 per cent; and
>   - (iii) Public grants and commercial loans, with collateral and/or partially covered by public loan guarantee schemes – 50 per cent.
> - (c) A total of 60 per cent of start-ups achieved break-even status within 15 months.

D. Common characteristics of SMEs

Unlike large enterprises, SMEs are more flexible and able to adapt to changing business environments. This agility is present in almost every facet of their business operations. In general, SMEs are able to avoid the rigidity and inertia common to established firms in their planning and strategy. They are an important source of innovation, both in products and in processes.[20] If they are not actively innovating, SMEs are more willing to adopt the best practices of others because their own routines are malleable. Their smaller size enables the management of human resources to be more informal than in larger companies. This allows flexibility in matching personnel to the myriad problems that SMEs face. Despite regional and country variations, SMEs have a range of common characteristics (AAMO, 2007; JSBRI, 2011; and Shane, 2008):

(a) Born out of individual initiatives, knowledge and skills – SME start-ups tend to evolve from a single entrepreneur or a small group of entrepreneurs – in many cases, leveraging a unique skill set;

(b) Greater operational flexibility – the direct involvement of owner(s), coupled with flat organizational structures, ensure that there is greater operational flexibility. As a result, decision-making is faster;

(c) Low cost of production – SMEs have lower overheads. This translates into lower production costs;

(d) Specialization in niche markets – successful SMEs concentrate on small but profitable markets in order to avoid battles with large enterprises as well as to ensure effective investment and utilization of their resources and expertise;

(e) A high propensity to adopt technology – SMEs show a propensity for adopting and internalizing new technology when given the proper incentives and learning;

(f) A high capacity to innovate – SMEs' capacity for innovation, improvisation and reverse engineering is extensive if the initial support is there;

(g) High employment orientation – SMEs are usually the prime drivers of job creation, in some cases creating up to 80-90 per cent of the total jobs in a country. SMEs tend to be labour-intensive and are able to generate more jobs for every unit of investment, compared with their larger counterparts;

(h) Utilization of locally available human and material resources – SMEs mostly utilize skills, manpower and resources available locally. This brings prosperity to the area where they operate; and

(i) Reduction of geographical imbalances – unlike large enterprises, SMEs can grow in developed and underdeveloped areas. This reduces geographical imbalances.

However, these characteristics of SMEs also have a downside. SMEs' small operational size and lack of resources (e.g., capital and human), skill/knowledge and network connections are a common feature. SMEs typically suffer from:

(a) Low bargaining power, both for sales and for procurement (i.e., low prices and high costs, leading to low income and less profit);

(b) Weak market access;

(c) Low technology adaptation;

(d) Lack of brand development;

(e) High debt structure;

(f) Weak management with less training;

(g) Weak human resource base with a low level of compensation; and

(h) Inadequate institutional support.

E. Contribution by SMEs

SMEs constitute an important segment of Asia-Pacific economies, and have made a laudable contribution to the economic development of various countries over the years. The role of SMEs is mainly to: (a) create employment; (b) nurture entrepreneurship, including that of women and youth; and (c) increase outputs with value-added. Thus, the development of SMEs contributes to increased GDP and poverty alleviation (ESCAP, 2009b).

In developing as well as developed economies, including those in the Asia-Pacific region, it is clear that SMEs dominate the classification for enterprises, in most cases constituting more than 99 per cent of all enterprises. Figure II.5 illustrates the constitution of the business environment in an emerging

---

[20] Innovation as a competitive advantage for SMEs naturally bolsters the national competitive advantage. For policymakers, the two greatest benefits of SME development for a country as a whole are innovation and job creation. Schumpeter (1942) viewed entrepreneurs as the catalyst for his famous "perennial gale of creative destruction" that would doom stodgy businesses but lead to technological and material advancement for society.

Figure II.5. Constitution of enterprises by size

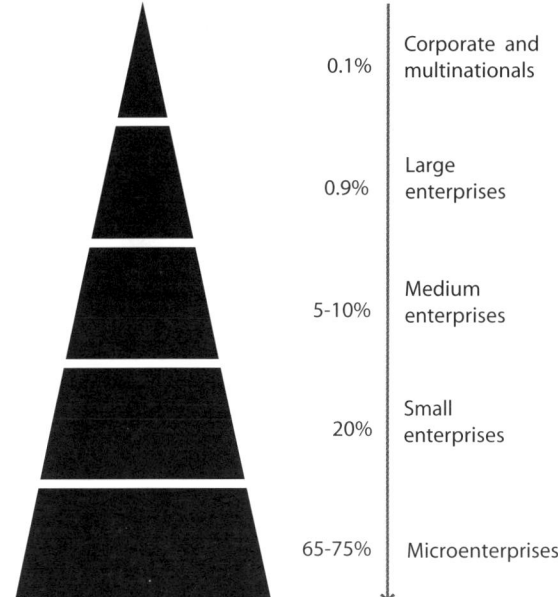

Source: IFC, 2009.
Note: Percentages represent the number of companies.

economy. The majority of firms are microenterprises and the next biggest sector is the SMEs. It is noteworthy that large enterprises and corporate multinationals typically only constitute a very minor percentage of the business environment.

SMEs generally employ 60 per cent or more of the enterprise workforce (table II.5) and account for a significant share of job creation. Small enterprises and non-manufacturing enterprises exhibit higher net job creation rates compared with large enterprises (ADB, 2009).[21]

Exporting is one of the major contributions made by SMEs to the national economy (as well as value-added). This consists of not only high export volumes but also diversified exports and technology and skill development, which are fostered through dealing directly with competitive, heterogeneous foreign markets. Export operations expand the base of domestic enterprises, which gain the ability to compete globally; thus, national competitiveness is enhanced alongside income generation. The share of SMEs'

---

[21] Large enterprises tend to move towards capital-intensive production facilities (e.g., assembly automation), with reduced dependency on labour but needing a skilled workforce.

Table II.5. Contribution of SMEs to exports/enterprises/workforce in selected economies of the world, and Asia and the Pacific, various years during 2001-2009

Region/country/area	Export share in GDP (1)	SME share in exports (2)	SME share of total enterprises (3)	SME share of total workforce (4)
Developed countries				
France	23.0	42.4	99.8	61.4
Germany	41.0	55.9	99.7	79.0
Japan	13.0	53.8*	99.7	70.2
Spain	23.0	68.5*	99.9	78.7
United Kingdom	28.0	45.9*	99.6	54.0
United States	11.0	22.2	99.9	55.8
European Union	n.a.	43.4	99.8	67.4
Asia and the Pacific				
China	27.0	69.2	99.0	74.5
India	20.0	40.0	n.a.	n.a.
Indonesia	24.0	20.0	99.9	99.6
Malaysia	96.0	19.0	99.2	59.0
Pakistan	13.0	30.0	97.9	78.5
Republic of Korea	50.0	39.0	99.9	87.7
Russian Federation	28.0	54.0**	97.6	60.9
Singapore	221.0	16.0	91.5	51.8
Taiwan Province of China	n.a.	17.0	97.8	77.2
Thailand	57.5	30.6	99.6	69.0
Viet Nam	68.0	20.0	99.9	77.3
Micronesia (Federated States of)	n.a.	n.a.	>90.0	20.0

Sources: World Bank, 2011a. Columns (2)-(4): ADB, 2001; Bank of Negara, 2005; European Commission, 2005 and 2009a; General Statistics Office of Viet Nam, 2011; Korean National Statistical Office, 2009; National SME Development Council of Malaysia, 2010; Organisation for Economic Co-operation and Development (OECD), 2005a and 2011; Office of SME Promotion of Thailand, 2011; Small and Medium Enterprise Administration, 2010; Tambunan, 2006 and 2009; USAID, 2004; and United States International Trade Commission, 2010.
* Value-added.
** Share of total sales revenue.

contribution to exports varies widely among countries in the Asia-Pacific region, ranging from 19.0 per cent in Malaysia to 69.2 per cent in China (table II.5). The varying ability of SMEs to export is an indication of how SMEs can or cannot compete in regional and global markets, where specific support measures may be needed to improve performance (UNCTAD, 2002).[22] SMEs' contribution to exports is generally higher in developed economies, such as those in the European Union, than in the developing economies of Asia and the Pacific.[23]

In summary, the contribution of SMEs is vital to the well-being of various countries in the region as they:

(a) Constitute over 99 per cent of all enterprises;
(b) Provide over 60 per cent of the private sector jobs; and
(c) Share more than 20-30 per cent of direct and indirect exports.

However, SMEs are still underdeveloped in many countries in Asia and the Pacific, although they have contributed to the economic development of the region. In particular, the SME sector remains relatively weak in Asia-Pacific developing countries, especially in least developed countries (LDCs) – even though the importance of SMEs in the national economy is well-recognized in terms of their substantial shares in the number of enterprises and their contribution to employment, income and exports.

Figure II.6 shows that developed countries possess a large number of SMEs, including microenterprises, with 63 enterprises per 1,000 people for developed countries in the Asia-Pacific region in 2001-2006. In contrast, the Asia-Pacific region's developing countries had only 27 enterprises and least developed countries only registered a paltry nine enterprises per 1,000 people. In addition, many enterprises in the region are in the informal sector, which governments neither tax nor monitor (ESCAP, 2009b). In countries with poor business environments, SMEs choose to remain informal due to the costs and procedural burden of joining the formal sector (World Business Council for Sustainable Development, 2007).

Figure II.6. Number of SMEs per 1,000 people, 2001-2006

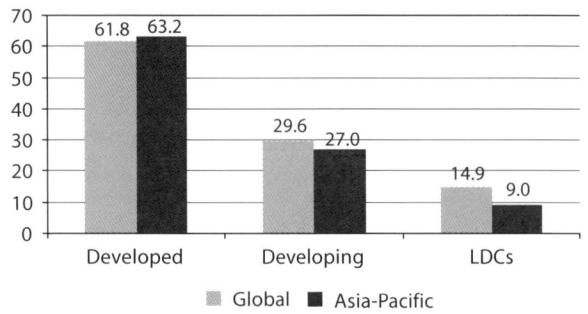

Source: ESCAP, 2009b.

F. Start-up, growth, maturity and exit[24]

SME development pertains to four stages in the SME 'life cycle': start-up, growth, maturity and exit. Some SMEs may encounter just one or two of these stages (i.e., start-up and exit), while others may experience all four stages (see figure II.3).

---

[22] This point may need to be revisited based on the fact that definitions of what constitutes a SME vary quite widely from country to country in Asia and the Pacific, and even within single countries. An extreme example is China, which defines medium-sized enterprises as those with less than 1,000 employees, while in Malaysia medium-sized enterprises are those with 150 or less employees. Developing economies in Asia and the Pacific typically define SMEs, including microenterprises, as commercial entities with less than 300 employees.

[23] For developed economies, exports are not relatively large components of GDP, while developing economies in Asia and the Pacific are reliant on exports as a significant source for GDP growth (e.g., Malaysia and Thailand) in line with their export-oriented developmental strategies. Generally speaking, a trend can be seen in that as nations rise to high-income status, their reliance on exports as a driving force of GDP growth is diminished – most likely the result of strong domestic demand growth. Additionally, SMEs appear to be the driving source of exports in developed countries, compared to developing countries (at least in the Asia-Pacific region).

[24] This section was extracted from ESCAP, 2009, unless otherwise stated.

Box II.3. Contributions by SMEs in Japan

In Japan SMEs make up 99.7 per cent of enterprises, more than two-thirds of employment and close to 50 per cent of manufacturing value-added, as shown in the pie charts.

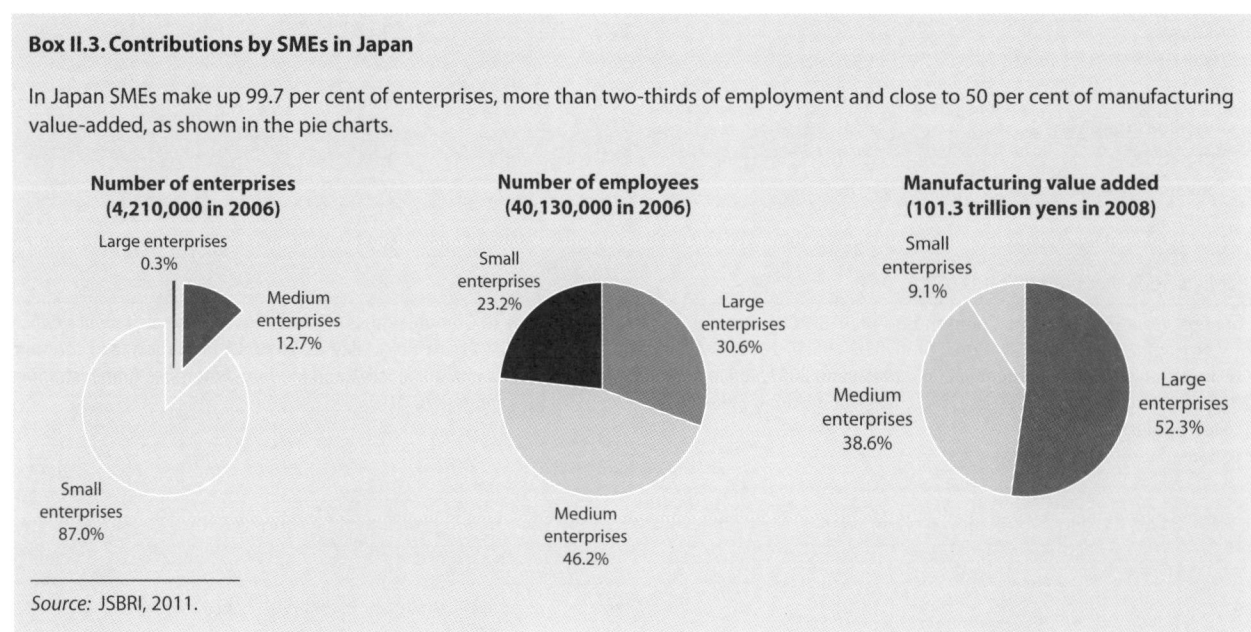

Source: JSBRI, 2011.

The first critical stage of an SME's development is that of "start-up", or market entry. This entails all the steps and procedures for starting a business, in compliance with the laws and regulations of the host country. There are typically two important factors in this regard: (a) the time it takes to start a business; and (b) the cost of doing so. If the time is too long or the costs are too high, this will serve as a major barrier for many potential new businesses as well as a potentially major loss for the economy, in terms of jobs foregone, income not generated etc. These are certainly not the only potential inhibitors to SME start-up rates. For example, if an entrepreneur is unable to gain access to the capital needed to finance the planned business venture, he/she may opt not to proceed. Some observers have argued that the start-up phase for an SME usually lasts around 3.5 years (or 42 months). If an SME passes that landmark date, then it has graduated beyond the critical period when most young companies tend to fail, and therefore can be regarded as a potentially sustainable business.

Once an SME has successfully entered the market and commenced operations, a number of other factors will be critical to its subsequent performance. These factors first determine whether it can sustain its business model beyond the short term, and then dictate whether it will grow to prosper as a competitive entity or simply be a survivor reaching the mature stage. This entails interplay between the SME itself and its wider enabling environment. In Japan, for example, key inputs include (but are not limited to) access to: (a) quality human capital; (b) a range of appropriate financial resources; (c) an adequate customer base; (d) accurate and timely market information and an ability to analyse that information in a meaningful way; (e) knowledge and technology; and (f) capable suppliers (JSBRI, 2011). The more conducive the enabling environment, the more likely an SME will thrive and not just survive.

Turning now to exits by SMEs, two scenarios need to be considered. The first is that an SME develops into a large enterprise, and therefore graduates beyond the SME sector.

For all concerned, this is perhaps the most welcomed outcome for an SME. Needless to say, not every SME goes through this growth path, as the failure rate of new businesses is considerably high. The second is the demise and closure of an SME, for whatever reason.[25] This is an unfortunate outcome, but it should not be dismissed as a policy irrelevance. It is inevitable that not all SMEs will be successful. Some will have an early demise, while others may close after considerable time. In general, at least one-third of all new companies around the world close within two years of commencing operations.[26] In Canada, for example, two-thirds of new businesses discontinue within five years (Ibrahim and Soufani, 2002). In New Zealand, enterprises' four-year survival rates are 50 per cent and 40 per cent in manufacturing and services sectors, respectively (OECD, 2011). The survival rate for small businesses, such as restaurants and retailers, is even lower at around 20 to 30 per cent in the first year, and only about half of those who survive the first year will remain in business during the following five years (Holland, 1998). New businesses face a particularly difficult time during their start-up period. According to the Japan Finance Corporation (JFC) (2009), in Japan, approximately 44 per cent of new companies are still losing money after being open for one year.

Considerable differences in entry and exit rates are also observed across industrial sectors. In the United Kingdom for example, while approximately one-third of enterprises close within three years, such sectors as hotels and restaurants, mining and utilities, transport and communications and wholesale and retailing experience higher exit rates than other sectors (Department for Business Innovation and Skills, United Kingdom, 2007). Figure II.7 highlights sectoral differences in Japan, which has experienced a large number

---

[25] As Headd (2003) noted, not all SME closures stem from business failure; some are the consequence of an orderly exit by the owner(s).
[26] Authors' calculation, based on the data of 17 OECD member and non-member countries obtained from the OECD Structural and Demographic Business Statistics Business Demography Indicators at http://stats.oecd.org/Index.aspx?DataSetCode=SDBS_BDI.

Figure II.7. Entry and exit rates, by industry, in Japan, 2004-2006

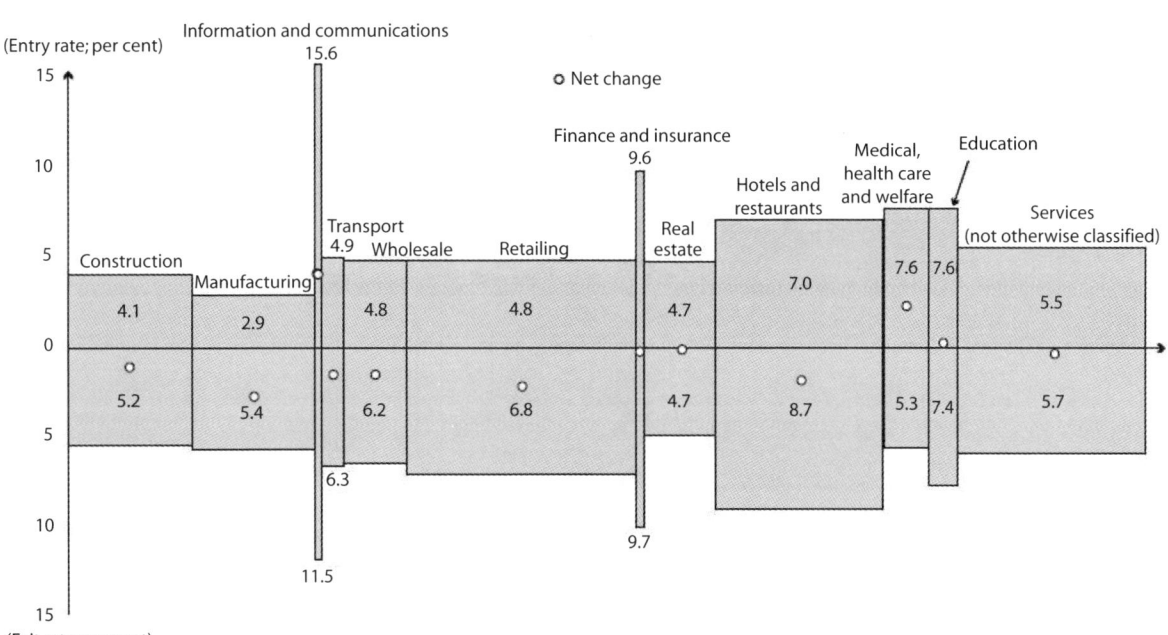

Source: JSBRI, 2011.
Note: The horizontal axis indicates the proportion of all enterprises in the beginning of 2004.

of entries in the information and communication sector as well as the medical, health care and wealth sector, exceeding their exit rates. The finance and insurance, hospitality and education sectors have attained both high entry rates and high exit rates (JSBRI, 2011).

Figure II.8 highlight the differences in entry and exit rates as well as survival rates of new businesses in Japan and the United States. A growing economy experiences more entries than exits, which is a useful indicator for policymaking and adjustment.[27] Entry and exit rates of the United States are both twice as much as those of Japan, strongly supporting a commonly shared belief about the dynamism of the American economy. As a result of these high entry and exit rates, one quarter of start-ups close within the first year of business and more than 70 per cent of start-ups close within 10 years in the United States (Shane, 2008). In contrast, less than 10 per cent of new businesses close within two years in Japan while approximately 70 per cent of new enterprises are still in business after 10 years.

The large differences between Japan and the United States in entry and exit of enterprises as well as enterprise survival could be, at least partially, explained by their different national cultures and attitudes toward entrepreneurship. Figure II.9 indicates that the Japanese appreciate steadiness and stability more than Americans. Compared with Americans, fewer Japanese consider themselves to have the opportunities, abilities or desire to pursue an entrepreneurial career, as they fear the consequences of failure. Cultural and attitudinal aspects can negatively (or positively) affect national entrepreneurship activities.

---

[27] In Thailand, the Office of SME Promotion (2010a) statistics show that while 63,000 enterprises were closed down in 2009, only 41,000 enterprises were newly founded, implying the adverse impact of the global economic crisis as well as the informal sector's considerable role within the country.

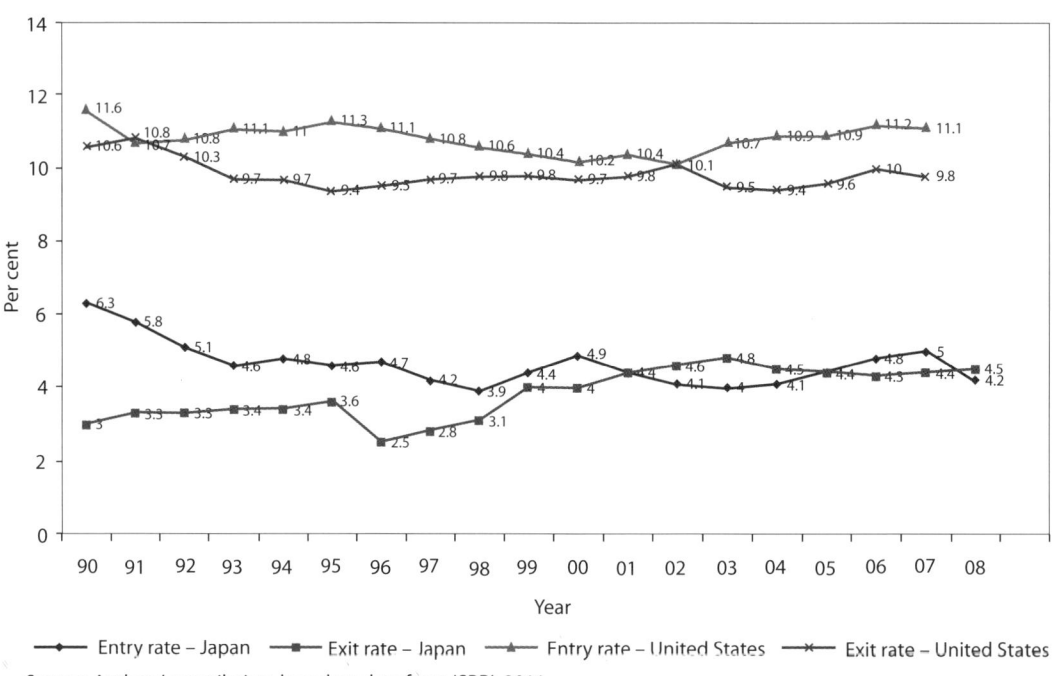

Figure II.8. Comparison of entry and exit rates between Japan and the United States, 1990-2009

Source: Authors' compilation, based on data from JSBRI, 2011.

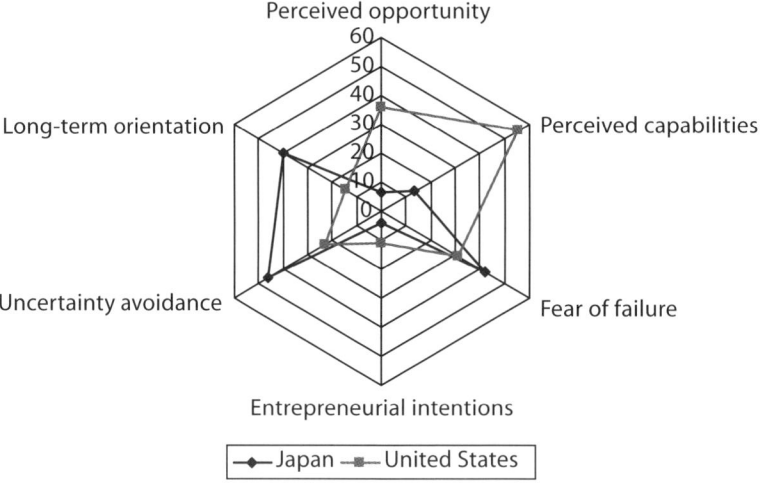

Figure II.9. National culture and entrepreneurship, Japan and the United States

Sources: GEM, 2011 and Hofstede, 1991.

Policymakers naturally want firms to stay in business and provide jobs; however, not all businesses can be saved. Most attention is typically paid by policymakers to the first stage – start-up or market entry – while relatively less effort is expended on the latter stages – exit or closure – for understandable reasons (Dannreuther, 2007). As a result, while countries are often quite zealous in recording and reporting company start-ups, they tend to be much less focused on recording company closures, particularly in Asia-Pacific developing countries.[28] There is little utility in allocating resources to prolong the life of a terminally-ill SME. It is better to allow failing SMEs to exit instead of trying to prop them up with scarce resources that can be used more efficiently elsewhere in the economy. Smooth bankruptcy procedures for troubled firms, allowing for exit with minimal cost, are an important feature of the SME development landscape. The important issue for policymakers is to ensure that their closure does not become a constraint on the emergence of new SMEs, and hopefully some of the lessons learnt are disseminated to the collective awareness of the local business community.

This asymmetry in the focus of most SME development can be misguided in some cases. For example, too much emphasis on removing market entry obstacles alone can, over time, result in diminishing returns for policymakers and development partners. Rather, there needs to be a balanced portfolio of interventions that can assist SMEs overcome obstacles throughout their development trajectory. Another inhibitor can also be found at the opposite end of the SME "life cycle" – exit or closure. If the regulations pertaining to shutting down a business or to bankruptcy are too onerous, then an entrepreneur may be unwilling to take the risk of establishing an SME. Given the risks that accompany every new business venture, this can be a serious factor in reducing start-up rates.

G. Microenterprises

Microenterprises are a subcategory of small enterprises and typically classified based on the number of employees, annual turnover and asset size.[29] A combined and comprehensive definition of a microenterprise is "a very small enterprise that is typically owner-operated and participated by marginalized segments, that sells a product or service through entrepreneurial methodologies and utilizing diverse organizational forms" (Munoz, 2010).

As can be seen from table II.6, the term microenterprise is perceived and utilized in different ways across countries and in some cases by sector. These differences may generate inaccuracy in the vertical comparison of microenterprises among these five countries (as well as others). However, some common points can be made, including: (a) microenterprises comprise the majority of all enterprises and are the main constituents of SMEs; and (b) apart from for Viet Nam and, to a lesser extent, Malaysia, the national percentage of microenterprises are comparable.

In more advanced industrial economies (Japan and the Republic of Korea), there are greater numbers of enterprises, with microenterprises comprising the majority, at 87.0 per cent and 87.9 per cent, respectively, than those seen in developing economies (except the Philippines). Specifically, Viet Nam and Malaysia both have lower numbers of microenterprises, i.e., 55.9 and 78.7 per cent, respectively. In addition, the variation seen within the three selected developing Asia-Pacific economies ranges from 55.9 per cent (Viet Nam) to 91.1 per cent (Philippines); this may be explained by the presence of the large informal sector and their weaker business environments.

Microenterprises share some common characteristics (Eversole, 2004; Larson and Shaw, 2001; Lee, 2008; and Tambunan, 2010):

(a) Usually owner-managed, with family members working in the enterprise;

(b) Many in the informal sector so no statistical record available;

(c) Often constrained by capital shortages;

(d) Lower market entry barriers;

(e) Largely situated in rural areas particularly as agriculture-related business;

(f) Feature high rates of start-ups and business termination; and

(g) Operated under flexible arrangements and locations according to market trends and customer requirements.

Due to the unique characteristics of microenterprises, the issues that have an impact on SME development also apply and, in some cases, are exacerbated. These constraints include:

(a) Gaps between rapidly-growing demands of microenterprises for capital, manpower and other resources, and government awareness and support;

(b) A lack of access to formal financial services, especially in rural areas where most of the microenterprises are located. This constraint is further aggravated by the low profit margins for banking institutions and the high-risk nature of microenterprises;

(c) A lack of access to business development services such as marketing, training in basic business skills, business incubation etc.; and

(d) Low bargaining power and vulnerability to economic shocks.

---

[28] OECD has developed a database of enterprise statistics called Structural Demographic Business Statistics for selected member and non-member countries, covering entry and exit rates of new enterprises together with their five-year survival rates (http://stats.oecd.org/Index.aspx?DataSetCode=SDBS_BDI).

[29] According to the European Union's definition of a microenterprise, the annual balance sheet or turnover does not exceed € 2 million and the total number of employees is less than 10 people (European Commission, 2003).

Table II.6. Share of microenterprises in selected Asia-Pacific countries, 2010

Country	Microenterprise definition	Number of enterprises	Number of SMEs	Number of microenterprises	Share of SMEs, excluding microenterprises	Share of microenterprises
Japan	Manufacturing: 20 or fewer employees. Trade and services: Five or fewer employees.	4 210 070	4 197 719	3 663 069	12.7	87.0
Republic of Korea	Manufacturing, mining, construction and transportation: Less than 10 employees. Other sectors: Less than five employees.	2 976 646	2 974 185	2 616 222	12.0	87.9
Viet Nam	All sectors: One to nine employees.	205 689	203 331	114 928	43.0	55.9
Philippines	Asset size less than P 3 million, or between one and nine employees.	780 479	777 357	710 822	5.5	91.1
Malaysia	Manufacturing, manufacturing-related services, and agro-based industry: Sales turnover of less than RM 250,000, or less than five full-time employees. Services, primary agriculture, information and communications technology: Sales turnover of less than RM 200,000, or less than five employees.	552 849	548 267	434 939	20.5	78.7

Sources: Department of Statistics (Malaysia), 2011; Department of Trade and Industry of the Philippines, 2011; General Statistics Office of Viet Nam, 2011; Ministry of Economy, Trade and Industry of Japan, 2011a; and Small and Medium Business Administration of Japan, 2011.

H. SME productivity

Firm productivity measures the efficiency of how a firm transfers inputs into outputs. Therefore the productivity of a firm is a reflection of both labour ability and technology. The main determinants of productivity include access to materials, quality and size of workforce, the capabilities of management, the organizational structure, the use of technology and the level of capital sufficiency.

In general, it is more difficult for SMEs to achieve the same productivity levels as those of larger firms due to several constraints (figure II.10). Apart from scale restrictions, SMEs tend to face higher costs of capital and fewer capital resources. The lack of new technologies and managerial capacities also reduce their abilities to raise productivity. SMEs tend to pay lower wages than large firms, preventing them from acquiring and keeping highly-skilled labour. All these elements add barriers to achieving high productivity in SMEs. As a result, SMEs often suffer from higher rates of failures and exits, compared with large firms (Berry, 2007). Microenterprises often operate in the informal sector, exhibit even lower labour productivity and generate less earnings for their owners and employees than small enterprises (figure II.11). Recent research suggests that many micro-entrepreneurs may not be "capitalists in waiting" (de Mel and others, 2010). On the other hand, given the relative scarcity of capital in economies, large firms achieve lower total factor productivity (TFP)[30] than SMEs – possibly because large firms use their capital less efficiently (European Commission, 2005).

As mentioned above, SMEs face more constraints and risks than large firms but they also have the potential to improve the aggregate productivity of the economy. Small firms often act as a major engine of innovation with their flexibility; therefore, growing SMEs can heighten competition by disrupting the "cozy relationships" within an industry, and more SMEs can increase the level of competition and cause those performing badly to exit (Mole, 2002). In this context, policy support could be a key factor in stimulating this progress. Empirical studies imply that properly aimed SME policies might have a significant positive effect on aggregate productivity by reallocating capital resources towards SMEs (Ibarrarán and others, 2009). Here, the policies refer to those aimed at increasing firms' productivity through the promotion of training, innovation, quality certification and facilitation of SME financing.

For example, Japan has a moderate tax credit for R&D investment of 20 per cent; the rate for SMEs can be higher by as much as 6 per cent (APEC, 2006a). As SMEs tend to be more sensitive to tax credits than large firms, this policy enhances innovations at SMEs, which are identified as a main source of productivity gain. Another example involves the Business Incubation Centre of Zhongguancun Haidian Science Park in Beijing, which provides comprehensive services such as business incubation, finance, technical consultation, logistics and recruitment to tenant high-tech SMEs. The resources and services provided by the centre augment the production and managerial efficiencies of the client SMEs, especially start-ups, and thus increase their productivity. To summarize, various resources must be available for SMEs to adopt new practices that increase their productivity, and policy must focus on ensuring SMEs' access to those resources for such a purpose (Mole, 2002).

---

[30] Total factor productivity (TFP) is the portion of output not explained by the amount of inputs used in production. As such, its level is determined by how efficiently and intensely the inputs are utilized in production; sometimes it can be viewed as a reflection of technology and managerial ability. TFP growth is usually measured by the Solow residual in a growth model, and the higher the TFP is the more efficient the firm will be (Comin, 2006).

Figure II.10. Productivity (value-added per worker) differentials by enterprise size (large enterprises = 100)

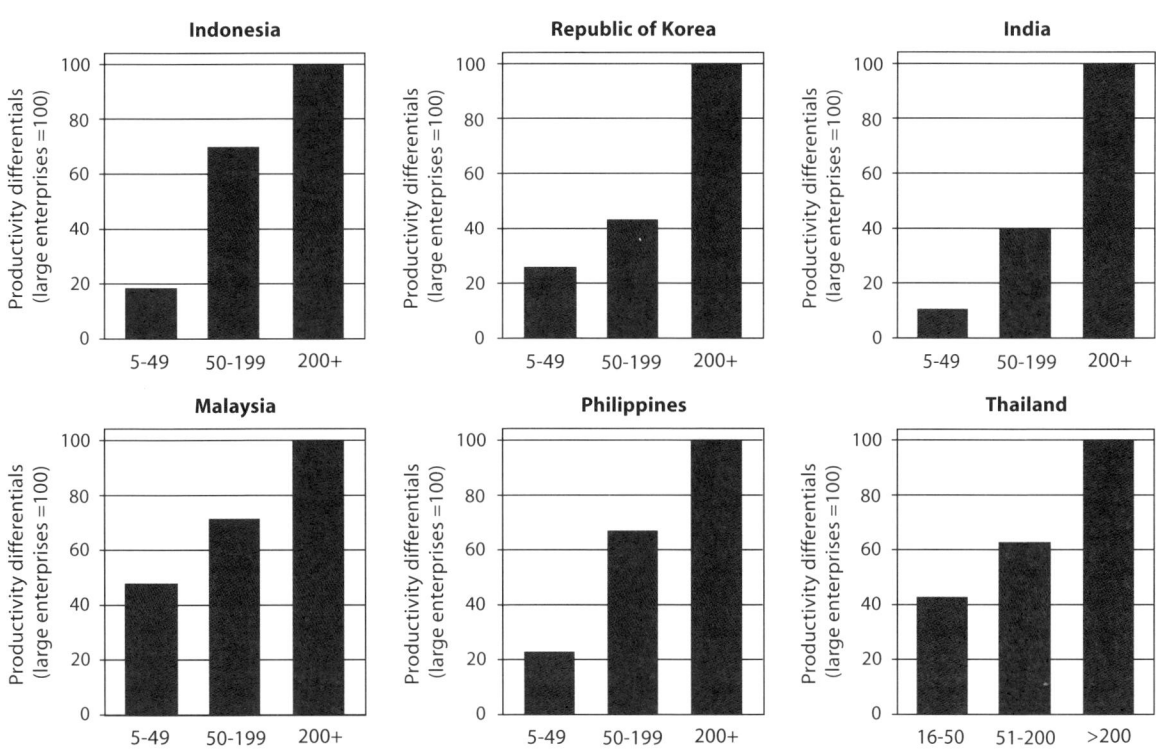

Source: ADB, 2009.
Note: Enterprise size is measured in terms of number of workers.

Figure II.11. Labour productivity of micro and small enterprises

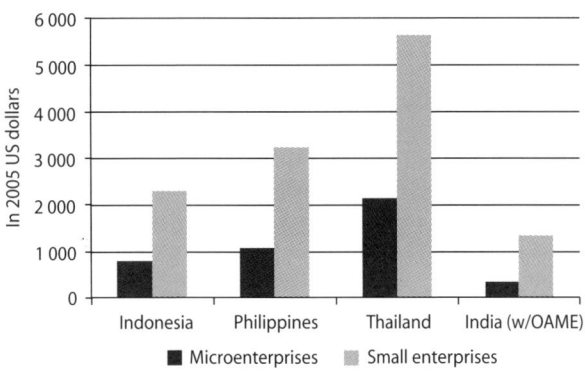

Source: de Mel and others, 2010.
Notes: OAME = Own-account manufacturing enterprise Microenterprises in Thailand are taken here to mean firms that employ 1-15 workers while the small enterprises are those that employ 16-50 workers.

I. Determinants of SME competitiveness

In order for any firm to survive, it must be able to compete. Policymakers constantly search for ways to assist businesses in honing their competitive edge. SME competitiveness can be defined as an SME's (or the national SME sector's) ability to compete for markets, resources and revenues, as measured by indicators such as relative market shares, growth, profitability or innovation levels (ESCAP, 2009b). In this context, competitiveness can be referred to as the relative performance of SMEs in a particular product (or service) market at the national, regional or global level as well as the capability to create new market niches. It reflects the ability of SMEs to sustain superior market positions and profitability, relative to their domestic and international competitors, by (a) producing goods and/or services of high quality and functionality for their customers at low cost and (b) by delivering in a timely manner or (c) for overall superior QCD (i.e., quality, cost and delivery) (ESCAP, 2009b). In addition to competitors and customers, Porter (2008) highlighted the fact that SMEs had to consider three other key market forces when enhancing their competitiveness, i.e., suppliers, potential entrants and substitute products, all of which shape the structure and the nature of competitive interaction within an industry or sector.

Many interacting factors, such as barriers and constraints, influence the competitive performance of SMEs, and they can be broadly divided into external (change or pace of change) or internal (lack of resources) factors (table II.7).

External problems are those principally beyond an entrepreneur's control. They generally involve change, or rates of change, in the business environment in which they operate. For example, a country's central bank may tighten the money supply, resulting in credit rationing that hurts SMEs. Other examples are new business statutes that adversely affect the ability to compete, or new fiscal policies that crowd out private business initiative or investment.

Internal problems are primarily under an entrepreneur's control. They typically arise from a lack of one or more resource, i.e., capital, management ability, technical ability or market knowledge. Also involved is the capacity of an SME to respond effectively to competitors, its flexibility in responding to changing circumstances and its capability to create new market niches. The outlook and capabilities of

Table II.7. Determinants of SME competitiveness

Determinants	Examples
External	
1. Market access.	Domestic markets; penetration of export markets; GSP treatment; trade and investment liberalization (e.g., regional trade agreements, bilateral trade agreements, bilateral investment treaties); and the establishment of foreign operations.
2. Access to resources.	People; skills; capital; finance; physical assets; technologies; knowledge; and supply of raw materials.
3. Regulatory framework which conditions business performance.	The processes of business registration and licensing; taxation; competition and bankruptcy laws; property and intellectual property rights; trade, fiscal, monetary and investment policy; legal system; customs procedures; and export/import procedures.
4. Supporting services provided by both public and private organizations.	The quality of physical infrastructure and logistics systems; formal and vocational education; training services; business development services; and professional services such as accounting and legal advice.
5. Consumer demand.	Change in consumer preferences.
Internal	
6. Management and personnel issues.	Lack of scientific management skills; labour shortages; low skills and education of staff; personal commitment and ambition.
7. Capacity to respond effectively to competitors.	Substitutes for products and services; diversified product and service lines; low cost structure; technical and operational discrepancies.
8. Capability and flexibility to respond to changing circumstances.	The availability to access key resources; capacity for process and product innovation; and flexible supply chains.
9. Contestable market power and capability to create new market niches.	Marketing capability and branding; culture of innovation; and customer/market orientation.

Source: Modified from ESCAP, 2009a.

the owner of an SME tend to drive these issues, as they play a crucial role in determining the success of smaller organizations such as SMEs. These internal problems are often an outcome of faulty managerial strategies or practices.

In addition to the above factors, general conditions such as natural resource endowment, macroeconomic conditions and microeconomic factors prevailing in their home countries, affect the competitive performance of SMEs. Figure II.12 illustrates the competitiveness framework, which covers the causal relationship between external and internal determinations of (a) competitiveness, (b) products and services with superior quality, cost and delivery (QCD), and (c) large market share and high profitability.

It is obvious that the national business environment plays a central role in the enhancement of the competitiveness of SMEs, as some nations have succeeded in attaining competitive advantages for their industries while many others have not. The relationship between the business environment and a nation's prosperity is symbiotic. On the one hand, an SME must understand both the advantages and disadvantages of operating in its home nation. These strengths and weaknesses affect its ability (or inability) to create and sustain a competitive advantage. On the other hand, a nation's standard of living in the long term depends on its ability to attain and sustain a high level of productivity among industries in which SMEs compete. In this context, the main goal of an SME's competitiveness strategy, both at the enterprise and the national levels, may be to upgrade current capacity by incorporating new skills and technologies for higher quality and efficiency. This should begin with an analysis of the strengths and weaknesses of the existing business environment, including SME policies, programmes and structures at all levels, i.e., micro, meso and macro. The results of such an analysis will help form the design of efficient policies and programmes needed for increasing the value that SMEs add to the economy.[31]

Competitiveness can also be assessed at the national level (Porter, 1990), where export performance is the single most important indicator, particularly in the Asia-Pacific region. SME competitiveness can be also defined as the SME sector's ability to produce goods and services that meet the requirements of international markets while simultaneously maintaining and expanding real incomes of the nation in the long term (President's Commission on Industrial Competitiveness, 1985). According to the World Economic

Figure II.12. Competitiveness framework for SMEs

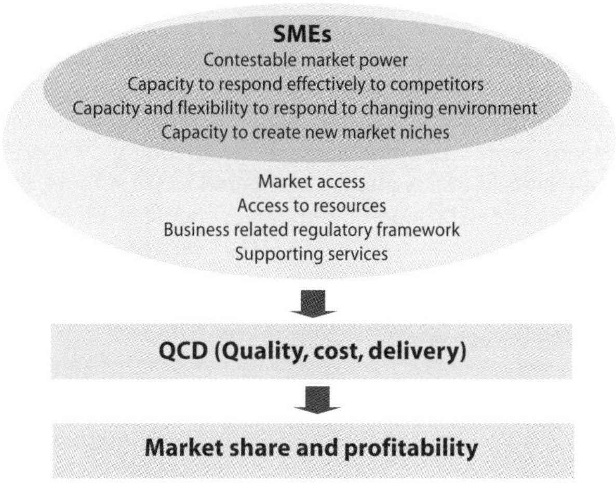

SMEs
Contestable market power
Capacity to respond effectively to competitors
Capacity and flexibility to respond to changing environment
Capacity to create new market niches

Market access
Access to resources
Business related regulatory framework
Supporting services

⬇

QCD (Quality, cost, delivery)

⬇

Market share and profitability

Source: Authors' compilation.

Forum's (WEF) (2011) Global Competitiveness Report of 2011-2012, two of the 10 most competitive countries are in the Asia-Pacific region, i.e., Singapore and Japan, compared with seven in Europe and the United States.[32] Greater competitiveness allows a developing country to diversify beyond dependence on a few primary-commodity exports and move up the skills and technology ladder, which is essential to sustaining rising wages, and to permit greater economies of scale and scope in production (UNCTAD, 2002). The ability to compete in international markets is usually thought to be dependent on (a) macroeconomic policies and conditions (trade policies, exchange rates etc.) as well as (b) a nation's comparative advantage, i.e., its factor endowment (land, natural resources, labour and capital) relative to other nations. Due to greater competitiveness, a nation may attain a positive balance of trade and rising incomes for its inhabitants. For example, Singapore became one of the most competitive countries in the world by adopting far-sighted policies that invested in institutions and human resources, and by attracting FDI in order to make up for its lack of natural resources and capital (UNCTAD, 2005a).

These determinants of SME competitiveness clearly point towards the important role that governments play in enhancing competitiveness by creating enabling environments, facilitating better market and resource access and providing pro-business regulatory frameworks and business support services (ESCAP, 2009b). A deeper examination of individual economies in the Asia-Pacific region reveals that some of them have not placed the development and growth of SMEs at the top of their national agendas. These economies will need to prioritize the development of SMEs to stimulate higher growth. This can be achieved by integrating SME development into the mainstream of national development plans. Therefore, a proper understanding of the SME sector, especially its values and roles, needs to gain urgency among policymakers and other stakeholders.

---

[31] Institutional frameworks for SME development vary from country to country. Various government offices in the fields of commerce industry, agriculture, enterprise development, investment and export promotion, quality standards etc. may handle portions of SME policy. There has been a trend to establish a sector-wide SME development agency to implement a coordinated and consolidated national SME development policy and relevant activities. These initiatives include Bangladesh's SME Foundation, Sri Lanka's National Enterprise Development Authority and Thailand's Office of SME Promotion, which the international donor community recommended. Such newly-established SME agencies often lack adequate resources, experience and effective mandates to conduct comprehensive and substantial SME development initiatives in collaboration with other ministries and are thus not fully able to achieve their objectives. For more details of these SME agencies, visit the websites at www.smef.org.bd, www.neda.lk/ and http://eng.sme.go.th/Pages/home.aspx.

[32] The Global Competitiveness Report is a yearly report published by the World Economic Forum. The 2011-2012 report covers 142 major and emerging economies. For more details, visit the website at www.weforum.org/reports/global-competitiveness-report-2011-2012.

In addition, governments could support institutional capacity-building and the development of human resources for new businesses through such policy actions as the provision of a quality formal education system, a technical and vocational education and training (TVET) system, business and technology incubation facilities, consultancy services and cluster development (see chapter VI). As SMEs are relatively disadvantaged compared to large firms, the aforementioned support programmes should all be geared towards facilitating activities for SMEs, which are working to improve their market (ESCAP, 2009b).

J. SME clusters

Industrial clusters have increasingly been recognized as an effective means of industrial development and promotion of SMEs. UNIDO (1999) defines a cluster as "a sectoral and geographical concentration of enterprises which produce and sell a range of related or complementary products and thus are faced with common challenges and opportunities". Another definition is "a group of firms that cooperate on a joint development project complementing each other and specializing in order to overcome common problems, achieve collective efficiency and conquer markets beyond their individual reach" (UNIDO, 1999). Clusters are often located close to equipment and raw material suppliers, independent component producers, subcontractors and final goods producers as well as ports and airports. Suppliers of key business services are also present as are buyers and their agents.

As a consequence of facing the common challenges and exploiting opportunities, SMEs within the cluster sharpen their own competitive advantage. Clusters can allow SMEs to escape the straitjacket imposed by a lack of economies of scale and benefit from a variety of spillover benefits, including access to a wider pool of relatively specialized labour and opportunities to learn about potentially profitable product lines and technologies. In short, participation in a cluster involves elements of both cooperation and competition. Spillovers of knowledge and other intangible benefits are a common byproduct of these firm interactions.

SMEs also see the following advantages in forming or joining a cluster (ESCAP, 2007b):

(a) Collective bargaining power will increase profitability among member firms;

(b) Collective efficiency based on scale will lead to greater supply in the global market;

(c) Collective efficiency based on specialization will increase productivity through product and process improvements, skill upgrades and market knowledge; and

(d) Joint action will lead to systematic collaborations and formation of associations that can provide better access to global markets.

Clusters have existed naturally in many countries and their development has become a policy priority in the past couple of decades in the developing world.[33] In Japan, based on a review of the history of 14 industrial clusters, Yamawaki (2001) noted several different factors that played key roles across different clusters. These include:

(a) The catalytic role played by the emergence of a large enterprise (for example, the general machinery cluster that emerged around Komatsu Corporation, a large producer of construction machinery);

(b) The presence of public research in a standards testing facility (for example, the establishment of a public technology centre in Hyogo in 1984); and

(c) The availability of a pool of workers (for example, the emergence of an apparel cluster in Gifu, which was helped by an abundance of part-time female labour).

Based on a survey of small enterprises in various clusters, Yamawaki pointed out that for many small firms, being part of a cluster had helped them to specialize, absorb new technologies and facilitate their procurement of inputs. Additionally, local government provisions for public testing facilities and research and technology development centres in the cluster were also helpful.

Being part of a cluster also appears to have helped SMEs in Indonesia. Clustering, together with subcontracting relationships with foreign firms, has played an important role in helping many SMEs become successful exporters of furniture and garments. In addition to enabling SMEs to establish links with foreign buyers, clusters also introduce them to a variety of process and product innovations. For example, the metal industry clusters in Ceper (Central Java) and in Pasuruan (East Java) generally meet the above criteria and are considered successful industrial clusters for SMEs (ADB, 2009). In contrast, small enterprises outside the clusters have not been as successful in either entering export markets or diversifying their product lines.

Zhejiang Province in the eastern coastal region of China is considered to have one of the most vibrant SME industrial clusters in China (ADB, 2009). Its growth was fuelled by the clustering of SMEs in specialized industrial zones. Many small towns in China depend on township enterprises for their economic growth. Such enterprises are expected to generate more employment opportunities for the rural surplus labour force (ADB, 2009). A small town's development must be supported by its industry and such support can come from SME cluster enterprises in secondary and tertiary industries. Clustering does not inevitably cause SME dynamism but it does increase its likelihood. Having an anchor firm or firms in the cluster is also crucial. The large enterprise(s) act as the hub of business links in the form of subcontracting, and drive innovation for the member firms.

The private sector should lead cluster development and governments should be a catalyst. Given the weakness of the private sector in many developing countries in Asia and the Pacific, the governments might initiate the process by establishing appropriate cluster support structures. A number of governments in the region are using assistance to clusters as a chief method to instill dynamism. This aid includes adequate regulatory frameworks, infrastructure and logistics, financial facilities as well as various programmes for capacity-building and cooperative technology development and

---

[33] Successful examples of SME clustering include the Sialkot Surgical Instruments Manufacturers Association and Sialkot Chamber of Commerce (Pakistan), the Tirupur Exporters Association (India) and the Penang Skills Development Centre (Malaysia).

innovation efforts. A package of policy interventions should be implemented based on a holistic approach for cluster development, including diagnostic study, trust-building, export promotion, marketing support, skills development, technology upgrading, establishing common facility centres and physical infrastructure upgrading.

K. Gender issues related to SME development

Women entrepreneurs, who often run SMEs, do not operate in isolation. They work under the same macro, regulatory and institutional framework as their male counterparts. It is necessary to explore how gender bias embedded in society limits women's mobility, interactions, active economic participation and access to business development services.

Within the Asia-Pacific region, gender equality remains an elusive goal. Women in many developing countries in Asia and the Pacific remain far behind men in enjoying basic human rights, let alone participating with men on an equal footing in economic activities. Even in countries where legal equality is granted to women, their participation in the social, political and economic life of the nation trails that of men. In this regard, UNDP developed the Gender Empowerment Measure[34] that attempts to capture the level of human development, the level of development of women and the extent to which women are free from discrimination in building their capabilities and in gaining access to resources and opportunities (ESCAP, 2005a). Within the Asia-Pacific region, there are disparities both within and between subregions in terms of the Gender Empowerment Measure (UNDP, 2009). The economies in South-East Asia and East and North-East Asia display a more conducive environment for women entrepreneurs to flourish compared to the Pacific and South and South-West Asia which clearly lag behind in terms of women empowerment (table II.8). A possible explanation may be the socio-cultural norms and values shared within a subregion (International Bank of Reconstruction and Development/World Bank, 2012). However, at the same time, clear differences can be seen within some subregions, such as South-East Asia – with Singapore, Viet Nam and Indonesia ranking sixteenth, sixty-second and ninety-sixth, respectively, in the world. These differences reflect the varying severity of challenges facing women entrepreneurs throughout Asia and the Pacific.

The business environment for women also reflects the interplay of different factors that ultimately result in the disadvantaged status of women in society. Accordingly, women generally have lower participation rates in the formal sector compared to men. However, within the informal sector, they often have higher rates of start-ups and growth. These women-led businesses have traditionally been in sectors that are crowded with competitors and characterized by low profit margins and productivity levels (ESCAP, 2006). They are typically small-sized businesses, employ few workers, compete in the light manufacturing sector and generally access fewer resources than male-owned SMEs.

Despite those statistics, women-led SMEs account for 35 per cent of all SMEs within the Asia-Pacific region (MasterCard Worldwide, 2010). On an individual level, women entrepreneurs tend to be highly motivated, focused and competent in finance, and have strong interpersonal skills, general business management skills, high internal control and a strong sense of achievement (Jalbert, 2000). These traits have been responsible for a steady but moderate growth of female-owned SMEs in East and South-East Asian developing countries during the past decade (figure II.13).

Despite these valuable entrepreneurial traits and the growth within the region, women entrepreneurs face additional gender-specific barriers to their enterprises, i.e., credit barriers, lack of experience and training, lack of relevant networks and societal position and difficulty in time management due to family responsibilities (Jalbert, 2000; and OECD, 2004a). The details are explained below:

(a) Credit barriers. Women in particular tend to seek small personal loans because, in general, they tend to start small businesses. Banks do not consider small businesses to be worthwhile because of their slender profit margins. In the best case scenario, banks do not make much money from lending to SMEs, and in the worst case scenario the SMEs fail and expose the bank to credit risk;

(b) Lack of experience and training. Highly-educated women mainly choose salaried positions; thus, less-skilled women are relatively more likely to be entrepreneurs. Once they do become SME owners, these women have no access to management and technical training;

(c) Lack of relevant networks and societal position. In general, women tend to have a lower social position than men in the Asia-Pacific region, affecting the type of networks available to them. They are less likely to have access to the critical resources, support and information needed to establish and foster enterprises. Yet, the importance of social networks has been acknowledged as a crucial factor underlying the success of new ventures; and

(d) Difficulty in time management. Another recurring theme for women entrepreneurs is competing demands for their time. Women are more prone to not have enough free time to develop either

Table II.8. Subregional rankings of gender empowerment measure

Subregions	Average Gender Empowerment Measure ranking
Developed economies	24.7
South-East Asia	66.9
East and North-East Asia	75.7
North and Central Asia	80.4
Pacific	95.5
South and South-West Asia	99.6

Source: UNDP, 2009.
Note: Refer to the Explanatory Notes at the beginning of this publication for subregional groupings and their economies in Asia and the Pacific.

---

[34] Gender Empowerment Measure ranks 109 countries based on the extent to which there is gender equity in economic and political representation. It also reflects gender equity in managerial decision-making, professional roles and economic activity (UNDP, 2009).

Figure II.13. Annual growth of female-owned SMEs (Per cent)

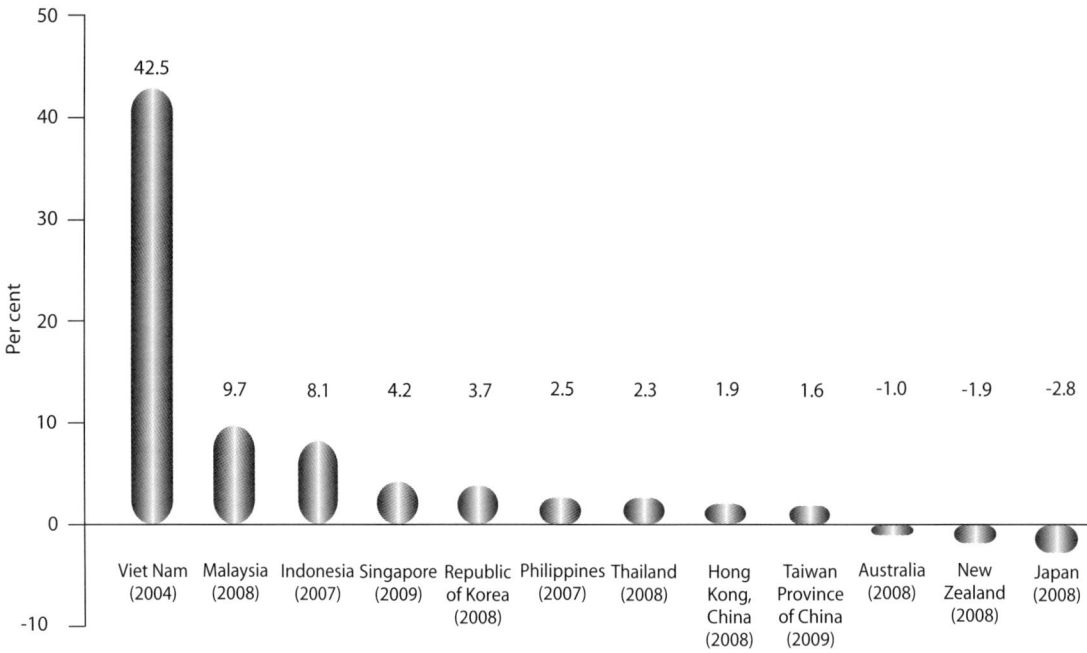

Source: MasterCard Worldwide, 2010.

their entrepreneurial skills or their businesses due to many domestic chores and raising children. Accordingly, they do not have time to meet with institutions and banks for advice and information on credit, attend training programmes to acquire skills or attain market information about potential customers and suppliers (figure II.14).

Overcoming these barriers would allow greater enterprise development among women, leading to their economic empowerment and hence giving them an equal opportunity to support their families and be partners for their progress. It is only in recent decades that policymakers in the region have recognized the importance of female contributions to national GDP and have therefore sought to involve women in public affairs (ESCAP, 2006). These government-led initiatives, while commendable, have often encountered difficulties in making a practical impact. In Viet Nam, for example, the gender equality law was passed in 2006 and came into effect in 2007. It has been found that many of the policies to promote women-led entrepreneurship and increase employment largely only exist on paper (Vietnam Women Entrepreneurs Council, 2007). Similar difficulties exist in Bangladesh where surveys have found that women entrepreneurs are often unaware of government initiatives to promote and support their development (Morshed, 2008).

In principle, opportunities must be the same and equally available to both sexes; however, differences exist in practice. Men are free to participate in all social and business activities, while many women remain with the family. Women entrepreneurs appear to have more difficulty in balancing work and family. Men are more tolerant of risks, while women are more careful and reluctant. Women now have higher levels of education and competencies. Some very successful entrepreneurs are women and their success could be attributed to family support, educational attainment, changing environments, motivation to succeed or the need

Figure II.14. A woman's quest to get a job or start a business

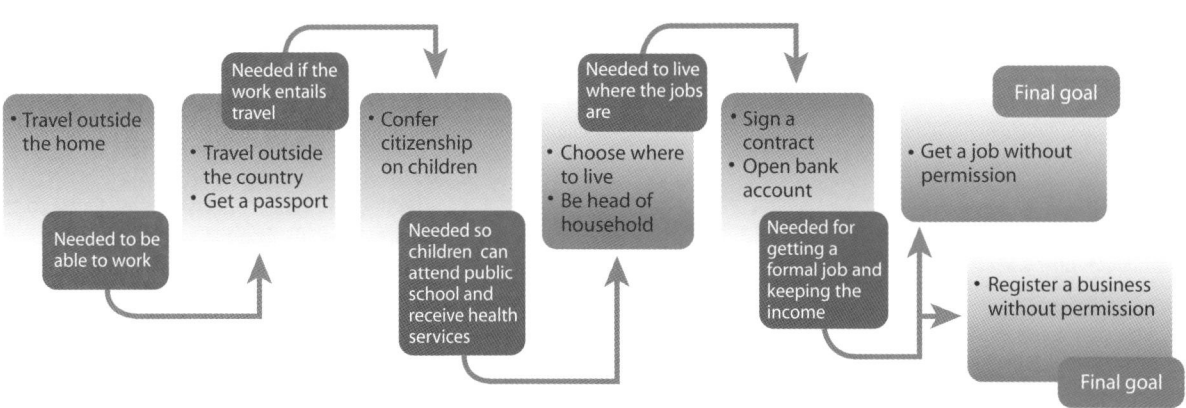

Source: International Bank of Reconstruction and Development/World Bank, 2012.

to sustain themselves and their families.[35] This issue is discussed throughout this publication where appropriate (e.g., women entrepreneurship in chapter IV).

---

[35] The fields of labour economics and entrepreneurship contain extensive literatures about women's opportunity to participate in the labour force and the travails they face when opening a business. Some relevant articles include: Brush, de Bruin and Welter, 2009; Burda, Hamermesh and Weil, 2007; Terrell and Troilo, 2010; and Weeks, 2009.

Box II.4. Assistance to women entrepreneurs in India

In India, the share of women entrepreneurs in cottage industries such as handloom weaving, handicrafts, coir products and sericulture is as high as 30 to 40 per cent. The Government of India has been promoting entrepreneurship among women, particularly with the aim of encouraging first-generation women entrepreneurs through various training and support services. For example, India has adopted a special strategy to assist women to establish self-employment ventures, providing both forward and backward linkages for marketing facilities. State-run banks are providing microfinance at concessional rates of interest to women entrepreneurs. The Government has also introduced special schemes to subsidize foreign travel for women entrepreneurs to participate in trade exhibitions abroad in order to promote their business in export markets.

Share of women-managed industrial enterprises (in total registered) in India

1987-1988	2001-2002	2006-2007
8% (44 784)	10% (137 534)	14% (215 000)

Source: Ministry of Micro, Small and Medium Enterprises, 2010.

Box II.5. Women entrepreneurship culture in Thailand

Thailand illustrates the important yet veiled role of women in the society. Women comprise 46 per cent of the labour force, 26 per cent of senior officials, legislators and managers and nearly 50 per cent of entrepreneurs in the country (Terjesen and others, 2007). A majority of women are running small enterprises while some lead large enterprises. In particular, women entrepreneurs were playing a significant role in service, tourism and manufacturing sectors in Thailand. Thai women have a more positive attitude towards entrepreneurship than do their male counterparts (Virasa and Hunt, 2007). While a majority of women-run businesses in Thailand are in the informal cottage sector, many are incorporated (36 per cent) and a few (1.4 per cent) are even listed on the stock exchange of Thailand.

Comparison of perceived entrepreneurship between Thai men and women, 2005

Survey results	Male (Per cent)	Female (Per cent)
Business started in the past two years	43	57
Perceive good start-up opportunities	40	60
Fear of failure prevented start-up	35	65
Had knowledge and skills to start-up enterprises	46	61
Entrepreneurship is a good carrier choice	39	61
Successful own business is high status	39	61

Source: Virasa and Hunt, 2007.

Box II.6. Corporate social responsibility and SMEs

The concept of corporate social responsibility (CSR) is aimed at addressing salient socioeconomic as well as environmental issues in a given society. The World Bank (2004) defines CSR as "the commitment of business to contribute to sustainable economic development – working with employees, their families, the local community and society at large to improve the quality of life, in ways that are both good for business and good for development".

For SMEs, the sincere implementation of CSR measures not only facilitates their socioeconomic and environmental responsibilities, but also has a positive impact on their competitiveness (Turyakira, Venter and Smith, 2010). While current evidence has to be viewed with caution, the implementation of CSR measures could stimulate entrepreneurial and innovative ideas, positive changes in the production process, higher motivation among the workforce, cost savings and an overall competitive advantage over SMEs that disregard CSR (Austrian Institute for SME Research, 2007).

Environmental issues particularly in the SME sector have acquired critical importance. As more than 90 per cent of all businesses worldwide fall into the category of SMEs (UNIDO, 2007), one can easily picture their impact on the environment.

It is not surprising that SMEs are found to be the most polluting agents in Asia and the Pacific (Institute for Global Environmental Strategies, 2006). Some of the economies in the region, aware of the consequences, have initiated various measures for tackling the growing problem. Creating adequate awareness and promoting due appreciation of CSR among SMEs are recent and very timely phenomena, as the belief that CSR is only applicable to larger corporations is still widely spread among the SME community. Localizing the CSR agenda also deserves emphasis. Dismissing the one-size-fits-all approach and convincingly demonstrating that a tailor-made CSR programme has the potential to meet the specific needs of SMEs could prove the above-mentioned belief wrong (UNIDO, 2007).

To explore the role of government in facilitating the uptake of CSR among SMEs, UNIDO convened an expert group meeting in 2007. The meeting pointed out that governments are mainly involved at three levels: the basic enabling environment; interventions aimed at promoting the spread of best CSR practices; and strategic partnerships (UNIDO, 2007). At each of these levels, governments have a specific role to play and are able to employ a number of tools and strategies to strengthen CSR. The World Bank outlined four of these roles and proposed the inclusion of a fifth (Ward, 2004):

Box II.6. *(continued)*

(a) Mandating – Laws, regulations, penalties and associated public sector institutions that are related to the control of some aspect of business investment or operations;

(b) Facilitating – Setting clear overall policy frameworks and positions to guide business investment in CSR, the development of non-binding guidance and labels or codes for application in the marketplace, laws and regulations that facilitate and provide incentives for business investment in CSR by mandating transparency or disclosure on various issues, tax incentives, investment in awareness raising and research and facilitating processes of stakeholder dialogue (although not necessarily in the lead);

(c) Partnering – Combining public resources with those of business and other actors to leverage complementary skills and resources to tackle issues within the CSR agenda, whether as participants, conveners or catalysts;

(d) Endorsing – Showing public political support for particular types of CSR practices in the marketplace or for individual companies, endorsing specific award schemes or non-governmental metrics, indicators, guidelines and standards and leading by example, such as through public procurement practices; and

(e) Demonstrating (proposed) – Public sector agencies can demonstrate leadership to business in the exemplary way that they themselves engage with stakeholders or promote and uphold respect for fundamental rights. They can demonstrate leadership by carrying out their activities with probity and free of corruption. In addition, they can show leadership in the way that they support transparency about their own activities in relations with external stakeholders.

While this World Bank approach was aimed at governments, UNIDO also worked directly with the SME community. Considering that SMEs constitute the overwhelming majority of all businesses in Asia-Pacific, UNIDO realized the potential positive social and environmental impact that the adoption of responsible business practices by SMEs could make. UNIDO started a triple bottom line demonstration project in 2001 in India, Pakistan, Sri Lanka and Thailand. In addition to facilitating market access for suppliers located in these countries, UNIDO created a framework for export-dependent SMEs that focused on their compliance with environmental and social requirements of global buyers and supply chain partners.

UNIDO also developed its very own CSR methodology called the responsible entrepreneurs achievement programme (REAP). REAP is a management and reporting tool tailored to SMEs that would like to implement CSR concepts and follow the triple bottom line approach. In applying REAP, the project has demonstrated that SMEs can improve their environmental and social performance in a manner that is financially advantageous due to reduced operational costs as well as increases in productivity and international export orders. It remains to be seen how REAP can reach scale and be adopted by a larger number of SMEs.

While the importance of the uptake of CSR among SMEs seems unquestionable due to their enormous cumulative socioeconomic and environmental footprint, the challenges and opportunities for policymakers in this area remain plentiful. Localizing the CSR agenda, policy advocacy and knowledge sharing with the important task of explaining the potential CSR for SMEs is no challenge. If enhanced competiveness and better access to international markets and integration into global supply chains are results of the incorporation of CSR measures into their business model, then more SMEs in Asia and the Pacific should be able to consider CSR, not only as an incentive but as a very valuable corporate strategy.

Box II.7. SME Corp of Malaysia policy framework

The Small and Medium Enterprise Corporation Malaysia (SME Corp) was established in October 2009 through a transformation process of its forerunner, SMIDEC, which was formed in May 1996 to be the premier organization in Malaysia for the development of progressive SMEs. Its main objective is to promote the development of competitive, innovative and resilient SMEs through effective coordination and provision of business support. As the coordinator of all related ministries and agencies, SME Corp provides various business support and information and advisory services for all SMEs in Malaysia. It also serves as the secretariat to the National SME Development Council (NSDC) (chaired by the Prime Minister) and is responsible for the management of data and the dissemination of information and research on SMEs.

In 2010, a total of 226 SME development programmes, with a financial commitment of RM 7.1 billion, were implemented by SME Corp together with related Malaysian ministries and agencies that benefited 614,242 SMEs across all sectors. These programmes are based on three main strategic thrusts that aim to: (a) strengthen the enabling infrastructure; (b) build the capacity and capability of domestic SMEs; and (c) enhance access to finance for SMEs.

Several programmes are provided by SME Corp:

(a) The SME Competitiveness Rating for Enhancement (SCORE) – a diagnostic tool used to rate and enhance competitiveness of SMEs, based on their performance and capabilities. The strengths and weaknesses of SMEs are identified through the SCORE model of the specific industries and recommendations are made for further improvements;

(b) The 1-Innovation Certification for Enterprise Rating and Transformation (1-InnoCERT) – a certification programme to recognize and certify innovative enterprises and SMEs, and to encourage entrepreneurs to venture into high technology and innovation-driven industries. Certified companies will be given fast track access to incentives, including funding for their projects;

Box II.7. *(continued)*

(c) The Annual SMIDEX Showcase – an annual event for SMEs to exhibit their products and services, and for large skills companies and TNCs to seek potential suppliers among SMEs. The yearly event also provides SMEs with opportunities to network regionally as well as exchange ideas and information on technology and innovation;

(d) The One Referral Centre – provides advisory services and information through business counselors, pocket talks, physical and virtual sources of information, product galleries and linkages to other relevant ministries and agencies;

(e) Business Accelerator Programme – designed specifically for the manufacturing, services and agro-industry sectors. After the SCORE assessment, eligible SMEs will receive advisory services from SME Corp that include managerial training, technical advice and consultation to strengthen core business and access to finance;

(f) Enrichment and Enhancement Programme (also known as E^2) – provides microenterprises with business and technical advisory services. It covers manufacturing and manufacturing-related services, services and agri-business;

(g) The National Mark of Malaysian Brand – encourages SMEs providing products and services with high quality, reliability and package standards by giving them the right to carry the Malaysian Brand;

(h) Enterprise 50 Award Programme – recognizes the achievements of Malaysia's SMEs;

(i) Malaysia-Japan Automotive Industries Cooperation (MAJAICO A-1) – for improving the competitiveness of SMEs in automotive industries;

(j) Brand Innovation Centre – provides awareness of the importance of branding and packaging, and training in branding and packaging to SMEs across the country;

(k) SME Expert Advisory Panel – strengthens technical advisory services for SMEs' export business;

(l) Skills Upgrading Programme – enhances knowledge of the SME owners in managing business and skills of their employees;

(m) SME@University Programme – provides a structured learning opportunity to the SME owners, conducted by universities;

(n) SME-University Internship Programme – provides an opportunity for undergraduates to offer advisory services for the improvement of SMEs; and

(o) Business matching – promotes competitive SMEs to become suppliers of parts and components, products and services to large enterprises, TNCs and state owned enterprises.

Source: SME Corp Malaysia, 2011.

L. Summary

SMEs are difficult to define, as different countries and organizations use different criteria, including employee headcount, amount of assets and sales turnover. The specification of SMEs can and does differ by industry sector; what counts as an SME in manufacturing may not be an SME in services. These differences underscore the point that policymakers should use this book as a general reference and tailor their policies to their unique country context.

A typology of SMEs demonstrates that they differ with regard to the stage of economic development in which they operate as well as their own market orientation and stage of the corporate life cycle, and their ability to innovate and use technology. This reinforces the need for policy customization. On the other hand, SMEs commonly face resource constraints due to their small size. These constraints are financial, technological and managerial and should form the basis for shaping SME policy.

Such a policy should focus on improving SME competitiveness and can address both external and internal issues (table II.7) that face small businesses. Of these two categories policymakers are better positioned to handle the former, as the latter is more firm-specific. Policymakers need to streamline the legal and regulatory environments, increase market access and remove uncompetitive practices and expedite access to resources such as financial capital.

Broader policy objectives include the development of SME clusters. Industrial clusters produce agglomeration benefits that spill over to member companies, both large established players and SMEs alike. Policymakers can help this process by providing a robust infrastructure and offering tax incentives to start up in a given area.

Additionally, the inclusion of women in the economy as entrepreneurs is a boon to economic development and women business owners provide the same benefits of productivity and job creation as their male counterparts. Policymakers in various Asia-Pacific nations must challenge and change a number of formal regulations and informal norms in order to allow increased female entrepreneurship. The realm of education is of particular importance; adequate schooling can help women obtain the skills and attitudes they will need to succeed as entrepreneurs.

In concluding this chapter, several key points should be emphasized. First, general agreement exists about the crucial areas for SME development: (a) enabling policy and regulatory framework and infrastructure; (b) entrepreneurship; (c) access to finance; (d) innovation and technology; (e) business development services; and (f) foreign market penetration. The difficulty is that not all donors, development agencies and policymakers adhere to such a comprehensive approach (cf., SME cluster development). Piecemeal activities dissipate scarce resources. In addition, collaboration among the bilateral and international development agencies has been weak and must be enhanced in most developing countries in the region in order to design larger, coordinated and project-supporting programmes; some progress has however been observed, particularly in South Asia (GTZ and Embassy of Japan, Bangladesh, 2006).

The main focus of policymakers on SME development will continue to be on reforms for attaining a business enabling environment, comprising improved policy and regulatory frameworks and an adequate supporting infrastructure. Providing accessible finance has been one of the most critical issues for desired SME growth in the region. Policymakers should also initiate direct support to enterprises on an experimental basis while utilizing SME associations and targeting priority sectors.

This direct support should encompass development of an entrepreneurial culture. Such a culture is essential for SME foundation and growth, but technical assistance often overlooks this factor. A comprehensive "entrepreneurship training programme" should be launched, particularly in rural areas. Special preferences could be given to women and youth entrepreneurs to further their development. Conventional technical assistance to SMEs also neglects innovation through technology development and adaptation, and thus puts SMEs at a competitive disadvantage. Business development services, including marketing support represent another area where assistance would be fruitful. SMEs require professional consultancy on building and maintaining a competitive advantage. Connecting SMEs to regional and global supply chains also merits the attention of policymakers. These chains are instrumental in upgrading human resources and management skills and SMEs benefit enormously when they become a part of such chains.

CHAPTER III
Business enabling environment

The Donor Committee for Enterprise Development (DCED, 2008) noted that BEE was an interplay of policy, legal, institutional, regulatory and physical conditions that facilitated business activities. It is critical to the economic development of a country as it provides the fundamentals of steady private sector development. It is an indispensable condition for competitiveness, the growth of individual enterprises and the development of the SME sector which is a particularly vulnerable and disadvantaged segment of the private sector. The aim of all BEE programmes is to help create a more effective environment for investment and business development.

The business environment influences the choice of entrepreneurs (and investors) in locating, operating and expanding their businesses. Uncertain economic policies or those that lack proper direction can hinder economic growth even when a country makes significant progress on other development fronts. Prevailing norms and customs, laws, regulations, policies, international trade agreements and public infrastructure can either facilitate or hinder the movement of goods and services along the value chain. At the national level BEE encompasses policies, administrative procedures, regulations and the state of public infrastructure. At the regional and international level, conventions, treaties, agreements and market standards shape BEE.

In addition to these formal factors, the informal factors (e.g., social norms, business culture ethics and local expectations) can be powerful forces that influence BEE. Understanding these unwritten societal rules is essential to fully comprehending the state of the business environment, particularly for SMEs, as BEE has significant impacts on the relative competitiveness of SMEs in domestic, regional and global markets through a number of factors. These factors and associated policy prescriptions are discussed in this chapter.

A. How does BEE matter?

As a basic requirement, a healthy business environment is fundamental to enabling firms to emerge, survive and grow. Such an environment must include:

(a) A transparent, open, fair and competitive business framework;
(b) Clear, independent rule of law for all firms;
(c) Easy establishment and dissolution of businesses; and
(d) Equal and stable legal treatment for national and cross-border transactions.

In other words, governments must develop and implement policies and regulations that will enable people to start (and dissolve) businesses, and remove barriers to help these businesses become more profitable and competitive. Without a healthy BEE, a nation's SME sector will not be able to thrive. Global competition has become so intense that exports will decimate SMEs if their nation's BEE handicaps them.

BEE can reduce costs on both the private sector and government, increase productivity, and promote growth. Burdensome and unpredictable regulations are costly in terms of the time and money required for compliance as well as lost business opportunities. Enhancing BEE not only allows SMEs to spend less time and money dealing with administrative red tape, but also helps them to focus on their core business operations (e.g., marketing their goods and services). Governments can spend fewer resources on regulating and monitoring the business sector, and invest more on infrastructure and business development services.

The primary theories underlying the importance of BEE are institutional economics and transaction cost economics. North (1990) characterized institutions as "humanly devised constraints on human interaction"; they are the "rules of the game" that give incentives (or disincentives) to firms to develop and grow. In North's view, institutions were either "formal" or "informal". Formal institutions are codified in law and carry official sanctions, whereas informal institutions are the norms and values governing society. Violations of norms carry penalties such as ostracism and censure. A nation's institutional framework exists on a continuum from informal to formal and they tend to be mutually reinforcing, i.e., a society's norms become the basis of its legal system, which in turn creates laws supporting those norms (North, 1990).

As economies develop, the complexity of interactions among actors necessitates the formation of formal institutions. In a small, less-developed society, trust can function to unite partners in business dealings. If trust is violated, the violators may find themselves alienated from the rest of the community and thereby unable to earn a living. Knowing this *a priori*, businesspeople transact with some certainty that they will not be cheated. When an economy is large and actors are relative strangers to one another, the temptation to defraud may be too much for informal sanctions and therefore contract law, enforceable by courts, becomes necessary to deter opportunistic behaviour. Constraining such behaviour lowers transactions costs (Coase, 1960; Williamson, 1985; and Jaffe, Carciente and Zanoni, 2007)

Informal practices based on trust as well as formal institutions such as the rule of law and property rights both serve to protect economic actors from expropriation of rents. Without strong institutions in communities with uncertain levels of trust, the cost of transacting business becomes too great and so there are disincentives to start new businesses or grow existing ones. For SMEs, which rarely possess the resources to undertake legal action, trust is particularly important. When few people can be trusted, transaction costs can be very high (North, 1990; and Casson, 1995).

In terms of formal institutions, property rights guard against "vertical" expropriation of rents by government, whereas rule of law (particularly contract law) protects SMEs from "horizontal" expropriation of rents by other citizens (Acemoglu and Johnson, 2005; and Troilo, 2011). Beyond property rights, policymakers should also consider corruption and excessive taxation as forms of vertical expropriation which stifle SMEs. Investigating graft and reforming the tax code are important ways policymakers can create a business enabling environment. Adopting international standards of contract law and implementing equitable and certain enforcement of those standards are ways that policymakers can help SMEs avoid horizontal expropriation of rents.

In many countries, expecially in less-developed ones, these transaction costs could be particularly substantial due to less favourable business environments. Most Asia-Pacific countries need to reform their laws because many governments have unfortunately been "controllers" rather than "facilitators" of SMEs. The consequence of this trend has been a hostile environment for the foundation and growth of SMEs, particularly for start-ups, micro and small enterprises as the attitude of control suffocates individual entrepreneurial initiatives. Moreover, those "controllers" often conduct their tasks under inadequate or unclear legal frameworks, making the situation more complicated and unpredictable for businesses. Figure III.1 presents an example of the levels of business regulatory compliance costs among different sizes of enterprises in Lao People's Democratic Republic. It indicates that SMEs, including microenterprises, have to pay proportionately higher costs for regulatory compliance per employee than large enterprises.

Improving the business environment by lifting constraints and filling the gaps in the regulatory and administrative framework is essential for enhancing SME competitiveness. Reforms in the regulatory and administrative framework can result in substantial benefits for an economy, including faster growth, job creation, income generation, increased exports, greater incorporation, less corruption and lower fiscal deficits. For example, after Viet Nam reduced the time and costs involved in registering businesses, new corporate registrations increased by 28 per cent (World Bank, 2006a).

The major benefits of improved BEE are evident in higher employment and income generation, increased trade and reduced corruption (World Bank, 2008a):

(a) Employment creation and income generation. BEE enhancement gives rise to the creation of additional employment and income generation, encouraging entrepreneurs to invest more in new or existing businesses. When regulations are fair and transparent, entrepreneurs are more willing to expand their business, since they will retain most of the profits. On the other hand, an ill-conceived regulatory regime often discourages people from making new investments. For example, tight regulation of labour markets, even though it is generally aimed at protecting labour rights, can discourage the creation of jobs in the formal sector and may increase the number of unprotected workers in the informal sector;

(b) Increased trade. BEE enhancement has a positive impact on trade by accelerating the movements of goods and services. Delays caused by excessive regulations across borders have an adverse impact on a country's exports, especially for time-sensitive goods such as perishable agricultural products; and

(c) Reduced corruption. Corruption can be reduced by eliminating unnecessary government interventions, and by increasing the transparency of government and business relationships. These measures, among others, can decrease the sources and opportunities where corruption manifests itself. With this in mind, the World Bank (2000) outlined a multi-pronged strategy to combat corruption and foster a competitive private sector, with components that include economic policy reform, competitive restructuring of monopolies, regulatory simplification for entry, transparency in corporate governance and collective business association.

B. Components of BEE

While acquiring competitiveness in the global market primarily depends on the entrepreneurs themselves, BEE has a large influence on their competitive performance. The particular BEE factors affecting the SME sector in any country are generally: (a) macro- and microeconomic policies, including monetary and foreign exchange management; (b) factor endowments including supplies, labour and land; (c) entrepreneurship culture; (d) technology; (e) regulatory and administrative framework; and (f) infrastructure. Figure III.2 illustrates those major components.[36]

Figure III.1. Business regulatory compliance costs by firm size, Lao People's Democratic Republic*

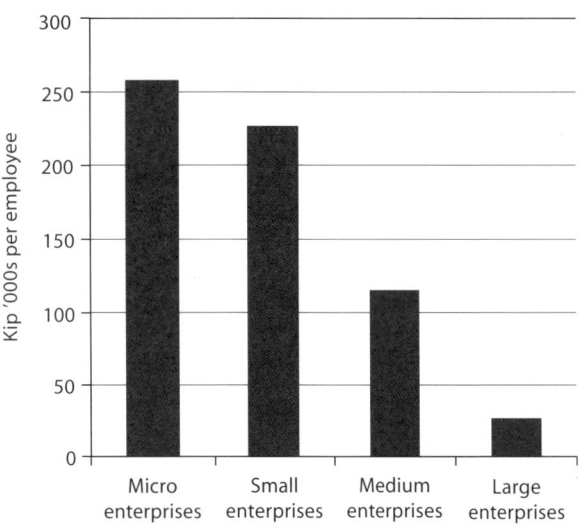

Source: ADB, 2009.
* Compliance cost per employee of the three main permissions required: enterprise registration, operational permissions and tax certificate.
Note: Microenterprises are defined as businesses with between one and four employees; small firms – between five and nine employees; medium-sized firms – between 10 and 99 employees; and large firms – 100 or more employees.

---

[36] Among those major components of BEE, this chapter mainly elaborates on the regulatory and administrative framework as the key issue for SME development in Asia and the Pacific, while supporting infrastructure is briefly discussed. Entrepreneurship culture and technology are discussed in chapters IV and VII, respectively.

Figure III.2. SME business enabling environment and its components

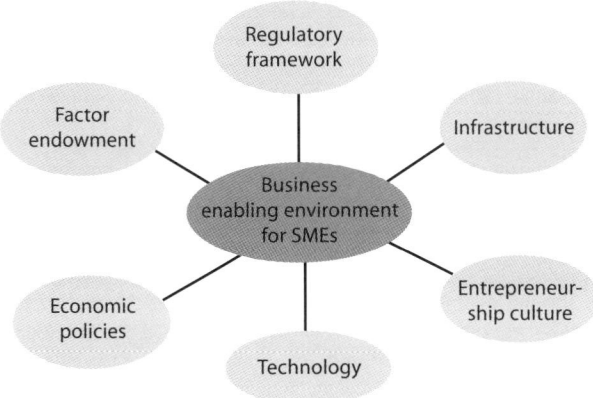

Source: Authors' compilation.

Economic policies are crucial. Sound monetary policy to control inflation preserves individual savings that are so often used as seed capital for SME start-ups. Openness to competition and investment prepare SMEs for the global economy and enable them to enjoy the benefits of overseas capital. As previously mentioned, taxation must be kept at a reasonable level, enough to provide infrastructure but not so high as to be confiscatory (see annex III.2 for a more detailed discussion on taxation for SMEs).

Factor endowments are closely related to economic policy. These endowments can be natural resources, human capital or an advantageous geographic location. In the absence of valuable natural resources (e.g., Hong Kong, China; or Singapore), a diligent, well-educated workforce, favourable geographical location and a well-trained civil service to direct industrial development can be ample compensation. Policymakers should develop their SME sector in conjunction with the specific factor endowments of their nation being mindful of comparative advantage in specific industries, i.e., low labour costs for producing textiles and garments.

Entrepreneurship culture is also critical. Certain attitudes and values, such as an appetite for risk, propels entrepreneurial activity. Other attitudes and values, such as fear of failure and the stigma attached to failure, hinder entrepreneurial activity. This topic is futher explored in the next chapter.

Chapter VII focuses on innovation and technology. Of particular importance is access to the Internet for all SMEs, regardless of whether they compete in a high-tech sector or not. Such access increases SME awareness of global trends and opportunities.

Infrastructure such as reliable roads, ports, electricity, water, and other such facilities are fundamental to business development and growth. Policymaking in this area should concentrate on transparency and integrity, competitive and open bidding for large projects, monitoring and prevention of corruption, sound financial planning etc. For the owners of many SMEs in developing economies, the struggle to obtain basic business necessities such as water and electricity often prevents them from surmounting subsistence levels of revenue (see box III.1).

So far, most BEE-related policy interventions and technical assistance activities have been conducted within the regulatory and administrative framework (JICA, 2006; and WEF, 2011) as the degree of control or ease of doing business enshrined in the regulatory and administrative framework determines the nature of BEE (World Bank, 2010a). Table III.1 lists the subcomponents of a regulatory and administrative framework.

Box III.1. Importance of infrastructure

Infrastructure plays a crucial role for SME development through the availability of roads, transportation services, electric power, water supply, drainage, telephone services and storage facilities. The term "infrastructure" also often goes beyond the boundaries of physical facilities to include related concepts such as management and services as well as comprehensive industrial development plans such as cluster development and industrial or technology parks (see chapter VIII for additional information).

In Asia-Pacific developing countries, SMEs have been typically operating for decades with insufficient infrastructure which can become a major source of environmental degradation. SMEs traditionally clustered around certain focal points due to homogeneity of industrial activity and proximity to their living places. This pattern gave rise to the unchecked and unplanned spread of industrial areas over the years with the haphazard growth gradually penetrating residential areas and giving rise to serious environmental problems (e.g., Old Dhaka of Bangladesh[37]). Providing basic infrastructure and better urban planning are primary responsibilities of policymakers as this can yield both economic and environmental benefits.

While some countries have made good progress by setting up well-planned industrial estates, technology parks and economic special zones, many have yet to realize that issues related to infrastructure development and cluster development are intertwined and should be addressed holistically. UNIDO (1999) has attached significance to cluster development as an "SME cluster" is complementary to physical infrastructure as well as a comprehensive concept of supporting infrastructure for small businesses (see the previous chapter). This entails the existing and planned development of the prospective clusters receiving the latest infrastructural support facilities and environmentally friendly management systems.

---

[37] For a more detailed discussion see ESCAP, 2011.

Table III.1. Subcomponents of a regulatory and administrative framework

Component	Content and function
Business registration	The complexities of business registration differ widely between countries,[38] but in general, there are three core functions: (a) controlling business incorporation with a unique name; (b) inscription of a commercial registry; and (c) registration with the tax authorities. Efficient and easy business registration is important for encouraging the establishment of new business.
Licensing	The system of business licensing is a major entry barrier for small businesses in many countries. As licensing is a key potential bottleneck in starting a business, the gains from licensing reforms stand to be significant. Many Asia-Pacific countries have greatly benefited from resolving with this bottleneck.
Labour regulation	Every country has enacted some form of labour laws and regulatory framework to protect the interests of workers. A good set of labour regulations should include employment, industrial relations and social securities. The regulation of labour markets aimed at protecting workers should also receive due attention. A proper balance between workers' rights and employers' needs must be maintained in order to create an effective BEE.[39]
Property registration	Entrepreneurs can obtain commercial loans by mortgaging their properties (e.g., land and houses) to start or expand their business. Banks typically prefer land and buildings as collateral. Efficient property registration reduces transaction costs and improves the security of property rights. This benefits all businesses, especially SMEs. Firms generally feel that their property rights are better protected in countries with a clearly-defined property registration system.
Credit regulation	Governments can help protect creditors and facilitate lending by establishing regulations for loss recovery. Lender's rights can be particularly protected through suitable credit guarantee schemes.[40] An effective collateral system may also create a smooth credit environment for SMEs. Removing legal restrictions without affecting necessary legal protection is yet another way to improve BEE.
Corporate governance	Good corporate governance in the business community can enhance BEE with a set of policies about how an enterprise is directed or administered. A critical theme of corporate governance is accountability and transparency which aims for the reduction and elimination of corruption. A clear corporate governance code is an essential tool for enhancing corporate governance practices at the national level, thus ensuring ethical behaviour of businesses and ultimately, promoting long-term sustainability of enterprises.
Tax administration[41]	Complicated tax administration gives rise to business operations in the informal sector. Tax compliance costs are often regressive and put a disproportionate burden on small players.[42]
Trade facilitation	Trade facilitation is critical for SMEs' penetration into regional and global markets. Such integration could be achieved by simplifying documentary requirements and customs procedures, including inspection modalities.[43]
Contract enforcement	Contract enforcement reforms have proved to be beneficial in many countries. Those reform measures include, among others, simplified procedures of commercial dispute settlements and the establishment of a judicial information system. For example, the reform of contract enforcement in 2007 helped Tonga to increase its global ranking from 126 to 26 in contracts enforcement efficiencies in the "Ease of Doing Business" survey. The reform was based on a computerized case management system which set time limits on delayed cases that allowed the judge to remain on top of the docket without becoming mired in the details of case administration (Ford and Lorenz, 2008).
Alternative dispute resolution	An effective mediation or arbitration system makes it easier to settle commercial disputes, saving time and money. While it should not be taken as a substitute to the formal judicial system, introducing mediation is one way of making the system more efficient for SMEs, which typically lack resources and knowledge.
Bankruptcy law/exit rule	The existence of clear and enforceable bankruptcy laws and exit rules plays an important role in promoting SME development in a country. Such a framework, which is nearly absent in developing countries in Asia and the Pacific, is important to ensuring fair and efficient dissolution of business with full transparency and thereby reduces the risk of entrepreneurial activities. The system must develop a pre-determined set of procedures concerned with the legal definition of insolvency.
Competition policy	Competition laws foster a culture of fair competition that ultimately benefits the society through better quality, price and service. Competition laws should provide a regulatory framework in order to maintain and improve efficiency in markets as well as monitor pricing practices to restrain unreasonable price rises.

---

[38] For details, visit the website at www.doingbusiness.org/.
[39] ILO provides useful resources to policymakers in this regard. More details are available at www.ilo.org/global/lang--en/index.htm for information.
[40] This issue is discussed further in chapter V.
[41] See annex III.2 for more information.
[42] For empirical studies of the impact of taxation on entrepreneurship, see Henrekson, Johansson and Stenkula , 2010, and Henrekson, 2007.
[43] Various technical materials related to trade facilitation in Asia and the Pacific are available at www.unescap.org/tid/publication/publicat.asp.

Table III.1. *(continued)*

Component	Content and function
Corruption	Public corruption, which increases the cost of business, is one of the biggest hurdles in the smooth growth of the SME sector across the developing countries in Asia and the Pacific.[44] Those countries need to restructure the law and regulatory framework to reduce abuse of discretionary power by enhancing transparency and minimizing uncertainty while maximizing compliance of rules.

Source: Authors' compilation.

Box III.2. Role of information and communications technology in SME development

Information and communications technology (ICT) applications can be used to help SMEs in developing countries overcome hurdles such as lack of infrastructure and deficient institutions. According to a survey conducted by Digital Philippines for the Asia Foundation, more than 90 per cent of respondent SMEs in three main Philippine cities believe that e-commerce is gaining importance to their business (Lallana, Pascual and Andam, 2002). The e-marketplace in the Philippines is dominated by BayanTrade, a B2B e-procurement hub jointly founded in 2000 by the six largest conglomerates in the Philippines. With a buyer base of 150 companies and suppliers of nearly 350 companies, BayanTrade now also caters to sourcing and procurement services rather than only focusing on e-commerce – covering a wide range of industries and markets in Philippines (BayanTrade, 2011).

Additionally, the encompassing adoption of mobile phone usage in some underdeveloped countries has made it the mainstream communication mode for conducting business. It enables SMEs with limited ICT resources to communicate with customers and suppliers in a short period at low cost or to transfer money between business partners through mobile banking. In particular, farmers in remote areas with poor electricity infrastructure or network unavailability can receive real-time market information on agricultural or fish prices on their mobile phones (Melchioly and Sœbø, 2010).

E-finance, which refers to "financial services delivered through the Internet" (UNCTAD, 2001a), has also helped to facilitate the development of SMEs. Generally speaking, it includes online brokerage, insurance, banking and other financial services. E-finance for SMEs in developing countries mainly consists of Internet banking and payment, e-trade finance and online credit information. In addition to flexibility, e-finance offers lower transaction costs to SMEs as well as greater access to financial information. Government investment in information technology infrastructure is therefore a cost-effective way to enable SMEs in developing countries to access capital via e-finance, particularly in remote rural areas (UNCTAD, 2001a).

Box III.3. Public-private partnership in perspective

Governments worldwide have sought to increase the involvement of the private sector in the delivery of public services. These initiatives have enabled the mobilization of private finance in the provision of public infrastructure and services as well as policy advocacy (HM Treasury of the United Kingdom, 2011). It is now generally recognized that public-private partnerships (PPPs) offer a long-term, sustainable approach to improving infrastructure, enhancing the value of public assets and making better use of tax revenue. PPPs have developed partly due to financial shortages in the public sector. They have also demonstrated the ability to harness additional financial resources and operating efficiencies from the private sector (IMF, 2011).

The concept of PPP originated in Europe and North America but has become more prominent in recent decades for the economic development of the Asia-Pacific countries. According to ADB (2011) "[t]he term 'public-private partnership' describes a range of possible relationships among public and private entities in the context of infrastructure and other services". The idea of PPP is to involve direct participation by private finance and management expertise in financing public sector infrastructure and to sustain it on a long-term basis. In broad terms, it encompasses a diversity of partnerships, but all PPPs involve at least one public and one private sector institution as partners in a cooperative venture. A PPP works as a contractual arrangement between a public sector agency and the concerned private sector, whereby resources and risks are shared for the purpose of delivery of a public service or development of public infrastructure. PPP arrangements are growing as an alternative and effective method to mobilize additional financial resources and to harness the benefits of private sector efficiencies.

Each type of PPP has inherent strengths and weaknesses that must be recognized and integrated into the project design. Each partner to a PPP has responsibilities. The benefits of PPPs will depend, to a large degree, on effective management and monitoring systems. The latter is particularly crucial as public funding will necessitate proper accounting and transparency, not only for the identification of additional funding sources but also to ensure more effective use of public funds. In addition, for a PPP to function properly, each participant should be a principal and thus capable of autonomous bargaining. This usually requires the public sector participant to be established as a special agency before collaboration becomes possible (Partnerships for Public Service, 2011).

PPPs can be useful for a number of activities especially in the areas of services, transport and logistics, trade facilitation and industrial parks. Government support for SME development is being provided increasingly through PPPs. The development of clusters to enhance the competitiveness of SMEs and their global reach (as discussed in box III.1) is also a key area for PPP involvement.

---

[44] The Global Corruption Report of Transparency International provides some useful insights in this regard. For more details visit the website at www.transparency.org/.

C. BEE surveys

There are a number of international surveys relevant to the assessment of business environments in the economies of Asia and the Pacific. Major business environment surveys include the "Ease of Doing Business and "Economic Freedom of the World Exercise" surveys, the Global Competitiveness Index and the Corruption Perception Index. Each is discussed briefly below.[45]

1. Ease of Doing Business survey

Although not specific to the SME sector, the World Bank's annual "Doing Business" rankings are perhaps the most comprehensive survey of economies (183 in its latest iteration) and their differing business conditions.[46] The exercise seeks to quantify and rate the ease of doing business in an economy, based on ten components: (a) starting a business; (b) dealing with construction permits; (c) getting electricity; (d) registering property; (e) getting credit; (f) protecting investors; (g) paying taxes; (h) trading across borders; (i) enforcing contracts; and (j) resolving insolvency. Although there is some debate about the methodology, the findings are useful for highlighting an economy's strengths and weaknesses in terms of doing business. A high ranking can indicate that a government has created a regulatory environment more conducive for business operation (ESCAP, 2009a). Table III.2 shows the Doing Business 2012 rankings for Asia-Pacific economies covered by the survey.

Figure III.3 presents the averaged survey results among five developing subregions of Asia and the Pacific: (a) East and North-East Asia; (b) North and Central Asia; (c) Pacific; (d) South-East Asia; and (e) South and South-West Asia.[47] The results show that South and South-West Asia ranked the lowest among the five developing subregions, while East and North-East Asia ranked the highest. For comparison purposes, the averaged ranks of three developed economies in the region (Australia, Japan and New Zealand) were included and unsurprisingly indicated a better business environment than in the developing economies.

Two components of the ease of doing business survey, "starting a business" and "trading across borders" which are critical to new businesses as well as export-oriented and supporting industry SMEs, are reviewed below to provide some detailed insights.

The information gathered for the "starting a business" indicator shows the bureaucratic and legal hurdles that an entrepreneur encounters while incorporating and registering a new firm. It considers the procedures, time and costs involved in launching a commercial or industrial firm with up to 50 employees and start-up capital of 10 times the economy's per capita gross national income (GNI) (thus fitting common categorizations of SMEs in many economies in Asia

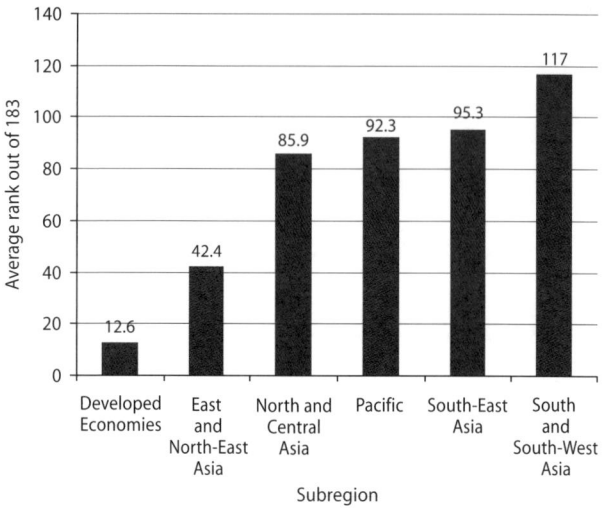

Figure III.3. Ease of doing business ranking, by subregion, in Asia and the Pacific

Source: World Bank, 2012a.
Notes: Developed economies comprise Australia, Japan and New Zealand. Taiwan Province of China is included in East and North-East Asia. Some Asia-Pacific economies (i.e., the Democratic People's Republic of Korea; Macao, China; Myanmar; Turkmenistan; American Samoa; Cook Islands; French Polynesia; Guam; Nauru; New Caledonia; Niue; Northern Mariana Islands; and Tuvalu) were excluded from this analysis due to the lack of survey data.

and the Pacific). Table III.3 shows the subregion averages for the four main sub-indicators:

(a) All procedures required to register a firm;
(b) Time spent completing the procedures;
(c) Official fees for legal or professional services for the procedures; and
(d) The minimum capital required as a percentage of income per capita.

The averaged results indicate that the South-East Asia subregion is the most difficult in which to start a business. Notably, although the averaged number of registration procedures is only slightly higher than in South and South-West Asia, the number of days needed to complete these procedures is more than double. Another interesting feature of this comparison is that while the East and North-East Asia subregion ranks relatively well in terms of the number of procedures, the amount of time needed for completion as well as the cost for these procedures, the minimum paid-in capital needed before and following incorporation is almost 30 per cent of the economy's income per capita. This is a significant, and perhaps prohibitive, initial input for potential entrepreneurs.

Ease of "trading across borders" is measured based on the procedural requirements for exporting and importing a standardized cargo of goods (see table III.4 for subregion averages). Every official procedure is counted, from the contractual agreement between the two parties to the delivery of goods, together with the time required to export or import goods. The survey specifically measured three main indicators for both exports and imports:

(a) The number of documents required;
(b) Time required; and
(c) Costs.

---

[45] Other major surveys include: IMD international's World Competitiveness Yearbook (available at www.imd.org/research/publications/wcy/World-Competitiveness-Yearbook-Results/#/); The Heritage Foundation and *Wall Street Journal* Index of Economic Freedom (available at www.heritage.org/index/Ranking); and the Global Entrepreneurship Monitor (available at www.gemconsortium.org).

[46] For the latest rankings, visit the website at www.doingbusiness.org/.

[47] See the Explanatory Notes in this publication for the detailed economies of Asia and the Pacific and their subregional groupings.

Table III.2. Ease of doing business in Asia and the Pacific, 2012

Economy	Overall Ease of Doing Business rank	Starting a business	Dealing with construction permits	Getting electricity	Registering property	Getting credit	Protecting investors	Paying taxes	Trading across borders	Enforcing contracts	Resolving insolvency
Singapore	1	4	3	5	14	8	2	4	1	12	2
Hong Kong, China	2	5	1	4	57	4	3	3	2	5	16
New Zealand	3	1	2	31	3	4	1	36	27	10	18
Republic of Korea	8	24	26	11	71	8	79	38	4	2	13
Australia	15	2	42	37	38	8	65	53	30	17	17
Thailand	17	78	14	9	28	67	13	100	17	24	51
Malaysia	18	50	113	59	59	1	4	41	29	31	47
Japan	20	107	63	26	58	24	17	120	16	34	1
Taiwan Province of China	25	16	87	3	33	67	79	71	23	88	14
Tonga	58	33	32	29	141	78	111	29	77	53	108
Samoa	60	22	68	32	26	126	29	66	96	80	145
Solomon Islands	74	110	36	42	168	78	46	25	86	108	115
Vanuatu	76	114	40	147	111	78	79	32	128	71	53
Fiji	77	119	73	110	52	67	46	80	113	64	126
Maldives	79	59	20	132	152	166	79	1	137	92	41
Brunei Darussalam	83	136	83	28	107	126	122	20	35	151	44
Mongolia	86	97	119	171	26	67	29	57	159	33	124
Sri Lanka	89	38	111	95	161	78	46	173	53	136	42
China	91	151	179	115	40	67	97	122	60	16	75
Viet Nam	98	103	67	135	47	24	166	151	68	30	142
Papua New Guinea	101	84	138	20	87	98	46	106	99	163	116
Pakistan	105	90	104	166	125	67	29	158	75	154	74
Marshall Islands	106	52	8	76	183	78	155	96	66	63	135
Nepal	107	100	140	99	24	67	79	86	162	137	112
Kiribati	115	141	106	159	69	159	46	6	85	75	183
Palau	116	124	39	80	20	182	174	97	124	144	61
Bangladesh	122	86	82	182	173	78	24	100	115	180	107
Indonesia	129	155	71	161	99	126	46	131	39	156	146
India	132	166	181	98	97	40	46	147	109	182	128
Philippines	136	158	102	54	117	126	133	136	51	112	163
Cambodia	138	171	149	130	110	98	79	54	120	142	149
Micronesia (Federated States of)	140	102	19	40	183	126	174	92	106	146	164
Bhutan	142	83	135	145	83	126	147	67	169	35	183
Afghanistan	160	30	162	104	172	150	183	63	179	161	105
Lao People's Democratic Republic	165	89	80	138	72	166	182	123	168	110	183
Timor-Leste	168	157	114	55	183	159	133	31	89	183	183

Source: World Bank, 2012a.
Note: Rankings out of 183 economies.

Table III.3. Starting a business, by subregion, in Asia and the Pacific

Subregion	Procedures (number)	Duration (days)	Cost (per cent GNI per capita)	Min. capital (per cent GNI per capita)
Developed economies	3.7	8.7	2.9	0.0
East and North-East Asia	6.4	14.2	5.1	27.3
North and Central Asia	4.9	14.4	6.9	3.6
Pacific	6.5	29.1	33.0	3.7
South and South-West Asia	7.1	23.1	21.58	19.1
South-East Asia	8.5	54.4	20.5	31.0

Source: World Bank, 2012a.
Notes: Rankings out of 183 economies. Developed economies comprise of Australia, Japan and New Zealand. Taiwan Province of China is included in East and North-East Asia. Some Asia-Pacific economies (Democratic People's Republic of Korea; Macao, China; Myanmar; Turkmenistan; American Samoa; Cook Islands; French Polynesia; Guam; Nauru; New Caledonia; Niue; Northern Mariana Islands; and Tuvalu) were excluded from this analysis due to the lack of survey data.

Table III.4. Facilitating international trade by developing subregions in Asia and the Pacific

Subregion	Documents for export (number)	Time for export (days)	Cost to export ($ per container)	Document for import (number)	Time for import (days)	Cost to import ($ per container)
Developed economies	5.3	9.6	941.7	5.0	9.3	971.3
East and North-East Asia	5.8	18.2	935.0	5.2	19.0	985.0
North and Central Asia	7.9	48.6	2 688.1	9.1	52.5	3 131.9
Pacific	6.7	24.1	1 006.4	7.3	25.7	1 032.2
South and South-West Asia	7.8	32.1	1 590.0	8.9	32.5	1 768.3
South-East Asia	6.2	20.0	768.7	7.2	20.5	835.1

Source: World Bank (2012a).
Notes: Rankings out of 183 economies. Developed economies comprise of Australia, Japan and New Zealand. Taiwan Province of China is included in East and North-East Asia. Some Asia-Pacific economies (the Democratic People's Republic of Korea; Macao, China; Myanmar; Turkmenistan; American Samoa; Cook Islands; French Polynesia; Guam; Nauru; New Caledonia; Niue; Northern Mariana Islands; and Tuvalu) were excluded from this analysis due to the lack of survey data.

Box III.4. Singapore's proclaimed business environment

Singapore, for the sixth year in a row, has again been ranked number one according to the World Bank's Ease of Doing Business survey in 2012. Of the ten major indicators, Singapore ranked in the top ten for eight of them: (a) starting a business (fourth); dealing with construction permits; (third), getting electricity (fifth); getting credit (eighth); protecting investors (second); paying taxes (fourth); trading across borders (first); and resolving insolvency (second).

Singapore introduced further reforms to make it easier to start and operate a business while also improving the banking system and permit attainment procedures. The simplification of the online procedures for business start-ups reduced the process to three days. Through increased Internet utilization, Singapore also cut the time it takes to issue a construction permit from 102 days to just 26 days.

The World Economic Forum's Global Competitiveness Report 2010-2011 (WEF, 2011) ranked Singapore as third. The report takes into account factors such as infrastructure, macroeconomic stability, health and education, labour market efficiency, technological readiness and innovation.[48]

In another survey conducted by a commercial rating agency, Business Environment Risk Intelligence,[49] Singapore was ranked second as the city with the best investment potential, a position that the city has maintained for 14 years. In particular, Singapore was ranked as first in the foreign trade and investment indicator, having been viewed as an attractive, tax-efficient SME location for conducting international business (Healy Consultants, 2011).

Based on the averaged results, the subregion with the lowest ease of cross-border trade is North and Central Asia. On average, this region requires the highest number of documents, takes the longest time, and is the most expensive in which to export and import. In contrast, the indicators for East and North-East Asia and South-East Asia are significantly more favourable in the region. Although South-East Asia requires more documents and takes longer than East and North-East Asia, the difference on average is slight. South-East Asia has the lowest costs for exporting and importing.

The World Bank (2012a), while collecting worldwide data for the 2012 Doing Business Indicators, recorded 245 reforms made between June 2010 and May 2011 by governments in 125 economies. Notably, in low, lower and middle income economies a larger portion of these changes were aimed at strengthening courts, insolvency regimes and investor protections than in the past. Reforms measured by the Doing Business survey have played an important role in enhancing the BEE in Asia-Pacific countries, which is illustrated by the policy response of the Government of Singapore in box III.4.

---

[48] For more details see the website at www.weforum.org/issues/global-competitiveness.
[49] The corporate profile of Business Environment Risk Intelligence is available at www.beri.com/aboutus.asp.

2. Economic Freedom of the World Exercise

The Fraser Institute's Economic Freedom of the World Exercise which has been running for more than 20 years and now spans 141 economies, conducts similar research to that by the World Bank. It is an index that seeks to use 42 data points to measure economic freedom in five broad areas that are pertinent to SMEs and the business sector as a whole. The five areas are: (a) size of government; (b) legal structure and security of property rights; (c) access to sound money; (d) freedom to trade internationally; and (e) regulation of credit, labour and business. The most recent report, published in 2011, analysed data from 2009. The rankings for some Asia-Pacific economies are shown in table III.5.

Table III.5. Economic freedom: Rankings of Asia-Pacific economies

Economy	Rank	Economy	Rank
Hong Kong, China	1	Fiji	77
Singapore	2	Malaysia	78
New Zealand	3	Azerbaijan	84
Australia	5	Indonesia	84
Japan	22	Viet Nam	88
Taiwan Province of China	26	Philippines	89
		China	92
Republic of Korea	30	India	94
Mongolia	36	Bangladesh	103
Kazakhstan	56	Sri Lanka	107
Papua New Guinea	61	Pakistan	114
Thailand	65	Nepal	129
Kyrgyzstan	70	Myanmar	140

Source: Gwartney, Hall and Lawson, 2011.

This survey considers the most relevant environmental factors to be:

(a) The size of government in business (which relates to "crowding out" issues);[50]
(b) Property rights protection;
(c) Legal enforcement of contracts;
(d) Freedom to hold foreign currency;
(e) Regulatory trade barriers;
(f) Taxes imposed on international trade;
(g) Commercial credit;
(h) Hiring and firing regulations;
(i) Price controls;
(j) Starting a business and licensing restrictions; and
(k) Bribes and extra payments.

For each of the 141 economies covered by the index, a detailed breakdown is conducted. More than 40 separate numerical ratings are applied, which allows: (a) a diagnostic to be undertaken of where a specific economy is faring less well; (b) cross-economy comparisons; and (c) monitoring of a single economy's performance over time, across any of the 42 elements that are measured by the index. For example, Viet Nam ranks relatively high in terms of "freedom to trade internationally" and "legal structure and security of property rights" however, it scores worse on the "access to sound money" component which drags down its aggregate ranking.

3. Global Competitiveness Index

Similar to the previous two indices, this index does not focus solely on SMEs but measures a range of issues that are highly pertinent to SME development, i.e., "the set of institutions, policies and factors that determine the level of productivity of a country" (WEF, 2010). As discussed in *The Global Competitiveness Report, 2011-2012*, the World Competitiveness Index tracks 12 pillars of economic competitiveness (WEF, 2011). These pillars are: (a) institutions; (b) infrastructure; (c) macroeconomic environment; (d) health and primary education; (e) higher education and training; (f) goods market efficiency; (g) labour market efficiency; (h) financial market development; (i) technological readiness; (j) market size; (k) business sophistication; and (l) innovation. Although the pillars are reported on separately, they are interrelated and the strength or weakness of one has an impact on others (WEF, 2011). Table III.6 shows the rankings for some Asia-Pacific economies included in the Global Competitiveness Index.

Table III.6. Global Competitiveness Index: Rankings for Asia-Pacific economies

Economy	Rank	Economy	Rank
Singapore	2	Sri Lanka	52
Japan	9	India	56
Hong Kong, China	11	Viet Nam	65
Taiwan Province of China	13	Kazakhstan	72
		Philippines	75
Australia	20	Mongolia	96
Malaysia	21	Cambodia	97
Republic of Korea	24	Tajikistan	105
New Zealand	25	Bangladesh	108
China	26	Pakistan	118
Brunei Darussalam	28	Nepal	125
Thailand	39	Kyrgyzstan	126
Indonesia	46	Timor-Leste	131

Source: WEF, 2011.

4. Corruption in Asia and the Pacific

With some exceptions (e.g., Singapore and Hong Kong, China), entrepreneurs routinely identify corruption as a significant constraint to doing business in the Asia-Pacific region (Gill and Kharas, 2007). Corruption raises the costs of doing business and creates a more unpredictable business environment, making it more difficult to plan ahead. It may also create an incentive for firms to stay informal, in order to escape the discretionary power of local officials. Opportunities for corruption are also greater where business regulations are numerous and overly complex.

---

[50] According to the survey, the extent to which countries use government-provided, rather than private, goods and services has a significant impact on the level of economic freedom, and thus fair competition. Government firms are not subject to the same rules as private enterprises. They do not depend on consumers for revenue, or investors for capital, and they often operate in protected markets. Consequently, the greater market share government firms hold, the less space there is for private enterprises and thus economic freedom is reduced (Gwartney, Hall and Lawson, 2011).

Transparency International, an NGO that monitors corporate and political corruption worldwide, developed the Corruption Perception Index which ranks almost 200 economies by the private sector's perceived levels of corruption in an economy (Transparency International, 2011). The rankings for Asia-Pacific economies are separated into subregional groupings and presented in figure III.4. There is a clear difference between subregions that are perceived as more corrupt and those that are less corrupt, based upon economic developments.

Figure III.4. Subregional corruption ratings in Asia and the Pacific

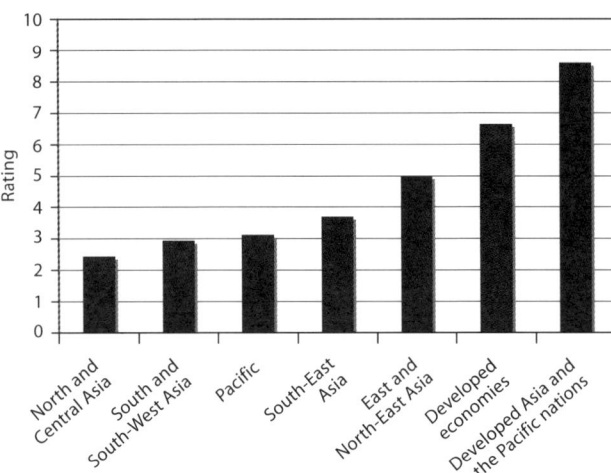

Source: Transparency International, 2011.
Note: Rating from 0 (highly corrupt) to 10 (very clean). Developed Asia-Pacific economies include Australia, Japan and New Zealand.

Developed Asia-Pacific economies, e.g., Australia, New Zealand, and Japan, have strong governance standards and regulations that serve to undercut corruption. In contrast, those scoring low on the Corruption Perception Index lack proper governance structures and feature excessive regulations foster corruption. Ancillary factors that serve to undermine anti-corruption efforts in the region, e.g., low public sector salaries, lack of disciplinary action and cultural tolerance of corruption, exacerbate these institutional-level shortcomings. Accordingly, SMEs in these developing economies are the most vulnerable to corruption.

A recent survey by the European Bank for Reconstruction and Development and the World Bank found that more than 70 per cent of SMEs worldwide perceive corruption as an impediment to their business (Transparency International, 2009). In this regard, SMEs face four main challenges: (a) ingrained bribery culture in the business community that SMEs are forced to acquiesce to; (b) poor knowledge of anti-bribery laws; (c) limited resources to deal with extortionists; and (d) the lack of an anti-corruption mechanism for SMEs to contact when faced with extortion. All of these factors make it difficult for SMEs to fight corruption (Transparency International, 2009).

5. Subnational surveys

An interesting, and relatively recent, development has been the creation of subnational indices, such as the provincial competitiveness index in Viet Nam, and a similar survey in Cambodia.[51] Such an approach recognizes that most SMEs have relatively limited relationships with national agencies. They interact with municipal or provincial bodies and conduct their activities largely or entirely within that sphere. The provincial competitiveness index seeks to measure and rank business conditions in the 64 provinces of Viet Nam. Such an exercise is highly pertinent to SME development as it focuses on the principal factors that impact SMEs, comprising:

(a) Cost of market entry;
(b) Access to land and security of tenure;
(c) Issues relating to the transparency of regulations and their enactment by provincial bodies;
(d) The time required to comply with regulations;
(e) Informal charges imposed;
(f) Bias towards state-owned enterprises;
(g) The proactiveness of provincial authorities in assisting firms;
(h) The provision of BDS;
(i) The availability of training for employees; and
(j) The quality of legal institutions.

In the case of Cambodia, a provincial business environment scorecard has been developed, spanning the country's ten most economically active provinces. Similar to the provincial competitiveness index in Viet Nam, ten sub-indices have been developed for measuring the enabling environment in the ten provinces. However the indices have also been tailored to suit the different conditions in Cambodia including, among others, tax administration, crime prevention and dispute resolution.

D. BEE reforms

Reforming BEE is characterized by an increasing and evolving set of interventions. These are distinct but often complementary to private sector development policies that primarily support the direct delivery of microfinance or business development services (IFC, 2008). Some BEE interventions are closely linked to the World Bank's Doing Business indicators and are viewed as "regulatory-based", such as business entry simplification, business licensing streamlining and administrative reform.[52] The goal of these BEE reforms is to reduce the burden of regulatory compliance for businesses (often coined as the "obstacles to doing business" and its associated compliance costs) while also safeguarding human health and security, environment, fair competition and other aspects of social welfare. The benefits that may accrue from this includes increased investment, productivity and employment as well as reduced corruption.

---

[51] The provincial competitiveness index in Viet Nam was developed by The Asia Foundation as part of the Viet Nam Competitiveness Initiative funded by the United States Agency for International Development. The Cambodia variant was also developed by The Asia Foundation, with support from the International Finance Corporation-Mekong Project Development Facility (MPDF), and the Australian Agency for International Development (AusAID).
[52] Import-, export- and sector-specific interventions are often also regulatory-based but are typically implemented as a part of larger private sector development interventions to improve trade facilitation and value chains for specific sectors.

These regulatory-based BEE interventions often have a defined measurable goal and objective and may involve elements of legislative change as well as administrative and procedural review. Another area of reform, alternative dispute resolution, centres on reforming the legal framework but in a different way, by focusing on the introduction of institutions and processes for alternative means of commercial mediation.

In order to achieve the set objectives of BEE reforms, specific functional aspects operate at four different reform levels – regional, national, subnational and sector levels (DCED, 2008).[53] Table III.7 sets out that these diverse functional areas and levels.

It is important for BEE reforms to be specialized to a particular level, or comprehensive enough to cover more than one level. At the regional level, for example, bodies such as ESCAP play

---

[53] The categories presented are not mutually exclusive. Development agencies may work at more than one level or even at all levels for BEE reforms. For example, improving BEE in a single sector can be done through one of the four functional areas or through all four. While the flip side is also true, institutional agreements can be reformed on one or all four reform levels.

Table III.7. Functional areas and levels of business environment reform

	Levels of business environment reform			
	Regional	**National**	**Subnational**	**Sectoral**
Key programme partners	Regional development bodies (e.g., African Union, ASEAN), regional economic communities (e.g., Southern African Development Community), World Trade Organization	Parliament, political parties, national government ministries, regulators, private sector representatives, business membership organizations, business media, worker organizations and consumer groups	Subnational legislatures, provincial, regional and local government authorities, local business associations and community-based organizations	Sector-specific business associations, regulators, government authorities and policies
Policy and legal framework	Improving policies and harmonizing laws and regulations that promote regional trade and investment	Improving national policies and laws that promote competition, open markets and general conditions for private sector development	Improving local policies for private sector development	Sectoral policies and laws often deal with promotional interventions and ways to enhance the value chain
	Trade policies, laws and regulations	Competition, tax, trade, labour policies and laws	Subnational policies for regional development, local economic development and private sector development	Sector development policies
Regulatory and administrative framework	Improving the regulations that hamper regional trade and investment	Improving national regulations that affect the establishment, operation and closure of private enterprises	Improving the regulations created by subnational authorities	Improving business regulations that apply to specific industry sectors or subsectors
	Trade regulations, customs administration	Business regulations; tax laws and administration; labour laws and regulation; trade regulations; customs administration	Business startup and licensing procedures	Sector licences and permits
Institutional arrangements	Supporting member states of regional bodies to design and implement reforms; improving public-private dialogue at the regional level	Improving dialogue between national government and private sector representative agencies (e.g., public-private dialogue)	Supporting local structures and processes for subnational public-private dialogue	Building and supporting sectoral business membership organizations to participate in discussions with government agencies on improving the business environment
	Trade facilitation and capacity-building	Regulatory governance and capacity building	Capacity-building	Capacity-building

Source: DCED, 2008.

> **Box III.5. Value chain approach for BEE reform**
>
> A value chain refers to all the activities and functions that bring a product or service from its conception and design through production to its end use in a particular industry or sector. It is so-called because of the value it adds to the product or services at each step of the business process (Porter, 1985). By taking a value chain approach to BEE reforms, all the major constraints and opportunities faced by the entities involved in every value-added step of the process can be analysed.
>
> The value chain approach provides both a context for assessing policy barriers and a framework for organizing and prioritizing reforms in a certain industry or sector. The value chain approach facilitates the identification of binding constraints faced by BEE. The selection process of interventions aids in the strategic prioritization of these potential reforms and assesses their impact on the chain's performance. Such assessments help avoid ad hoc decision-making and promote thorough analysis of which reforms will change investment behaviour. Working within a value chain context further allows the impact of reforms to be identified and quantified easily in the steps of a specific sectoral or industrial business process.
>
> This type of analysis contrasts with others, such as national policy studies, which do not necessarily reveal the contribution of a reform to the growth of specific sectors or industries (Kleinberg and Campbell, 2008). BEE opportunities for specific value chains to become more competitive may influence the selection of the value chains targeted for national development; thus, the value-chain approach can be further used to develop competitiveness enhancement strategies. This approach can also be applicable to analysing cross-border business processes, which are often known as international production networks or global or regional value chains.

an important role in stimulating the demand for reform by promoting good practices as well as quality policies, laws and regulations. At the national level, these regional associations can work with national agencies and ministries in reforming the current business environment. These reforms can have a significant impact on BEE by creating a business-friendly regulatory framework and reducing obstacles to doing business, e.g., easing business regulations, labour laws, customs, regulations etc.

At the subnational level, policymakers must recognize variations exist across subnational business environments and ensure their reforms cover this diversity. Reforms that remove constraints to growth, improve local market competition and strengthen local systems, procedures, skills and institutions would assist in the development of the subnational BEE. Sector-specific policies that promote BEE can be important drivers of economic performance by addressing obstacles to business (DCED, 2008).

E. Role of government and policymakers in BEE reforms

There is an important role for governments in making the BEE more SME-friendly. As mentioned above, many governments in Asia and the Pacific are still playing the role of a "controller" rather than a "facilitator". To increase the competitiveness of the Asia-Pacific SME sector, governments must design a vibrant BEE and continue reforms to keep pace with changing market conditions. Some major recommendations to governments and policymakers are:

(a) Identify the challenges and opportunities for SME sector growth focusing on capacity-building.
(b) Design effective public policies based on an understanding of the constraints faced by SMEs.
(c) Determine the factors of market failures and recognize the need for early warning signals.
(d) Implement specific programmes enabling SMEs to overcome marketing constraints.
(e) Invite the representatives of SME associations to interact with policymakers at regular intervals.
(f) Evolve support programmes for SME using PPPs.
(g) Design an outward-oriented trade regime. The macroeconomic environment would need to be stable and predictable from the perspective of small firms.
(h) Put in place economic and financial safety nets for SMEs to insulate them from the ill-effects of a possible future economic crisis.
(i) Design a fair and transparent legal and regulatory regime for SMEs.
(j) Promote FDI policies aimed at facilitating the integration of domestic SMEs into global supply chains consistent with an economy's comparative advantage and development.
(k) Create a business-friendly environment for SMEs by:
    (i) Providing for relative ease of entry and exit of small firms, particularly for young entrepreneurs;
    (ii) Streamlining bureaucratic rules and procedures;
    (iii) Assessing the costs and benefits of specific regulations and eradicating the roadblocks; and
    (iv) Simplifying import-export procedures.
(l) Reform the government's procurement system, perhaps to include e-procurement.
(m) Bestow adequate attention on trade facilitation measures and address legal and regulatory obstacles.
(n) Identify gender imbalances and make suitable provisions for encouraging female entrepreneurship.
(o) Give priority and incentives to R&D, innovations, high-risk projects and intellectual property rights (IPRs) issues in the regulatory framework.
(p) Reduce social stigma for SMEs going bankrupt and provide suitable exit routes.
(q) Provide incentives for providers of business development services.
(r) Reduce government control and interventions.

One clear problem, particularly in the developing countries of Asia and the Pacific, is the lack of government skills and knowledge needed to develop appropriate policies. There are good resource and knowledge centres within countries, such as universities and research institutions, but governments often ignore their expertise and invite foreign resource persons who may have an inadequate understanding of local conditions. However, there are also promising signs of innovation and reform as highlighted in the following cases (boxes 6-8).

Box III.6. Cambodia's reform in enterprise registration

In 2004, the Government of Cambodia reformed its enterprise registration. At that time, such registration required a minimum amount of capital of $ 5,000, and on average took 94 days, involved 11 procedures, and cost more than five times per capita GDP. This cost was among the highest in the Asia-Pacific region in terms of both time and financial demands, which motivated many firms to remain informal.

The Government took steps to lower barriers to enterprise registration in August 2004. The cost of registration was reduced from $ 650 to $ 177 while the minimum capital requirement for incorporation was reduced from $ 5,000 to $ 1,000. In addition, the number of documents necessary to apply for registration was also reduced. Those efforts paid off immediately as the average number of enterprise registration doubled from 61 to 129 per month after late 2004 (figure III.5).

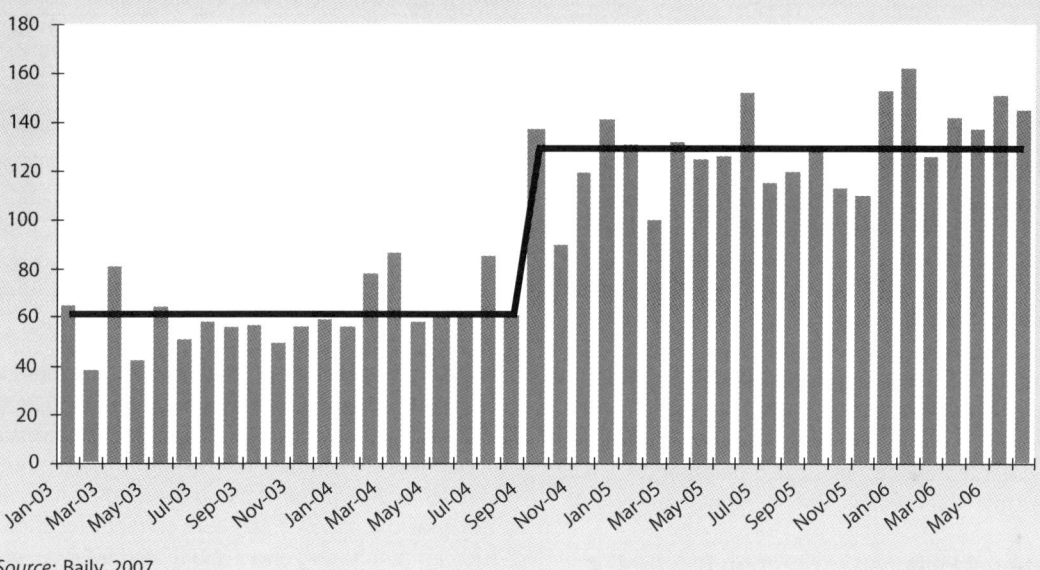

Figure III.5. Monthly enterprise registrations, 2004

Source: Baily, 2007.

Box III.7. Streamlining business permits and licensing procedures in Ormoc City, The Philippines

In order to improve the business environment at the municipal and provincial levels, the Philippine Department of Trade and Industry and GTZ provided technical assistance to Ormoc City to simplify the business permits and licensing procedures. The specific objectives of the project were to monitor and evaluate the business permit procedures, recommend ways of improving the current licensing procedures and encourage other subnational governments to do the same. The project, which was implemented from December 2004 to April 2006, included assessment, planning, implementation and evaluation.

The reform reduced the process of business registration from 17 steps to 5 steps, and the time required from 17 days to 2 days. This led to a 25 per cent increase in the number of registered businesses in Ormoc from 2005 to 2006. The Philippine Chamber of Commerce and Industry awarded Ormoc City the title of the "Most Business Friendly City for Visayas" in 2006. Other municipal and provincial governments have reviewed and improved their business permit and licensing systems guided by the Ormoc model.

Source: Keppel, Buh and Spatz, 2006.

> **Box III.8. Reform of public procurement system**
>
> State agencies are important customers and major sources of revenue for enterprises, particularly in Asia-Pacific developing countries where the private sector is often at a nascent stage of development (ESCAP, 2009b). However, SMEs typically struggle to qualify as suppliers to the state agencies. Governments, SME development agencies in particular, could do much to make public procurement policies more accessible to SMEs by informing them about the criteria and processes to become an approved government supplier. The state agencies should streamline their procurement policies and processes to yield efficiency, thus cost-saving and ensure that procurement policies do not discriminate against SMEs.[54]
>
> At the international level, the WTO Agreement on Government Procurement (GPA) provides an international legal framework for the liberalization and governance of public procurement markets (Anderson, 2010). Some of the main GPA features are:
>
> (a) Guarantees of fair national treatment and non-discrimination;
>
> (b) Minimum standards regarding national procurement processes to fair competition;
> (c) Various transparency requirements;
> (d) Procedures dealing with modifications of commitments;
> (e) Requirements regarding bid challenges;
> (f) Application of WTO Dispute Settlement Understanding; and
> (g) A 'built-in agenda' for improvement of the Agreement.
>
> Not all WTO members are bound by the GPA however, in recent years the trend has been for new WTO member countries to also seek accession to the GPA. The text and coverage of the agreement are also under ongoing negotiations as the GPA has become an increasingly important and visible international economic policy instrument (Anderson, 2010).

F. Toolkits for BEE reforms

Given existing regulatory and administrative frameworks, policymakers should prioritize when designing a beneficial BEE for SMEs in the Asia and the Pacific. Not all components of BEE are equally important, nor should all reforms be attempted simultaneously. Within this context, some multilateral and bilateral development agencies have created toolkits (e.g., handbooks/guidebooks, manuals, training modules) for BEE reforms. This section reviews four major toolkits by the International Finance Corporation (IFC), ADB, ILO and the Japan International Cooperation Agency (JICA).

1. International Finance Corporation BEE toolkit

The International Finance Corporation (IFC), a private sector development arm of the World Bank, has published more than a dozen toolkits and guidebooks for practitioners and policymakers who want to improve their business environment. The aim of the IFC toolkits is to promote reforms that support private sector development by targeting the most critical areas affecting local businesses and by bringing small businesses into the public-private dialogue. The specific actions include (IFC, 2008):

(a) Supporting the operating environment by creating a market-oriented economy where private firms can operate efficiently and effectively without hindrance;

(b) Influencing policy and legal reforms in order to reduce direct and opportunity costs of doing business without removing the protection necessary for human health and safety as well as the environment; and

(c) Strengthening institutions to ensure that reforms in the business environment are properly designed, implemented and enforced in a transparent and equitable manner.

The IFC's knowledge centre website[55] provides information on the implementation of business environment reform. The IFC has collected and analysed data on the success and failure of business environment reform efforts throughout the world in order to develop practical guides for their successful design and implementation. The guides currently focus on key topics such as: monitoring and evaluation (M&E); tax systems and SME taxation; communications; public-private dialogue; alternative dispute resolution; business inspections; business licensing; business start-up; import and export procedures; collateral reform; subnational regulation; and business advocacy (IFC, 2011a).

Currently, the following guides are available online:

(a) Monitoring and evaluation – a handbook for business environment reform;

(b) Subnational regulations – simplification of business regulations at the subnational level;

(c) Public-private dialogue – handbook for business environment reformers;

(d) Communications for business environment reforms;

(e) Business advocacy – building the capacity of business membership organizations;

(f) Alternative dispute resolution manual – implementing commercial mediation;

(g) Good practices for business inspection – guidelines for reformers;

(h) Business licensing reform toolkit;

---

[54] SPRING provides a good example of providing SME-support services, including its user-friendly guide to SMEs on public procurement. SPRING is the main agency for enterprise development, and is the national standards and conformance body under the Ministry of Trade and Industry of Singapore. Its objective is to enhance the (a) competitiveness of enterprises through nurturing a pro-business environment and (b) innovation and enterprise capabilities of SMEs. More information is available at the website www.spring.gov.sg/Pages/Homepage.aspx.

[55] For more details see the website at www.ifc.org/ifcext/sme.nsf/Content/BEE+Toolkits.

(i) Business start-up – reforming business registration regulatory procedures at the national level;

(j) Import and export procedures – reforming regulatory procedures for imports and exports;

(k) Reforming regulatory procedures for import and exports;

(l) Collateral reforms – reforming collateral laws to expand access to finance; and

(m) SME taxation – tax administrations and SMEs in developing countries.

These IFC toolkits offer guidance for successful BEE reforms by expounding the good practices and lessons learnt from the experiences of nations that have undertaken such reforms. The information has been developed through consultation with various government and non-government agencies and through IFC's experience in the field.

2. International Labour Organization BEE toolkit

The BEE toolkit developed by ILO is designed to create a policy environment conducive to starting and sustaining small enterprises. The specific focus of the ILO toolkit is the employment creation function of SMEs.

In the toolkit the ILO has identified six elements related to the environment in which small enterprises operate, such as the policy and legal framework, market opportunities and the availability of resources. Among the elements, the policy and legal framework is the most important one as it has an impact not only on the small enterprises but also on the other elements. Governments and other stakeholders can improve this framework to achieve the desired economic and social outcomes.

Government activities that shape the policy and legal framework for small enterprises are divided into three layers: (a) policies and laws; (b) regulations and procedures, and (c) administration. This three-layer system describes a complete procedure of policy direction setting, implementation, management and monitoring. On the basis of this model, ILO has listed the possible causes of problems, relevant reform areas and a checklist for good actions for each layer. Policymakers can design and evaluate their BEE reforms in accordance with this specific and practical information. Some specific policies on small enterprise development are also provided to address corresponding issues, such as risk management or entrepreneurship promotion, among target groups.

The importance of policy analysis is also highlighted in this toolkit. As a continuous activity, policy analysis should be conducted during the whole reform process to detect possible reform areas and to regularly assess the policy impact. This analysis procedure requires the involvement of the key stakeholders, including representatives from the public, private, labour and community sectors. ILO proposes three key tactics to enhance the cooperation among different stakeholders: (a) dialogue; (b) collaboration; and (c) coordination (ILO, 2003a).

3. Japan International Cooperation Agency (JICA) BEE toolkit

The "Effective Support Approaches for Small and Medium Enterprises by Development Stages" programme, overseen by JICA (2006), aims to provide a practical guide to BEE reformers for formulating programmes to aid SME development in target countries. The programme is aimed at analysing generic processes of SME development in developing countries, assess their development with a set of clear criteria, and develop and implement technical assistance programmes customized to the particular situation or stage of SME development (table III.8).

Within this context, JICA focuses on the five core issues of: (a) general business environment; (b) policy, institutional and operational framework; (c) business development services; (d) SME finance; and (e) technology, which serve as the primary factors affecting BEE. Each factor is reviewed, its key elements identified, and specific constraints of the factors and their specific development stages identified with a comprehensive checklist to monitor the progress of SME development. Once such constraints and development stages are identified, action plans can be developed based on assessment criteria (e.g., relevance, effectiveness, efficiency, impact and self-sustainability). The specific action plans are then combined into a five-year programme that serve as policy recommendations for a client developing country. The end result is the identification of main constraints and the development of action plans, catered specifically to local environments and factors.

JICA has implemented this BEE toolkit in a number of Asia-Pacific nations, and serves as a guide to create a BEE for Japan's export industries (especially in nations where Japan has vested business interests). For example, through this programme, JICA offered its technical expertise to assist in the development of Sri Lankan SMEs by offering policy recommendations and action plans for the Government of Sri Lanka (JICA, 2009).

4. Asian Development Bank BEE toolkit

Similar to the initiatives of IFC and JICA, ADB has developed toolkits to assist developing counties in fostering an enabling environment for SMEs. A good example to illustrate ADB's approach in detail is "The SME Development Framework (2005-2010)", which is specifically designed for the Ministry of Economy and Finance of Cambodia (MEF) (2005). First, the toolkit analysed major constraints that policymakers should address to support the growth of the SME sector. Second, those constraints – regulatory and legal framework, access to finance, SME support activities and implementation of SME policy framework – were broken down into subcategories. Each subcategory (e.g., credit information sharing, collateral and titling, leasing and business development services) led to clear-cut objectives of BEE reforms in Cambodia and specific recommendations and action plans were developed. In particular, Cambodian SMEs' effective penetration of international markets became a primary objective.

Table III.8. Development stages of SMEs

Stage 1	(a)	Microenterprises and the informal sector dominate the economy and productivity is low;
	(b)	Most businesses are small and family-based. With low educational levels, they have difficulties even with bookkeeping. They have never received any vocational training and thus do not have sufficient knowledge to identify and solve their problems;
	(c)	With the businesses' limited cash flow, major capital investment is not expected, while access to the formal financial sector is practically impossible due to the businesses' informality; and
	(d)	There are neither vertical nor horizontal linkages between businesses.
Stage 2	(a)	Although microenterprises and the informal sector still dominate the economy, quite a few companies have been formalized;
	(b)	Although the nation's educational level is relatively good, employment opportunities are still limited;
	(c)	Although access to financing is still limited, informal financing is complementing the formal financing to some extent; and
	(d)	Some cases of vertical and horizontal linkages between businesses are observed.
Stage 3	(a)	Formal SMEs are playing a certain role in the economy;
	(b)	Although SMEs have minimum technical expertise and knowledge to survive in the economy, they lack managerial skills including marketing knowledge, production and quality control skills;
	(c)	Although SMEs have access to formal financing, many of them cannot fulfill the conditions to borrow money; and
	(d)	Although various linkages between companies are observed their effectiveness is limited.
Stage 4	(a)	A significant number of SMEs are growing into large companies or are securing a certain segment of the domestic market;
	(b)	Although there are SMEs that have strong technical expertise, their products are not yet competitive in the global market in terms of quality and price;
	(c)	There are no significant impediments in access to the financial sector for those SMEs that have sufficient skills and are producing competitive products; and
	(d)	A significant number of SMEs have increased their competitiveness by forming clusters and networks.
Stage 5	(a)	There are a large number of competitive SMEs, and many of them supply their products in international markets;
	(b)	Quite a few SMEs with high-level technical knowledge and expertise are manufacturing products at a level which meets international standard;
	(c)	Access to financing is adequate; and
	(d)	Many SMEs constitute supporting industries to large enterprises or are taking part in global supply chains.

Source: Modified from JICA, 2006.
Note: Stage criteria: (a) significance of SME sector in an economy; (b) SMEs' educational and technical level; (c) access to financing; and (d) linkage between companies.

Box III.9. Limited liability partnership in India

A law to allow "limited liability partnerships" (LLPs) in India was enacted by the Indian Parliament in 2008. An LLP is an alternative corporate business entity that provides the benefits of limited liability of a company but allows its members the flexibility of organizing their internal management on the basis of a mutual agreement, as is the case in a partnership firm. Under the bill, an LLP is a corporate body and a legal entity separate from its partners, having perpetual succession. While an LLP is a separate legal entity, liable to the full extent of its assets, the liability of the partners would be limited to their agreed contribution in the LLP. No partner would be liable on account of the independent or unauthorized actions of other partners, thus allowing individual partners to be shielded from joint liability created by another partner's wrongful business decisions or misconduct. An LLP entity can be registered online with the centralized registrar of LLPs, and the registration certificate can then be printed.

This reform is expected to bring relief to SME owners and will allow greater flexibility of their operations. It is particularly useful for SMEs in the service sector, including professionals and knowledge-based enterprises. So far about 6,000 LLPs have been registered in the country; however, SMEs have yet to understand fully the benefits offered under these acts and more education is necessary.

According to a recent report in the Economic Times of India, foreign investors may soon be able to set up LLPs as the Government is willing to allow FDI in selected sectors. The Government intends to cap FDI at 49 per cent of LLPs even in sectors where companies are allowed to receive 100 per cent capital from FDI (Sikarwar, 2010).

Source: Limited Liability Partnership, 2009.

Finally, it was suggested that the Government could approach major donors (e.g., ADB, JICA and the World Bank) for funding and technical assistance. Annex III.1 provides the details of "The SME Development Framework (2005-2010)" for Cambodia.

G. Lessons learnt from BEE reforms

While there is no standard process for BEE reforms, some lessons in general can be learnt from experiences in the region – covering technical, political and institutional issues. Those lessons include:

(a) Develop a strong political will to undergo changes;

(b) Identify specific constraints affecting BEE from sources such as the World Bank's Doing Business indicators;

(c) Identify priorities;

(d) Be receptive to best practices;

(e) Focus on regulatory, financial and investment frameworks, with special emphasis on fair competition;

(f) Make BEE business-friendly, especially for SMEs; and

(g) Be accountable and transparent.

H. Summary

The BEE is critical for economic development and influences the decisions of entrepreneurs to open, locate, operate and expand their businesses. It also has a profound effect on investors, as financial capital will be in short supply in environments where expropriation is rife and regulations are opaque. It is equally important to have bankruptcy proceedings that are clear and impart no stigma on failing firms. The orderly dissolution of SMEs is a nuance of policy often overlooked. This is an area of potential improvement in the Asia-Pacific region that can minimize the expenditure of scarce resources.

The BEE includes both formal and informal channels of rules, norms and support. The concept of a business enabling environment as the central result of various development agents typically covers: (a) regulatory and administrative frameworks; (b) institutional support frameworks; (c) access to finance and taxation; (d) market access; (e) technology; (f) business development services; and (g) PPPs. The role of culture and norms is discussed in the next chapter.

A number of surveys, such as the World Bank Doing Business Indicators. have demonstrated a wide variation in performance in the region. Some nations, such as Singapore and New Zealand, are exemplary while others need to improve in almost all categories. Businesses turn to governments for a wide variety of services, from customs clearances to business licences to dispute resolution mechanisms. Today, the time needed to obtain these services and, in some cases, the lack of transparency in the process (thus leading to corruption) can and often does thwart SME efforts to compete effectively (UNDP Asia-Pacific Development Information Programme, 2007).

Beyond the evidence in these surveys, the role of government and policymakers in BEE reforms have been specified. Some effective policies have been illustrated in a number of cases detailing the streamlining of permits in the Philippines and Thailand and BEE reforms in Viet Nam. Table III.9 proposes the BEE policy focus according to level of economic development.

All of the above are applicable. Some are, however, relatively more salient than others at a given stage of development. For example, financing is crucial for SMEs in all economies, but until the legal system is somewhat impartial it is difficult for capital to flow both to large companies and to SMEs. The risk of expropriation can be too great for investors to commit funds.

Information has been provided about several toolkits from IFC, JICA and ADB for guiding government officials. Countries may adapt these toolkits to their specific context with the clear objective of encouraging SME development and, by extension, national economic development. The BEE toolkits can provide some useful models to serve as a comprehensive guideline for policymakers and supporting institutions in designing and developing a business environment that is friendly for SMEs. It is important for policymakers to recognize that there may be local experts who can help. Often, policymakers look externally for assistance in improving BEE, while relevant resources in their own universities and think tanks are neglected. The search for expertise should be both global and local.

Table III.9. BEE policy focus by level of economic development

Stage of economy	Policy objectives	Policy recommendations
Developing	<ul><li>Provide basic infrastructure.</li><li>Ensure legal system is fair.</li><li>Create competitive markets.</li><li>Encourage female participation.</li></ul>	<ul><li>Earmark budgets for basic infrastructure.</li><li>Reform regulations to encourage new entrants.</li><li>Refrain from government intervention.</li><li>Provide more education to girls and remove roadblocks to female participation in the economy.</li></ul>
Middle	<ul><li>Provide financing.</li><li>Expand market access.</li></ul>	<ul><li>Ascertain financing needs of SMES and fulfill them (see chapter V).</li><li>Educate SMEs about exporting and other forms of participation in the global economy (see chapter VIII).</li></ul>
Advanced	<ul><li>Adopt technology.</li><li>Spur innovation.</li></ul>	<ul><li>Provide incentives for learning about latest technologies and innovations (see chapter VII).</li></ul>

Source: Authors' compilation.

Annex III.1

Cambodian enabling environment toolkit for SMEs

The SME Development Framework (2005-2010)

An overall vision: Develop a conducive business environment, which will lead to a competitive SME sector contributing to the creation of quality employment and improve the range of goods and services available to the people of Cambodia.

Major issues	Phase I (2005-2007) Establish the framework for and enabling environment for SME development	Phase II (2008-2010) Enhance and expand the framework for enabling environment for SME development	Future consideration: Foster Competitiveness of SMEs through integration into the world economy	Major donor activities
I. Regulatory and Legal Framework **Vision:** To reform the regulatory and legal framework for the purpose of creating and enabling business environment based on the rule of law and designed to minimize the impacts of government interventions on the private sector while providing the necessary protection of public goods.				
(A) Company registration Objective: Reduce the barriers and build the necessary system of effective registration.	• Reduce administrative and cost barriers in registration, including reduction of minimum capital requirement. • Engage in public-awareness campaign, including issuing a manual on registration process and a series of necessary templates. • Conduct pilot decentralization of company registration outside Phnom Penh.	• Commence full decentralization. • Plan for online registration system. • Link business registration at the Ministry of Commerce with tax and VAT registration at MEF and eventually merge into one procedure.	• Implement the online registration. • Expand registration to a wider segment of economy by further developing practical thresholds for firms to register.	• ADB – Cambodia SME Development Programme (CSDP) • World Bank review of investment climate and reform strategy
(B) Regulatory review and recourse mechanism Objective: Reduce regulatory compliance costs by enhancing governance and responsibilities of the relevant state agencies.	• Establish regulatory review process for existing and proposed licences and remove or streamline the requirements for both operating and regulatory licences. • Formulate a recourse mechanism to appeal administrative decisions. • Plan for a pilot programme for one-stop window for all relevant business licences.	• Continue to evaluate and remove unnecessary licences. • Implement a comprehensive system for issuance of new licences and recourse mechanism. • Develop a comprehensive programme for one-stop window for all relevant business licences.	• Continue to implement the reforms as outlined. • Expand the one-stop window programme for licensing of SMEs.	• ADB – CSDP

Chapter III

54

Major issues	Phase I (2005-2007) Establish the framework for and enabling environment for SME development	Phase II (2008-2010) Enhance and expand the framework for enabling environment for SME development	Future consideration: Foster Competitiveness of SMEs through integration into the world economy	Major donor activities
(C) Commercial legal framework Objective: Develop basic legal infrastructure needed for businesses and strengthen the rule of law.	• Enact draft laws on commercial enterprises, insolvency, secured transactions and contracts, among others, and harmonize them with the civil code. • Enact legal framework necessary to create a specialized court to resolve commercial disputes and strengthen training of judges.	• Engage in extensive capacity-building programmes for the commercial court system. • Enact legislation to establish commercial arbitration. • Implement anti-corruption legislation to improve transparency and fairness, and adopt code of ethics.	• Establish small claims court to strengthen contract enforcement for SMEs.	• JICA – Civil Code and Procedures • World Bank Contract Law • Canada International Development Agency (CIDA) – Law on Commercial Arbitration, and Law on Commercial Court

II. Access to Finance

Vision: To ensure that SMEs have access to necessary working capital as well as medium- and long-term finance by strengthening the collateral system and by providing a greater range of products from a wider variety of financial institutions.

Major issues	Phase I (2005-2007)	Phase II (2008-2010)	Future consideration	Major donor activities
(A) Collateral and land titling Objective: Establish secure titling to improve collateral base, and effective mechanism of enforcement of the land law.	• Issue the legal framework for secured transaction and land registration. • Initiate the registration system for both movable and immovable properties.	• Develop and implement support programmes for banks and other financial institutions for effective collateral valuation.	• Expand the online registration systems on a nationwide basis.	• ADB – Financial Sector Programme Loan (FSPL) • Mekong Project Development Facility (MPDF) – Bank Training Institute • ADB – TA 4181 on Land Law (phase II) • World Bank and other donors – land titling project
(B) Leasing Objective: Create an enabling framework for banks to provide finance leasing	• Amend the tax law so as to enable finance leasing to occur. • Issue the legal framework on leasing covering both financial and operating leases.	• Issue IAS – 17, specifying best accounting practice for leasing. • Develop and implement training and information programmes for banks, SMEs, and equipment suppliers that promote leasing.	• Promote joint ventures or stand-alone finance or operating leasing companies.	• ADB – CSDP • ADB – FSPL • International Finance Corporation (IFC) – review of leasing industry
(C) Credit Information sharing Objective: Facilitate enhanced access to finance by reducing the risks associated with limited information on potential borrowers.	• Implement the private credit information sharing system. • Establish an enabling legal framework for operation of the system to protect the rights of borrowers.	• Expand the credit information system by providing historical and other information. • Facilitate the establishment of a private credit bureau. • Develop and implement a plan to include other financial institutions to participate in the system.	• Continue to implement the plan for expanded credit information system and inclusion of non-bank financial institutions. • Draft a plan for the feasibility of developing new information products such as credit scoring.	• ADB – CSDP • ADB – FSPL • Agence Francaise de Development (AFD) – capacity-building for microfinance institutions • Kreditanstalt fur Wiederafbau (KfW) – capacity-building for commercial banks • MPDF – Bank Training Institute

Chapter III

Major issues	Phase I (2005-2007) Establish the framework for and enabling environment for SME development	Phase II (2008-2010) Enhance and expand the framework for enabling environment for SME development	Future consideration: Foster Competitiveness of SMEs through integration into the world economy	Major donor activities
(D) Simplified accounting and taxation systems for SMEs Objective: Facilitate enhanced access to finance by reducing the risks related to lack of appropriate financial information.	• Issue simplified SME accounting guidelines (including the related templates). • Develop a simplified tax-reporting system for SMEs operating as companies. • Engage in extensive training programmes to both accounting professionals and SMEs (through private sector representatives).	• Continue to support the development of the accounting professionals. • Issue guidelines and specific requirements to assist the SMEs in adhering to the formal tax system.	• Develop corporate governance guidelines and disclosure requirements on financial information.	• ADB – CSDP • ADB – FSPL • ADB and IMF – public financial management programme.

III. SME Support Activities

Vision: Create a dynamic market for SME support service. Assure that services are supplied in the most efficient means possible by the private sector and government. Encourage suppliers of services to respond to market signals and cater to a range of enterprise size. Finally, create a market place where SME are aware of the benefits and range of services available.

Major issues	Phase I (2005-2007)	Phase II (2008-2010)	Future consideration	Major donor activities
(A) Business development services (BDS) Objective: Create a dynamic market for BDS supplies as private goods and offering a range of serviced demanded by SMEs.	• Identify existing BDS suppliers and demand for services and develop a registry by district of BDS suppliers and make it available to SMEs. • In cooperation with BDS facilitators (NGOs, donors, and business associations), identify BDS needs of SMEs and barriers to greater use.	• Develop and implement education campaign for SMEs on the benefits of BDS. • In cooperation with BDS facilitators, encourage new BDS suppliers into the market. • Encourage existing institutions to enter the BDS market or link with existing BDS providers to improve their services (for example, linkages between educational institutions and BDS providers can improve quality). • To stimulate supply and demand, encourage third parties to deliver pilot projects for voucher schemes.	• Develop in public private partnership new BDS products. • Facilitate the replication of successful BDS providers. • Encourage a BDS provider association to develop a code of ethics and independent certifications of BDS providers. • Direct delivery of BDS should be avoided by the government however, when it does occur, some cost recovery components should be introduced.	• Australian Agency for International Development (AusAID) – BDS for agriculture • JICA – BDS development • MPDF – business advisory assistance

Major issues	Phase I (2005-2007) Establish the framework for and enabling environment for SME development	Phase II (2008-2010) Enhance and expand the framework for enabling environment for SME development	Future consideration: Foster Competitiveness of SMEs through integration into the world economy	Major donor activities
(B) Access to markets Objective: Improve SMEs access to domestic and export markets through better access to information, market research, product development and promotional activities.	• Design and implement an education programme on utilizing information for access to markets. • Encourage and assist SMEs to participate in trade fairs and exhibitions. • In cooperation with SME associations develop multi-purpose facilities. • In conjunction with other stakeholders, link buyers with SMEs for clusters of SMEs.	• Develop and implement a strategy for regional SMEs to have improved access to the internet. • Facilitate better flow of useful information between public institutions, such as technical colleges and universities, and SMEs • To improve access to export market, facilitate linkages between local and international business associations.	• To enhance the use of the internet, a legal and regulatory framework for e-commerce should be implemented. • Facilitate trade fairs and product exhibitions in partnership with the private sector. • Develop and implement a matching grant scheme for SMEs to access export markets.	• ADB – TA 4121 (Garment Sector Study) • European Union – WTO assistance • European Union – export development • GTZ – trade promotion • New Zealand Agency for International Development – trade policy in agriculture • ESCAP – WTO assistance • UNIDO – market access support • World Bank – supply chain and trade facilitation
(C) Technology and human resource upgrading Objective: Improve availability and awareness among SMEs of technology and technical and managerial training.	• Review current technology and training needs, incentive structures and barriers. • Coordinate with providers of vocational training to identify needs and develop links with SMEs. • Strengthen the capacity of current research institutions and foster linkages with the private sector (including academic institutions).	• Develop an action plan for implementing opportunities identified in the phase on review. • Coordinate and work with training institutions and donors to develop toolkit packages for training and capacity building in SMEs.	• Encourage quality standards in SMEs through ISO 9000 certification process. • Encourage linkages between training and research institutions and SMEs.	• ADB – garment sector study • Government of India – vocational training • GTZ – vocational training • JICA – training centre • UNIDO – industrial standards
(D) Linkages Objective: Assist SMEs to work together and cooperate in integrated networks to improve their competitiveness and access to local and international markets.	• Review relevant regulations and procedures for the registration of associations and make recommendations for improvements. • In cooperation with other stakeholders, develop and implement an action plan for encouraging the formation and strengthening of associations. • Take an inventory of clusters, including identifying number, size, type, and location.	• Encourage the development and use of media outreach programmes for raising awareness of issues related to SMEs. • Develop, in cooperation with donors and associations, common service provisions and other related support for clusters.	• To help improve the competitiveness of clusters, encourage linkages between local clusters and international organizations. • Working together with other stakeholders, assist SMEs in clusters to become integrated in global supply chains. This can include promoting learning networks, joint international marketing, as well as a range of other services.	• ADB – FSPL • ADB – garment sector study • World Bank – trade facilitation and supply chain • JICA – feasibility of export processing zone to build backward linkages to SMEs • USAID – capacity-building for business associations

Chapter III

Chapter III

Major issues	Phase I (2005-2007) Establish the framework for and enabling environment for SME development	Phase II (2008-2010) Enhance and expand the framework for enabling environment for SME development	Future consideration: Foster Competitiveness of SMEs through integration into the world economy	Major donor activities
IV. SME Policy Framework – Implementation Process Vision: Develop a specific framework and institutional arrangements for effective policy formulation and implementation as well as monitoring of its impact. Involve the private sector representatives and obtain donor support to ensure its overall success.				
(A) Government Organizations Objective: Develop an institutional arrangement among key government agencies for effective and coordinated policy formulation and implementation.	• Formulate and implement the First SME Development Framework based on public private partnership. • Establish a secretariat for the National SME Subcommittee with a detailed work plan. • Develop and implement a plan to provide and collect information to and from SMEs. • Publish a report on the state of the SME sector and the achievements of the First SME Development Framework. • Develop a specific plan for capacity-building programmes for the government officials and private sector representatives. • Ensure that the implementing agencies are allocated sufficient resources to undertake the reforms as outlined in the SME Development Framework.	• Formulate and implement the Second SME Development Framework based on public private partnerships. • Expand the system to provide information to and collect from SMEs. • Publish a report on the state of the SME sector and the achievement of the Second SME Development Framework. • Expand the specific plan for capacity-building programmes for the government officials and private sector representatives.		• ADB – Cambodia SME Development Programme (CSDP) • World Bank review of investment climate and reform strategy
(B) Promotion of public private partnership Objective: Support the development of active private sector representation in policy advocacy.	• Develop a specific consultation process with business associations and other stakeholders to foster public-private partnerships. • Formulate a plan to enhance the capacity of business associations to provide policy advocacy on behalf of SMEs.	• Facilitate the establishment of private policy research institutions for support in policy formulation, evaluation, and monitoring of their impact.		• USAID – Capacity-building for business associations • MPDF

Source: MEF, 2005.

Annex III.2
SME Taxation

A. Taxation for SMEs

SMEs do not add significantly to tax revenue because they are small and fragmented, typically less profitable than large enterprises, and more likely to operate in the informal sector in any given economy (International Tax Dialogue, 2007). As such, tax morale plays a significant role in determining the tax revenue contributions from SMEs and the size of the informal sector (Schneider and Torgler, 2007).

SME owners usually have limited knowledge about tax codes and information on tax policies and procedures can be difficult to attain. Tax compliance costs are an additional burden for SMEs. These hindrances discourage entrepreneurship and deter SMEs from entering the formal sector. Governments and policymakers can alleviate these factors by outlining clear and straightforward taxation policies.

Tax incentives such as reduced tax rates and tax relief can also be a useful tool to alleviate SMEs' competitive disadvantage compared with large enterprises. Well-designed tax incentives could facilitate SMEs' investment to improve their capacity while increasing their cash flows. Spillover effects through SMEs could foster broader economic growth.

1. Tax compliance and business formality

As discussed above, there is association between the informal sector and the level of non-compliance with the tax code (Schneider and Torgler, 2007). The tax system is one of the key reasons for the growth of the informal sector. Non-compliance with the tax system might give a competitive advantage to SMEs as they will be able to offer their goods and services at lower price than their competitors in the formal sector. However disadvantages resulting from non-compliance with the tax system may exceed potential benefits. Annex table III.1 discusses the advantages and disadvantages of tax system non-compliance.

2. Tax compliance cost

A tax burden is not only the result of higher tax rates but also tax compliance costs that are associated with businesses. Tax compliance costs have both monetary and non-monetary elements, which can be classified under three main categories: monetary costs; time costs; and psychological costs (Annex table III.1).

Tax compliance costs have been a policy issue for the past two decades; OECD nations regularly calculate them via surveys. Discovering these costs is a recent process in

Annex table III.1. Advantages and disadvantages of tax non-compliance on various entities

Advantages of non-compliance	Disadvantages of non-compliance
Business: (a) Comparative advantage due to possibility of offering products at lower price; (b) Less harassment from tax officers; and (c) Avoidance of high compliance costs. Tax administration: (a) Lower administrative costs; and (b) Possibility of allocating scarce resources to administrating high-potential taxpayers.	Business: (a) Inability to obtain formal licences and permits from local and other government agencies; (b) Difficulty in securing credit from formal sources; (c) To avoid attracting the attention of the authorities, informal business needs to maintain a low profile. This precludes advertising, which will likely result in lost sales; (d) Vulnerable to corruption. Officials may need to be bribed to overlook the informal status of the enterprise; (e) Impediment to trading with the formal sector, which may only buy from registered VAT taxpayers; and (f) Inability to claim legitimate tax deductions and exemptions. Government: (a) Incorrect estimation of revenue potential of SME segment; (b) Violation of tax equity; (c) Risk of erosion of general compliance attitude; and (d) Non-compliance with the tax system creates risks of being associated with non-compliance with other laws, e.g., environmental and safety standards. Public: (a) Less tax revenue available for public services; and (b) Less government accountability.

Source: IFC, 2007.

Annex table III.2. Monetary and non-monetary elements of tax compliance costs

Monetary costs	Time costs	Psychological costs
Fees paid to tax advisers, lawyers and accountants	Time spent on studying tax laws, procedures and filing returns	Stress and anxiety arising from complying with a specific tax or with tax-related activities
Salary of staff working on tax returns and tax accounting	Time spent on preparing the tax audit	Frustration as a result of taxpayer harassment
Tax literature and software	Time spent on preparing appeals	
Operational costs (telephone calls, travel and postage)		

Sources: Pope, Fayle and Chen, 1991; and Sandford, Godwin and Hardwick, 1989.

Annex figure III.1. Factors responsible for high tax compliance in New Zealand, 2003 (percentage of respondents)

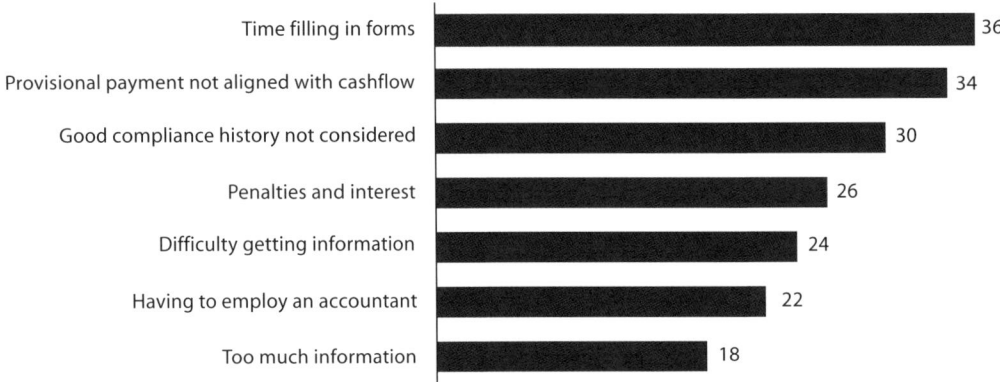

Source: IFC, 2007.

developing countries and, as a result, little data is available for policymakers. The OECD country data on tax compliance indicate the disproportionate burden on SMEs; nearly all studies find a regressive pattern of tax compliance cost for smaller firms (Evans et al., 1997). A 2003 survey carried out in New Zealand outlined some factors responsible for high tax compliance including time requirements, lack of information and others (annex figure III.1).

3. Tax incentives for SMEs

Despite the importance of SMEs to economic prosperity, they are at a competitive disadvantage compared to large enterprises and TNCs. Most governments and policymakers are therefore in agreement that special incentives should be provided to SMEs in order to foster their growth. One way to achieve this is by providing tax incentives for SMEs. Tax incentives are useful due to their spillover effects through SMEs to the broader economy. This is especially the case since SMEs provide the bulk of the employment with required labour training and skill development, and are an important source of innovation. Providing tax incentives to foster and support the growth of SMEs will add value to the broader economy. SME tax incentives can mitigate the tax compliance burden of SMEs and promote inclusion into the formal sector.

Policymakers have to be careful in designing a tax incentive programme that provides the best results for specific objectives. A programme can be designed for different development stages, starting from initial investment to daily operation to re-sale or closure. In the following section we will look at various tax incentives that SMEs can get at the different stages, mainly using examples from developed countries:

(a) Reduced tax rate. Considering the high tax compliance cost for SMEs, governments can consider reducing statutory tax rates on profits earned by SME, in order to promote entrepreneurship. For example, Japan reduced its corporate tax (from 22 per cent to 18 per cent) for SMEs in 2009 to protect its SME sector from the global economic crisis (ASG Tax Corporation, 2009);

(b) Investment in depreciable assets. Since SMEs have limited access to necessary capital to invest in assets or for developmental activities, investment tax credit can lighten the financial burden and help build the required fixed assets for the SMEs. In Japan, SMEs acquiring depreciable assets (machines and equipment) can benefit from a special initial depreciation of 30 per cent of the billing cost, or a special investment tax credit of 7 per cent. Furthermore, in South Africa, SMEs can write off 100 per cent cost of the machinery and equipment (OECD, 2009a);

(c) Investment in research and development.[56] Innovation is the key for any business to be successful, and tax policies can be of great help by providing tax concessions for costs incurred on

---
[56] Also see the detailed discussion on the R&D tax issues in chapter VII.

Annex table III.3. SME taxation criteria

Criteria	Problem
Business turnover	(a) With high volume of cash transactions and low recordkeeping standards, determining the correct amount of turnover is difficult; (b) Turnover under-declaration is widespread among SMEs.
Tax paid or tax liability	(a) Losses result in zero tax liability, including for some very large businesses; (b) Fails to account for tax holidays.
Number of employees	(a) Some industries may be very labour intensive but have low productivity, and hence low profitability and tax liabilities; (b) Some capital- or technology-intensive sectors with few employees may be highly profitable.
Capital base	(a) Not all capital-intensive industries remain profitable, particularly in declining or subsidized sectors; (b) The burgeoning, and often highly profitable, service sectors may have minimal capitalization.
Entity type	(a) While many large taxpayers are incorporated, not all corporations are large; (b) There could be some unincorporated enterprises that are quite large.
Industry type	Major taxpayers may be common in highly regulated (banking or capital intensive) industries but the businesses that service these sectors may range widely in size.
International transaction	Economic globalization is now affecting businesses of all sizes, particularly importers, exporter and certain service sectors.

Source: IFC, 2007.

R&D activities. The *Durfkapitaal* scheme in the Netherlands is an example of such an incentive programme. Under this scheme, any SME that includes a R&D facility can get tax compensation up to € 50,000 (Internationaal Ondernemen, 2011);

(d) Incentives on employability. Tax policies can also promote employability by favouring SMEs that employ more people in a particular period, through specific tax relief. In this case, governments have to keep check on the duration of employment to make sure the incentives are used properly and not manipulated. In Belgium, for example, SMEs receive an allowance of $ 6,292 in each tax year for each additional staff member employed (OECD, 2009a); and

(e) Incentives for SMEs on capital gains and capital losses. Tax incentives can be provided on capital gains or capital losses from non-inventory assets (e.g., stocks and bonds) to promote greater participation by shareholders and venture capitalists in the SME sector. This will help SMEs' cash flow and enable them to expand. For capital losses, tax policies could make provisions to carry over the loss during several years, so that an SME can withstand the initial start-up process and potential losses (Irish Tax and Revenue, 2011).

B. Criteria of SME taxation

A key issue with SME taxation is that the definition for SMEs varies from one country to another and so do the applicable tax policies. Despite these differences, tax laws for SMEs have one thing in common – they specifically define the eligibility criteria for incentives aimed at SMEs. The main criteria, and main issues related to them, are presented in annex table III.3.

Business turnover is one of the most accepted criteria in determining tax rules for SMEs as there are separate definitions of it for tax purposes. This allows more targeted tax incentives and simplified tax regimes for businesses requiring special considerations, e.g., SMEs (IFC, 2007).

C. Valued-added tax reforms for SMEs

The value-added tax (VAT) threshold determines the level of turnover a business should generate in order to be exempt from VAT. Policymakers have to consider the VAT system carefully since compliance with VAT can be particularly difficult for SMEs. Various studies (Nemickas, Senchuk and Babanin, 2002; and Skatteverket, 2006) have indicated that compliance with VAT is the most problematic form of tax for SMEs.

In order to encourage SME development and their inclusion into formal markets, it is essential for policymakers to consider a proper VAT registration threshold for SMEs. Some developing countries are already reforming their policies with assistance from international organizations, e.g., IMF and the World Bank (OECD, 2007a). Some simplification processes for VAT systems are:

(a) Choosing optimal threshold. The VAT threshold varies considerably from one nation to another, mainly due to each nation's non-uniform definition of SMEs. The mean global VAT threshold is in the range of $ 90,000; in Singapore it is as high as $ 700,000 (OECD, 2009a). The appropriate threshold for a given country requires a thorough analysis of many factors, including the number of taxpayers, their expected contribution to overall VAT revenue yield per turnover band, structure and characteristics of the SME community and the level of administrative and compliance costs per turnover band (IFC, 2007). Alternatively, IMF (2001), in its publication *The Modern VAT – 2001*, proposes a formula, taking into account of the rate at which VAT is levied, valued-added per unit output, administration costs, compliance costs and the net loss to a government, for adjusting the VAT ceiling for SMEs to an optimal level;

(b) A simple VAT rate structure. Most developing countries operate with multiple VAT rates for the SME sector. This system not only increases compliance costs but also increases administration burdens. A study of VAT compliance cost conducted in Sweden established a direct correlation between compliance cost and the multiple tax rates (Skatteverket, 2006). Simplifying VAT, e.g., having a comprehensive, single VAT rate structure, can streamline SMEs into the formal sector;

(c) Cash accounting for SMEs. Most SME's problems are based on their inability to maintain cash flow. VAT is based on accrual accounting, which requires VAT to be remitted on taxable sales where the cash has not yet been received (accounts receivables[57]). When using cash accounting, VAT is paid on sales only when the cash is received and input tax credits are claimed only when cash is paid on a purchase. Cash accounting is specifically helpful to SMEs as it mirrors their daily operations;

(d) Frequency of tax return filings. In most countries utilizing the VAT system, tax returns are filed monthly and add to compliance costs. Policymakers should decrease the frequency of SME VAT returns, thus allowing SMEs to have extra cash flow. Examples can be drawn from countries such as Austria, Australia, Canada, New Zealand and Sweden on how reducing the frequency of tax filing will lead to extra cash flow for SMEs. In New Zealand, businesses submit VAT returns every six months if their turnover is less than $NZ 250,000. For businesses having a turnover of between $NZ 250,000 and $NZ 24 million, the VAT return is filed once every two months rather than on a monthly basis. Similarly, Canadian SME businesses with a turnover of less than $C 6 million but above $C 500,000 qualify for quarterly filing, while those with a turnover less than $C 500,000 qualify for annual filing with quarterly installment payments (IFC, 2007; and OECD, 2009a).

It is also important to understand the overall advantages and disadvantages these processes can have for government bodies and a business itself:

(a) Advantages of VAT reforms:
  (i) Significantly reduced compliance costs;
  (ii) Increased cash flow for the SMEs;
  (iii) Less administrative costs for government bodies;
  (iv) More entry of SMEs into the formal economy.

(b) Disadvantages of VAT reforms:
  (i) Under-reported turnover in order to take advantage of exemptions;
  (ii) Deterioration of business credibility because suppliers generally prefer dealing with clients with a registered VAT number.

D. Increasing popularity of presumptive taxation

The general taxation regime works in those countries where most SMEs operate in the formal sector. In developing economies it is almost impossible to have a general taxation regime since a considerable portion of SMEs operate informally. Because of such non-compliance with obligatory bookkeeping and accounting practices, presumptive taxation[58] is very popular in order to bring existing or new SMEs into the formal sector. Presumptive taxation does not follow a fixed manner; it is flexible and convenient in terms of operation and the scope of application. This system is generally welcomed by SME communities due to its convenience, usage and simplicity (IFC, 2007).

The presumptive tax system can be planned based on the following criteria (IFC, 2007):

(a) Turnover or gross income of the company
  (i) Tax rate based on standard percentage of turnover;
  (ii) Progressive turnover tax rates.
(b) Indicators
  (i) Number of employees;
  (ii) Energy (e.g., electricity) consumption.
(c) Combination of turnover and indicator base.
  (i) Turnover plus number of employees;
  (ii) Turnover plus energy consumption.
(d) Professional patent
  (i) Small machinery;
  (ii) Carpenter and woodworker;
  (iii) Hairdresser and barber services etc.

There are possible advantages and disadvantages connected with some types of presumptive taxes as shown in annex table III.4.

In addition to the above, certain general disadvantages associated with this tax system should also be noted (IFC, 2007):

(a) In cases of losses suffered by SMEs, the government or tax office will not be able to provide any immediate help;
(b) There is a risk of the tax system being abused by entrepreneurs and SME proprietors;
(c) The presumptive tax system discourages the growth aspect of SMEs and entrepreneurs, and will negatively affect their long-term planning.

Annex table III.5 provides comparative information on Asia-Pacific countries with regard to VAT percentage, VAT

---

[57] Money owed by customers (individuals or corporations) to another entity in exchange for goods or services that have been delivered or used, but for which payment has not yet been received. Receivables usually come in the form of operating lines of credit and are usually due within a relatively short period, ranging from a few days to a year.

[58] Presumptive taxation involves lump sum levies on certain small-scale business activities. The assessment of taxes through indicators or proxies helps in estimating a taxpayer's income (estimated income), and the estimation of minimum income irrespective of a taxpayer's actual level of business activity (presumptive minimum income).

Annex table III.4. Advantages and disadvantages of presumptive tax systems

Type of system	Advantages	Disadvantages
Patent	Simplicity. Low tax compliance and administration costs.	Imposes a relatively high tax burden on firms with relatively low turnover. Imposes a relatively high tax on profits during downturns when profits are low or negative.
Indicator-based tax	Less easy to misreport. May offer substantial savings in tax compliance and tax administration costs. Does not factor in tax revenues and thereby discourage income growth accompanying increased work effort.	May discourage investment in buildings and/or the hiring of additional workers.
Turnover tax	Avoids the competitive distortions of profit-insensitive taxes. Facilitates the adjustment of firms to a regular income tax system by requiring the maintenance of cash accounts measuring turnover.	Imposes a relatively low effective tax rate on business that are more profitable than others. Tends to discourage the allocation of capital to business activities where profit margins are relatively thin.

Source: OECD, 2007.

Annex table III.5. VAT and presumptive tax threshold comparison for Asia-Pacific countries

Country	VAT rate	VAT registration threshold	Presumptive tax threshold (VAT exemption)
Australia	10 per cent	$A 75,000	Convenient tax paying system for turnover under $A 75,000
China	Standard rate: 17 per cent Small entrepreneur: 3 per cent	RMB 800,000	Turnover not exceeding RMB 800,000 (6 per cent standard tax rate)
Cambodia	10 per cent	CR 125 million	n.a.
India	State level rates of 1 per cent, 4 per cent, 5 per cent and 20 per cent	Varies according to state (Rs 2,500 - Rs 2 Crore)	Turnover not exceeding Rs 4 million (8 per cent standard tax rate)
Indonesia	10 per cent	Rp 600 million	Turnover not exceeding Rp 600 million
Japan	5 per cent	¥ 10 million	Separate tax slab available for SMEs
Lao People's Democratic Republic	10 per cent	NK 400 million	Turnover below NK 100 million
Malaysia	6 per cent	RM 500,000	Separate tax slab available for SMEs
New Zealand	15 per cent	$NZ 60,000	Turnover below $NZ 60,000
Russian Federation	Standard rate: 18 per cent Reduced rate:* 10 per cent	No threshold	Up to 1,000 employees plus turnover below R 11 million
Republic of Korea	10 per cent	n.a.	Separate tax slab available for SMEs
Singapore	7 per cent	$S 1 million	Turnover not exceeding $S 500,000
Thailand	7 per cent	B 1.8 million	Different tax rate slab available for SMEs.
Viet Nam	10 per cent	No threshold	Based on turnover, which varies according to business sector and location.

Sources: TMF Group, 2009; ATO, undated; Ministry of Finance, Japan, 1999; ASG Tax Corporation, 2009; KPMG, 2012; AAJ Associates, 2010; GST Malaysia, undated; PWCCN, 2012; ADB, 2012a and 2012b; Hauerstein and Niemann, 2002; Revenue Department, Thailand, 2008; Inland Revenue Authority of Singapore, 2011; and New Zealand Institute of Chartered Accountants, 2010.
* Reduced rate for foodstuff, medical and clothing materials.

registration thresholds for business, and presumptive tax thresholds. In cases where a number of businesses are unable to register for VAT, governments may take measures to introduce presumptive tax. This will help to control the informal sector and maintain proper data on the SMEs in the long term. It will also serve as a guide for policymakers in reforming SME taxation policies.

E. Tax administration

Tax administration, particularly in developing countries, generally does not focus much on tax compliance by SMEs; a small number of major taxpayers contribute the majority of tax revenue. Attention given to small businesses is limited, with some tax administrations even discouraging the inclusion of small businesses in the tax net because of the high administrative cost-benefit ratio[59] (Bahl, 2003).

IFC, in its report "Designing a tax system for micro and small businesses," provides certain guidelines for comprehensive tax administration that includes SMEs (IFC, 2007):

(a) Tax administration reform must accompany tax policy reforms;

(b) Given the special compliance problems and service needs of small taxpayers, creating dedicated administrative structures within the tax administration to manage small taxpayer compliance and satisfy service needs is a promising reform. Similar to the operation of large taxpayer offices existing in many countries, specialized small taxpayer offices could be created;

(c) In a number of countries, the registration of businesses for tax purposes remains a slow, cumbersome and often costly process. Streamlining taxpayer registration is an important administrative reform, and should be linked to the reform of business registration requirements on a broader base. Ideally a one-stop approach to registration should be adopted;

(d) Small taxpayers have special service and information needs. These concern both the content and mode of delivery. As the use of information technology is becoming more widespread in small business communities, its use should also be considered for service and information purposes to facilitate compliance (e.g., filing and payments);

(e) Cooperation with the private sector, particularly with small business and SME associations, is important for successful compliance management. Consideration could be given to introducing some elements of associational taxation and to involving those associations in the tax collection process; and

(f) Close cooperation with local governments should be established for information sharing on tax policies and the tax regime.

---

[59] Administrative costs per United States dollar of collection rise considerably with efforts to increase the compliance rate beyond a given point, which is determined by tax administration capacity as well as the size and structure of the group of potential taxpayers (Bahl, 2003).

CHAPTER IV
Entrepreneurship development

Economic growth hinges upon entrepreneurship. A vibrant entrepreneurial climate provides new jobs, increases competitiveness, and produces novel goods and services. It is not surprising, therefore, to learn that policymakers attempt to increase entrepreneurial activity in numerous ways. They may reform the regulatory environment in order to reduce the number of permits and licences required to start a business. They may make more capital available to new firms via loans, subsidies or tax incentives. They may also increase the amount of resources devoted to education in general and business education in particular, in order to create a set of attitudes and skills in the populace that is conducive to entrepreneurship. Indeed, a dearth of entrepreneurial and managerial skills is a major impediment that less-developed economies face.

This chapter first establishes a definition of entrepreneurship and entrepreneurs and briefly considers the institutional context in which these developments take place. It then examines the contribution that entrepreneurial activities make at different stages of economic development. Some of the key factors of success, and the main entry barriers for entrepreneurs are also examined. Creating awareness and knowledge about the potential benefits of entrepreneurship is essential to its development and this chapter highlights the important role that education can play in facilitating this process.

While there are many players in entrepreneurship development, this chapter pays particular attention to the subsectors of women, youth and rural entrepreneurs. Finally, this chapter briefly discusses the value of the emerging trend of social entrepreneurship. It concludes with some key policy considerations.

A. Entrepreneurship and entrepreneurs: Definitions and concepts

Entrepreneurship generally refers to the rapid growth of new and innovative businesses, based on the ability to recognize business opportunities or combine resources in novel ways. There are a number of accepted definitions of entrepreneurship (and entrepreneurs). It can be understood as "the ability to amass the necessary resources to capitalize on new business opportunities" (Kayne, 1999). Entrepreneurship may also be "the act of creation requiring the ability to recognize an opportunity, shape a goal, and take advantage of a situation" as "[e]ntrepreneurs plan, persuade, raise resources, and give birth to new ventures" (Bodell, Rabbior and Smith, 1991). According to the National Knowledge Commission of India (2008), entrepreneurship is "the professional application of knowledge, skills and competencies or monetizing a new idea, by an individual or a set of people, by launching an enterprise *de novo* or diversifying from an existing one (distinct from seeking self-employment as in a profession or trade), thus to pursue growth while generating wealth, employment and social good". In academia, a common definition of an entrepreneur is "one who organizes, manages and assumes the risks of a business or enterprise" (Greve and Salaff, 2003). This definition encompasses many types of entrepreneurial activity, and is therefore more inclusive than the first three definitions.

Many scholars, however, focus on innovation and firm growth as key aspects of entrepreneurship. While an entrepreneur can be a small-business person, all small-business persons need not be entrepreneurs. Entrepreneurial enterprises focus on new and innovative products, services and processes. They are growth-oriented and aggressively strive to capture market share. Entrepreneurial enterprises may begin as small businesses but often grow to be large firms, as they frequently reinvest their earnings to either expand their original enterprise or to create new ventures.

The authors define entrepreneurship as the individual or team process of doing something new or different to add value to society through calculated risk-taking behaviour for future gains. The term "calculated risk" is often associated with danger; however, in the context of entrepreneurship, it can be defined as the entrepreneurial spirit of taking financial and social risk where opportunities have been clearly identified, and where as much control as possible is exercised over the outcome.

Camp (2002) also observed that entrepreneurship was a multifaceted concept with components related to:

(a) Cognitive mindset – thinking "entrepreneurially";
(b) Behavioural process – starting new businesses;
(c) Economic and sociological events – new firm formation; and
(d) Approach to general or strategic management – organizational innovation and growth.

Policymakers should recognize from this discussion that there are different categories of entrepreneurship based on their motivations for starting a business and their growth aspirations. GEM uses the designations of "opportunity," or "improvement," versus "necessity" entrepreneurship. Opportunity entrepreneurs start businesses because they want to exploit an opportunity, whereas necessity entrepreneurs start firms because they see no better economic alternatives. GEM also characterizes nascent entrepreneurs by the number of jobs they expect to create, the degree of exporting they anticipate, and the level of market expansion and innovation they hope to achieve (GEM, 2007). Entrepreneurs hoping to create 20-plus jobs in five years are labelled "high-growth aspiration," as are entrepreneurs who expect "significant" or "profound" market expansion.

Entrepreneurial activities do not take place in a vacuum; and it is important to consider the specific institutional context in which they operate. Within the wider social, cultural, and political contexts, GEM's entrepreneurship model (figure IV.1) highlights the fact that there are basic requirements (e.g., institutions, infrastructure, macroeconomic stability and education), efficiency enhancers (e.g., higher education, technological readiness and market size), and a number of innovation and entrepreneurship conditions that all contribute to firm expansion, entrepreneurship development and,

Box IV.1. Think big, start small: The Cathay Pacific story

"It all began with the entrepreneurial vision of two former World War II veterans, American Roy Farrell and Australian Sydney de Kantzow. After World War II, Roy and Sydney spotted an opportunity to start passenger and cargo flights out of Shanghai. Early in 1946, they moved their enterprise to Hong Kong and in September of the same year, paid $HK 1 apiece to register the airline. They named it Cathay Pacific Airways. Cathay, the ancient name of China, and Pacific, because the far-sighted Farrell speculated that one day the airline might fly across the ocean.

The fledging airline consisted of just two United States Army surplus DC3 aircraft, Betsy and Nikki, but Cathay continued to grow. In 1949, the airline acquired its first four-engine aircraft, a Douglas DC4. The 1970 decision to equip the airline with Boeing 707s opened the door to long-range flights. Cathay Pacific was the world's first airline to take delivery of Rolls-Royce-powered B747-400 in 1989, bringing destinations such as Vancouver, London and Los Angeles within non-stop range. In 2002, the airline introduced its first ultra-long-haul Airbus A340-600 and is currently expanding its fleet with the purchase of 30 Boeing 777-300 ER "Extended Range" aircraft that will form the backbone of its long-haul passenger fleet in the years to come". The rest is history.

Source: Extracted from *Discovery*, the Cathay Pacific in-flight magazine, September 2011, p.108.

Figure IV.1. Institutional context and its relationship to entrepreneurship

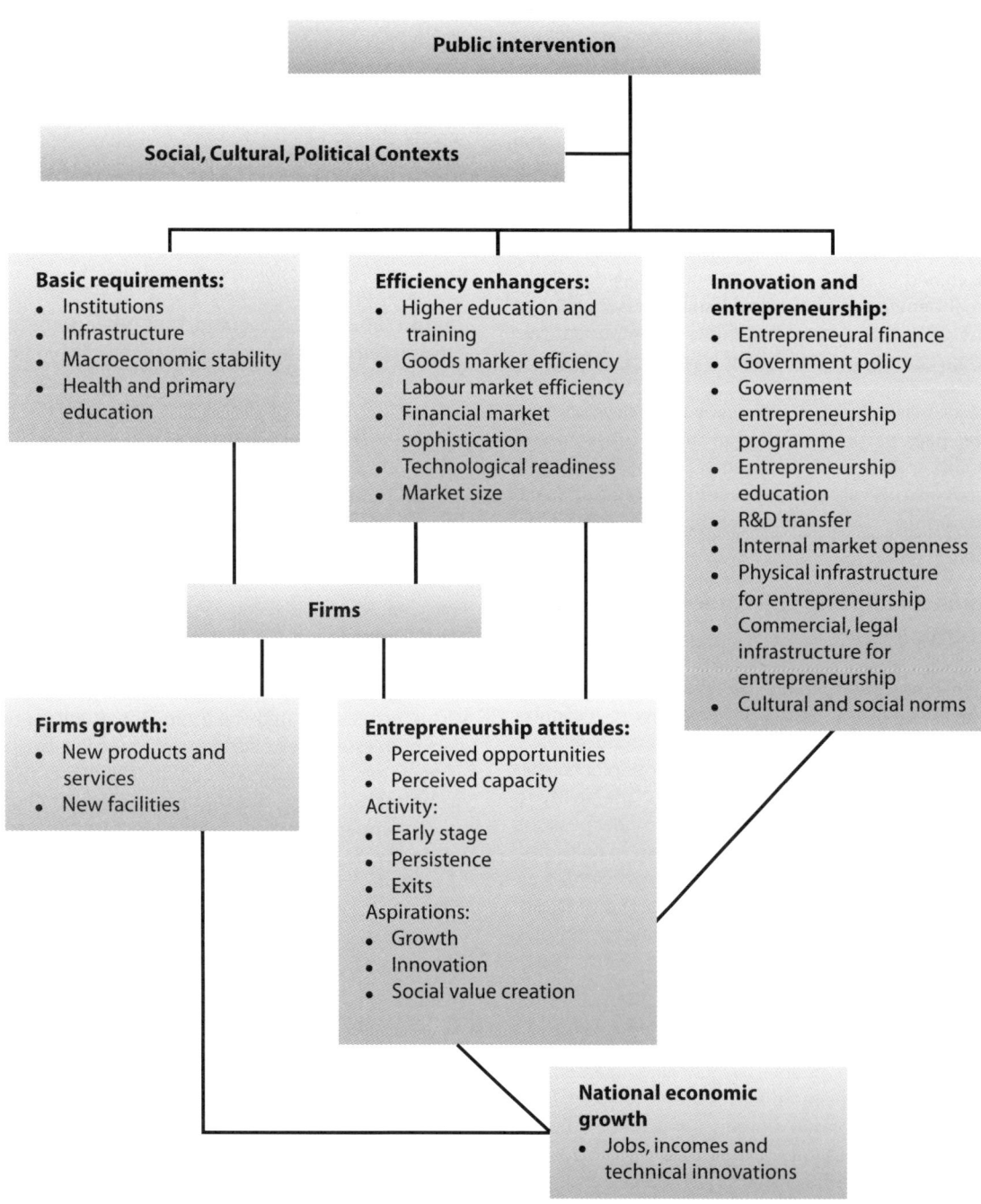

Source: Modified from GEM, 2010.

eventually, national economic growth. While these factors also have an impact on established firms, new entrepreneurs are particularly sensitive and the presence of these conditions can have a significant positive impact on their development.

Given this framework, policymakers have to choose suitable policy instruments in order to stimulate positive entrepreneurial attitudes within a society, and encourage entrepreneurs to recognize valuable business opportunities and pursue skills to capitalize on them. Most importantly, governments need to encourage entrepreneurs' aspirations to grow, innovate and help entrench these social values in order to promote sustainable competitiveness. Through the provision of supportive resources and policies, policymakers can help increase entrepreneurship activities for greater national competitiveness and sustained economic growth.

B. Role of entrepreneurship in different phases of economic development

The World Economic Forum (2011) classifies entrepreneurial activities according to three stages of economic development – factor-driven, efficiency-driven and innovation-driven. Factor-driven economies are largely extractive, whereas efficiency-driven economies and innovation-driven economies add increasing amounts of value in their production of goods and services. The hallmark of efficiency-driven economies is scale, whereas that of innovation-driven economies is creativity. Table IV.1, drawn from GEM (2012), uses these groupings to present entrepreneurial activities in select Asia-Pacific countries. It is notable that the entrepreneurship percentage is generally higher in the factor-driven economies than in efficiency and innovation economies, not only in the region but on average overall.

Taken together, the numbers in table IV.1 provide a picture of the characteristics of overall entrepreneurial activity for each country. The results indicate large variations among the sample countries due to different economic and social conditions. One of the principal measures is early-stage entrepreneurial activity (TEA), which represents the proportion of people aged 18-64 years who conduct entrepreneurial activity as a nascent entrepreneur or as an owner-manager of a new business. By further disaggregating the data, it can be seen that TEA rates are lowest in innovation-driven economies and fairly similar in factor- and efficiency-driven economies. The rate of established business ownership among the factor-driven economies is relatively low in relation to TEA. Within the group of efficiency-driven economies, Thailand can be considered an outlier, as the ownership rate is far higher than its TEA rate, which is not the case for any of the other economies in this category. As economies move towards higher development levels, the number of businesses that discontinue decreases. This inverse relationship should not be surprising given the higher share of TEA in factor- and efficiency-driven economies. This trend may indicate a more stable environment for businesses in developed than developing nations (GEM, 2011).

Table IV.1. Entrepreneurial activity in selected Asia-Pacific countries in 2011, by phase of economic development

	Nascent entrepreneurship rate	New business ownership rate	Early-stage entrepreneurial activity (TEA)	Established business ownership rate	Discontinuation of business	Necessity driven (per cent of TEA)	Improvement driven (per cent of TEA)
Factor-driven economies							
Bangladesh	7.1	7.1	12.8	11.6	2.5	27.3	50.0
Iran (Islamic Republic of)	10.8	3.9	14.5	11.2	6.4	53.0	31.5
Pakistan	7.5	1.7	9.1	4.1	1.6	46.9	24.7
Average (unweighted)[a]	9.2	4.8	13.4	5.6	5.7	37.0	38.5
Efficiency-driven economies							
China	10.1	14.2	24.0	12.7	5.3	40.6	29.0
Malaysia	2.5	2.5	4.9	5.2	2.6	10.2	71.8
Russian Federation	2.4	2.3	4.6	2.8	1.5	26.9	41.9
Thailand	8.3	12.2	19.5	30.1	4.5	18.9	66.8
Turkey	6.3	6.0	11.9	8.0	3.9	31.6	44.8
Average (unweighted)[b]	8.4	5.9	14.1	7.2	4.3	28.2	41.7
Innovation-driven economies							
Australia	6.0	4.7	10.5	9.1	4.3	15.0	73.1
Japan	3.3	2.0	5.2	8.3	0.7	24.9	63.5
Republic of Korea	2.9	5.1	7.8	10.9	3.2	41.5	36.2
Singapore	3.8	2.8	6.6	3.3	2.1	16.2	52.6
Taiwan Province of China	3.6	4.4	7.9	6.3	4.9	17.5	49.8
Average (unweighted)[c]	4.0	3.0	6.9	7.2	2.7	17.6	57.0

Source: GEM, 2012.

[a] Average refers to all factor-driven economies covered by the GEM 2011 adult population survey, not only the listed economies from Asia and the Pacific.

[b] Average refers to all the efficiency-driven economies that are covered by the GEM 2011 adult population survey, not only the listed economies from Asia and the Pacific.

[c] Average refers to all the innovation-driven economies that are covered by the GEM 2011 adult population survey, not only the listed economies from Asia and the Pacific.

Box IV.2. Realities of entrepreneurship

- People are more likely to start companies in places that are poorer or with high rates of unemployment than in places that are richer and with low rates of unemployment.
- The typical startup is an ordinary, barely innovative, home-based business that starts and stays tiny.
- Entrepreneurs do not select industries because they are good for startups but rather because they know these industries and because it is easy to start businesses in them.
- The typical entrepreneur, who is a middle-aged person, starts a business because they do not like working for someone else and because they are just trying to make a living.
- People are more likely to go into business for themselves if they are unemployed, work part-time, have changed jobs often and make less money.
- Obtaining higher levels of education makes people more likely to start businesses.
- Studying fields or subjects that correspond to occupations in which many people run their own businesses is likely to increase a person's chances of starting a business.
- Most entrepreneurs do not systematically search for, or evaluate, their new business ideas, offering instead the same, or similar, products to the same, or similar, customers as their previous employers. More people even start companies before they have identified a business idea than the other way around.
- The typical business is started by a single person alone and when more than one person is involved in starting a business, it is usually two spouses working together.
- It does not take a large amount of money to start a business; the typical new business established in the United States requires less than $ 25,000 in initial capital.
- The most common source of capital for a new business is personal savings. Many entrepreneurs borrow personally to finance their new businesses, with personal bank loans being the most important source of personal debt for new businesses. About half of all new businesses are financed with debt and half with equity.
- One of the most overlooked reasons why some entrepreneurs get external financing is simply that they ask for it.

Source: Shane, 2008.
Note: Venture capitalists provide money to less than one-tenth of 1 per cent of all start-ups, and account for less than 2 per cent of all small business financing.

There are also differences in the percentages of necessity-driven or improvement-driven entrepreneurial activities in different phases of economic development. A necessity-driven entrepreneur is one who starts a business due to a lack of job opportunities (GEM 2011). In contrast, improvement-driven opportunity entrepreneurs are those who start businesses because they identify an opportunity to increase income and independence (GEM 2011). The above illustrates that in factor-driven economies there is a balance between necessity and improvement-driven entrepreneurs. As economic development increases there are more improvement-driven entrepreneurs and less necessity-driven entrepreneurs. In innovation-driven economies, nearly two-thirds of participants in the GEM survey indicated that improvement opportunity and not necessity was the key motivating factor for engaging in entrepreneurial activities.

C. Key factors for success of entrepreneurs

While it is not possible to compose an exhaustive list of all the factors that determine the success of entrepreneurs, it is possible to identify a number of factors that successful entrepreneurs have in common. The main elements include: adequate education; relevant experience; deep market knowledge and professional networks; and a marketable idea. In order to manage the whole business process, successful entrepreneurs should also have solid command of management skills covering marketing, cost control, cash flow management and certain knowledge of legal requirements (e.g., business registration).

Resources are another crucial factor influencing the success of new business ventures, with the most important being financial, technological and human. Entrepreneurs need to guarantee adequate start-up funds from their own capital, family support or external financial supporters, such as "angel investors".[60] Among other factors, human resources are the foundation of a successful and well-functioning enterprise while technological expertise is essential to the realization of ideas.

A unique and well-developed business plan is essential in competitive markets as it is an assessment of all factors and coordinates entrepreneurs' strengths and available resources. Successful business plans consist of clearly-defined corporate missions, strengths and weaknesses, and competitive products and services (see annex IV.1 for detailed exercises for business plan development). During the implementation of business plans, successful entrepreneurs should always pay close attention to: (a) the trends of the market and customer needs; (b) policy changes, including public spending and procurement; (c) advancement of technologies; and (d) economic volatilities (boom or decline).

While entrepreneurs can exercise influence on many of the aforementioned factors for success, the external environment in which entrepreneurial activities take place is beyond their control. The external environment includes factors such as the overall macroeconomic stability, the existence and efficiency of institutions and infrastructure as well as appropriate levels of health and education (figure IV.1). A favourable external environment will play a key role in determining the likelihood of entrepreneurial success. Entrepreneurs also benefit from a being highly aware of the specific social, cultural and political context in which they are operating. An adequate understanding of these dimensions helps them obtain market insights and develop context specific products or services. Figure IV.2 illustrates the overall framework of key factors for successful entrepreneurs.

---

[60] An "angel investor" is an affluent individual who funds business start-ups in exchange for ownership equity or future repayment of loans. For more details see chapter V.

Figure IV.2. Key success factors of entrepreneurs

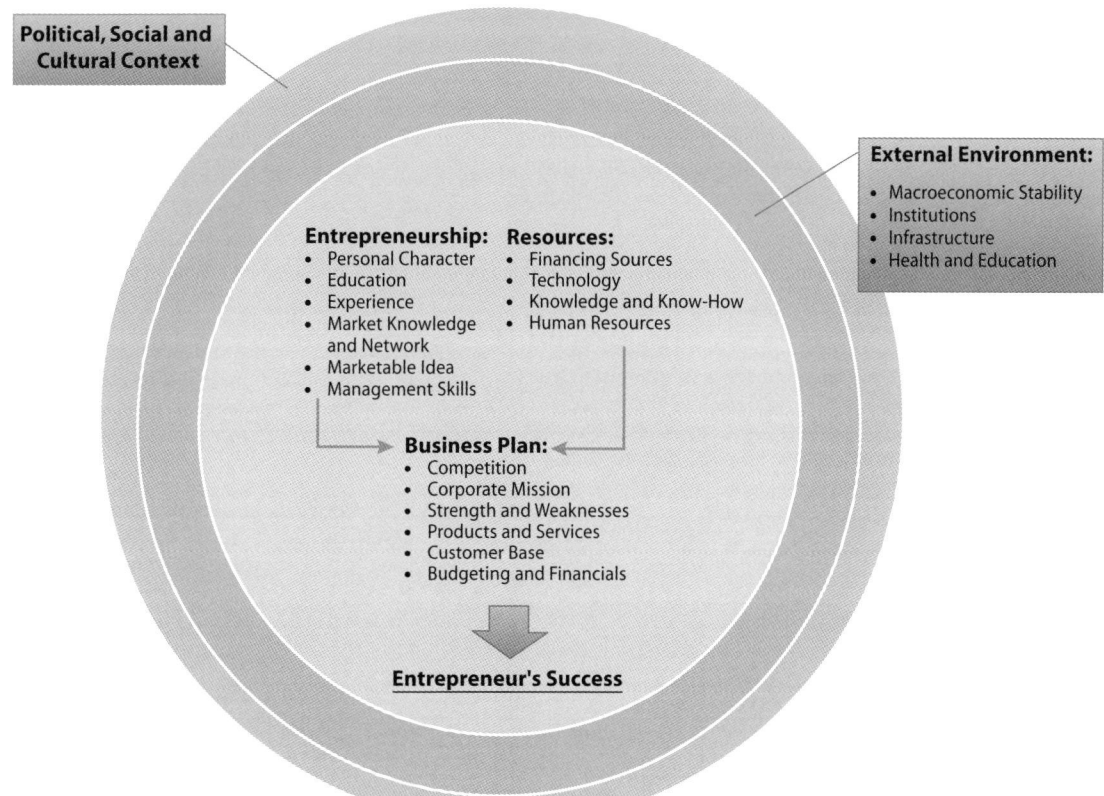

Source: Authors' compilation with elements from the Entrepreneurship Model (GEM, 2011).

D. Entry barriers to entrepreneurship

The 'fear of failure' is the paramount entry barrier to entrepreneurship in the Asia-Pacific context. In a number of nations, for instance, any kind of failure carries strong stigma (GEM, 2009). The "fear of failure" is not simply an internal mindset; it is influenced by the following socioeconomic and cultural factors:

(a) Negative peer pressures (e.g., parents, relatives and friends);
(b) No respectable exit route without economic punishment;
(c) Social stigma;
(d) Lack of confidence due to inadequate skills and knowledge; and
(e) Low aspirations.

In addition, cumbersome procedures as well as high monetary costs and poor market access often prevent potential entrepreneurs from either starting their businesses or from registering them formally. Research on the differential regulatory burden faced by entrepreneurs would be useful, both in understanding which procedures impose particular costs on entrepreneurs and the best way to mitigate those costs (World Bank, 2012a). The Asia-Pacific region is home to some of the best business environments (e.g., Singapore, the Republic of Korea and Hong Kong, China) as well as some of the most difficult. According to the most recent World Bank Doing Business "starting a business" indicators, Cambodia (171 out of 183 countries) is the lowest ranked of all countries in the region. The nine required procedures take an average of 85 days to complete and cost 109.7 per cent of the economy's income per capita (World Bank, 2012a). India (166) also has a low ranking for starting a business, as does the Philippines (158), Timor-Leste (157), Indonesia (155) and China (151). All of these countries, with the exception of India and Indonesia, dropped in the "starting a business" rankings in the past year (World Bank, 2012a).

E. Cultural aspects and their impacts on entrepreneurship

Culture is another important factor that explains cross-country differences in SME development as entrepreneurs' decision-making is influenced by their cultural backgrounds. The term "culture", as discussed here, is defined as "the collective programming of the mind that distinguishes the members of one group or category of people from another" (Hofstede, 1991). On the basis of this definition, Hofstede (1980 and 2001) proposed a five-dimensional model for analysing national cultures (table IV.3).

Abundant empirical literature has demonstrated the relationship between entrepreneurial activities and cultural dimensions, and has found similar results. In general, low power distance, individualism, low uncertainty avoidance, and long-term orientation are associated with entrepreneurial activities and innovation (Shane, 1993, 1995; Thomas and Mueller, 2000; and Jones and Davis, 2000). Collectivism can be a good support to subsequent implementation after invention (Nakata and Sivakumar, 1996). Masculine cultures emphasize the value of performance, competition and success, while feminine countries may be more successful in the service sector due to the strong focus on relationships (Luczak and Mohan-Neill, 2009).

Box IV.3. Entry barriers to entrepreneurship for youth in the Greater Mekong Subregion

In 2009, the Entrepreneurship Development Institute of India conducted a research survey of the entry barriers to entrepreneurship in the Greater Mekong Subregion (GMS), which comprises of Cambodia, the Lao People's Democratic Republic, Myanmar, Thailand and Viet Nam as well as two southern provinces of China (Yunnan and Guangxi). The objective of the study was to understand the perception of students and young employees regarding entrepreneurship as a career option in the GMS. The study particularly delineated the factors that influence career choices of youth, which helped in identifying barriers to entrepreneurship.

The selection of all the respondents (254 students and 253 employees) from the GMS countries was based on the convenient sampling method. The coverage of respondents, the sample size and inclusion of regional variations lend validity to the findings. In order of the greatest to the least influential factor, the following four entry barriers were identified:

(a) Attitudinal (no interest in owning one's own business; preference for employment over self-employment);

(b) Lack of confidence in business;

(c) Disapproval of family or friends; and

(d) Desire to wait for some more time.

It is necessary to sustain the morale and motivation of those who are willing to venture into self-employment and entrepreneurship, and it is useful to know whether they do so immediately after completing studies or after a few years of working as an employee. Although nearly 63 per cent of the sample employees in the study were not very keen to take up entrepreneurship, it is heartening to note that 41 per cent of them might consider entrepreneurship, provided the right kind of encouragement, environment, support and motivation are available. This is an opportunity for action by policymakers concerned with entrepreneurship development in the GMS. However, this interest may decline as employees take up other opportunities; and so requires the timely attention of policymakers.

Table IV.2 proposes a framework for dealing with these barriers. This framework is not all-inclusive; rather, it suggests possible areas of focus to policymakers. The point is to stimulate thoughts about necessary policies to overcome the identified hurdles to entrepreneurship in the GMS.

Table IV.2. Minimizing the barriers: A suggested framework

Entry barrier	Reasons for not starting the venture	Measures to cross the entry barrier
Lack of self-confidence	• To gain experience. • To arrange for finance. • To seek social security by working first.	• Managerial skills and vocational training. • Ensuring timely access to finance. • Changing the mindset.
Resistance from peers and conflicting social values	• Lack of connections to the business community. • No family business experience. • Bad experiences from founding firms in the past. • Limited capacity of the family to bear the risks.	• Counselling for confidence-building. • Demonstration of cases of successful first-generation entrepreneurs. • Provision for social security and fellowship for those opting for an entrepreneurial career.
Lack of expertise, weak will to compete and inadequate knowledge and information.	• Lack of knowledge of business opportunity. • No institutional linkages. • Lack of knowledge about the procedures and formality involved in launching an enterprise.	• Business opportunity guidance and entrepreneurship education. • Information on organizations, procedures, and sources of assistance. • Behavioural training. • Business incubation programmes.
Attitudinal – no interest in setting up own business; distinct preference for employment or salaried job.	• Satisfied with current position. • Lack of business aptitude. • Desire to have a secure job. • Unwillingness to risk loss of money and social stigma.	• Inculcating entrepreneurial values and behavioural training. • Skills training and counselling. • Facilitate risk management; loss insurance.

Source: Authors' compilation.

Table IV.3. Five dimensions of national culture

Dimension	Definition
Power distance	The degree of inequality among people that the population of a country considers as normal.
Individualism versus collectivism	The extent to which people feel they are supposed to take care of, or to be cared for by, themselves, their families or organizations to which they belong.
Uncertainty avoidance	The degree to which people prefer structured over unstructured situations.
Masculinity versus femininity	The extent to which a culture is conducive to dominance, assertiveness and acquisition of things versus a culture that is more conducive to people, feelings and the quality of life.
Long-term versus short-term orientation	Values to concentrate on the future and focus on long-term relationships, such as saving and persistence versus values oriented towards the past and present, such as fulfilling social obligations and transaction-based relationships.

Source: Hofstede, 1980 and 2001.

According to Didero and others (2008), the Asia-Pacific region is generally characterized by high-power distance, high collectivism and long-term orientation. Some countries (e.g., Japan) are marked as masculine with high uncertainty avoidance, while the others (e.g., Thailand) are associated with femininity and low uncertainty avoidance. This conclusion implies that Asia-Pacific countries may lack certain cultural elements for entrepreneurial activities and innovation, even though they do have some positive cultural dimensions to support the development and maintenance of business. Table IV.4 summarizes the results of the national culture survey by Hofstede (2001), which was conducted in 53 countries.

Table IV.4. Values of Hofstede's cultural dimensions

Region	Country/area	Power distance[1]	Uncertainty avoidance[2]	Individualism[3]	Masculinity[4]	Long-/short-term orientation[5]
Asia-Pacific	Australia	36	51	90	61	31
	Hong Kong, China	68	29	25	57	96
	India	77	40	48	56	61
	Indonesia	78	48	14	46	n.a.
	Iran (Islamic Republic of)	58	59	41	43	n.a.
	Israel	13	81	54	47	n.a.
	Japan	54	92	46	95	80
	Malaysia	104	36	26	50	n.a.
	New Zealand	22	49	79	58	30
	Pakistan	55	70	14	50	0
	Philippines	94	44	32	64	19
	Singapore	74	8	20	48	48
	Republic of Korea	60	85	18	39	75
	Taiwan Province of China	58	69	17	45	87
	Thailand	64	64	20	34	56
	Turkey	66	85	37	45	n.a.
Arabia	Arabic countries	80	68	38	53	n.a.
Africa	East African countries	64	52	27	41	25
	South Africa	49	49	65	63	n.a.
	West African countries	77	54	20	46	16
Europe	Austria	11	70	55	79	31
	Belgium	65	94	75	54	38
	Denmark	18	23	74	16	46
	Finland	33	59	63	26	41
	France	68	86	71	43	39
	Germany (former West Germany)	35	65	67	66	31
	Greece	60	112	35	57	n.a.
	Ireland	28	35	70	68	43
	Italy	50	75	76	70	34
	Netherlands	38	53	80	14	44
	Norway	31	50	69	8	44
	Portugal	63	104	27	31	30
	Spain	57	86	51	42	19
	Sweden	31	29	71	5	33
	Switzerland	34	58	68	70	40
	United Kingdom	35	35	89	66	25
	Yugoslavia	76	88	27	21	0
North America	Canada	39	48	80	52	23
	United States	40	46	91	62	29
Latin America	Argentina	49	86	46	56	n.a.
	Brazil	69	76	38	49	65
	Chile	63	86	23	28	n.a.
	Colombia	67	80	13	64	n.a.
	Costa Rica	35	86	15	21	n.a.
	Ecuador	78	67	8	63	n.a.
	Guatemala	95	101	6	37	n.a.
	Jamaica	45	13	39	68	n.a.
	Mexico	81	82	30	69	n.a.

Table IV.4. *(continued)*

Region	Country/area	Dimensions				
		Power distance[1]	Uncertainty avoidance[2]	Individualism[3]	Masculinity[4]	Long-/short-term orientation[5]
	Panama	95	86	11	44	n.a.
	Peru	64	87	16	42	n.a.
	Salvador	66	94	19	40	n.a.
	Uruguay	61	100	36	38	n.a.
	Venezuela	81	76	12	73	n.a.

Source: Hofstede, 2001.
Notes: Arabic countries include Egypt, Iraq, Kuwait, Lebanon, Libya, Saudi Arabia, United Arab Emirates; East African countries include Ethiopia, Kenya, Tanzania and Zambia; West African countries include Ghana, Nigeria and Sierra Leone.
[1] Power Distance: higher number = large power distance
[2] Uncertainty Avoidance: higher number = higher uncertainty avoidance
[3] Individualism: higher number = individualist
[4] Masculinity: higher number = masculine
[5] Long-/short-term orientation: higher number = longer-term orientation

To address cultural impacts on entrepreneurship, the interrelationships among culture, policy, and entrepreneurial development must first be considered. As illustrated in figure IV.3, there will be changes in policy results, based on different combinations of policy and culture. If both variables favour the development of entrepreneurship, the yield will be a virtuous circle for entrepreneurial activities (quadrant Entrepreneurial). If the opposite happens, the result will be few entrepreneurs and little entrepreneurship (quadrant Stagnant). The two remaining quadrants are more complex because they involve mismatches between the two variables. A favourable policy with an unfavourable culture produces the "Led" quadrant: a government leads the public to greater acceptance of, and support for entrepreneurship, thereby towards more entrepreneurial behaviour and outcomes. The opposite quadrant, "Repressed", represents the scenario in which a government attempts to resist public inclinations for more supportive entrepreneurial environment (Dennis, 2005).

Figure IV.3. Relationships among culture, policy and entrepreneurship

	Policy	
	Favourable	Unfavourable
Culture Favourable	Entrepreneurial	Repressed (bottom up)
Culture Unfavourable	Led (top down)	Stagnant

Source: Dennis, 2005.

This model highlights the changeable nature of entrepreneurial activities in a geographical area as well as the impact of both culture and policy on this issue. To promote entrepreneurship, a favourable culture needs to be shaped, even though progress may be slow. In addition, cultural differences within the country concerned should also be taken into consideration during the policymaking process.

Because the specific groups or geographical areas may start at different points, the effects of the same policy may also vary. For example, in Malaysia, the Chinese Malays and, to some extent, the Indian-Muslims have long had a tradition of entrepreneurship, while the Bumiputra community did not have a similar tradition. As a result, the same SME policies did not lead to significant improvement of Bumiputra entrepreneurship despite the prosperity of other groups. Consequently more targeted government initiatives have been needed (Agensi Inovasi Malaysia, 2011).

The above analysis indicates that the policy objective of shaping culture is not to overtake it but to capitalize on the positive sides and to introduce the missing elements for entrepreneurship and innovation. To foster such a culture, the OECD (2007b) provided some general measures including:

(a) Increase awareness of entrepreneurial opportunities;
(b) Intensify enterprise education and awareness campaigns;
(c) Create identifiable role models and champions;
(d) Establish mentor and patron relationships;
(e) Incentives and support for business succession;
(f) Create incentives for SMEs to train apprentices; and
(g) Enhance entrepreneurship within existing businesses.

F. Creation of entrepreneurship awareness

Governments and their agencies can promote awareness about the importance and role of entrepreneurship through a variety of programmes. Before embarking on such programmes, policymakers must recognize the social and cultural values and norms, including family traditions, which might inhibit entrepreneurial awareness. As reviewed in the previous section, the "fear of failure" needs to be addressed. Utilizing educational networks, mass media, confidence-building programmes that include easy and non-punitive exit-route legislation as well as financial assistance schemes for rehabilitation or closing failed ventures, are all worthy tactics. These measures would promote an entrepreneurial culture in an economy.

While a number of Asia-Pacific economies have initiated awareness creation programmes, it has not yet become a region-wide practice. According to a study by APO (2007), countries with successful awareness creation programmes include Bangladesh, India, Indonesia, Malaysia, Nepal, Pakistan, the Philippines and Viet Nam. With the changing needs of society, countries that are already operating the programmes may need to revisit the contents and make adjustments accordingly. Ongoing programmes in India and Pakistan exemplify government efforts in creating entrepreneurship and offer ideas about how countries should design programmes that can keep pace with social, economic and cultural development.

Entrepreneurship awareness creation has been integrated into India's educational training programmes since the establishment of the Entrepreneurship Awareness Camps in 1982. The three-day camps are conducted by specialized institutions with the aim to create awareness among students about entrepreneurship as an alternative career option. More than 100,000 students have been provided with in-depth knowledge about entrepreneurship, especially in the areas of science and technology. In addition, entrepreneurship is now offered as a postgraduate subject in major Indian institutes, such as the Indian Institute of Management, as well as the commerce departments of some universities (APO, 2007).

Past entrepreneurship awareness programmes run by the Government of Pakistan were not comprehensively designed and had limited impacts on promoting entrepreneurship among educated Pakistani youth. With a new direction to create awareness and to provide support, the Small and Medium Enterprise Development Authority offers training on business development and new business start-ups to potential young entrepreneurs and students aged between 18 years and 32 years (APO, 2007).

G. Education and training for entrepreneurship development

Generating a critical mass of entrepreneurs oriented towards high levels of growth depends on the quality of education and training provided as well as the presence of an environment fostering innovation. The three interconnected areas – education and training (especially quality vocational training and skills development), innovation (generating commercial value through new and creative ideas) and entrepreneurship – provide possibilities for mutually beneficial synergies through the flow of ideas and wealth. Education and training are indispensable for skills development, while the ability to innovate and generate commercially valuable new products and processes can only take place in environments that encourage experimentation and value addition.

According to the Global Entrepreneurship Monitor Report (GEM, 2011), primary education is a basic requirement for enabling entrepreneurship in factor-driven economies and thus should be given priority. Beyond primary education, policymakers should devote attention to entrepreneurial instruction, i.e., cultivation of people's ability to recognize opportunities and to exploit them. Such an education would deliver the knowledge necessary to identify and capitalize on opportunities that offer economic advantages. It would equip the entrepreneur with an ability to apply knowledge to maximize gains, useful business skills, leadership qualities and, above all, the self-confidence required to execute all these actions.

Organizations such as ILO and SDC offer examples of success stories in this regard. They have supported a number of countries in the Asian and Pacific region in their endeavours to train their youth for entrepreneurship, not only by introducing the *Know about Business (KAB)* curriculum in the education system but also by capacity-building through the establishment of educational institutions.[61] Countries such as China, Indonesia, the Lao People's Democratic Republic, Papua New Guinea, the Philippines, Sri Lanka and Viet Nam have either introduced or are in the process of introducing entrepreneurship education at secondary, post-secondary, vocational and technical schools, and in higher education. For example, entrepreneurship education within all educational institutions has been a high-level priority in Indonesia as reflected in that country's medium-term development plans (Ministry of National Development Planning, 2010).

Education and training for entrepreneurship development also should be geared towards both youth and women in the population. Training, motivation and guidance of youth and women towards entrepreneurship and self-employment provide the best solution for controlling unemployment and fostering growth. The issue of women, in particular, is considered in greater detail later in this chapter.

H. Main players in entrepreneurship development

Several economies in the Asia-Pacific region have designed and put into operation entrepreneurship development programmes. The main players are government, academia, the private sector and the media.

Most of the policy programmes for SME development conducted by governments feature entrepreneurship development as an important component. Various agencies have placed SME and entrepreneurship development at the centre of their agendas and oversee these programmes at the national level.

Several institutions, universities and R&D centres across Asia and the Pacific are designating entrepreneurship development as their core function. Over the years, many of these agencies have emerged as centres of excellence. The private sector as well as NGOs play a vital role in promoting entrepreneurship in various countries.

In this context, the role of the media assumes great importance. The media provides a powerful means of creating an entrepreneurial culture in society, particularly through its influence on collective and individual perceptions and attitudes. The media educates and enhances entrepreneurship by conveying positive messages and knowledge that are crucial in building supportive social attitudes (and even systems) towards generating entrepreneurial activity (Hang and van Weezel, 2007).

---

[61] For more details, visit the website of ILO's International Training Centre at http://kab.itcilo.org/en.

Box IV.4. Technical and vocational education and training

Technical and vocational education and training (TVET) is concerned with the acquisition of knowledge and skills for employment. It aims to import specific job-relevant skills that can make the worker suitable for a given job. TVET includes at least two major forms: vocational and technical education in formal education systems (lower and senior secondary schools, post-senior secondary but less than college level institutions like polytechnics, and colleges at tertiary level), and training outside formal system of education (pre-employment training and on-the-job-training). The latter form also includes apprenticeship-training systems, non-formal training centres, enterprise based training, etc.

In addition to basic and occupational skill development, TVET can be a channel to deliver entrepreneurship education by adding relevant elements. Awareness of entrepreneurship should be integrated into the whole training process to encourage students to see self-employment as a valuable career path. The specific skills needed for successful entrepreneurship such as business plan drafting, accounting and marketing skills, knowledge of commercial laws, and the administrative procedures for starting a business should be covered by the courses.

Some countries in Asia-Pacific have taken steps in this direction. For example, in collaboration with the Colombo Plan Staff College for Technician Education, the Ministry of Vocational Education and Training Government of Sri Lanka has developed a TVET programme to promote entrepreneurship. Figure IV.4 illustrates the course structure, training process, and expected outcomes of this programme, which provide a comprehensive framework of knowledge and skills needed in entrepreneurial activities.

Source: Colombo Plan Staff College for Technician Education, 2007.

Figure IV.4. Overview of the TVET programme for entrepreneurship in Sri Lanka

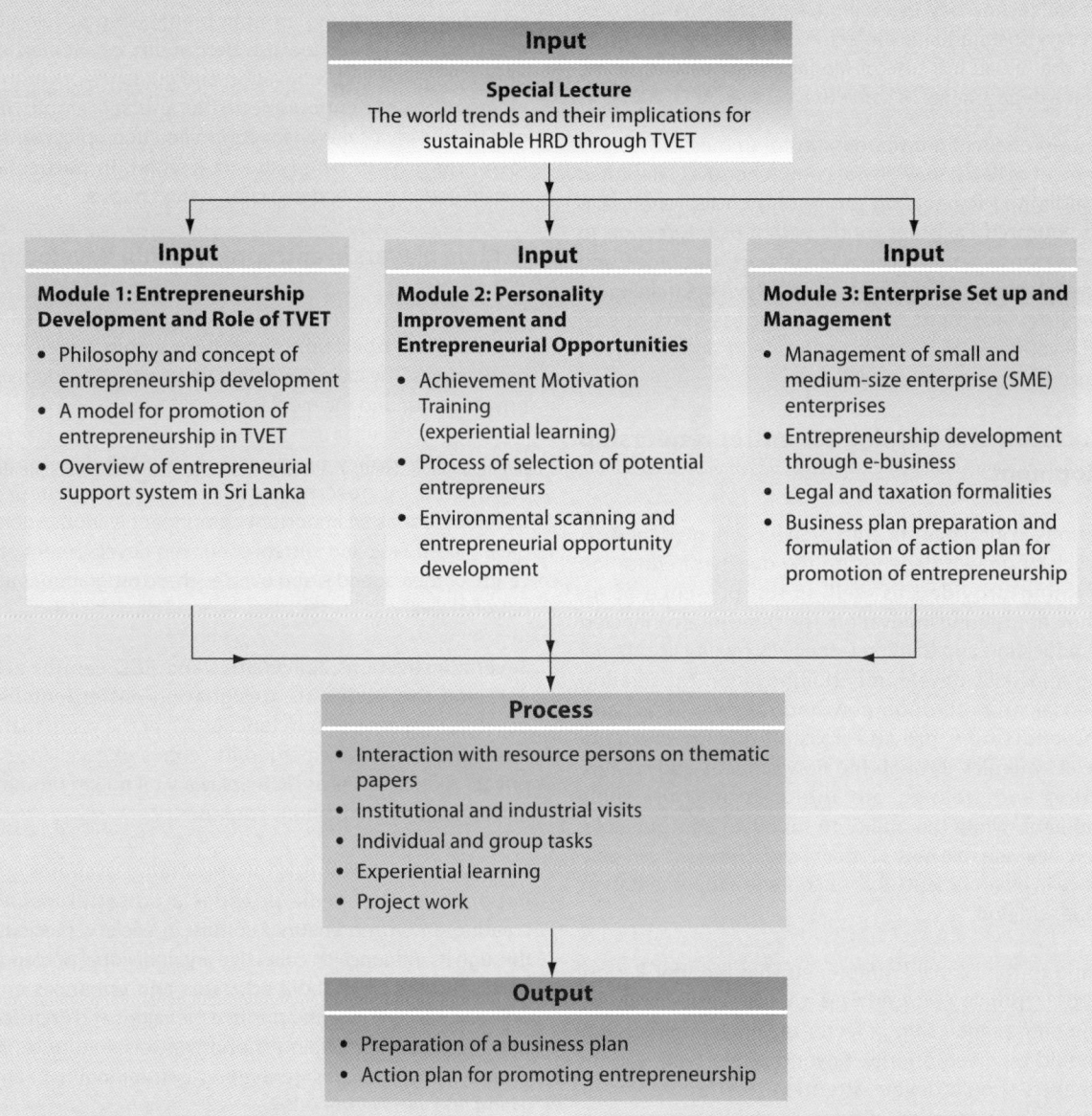

Source: Tilak, 2002; European Commission, 2009b; and the Colombo Plan Staff College for Technician Education, 2007.

I. Women entrepreneurs

Empirical studies of economic development consistently demonstrate a strong positive correlation between the degree of women's participation in the economy and economic growth (Tansel, 2001). Women entrepreneurs, as a group, have demonstrated impressive business acumen over the years. They have emerged as reliable borrowers (e.g., microfinancing) and contributors to family income and the national economy at large. They are particularly active in the agricultural, food processing, light manufacturing, service and entertainment sectors.

A study by the Kauffman Foundation (Cohoon and Mitchell, 2010), based on data collected during 2008-2009 from 549 respondent business women (about 40 per cent of the female founders from randomly selected high-tech companies), identified the five top factors that motivate women to become entrepreneurs (Cohoon and Mitchell, 2010):

(a) A desire to build wealth;
(b) Wish to capitalize on the business ideas;
(c) The appeal of start-up culture;
(d) A desire to have their own company; and
(e) Working for someone else does not appeal to them.

Box IV.5. Women entrepreneurs in the food-processing industry

Women have traditionally played a vital role in the agricultural and light manufacturing sectors in the developing countries of Asia and the Pacific. They dominate various subsectors – for example: (a) textiles, clothing and leather; (b) food, beverages and tobacco; and (c) wood and wood processing – making up more than 80 per cent, 75 per cent and 60 per cent of employees, respectively (UNIDO, 1995). Due to their greater participation in the above subsectors, women entrepreneurs are at an advantage when starting businesses. In fact, it is common for women to act as microentrepreneurs and traders of agricultural products in rural areas in many Asian and Pacific countries.

Food processing is particularly popular among home-based women workers and self-employed women entrepreneurs, as it is an extension of their domestic duties. For example, Laoganma Special Flavour Foodstuffs Co., Ltd. is famous for its product brand "Laoganma" chilli sauce and the story of its female founder Huabi Tao in China. Tao was a street vendor selling home-made noodles when she noticed that it was her own, specially formulated chilli sauce seasoning that kept customers coming back for more. With her business acumen, she founded Laoganma in 1989. Today, over 1,000 Laoganma staff and workers produce 430,000 jars of chilli foods per day, achieving an annual turnover of $ 50 million. The products have been exported to 30 countries and regions, and Tao has become one of the most successful women entrepreneurs in China.[62]

When given a level playing field, women have displayed entrepreneurship skills and achieved success. The study observed that "successful men and women entrepreneurs share similar motivations, view the reasons for their success in largely the same way, secure funding from the same types of sources, and face many of the same challenges". Thus, both men and women can be equally successful entrepreneurs under the same conditions (Cohoon and Mitchell, 2010).

Until recently, policymakers have not taken into consideration the particular obstacles that women may face in starting a business. These include cultural attitudes that limit women's involvement in business, laws prohibiting female ownership of property, lack of capital or information due to membership in social networks that are not as robust as those of men, and generally inferior education. Many governments still need to address these issues, fill the gaps and remove the operational roadblocks confronting women entrepreneurs. Addressing these issues will not only increase economic productivity, it will also improve the general social status of women.

Given the above points, policymakers should pay attention to empowering women in business. To do so, the financial instrument of micro lending has gained worldwide attention. Popularized by Dr. Muhammad Yunus, the 2006 Nobel Laureate and founder of the Grameen Bank in Bangladesh, micro-lending enables women to start their own modest firms, in order to support their families. Micro-lending targets women not only with the objective of empowering them but also for a practical reason as women are considered to be a better credit risk than men. The rate of interest on micro-loans, while high by developed country standards, is generally much lower than what an entrepreneur could obtain from a loan shark, the typical source of credit in a rural village. For all of these benefits, however, it must be noted that few large-scale empirical analyses of the efficacy of micro-lending have been undertaken. Much of the evidence of the benefits of micro-lending is anecdotal (Morduch, 2002).

J. Rural entrepreneurship

Rural development is closely linked to entrepreneurship as individuals and institutions that promote rural development have to stress the need to create and grow rural enterprises. Rural entrepreneurship is viewed as the central force of local economic growth with enormous employment potential, particularly for youth. It utilizes local and regional raw materials and resources, and decreases vulnerability of the rural economy to financial shocks. Farmers welcome it as an instrument for improving agricultural earnings. It also provides home-based jobs for women. Rural entrepreneurship develops the countryside economically, socially and environmentally (Petrin, 1994).

To strengthen rural entrepreneurship, policymakers should start by identifying local and regional assets and resources. Officials can advertise them to attract entrepreneurs who will, in turn, convert entrepreneurial activities into actual economic benefits. For this conversion to be successful a number of conditions must be present, including: adequate

---

[62] For more details, visit the company's website at www.laoganma.com.cn/english/e_index.jsp.

local infrastructure, an organized and supportive rural community, and systems that ensure the cultivated rural entrepreneurs remain in their communities (OECD, 2011b).

At the beginning of the 1980s, a good example occurred in China of how effective rural entrepreneurship can be. At that time China was starting the transition from a centrally-planned economy to a market economy. In the interest of not shocking the economy with too many reforms at once, but also to gain the most benefit for the greatest number of people possible, the Government of China instituted reforms in the agricultural sector (CIA World Factbook, 2011). Local government officials encouraged farmers to sell surplus produce at market prices, and also supported the establishment of new firms known as township-village enterprises. After an initial decline in agricultural output, the amount of farm production skyrocketed in 1984 (ITC, 2011). From 1978-1984, the number of rural enterprises increased fourfold in China, as did the value of gross output. The average annual growth rate of rural industrial output was about 27 per cent, nearly three times that of national GDP, while the average asset scale of township-village enterprises boomed tenfold with an average annual growth rate of 25 per cent (Zou, 2003).

K. Social entrepreneurship and social enterprises

The development and recognition of social entrepreneurship and social enterprises has gained momentum during the past few years. While both have the objective of addressing salient socioeconomic as well as environmental issues in a society, it is worth clarifying the two terms. With regard to social entrepreneurship, Boschee (2009) from the Social Enterprise Alliance emphasized the individual, who as a social entrepreneur seeks to solve a social problem. Borstein (2004) described social entrepreneurs as a transformative force for social change with bold ideas, who seek to inspire and move people at large. Contrasting business entrepreneurs and social entrepreneurs, the former are as important to the economy as the latter ones are to social value creation and change (Bornstein, 2004). The social entrepreneur can pursue this goal within a not-for-profit organization (NPO); however, social entrepreneurs and, by extension, social entrepreneurship can also be located within conventional businesses and government organizations where they take on the role of a change-seeking entrepreneur (Boschee, 2009).

Having recognized that organizational forms such as NPOs and philanthropic foundations have their limitations in addressing social and environmental challenges, an increasing number of social entrepreneurs are searching for a more suitable organizational type. Therefore, the social enterprise model may offer a viable alternative (Boschee, 2009). A plethora of definitions of social enterprises exist. Although there is not one universally agreed-upon definition, numerous studies mention several salient characteristics.[63] Ming and Shahnaz (2009) assessed both the contexts of, and opportunities for, social enterprises in Asia and the Pacific as follows:

(a) A specific positive social impact is the primary reason for the entity's existence (versus ancillary or secondary development such as a company's CSR programme);

(b) The business model reflects responsible entrepreneurship and growth for all stakeholders: staff and overseers, beneficiaries, customers, the overall community and the environment;

(c) The enterprise has a market orientation; and

(d) It embraces for-profit as well as not-for-profit approaches.

While this definition captures the essence of a social enterprise, the impact of social enterprises can be broad, embracing positive social, environmental and cultural purposes. Social enterprises create positive change by applying business methods in various fields, ranging from education, health and environment to enterprise development.

In order to shed further light on this emerging trend and to profile the people behind social enterprises around the world, the GEM published a special report on social entrepreneurship in 2009. The GEM report applies a broad definition of social entrepreneurship, referring to individuals or organizations engaged in entrepreneurial activities with a social goal. Among the 49 nations participating in the survey, an average 1.8 per cent of the adult population was involved in early-stage social entrepreneurial activity (with a range of 0.1 per cent – 4.3 per cent). While more men than women start social enterprises, there is a relatively high prevalence of female social entrepreneurs in the age bracket of 25-34 years with a diverse educational and work background. Figure IV.5 shows social entrepreneurial activity by country, including some Asia-Pacific economies.

Governments have noticed the emergence of social entrepreneurship. For example, the Government of the United Kingdom has been particularly accommodating and progressive with its policies towards social enterprises. In February 2011, the Government released a vision and strategy for expanding the social investment market (Cabinet Office, 2011a). The centrepiece of this vision is Big Society Capital (formerly Big Society Bank), a financial institution that aims to provide greater access to financial resources and technical advice particularly to social enterprises, charities and voluntary organizations (Cabinet Office, 2011b).

Governments in Asia and the Pacific have also started to recognize the value and importance of social entrepreneurship and are implementing their own policy programming. The Government of Thailand, for example, installed the national committee of social enterprise development in 2010 and later transformed the committee into the permanent Thai Social Enterprise Office in 2011. The Government empowered the office to design specific criteria to assess social enterprises for their eligibility to receive tax and other benefits (Social Enterprise Network Asia, 2010).

In Singapore, the Government is also trying to foster the development of its social enterprise sector. In 2006, the Minister of Community Development, Youth and Sports requested the formation of the social enterprise committee with the objective of analysing possible growth strategies. A specific example of the Government's interest in social enterprises is its support for an organization called Impact

---

[63] For a clarification between social enterprise and social entrepreneurship, see Boschee, 2009.

Figure IV.5. Social entrepreneurial activity by country

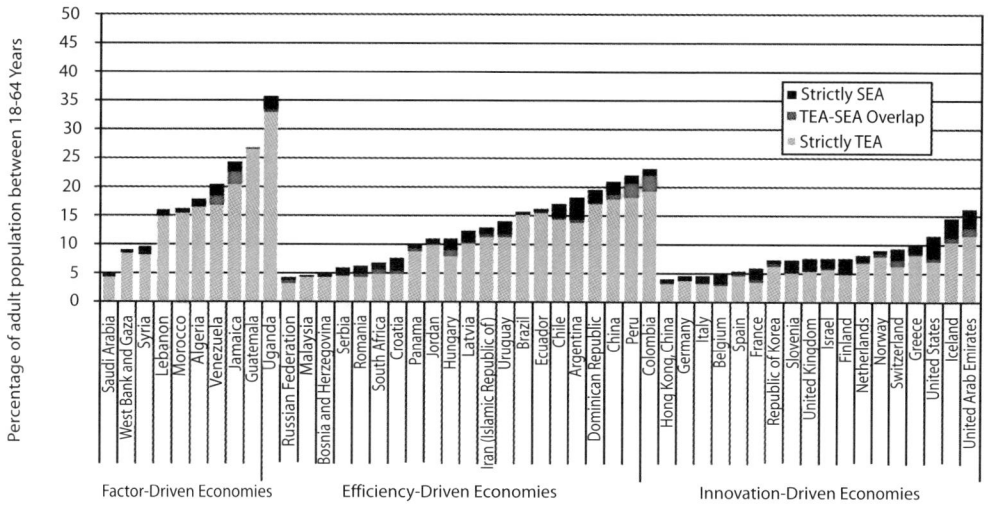

Source: GEM, 2009.

Investment Shujog. While Impact Investment Shujog provides capacity-building services for social enterprises, its sister company Impact Investment Exchange Asia is building the region's first social stock exchange focused exclusively on the financial needs of social enterprises. Together, they seek to expand the sector, which was established as one of the goals of the Government of Singapore.[64]

It is no coincidence that many of the policies targeting social enterprises resemble those focusing on SMEs. Social enterprises commonly fall into the category of SMEs, measured either by turnover, number of employees or capital investments. Many of the frequently cited main obstacles faced by SMEs (see chapter II) are of relevance to social enterprises.[65] Social enterprises are mostly SMEs facing very similar challenges, but they have the additional expectation of solving a social, environmental or cultural problem while operating in a financially sustainable way. Referring to the previously mentioned feature of a social enterprise – the specific positive social impact is the primary reason for an entity's existence – policymakers who choose to support SME development would be well-advised to pay close attention to the specific needs of social enterprises, as they are similar but not necessarily identical to those of SMEs.

L. General recommendations

1. Offering 'single window' assistance

State policies and financial support schemes should be more entrepreneur-friendly. The "single window" concept is aimed at helping entrepreneurs to obtain all approvals as well as related documents and information from governments at one focal point, and financial assistance, both long term and short term, if possible from one financial institution. This initiative not only expedites administrative procedures but also reduces the chance of corruption. In the Asia-Pacific context,

---

[64] For more details visit the website at http://shujog.org and http://www.asiaiix.com.
[65] For a comparison, see ESCAP, 2003.

single-window assistance is operated in Malaysia; Singapore; China; Hong Kong, China; India; Japan, and others. These and further case studies on the single window are available at the online UN/CEFACT Single Window Repository website, www.unece.org/cefact.

2. Reformation of business registration process

Many countries have undertaken business registration reforms, often as part of a larger regulatory reform programme. This has resulted in greater firm satisfaction and savings, and more registered businesses, financial resources and job opportunities. A number of studies (see, for example, Barseghyan and DiCecio, 2009, and World Bank, 2006b) have shown that economies with higher entry costs are associated with a larger informal sector and a smaller number of legally registered firms. For example, in Egypt the reduction of the minimum capital requirement in 2007 and 2008 led to a more than 30 per cent increase in the number of limited liability companies (World Bank, 2011b). More streamlined business registration regulations also lead to greater tax revenues in government coffers.

3. Facilitating access to seed capital

As mentioned above, one of the biggest obstacles to starting up a business is a lack of initial capital. A financial gap exists between entrepreneurs' financial needs and formal financing to support them. Public sector interventions could be effective in narrowing this gap. One technical issue for term loans is how to meet commercial banks collateral requirements. Based on proper risk evaluation, and in cooperation with commercial banks and business associations, developing public credit guarantee schemes and seed capital funds could be considered.

4. Ensuring formal property rights

In many cases, banks request property as collateral against loans. Without assigning property rights correctly, the potential borrower is not able to prove his creditworthiness and will be denied access to finance. This is one of the reasons why ensuring formal property rights are of utmost importance (World Bank, 2011b).

Within the area of property rights management, effective administration of land is particularly important. If the modalities of transferring formal property are overly complex and expensive, there might be a risk that formal titles will turn informal again. In the past six years, 105 economies have undertaken 146 reforms to make it easier to transfer property. Globally, the time required to transfer property fell by 38 per cent and the cost fell by 10 per cent during that period. The most popular feature of property registration reform, implemented in 52 economies, was lowering transfer taxes and government fees (World Bank, 2011b). Accurate recording of property titles can increase property tax revenues, and can also improve the development and liquidity of capital markets (De Soto, 2000).

5. Simplification of tax collection procedures

Simplified tax codes encourage entrepreneurs to stay in the formal economy. It has been observed that more efficient filing and payment methods (e.g., online systems) have a positive effect on the number of payments made (IFC and PricewaterhouseCoopers, 2011) and at the same time, facilitating the public sector's formal assistance to those entrepreneurs and SMEs. Such a system can have a positive impact on businesses by reducing transaction costs. For example, Colombia introduced a new electronic system for social security and labour taxes in 2006, and by 2008 the social security contributions collected from SMEs had risen by 42 per cent (IFC and PricewaterhouseCoopers, 2011).

6. Provision of credit information systems

Accurate, current credit information is important in helping entrepreneurs gain access to credit. It also assists credit providers to assess potential borrowers and reduce risk. China created a national online registry for pledges of receivables. From January to May 2010, China's Credit Information Centre reported more than 57,000 registrations, representing loans with an estimated value of about $ 1.5 trillion. More than 30,000 SMEs benefited by being able to access credit and secure their loans against account receivables (World Bank, 2011c).

7. Stronger investor protection

Stronger investor protection matters with regard to the ability of companies to raise the capital needed to expand, innovate, diversify and compete. This is crucial in times of financial crisis when entrepreneurs must navigate difficult environments to finance their activities. For example, Indonesia has consistently and extensively improved its investor protection laws since the start of this millennium and the payoff has been striking.

8. Provision of exit channels

Another obstacle to entrepreneurship is a strong "fear of failure" among potential entrepreneurs, which is generally influenced by national culture and social norms. One solution is to offer a respectable exit channel for failed entrepreneurs and firms by minimizing financial punishment. A well-developed bankruptcy law as well as its proper enforcement is necessary.

9. Creation of positive attitudes towards entrepreneurship

One of the most serious entry barriers to entrepreneurship is disinterest in an entrepreneurial career. Knowledge about the attitudes towards the desirability of such a career can help policymakers address this issue. As mentioned above, the "fear of failure" inhibits people who see opportunities for, and are suited to, starting a business (GEM, 2010). Policymakers could address this by prioritizing the introduction of entrepreneurship courses on the benefits of self-employment. The curriculum to achieve these objectives could consist of inculcation of entrepreneurial values through success stories of achievers from different walks of life and discussions about business achievers. In addition, creating awareness and knowledge about the potential benefits of entrepreneurship would be useful, perhaps through cooperation with the mass media.

10. Institutionalization of entrepreneurial education and skills development

As previously highlighted, education and training for entrepreneurship is of critical importance in stimulating and expanding entrepreneurial activities. Policymakers should carefully develop a well-structured and holistic approach to entrepreneurial education and skills development. Schools, technical and vocational training and education institutions as well as universities would be well-advised to incorporate entrepreneurship-focused courses in their respective curricula (OECD, 2010a). Having recognized the benefits of such policies for students, numerous European countries have already designed specific policies to further entrepreneurship education. By including entrepreneurship at all its educational levels, the Government of Norway aims to equip students with the necessary knowledge and skills for entrepreneurship, nurture their self-confidence and competencies in self-employment, and promote entrepreneurial values and culture (OECD, 2010a). Moreover, as strong growth potential and scalability are among the most desirable characteristics of new enterprises, entrepreneurial education should ensure the development of a specific skill set that will enable entrepreneurs to navigate through growth-related challenges.[66] Such skills include:

(a) Opportunity identification;
(b) Risk-taking;
(c) Strategy-making;
(d) Leadership;
(e) Negotiation;
(f) Networking;
(g) Building strategic alliances; and
(h) Intellectual property protection.

Also, while mastering traditional business management skills (such as managing cash flow and developing a business plan) remains important, entrepreneurs will greatly benefit from

---

[66] Several examples of modules for entrepreneurship training are provided in annex IV.2.

learning how to manage cross-functional problems, as these are the types of challenges they will have to face in practice (OECD, 2010a). By sowing the seeds of entrepreneurship at an early stage and ingraining it into the various levels of education, a more conducive environment for new firm formation and an increasing number of successful entrepreneurs will be the result. In order to pursue such a policy change, more resources need to be allocated for example, to the training of trainers and the development of entrepreneurship teaching materials. Possible modules for entrepreneurship training are also given in annex IV.2.

11. Pay special attention to innovative and growth-oriented entrepreneurships

One of the key policy options related to entrepreneurship is to foster more innovative and growth-oriented entrepreneurs who have the potential to be the future business leaders as well as expand their enterprises into large companies. Such innovative companies would also have high potential to be exporters, and they would be important partners to large enterprises and TNCs. Specific technical assistance from policymakers would be useful here.

12. Encourage female, youth and rural entrepreneurs

The positive correlation between female participation in the economy and economic growth has been highlighted. Policymakers can support women entrepreneurs in many ways in addition to their interventions to encourage the development of youth and rural entrepreneurship. One area is property rights. Officials should break down barriers to women owning property, whether these barriers exist in the laws or the customs of a society. Another area is capital. Policymakers can provide subsidies or promote microfinance for nascent female-owned enterprises until they become self-sufficient. Young entrepreneurs require adequate education and training. Furthermore rural entrepreneurship can contribute significantly to averall economic growth.

M. Summary

This chapter began with a discussion of the definitions and concepts of entrepreneurs and entrepreneurship. Entrepreneurs are creative and innovative, and recognize opportunities where others do not. They create value where none previously existed by recombining inputs in novel ways. The most common expression of this creativity is new firm formation. Policymakers need to understand that entrepreneurship occurs in different ways owing to the different motivations of new business owners.

Next, key factors for entrepreneurial success as well as entry barriers were considered. Given the discussion on infrastructure and the regulatory environment in chapter III, the focus in this chapter has been on some of the "soft" elements of BEE, i.e., the attitudes, traits and norms that can help or hinder an entrepreneurial culture. Lack of self-confidence, stigma associated with failure and general disinterest in owning businesses are all common problems in the Asia-Pacific region.

A key theme of this chapter is education and training in entrepreneurship. Often, people shy away from entrepreneurship because they feel ill-equipped to run a business, or perhaps the idea of running a business has never been suggested to them. The example of TVET schools in Sri Lanka has been highlighted, and examples of modules for entrepreneurship training are provided in annex IV.2. In the case of primary and secondary education, policymakers need to incorporate the idea of entrepreneurship as a viable career, and to formulate plans for practical study at the secondary and tertiary levels.

Given the varieties of entrepreneurs, there are subsets of particular importance. As pointed out in chapter III, women entrepreneurs are one such group. This issue has been further considered in this chapter by highlighting the fact that, with proper training and lower social barriers, women can create jobs and wealth. Rural entrepreneurship is another special area, especially for developing nations. China is an excellent example of how fostering entrepreneurship in the countryside can spur national growth and development.

Social entrepreneurship is a recent phenomenon that is rapidly gaining importance. Together with the notion of corporate social responsibility (see box II.5), attempts to harness the profit motive to the furtherance of the common good – be it the environment, public health, education or enlightened labour practices – will be essential. The Government of Thailand is providing incentives to social enterprises in the form of tax concessions and other benefits via the Thai Social Enterprise Office. This is a useful model for other nations in the Asia-Pacific region to consider.

The chapter concluded with a list of general recommendations. Many of those leading the list focus upon the formal aspects of BEE: permits, property rights, regulations, investor protection and access to credit. The final few recommendations, which focus on education, attitudes, and women entrepreneurs, are less tangible and more difficult to achieve. Policymakers will need to cater to the needs and interests of a wide range of stakeholders in order to improve attitudes and perceptions about entrepreneurship.

Annex IV.1
Business plan development

Writing an effective business plan is an integral part of starting or expanding a business. One of the objectives of a business plan is to help the entrepreneur transform a business idea into executable actions. It provides an overall map about the whole business including sales, supply chain and financial plans.

To create a business plan, the "Plan-Do-See" exercise is recommended. An initial business plan is developed first ("Plan") and business activities are conducted following the plan ("Do"). The business plan also needs to be evaluated and improved according to the operating environment and the market reaction during implementation ("See") to ensure its feasibility and the competitiveness of the business.

As a business plan may have various users, the specific needs of those users should be considered in the development process. Entrepreneurs use business plans to refine their business ideas. They require their plans to be clear-cut and executable. A business plan is also important for employees and suppliers who need to define a clear corporate direction. For the public and commercial financial institutions, a business plan can be also be used as a supporting document for grants or loans in order to evaluate their feasibility for funding consideration.

While there are many obstacles to gaining access to institutional finance, entrepreneurs can help themselves by preparing a competent business plan before approaching the financial sector for assistance. Financial institutions must see a "feasible and viable" business plan that projects a pattern of cash flow sufficient to service the loan (known as debt: service ratio) after meeting all the liabilities by the borrower. The plan also needs to demonstrate that the entrepreneur has basic general and financial management skills, including cash flow management, book-keeping and accounting.

Annex table IV.1 details the basic components of a business plan. To create a comprehensive plan, entrepreneurs need to consider each of the components listed in annex table IV.1. Among all these components, the sales forecast could be a difficult part, especially for the startups. In this part, uncertainty and seasonal factors along with the characteristics of the market and the product or the service should be carefully considered, and ideally, the sales forecast should be developed with three scenarios, namely conservative, most likely, and ambitious. In the funding plan, it is also necessary to note that the funds needed and fund raising must be balanced.

Annex table IV.1. Basic components of a business plan

Basic components	Details
Business idea	Idea creation is the art of business
	Review available resources
	Identify unrealized needs
	Get a novel idea through knowledge and experience
	Copying and modifying something marketable
Marketing plan	To whom: customers
	What: products and services
	How: channels and distributions; Internet; price schedule and sales terms; volumes
	Where: country, city, area, and shop
	By whom: employees, agents, franchisees, etc.
	When: business hours
Sales forecast	Three scenarios of revenue (ideally):
	(a) Conservative;
	(b) Most likely;
	(c) Ambitious.
	Different methods by sector:
	(a) Retailer – expected sales amount per square metre
	(b) Services – sales per customer x number of seats x turnover rate (e.g., restaurants, barbers and beauty shops)
	(c) Labour-intensive sector – sales amount per labour x number of employees (e.g., auto sales, cosmetics and building cleaning)
	(d) Asset intensive sector – capacity of assets x number of facility utilization (e.g., manufacturing, printing and transportation)
Procurement plan	What: materials, components, labour and services
	Where: suppliers and supply markets
	When: lead time
	How: price and payment terms
	How much: volume, quantity and duration

Annex table IV.1. *(continued)*

Basic components	Details
Production plan (if needed)	What: products and services Where: factories and warehouses When: lead time How: methods, technology, machinery and equipment How much: volume, quantity

Funding plan	Funds needed for a start-up:
	   (a) Facilities and equipment (factories, warehouses, shops, machinery, goods and automobiles)
	   (b) Operating costs (supplies, salaries, rents and interest) – at least for an initial two to three months after launching the business
	 Fund raising:
	   (a) Own capital (ideally, more than 50 per cent of total funds)
	   (b) Support from family, relatives, friends and others
	   (c) Public grants
	   (d) Public loans (normally collateral is required)
	   (e) Commercial loans (collateral required)

Source: Authors' compilation.
Note: Funds needed and funds raised must be equal.

Annex figure IV.1 provides an example of a simplified business plan that is widely used in Japan.[67] This two-page plan consists of two parts: (a) a business proposal and (b) financial planning. The business proposal provides a concise but comprehensive business analysis that includes company information, products and services, market, business process and competitiveness analysis. The financial planning contains capital requirements, funding plan and income forecast, describing the source of funding and the profitability of the business.

There are several criteria to be considered in evaluating the feasibility of the business plan and the sustainability of the business. First, the two parts of the business plan (business proposal and financial plan) should be consistent (e.g., activities versus funding requirements). Furthermore, the funding plan needs to support both the initial asset investment and operating expenses (at least for the initial two to three months). Generally, the start-up business should plan to be in the black after the first year. Entrepreneurs need to plan carefully to ensure they have made adequate provision for loan installments or something similar.

In addition to the example provided here, the International Finance Corporation (IFC) and Small Business Administration (SBA) of the United States have also developed models of business plans,[68] which could be useful starting points for SMEs. Both of these models provide a computer-based learning exercise, explain how to generate business plan electronically and cover basic financial forecasting.

Annex box IV.1. Checkpoints for start-ups

The following are examples of some pertinent checkpoints that can help a potential entrepreneur think about the range of requirements for achieving success. While this can be an informal process, and the answers need not be specific and executable strategies, at minimum they should trigger consideration. It is also recommended that entrepreneurs refer to this checklist at various stages to ensure nothing is overlooked.

1. Entrepreneurship
   Do you really want to run a business? Why?
   Are you confident you will be successful? How?

2. Management skills
   Do you have any business experience? If yes, describe it.
   Have you forecasted sales, costs and profits? If yes, describe it.

3. Resources
   Will your family support your plan? How?
   Have you secured adequate start-up funds, What are your sources? How much?
   Have you hired adequate and quality employees? How many? What are their roles?

4. Business plan
   Do you know customers and the market well? Who are the customers?
   Can you provide competitive products or services? What are they?
   Have you decided where you will run the business? Describe.
   Have you completed a business plan?

---

[67] A Japanese language version is available at the Japan Finance Corporation website www.jfc.go.jp/k/pfcj/pdf/kaigyou00_110401.pdf.

[68] IFC's tool kit is available at www.smetoolkit.org/smetoolkit/en while the SBA template can be found at http://web.sba.gov/busplantemplate/GenRpt.cfm#.

Annex figure IV.1. Simplified business plan

| **Business plan** | Date: _____ |
| | Company name: _____ |

A. Business proposal

Line of business		Expected date of start-up		Location of business	
Objectives and opportunities					
Business experience	☐ I have no experience running a business. ☐ I established a firm before, and I still manage it. ☐ I ran a business before, but I already closed it. If so, when did you close it? ( )			
Relevant experience, education, certificates and personal background					
Detailed products and/or services					
Strengths					
Challenges and weaknesses					

Customers (including channels and distribution)	Suppliers
Executives and employees	

B. Required funds and fund-raising

Required funds		Amount (US$)	Fund-raising	Amount (US$)
Assets purchase/leasing	Shops, factories, machinery, equipment and automobiles *(details)*		Own capital	
			Loans from family, relatives and friends *(Details and loan terms)*	
			Public grants *(Details and conditions)*	
Operational funds	Materials, supplies, salaries, rents, miscellaneous for at least an initial three months. *(Details)*		Loans from commercial banks and/or other financial institutions *(Details and loan terms)*	
Total (A)			Total (B)	

Note: Totals (A) and (B) must be equal.

Income forecast (monthly average)

		Start-up (US$)	One year later (US$)	Details of revenue, costs of products, and operational expenses
Revenue (1)				
Costs of products (2)				
Operational expenses	Salaries			
	Rent			
	Interest/installments			
	Others			
	Sub-total (3)			
Income before tax (1) – (2) – (3)				

Source: Modified from Japan Finance Corporation, 2012.

Annex box IV.2. Creating business ideas

To be successful, entrepreneurs have to come up with business ideas that fulfill unmet market needs. They have to create ideas of something marketable by analysing market intelligence using their knowledge, experience and network. Five tools and techniques are introduced below to facilitate the development of business ideas (as well as a business plan) for entrepreneurs to make their new businesses sustainable.

A. Three critical factors

Three factors are particularly critical for entrepreneurs to decide on their business, including the line of business, products or services, target customers, location etc. The factors are: (a) personal interest or desire; (b) capabilities; and (c) market needs (see below). Before moving on (e.g., business plan development), it is highly recommended that entrepreneurs evaluate the three factors.

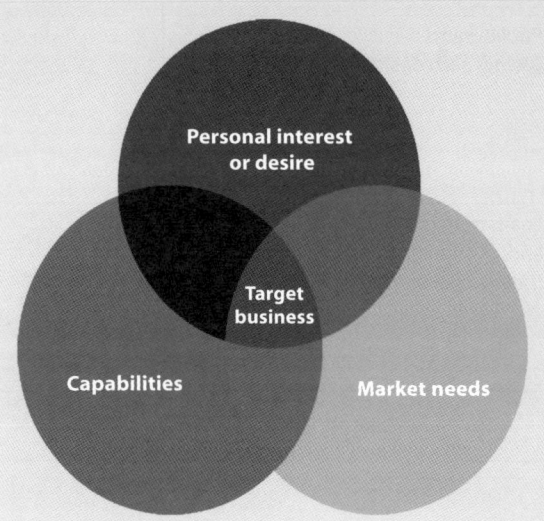

B. SWOT analysis

This analysis has probably been the most popular technique under modern corporate management. It facilitates deep analysis of external environment, internal capabilities, available resources and requirements. The framework of the SWOT analysis is simple, requiring an entrepreneur to evaluate four critical factors around their business: (a) strength; (b) weakness; (c) opportunity; and (d) threat (SWOT). All four components are included in the simplified business plan template introduced in this annex.

	Positive	Negative
Internal	(**S**trength) ○○○○	(**W**eakness) △△△△
External	(**O**pportunity) □□□□	(**T**hreat) × × × ×

C. Reviewing available resources

This is a supply-side technique. It encourages entrepreneurs to evaluate various resources that are available to them, such as human resources, capital, tangible and intangible assets, and personal networks such as customers and suppliers. Their knowledge, experience, education and training can also be considered as resources.

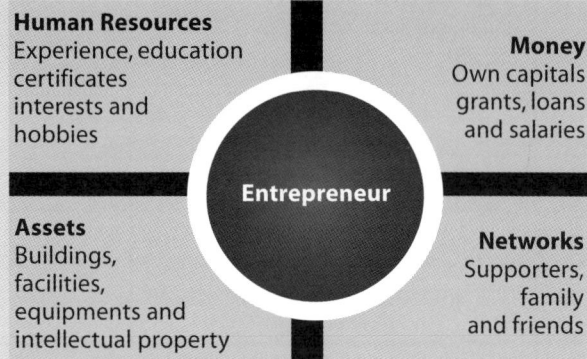

D. Negative keyword method

This is an unconventional method for identifying a new idea by identifying market needs that are unmet by existing products or services. In particular, it uses negative keywords for such needs identification. The negative keywords could include:

(a) Expensive/poor;
(b) Inconvenient;
(c) Lacking/inadequate;
(d) Late/slow;
(e) Old/outdated;
(f) Unstylish;
(g) Complicated; and
(h) Unreliable.

This technique may be able to identify some business ideas rather quickly, particularly adaptable to the services sector.

E. Who-what-how method

This is a conventional method for identifying business ideas. It is a market-driven approach starting from targeting potential customers, then planning the right product or service for the segmented customers, and development of a plan or way to reach the segment.

Who	What	How
Customers	× Products/Services	× Channels and Distributions

☐ Examples

Female professionals	× Stylish dresses	× High-end specialized shop at a prestigious location
Middle aged citizens	× Healthy foods	× Restaurant with low calorie dishes
Pre-school children	× Conversational English	× Bilingual kindergarten

Sources: JFC, 2008; and Sagamihara City Hall Economy Department, 2008.

Annex IV.2
Modules of entrepreneurship training

A. Babson College

As one of the pioneers of entrepreneurship education, Babson College has provided experience-based learning courses. The college focuses on the following eight key issues in its entrepreneurship education:

(a) Women's leadership;
(b) Family enterprising;
(c) Corporate entrepreneurship;
(d) New venture creation;
(e) Social entrepreneurship;[69]
(f) Entrepreneurial finance;
(g) Technology; and
(h) Public policy.

An example of Babson's entrepreneurship courses is an intensive ten-week programme entitled "Entrepreneurs Develop Businesses". The programme offers an environment that supports the startups including:

(a) Open workspace which allows teams to network, assist one another and share resources;
(b) Dormitories where many teams live so they can work around-the-clock to refine their ventures;
(c) In-house counselling from the programme director and meetings with entrepreneur-mentors at least once a week;
(d) Idea-sharing among teams through meetings, presentations and feedback; and
(e) Brown-bag luncheons with featured professors and business guest speakers.

The programme concludes with each team's presentation of its business plan in front of professional investors and the Babson community.

Source: Babson College, 2011.

B. 'Know about Business'

The International Labour Organization has developed the "Know about Business" (KAB) package, a set of training materials for entrepreneurship education. One of the objectives of the package is to create awareness of entrepreneurship and self-employment as a career option for students in secondary education as well as for trainees in vocational and technical training institutions. The trainees are from secondary, vocational, technical training and higher education institutions, and are taught about business practices and procedures, business opportunities and challenges, and skills needed for entrepreneurship. KAB has reached youths in more than 55 countries, and has helped to shape their attitudes toward entrepreneurship, and has increased their skills and employability.

Below is an excerpt from the curriculum of the "Know about Business: Entrepreneurship Education in School and Technical Vocational Training Institutions, 2005 edition." There are nine modules, totalling 134 hours.

---

[69] Babson College (2011) defines social entrepreneurship as "[t]he process of identifying opportunities, organizing resources and providing leadership to solve 'people and planet' problems while generating societal and economic values."

Annex box IV.3. Curriculum of the Know about Business package

Module 1: What is enterprise? (9 hours)
(a) Meaning and scope of enterprise
(b) Different forms of enterprises
(c) Roles people play in enterprises
(d) Small enterprises

Module 2: Why entrepreneurship? (11 hours)
(a) Entrepreneurship defined
(b) Reasons for entrepreneurship in business
(c) Importance of entrepreneurship in society
(d) Self-employment

Module 3: Who are entrepreneurs? (22 hours)
(a) Assessing entrepreneurial potential
(b) Identifying entrepreneurial characteristics
(c) Entrepreneurs as leadership
(d) Entrepreneurial decision-making
(e) Risk-taking

Module 4: How do I become an entrepreneur? (13 hours)
(a) Competencies for successful entrepreneurship
(b) Key success factors in setting up a small business
(c) Entrepreneurial decision
(d) Being involved in an enterprise

Module 5: How do I find a good business idea? (7 hours)
(a) Generating ideas
(b) Identifying and assessing business opportunities

Module 6: How do I organize an enterprise? (19 hours)
(a) Selecting a suitable market
(b) Selecting a business location
(c) Legal forms of business ownership
(d) Money needed to start an enterprise
(e) Ways of getting into business

Module 7: How do I operate the enterprise? (22 hours)
(a) Hiring and managing people
(b) Managing time
(c) Managing sales
(d) Selecting suppliers
(e) Using technology in small business
(f) Knowing the costs of an enterprise
(g) Managing money
(h) Using financial statements

Module 8: What are the next steps to becoming an entrepreneur? (22 hours)
(a) Sources of information and assistance
(b) Preparing a business plan
(c) Maintaining an entrepreneurial outlook
(d) Evaluating factors in starting an enterprise
(e) Beyond this package

Module 9: How to elaborate one's own business plan (9 hours)
(a) Standard business plan
(b) How to elaborate the business plan
(c) How to interpret the findings of the business plan

Source: ILO, 2005.

C. Japanese SME Agency

The Organization for Small and Medium Enterprises and Regional Innovation, Japan (SMRJ), which implements national SME support policies and activities, has established nine regional SME universities throughout Japan since the early 1960s. The SME universities offer a variety of training programmes to develop capable entrepreneurs and SME managers.

The ten-month, full-time university entrepreneurship training course covers the following topics:

(a) Business environment;
(b) Overview of management skills;
(c) Entrepreneurship;
(d) Strategic management;
(e) Marketing;
(f) Finance and accounting;
(g) Human resource management;
(h) Organizational behaviour;
(i) Information and communication systems;
(j) International business; and
(k) Business law.

The training course is conducted by using various teaching methods, including case studies, group activities, management games and simulations as well as internships. Thesis writing is required at the end of the course. The size of a class is limited to 20 young business persons, providing a networking opportunity, and is particularly popular among the successors of SME owners for brushing up their managerial skills. A state agency provides grants to encourage SME participation in the training course.

Source: www.smrj.go.jp/english/index.html.

D. SMEs management and development by the Galilee International Management Institute

The Galilee International Management Institute is a public, international management-training institution. Its programme is aimed at providing participants with strategic thinking skills and administrative techniques for appropriately allocating public resources in order to stimulate local entrepreneurs to invest in, and manage, new businesses and industries that will efficiently compete in national and international markets. The programme is specifically designed for decision-makers in local and national governments, economic development corporations and banks.

The programme comprises the following subjects:

(a) Supply chain for business;
(b) Access to financing – microfinance;
(c) Assessment criteria for the servicing of SMEs and microfinance Institutions;
(d) Human resource development and management;
(e) Project management:
   (i) Concept development;
   (ii) Planning and budgeting;
   (iii) Financial analysis and evaluation;
   (iv) ICT applications;
(f) ISO 9000;
(g) Total quality management;
(h) Business plan development;
(i) Forecasting;
(j) Production planning and industrial engineering techniques;
(k) Marketing research and marketing strategy;
(l) Small businesses in tourism; and
(m) Globalization of the world economy.

The programme is based on both experiential and participatory activities. Lectures will be supplemented by study tours, case study analyses, small group discussions, games and simulations facilitated by faculty and guest lecturers.

Source: www.galilcol.ac.il/.

CHAPTER V
Financing a business

While not every SME turns into a multinational enterprise, they all face a similar issue in their early days: finding the right type of finance at an affordable cost to start and grow the business. The ability of SMEs to develop, grow, sustain and strengthen themselves is heavily determined by their capacity to access and manage finance. Unfortunately, SMEs in the region consistently cite the lack of access to finance as a serious obstacle to their development. Therefore, this chapter addresses some of the key issues concerning the financing of SMEs.

This chapter begins by describing the current situation of SME financing in the region and the financing needs of SMEs at different stages of growth. Working capital management, obtaining credit and other financial instruments are discussed, as these issues have the most direct impact on SMEs' cash flow. The myriad ways that SMEs can obtain capital and the relationship between the bank and the borrower are reviewed, together with observations about raising capital. The chapter concludes with policy prescriptions.

The importance of cash flow for small businesses can never be over-emphasized; even profitable firms will fail if they cannot collect the cash that is due to them. Policymakers can have a significant positive impact on SME survival if they articulate and enforce a coherent programme of creditor rights.

A. Raising capital

Raising capital is one of the most critical issues for SMEs' growth and survival. While the gap in financing SMEs is significant both in developed and developing countries, some differences in characteristics exist.

While an OECD (2006) survey of SME financing indicated large financing gaps in both OECD and non-OECD countries, the overall situation was more severe in non-OECD countries (figure V.1). Further, OECD and non-OECD countries differed significantly on the matter of debt financing: only 30 per cent of the firms in the OECD counitres felt a gap existed in debt financing while 70 per cent of non-OECD countries felt the same. This difference strongly the firms in suggests an underdeveloped banking sector, which is the main provider of debt financing, in non-OECD countries. The equity financing gap was more similar among the two groups, at 75 per cent and 60 per cent, respectively, perhaps indicating a large demand for equity financing by advanced SMEs in the OECD countries.

The disadvantages in SME financing in developing countries also exist in the lending policies of commercial banks, the most important source for SMEs' external financing (Park, Lim and Koo, 2008). The results of the survey conducted by Beck, Demirgüç-Kunt and Peria (2008) suggested that the financing gap was greater between countries than between firms of different sizes. In developing countries, commercial banks require more collateral for loans (figure V.2) than those in developed countries, regardless of firm size (also see the annex to this chapter). The interest rates for loans almost doubled in developing countries even though the portion of non-performing loans was higher in developed countries (figure V.3).[70] The combination of lower risk and higher borrowing costs implies a high transaction cost in the commercial banks of developing countries, adding further challenges for SME financing in such countries.

Figure V.1. SME financing gaps in OECD and non-OECD countries

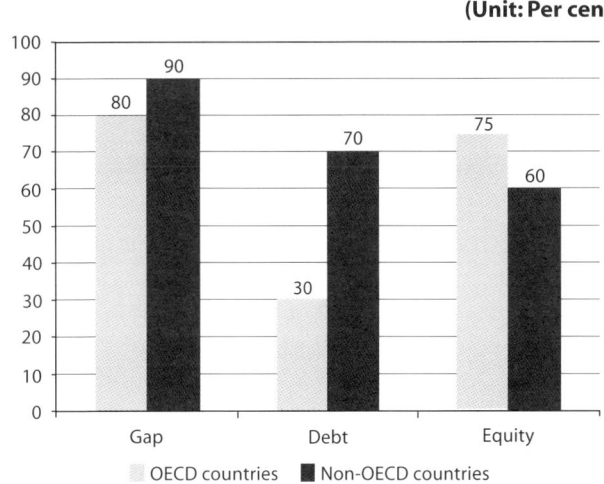

Source: OECD, 2006.
Note: The results are based on a survey in 20 OECD countries and 10 non-OECD countries.

Figure V.2. Collateral requirement in developing and developed countries

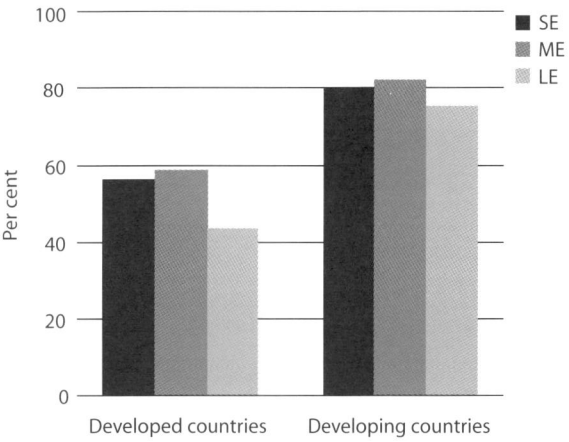

Source: IFC, 2009.

---

[70] It should be noted that the smaller the size of the enterprises, the higher was the portion of non-performing loans.

Figure V.3. Interest rates and non-performing loans in developing and developed countries

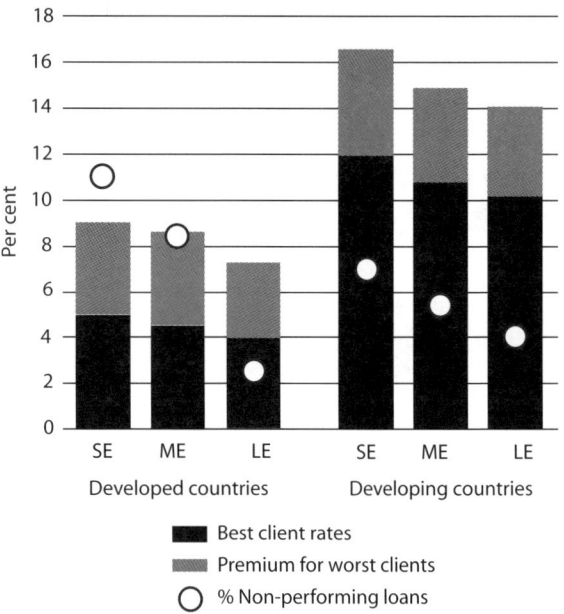

Source: IFC, 2009.

The World Bank's Ease of Doing Business survey measures the level of enterprises' credit access in a country. Table V.1 shows the four main indicators of facilitation of access to financing and availability of credit information:[71]

(a) Legal rights – the degree to which collateral[72] and bankruptcy laws facilitate lending;

(b) Depth of credit information – rules and practices affecting the scope, access to and quality of credit information;

(c) Public credit registries' data coverage of borrowing history, thus credit worthiness, of individuals and firms; and

(d) Private credit bureaus' data coverage of borrowing history, and thus credit worthiness, of individuals and firms.

---

[71] A more detailed explanation of the indicators concerning getting credit can be found in World Bank, 2011a, p. 48.
[72] The typology of collateral is given in annex V.1.

As shown in table V.1, developed economies rank the highest in terms of strength of legal rights and depth of credit information within the region. They have also developed private credit bureaus that provide credit history for almost the entire adult population. East and North-East Asia ranks second for the first two indicators. The credit information coverage in these countries is relatively comprehensive with the combination of public registries and private bureaus. The strength of legal rights indicator for the other four subregions is not far behind the two leading subregions; however, the lack of public and private credit information is likely to be a major obstacle for getting credit in those countries, especially in the Pacific, and South and South-West Asia.

B. Business life cycle and the need for cash

Throughout the SME life cycle, each stage – start-up, growth, maturity, decline, transition and exit – will have varying cash flow needs. SMEs may obtain equity capital and debt financing from various sources at each of those stage. (Sridhar, 2008). Figure V.4 shows that the particularly crucial periods of cash drain occurs during the start-up, growth and transition stages.[73]

Figure V.4. SME business growth stages and cash flow

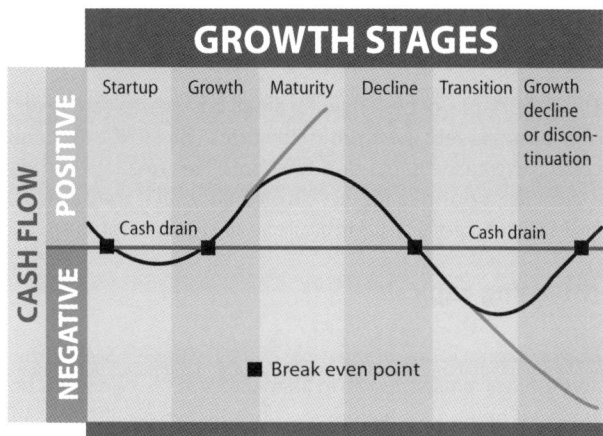

Source: Authors' compilation.

---

[73] This is a simple generalization, though, as real life cycles differ between individual companies, between growth and non-growth sectors, and between new and traditional industries (Johnsen and McMahon, 2005).

Table V.1. Ease of getting credit by subregion

Subregion	Legal rights*	Depth of credit information*	Public registry coverage (per cent adults)	Private bureau coverage (per cent adults)
Developed economies	8.7	5.3	0.0	92.0
East and North-East Asia	7.3	4.5	20.8	41.3
North and Central Asia	5.1	4.0	3.6	14.3
Pacific	6.2	0.7	0.0	4.8
South and South-West Asia	5.1	2.6	4.7	7.7
South-East Asia	5.8	2.7	11.4	20.4

Source: World Bank, 2011a.
* Based on a 0-10 scale with 10 being the most developed.
Notes: (a) Ranking out of 183 economies; (b) developed economies include Australia, Japan and New Zealand; (c) Taiwan Province of China is included in East and North-East Asia; (d) some Asia-Pacific economies (Democratic People's Republic of Korea; Macao, China; Myanmar; Turkmenistan; American Samoa; Cook Islands; French Polynesia; Guam; Nauru; New Caledonia; Niue; Northern Mariana Islands; and Tuvalu) were excluded from this analysis due to a lack of survey data.; and (e) explanatory notes show all countries by subregion.

The first period (start-up) involves a high mortality rate for SMEs if they cannot find enough initial capital, even though the scale of their needs may not be large. In addition to the slow sales that they often face during this stage, it is common for (even profitable) SMEs to fail because, while they may have profits on paper, they do not have the cash in hand from their customers to pay bills or to cover operating costs (figure V.5). This time gap is difficult for start-up businesses to avoid, and survival can depend on a firm's ability to raise additional working capital. The inability to survive the time gap between cash inflows and outflows is a primary cause of business failure throughout an SME's entire life. Apart from personal assets and loans from family and friends, during the start-up stage SMEs may get funds from seed capital, venture capital, business angels and/or government or institutional sources.

Figure V.5. Main reason for SME failure: Time gap between receivables and payables

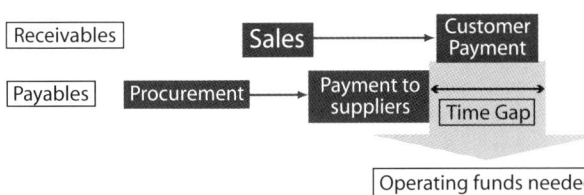

Source: Authors' compilation.

In the second period (growth), SMEs pass the break-even point and start making money. At this point, they normally require additional financing, such as a large amount of working capital as well as investment in production facilities and human resources. While such financing for growth could be supported by short-term loans and working capital generation from their daily business, long-term loans from commercial banks are usually preferred in order to ensure long-term investment and maintain adequate working capital. Venture capital funds may also become an important resource for expansion. The availability of other funds could also increase at this stage with local, national and international financial sources. Entrepreneurs typically experience difficulty raising funds at this critical stage. Commercial banks do not lend easily to those who still have no, or limited, credit record, and venture capital is not readily available for small-scale investment in new businesses, particulary in developing countries.

In the third period (transition), it is necessary for SMEs that are losing money to undertake measures to improve profitability, either by increasing sales or by reducing costs. While long-term financing or working capital generation is necessary for continuous enterprise growth and development, immediate short-term financing, perhaps through commercial debt financing, is often critical for SMEs during cash-drain periods.[74]

C. Overview of SME financing

SME financing refers to a range of mechanisms for funding the development of SMEs. There are a number of notable features to SME financing. The ability to increase capital relatively quickly in response to growth is a key feature. Another salient characteristic is complementarity: SME financing augments traditional sources of financing in many contexts. Effective financing mechanisms also contribute to sustainability as the financing of successful and profitable SMEs generates additional capital for future SMEs, thereby creating a virtual cycle. SMEs' financing needs (as both debt and equity) may vary (Johnsen and McMahon, 2005; and Zavatta, 2008) depending on such factors as:

(a) Home country;
(b) Industrial sectors;
(c) Perceived business risk;
(d) Asset structure (e.g., tangible versus intangible; capital-intensive versus less capital-intensive; and high or low fixed assets);
(e) Debt-to-equity ratio;
(f) Growth rate; and
(g) Profitability.

SMEs can obtain the necessary funds from a number of different financial instruments. These instruments can be broken down into the six general categories listed in table V.2.

Informal finance refers to all transactions, loans and deposits occurring outside the regulation of a central monetary authority (Atieno, 2001). Such funds may come from personal savings, borrowing from relatives or trade credits. Internal

Table V.2. Different SME financing sources

Category	Examples
Informal financing	Personal savings Borrowing from family or friends Borrowing from money lenders Trade credit
Internal financing	Retained profit Internal savings Working capital Sales of assets
Debt financing	Short-/long-term loans Line of credit Promissory notes Credit cards Overdraft Corporate bonds
Equity financing	Seed capital Angel finance Venture capital IPOs
Asset-based financing	Factoring Invoice discounting Inventory financing
Leasing	Capital leasing (hire-purchasing) Operating leasing
Government grants and subsidies	Grants Interest subsidies Credit guarantees scheme Loan insurance schemes Loan schemes

Source: Authors' compilation.

---

[74] In financial terms, short term is a period of a year or less while long term represents more than one year.

financing is the method of generating funds through a company's core business, such as through profits and working capital (Wilson, 2011). In developing countries, including those in Asia and the Pacific, informal and internal financing typically dominates SMEs' financial sources, particularly for start-ups and micro and small enterprises.

Debt financing, which is also a major financial source for SMEs, typically takes the form of credit lines and term loans that must be repaid over time, usually with interest (Helms, 2006). Most of the debt financing is provided by banks, but it also includes corporate bonds.

Equity financing takes the form of money obtained from investors in exchange for an ownership share in the business (Helms, 2006). It includes a wide range of financing sources such as business angels, venture capital and initial public offerings (IPOs).

Asset-based financing is defined as obtaining funds by pledging a subset of the firm's assets as collateral or as the primary source of repayment (Berger and Udell, 2005). The most common types of asset-based financing are factoring, invoice discounting and inventory financing (Business Owners Toolkit, 2012a).

Leasing is a common method of financing equipment. It can be defined as a rental contract specifying the payment schedule for the lessee (the borrower) in exchange of the right to use the fixed asset bought by the lesser (lender) (Berger and Udell, 2005).

The public sector actively promote the development of SMEs by providing grants and subsidies. This financial support has many flexible forms and is usually delivered to the SME via financial institutions or government line agencies (RAM Consultancy Services, 2005). Some of the major financial instruments for SME development are further reviewed in the following section.

D. Forms of finance

Figure V.6 shows major instruments of SME financing (Berger and Udell, 2005; IFC, 2009; Szabó, 2005; Women's World Banking, 2004; and Zavatta, 2008). The figure was developed to present a comprehensive set of SME financial instruments, whose features are relevant to the size and credit history of individual firms. These financial instruments can also be categorized based on creditors' perceptions on risk and return as well as the level of financial sector sophistication in an economy. These financial instruments are not exclusive and policymakers often use various instruments in concert to support SMEs. A discussion of these instruments, beginning with the financial instruments with the lowest financial sector sophistication and progressing to the highest level, follows.

Box V.1. Development of an SME financing support system in China

"Development of an SME financing support system" is an ADB project for developing the comprehensive institutional and regulatory framework of SME financing in China. The main objectives of this project are to: (a) increase the total amount of equity and debt financing available to SMEs; (b) attract private sources of SME financing; and (c) encourage investment by increasing the profitability and reducing the risk of loss to the lending institutions. After analyzing the existing strengths and weaknesses of SME financing in China, ADB proposed the following four main policy recommendations to make the Chinese SME financing system more effective:

1. Equity financing for SMEs in traditional sectors

SMEs in traditional sectors such as food processing, retailing and consumer services are important due to their job-creation function. They generally face difficulties in attracting investors who believe that the potential return on investment is not high enough to justify the risk of loss involved. Government intervention has to focus on either increasing the potential profit of businesses or reducing the risk of loss while providing direct equity financing. To ensure the success of the public equity funds, specific measures are recommended including: (a) introducing private co-investors and profit-driven fund managers; (b) increasing the share of return for private investors; and (c) limiting the investment coverage strictly to SMEs.

2. Legal and regulatory framework

The absence of supportive laws and regulations in China severely limits the availability of financing for SMEs, especially from private and foreign sources. ADB identified many principal barriers of investment in SMEs in the existing legal and regulatory framework of China. Taking private investment funds as an example, company laws in China had strict limitations in investment percentage, organizational structure and fund operations, which severely inhibited the development of the private venture capital industry. ADB proposed drafting new laws or making legislative changes in laws relating to the following aspects:

(a) Organizations and operations of private investment funds and public credit guarantee agencies;
(b) Company laws; and
(c) Bankruptcy and security legislation.

3. Equity financing for technology-based enterprises

More than 200 public funds for technology-based enterprises had been established by regional and local governments but most of them lacked efficiency and had a low level of return on investment. To solve this problem, ADB recommended several measures for funding operations, including hiring skilled and profit-motivated fund managers, and focusing on investing in start-ups and SMEs. In addition, ADB recommended competition among fund receivers as well as transparency in the whole selection and operation processes.

4. Credit guarantee for bank loans to SMEs

Debt is an important source of SME financing. The establishment of a credit guarantee programme can facilitate SMEs' debt financing by sharing the risk with lenders. ADB presented a comprehensive framework for a loan guarantee programme covering legislation, regulation, operating procedures and service and liquidation operations. It has also provided some risk management procedures for such a programme.

Source: ADB, 2002.

Figure V.6. Forms of finance for SMEs

Creditor/investor's perception on risk and return	Forms of Finance	Financial sector sophistication
High	Angel finance · Venture capital · IPO/Stock market · Seed capital · Corporate bond	High
Medium	Microfinance · Long-term loan · Credit guarantee · Short-term loan · Factoring · Leasing	Medium
Low	Trade credit · Working capital · Personal saving	Low
	Micro, start-up (No credit record) · Small (Limited credit record) · Medium (Moderate credit record)	

Source: Authors' compilation.

1. Personal net worth or saving

The first step in accessing capital is to fund the venture with the entrepreneur's own assets, e.g., savings. After investing his/her own money the entrepreneur then typically turns to family and friends (or banks) for personal loans (Shane, 2008). It is important to highlight for policymakers the fact that entrepreneurs and small business owners will generally go to formal financial institutions only if personal sources have been exhausted. They will finance their businesses from personal savings first; thus, policies that protect individual wealth, such as tax reforms[75] and property rights, indirectly assist the financing of SMEs.

2. Working capital

Working capital represents the excess of current assets over current liabilities such as debt, where "current" is a time span of a year or less. A high level of working capital indicates significant liquidity, and it is frequently used to measure a firm's ability to meet current obligations (Scott, 1997). Positive working capital requires the maintenance of steady operating cash flows.

Working capital is a necessity for enabling all businesses to continue functioning, particularly new businesses. This is commonly overlooked in business planning. For example, growth intentions are often not supported by sufficient working capital. Rapid growth needs high inputs of capital, which can be difficult for SMEs to secure and sustain. It is essential that each firm has proper working capital management (ESCAP, 1997).

Prior to borrowing from the financial sector, SMEs can manage their working capital to generate cash for operations. This is particularly important for SMEs because they often do not have easy access to financing from external sources. SMEs' skilful management of working capital can increase cash flows and minimize the short-term need for external debt financing (see figure V.7). For example, SMEs could delay paying vendors while also collecting their receivables more actively in order to increase available working capital (this is called trade credit; see the next subsection for more details). They could also attempt to minimize their inventory and/or reduce operating costs, or sell unnecessary or unproductive assets to gain needed cash. Financial institutions, in addition to providing funds to SMEs, can offer SMEs consulting services in working capital management, including techniques of cash flow forecasting, and rescheduling or refinancing of existing loans.

Figure V.7. Examples of working capital management

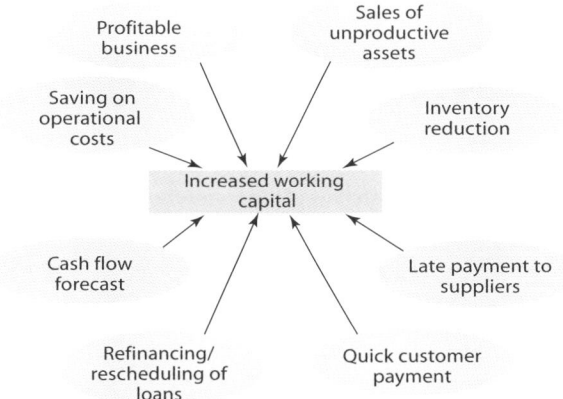

Source: Authors' compilation.

---
[75] Refer to annex III.2 for further discussion on this aspect.

3. Trade credit

Trade credit, or buyer's credit, is an important source of capital and is the second largest funding source for SMEs after banks and private lenders (Campbell, 2009). Trade credit is an arrangement between businesses to purchase goods or services on account without making immediate payments. The agreement is provided by suppliers to buyers to bill the buyer for payment at a later stage. A specific fixed period (e.g., due between 30 days and 90 days after the invoice date) is agreed upon within which the customer is required to make full or partial payment. Trade credit conditions are usually industry-specific; however, it is underpinned by collaboration between businesses to make the use of capital more efficient and effective.

Trade credit serves as a valuable source of finance especially in the developing world. The "buy-now-and-pay-later" mechanism, in particular, holds many advantages for SMEs. One of the most important advantages is that it helps to increase working capital by postponing the amount of monetary expenditure in order to create positive cash flows (figure V.8) while reducing capital investment requirements (Tradecredit, 2008). A further advantage is that it allows businesses to focus on growth and other productive activities with the assurance of sufficient investment and without restrictions on their development and expansion (Tradecredit, 2008).

Figure V.8. Trade credit

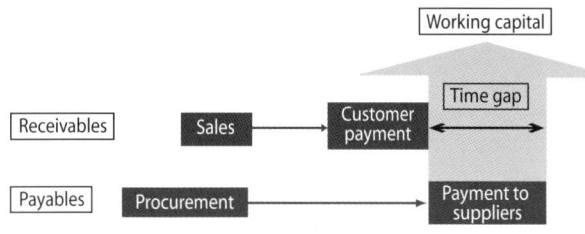

Source: Authors' compilation.

4. Leasing

In order to help small borrowers, some banks, non-banking finance companies and other financial institutions offer leasing. Leasing is a convenient option to assist SMEs in obtaining business equipment for a smaller cash outlay than an outright purchase. The SME can finance up to 100 per cent of the equipment value without collateral. Repayment schedules can be adjusted according to cash flow. Documentation requirements and approval time are relatively simple and short.

There are two basic types of lease: capital and operating. A capital lease, or hire-purchase, treats the leased equipment as an asset owned by the lessee (an SME), whereas an operating lease does not. Both types of leases can be useful for increasing the cash flow of the lessee, but only the capital lease confers ownership of the asset on the lessee at the end of the lease period.

A leasing arrangement typically involves the following (CIMC, 2011):

(a) The lessee (borrower) selects an asset (e.g., equipment, vehicle or software) that the lessor (the finance company) owns or will buy for renting to the lessee;

(b) The finance company is the legal owner of the asset during duration of the lease;

(c) The lessee has the control of that asset to use during the lease period;

(d) The lessee pays monthly rental or installments for the use of that asset;

(e) The lessor recovers a large part or all of the cost of the asset plus earns interest from the rentals paid by the lessee; and

(f) At the end of lease period, the lessee has the option to acquire ownership of the asset (i.e., transfer of title after paying the last rental or bargain option purchase price).

5. Factoring

Factoring is a relatively new form of asset-based financing for increasing working capital in Asia and the Pacific, and refers to the sale of accounts receivables by a company to a third party (called a factor) for immediate money and finance (Sridhar, 2008). A bank or a specialized financial institution may purchase accounts receivable from an SME with adequate trustworthiness for cash at a discount from the face value, thus assuming the risk on the ability of the buyer to pay and handling collections on the receivables. This practice, called factoring, may increase SMEs' short-term cash flows, while reducing administrative costs of accounts receivables (Sridhar, 2008).

There are three main differences between factoring and bank loans. First, the emphasis is on the value of the receivables instead of the firm's creditworthiness. Second, factoring is a purchase of financial assets rather than a loan. Finally, factoring involves three parties (i.e., a firm, a buyer/customer and a factor) while a bank loan only involves two (i.e., a firm and a bank) (EURO-Phoenix, 2011).

SMEs, especially start-ups and those with poor credit histories, may find factoring attractive because it places less reliance on collateral. The key value of factoring is that underwriting is based on the risk of the receivables (e.g., the buyer) rather than the risk of the seller (Klapper, 2006). Factoring may be particularly suited for those SMEs holding account receivables from large or foreign firms whose credit risk is far lower than the sellers themselves (Sridhar, 2008).

Factoring is an expensive form of financing in comparison to bank loans and therefore may not be the ideal choice when other sources of financing are viable. The rate of return should be considered in advance and factoring may be adopted only when the expected return of capital is higher than the cost. Factoring often requires the endorsement of, or notification to the buyers in advance; this may signal financial weakness.[76]

---

[76] Invoice discounting is a similar asset-based instrument as factoring, in that the invoice discounter advances an agreed percentage of the invoice value (receivables). The main difference is that invoice discounting allows SMEs to continue administering their sales ledger rather than transferring this responsibility to the factor, and the service is usually undisclosed to customers (Asset Based Finance Association, 2011).

6. Short- and long-term loans

Short- and long-term loans, especially from commercial banks, are a very common form of financing for SMEs. The length of the loan generally depends on the collateral, guarantee or credit history of the borrower.

Short-term loans are the most common form of bank loans for start-ups and small businesses, as commercial lenders are generally less willing to take large risks with new companies. They have a maturity of one year or less, although many are repaid within a shorter timeframe (Peavler, 2012). They are usually taken out for a specific expenditure, for example, to purchase a piece of equipment or to pay a particular debt. In this context, a fixed amount of money is borrowed for a set time with a fixed interest rate (Business Owner's Toolkit, 2012b). In general, the sources of short-term financing for SMEs include a line of credit, promissory notes, other short-term banking instruments (credit cards and overdrafts) and loans from other financial companies.

Short-term financing is easier to arrange, has lower costs and is more flexible than long-term financing. However, short-term financing is more vulnerable to interest rate swings, requires more frequent refinancing and requires earlier payment. Compared to long-term financing, short-term financing allows a business to operate with more flexibility and sufficient freedom, and it is usually less expensive. Therefore, SMEs can rely on short-term loans to operate on thin cash reserves, to meet sudden financial needs or to gain additional working capital, especially in such situations as a temporary cash crisis or delay in an expected payment from a debtor (ShortTermLoans, 2011). In addition, one source may be more suitable than the others because of differences in their interest rate and collateral requirements; thus, SMEs may consider using one or more short-term sources in a given circumstance.

A related form of short-term borrowing, which is typical in developed countries, is a line of credit that sets a maximum amount of funds available from the bank to be used when needed for working capital or other cash needs. This allows the business to borrow funds quickly up to a certain limit with floating interest, which they pay only on the outstanding balance (Business Owners' Toolkit, 2012c). If the business does access this credit, it must make monthly payments of interest and principal towards the debt. A line of credit gives SMEs flexibility and typically lasts for three years, subject to renewal.

Beyond lines of credit, another typical short-term borrowing instrument that is common in some Asia-Pacific countries (e.g., India, Japan and the Republic of Korea) is a promissory note, a negotiable instrument payable to the bearer on demand. It details the terms of a promise by one party (the borrower, sometimes also called the maker, obligor, payer or promisor) to pay a sum of money to the other (the lender, or sometimes payee, obligee or promisee) (Self-Counsel Press, 2009). An SME with adequate creditworthiness can issue the note and will repay the principal in a fixed future time, e.g., three months later, according to the demand of the lender together with interest, or may make interest payments according to a pre-determined schedule, such as monthly or quarterly. The clauses of a promissory note are simpler than those of a loan agreement; therefore, a promissory note is more flexible and negotiable than loan agreements.

Credit through credit cards, which are often used by SME owners, are also a form of short-term loans. Credit cards are a convenient means of making payments and tracking expenses but have higher interest rates than other forms of short-term borrowing. Sometimes it works as a substitute for other types of loans by SMEs, because small firms and start-ups usually have little credit history to ask for commercial loans. In addition to a personal credit card, there are business cards with more specific functions for business operations but which can more expensive and more difficult to qualify for (Dratch, 2011). Based on a survey in the United States, a personal credit card was widely used among the smallest firms, while the use of business credit cards generally increased with firm size (Mach and Wolken, 2006).

Overdraft financing is provided when businesses make payments from their business current accounts that exceed the available cash balance (Touch Financial, 2000). The overdraft limit needs to be negotiated with banks, and the amount borrowed is repayable on demand by the bank. Depending on the size of the overdraft, a bank may require the SME to provide some collateral.

Long-term commercial loans usually refer to those repaid beyond one year and up to three years (Business Owners' Toolkit, 2012d). This type of loan enables businesses to invest and expand their business with less risk of financial uncertainty, and increases working capital while reducing the amount of installments. Longer-term commercial loans are used for a variety of purposes, such as purchases of major equipment and plant facilities, business expansion or acquisition costs. Lenders require significant collateral because the risk increases with the term length.

It is more difficult for SMEs to obtain long-term loans due to the lack of adequate assets to use as collateral and the insufficient supply of such long-term loans, particularly in developing countries (IFC, 2009). The obvious consequence of a long-term loan shortage is that SMEs are unable to plan on a long-term basis, thereby constraining growth plans and long-term investment decisions (Obamuyi, 2007). One solution involves government intervention through mechanisms such as credit guarantees (see next subsection) or direct long-term loans.

Some government agencies and international institutions are also devoted to helping to solve this problem. An apt example is two-step loans. These are often designed to support development in specific sectors in developing countries. It takes its name from the process whereby funds are first provided by the public sector to a local financial institution and are then disbursed to multiple end-beneficiaries (Association for Promotion of International Cooperation, 2011). In general, the maturity of this type of loan is quite long and the interest rate is lower than the market rate (Okuda, 1993).

7. Credit guarantee

Loan credit guarantee schemes (CGS) have been recognized as one of the most effective ways of providing assistance to SMEs' debt financing.[77] Various governments, often in cooperation with international financial institutions, employ CGS to serve as long-term mechanisms for SME support by cushioning banks from the risks associated with lending to small businesses. These schemes help entrepreneurs to secure both short-term and long-term credits with less collateral or even without collateral. Another policy objective of the schemes is to provide an opportunity for banks to learn more about SMEs – their problems and operations – and to help improve handling of their SME loan portfolios. Through their direct association with SMEs, financial institutions can gradually learn how to lend independently to SMEs.

Levitsky (1997) analyzed various types of CGS and found that most schemes had guarantees for between 60 per cent and 80 per cent of the loan amount; the key factor underpinning their success was a strong cooperative relationship between guarantors and lenders. Apart from the benefits already mentioned, one of the major arguments in favour of these guarantee schemes is that these funds can reach important levels of leverage (five times or more in developed countries) (Levitsky, 1997). In practice, the credit guarantee is often a soft loan.[78]

While many countries in the Asia-Pacific region have been operating CGS, some for many years, the operational experiences of these schemes have been mixed. Despite the best intentions of policymakers, CGS have often failed to inspire confidence among banking institutions. Issues surrounding the system of guarantee include: (a) moral hazard; (b) high administrative costs due to complicated procedures and fragmented clients; (c) staff reluctance to deal with SME loan portfolios; (d) delays in paying claims; (e) low demand by SME borrowers; and (f) limited outreach by banks. As such, experience shows that banks have not always chosen to utilize these schemes and sometimes have had to be forced by the government into cooperating. Some of the problems identified above could be resolved if staff were better trained and motivated to deal with SMEs. The administrative costs of credit appraisals and monitoring SMEs could also be reduced by outsourcing these activities to providers, such as chambers of commerce and federations of industries. Last, the risk of moral hazard/non-repayment might be reduced via relationship development and/or lower loan guarantees.[79]

---

[77] Other major pubic support schemes for facilitating SME debt financing include interest subsidies, credit insurance schemes and promotion of promissory notes, which are delivered to the SME sector either via commercial banks or non-banking financial institutions (RAM Consultancy Services, 2005).

[78] Soft loans are provided by the public sector at lower-than-market interest rates.

[79] However, lower loan guarantees may discourage financial institutions to participate in the guarantee schemes.

Box V.2. Japan's SME credit guarantee schemes

The Credit Guarantee Corporation (CGC) of Japan, which was established in 1937, aims to help SMEs raise funds from financial institutions by providing credit guarantees on commercial loans. The National Federation of Credit Guarantee Corporations comprises of 52 local CGCs, with at least one in each of the 47 prefectures of Japan, which engage in activities that support local businesses, promote standardized guarantee systems and respond to specific local needs.

Japan's credit guarantee scheme is characterized by two key functions: (a) a credit guarantee function; and (b) a credit insurance function. The credit guarantee function is illustrated in figure V.9 with nine steps. Following the submission of the SME loan application (1) and its corresponding creditworthiness check (2), a guarantee certificate is issued to the financial institution (3), and the SME is then required to pay a guarantee fee to the CGC before the loan is extended (4). Successively, the

Figure V.9. Credit Guarantee Corporation's credit guarantee function

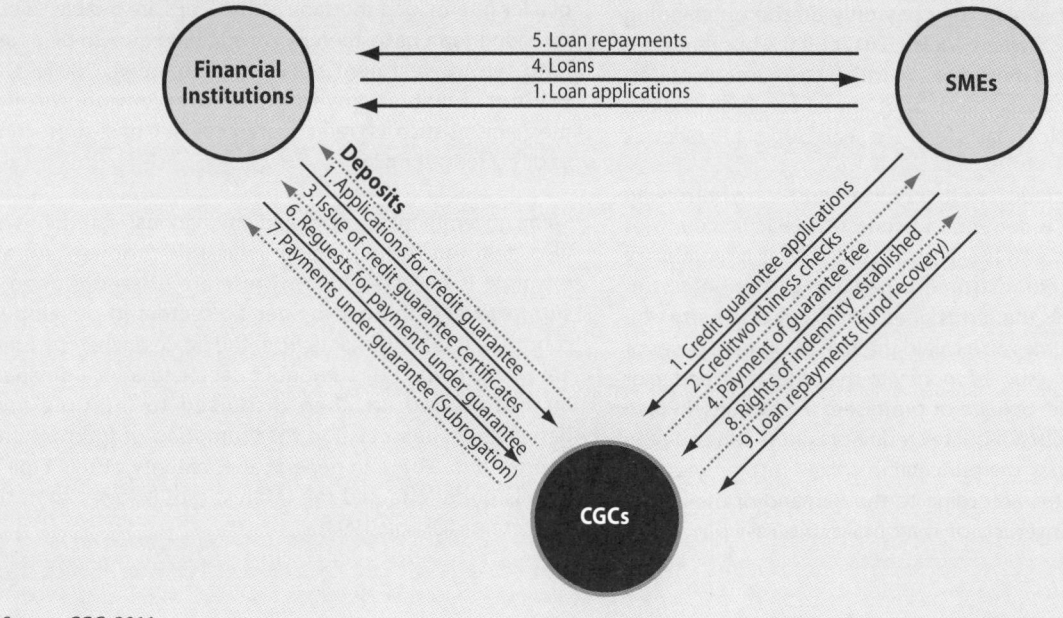

Source: CGC, 2011.

Box V.2. *(continued)*

SME is required to make repayments according to the agreed terms and conditions of loan with the financial institutions (5). However, in the event that the SME is unable to make all or part of the repayments within the agreed term, the financial institution can request the payment from CGC under the guarantee (6 and 7). Afterwards, CGC will obtain the right of indemnity against the SME (8) and recover the loan repayment, often through assisting the SME to rebound (9). To facilitate the process, CGCs place certain deposits with the participating financial institutions.

To spread the risk, a loan is automatically insured by Japan Finance Corporation (JFC) when a CGC approves a credit guarantee. This serves as the credit insurance function of the credit guarantee and is maintained by public funds. CGC pays a credit insurance premium to JFC and will get a subrogated amount from JFC if it makes payments on behalf of an SME under the guarantee scheme.

While the operations of CGCs are financed primarily by the guarantee fee and capital gains on CGCs' assets, the national and local governments also provide financial support to the National Federation of Credit Guarantee Corporations and CGCs to promote their operations and enhance the management base. As figure V.10 shows, the national and local governments and JFC provide credit insurance funds, various subsidies, deposits and compensation for losses. With the active engagement of CGCs and the support from government organizations, more than a million cases were approved by CGCs in the fiscal 2010, to the amount of ¥ 14.17 trillion (approximately $ 13 billion).

Figure V.10. Institutional framework of Japan's credit guarantee schemes

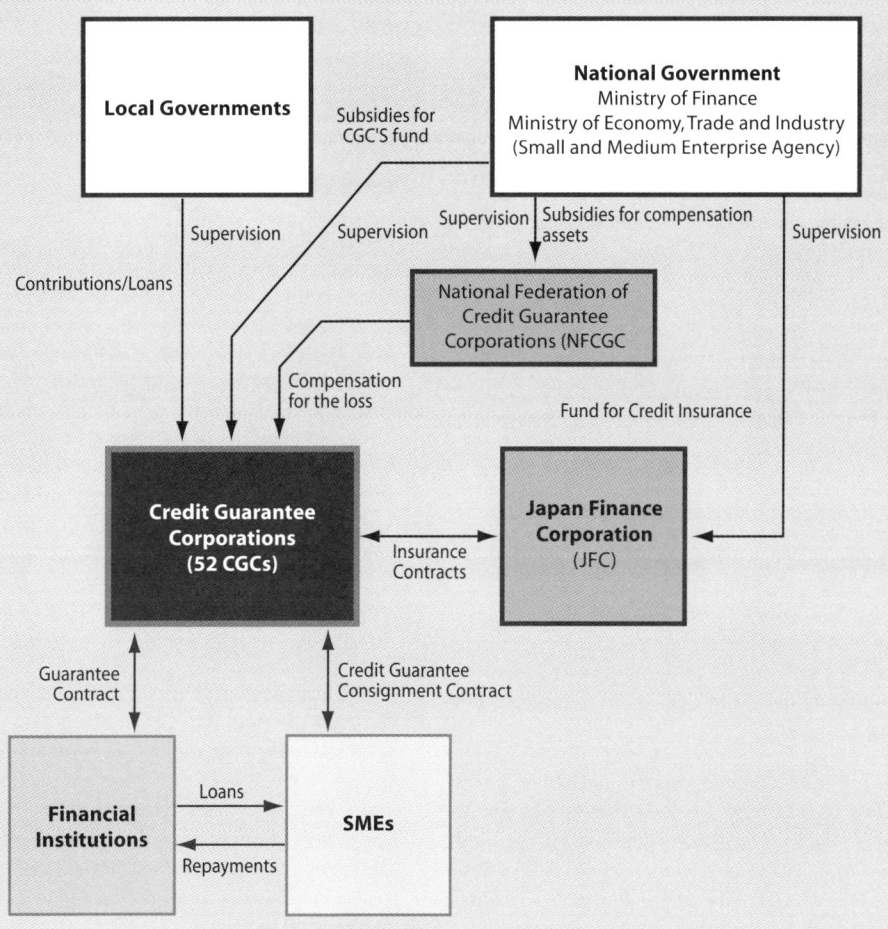

Source: CGC, 2011.

8. Microfinance

Microfinance, as described by the Consultative Group to Assist the Poor (2011), comprises a wide range of financial services geared towards the poor and low-income group as well as micro, small and start-up enterprises. Microloans, savings and micro-insurance are examples of such financial services, which are aimed at providing access to formal finance and facilitating financial inclusion for these businesses. The Microfinance Information Exchange (2010) reported that as of 2010 there were 15.8 million active borrowers and 5.8 million depositors in select developing countries in East Asia, South-East Asia and the Pacific[80] with an average loan balance of $ 306.5 per borrower. In contrast, the average loan balance in South Asia[81] is only $ 144 per borrower, but there are 53.7 million borrowers and 26 million

---
[80] Those countries include Cambodia, China, the Lao People's Democratic Republic, Malaysia, Papua New Guinea, Philippines, Samoa, Thailand, Timor-Leste, Tonga and Viet Nam.
[81] South Asia comprises of Afghanistan, Bangladesh, Bhutan, India, Nepal, Pakistan and Sri Lanka.

Box V.3. Examples of credit guarantee schemes: India, Pakistan and Turkey

A. Credit guarantee fund for micro and small enterprises, India

The micro and small enterprise (MSE) sector in India includes an estimated 26 million enterprises, providing employment to approximately 60 million people. Despite the size and importance of this sector, access to bank finance is often very low due to the perceived high risk of default. To protect themselves from defaults, banks insist on collateral; SMEs struggle to provide it. In order to facilitate collateral-free credit and make it available to the MSE sector, the Government of India launched the credit guarantee fund for SMEs in 2000. As of March 2010, there were 112 participating lending institutions registered with the fund, comprising banks, institutions and corporations.

This fund offers both term loans and working capital facilities up to Rs 10 million (approximately $ 190,000) per borrowing unit, which can be extended without any collateral security or third-party guarantee to a new or existing unit in the MSE sector by a single lending institution. Any credit facility covered under the scheme is not eligible for additional coverage. The extent of credit guarantee ranges from 62.5 per cent to 85 per cent, depending on the borrower category and the credit facility. The guarantee under the scheme runs through the agreed term loan/composite credit, and has a tenure of five years or as five-year blocks, depending on whether the working capital facility is standalone or not.

In 2009-10, 151,387 credit guarantee proposals were approved with a total credit amount of Rs 68,751.1 million (approximately $ 1,317 million). The cumulative number of proposals since the establishment of the scheme in 2000 is 303,982, which accounts for Rs 118,354.1 million (approximately $ 2,270 million) guaranteed for SME loans.

Source: Ministry of Micro, Small and Medium Enterprises, 2011.

B. SME Credit Guarantee Fund, Pakistan

The SME Credit Guarantee Fund (CGF) of Pakistan was incorporated in 1984 as a public-private partnership company. As a subsidiary of the Small and Medium Enterprises Development Authority of Pakistan, CGF aims to facilitate SME access to finance.

The endowment fund of CGF was created by pooling equity investment of PRs 10 billion by the Government and partner banks on 1:1 basis. Funds are invested in deposits and securities. Returns are used to meet the operational expenses and offset subrogation losses of CGF. The upper limit of guarantee exposure may be up to 10 times that of the endowment fund (e.g., PRs 100 billion).

CGF provides credit guarantees for both working capital financing and capital investment. Guarantees are primarily given to the following: (a) individual SMEs on a retail basis; (b) overall portfolios for SMEs; portfolios earmarked for a priority sector; and (c) programme lending schemes for specific clusters. In general, guarantees issued by CGF are only partial in nature. Proportions of risk to be borne by the respective parties are 50 per cent for CGF, 30 per cent for banks and 20 per cent for SMEs through collateral. CGF may also issue full guarantees, in line with the specific needs of disadvantaged regions and sectors.

CGF works closely with its partner banks in ensuring that processes have minimal potential risks. First, banks carry out credit checks and risk assessments of all applications. Following this due diligence by banks, applications are forwarded to CGF for their own processing. If the application passes both processes, a guarantee will be issued by CGF and forwarded to its partner bank.

Apart from CGF, the Credit Guarantee Scheme, offered by the State Bank of Pakistan, is implemented to endorse accessibility of financing for low-end fresh and collateral deficient borrowers.

Source: Presentation by the Small and Medium Enterprise Development Authority, 29 June 2011, Bangkok.

C. Credit guarantee fund, Turkey

In 1993, Turkey established its credit guarantee fund under the auspices of the Small and Medium Industry Development Organization – one of the major organizations responsible for the SME policy of Turkey and a major stakeholder in the fund. The other main shareholders include the Union of Chambers and Commodity Exchanges of Turkey and 20 major banks in Turkey.

The main objective of the fund is to support SMEs by providing a guarantee for their financing and by increasing their credit usage in general. The guarantees are targeted at supporting youth and woman entrepreneurs, promoting innovative investments and high-tech SMEs, encouraging exports, increasing the rate of employment and contributing to local development. Since its foundation, the fund has helped nearly 10,000 SMEs with guarantees of more than $ 1 billion.

Apart from the credit guarantee fund, the Small and Medium Industry Development Organization also provides direct loans under its loan programmes. The key features of the programmes are zero interest rates, easy payment periods, clear non-payment terms and pre-defined maximum limits. These loan programmes are mainly conducted in the areas of export promotion, new employment, digital infrastructure, relocation of the leather sector in industrial zones and machinery and equipment credit for the food sector.

Source: Republic of Turkey Small and Medium Enterprises Development Organization (undated).

---

depositors. Overall, the microfinance sector in Asia and the Pacific showed impressive growth rates during the past few years, with an increase in borrowers of more than 100 per cent from 2005 to 2010. Three of the top five countries of microfinance recipients in 2010 were Asian nations: China ($ 14 billion borrowed), India ($ 5 billion borrowed) and Viet Nam ($ 5 billion borrowed) (Microfinance Information Exchange, 2010). Another feature of microfinance in Asia and Pacific is that microfinance institutions specifically set women as a target client group. In 2010, the percentages of female clients in East Asia (and the Pacific) and South Asia were 56.76 and 91.54 per cent, respectively (Microfinance Information Exchange, 2010).

Among the notable large-scale microfinance projects in the region the Microfinance Initiative for Asia stands out (IFC,

2012a). Under the Microfinance Initiative for Asia, the KfW Development Bank of Germany and the International Finance Corporation (IFC) agreed in 2007 to invest $ 1 billion during the course of three to five years. Using debt and equity investments, structured finance and consulting services for Asian micro-financing institutions (MFIs), the Microfinance Initiative for Asia targets two main objectives: (a) the creation and enhancement of the institutional capacity for sustainable microfinance delivery; and (b) the strengthening of linkages between domestic and international capital markets.

Many types of organizations provide microfinance. Among MFIs, not-for-profit organizations, self-help groups, state-owned banks and commercial institutions can be found. While these organizations differ considerably in their operating models, they often share one important common characteristic: high repayment rates. By applying innovative solutions, such as a shared liability model and collateral-free lending, MFIs are able to keep the average default rates as low as 2.4 per cent worldwide (Microfinance Information Exchange, 2010). An apt example is the Group Model applied by the Grameen Bank. In this model, the borrowers are divided into five member groups and each group jointly assumes debts. Consequently, peer pressure and collective responsibility can help to control the default risk (Grameen Bank, 1998). Many MFIs have successfully proved that the poor are "bankable" and that the base of the pyramid, e.g., the poor and micro enterprises, is a financially viable market.

The nominal interest rates charged by most MFIs in the Asia-Pacific region range from 30 per cent to 70 per cent per year, which are very high compared with the rates of commercial banks and subsidized lending organizations (Fernando, 2006). The high nominal interest rate is mainly due to the high cost of funding, inflation and high cost of administration and operation associated with MFIs (Microfinance Information Exchange, 2010). Microfinance remains attractive to SMEs because it specifically caters to this sector, is more accessible and most loans are still cheaper than informal or black market financing sources. More recently, the debate about whether it is ethically justifiable to profit from the poor (Grameen Foundation, 2010) and the serious problem of market saturation and over-indebtedness have led to more stringent scrutiny of microfinance (Kappel, Krauss and Lontzek, 2010). Nonetheless, microfinancing remains a powerful tool for financial inclusion, particularly for SMEs.

9. Corporate bonds

A corporate bond is a debt instrument issued by a corporation, the holder of which receives interest from the corporation periodically for a fixed period and repayment of the principal together with the interest due at the end of the maturity period (Securities and Exchange Board of India, 2010). Corporate bonds are a good source of longer-term debts, with medium and long-term maturities. Compared with bank loans, corporate bonds are more flexible because a company can determine the terms and the date to maturity. Another advantage is that the issuance of corporate bonds can raise funds without affecting shareholders.

It can be difficult for SMEs, particularly in developing countries in Asia and the Pacific, to issue bonds. Investors are not interested in bonds when disclosure of financial information is lacking and the national bond market is not developed. Furthermore, the bond market is not always accessible to SMEs, or simply does not exist.

Corporate bonds have substantial issuance costs, including a large fixed-cost component (Altunbas, Kara and Marques-Ibanez, 2010) (table V.3 for detailed cost items). The scale of debts for a single SME may not be large enough for achieving cost efficiency and the issuance costs therefore become a major obstacle for accessing such a financing instrument.

Table V.3. Issuance costs of corporate bonds

Recipient	Typical cost item
Regulator or government	Stamp duty, issue licence fee (may take the form of a prospectus reviewing fee, securities registration fee and so on)
Stock exchange	Listing fee
Intermediaries	Underwriting, management and placement fees ("gross spread"), trustee fee, payment agent fee, listing agent fee and intermediaries' out-of-pocket expenses
Professionals	Legal fee, accountant's fee and rating fee
Miscellaneous	Prospectus printing expenses, road show expenses and staffing costs

Source: Endo, 2008.

A plausible solution to the inherently higher credit risk and the scale problem may involve pooling a group of SMEs for corporate bond issuance (Park, Lim and Koo, 2008). The combination of SMEs with various degrees of risk exposure to the economic cycle may lower the risk to an acceptable level for investors. The high issuance cost could also be lowered with a sufficiently sized deal.

10. Seed capital

For entrepreneurs, seed capital – the financing of direct equity capital for start-ups – is needed to establish their business. It can come from various forms of equity and debt such as convertible equity loans and soft loans.[82] The main underlying characteristic of this form of financing is that the capital provider may not seek high rates of return and may be satisfied with modest returns on investment. This is usually the case with public agencies that have the mandate to provide seed capital for business start-ups (UNCTAD, 2001b).[83]

The providers of seed capital have evolved into partnerships between governmental agencies and banks, with the former acting as a mediator and the latter as a source of lending capital. Banks usually allocate a certain amount of seed capital through funds designated for SME development; however, these funds usually do not provide enough variety of financing packages, nor the full capital, needed by the SMEs (UNCTAD, 2001b). Therefore, public sector assistance is often needed to fill this gap.

---

[82] However, seed capital typically comes from entrepreneurs' savings and/or informal loans from their associates.
[83] There are dangers of moral hazard if policymakers extend soft loans as well as exposed risks taken by public agencies.

For example, ING Bank of the Netherlands has established a seed capital fund that exposes the bank to only 50 per cent participation in the financing of any SME. Another example is of the partnership between Enterprise Ireland and the Bank of Ireland, with the Enterprise 2000 Seed Capital Fund, that offers a combination of equity loan financing (in a 1:3 ratio) to start-ups. The loan amount ranges from € 32,000 to € 125,000. The fund, a partnership between the State and private funds, does not require personal guarantees, but does require a post investment follow-up (European Commission, 2000). In India, the State Bank of India (SBI) provides interest-free seed capital of up to Rs 1 million to entrepreneurs under a scheme aimed at encouraging SME development in India. The scheme offers the matching seed capital for entrepreneurs to secure traditional banking loans for their business, and has a five-year moratorium on repayment of that initial seed capital (Sikarwar, 2010).

Direct government support for equity financing typically experiences difficulties in making equity investments effective. The issues include unclear SME beneficiaries, lack of business expertise, inappropriate organizational structure and cultural mismatch between government and business.

11. Angel finance

At the very early stage of the business life cycle, SMEs without a proven track record can find it especially difficult to access finance. In such cases, angel finance can be a potential source of funding worthy of exploration. Angel investors are described as high net-worth individuals with extensive entrepreneurial experience, who provide seed capital for early-stage ventures in return for convertible debt or an equity stake (Freear, Sohl and Wetzel, 1994; and Avantage Ventures, 2011).

Unfortunately, as Scheela and Isidro (2009) pointed out in their study on business angels in emerging Asia-Pacific economies, there is a dearth of well-documented reports on this particular topic. Due to the absence of reliable quantitative data on business angels in the Asia-Pacific region, an accurate assessment of indicators such as availability of funds and number of deals is lacking. However, considerable descriptive and anecdotal data exists that provides valuable insights into this field. Among other things, the field of angel finance is frequently characterized as being financially risky, with only 10 per cent to 20 per cent of the investments bringing a return. In the assessment of the prospective investee, the angel investor demands a solid business plan, entrepreneurial leadership and growth potential (SPRING Singapore, 2011b). In addition to the financial incentive, SMEs should not overlook the great benefit of having an angel investor as a mentor and who can gain access to the investor's network.

In striving for a more organized and professional approach to angel finance, a number of local and regional business angel networks have been set up in Asia and the Pacific during the past decade. The Business Angel Network South-East Asia (BANSEA) is among the more established and prominent networks of angel investors in the region. Based in Singapore, BANSEA was founded in 2001 and has about 50 members. With a vision of "fostering a vibrant start-up ecosystem in which angel investors fund entrepreneurs who eventually become angels themselves," the members have invested about S$ 18 million in almost 80 start-up enterprises (BANSEA, 2012). The early stage companies that manage to pitch successfully to investors receive funds in the range of S$ 100,000 to S$ 1 million (BANSEA, 2012). While not every SME will meet the investment criteria of business angel networks or individual angel investors, angel finance represents an increasingly important source of funding for a selected number of SMEs in Asia-Pacific.

12. Venture capital

Venture capital is a form of investment finance designed to provide equity or quasi-equity funding to private SMEs, where the primary return to investors is from capital gains rather than from dividend income. Venture capitalists are actively involved in the operations and management of such SMEs to ensure the success of their investments. They generally possess experience with investing in previous start-ups and general business expertise – as such venture capital which is a long-term risk finance operation (Ross, Westerfield and Jordan, 2008; and UNCTAD, 2001b). Investors are attracted to venture capital investments due to the potentially large gains from future sales of shares of the company and are therefore willing to accept the higher risks involved, compared to traditional banks (UNCTAD, 2001b). It is not uncommon that in a portfolio of 20 companies only one will return anything to the venture capitalist;[84] the hope is that the one company will provide a big payoff.

A distinction is usually made between seed capital and venture capital, with seed capital referring to the financing of direct equity capital for start-ups in the initial stages to supplement the shortfall in capital needed by the firms. On the other hand, venture capital refers to the next one or two phases of finance needed to achieve company stability and ensure strong growth potential (UNCTAD, 2001b). Venture capitalists do not necessarily invest their own money (Thunderbird Angel Network, 2010).

A venture capital fund would typically invest in an SME within a high-growth sector that seeks to expand its operations. Alternatively, they can also partake in buyouts of more established companies. The duration of involvement of a venture capitalist is usually between two and four years, after which the venture capitalist will typically sell the shares of the company on a stock exchange (e.g., an IPO), as a trade sale to other companies, through a management buyout to transfer managerial control or by selling the whole stake in the company to a more established competitor or other venture capitalists.

To lower their risk exposure, venture capitalists typically provide financing in stages, with each installment sufficient enough to reach the next development stage (Ross, Westerfield and Jordan, 2008; and Zavatta, 2008):

 (a) Start-up – additional funding for marketing and product development expenses for an early-stage firm;

---

[84] In the authors' interviews with venture capitalists, the typical outcomes they described for a 20-firm portfolio was that 5 would lose money, 14 would either break even or produce modest profits, and only one firm would be "successful, i.e., yield the type of return they seek.

(b) First round – financing for prototype production and manufacturing plans;

(c) Second round – major investments needed in order to begin manufacturing, marketing and distribution of product;

(d) Third round, also called the mezzanine level – the expansion funds required for a newly-profitable company; and

(e) Fourth round, also called bridge level – intended to finance the "going public" or IPO process.

Venture capital has the potential to offer valuable sources of finance that complement the more traditional credit finance provided by commercial banks. Some of the factors hindering SMEs' access to capital from traditional credit institutions are less important to those venture capitalists willing to take on greater risks. Some of the advantages for venture capitalists for SMEs are (UNCTAD, 2001b):

(a) Venture capitalists are willing to accept higher risks than traditional banks in exchange for potentially large gains from the future sale of shares of the company;

(b) Venture capitalists do not require collateral from borrowers;

(c) Operating costs are lower due to the absence of high interest rate payments;

(d) Venture capital is a long-term or at least medium-term capital commitment in contrast to short-term loans from banks; and

(e) The managerial know-how provided by venture capitalists can, in some cases, be more valuable to the start-ups than the actual financing.

However, there are also some disadvantages:

(a) Because of the high-risk nature of venture capital and the timeframe for returns as well as a lack of adequate skills and corporate information, finding initial investors may be difficult, particularly in Asia-Pacific developing countries; and

(b) The need for highly-liquid capital markets is not as pressing, compared to open-ended funds or mutual funds, since venture capital funds have a long-term involvement in their target companies. Nevertheless, an exit mechanism is necessary for venture capitalists to benefit from capital gains. This is difficult in almost all developing countries in Asia and the Pacific, except those with fairly developed stock markets. Other mechanisms such as guaranteed buy-backs are not realistic for SMEs.

The United States pioneered the use of venture capital and is still the world leader in terms of money invested and number of deals, but other countries are now developing their own venture capital funds (UNCTAD, 2001b). Venture capital is a familiar source of funding for SMEs in Europe and Israel, and the amount of venture capital utilized in China has risen tremendously during the past five years (Zero2IPO, 2010). Some countries, such as India, have set up sector-specific venture funds for the ICT industry and biotechnology sector (Small Industries Development Bank of India, 2011).

13. Stock market and initial public offerings

The stock market is a financial source for SMEs at a later stage of development, and an IPO is the main way to go public. Access to the stock market is a key stage in the growth of SMEs, especially for the high-tech, high-growth firms. In an IPO, a company raises capital by issuing shares to investors for the first time and subsequently becomes listed on a stock exchange (Government of Canada, 2003). In these transactions, shares are sold to investors to provide equity capital for the company in return for company ownership. Going public through an IPO gives SMEs access to a pool of capital that is much larger than a relatively small group of original owners and investors. It provides an alternative way to raise long-term capital instead of debt financing.

IPOs give extra credibility to suppliers and customers, help boost employees' morale, and may attract other financing sources. More importantly, an IPO is by far the most preferred exit mechanism for early stage investors such as business angels and venture capitalists (Zavatta, 2008). An efficient IPO mechanism can encourage risk-taking investments and more capital flows into innovative, high-growth-potential firms (Riding, 1998).

Box V.4. Pros and cons of equity financing for SMEs

Equity finance is raising funds for enterprise activities by selling shares to individuals or institutional investors who receive ownership interests in the enterprise. It is notable that there is a trade-off between the benefits and potential shortcomings of equity finance.

A significant advantage of equity finance is that it does not need to be repaid and there is no interest rate on the money. Investors can also bring with them valuable skills, networks and experience, and assist with developing business strategies and decision-making. Moreover, as the business grows, it can be supported with follow-up funding by investors already involved and knowledgeable about the firm (Business Link, undated). In addition, equity finance can help SMEs to reach the minimum equity requirement set by banks, thus increasing the opportunities to obtain bank loans (Sridhar, 2008).

However, raising equity finance can be costly and time-consuming, particularly for small businesses, and may take management focus away from the key business activities. Also, management time has to be invested to provide regular feedback to investors as part of the monitoring process. Moreover, a certain amount of control over the management and decision-making has to be shared with investors (Business Link, undated). In general, equity investment is associated with high risks; therefore, equity investors would expect a rate higher than publicity trade investors, even though the expected return of equity injection declines for each round as the risk becomes lower (Sridhar, 2008). This characteristic may reduce the possibilities for SMEs in conservative lines of business to access the equity sources in the early stages.

Note: Specific forms of equity financing can be found in Zavatt, 2008.

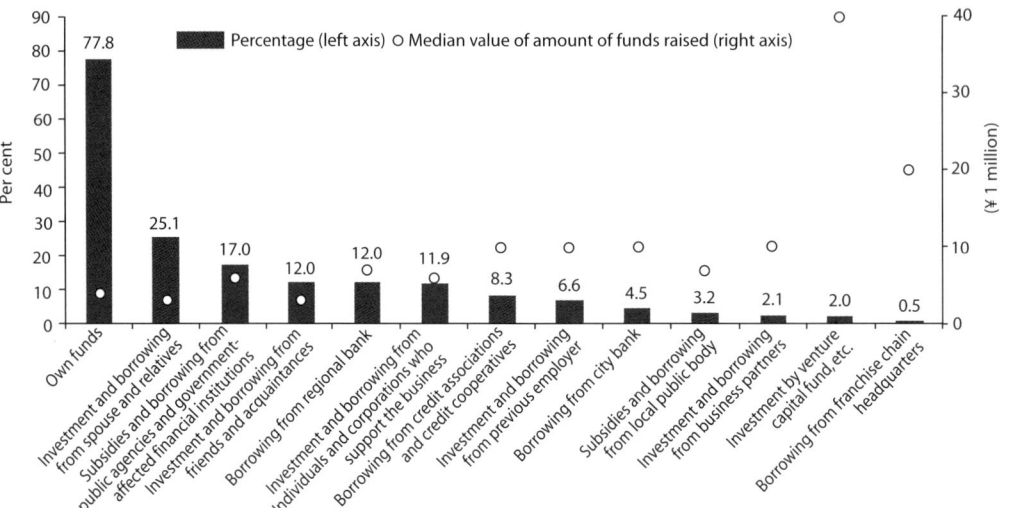

Figure V.11. Sources of start-up funds in Japan

Source: JSBRI, 2011.

Going public also brings new challenges to SMEs. They must report to the public because of the new management structure, and maintain high growth potential to avoid undervaluation of their stock and poor medium-term returns. Considerable costs are also associated with IPOs, including significant time and money invested in both the initial process of issuing shares and the ongoing requirements for disclosure and shareholder relations (Riding, 1998).

To take full advantage of this approach, the prerequisite is to have adequately developed capital and stock markets in terms of depth and liquidity (Park, Lim and Koo, 2008). An expanded venture capital market and financing would, in turn, encourage more IPOs because venture capital supports the growth of firms to a later stage and provides adequate financing resources for IPOs (Government of Canada, 2003). Governments and SME agencies may also facilitate this approach by establishing information sharing systems to improve investment information transparency and by providing consultation services to reduce issuance costs.

E. Sources of funds

While commercial banking plays a key role in formal SME financing, informal financing such as own funds as well as loans from relatives and associates, and internal financing such as retained earnings and trade credit, dominate the financial sources of SMEs. For example, in ASEAN countries 75 per cent to 90 per cent of SMEs rely on informal financing and internal financing (RAM Consultancy Services, 2005). In China, entrepreneurs' personal savings provide between 50 per cent and 80 per cent of start-up capital, while approximately 20 per cent and 15 per cent of capital comes from bank loans and borrowing from friends, relatives and other individuals, respectively (Hussain, Millman and Matlay, 2006).

This section provides some quantitative evidence of major financial sources for SME development. For this purpose, two countries from Asia and the Pacific (i.e., Japan and Malaysia) and one country and one regional grouping from outside the region (i.e., the United States and the European Union) are taken as examples.

The sources of start-up financing in Japan, including the amounts involved, are presented in figure V.11. Informal financing (e.g., own funds; loans from relatives and friends) is the major source of finance for supporting the capital needs of entrepreneurs, although the amounts are relatively small. Public support also provides substantial amounts of funds to start-up businesses in Japan, reflecting its well-developed public assistance to entrepreneurs. While commercial loans from the banking sector play a smaller role, they provide relatively large amounts of funds to start-ups. It is noteworthy that venture capital provides by far the largest amounts of funds among financial sources although coverage is still limited.

Table V.4 illustrates the financing sources for Malaysia SMEs in different life cycle stages. Almost 68 per cent of SMEs in the sample make use of self-financing during their start-up period but this falls quickly with the growth of the firms. Venture capital shares a similar trend as self-financing,

Table V.4. Financial sources for Malaysian SMEs, 2004

(Unit: Per cent)

Phase of life cycle/financing sources	Start-up	Established	Mature
Self-financing	68.0	21.0	25.0
Government schemes	7.8	13.0	9.0
Venture capital	10.8	8.5	4.5
Short-term loans from banks	20.8	28.6	23.1
Medium-term loans from banks	10.4	32.6	21.8
Long-term loans from banks	7.4	23.7	37.2
Non-bank financial institutions	8.7	7.1	10.9

Source: Rozali and others, 2006.
Notes: Short term loan is granted for less than one year; medium term loan is for one to three years; and long term loan is for more than three years. As multiple choices can be selected, total exceeds 100 per cent.

even though the percentage is much lower. In comparison, long-term loans become more and more accessible to established and mature SMEs, and bank loans are the most important source for them. Other financial sources such as government schemes and non-bank institutional financing are equally distributed among SMEs in each stage of development at around 10 per cent.

Table V.5 compares financial sources used by small businesses in the United States in 1998 and 2003. In the United States, the banking industry is highly developed; thus, small businesses can access a wide range of credit services (e.g., line of credit, term loans and credit cards). Trade credit is also a main source for small business finance, and more than 60 per cent of SMEs employ it to finance their businesses. Around 30 per cent of business owners use their own assets as a key financing source. Only 8.7 per cent of small business received capital lease services in 2003.

Figure V.12 shows the major institutions used by Europe Union-based SMEs to obtain capital. Banks are by far the most popular financial institution when SMEs need financing. Close to 8 out of 10 companies surveyed went to a bank in order to obtain capital (79 per cent). Around à quarter of SMEs approached leasing or renting companies (24 per cent), and 1 in 10 go to public institutions supporting investment (11 per cent) (EOS Gallup Europe, 2005).

Another study supports this trend in the European Union. Figure V.13 shows the employment of financial sources by SMEs in the European Union. Debt financing through commercial banks (via overdrafts, lines of credit and bank loans) is the most important source of SMEs' external financing. Trade credit, an informal financing instrument, is also adopted by more than 25 per cent of SMEs. Moreover, the usage of other financial instruments such as leasing, hire-purchase and factoring increased from 2009 to 2011 is now used as frequently as bank loans.

Table V.5. Financial sources of SMEs in the United States, 1998 and 2003

(Unit: Per cent)

Year	Line of credit	Loan			Credit card		Leasing	Loan from owner	Trade credit
		Mortgage	Vehicle	Equipment	Personal	Business			
2003	34.3	13.3	25.5	10.3	46.7	48.1	8.7	30.3	60.1
1998	27.7	13.2	20.5	9.9	46.0	34.1	10.6	28.1	61.9

Source: Mach and Wolken, 2006.

Figure V.12. Institutions used by European Union-based SMEs to obtain capital, 2005

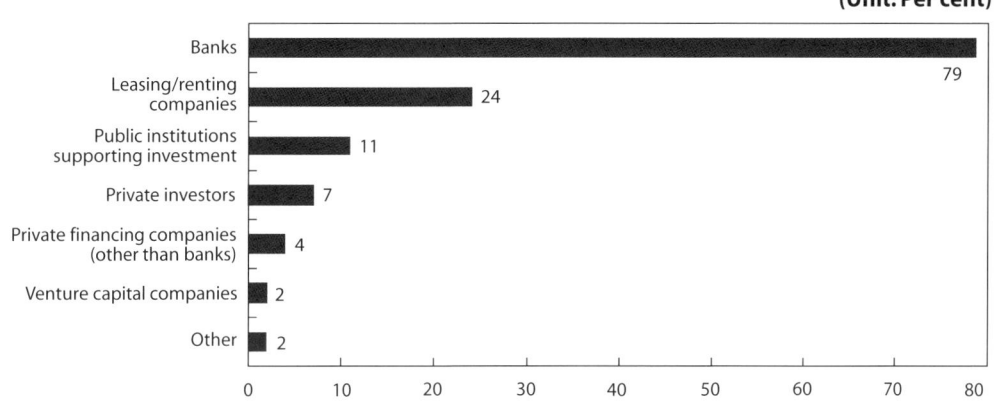

Source: EOS Gallup Europe, 2005.
Notes: Percentage of respondents; conducted in 15 European countries, namely Belgium, Denmark, Germany, Greece, Spain, France, Ireland, Italy, Luxemburg, Netherlands, Austria, Portugal, Finland, Sweden and the United Kingdom.

Figure V.13. External financing sources of European Union-based SMEs, 2009-2011

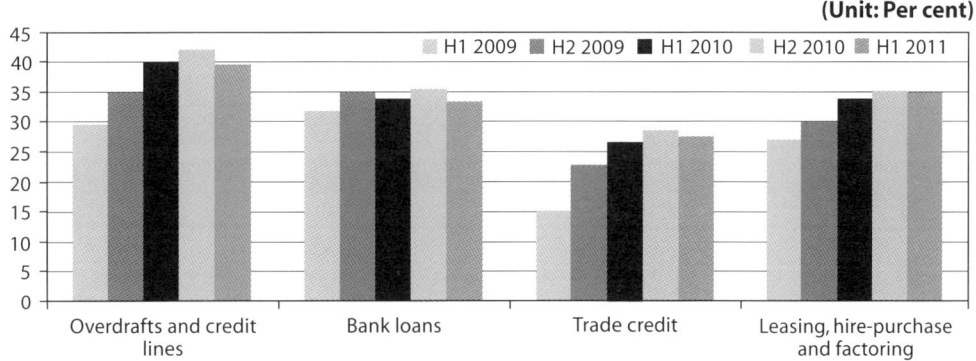

Source: European Central Bank, 2011.
Notes: Data for the preceding six months and percentage of respondents. The data are a survey conducted in Austria, Belgium, Cyprus, Estonia, Finland, France, Germany, Greece, Ireland, Italy, Luxemburg, Malta, Netherlands, Portugal, Slovakia, Slovenia and Spain.

F. Financial institutions for SMEs and their challenges

In the Asia-Pacific region, depending on the economic status of the country, the financial sector contains various financial institutions.[85] Some of the main institutional providers of SME financing consist of the following (Fliiby, 2009; World Bank, 2005):

(a) Development financial institutions (DFIs) for long-term loans;

(b) Commercial banks extending both long–term loans and short-term finance for daily operations;

(c) Specialized financial institutions (usually licensed for limited operations, activities, or services to differentiate them from full-service commercial banks), such as export and import banks that provide trade finance and export credit,[86] as well as rural banks, microfinance banks and non-bank finance companies;

(d) Government programmes or agencies for rural finance, microfinance or SME finance;

(e) Membership-based cooperative financial institutions (CFIs);

(f) Postal savings banks (PSBs) or institutions; and

(g) Public and private credit guarantee institutions.

Some Asia-Pacific countries have opted to set up apex banks for SMEs, generally known as SME banks, exclusively to cater to the needs of the SME sector. Non-banking/non-profit financial institutions and microfinance institutions have also cropped up to serve select sectors and categories of small borrowers. Some DFIs have also become more active in providing short-term loans and micro-lending in recent years.

International financial institutions, such as the World Bank and ADB, also devote resources to specialized financial institutions for lending to SMEs. International financial institutions have become particularly active in the region. For example, the International Finance Corporation (IFC) in 2010 committed $ 86.3 million to micro, small and medium-sized enterprises in South Asia. By the end of 2009, IFC's SME financial institution clients had taken out 374,000 loans in the region, totalling $ 10.7 billion (IFC, 2010b). In East Asia and the Pacific, IFC has committed $ 416.6 million in 2010, and SME financial institution clients had taken out 86,000 loans, totalling $ 17.2 billion by the end of 2009 (IFC, 2010c).

While financial institutions supporting the development of SMEs in the Asia-Pacific region have become increasingly active in the past few years, the banking sector remains the most important source of external financing for SMEs (Park, Lim and Koo, 2008). Banks offer diversified loans with different terms and various supplementary financing instruments such as export credit and discounting. Commercial banks in some countries also provide special loans targeted at priority sectors and key segments of the population as identified by the government, including SMEs.

However, SME development funds through commercial banks and financial institutions are not typically successful. Small bank loans and loans to SMEs as a percentage of total lending declined the past decade (Hall, 2009). Table V.6 contains data based on a global survey of 91 banks in 45 countries, conducted in 2008. It indicates that SMEs are strongly discriminated against by banks during loan issuance (also Table V.3). The survey result supports a commonly shared idea that the smaller the size the higher the risk. It partially rationalizes banks' discriminatory behaviour towards SMEs.

From the banks' perspective, the scarcity of funds for loans, especially in developing countries, means there is less incentive to seek out the profitable SMEs when larger and more qualified clients are available. Formal financial institutions often face higher transaction costs when dealing with the rather fragmented SME sector because the credit monitoring process requires an extensive branch network with more staff. The poor accounting system of many SMEs and insufficient collateral due to limited fixed investment also create obstacles to meeting the terms and conditions for borrowing from banks (ESCAP, 1997). Lack of risk management skills related to SME lending has contributed to significant non-performing loan problems in the past, demonstrating an inconsistency between commercial banks and SMEs, and discouraged banks from further lending to SMEs.

In addition to the general case shown in the last two right-hand columns of table V.6, the Asia-Pacific region has also seen a rising percentage of non-performing SME loans in the past few years. In China, the China Banking Regulatory

---

[85] For those financial institutions and their characteristics, see Reserve Bank of Australia, 2010, at http://www.rba.gov.au/fin-stability/fin-inst/index.html#funds.
[86] Trade finance is discussed in chapter VIII.

Table V.6. Different bank loan features of different-sized enterprise, 2008

	Share of total loans (per cent)		Loan fees (per cent of size of loan)		Share of non-performing loans (per cent of total loans)	
	Mean for developed countries	Mean for developing countries	Mean for developed countries	Mean for developing countries	Mean for developed countries	Mean for developing countries
Small enterprise	12.0	2.5	0.4	1.2	11.0	7.0
Medium enterprise	10.1	13.7	0.4	1.0	8.4	5.5
Large enterprise	27.9	32.8	0.2	0.8	2.5	4.1

Source: Developed from Beck, Demirgüç-Kunt and Peria, 2008.

Commission reported that non-performing loans (NPLs) to SMEs hit 22.1 per cent by the end of July in 2008, about two times the average 14.7 per cent of China (Xinhua Economic News, 2008). The State Bank of India, the country's largest lender, also reported that NPLs were rising, particularly in the SME sector (Choudhury and Rodrigues, 2010). The State Bank of Pakistan reported that NPLs in the SME sector increased by PRs 5.1 billion to PRs 96 billion by the end of 2010 (Daily Times, 2011).

The need for financial institutions to provide more suitable products and services for SMEs, develop comprehensive risk management skills and improve information transparency has been recognized. A number of financial institutions have also moved to offer non-financial assistance to SMEs for their capacity-building to enhance their profitability. For example, the SME Bank of Pakistan offers a range of business development services in the areas of marketing, accounting, product design and business planning (SME Bank Pakistan, undated). The SME Bank in Malaysia (also known as the Bank Perusahaan Kecil & Sederhana Malaysia Berhad) specifically targets SMEs and provides comprehensive advisory services to complement products offered by commercial banks. Some examples of these services are in-depth entrepreneurship training programmes for graduates, vendors, mentors and women (Bank Perusahaan Kecil & Sederhana Malaysia Berhad, 2012). Indonesia Eximbank, an export financing institution in Indonesia, has also developed technical assistance that includes quality improvement of products, product processing, packaging and marketing. Korean Eximbank assists stakeholders with capacity-building in the form of training and guidance in connection with export and trade financing activities (Korea Eximbank, 2011). The Korean Development Bank (KDB), a state-owned DFI in the Republic of Korea, facilitates the management and normalization of troubled corporations through corporate restructuring and consulting services that covers public, development and overseas projects (KDB, 2010).

Box V.5. SME finance in Sri Lanka

The present financing structure of SMEs in Sri Lanka is shown in figure V.14. Debt institutions, e.g., DFIs and commercial banks, are the major providers of financial services to SMEs but the emphasis of each type is different. DFIs such as DFCC Bank and the National Development Bank offer longer-term, project-based credits for SMEs with relatively low interest rates. Medium-term financing providers consist of NGOs, cooperatives and government institutions. A large number of local and international NGOs are engaged in microfinance activities, and some have now transformed their microfinance operations into separate entities.

Thrift and Credit Co-operative Societies and other cooperatives advance loans largely from mobilized savings. Government institutions, such as the Central Bank of Sri Lanka and Industrial Development Board, do not provide credit directly to SMEs but facilitate the lending process with credit guarantee schemes and technical expertise for SME lending. Commercial banks mainly offer short-term loans to SMEs because of the short-term nature of their deposits. Several commercial banks function as participating credit institutions in implementing SME credit schemes and provide their own schemes to assist SMEs. In addition, equity market, debenture market and venture capital companies act as supplements in SME financing by providing equity and debt financing to SMEs and start-ups; however their influence is limited.

Figure V.14. Present institutional financing structure of SMEs in Sri Lanka

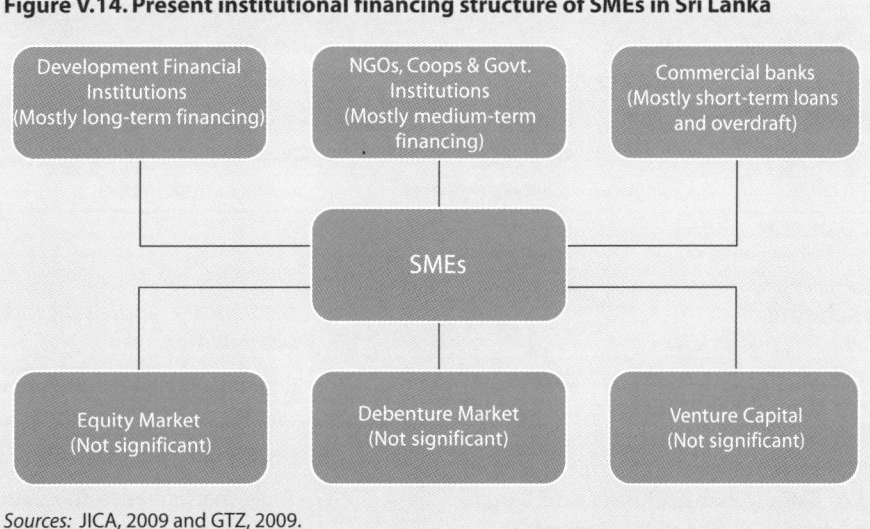

Sources: JICA, 2009 and GTZ, 2009.

Box V.6. Challenges of development finance institutions

For decades, DFIs, which are specialized financial institutions established by governments with specific development mandates, have played a significant role in the development of emerging and advanced economies. DFIs can provide SMEs with a range of specialized financial products and services in the form of medium and long-term loans, equity capital and guarantees for loans (Bank Negara Malaysia, 2012). They help small businesses to graduate to become medium-sized enterprises where feasible, and then large enterprises.

Table V.7 provides a comparison of the key differences between DFIs and commercial banks. Compared to commercial banks, one significant difference of DFIs is that they do not restrict themselves to providing only credit but also offer technical consulting and advisory services for the development of SMEs (Bank Negara Malaysia, 2012). Instead of basing the lending criteria solely on the financial viability of a proposal, DFIs pay considerable attention to the socioeconomic impact of their financing operations. Furthermore, DFI consideration is given largely to government economic strategies, rather than simply the maximization of profits (Malik, 2008).

While DFIs have many valuable strengths compared to commercial banks, there are also some difficulties and shortcomings. First, DFIs have come under rigorous challenge from commercial banks, which increasingly aim to become universal banks, and have gradually entered into the realm of long-term lending that was traditionally the domain of DFIs (Benston, 1994). Furthermore, DFIs lack a diversified range of institutional products and services. In addition, due to their shortage of adequate and independent resource bases, their lending resources are much more limited than those from commercial banks (Wattanapruttipaisan, 2003). DFIs also have experienced difficulties in raising resources at competitive rates compared with those offered by commercial banks (AAMO, 2007).

In response to these challenges, some DFIs have transformed themselves into commercial banks in order to be able to mobilize more funds, both for short- and long-term lending. In India for example, the Industrial Credit and Investment Corporation of India Bank (undated), a former development financial institution, moved towards universal banking in the 1990s to offer more diversified financial services. Similarly, the Industrial Development Bank of India (undated), after serving as a DFI for 40 years, decided to function as a commercial bank in addition to its original role of a DFI in 2004. Furthermore, the Industrial Finance Corporation of India (2008), the first development financial institution in India, transformed in 1993 from a statutory corporation to a company to fulfill its need for funds and direct access to capital market.

The risk and uncertainty of commercial banks' common policy "borrowing short and lending long", and DFIs' unique contribution of more comprehensive, long-term contributions to SMEs, including non-financial measures, suggests that DFIs converting themselves into commercial banks may not be ideal for SME financing; similarly, neither is commercial banks playing a dual role (AAMO, 2007).[87] Policymakers should strive to promote a vibrant commercial banking sector as well as sound DFIs.[88]

Source: Persaud, A. (2011) "Our future financial salvation lies in the direction of Basel". London, Centre for Economic Policy Research.

Table V.7. Comparison of commercial banks and development banks

	Commercial banks	Development financial banks
Driving force	Market	Government
Primary goal	Maximization of profit	Overall socioeconomic development
Product and service	Diverse	Limited
Loans	Short term	Medium and long term
Interest rate	High	Low
Resource base	Extensive and independent	Dependent and inadequate
Lending criteria	Financial viability of proposal	Socioeconomic impact

Sources: Malik, 2008, and Wattanapruttipaisan, 2003.

G. Credit rating scheme

Some countries in Asia and the Pacific, such as Malaysia and Singapore, have facilitated loans to SMEs via credit ratings. This encourages greater transparency about the SMEs' credit risks, thereby instilling more confidence in financial institutions to lend to SMEs (Alhabshi, Khalid and Bardai, 2009). A standardized process of rating SME credit results in greater consistency and reliability in lending. The credit rating process consists of:

(a) A comprehensive assessment of the overall condition of an SME;

(b) A review of the financial condition and several qualitative factors that have bearing on the creditworthiness of an SME (e.g., management skills; and reputation and goodwill);

(c) A composite appraisal/condition indicator and size indicator;

(d) Categorization of an SME, based on industry and size, for evaluation against its peers;

(e) Quality and characteristics of leadership; and

(f) Tools that enhance the market standing of an SME among trading partners and prospective customers (e.g., technologies, production facilities, knowledge and distribution channels).

---

[87] Basel III has however recently introduced a fundamental reform that requires banks to be better insulated from periods of financial market illiquidity and a better matching of maturities of lending and borrowing (Persaud, 2011).

[88] Potential new areas for DFIs are: social infrastructure development, environmental protection and support for SMEs, in addition to the traditional financing to conventional industries.

In the Asia-Pacific region, India has recently been proactive in formalizing a credit rating scheme for SMEs. Businesses with both the highest operating performance and financial stability are entitled to a reduction of 100 basis points (1 per cent) from the annual interest rate on their borrowing if they participate in the credit rating scheme, while those with strong performance and stability are rewarded with a reduction of 0.5 per cent (Petkar, 2010). The Government is subsidizing up to 75 per cent of the cost of the credit rating scheme in order to encourage SMEs to improve performance and credit rating. The SME Rating Agency of India Ltd. was jointly set up by National Small Industries Corporation Ltd., financial institutions, commercial banks and other stakeholders as the country's first rating agency that focuses primarily on the SME sector (SME Rating Agency of India, undated).

H. Financial support during economic downturns

SMEs are generally more vulnerable during economic downturns (e.g., the Asia financial crisis in 1997-1998 and the global economic crisis in 2008-2009). In addition to the direct shock of decreased demand, SMEs suffer from liquidity and credit problems due to tight money supply. Delinquent accounts receivable hit SMEs more severely than large enterprises as SMEs typically have higher debt-equity ratio and less cash on hand. Export-oriented SMEs are also vulnerable to variations in exchange rates. All these factors tighten cash flows and trap them in financial difficulties, which make financing SMEs one of the most important issues during an economic crisis.

This problem cannot be solved by market mechanisms alone due to the shortage of capital in most SMEs and the frailties of the banking sector. On one hand, the lack of transparency of financial conditions and managerial/marketing skills marks SMEs as high-risk clients. On the other hand, banks in crisis suffer their own financial problems and tend to be more risk-averse in issuing credit to the high risk and low profit segments of their clientele such as SMEs. These two factors combine to produce an environment where there is a disincentive for banks to lend to SMEs. This situation thus requires government intervention to ensure SMEs' survival.

Almost all governments are aware of SMEs' financial difficulties, and financial support measures have been adopted to boost their capital. The single most vulnerable area affected due to adverse economic conditions relates to quick access to finance in adequate quantities. Within this context, some governments have taken post-crisis measures such as increases in credit guarantee coverage, extension of credit guarantee terms, rehabilitation credits and more liberal trade/export credits. One effective policy measure may also be to introduce incentives for lending to the SME sector, especially export credit to recapture global markets. These measures must be accompanied by rigorous monitoring mechanisms to prevent the misuse of such incentives.

As a response to the 1997 Asian financial crisis, for example, a number of the Asia-Pacific governments issued laws and decrees, and shored up governmental agencies to improve the financial conditions of SMEs. Typical cases involve the new SME basic laws in the Republic of Korea and in Japan, the credit guarantee scheme for small businesses in Thailand and specialized SME banks in a number of countries in the region (Ying, 2009).

Direct financial support, including additional credit lines and loan guarantee schemes, are widely used to facilitate the financing of SMEs, and greater budgets are generally allocated to these schemes during a financial crisis. For example, the Government of Kazakhstan allocated 25 per cent of its emergency spending, amounting to approximately $ 956 million, to SMEs in response to the global financial crisis of 2008 (Pasadilla, 2010).

Indirect financial support, such as tax incentives and lower interest rates, are also common steps taken by governments to increase the cash flows of SMEs. Tax-related policies mainly include tax credits, cuts, deferrals and refunds. During a financial crisis, temporary tax measures are taken and tax

---

Box V.7. Japan's comprehensive policy framework to support SMEs during the global economic crisis, 2008 and 2009

The Lehman crisis of September 2008 seriously affected Japanese SMEs by sharply limiting their financing channels and severely reducing the demand for their exports. The Small and Medium Enterprise Agency (SME Agency) of Japan played an important role in the recovery of SMEs by easing their financial burden.

In October 2008, the SME Agency, in collaboration with the Japan Finance Corporation and Shoko Chukin Bank, launched emergency guarantee and safety-net (soft) loan programmes to support SMEs whose business stability was threatened by external factors (e.g., reduced orders from major customers, delayed payments and/or bankruptcy, the impact of a disaster, failure of the main bank etc.). Additional credit guarantees were made available with a total budget of ¥ 36 trillion used to guarantee loans to SMEs in all industries – raising the coverage from 80 per cent to 100 per cent of loan losses (CGC, 2011). It also issued safety-net loans to SMEs temporarily facing cash-flow problems due to a radical change in the business environment with a budget of ¥ 21 trillion. The regular corporate income tax rate was also lowered for SMEs from 22 per cent to 18 per cent for two years during the global financial crisis (Deloitte, 2010).

The SME Agency also provides emergency employment subsidies, designed to prevent SME employees from losing their jobs and to stabilize employment, amid the deterioration of employment conditions with the rapid economic downturn. The subsidies include a temporary layoff allowance or wage equivalent per person per day, training expenses and a temporary transfer allowance, all of which can be claimed for up to 300 days within three years.

Another SME Agency measure is the provision of information and consultation services for SMEs. During the financial crisis, the SME Agency offered information and advice on various tax and accounting measures to help SMEs take advantage of new tax incentives. Specifically, it provided information and advice related to the new Companies Act, including programmes such as the accounting adviser system, that significantly benefitted SMEs' financial management.

Sources: JSBRI, 2010, and SME Agency of Japan, undated.

rebates are often used to promote exports. For example, China increased its tax rebate seven times within 10 months from August 2008. The experience of OECD countries indicates that governments should consider cutting "profit-insensitive" taxes that are paid regardless of whether SMEs are recording a profit or loss (e.g., payroll taxes, licensing fees and capital taxes). Thus, the ability of SMEs to finance working capital internally will increase (OECD, 2009b). Related to this, an interest rate decrease would also reduce the cost of SME financing. With this in mind, the Central Bank of Indonesia gradually decreased its benchmark interest rate from 9.5 per cent in November 2008 to 7 per cent in June 2009 (Bank Indonesia, 2011).

Governments may also consider measures to reduce risks and transaction costs for banks, and provide them with centralized SME credit information and technical assistance needed for lending SMEs. Other measures include: (a) simplifying the application and grant procedures; (b) developing more efficient procedures to evaluate SME credit risks; (c) providing more assistance to government agencies and other service institutions for SMEs; and (d) exploring new channels for SME financing, such as equity financing and asset-based financing, as discussed above.

SME financing policies should also pay more attention to helping SMEs achieve long-term survival and competitiveness. Even though short-term measures, e.g., soft loan schemes mixed with expanded credit guarantee coverage, help alleviate the immediate financing problems of SMEs and increase their immediate cash flows, such emergency fund provisions are unsustainable and may be detrimental to the long-term interest of SMEs. For example, data from the SME Bank of Thailand (2003) indicates that 40 per cent of the non-performing loans to SMEs came from loans provided during the Asian financial crisis years (1997-2001) in support of the government policy to resolve liquidity problems in the financial system. In this sense, long-term measures are

---

Box V.8. Urgent policy interventions by Japan and Thailand for SME rehabilitation in disaster-hit areas, 2011

A. Japan

In addition to enormous human and physical damage, the Great East Japan Earthquake in March 2011 inflicted damage to approximately 740,000 SMEs within the affected prefectures. In addition, the earthquake had an impact on SME operations nationwide due to supply chain disruptions and electricity shortages, leading to decreased production and exports. At the same time, the demand side of the economy was weakened by radiation leakage rumours related to the nuclear power plant accidents and this led to a subsequent decline in consumer confidence.

Specific measures, which mainly focused on financial and employment support, were quickly undertaken to maintain SMEs' liquidity and to revitalize the private sector. As for financial support, the Japan Finance Corporation and Shoko Chukin Bank jointly established a special recovery loan programme with a separate credit line, extended grace and repayment periods and reduced interest rates, particularly for small businesses.

Credit guarantee corporations also established a special guarantee programme, with a 100 per cent credit guarantee to support emergent working capital needs of SMEs that had received a disaster victim certificate. These were issued by the local municipalities, certifying that an SME was partially, extensively or completely damaged by the earthquake or the tsunami. Employment support included special unemployment benefits for disaster-affected employees, subsidies to maintain SMEs' employment and job fairs for new graduates in the regions that were affected by the disaster.

Sources: JSBRI, 2011, and Ministry of Economy, Trade and Industry of Japan, 2011b.

B. Thailand

The flooding disaster in central Thailand in 2010 was one of the worst in Thai history, with one-fifth of the country becoming inundated, including several major industrial estates. The unprecedented level of flooding not only threatened the supply chain and food security, but also seriously affected a large number of SMEs. To restore the country's stability and prosperity, the Government prepared a three-phase strategy (i.e., immediate phase, short-term phase and long-term phase) with a budget of more than $ 10 billion to promote the economic recovery.

The objective of the immediate phase was to help people and businesses adjust to the flood situation within two months. In addition to rehabilitation activities, several economic measures were introduced, consisting of developing the skills of labour, restoring infrastructure, regulating prices and water management.

The short-term phase lasts for one year. The focus of this phase is to provide financial support to people and businesses affected by the floods and investment incentives and other measures to facilitate affected business operations. The specific measures include:

(a) Individual and enterprise loans for reparation of residences and reconstruction;

(b) Loans for the development of flood-protection systems for industrial estates and manufacturers;

(c) SME loans and credit guarantees from the Small Business Credit Guarantee Corporation;

(d) Two-step loans and safety-net loans with guarantees provided by the Japan Bank for International Cooperation for the recovery of businesses, especially SMEs;

(e) Consideration by the Board of Investment of Thailand on the extension of the incentive period and the investment benefits for affected investors;

(f) Facilitation of visa applications and employment licensing procedures; and

(g) A plan of action for the removal of water and quick reconstruction of the affected industrial estates.

The long-term phase provides a comprehensive framework of water management and flood prevention. Through the development of a water management system, flood warning system and a better infrastructure design, the Government is determined to ensure industrial confidence and economic development in the long term.

Source: Thailand Today, 2011.

needed to ensure the survival of SMEs, including: (a) identifying new markets; (b) investing more in research, development and innovation; (c) the provision of consultancy and information, especially on operations and financial management; (d) supporting education and training (e.g., TVET); and (e) building up comprehensive legal, tax and regulatory frameworks for an enabling business environment (Eurofund, 2011).

I. SMEs' view of major constraints

Despite various financial schemes and informative mechanisms, access to "timely and adequate" credit and establishing a good relationship with bankers are two persistent major problems for SMEs. According to a 2009 Asian Development Bank survey of SMEs in 13 countries, obtaining capital is the top constraint for firm formation and growth (ADB, 2009). There are several reasons why this is so.

Recent market developments and trends show that in the name of single window assistance many banks, including DFIs, have entered the arena of term lending, including short-term loans to SMEs. Despite this progress, there is a wide time lag between the approval of SME loans and the disbursement of funds. Since a portion of these loans pays for operating expenses, SMEs barely manage to survive while they wait. This scenario again underscores the importance of cash flow.

Although most of the governments in the Asia-Pacific region have formulated well-structured policies and placed well-developed institutional financing agencies on the ground to meet the needs of SMEs, there is a gap in the actual implementation of these policies. Bank management may not appreciate the dire need that SMEs have for cash. Banks may be willing to help but their SME clients get lost in the shuffle as bank management caters to larger, wealthier customers. Unfortunately, the SME-banker relationship may then become adversarial, further defeating the best intentions of policymakers. Part of the intransigence often lies with the owner of the SME, who may not be able to communicate effectively with the banker or present their needs in a way that would give incentives for the bank to cooperate.

Entrepreneurs also face various constraints to source financing, including specific problems related to short- and long-term loans.

(a) Specific problems related to short-term loans:
  (i) Delays in sanction and inadequate limit sanction;
  (ii) Inordinate gap between commissioning of the project and availability of working capital;
  (iii) Complex and lengthy documentation;
  (iv) Improper mix of fund-based and non-fund based facilities;
  (v) High cost of credit; and
  (vi) Insistence on high margins and collateral.

(b) Specific problems related to long-term loans:
  (i) Delay in appraisal of projects;
  (ii) Rigid and complex procedures;
  (iii) High cost of credit;
  (iv) Delays in disbursements;
  (v) Unwillingness to exercise delegation of powers by functionaries;
  (vi) Insistence on higher margin money;
  (vii) Insistence on more than 100 per cent collateral; and
  (viii) Non-availability of working capital sanction letter from commercial banks.

As shown in figure V.I5, the growth ability of small firms tend to be more vulnerable to financing constraints than those of large firms. When facing the same financing problems, the reduction of growth is more severe if the size of an enterprise is small. In general, financing obstacles result in an average decline of ten per cent in growth for small firms compared with six per cent for their larger counterparts. The figure also indicates that for bank requirements and conditions for financing, together with access to different financing modes, small firms still report a larger decrease in growth than larger firms in each situation.

Figure V.15. Effect of financing constraints on growth

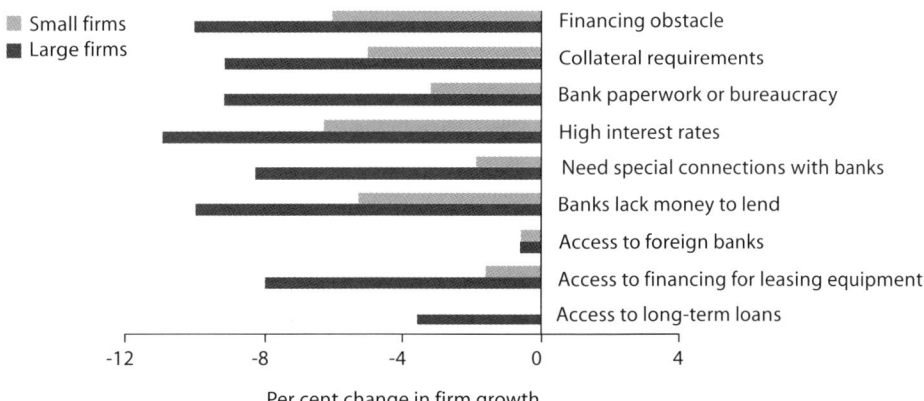

Source: ADB, 2009.
Note: This figure shows the effect of different financing obstacles on firm growth for small and large firms, measured at the average constraint for the two group sizes.

J. Potential market distortion by public interventions in SME financing

Many governments use direct and indirect public interventions to promote SME financing. Direct interventions made by governments are typically in the form of grants, subsidies and tax breaks, and are often delivered through dedicated governmental agencies. Some governments also provide financing assistance via commercial or state-owned banks and non-financial institutions including cooperatives and governmental agencies. This assistance can be in the form of soft loans, interest subsidies and ceilings, credit guarantees and credit insurance, seed capital, venture capital, loan quotas, loan waivers and through the promotion of promissory notes (RAM Consultancy Services, 2005). Additionally, there are measures for facilitating SME financing that do not provide direct credits but concentrate on strengthening the financial regulatory framework, building financial infrastructure and enhancing SME capacity-building and creditworthiness (IFC, 2011b).

The rationale for government intervention is to address deficiencies and market failures in the SME finance space. Well-designed government interventions can improve financial regulatory frameworks and financial infrastructure. It is also necessary when there is a lack of financial resources for particular groups (e.g., start-ups with little collateral and credit history, and women entrepreneurs) that cannot be easily solved by the markets. As discussed above, interventions are also warranted during periods of instability and crisis, where there is an actual or potential collapse of financial intermediation by private agents (IFC, 2010a).

Public interventions in SME financing may cause negative market distortions and long-term losses to the financial sector. First, it is often difficult to ensure that financial support reaches the target group. This is especially problematic when the target group cannot be well defined, which is often the case with the SME sector in the developing countries in Asia and the Pacific. Thus, the fiscal costs of the support could be high – often much higher than predicted before implementation (World Bank, 2008b).

Second, public interventions may lead to weaker financial discipline in the SME debt market because with grants and subsidies both lenders and borrowers suffer less direct losses when defaulting (Hallberg, 1999). As a result, a "non-repayment culture" may be created among beneficiary enterprises. "Moral hazard" may also be created and inhibit financial institutions from implementing and improving risk management techniques.

Third, such measures may distort competition in the financial market and result in a "crowding out" effect, as they discourage firms from using non-subsidized financial institutions (i.e., private financial providers if the subsidies are exclusively for DFIs) and non-subsidized forms of financing (e.g., personal savings) (Hallberg, 1999). This "crowding out" effect may lead to significant long-term losses that give few incentives both to SMEs to operate transparently, and to financial institutions to lend to SMEs.

The role of government intervention is important in expanding SME finance spaces. This is especially relevant in developing countries as they usually have less efficient financial markets compared to their more developed counterparts. However, it is equally important to minimize the potential distortions brought along by improper actions. Governments should keep in mind the fact that the goal of government intervention is to achieve an efficient market (Ganbold, 2008). Identifying the market failure and setting intervention boundaries is the key prerequisite to designing an appropriate strategy. In all cases, government intervention should be carefully designed to avoid any disincentive for private sector providers of financial services to serve the SME segment. They also need to be evaluated carefully to measure achievements in terms of outreach and leverage (IFC, 2011b).

State-owned financial institutions, including state-owned banks and development financial institutions, are widely used to serve SMEs as they have more incentives and willingness to serve certain segments of the market. Compared to their private counterparts, some state-owned financial institutions have less-developed SME lending technologies, lower levels of profitability and higher costs (Rocha, 2011). The failure of many state banks can be also explained by political interference, excessive risk exposure due to irrational development goals and internal operational inefficiencies (IFC, 2011b). To take advantage of state-owned financial institutions for SME financing, independent corporate governance, efficient operation and proper SME lending and risk management technologies are essential. A less distorted solution to the SME financing problem may be a well-designed credit guarantee scheme with an adequate capital base (IFC, 2012b).

Direct lending as well as programmes collaborating with other financial institutions in the form of soft loans, lines of credit, co-financing and equity funds will likely continue to be a popular interventions for SME financing in developing countries, due to their simple structure and fast rate of implementation (IFC, 2012b). Such programmes should also be carefully designed to minimize the subsidy component, political interference and crowding-out effects on the private sector. A good financing programme requires precisely defined performance targets, an independent governance structure, clear selection criteria for both beneficiaries and collaborating institutions, and a management team of very high quality (Levy, 2002). The operation of the programme needs to be market-oriented and a commercial interest rate should be applied. The mission and products of the programme should be flexible and adapted according to market maturity (Levy, 2002).

Most of the related literature emphasizes that the key role of government in improving access to finance is to offer a policy environment that allows competitive and diverse financial service providers to flourish (Ganbold, 2008). For SME financing, the least distortionary method may be that government performs a market facilitation role to narrow the gap between SMEs and the financial sources. The primary objective for the government is to create an overall enabling environment that offers incentives for financial providers to fill the SME finance space. This requires a proper regulatory and supervisory framework that balances the risk and benefits of providing innovative SME financial products while narrowing the existing financial gaps.

Governments also have the responsibility to build reliable and comprehensive financial infrastructure, such as accounting and auditing standards, and credit information systems, in order to reduce the information asymmetries and legal uncertainties in SME financing (World Bank, 2009a). In addition, governments and SME agencies may facilitate SME capacity and creditworthiness by providing localized training and consultation services in collaboration with local financial service providers to meet the specific needs of both the supply and demand sides (IFC, 2011b). Increasing government procurement from SMEs, instead of direct financing support, is another effective measure to enhance SME credit-worthiness and viability by avoiding delays in receivable payments and by increasing cash flow (IFC, 2011b).

K. Major issues for policy interventions

While a number of schemes exist that address SME financing gaps, they are contingent upon: (a) an attitudinal environment that welcomes innovation and entrepreneurship; (b) formal legal institutions that protect property rights; and (c) institutional financing procedures that are consumer-friendly. Policymakers therefore need to ensure that the existing overall business climate is conducive for people to engage in entrepreneurial activities with adequate and timely financial assistance. To achieve this, the following topics are suggested for consideration in the light of global best practices.

1. Maximizing working capital

In a number of developing countries in Asia and the Pacific, the sophistication of their financial sector still remains low, and capital and equity markets have yet to be developed adequately; thus, formal, institutional financing is difficult for SMEs to access. For those economies (e.g., least developed countries), one of the most effective policy options in the short term would be to maximize working capital of SMEs through the effective utilization of both informal and internal financing.

Informal financial instruments, including entrepreneurs' own savings and assets as well as borrowing from parents, relatives and friends are particularly important for new and small businesses during their seed and start-up phases. Trade credit or buyer's credit, another informal financial instrument, has been a major financial source for SMEs in developed countries and could be used by SMEs in the Asia-Pacific developing countries to increase their cash flows.

Internal financing refers to the generation of funds through an enterprise's retained earnings, which requires a profitable business model. Such internal fund-raising could be achieved by various measures, such as increasing sales, reducing operational costs, minimizing inventory and physical assets, forecasting cash flows properly and reducing external debt financing.

Neither informal financing nor internal financing requires external creditors and investors' involvements to raise funds for SMEs, so the existence of well-developed capital and equity markets is not necessary. Such financial instruments could provide large flexibility to SMEs' working capital management mainly by reducing the needs of external financing (e.g., bank loans). Policymakers can encourage SMEs to use those financial instruments in order to maximize their working capital by: (a) cultivating entrepreneurship culture; (b) developing a pro-business regulatory framework and tax system; (c) protecting property rights; and (d) improving managerial skills of entrepreneurs and SME owners. Within this context, policymakers may wish to collaborate in providing services and training through an existing web of business associations such as local chambers of commerce and industry.

2. Narrowing the gap in SME financing

Some agencies have pointed out that in developing countries the financial gap has been growing between commercial debt financing and microfinance (IFC, 2010a; and JFC, 2011). They argue that micro and small enterprises, including start-ups, have been in a disadvantaged position to access institutional debt financing. While the traditional term loans have focused on financing large firms or SMEs with relatively healthy performance and sufficient financial records, microfinance targets the poor, low-income groups and the informal sector with small-sized loans as well as high interest rates. Between those target groups of commercial banks and microfinance institutions, small (and micro) enterprises are growing. They have difficulty in raising funds from commercial banks because they have inadequate collateral and financial record, yet they are not satisfied with microfinance loans due to small loan size and high interest rate. Figure V.16 illustrates the financial gap in SME financing.

Figure V.16. Financial gap in SME financing

Source: Modified from JFC, 2011.

To narrow the gap, policymakers may consider some options. First, microfinance, as it has been growing rapidly in the region and may expand its operations to target small businesses, providing large-size loans with discounted interest rate. Second, commercial banks may wish to extend their financial services to those small players perhaps in cooperation with public credit guarantee agencies, where public support is required. Third, governments could launch and further develop various forms of financial assistance to them.

3. Develop and balance both debt and equity markets

Although the roles of debt and equity markets are theoretically clear, in practice these two financial systems differ widely across countries in Asia and the Pacific. In general, countries with bank-centred debt financing systems tend to be less conducive than stock market-centred systems to entrepreneurial activity. However, a bank-centred system may be a preferable option for countries with poor information infrastructures. On the other hand, stock markets take more time to develop but tend to encourage more entrepreneurial, high-growth ventures (based on the experience of developed countries). The majority of the innovations by SMEs have been successfully commercialized through stock markets, especially in the United Kingdom and the United States. In contrast, other developed countries rely more heavily on their banks – with Germany and Japan as prime examples (Benston, 1994). Within Asia-Pacific, some of the major stock markets (i.e., China; Hong Kong, China; Indonesia; India; Republic of Korea; Singapore; Sri Lanka; Taiwan Province of China) are well established, while other developing economies are working hard to strengthen their stock markets. Policymakers in most Asia-Pacific countries should focus on SME access to debt primarily through their banking sector, but with an eye towards establishing the regulations essential to a functional stock market (e.g., financial reporting requirements and statutes protecting minority shareholders).

SMEs list on stock exchanges for a variety of reasons, including gaining access to funds outside traditional sources (e.g., commercial banks), to spread the risk of high growth strategies and to increase corporate profiles (Pacific Economic Cooperation Council, 2003). As such, the following example from New Zealand illustrates a successful initiative undertaken by policymakers to incorporate SMEs into the equity markets.

Small New Zealand companies, with high-growth potential, face difficulties in listing on the main local stock exchange, the NZX Limited. To ease their burden, policymakers in 2005 initiated a new stock market, the New Capital Market, to address the equity needs of SMEs by providing a structured, cost-effective and fast initial public offering mechanism (NZVIF, 2011; PECC, 2003). The Seed Co-Investment Fund in New Zealand was also established to support SMEs with strong potential for high growth (Ministry of Economic Development, 2009). Overseen by the New Zealand Venture Investment Fund Ltd., the Seed Co-Investment Fund aims to accelerate the seed capital market for start-up companies to the point of self-sustainability and to foster investment inflows into innovative start-up firms. Some of the key provisions include (NZVIF, 2011):

(a) Co-investment with accredited investment partners, in a 50:50 matching scheme;

(b) Investment into the seed- and start-up stages of businesses; and

(c) Investments must be made into New Zealand businesses.

As of November 2011, the Seed Co-Investment Fund had a capital allotment of $ 48 million and 13 accredited Seed Co-Investment Partners. The fund and its investment partners have invested, on a one-to-one basis, in 64 New Zealand companies that have successfully established their business operations. These 64 SMEs are part of a diverse group of industries, ranging from biotechnology, information technology, marine safety, bottling and semiconductors to commercial cleaning services (NZVIF, 2011).

4. Reduce information asymmetry

Inadequate or insufficient information is one of the main obstacles hampering financing for SMEs. With information asymmetry, banks cannot be sure of the creditworthiness of SMEs, and potential equity investors may forego the equity offerings of SMEs unless policymakers implement expensive safeguards. It is costly and inefficient for individual lenders or investors to collect the information. SMEs, however, usually lack financial administrative skills to provide this information, or may even lack the basic knowledge about what type of information should be prepared.

Policy intervention can be essential in addressing this issue. The possibility for SMEs to obtain financial support from institutional lenders and equity investors should be increased to provide enough incentives for SMEs to produce credible accounts and operate transparently (OECD, 2006). Policymakers not only need to educate SMEs about related regulations, standards and practices, they must also strive to streamline them. There is a careful balancing act that policymakers must consider between the needs of creditors and investors to feel secure and informed, and the ability of SMEs to meet these needs.

Governmental organizations and SME agencies also need to initiate or pursue a dialogue with financial industries at the national level about methods for achieving better understanding, e.g., possible codes of conduct or specific information tools. Policies are needed to promote transparent lending terms and conditions of financial institutions. Training and information programmes, based on different information requirements of various financial institutions and investors, can also be implemented to assist SMEs in dealing with financing issues.

The credit history of SMEs is also an important piece of financial information. The credit rating scheme discussed above can provide effective indicators for the credit history of SMEs. An information-sharing mechanism among institutional lenders and investors, such as databases containing SME credit information and borrowing history, could be adopted by policymakers to increase information sharing and transparency. Such measures may automatically reduce the default risk of SMEs, because they need to maintain good credit records to further access financial resources.

5. Facilitate equity funding

Many governments have programmes for the direct injection of equity (or start-up capital) into SME ventures; however, the operational results of such programmes are not encouraging. Direct government programmes generally lack both the appropriate incentive structures and the expertise to administer the programme in a professional manner (OECD, 2009b). A better alternative is for policymakers to work alongside private sources of equity, such as the Business Angel Network South-East Asia (BANSEA),[89] in order to meet SME needs, while building the institutional capacity of equity markets with pro-business securities regulation. Transparency and shareholder protection allow higher-end types of financing, such as venture capital, to flourish while being comprehensible enough to invite SME participation, albeit often with professional legal counsel.

Within this context, the public sector is expected to serve as a conduit for building trust between SMEs and private capital.

---

[89] For the details of BANSEA see the earlier section in this chapter on angel finance.

For example, the Business Development Bank of Canada (BDC), a state-owned specialized development bank, focuses on leveraging private sector funding by running various equity and non-equity programmes (BDC, 2011). The most notable feature of BDC is its cooperation with the venture capital industry in Canada in addition to providing direct equity investment to SMEs. Good examples involve capital injection into private equity funds that target certain objectives (e.g., high-tech, life science and start-ups), supporting angel groups to professionalize their industry and helping venture capital to develop global networks and connect with potential stakeholders (BDC, 2011).

A more comprehensive programme, such as the European Risk Capital Action Plan, to improve entrepreneurs' access to risk capital finance could be an effective way of dealing with fragmented equity markets (European Union, 2006). Compared to the BDC, the Plan does not provide funds directly, but encourages investment from stakeholders by creating a favourable equity investment environment. The Plan concentrates on introducing a modern and flexible set of legal and administrative rules, designing appropriate tax regimes, facilitating the establishment of public risk capital and investment funds at all levels, and developing innovative sources of investment such as angel investors and employee financial participation (European Commission, 2003).

6. Combine financial services and business development services

Banks tend to charge SMEs higher interest rates and demand collateral relative to the asset base as a risk management technique (Beck, Demirgüç-Kunt and Peria, 2008). As mentioned above, this is a response to the lack of transparency regarding the creditworthiness of SMEs. Beyond credit rating schemes, policymakers should encourage SMEs to seek BDS providers, including various business associations such as chambers of commerce and federations of industries, and to work with banks to resolve financial and operational issues. A suitable combination of financial and non-financial services for SMEs is the most needed support. In this regard, financial institutions should consider: (a) developing capacities to provide information on markets and training facilities; (b) evaluate joint venture proposals; (c) assist in the development of business expansion plans; (d) guide financial and taxation matters; and (e) advocate the cause of SMEs at appropriate forums. Such an approach would obviate many difficulties in the SME sector.

Over time, BDS providers can also add value to bank lending and SME development due to their proximity to their clients as well as their direct knowledge of the enterprises' financial status and past performance. BDS providers are often better

Box V.9. SME financing through public-private partnership in Japan

A number of city-level chambers of commerce and industry in Japan have provided non-collateral loans to their small business members in collaboration with state financial institutions. For example, the Kyoto Chamber of Commerce and Industry facilitates the engagement of its small-sized business members (with no more than 20 employees) with JFC for long-term loans of up to $ 200,000 or equivalent. Such SME loans can be provided without any collateral and personal guarantee, and with a discounted interest rate for both working capital and asset investment. In addition to their good financial record, one of the major requirements for small businesses is that they have to receive training and counselling by the chamber before receiving loans. The advantages of this system are that the chamber can understand the conditions of small business members better than financial institutions, thus securing their repayment without collateral, while improving the capacity of the members. The institutional framework of the partnership is illustrated in figure V.17.

Figure V.17. Institutional framework of public-private partnership in Japan

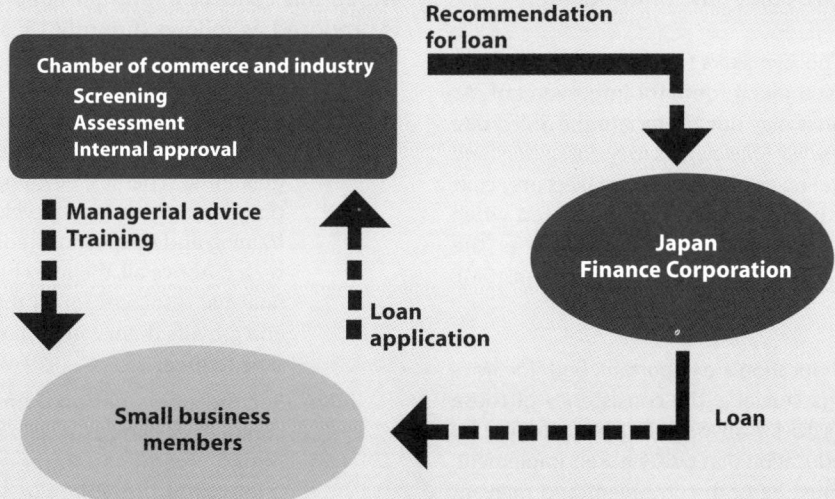

Sources: Kyoto Chamber of Commerce and Industry, undated; and JFC, 2011.

placed than financial institutions for identifying potential clients, ascertaining their creditworthiness, imparting professional financial and accounting techniques and other services germane to lending and repayment of debt. This complementary nature between BDS providers and financial services helps to minimize both the risk and transaction costs to creditors and investors, and makes access to credit and equity less costly and cumbersome for SMEs. Business development services are the central focus of the next chapter, which addresses many of these key issues in greater detail.

A number of BDS programmes, such as EMPRETEC – the Spanish acronym for *emprendedores* (entrepreneurs) and *tecnología* (technology) – address the business development requirements of SMEs. EMPRETEC is a capacity-building programme established by UNCTAD to promote the creation of sustainable support structures that help promising entrepreneurs build innovative and internationally competitive SMEs (EMPRETEC, 2008). The central product of this programme is entrepreneurship training workshops that provide participants with an opportunity to learn from successful entrepreneurs and apply these lessons to their own business behaviour. The core goal of this entrepreneurship training is for SMEs to improve their creditworthiness and attractiveness to potential investors from venture capital funds and financial institutions (UNCTAD, 2001b).

Enterprise Africa, a UNDP programme modelled on EMPRETEC, also encourages the private sector, such as large corporations, banks and consulting firms, to support SMEs through activities such as providing financial contributions, enhancing access to credit and contributing to training and post-training programmes and services (United Nations, 2011). A key feature of this programme is the joint credit delivery scheme whereby Enterprise Africa provides support and capacity-building services, and assumes responsibility for loan referral and monitoring – thus reducing lending costs for partner financial institutions and improving SMEs chances of securing access to finance (UNCTAD, 2001b).

7. Strengthening the bank-SME relationship

Despite the efforts of policymakers to enable SMEs to access bank loans, there is still much room for improvement. As mentioned above, banks may not appreciate the SMEs' dire need for quick capital, while SME owners may not understand bank policies for mitigating risk. While policymakers may craft effective strategies, their efforts may be frustrated when applied in practice. Intermediaries may lack either the incentives or the competence to build and sustain bank-SME relations.

Communication and education are important, both for SMEs and for banks. What is crucial is the consistency of these efforts. There needs to be an ongoing programme of communication and education that policymakers implement. Such a programme must be both convenient and relevant to both SMEs and banks in order to be credible. For example, a research programme has been conducted in Sweden since 1999 to foster better relationships between the credit sector and SMEs through interactions and information exchange between the two groups: (a) banking representatives, SMEs, auditors and tax authorities; and (b) academic representatives (European Commission, 2007). Another example involves the SME Centre for Asia in the Philippines, which provides a training framework for financial institutions dealing with the SME sector, comprising seminars, exhibits and a venue for banks to build linkages with SME entrepreneurs (SME Centre for Asia, 2011).

The following recommendations are made for designing a capacity-building training programme:

(a) Research, identify and review existing training materials;

(b) Adapt materials and prepare draft training packages;

(c) Field-test draft packages by running a few pilot programmes;

(d) Evaluate and refine programme contents based upon the field test;

(e) Run training-for-trainers programmes;

(f) Collaborate with selected trainers from developing countries in their first programme; and

(g) Disseminate training packages and obtain feedback on their utility for further refinements.

The key issues and suggestions for strengthening bank-SME relationships are summarized in table V.8.

8. Introduce a four-tier national financial system

Today's global economy exhibits unparalleled dynamism and experiences rapid changes. These changes affect SMEs more than larger firms due to the fact that they have fewer resources to cope with the volatility. In addition to the traditional forms of term loans and working capital, they require new forms and instruments to remain competitive. In this environment, national economies must hasten to keep pace and realign their own financial system accordingly; otherwise countries will start to lag behind.

Within this context, a four-tier national financial system is proposed as follows (figure V.18; see also figures II.5 and V.6):

(a) First tier – an apex bank (or agency) for SMEs that oversees policy prescriptions, credit guarantee schemes, new financing schemes and programmes, business development services and training and the flow of credit (and equity) to the sector. Above all, the apex bank should augment financial resources for all the concerned players and provide them with institutional support from time to time;

(b) Second tier – national financial institutions, commercial banks, specialized DFIs such as exim banks, credit guarantee agencies, credit information providers (e.g., credit registries), venture capital associations/networks and support institutions, such as national BDS provider associations/networks and national chambers of commerce and industry, should play the role of credit providers or facilitators to the organized sector of SMEs. In addition, corporate

Table V.8. Issues and suggestions for strengthening bank-SME relationships

Issue	Bank	SME
Insufficiency of credit	• Fear of non-payment should be addressed via proper assessment of risk and moral support from relevant government agencies. • Update credit databases to include SMEs. • Joint appraisal with commercial banks/DFIs and BDS providers.	• Careful planning for credit needs based on a specific, workable business plan. • Supporting documents for verification should be kept ready. • Be open to banks in discussing all financial problems. • Prepare thoroughly for presentation, interview etc.
Delays in credit sanctions	• All data requirements for credit appraisal should be communicated to SMEs in one installment. • The appraisal process should be explained in the initial interview. • The appraisal should continue even if a credit officer goes on leave but one person should ultimately be accountable for each SME application. • A single-window approach should be followed for appraisal. • The appraisal process should be focused on continuous improvement, including the models used for risk measurement.	• Produce all data requirements and documents in one installment. • Keep financial records current and accurate. • Extend cooperation to the bank in complying with the head office guidelines.
Collateral requirement is too high	• Get a second opinion on need for collateral, perhaps from a BDS provider. Consider future cash flow as the primary security for SMEs.	• Work with the bank and BDS providers to reduce risks. • Offer some collateral if feasible.
Information requirements are too high or not available	• Checklist of information on requirements to be prepared for SMEs with due care. • Use of computers for data storage and analysis. • Standardize the data requirements for loan applications across different institutions.	• Keep financial and operating records current and accurate. • Use computers where feasible. • Appreciate data needs of the bank.
Compliance with loan agreement, including audits	• Arrange audits to minimize inconvenience to borrowers. • Explain timing and procedures for loan compliance.	• Cooperate with the bank since post-sanction formalities are also for their benefit. • Regular submissions of statements and returns.

Source: Asian Association of Management Organizations (AAMO), 2007.

Box V.10. Methods and criteria for bank loan appraisal

There are two major appraisal methods for loan applications – transaction lending and relationship lending. The main difference between the two methods is that the former is primarily based on quantitative data (e.g., financial statements, bank accounts, credit scores, size of equity, assets and cash flow prediction) while the latter is based on qualitative data (e.g., management skills, leadership, owners' characters, banking relationship, reputation and quality of human resources) (RAM Consultancy Services, 2005).

In practice, particularly in developing countries in Asia and the Pacific, these two methods are often used by commercial banks in a mixed way to fit in with their unique operating environment. The World Bank's global survey on the banking sector reveals that banks consider specific factors in evaluating commercial loan applications (Beck, Demirgüç-Kunt and Peria, 2008). In general the following criteria are used:

(a) Financial assessment of the business;
(b) Firm's credit history with the bank;
(c) Characteristics of the firm's owner (age, sex, leadership, managerial skills etc.);
(d) Purpose of the loan;
(e) Collateral;
(f) Firm's credit history from a credit registry; and
(g) Size of the loan.

---

bond markets (and stock markets in an extreme case) also fall within this category for open market borrowing (and share offering);

(c) Third tier – subnational development financial institutions, regional banks, BDS providers, and local chambers of commerce and industry have a manageable specified region or a command area for serving the specific sector; and

(d) Fourth tier – at the base of the pyramid, MFIs cover the unorganized microenterprises and self-help groups through the provision of microcredit. MFIs have been placed at the base of the system because they have to cover the biggest segment as well as largest number of enterprises and individual entrepreneurs in the field. The MFI system is experienced and best-suited to keeping close contact with clients and to ensuring full recovery of loans. It is also equipped to give non-financial support to entrepreneurs.

Figure V.18. Four-tier financial system for SMEs

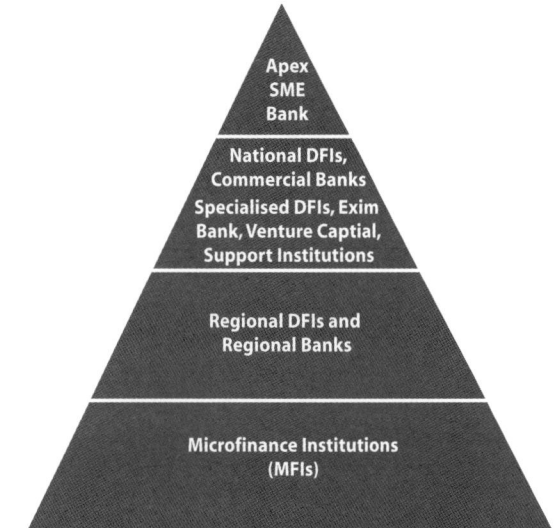

Source: AAMO, 2007.

The suggestions made above establish the significance and importance of restructuring the institutional network of the financial sector into a simplified framework for clear division of labour, so that its reach and institutional coordination are further improved. In addition to having the apex bank for SMEs, the role of MFIs in this framework also assumes greater importance. They should be given national recognition and legal status in the country's financial system to enable them to serve an increasing number of microenterprises.

A central question emerges regarding what limits access to, and use of the formal financial institutions by SMEs for the provision of financial products. Among the factors that hinder SMEs from accessing formal financial institutions are: (a) lack of transparency in SME management; (b) information asymmetry; (c) low managerial capacity; (d) low collateral; (e) small capital base; (f) small economies of scale; and (g) high transaction costs.

Lack of trust looms large in the minds of both banks and SMEs. The scarcity of term loans from banks and higher loan default rates by SME customers compound this attitude. However, policymakers can facilitate re-building this trust. Merely exhorting the financial sector to innovate, change and lend liberally will not make the SME sector thrive. Success lies in a "two-way" traffic system of promoting mutual trust and cooperation.

Giving support to DFIs and BDS providers, both at the national and regional levels is a good start. These institutions will have to project an image of member SMEs as: (a) profitable; (b) dependable; (c) creditworthy, with economic viability; and, above all, (d) timely repaying entities. This will help to build adequate confidence among lending institutions in giving financial support while enhancing their relationship-building with the SME sector, based on mutual trust.

9. Other policy responses: What works and what does not?

The policy reviews in this chapter provide guidance on how policymakers can approach issues of access to finance by SMEs. Some of the key observations are set out below:

(a) The public sector and financial institutions must understand the corporate life circle and associated cash requirements of SMEs. They need to place emphasis on the policies that assist in financing SMEs during their cash drains and to take measures to ease funding constraints due to the time gap between receivables and payables by employing various financing instruments;

(b) Governments should provide a knowledge-sharing and communications platform for different stakeholders (e.g., government, SME agency, financial institutions and SMEs) in order to increase mutual understanding and to share experiences;

(c) Governments need not operate financial assistance programmes for the SME sector directly, but they should work as a facilitator. In particular, policymakers should avoid introducing direct lending and credits at subsidized rates. Such programmes can go through the process of financial intermediation;

(d) Commercial banks have been found to incur large losses on account of publicly subsidized interest rates and non-payment by borrowers;

(e) Loan waivers by governments eventually distort the credit culture;

(f) Market failures should not be tackled with government finance. Governments should intervene and work with/through commercial forces to correct the distortions;

(g) Policymakers must give adequate attention to the protection of creditors' rights by introducing a suitable set of laws that protect lenders from non-payment. Without creditors' rights, the market for credit can be expected to remain underdeveloped;

(h) Governments should promote a collateral and third-party guarantee-free or reduced lending system, suitably backed by credit guarantee schemes or cash flow-based financing to encourage lenders to assist SMEs;

(i) Governments should concentrate policies on promoting the availability of risk capital to innovative, high-growth SMEs, mainly during the early stages of financing;

(j) Public sector funds could still be used to leverage private sector financing in order to reduce the financing gap;

(k) Policymakers should recognize the need for proximity between lenders and borrowers, particularly in the case of small-scale loans.

Table V.9. Matrix of policy measures facilitating access to finance by SMEs

Policy measure	Type	Intervention
SME Act	Legal	Introduce a national Act for development of SME sector.
Property rights	Legal	Proper property registration facilitates loans with collaterals.
SME development regulations	Regulatory	Suitable regulations create enabling environment for SMEs.
Financial sector reforms	Regulatory	Financial sector reforms facilitate timely and adequate finance to SMEs.
Central banking directives	Regulatory	Central Bank directs banks and financial institutions to support SME sector as priority sector.
SME development policies	Regulatory	A set of comprehensive development policies and programmes including financial support and exit policies for SMEs.
Fiscal incentives	Indirect government support	Fiscal and taxation policies increasing working capital and encouraging SME investments.
International cooperation for fund support and FDI	Indirect government support	Encourage international funds and TNCs for lines of credit and FDI.
Capital market and stock exchange development	Regulatory	Encourage SMEs for market borrowing and equity support.
Information and credit scoring	Financial intermediation	National network for credit and credit scoring of SMEs.
Financial intermediation development	Financial intermediation	Specialized financial institutions for assisting SMEs, such as SME banks, EXIM banks, venture funds, MFIs etc.
Financial services package	Financial intermediation	Enabling government policies encourages the financial system to offer a full range of financial services including debt, equity and innovative finance to SMEs and to offer BDS.

Source: Authors' compilation.

Regional and local equity initiatives (e.g., subnational funds) are appropriate for such types of lending;

(l) Governments should take emergency measures and facilitate extra credits to help SMEs through economic downturns. In addition, they should take measures to help SMEs build up long-term survival capacity and enhance long-term competitiveness;

(m) Governments must carefully design all the intervention policies to avoid market distortion;

(n) Policymakers should provide information and consultation services for SMEs to obtain funds (focusing on available sources of financing, understanding and meeting different criteria for different sources and dealing with legal and contract issues);

(o) Governments should provide training on accounting and financial management skills while raising SMEs' awareness of the importance of cash flow management; enhance their ability to obtain funds; help them use different financing sources efficiently;

(p) Governments should facilitate the designing of financial services that are suitable for SMEs;

(q) Governments should facilitate FDI to the SME sector; and

(r) Governments should, in association with private sector associations, chambers of commerce and BDS providers, encourage small businesses to maintain and report reliable information. This will help to reassure financial institutions to lend to SMEs.

A brief summary of general policy measures for SME financing is provided in table V.9.

L. Summary

Financial capital is a critical input for businesses in general, and SMEs in particular. Without adequate and timely finance there can be no start-up, much less expansion or long-term sustainability. This chapter began by emphasizing the need for cash. An SME can show legitimate profits on its books but will ultimately fold if it is not collecting the cash from customers. While this may seem obvious, collecting cash is a tedious process that new business owners often fail to consider in their planning. They assume that as long as they offer a product that consumers want, the cash will simply appear; however, the reality is that extensive follow-up may be required to get the cash from the sale. The rule of thumb for policymakers is to favour policies that provide quick cash to SMEs as opposed to policies that offer deferred benefits.

This need for cash was then linked to the life cycle stages of the firm. Entrepreneurs may obtain the funds necessary for start-up from their own savings or loans from family and friends, but the crucial period occurs soon after operations begin. There is a gap between when suppliers must be paid and receivables are collected; this gap is the foundation of working capital management (figure V.4). Policymakers at the local level need to educate new business owners about the necessity of working capital management; this should be included in business and entrepreneurship curricula.

The various financing options available to SMEs were then discussed. In addition to informal and internal financing, such as personal savings, working capital and trade credit, the traditional way involves using the banking system for debt financing. When new business owners cannot find the capital to expand within their own networks, they turn to banks. The usually tense relationship between banks and SMEs is noted, as both parties are often insensitive to the needs of each other. There is ample room in such a situation for the involvement of policymakers, primarily as facilitators. Banks need credit guarantees and other forms of risk mitigation. The most effective policies make credit information available for markets to use. Direct intervention (e.g., government loans and blanket guarantees) generally suffers from moral hazard and high administrative costs and is therefore less effective. However, on occasions, such direct intervention can be necessary; this is highlighted by the given examples of successful credit guarantees provided by the Governments of India, Japan, Pakistan and Turkey.

Additional financial measures include leasing, factoring, corporate bonds and seed capital as well as equity financing such as angel finance, venture capital and IPOs. These methods are common in advanced economies and are gaining traction in the Asia-Pacific region. Naturally they require the highest level of investor protection policies and rule of law as well as sophisticated capital and equity markets. As a matter of systemic improvement, policymakers should strive to balance the use of debt and the use of equity for supplying capital to their nation's businesses. Over-reliance on the banking sector is a hallmark of the Asia-Pacific region; future development should see more of a mix.

Beyond the balance of debt and equity, the chapter proposes other major areas of policy intervention. SMEs can increase working capital by improving their managerial capacity and utilizing financial techniques such as trade credit, thus reducing their need to borrow money from external sources. Reducing information asymmetry is a key; often SMEs do not know what financing options are available or how to access them. Financial institutions have difficulty gauging the creditworthiness of SMEs. Policymakers need to bridge these knowledge gaps. It is not sufficient to provide financing, as lack of managerial know-how can lead to wasting loans. Policymakers should package financial capital with business development services, an issue that is addressed in greater detail in chapter VI.

The relationship between banks and SMEs was explored in table V.8. It is noted that there is a role for both commercial banks and DFIs in supporting SMEs; policymakers should not favour one at the expense of the other. Robust competition in the financial sector will help SMEs and the overall economy. The authors suggest that the national financial system should follow the AAMO (2007) four-tier model depicted in figure V.18, with an apex SME bank supported by various levels of DFIs and banks and a foundation of microfinance.

The chapter concluded with a review of policy responses: what works and what does not? Table V.9 sets out a matrix of policy measures facilitating access to finance by SMEs. It is re-emphasized that government officials should adapt these general recommendations to the unique circumstances of their respective countries.

Annex V.1
Typology of collateral

Collateral is usually requested by lenders to serve as credit enhancement to reduce the risk of a borrower's default. The main types of collateral that the borrowers can use are:

(a) Property – a borrower may pledge property as security for a loan. If the loan is not repaid at maturity, these securities may be sold to reimburse the lender. Acceptable property and financial assets include any or a combination of real estate, equipment, inventory and precious metals (Holdsworth, 2009);

(b) Financial assets – it is possible to get a loan by assigning financial assets to the bank. In this situation, the bank keeps the assets until the borrower has repaid the loans. Common financial assets used for this purpose include savings accounts, certificates of deposit, stocks and bonds (SBA, 2009);

(c) Accounts receivable – sometimes banks lend money against accounts receivable. The borrower can select some of the larger and better accounts receivable and assign them to the bank or the financial institution. The purchaser may pay through the borrower or directly to the bank depending on the contract arrangements (SBA, 2009);[90]

(d) Life insurance – the cash value of a life insurance policy serves as collateral. The borrower can get credit from the insurance company directly or assign the policy to a bank (SBA, 2009); and

(e) Third-party loan guarantee – under a third-party guarantee agreement, the guarantor has an obligation to pay the lender the amount owed if the borrower defaults on the loan (Rocks, 2010). In some cases, several guarantors are required by the bank to co-guarantee one loan to ensure the safety of the credit; and

(f) Public credit guarantee – government agencies provide public credit guarantees to target groups (e.g., SMEs). Generally, the borrowers need to satisfy several criteria to obtain the guarantees, so that participating banks can issue corresponding credits to the successful borrowers.

---

[90] For more detailed information, see the discussion on factoring in this chapter on page 92.

CHAPTER VI
Business development services

SMEs not only need financial support but also BDS to stimulate growth. As reviewed briefly in the previous chapter, BDS are critical supplementary and complementary inputs to finance.

These capacity-building inputs are mainly targeted at enhancing the performance of an individual business, increasing access to markets, and improving their competitiveness and profitability (Committee of Donor Agencies for Small Enterprise Development, 2001). They include a wide range of non-financial support services concentrated in the following categories: market access, infrastructure, policy advocacy, bookkeeping/accounting, legal advice, consulting, input supply, training and technical assistance, technology and product development, and alternative financing mechanisms as well as business incubation (ILO, 2003b). In supporting the development and sustainability of SMEs, these services help to increase employment; generate higher incomes and provide economic security. Such interventions at the micro-level contribute to the alleviation of poverty and empower vulnerable groups by the means of economic development and growth (UNDP, 2004a). BDS interventions at the micro-level can lead to greater economic security and income generation, as SMEs create employment, innovation, value-added goods and services, and flexibility in response to dynamic markets (UNDP, 2004b).

While the objectives are similar, country experiences differ in the operational modalities of BDS. Various channels include governmental agencies, private sector BDS operators, independent consultants, chambers of commerce or federations of industries. In the Asia-Pacific region, BDS outcomes are mixed. Some countries have been successful in designing and implementing BDS programmes while others have faltered (APO, 2007).

This chapter begins with a discussion of the objectives and types of BDS. It then considers two distinct channels of BDS – traditional and market-oriented. Some BDS tools are then suggested for enhancing SME competitiveness (including business and technology incubators) as well as some advice for improving the BDS-SME interface.

A. Design and objectives

BDS is a comprehensive concept that covers the identification of business opportunities, delivery of updated and reliable information, support in the development of business plans, hand-holding during the process of setting up businesses by SMEs, and marketing of the products and services. R&D, innovations, and modernization are also critical components of effective BDS design. Since BDS designs and frameworks differ from country to country, no "one-size fits all" model can be recommended. Each country will have to customize their BDS depending on local conditions, requirements of the sector and other entrepreneurs.

The main objectives of BDS are:

(a) Provide non-financial services (e.g., accounting and legal advice) to SMEs at affordable costs, supplementing the role of financial services;

(b) Support SMEs in their promotion, development, and sustained growth; and

(c) Facilitate SMEs' development of competitive advantages.

The scope of BDS is wide, encompassing operational, advisory and advocacy roles. Operational services address daily routines of the business, whereas advisory services focus on medium-term or long-term issues. Advocacy services work for improving business environment through policy enhancement (table VI.1).

Table VI.1. Three core segments of BDS

	Operational	Advisory	Advocacy
Services	Short-term support services and hand-holding such as accounting, legal and regulatory advice, accessing technical information, labour management and secretarial services	Long-term development services, such as training, strategic management, marketing assistance and knowledge transfer.	Services to improve business environment through policy advocacy and infrastructure development.
Target clients	Individual firms	Individual firms	Public sector, business associations

Source: Authors' compilation.

Operational BDS typically include accounting, legal and regulatory advice, logistics and warehousing, labour-related requirements and ICT. Advisory BDS consist of services used to improve the competitiveness of the enterprise in the long term, including training, consultancy and advocacy roles, strategic management, marketing assistance, and transfer of knowledge and technical skills (ADB, 2006). Some countries have also offered innovative services such as environmental consulting and political risk consulting. Some BDS also target policy advocacy through the public sector or business associations as opposed to individual firms. Those advocacy initiatives include strengthening the financial sector, lowering or removing barriers to market entry, advising the government on procedural issues, intellectual property right issues, and promoting pro-business infrastructure development.

Table VI.2 Types of advisory and advocacy BDS

	Advisory	Advocacy
Market access and development	Marketing research, intelligence, and strategy development. Emerging opportunities and trade enquires, including niche markets and regional and global markets. Market/trade barriers, trends and competitors. Trade fairs, product exhibitions and B2B contacts. Development of samples and promotion tools and materials. Showrooms and packaging. Advertising. New product development.	Regulatory framework for subcontracting and outsourcing. Common brand and consortium approach. Trade missions and meetings. Forging TNC-SME linkages. Free trade and investment agreements. Non-tariff barriers. Trade and logistic facilitation.
Supporting infrastructure	Storage and warehousing. Transport and distribution. Business incubators. Telecommunications. Computer services.	Physical infrastructure (e.g., roads and ports, power supplies and utilities). Industrial estates. Easy money transfer. Internet access.
Supplies	Linking SMEs to input suppliers. Suppliers' capacity to provide quality inputs.	Establishment of bulk buying groups. Information on input supply sources.
Technical assistance and training	Mentoring, counselling and advisory services. Feasibility studies and business plan development. Technical training and capacity building in the fields of legal issues, finance and taxation, accountancy and bookkeeping, production and research and development.	Exchange visits and business tours. Regulatory framework for franchising/joint ventures.[91] E-commerce policy.
Technology and product development	Technology and innovation incubation. Linking SMEs and technology suppliers. Technology procurement. Technology sources and pricing. Technology transfer and commercialization. Cost and energy-efficient technologies. Productivity improvement. Equipment leasing and rental.	Quality assurance programmes. International standards and quality certifications. Design centres. Common tool facilities. National innovation incubation.

Source: Modified from ILO, 2003b.

In general, BDS operational services are more developed than BDS advisory and advocacy services due to regulatory requirements; thus, there is a sustained demand for them by SMEs (e.g., accounting services for tax purposes). In contrast, despite being the main focus of most donors, interventions in advisory and advocacy BDS have largely failed or been short-lived (UNDP, 2004a). Additionally, the market for operational BDS already exists, whereas an excess of third-party involvement in advisory and advocacy support has dulled the ability of SMEs to absorb what they need to learn and to apply it. In many cases a culture of dependency often develops. Some of the forms of advisory and advocacy BDS that could help in improving the competitive strength of SMEs are briefly presented in table VI.2.

B. Channels for delivering BDS: Traditional versus market-oriented

The traditional channel for delivering BDS in developing countries is typically through government agencies, such as SME development agencies. The public agencies, including donor-driven programmes and NGOs, deliver various forms of BDS directly to the SME sector, usually gratis or at a significantly reduced cost (figure VI.1). Public interventions, in various forms, have made important contributions to SME growth in conditions of economic reconstruction, transition or development (Phare, 2000). In Indonesia, for example, an ADB survey found that while private BDS providers dominated, government agencies and research institutes provided 10-15 per cent of BDS, and were particularly active in technology-related training and advice (Niemann, 2002). Furthermore, private providers tended to primarily serve

---

[91] BDS may also be provided to develop franchising and/or joint venture partnerships. Those services include: (a) the identification of franchising/joint-venture objectives and needs; (b) identification of potential franchising/joint-venture partners; (c) evaluation of the partner as well as the technology and know-how offered; (d) evaluation of other offers such as equity and marketing support; and (e) the legal aspects of the franchising and joint venture.

Figure VI.1. Traditional business development services approach

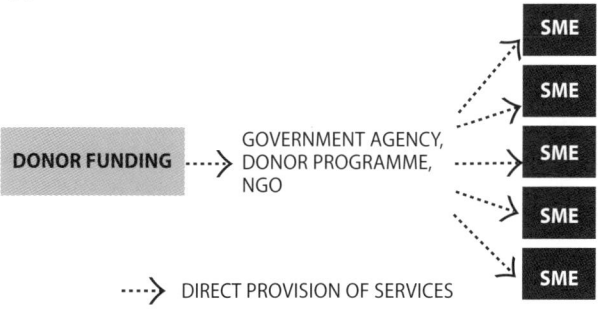

Source: Modified from DCED, 2001.

urban areas, whereas NGOs operated in rural and peripheral locations (Niemann, 2002).

Although the intent of lowering the cost of such services is admirable, the effect on SMEs is questionable. Evaluation studies in many countries have found a number of unintended negative consequences (UNDP, 2004a), leading to BDS programmes becoming unsustainable. These include:

(a) The government institution providing BDS can gain monopolistic power in the country, hindering commercial BDS providers from thriving;

(b) The provision of subsidized services adversely affects the quality of services rendered;

(c) All BDS activities become supply-driven rather that demand-driven, and there is insensitivity to market signals; and

(d) Subsidies create a culture of dependency at both firm and government levels. SMEs fail to learn independence and initiative, while national BDS development programmes stop innovating and rely on international aid or grants.

To remedy these deficiencies, a number of governments have turned to private suppliers to deliver BDS to the SME sector (UNCTAD, 2005a) (figure VI.2). Since these firms are in direct competition with one another, there is little chance that one of them can attain a monopolistic position without having government concessions. This market-development approach seeks to facilitate the sustainable increase in both supply and demand of services, while replacing subsidies with private payment for services. The ultimate result of this approach is that SMEs are able to select the BDS most applicable to their needs from a wide array of products offered by private sector suppliers (UNDP, 2004a).

This approach maximizes the number of providers and their competition. The profit motive gives the providers the incentive to offer BDS in a sustainable and high-quality manner in line with the development agenda of governments and donors. Within this context, donor emphasis has focused more on technical assistance to pre-delivery BDS activities, such as capacity-building, awareness raising, information dissemination, test marketing and service development as well as post-delivery BDS activities, such as client feedback and monitoring and evaluation (UNDP, 2004a).

Table VI.3 details the differences between the traditional and market-oriented approaches.

While market-oriented channels are preferable to traditional public sector driven channels, policymakers should recognize that the former may only be an option once a certain stage of economic development has been reached. Some developing nations simply lack the human resources necessary to support a thriving sector of private BDS

Figure VI.2. Market-oriented business development services approach

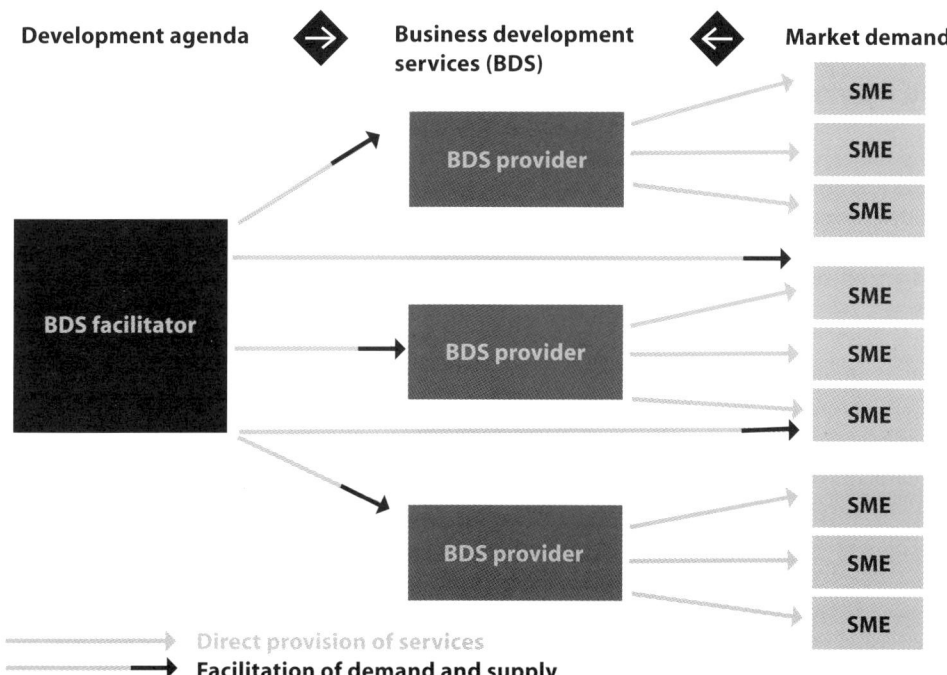

Source: Modified from McVay and Miehlbradt, 2001.

Table VI.3. Distinctive features of traditional and market-oriented channels

Core area	Traditional approach	Market-oriented approach
Management	Government-managed.	Private-sector managed, but facilitated by the government.
Objective	To provide supply-driven BDS.	To provide market-based, demand-driven BDS.
Resources	Subsidy and/or donor funded.	BDS paid for by the users.
Sustainability	Not sustainable in the long term as the subsidies are withdrawn.	Sustainable in the long term, even without subsidies.
Effectiveness	Supply driven BDS are not relevant at times – with the agency gaining a monopoly.	Numbers of BDS providers from private sector make the programme relevant and competitive – the scheme is diversified.
SMEs payment capacity	SMEs can get support without payment but not for long.	SMEs in the developing economies, and smaller-sized firms, may initially find it difficult to pay for the services.

Source: UNDP, 2004a.

providers and support from government and donor agencies may be the only feasible option. Start-up BDS providers in developing countries need support during their infancy stage as they find it hard to even raise the initial financial resources needed to set up their enterprises.

When the BDS market is underdeveloped and BDS are not commercially affordable for SMEs, some cases of market failure are observed. SMEs cannot afford expensive BDS; however, low-cost BDS may mean low-quality services. To address this issue, the support of BDS providers should be considered within the national policy framework (UNDP, 2004a). Governments, in collaboration with donor and development agencies, could support commercial BDS providers initially through subsidies to provide low-cost services to SMEs. Once SMEs become more profitable, they should be weaned from government/donor subsidized services and moved to a market-based BDS system. Governments have an important role to a play in mitigating any dependency issues that may arise during this transition process (ESCAP, 2001a).

C. BDS actors and their roles

BDS actors have varied roles, depending on their different perspectives, mandates and capabilities. DCED (2001)[92] offers an overview of the different actors and their roles:

(a) SMEs – demand-side, potential clients of BDS providers;

(b) BDS providers – national or subnational government agencies, business and industry associations, enterprises, individuals and NGOs who provide services directly to SMEs;

(c) BDS facilitators – NGOs, industry and employers' associations, government agencies (e.g., SME development agencies) and donors who support BDS providers through product development, capacity-building, promoting good practices, external evaluation and quality assurance;

(d) Donors – individuals, organizations or government agencies that provide funding for BDS projects and programmes; and

(e) Governments – play the principal role in creating enabling policy, legal and regulatory frameworks so that SMEs and BDS providers can function effectively together. They provide basic public services, such as infrastructure, education and information services.

Figure VI.3 offers a synopsis of BDS players and their interface with SMEs.

BDS donors have become increasingly diversified and sophisticated over the past few decades. The importance of BDS to the performance and competitiveness of SMEs has been increasingly recognized, which has increased the variety of key players. Furthermore, attempts have been made to raise the cost-effectiveness and sustainability of such services. An example is the DCED BDS Bluebook.

Business start-ups, especially in developing economies, often do not have enough resources to buy BDS from private providers, so governments are required to provide BDS or funding, at least in the start-up phase of SMEs (UNDP, 2004a). Public agencies should therefore collaborate with local private institutions to provide efficient and sustainable services for SMEs (UNCTAD, 2005a). Governments should not limit or fix the number, size or fee of BDS providers. In particular, governments should maximize the competition among BDS providers, wherever possible, while encouraging qualified providers to enter into the BDS market (UNDP, 2004a). This is the best way of ensuring low prices and high quality. Officials should avoid imposing market-entry constraints on new organizations in this sector and avoid tying professionals to certain organizations.

Another key issue is the involvement of subnational governments in the BDS framework. As they can work closely with the local BDS providers and the client SMEs and they understand local conditions, the subnational bodies are in a better position than national governments to facilitate BDS

---

[92] Also known as the BDS Bluebook, which was developed by DCED for donor interventions aimed at improving the effectiveness, outreach and sustainability of BDS interventions. See DECD's activities at http://www.enterprise-development.org/.

Figure VI.3. Business development services actors and their roles

Private BDS providers
rendering direct services to the SMEs. They may be individuals, NGOs, for profit companies, industry associations, etc.

BDS facilitators
giving support services to the BDS providers. They are generally government agencies such as SME development office, extension agencies, support institutions with development agenda and advocacy agenda, etc.

SMEs as Users of BDS

Donors
giving donations, grants and subsidies to the governmental agencies, BDS service providers and SMEs for using the BDS

Governments
providing budgetary support, creating enabling environment, basic public goods, etc.

Source: Modified from AAMO, 2007.

at the local level. However, subnational officials generally lack the capacities and skills to foster BDS efficiently. Technical assistance by the national government or donors to subnational governments would therefore be useful.

SME-oriented NGOs, including businesses and industry associations, could also be an effective instrument to provide the required service to the SME sector as they work closely with SMEs and understand their needs well. These NGOs should receive support and encouragement from policymakers. Irrespective of the type of BDS providers (government, private, NGO or international), they must help the SMEs build their own competencies and avoid a culture of dependency.

Box VI.1. Role of SME development agencies in business development services facilitation

SME development agencies are responsible for the coordination of policy formulation and implementation for SME development. They offer SMEs multidisciplinary assistance enabling them to address several issues in one place. This approach differentiates the SME development agencies from other governmental organizations. They can also provide BDS for SMEs that lack the wherewithal to pay or where such services are otherwise not available.

Although the focus of SME development agencies may differ according to their national development context, the areas of their services to SMEs generally include six main categories: (a) information collection and dissemination (e.g., national/subnational SME databases, market intelligence, SME portal etc.);

(b) capacity-building training; (c) consulting and business advisory services; (d) assistance in hands-on management; (e) financial support and incentives (including direct, indirect and risk sharing with banks); and (f) development of infrastructure (e.g., SME parks).

As BDS facilitators, SME development agencies can work on the demand side by educating SMEs about the potential benefits of services or by providing incentives for them to try BDS. Other facilitating roles include the external evaluation of the impact of BDS, quality assurance of BDS and advocacy for a better policy environment for the local BDS market.

Source: EURADA, undated.

Box VI.2. Highlights of SME development agencies in Asia and the Pacific

A. Office of Small and Medium-sized Enterprises Promotion, Thailand

In order to promote the IT sector in Thailand, the Office of SME Promotion runs a programme called WebsiteSpark in cooperation with Microsoft. This is a good example of how SME agencies can work with TNCs in specific fields. Available at www.sme.go.th/pages/home.aspx.

B. Small and Medium Enterprise Corporation of Malaysia

The National Mark of Malaysia Brand and the Enterprise 50 Award both aim to encourage Malaysian SMEs to improve the quality, reliability and reputation of their products and services, and foster competition between each other. Capacity-building programmes and financial assistance encourage competition among local SMEs to become suppliers of international companies. The SME Competitiveness Rating for Enhancement (SCORE) diagnostic tool was also introduced to enhance the competitiveness of SMEs. Visit the website at www.smecorp.gov.my/.

C. Bureau of SME Development, Department of Trade and Industry, Philippines

As a central office for SME development, the Bureau of SME Development provides full-scale information about BDS conducted by all other offices and bureaus under the Department of Trade and Industry. Available at www.dti.gov.ph/dti/index.php?p=79.

D. General Department of Industry, Cambodia

The General Department of Industry offers a joint financing scheme with HwangDBS Commercial Bank to provide SMEs with different loan options. Available at www.gdi.mime.gov.kh/.

E. SPRING, Singapore

SPRING runs many scholarships and programmes to support the training and development of future business leaders and executives. Financing schemes offered by SPRING are a combination of different schemes for the different needs of individual SMEs, such as loans for working capital, trade financing, and purchases of equipment and assets. SPRING provides a platform that helps to match the financial needs of entrepreneurs and existing funding sources. Available at www.spring.gov.sg/Pages/Homepage.aspx.

F. International Enterprise, Singapore

While SPRING is the agency working for the capacity-building of Singaporean companies, International Enterprise aims to help SMEs to compete on the international stage. International Enterprise offers programmes and services to encourage Singaporean SMEs to export and to cooperate with foreign companies. Available at www.iesingapore.gov.sg/wps/portal.

G. Agency for Enterprise Development, Ministry of Planning and Investment, Viet Nam

The Agency for Enterprise Development provides detailed and comprehensive information and step-by-step instruction on how to run an SME in Viet Nam. Both the national trade promotion programme and the national trademarks development programme are intended to help the development of strong national brands and trademarks in Viet Nam. Available at www.business.gov.vn/index.aspx?LangType=1033.

H. SMEs Department, Ministry of Industry and Information Technology, China

Rather than being an office conducting programmes for SMEs' development, the SMEs Department acts more as an interactive platform encouraging communication among SMEs, either buyers or sellers, to exchange information online. For financial support, it announces financial and investment incentive schemes in China, providing online applications systems. It also has an online forum for recruiters and job hunters to make these processes more efficient. Available at www.sme.gov.cn.

I. Small and Medium Enterprise Agency, Ministry of Economy, Trade, and Industry, Japan

The Agency of Japan is the only agency mentioned here that runs SME financing schemes to alleviate the impacts of the global economy crisis in 2008, such as emergency guarantee programmes. More details are available at www.chusho.meti.go.jp/sme_english/index.html.

J. Small and Medium Business Administration, Republic of Korea

The Small and Medium Business Administration (SMBA) is the government body for SME development in the Republic of Korea. It was established in 1996, and has developed and implemented a SME promotion system that combines financing, marketing, technology and support for start-ups and micro-enterprises (SMBA, 2009). In 2006, SMBA launched the SPi-1357 system to deliver policy information online, and offline to improve dissemination of SME policy knowledge and innovation (APEC, 2006). The system consists of an online policy information component and an offline counselling service (APEC, 2006). More information available at http://eng.smba.go.kr/main.jsp

K. National Small Industries Corporation, Ministry of Micro, Small and Medium Enterprises, India

The National Small Industries Corporation (NSIC) promotes SME participation in trade fairs, exhibitions, and buyer-seller meetings at the national and international levels. NSIC also promotes the upgrading of technologies and technical training of personnel. NSIC's national networks identify business opportunities and offer technical assistance to rural SMEs through their sites. For details refer to www.nsic.co.in.

D. Levels of BDS interventions

There are numerous levels for BDS interventions in any market, including those in Asia and the Pacific. Within this context a solid interchange is needed among the micro-, meso- and macro-levels of an economy for successful BDS to support SMEs. Each stakeholder, such as government, donor, business association or NGO in the BDS sector, needs to be aware of this interconnected environment in order to implement its services efficiently and to attain the development of the SME sector. The Committee of Donor Agencies for SME Development (1998) report on BDS provides a detailed outline of the key interventions at each level, which are briefly summarized below.

1. Micro-level

(a) Training

Training, the most common form of BDS intervention, covers a range of teaching activities for facilitators, trainers and groups of trainees. The aim is to develop SMEs' knowledge and skills in operational areas (e.g., marketing, accounting, finance, production and product development), in dealing with problems (e.g., attracting new pools of customers and lowering operating costs), and in finding useful partners (e.g., customers, suppliers and collaborators).

(b) Extension, consultancy and counselling[93]

This form of BDS intervention provides customized actions for individual SMEs. Each of the three forms has varying advantages and disadvantages, and are usually structured to cover the diverse SME field. Of the three, consultancy is the traditional instrument of SME promotion and is typically tied to pre-investment activities and loan schemes.

(c) Technology development and transfer

There are two general views – corporate and indigenous – that determine the type of BDS that is provided for technology development and transfer. The former view emphasizes the importance of professional technical expertise in technology development and transfer in a demand-driven process with strong marketing systems, to ensure the greatest effect. In the latter view, SMEs develop their own technologies through their own capacities or adopt new technologies through SME-led inter-enterprise learning. This topic is covered extensively in chapter VII.

(d) Access to market information

SMEs typically lack access to pertinent information on ever-changing markets. To combat this, a number of donor-supported activities have attempted to improve the information environment of SMEs. These activities include interventions to improve information flows from business associations, funding for attendance at trade fairs and exhibitions, and dissemination of information for SMEs. With greater market information, SMEs can respond more readily to market changes, pursue new market opportunities, and ultimately become more competitive.

(e) Business linkages

BDS interventions to improve commercial linkages between SMEs and large enterprises are focused on three main types: subcontracting, franchising and business clusters. These approaches are aimed at linking or incorporating SMEs into the operations of large enterprises. Subcontracting involves a large enterprise contracting work to smaller suppliers, upon which those suppliers can subcontract work to other small firms. As such, a number of BDS organizations, especially UNIDO, have promoted subcontracting in aiding SMEs. The second type, franchising, refers to when one enterprise sells the right to produce or sell a commodity under certain standards and procedures to another enterprise. The third type, business clusters, involves production and supply arrangements in specific sectors and/or geographic areas that involve a wide range of firms and organizations, such as business associations, research and development networks, and specialist service providers.

2. Meso-level

The majority of funding from donors is no longer delivered directly to enterprises but is directed to local and national BDS providers; as seen in figure VI.2. Accordingly, there is growing consensus on developing the capacity of BDS providers to deliver support services to SMEs. The objective of meso-level interventions is to improve the capacity of BDS providers to develop better services, add new products, expand their target groups, strengthen their organizations or develop networks of providers. These meso-level organizations can be divided into two categories: membership organizations and service delivery organizations. Membership organizations are created or owned by SMEs to represent their interests and provide services for the members, which include business associations, chambers of commerce, and cooperatives. Service delivery organizations are owned and operated by agents and provide specific services to SMEs. These include government organizations, NPOs or NGOs, and private enterprises, such as consulting firms and training institutions.

These types of meso-level interventions have both strengths and weaknesses. While membership organizations, such as business associations, are closest to SMEs and have proven potential to represent the interests of SMEs, their capacity can be underdeveloped. They can also be captive to large enterprises, ignoring the needs of their smaller members even though the latter constitute the membership majority. Among service delivery organizations, governmental organizations are less effective as BDS providers as they can be subject to political and bureaucratic interference. On the other hand, NPOs and NGOs have proven their effectiveness as BDS providers in the market; however, their charity orientation may conflict with their business-oriented decisions. As such, commercial organizations, with their business-approach and independence from political and bureaucratic interference, have the potential to be the most successful providers of BDS to SMEs. However there is a risk that profit-oriented BDS providers will focus on specific

---

[93] Extension is the delivery of advice or material assistance outside a classroom, typically at a client's place of business. Consultancy is expert advice on specialized technical and managerial issues. Counselling is the guided process of self-discovery or self-teaching (DCED, 2001).

Box VI.3. Roles of business associations

The roles of business associations, which comprise private enterprises in one industry or sector or from various industries or sectors, can be grouped under one of four types depending on their primary focus: market enhancing activities; market complementing activities; associational activities; and others. Each of these are briefly summarized below (Brimble, 2000; and Doner and Schneider, 1998).

A. Market enhancing activities

This involves indirect support for the functioning of the market. Activities include:

(a) Advising the public sector on the formulation of policies and strategies;

(b) Lobbying for the improvement of property rights and regulation;

(c) Pressuring the public sector for addressing critical infrastructure; and

(d) Playing a civil society role through working more closely with domestic policymakers, i.e., pressuring government for transparency and accountability.

B. Market complementing activities

These activities will strengthen the capacities of business association members to deal with market challenges by providing BDS. Activities include:

(a) Sharing best practices in management and specific technologies;

(b) Ensuring that members adhere to a quality standard;

(c) Providing market information and related promotional activities;

(d) Conducting training and meetings for skill and capacity development;

(e) Providing guidance for funding access; and

(f) Establishing recognized and accredited qualifications.

C. Associational activities

This relates to social networks, which may lead to members' engagement and more trusting attitudes towards suppliers, BDS providers, investors, TNCs, financial institutions, government offices and NGOs. The activities include:

(a) Providing a mechanism for dialogue with policymakers at the domestic and regional levels;

(b) Managing technology transfer through inter-firm cooperation;

(c) Organizing seminars, exhibitions and trade fairs, and missions;

(d) Serving as the communications channel for the private sector, including TNCs and foreign investors, around the globe; and

(e) Reducing unintended negative impacts of members' operations on local communities such as unwanted cultural changes or unsustainable competition among local firms.

D. Others

This type includes:

(a) Conducting CSR activities, such as community services;

(b) Promoting good corporate governance among members;

(c) Sharing the best practices of labour relations; and

(d) Promoting the image and reputation of business associations.

Three approaches are available for further enhancing the roles of business associations: (a) strengthening business associations; (b) developing activities and services; and (c) influencing policies and regulations.

(a) Strengthening business associations

One way is to provide sufficient resources to business associations to enable them to offer a higher level of services to their members and related parties. The inputs should include staff strengthening and training, facilitating development support such as ICT, advisory support on strategic development (i.e., how to best manage the organization and activities), and membership development assistance. A comprehensive needs assessment should be conducted to receive accurate inputs from business associations and their SME members.

(b) Developing activities and services

The development of activities and services should reflect the usefulness of the business associations to stakeholders. Members should value their membership and view it as a valuable asset for their future development. The services should include the provision of information such as a business guide, international business information and training, including short courses in specific topics and new technology.

(c) Influencing policies and regulations

Business associations will gain greater credibility when they become more involved in providing relevant information and participate in government development processes on regulation or trade policies that affect business.

Source: UNCTAD, 2005a.

service areas and ignore others that SMEs need. This will depend upon the level of development in different countries or within a country, e.g., urban and rural areas.

3. Macro-level

All stakeholders in an economy agree on the importance of macro-level policy and regulation in the development of SMEs. The macroeconomic environment that is conducive for BDS is based on four main pillars: (a) a stable macro-economy; (b) a competitive micro-economy; (c) global linkages; and (d) investment in people (DCED, 1998). Within this framework, a number of BDS instruments have been used to build the capacity of SMEs, including but not limited to:

(a) Setting up national SME agencies;
(b) Strengthening the capacity of business associations;
(c) Developing an environment conducive to SME development; and
(d) Supporting microfinance institutions.

E. Business and technology incubation

One of the best BDS for promoting growth-oriented SMEs is through the concept of "incubators". Business and technology incubation has been adopted worldwide as an effective means of promoting and supporting SMEs in becoming innovative entrepreneurs in transforming technological results into new products and services. Business and technology incubation is a relatively recent system. It is derived from the conventional BDS to SMEs, such as consultancy, counselling and training, but has other distinctive characteristics. A business and technology incubator is defined as an organization that develops, provides and maintains controlled conditions to assist in the cultivation of new growth-oriented or innovation-driven enterprises.[94] The National Business Incubation Association (NBIA) (2012) has estimated that there are approximately 7,000 business and technology incubators worldwide.

A business and technology incubator can be either a profit or a non-profit organization managed by public, private or academic institutions, or through a public-private partnership. Although incubators can target a variety of business lines, many of them are moving to technology-led businesses and tailored service offerings, e.g., ICT, bio and life sciences, energy, advance materials and agri-business (NBIA, 2009; and Zablocki, 2007). This is understandable, as many sponsors of incubation programmes aim to accelerate industry growth and job creation through innovation and technology commercialization. Some incubators also target minority groups, women or young entrepreneurs.

An incubator provides the following services (ESCAP, 2004; and NBIA, 2009):

(a) Office spaces and business equipment;
(b) Business plan development;
(c) Technical support;
(d) Marketing assistance;
(e) Financial management;
(f) Access to capital;
(g) Linkage with university/corporate partners/inputs providers;
(h) Business training;
(i) Mentoring and coaching; and
(j) Export operations.

The incubators facilitate business creation and assist entrepreneurs until their "graduation," when they have the capacity to "survive" in the external competitive environment (ESCAP, 2004). Incubators provide local, on the-spot diagnosis and treatment of business problems in addition to facilitating access to capital, thus dramatically lowering the early stage failure rate and enhance their performance (NBIA, 2009). Figure VI.4 illustrates the objectives and framework of incubation programmes.

Access to basic infrastructure such as office space and equipment at lower than market rental rates is essential, especially for start-ups and technologically-driven SMEs.

Figure VI.4. Objectives of incubators[95]

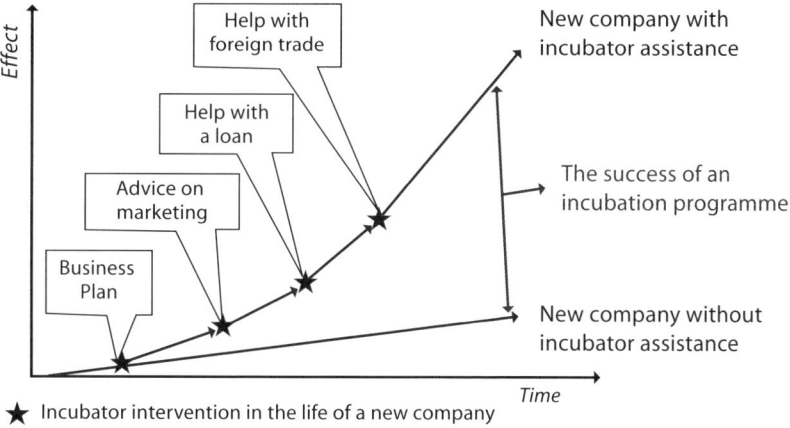

Source: NBIA, 2009.

---

[94] Proposed by the authors, based on Smilor and Gill, 1986.
[95] Refer to annex IX.1 on monitoring and evaluation, particularly the standard for results measurement that was proposed by the Donor Committee for Enterprise Development.

Box VI.4. Tianjin women's business incubator

China has worked extensively in the area of business and technology incubation. An example of a successful project is the Tianjin women's business incubator (TWBI) based in China's third-largest city. TWBI is a non-profit organization focused on assisting female entrepreneurs and fostering growth in the employment of women. Established in 2000 with financial assistance from the Tianjin Municipal Government, the Tianjin Women's Federation and other local government authorities, TWBI was China's first female-focused business incubator. Entrepreneurs received low-rent facilities, technical assistance, consultancies and training, including business plan development. TWBI also facilitates an on-site, micro-credit programme, which receives seed funding from UNDP and the Tianjin authorities. Incubator managers of TWBI have travelled abroad extensively to learn from other advanced incubators, and draw extensively on the National Business Incubator Association website for information.[96]

TWBI currently has a building area of 5,000 m^2 with 54 on-site and 16 off-site tenants. By the end of 2011, TWBI had graduated 29 companies. Directly and indirectly, TWBI has been responsible for providing employment opportunities for an estimated 2,000 people, which may be more than the opportunities generated by comparable incubators in developed countries. Operating at full capacity, TWBI has almost developed financial self-sufficiency by charging for office rent, business services and external training courses for participating entrepreneurs.

Source: Tianjin Women's Business Incubator, undated.

Box VI.5. Supply chains, SMEs and business development services

SMEs can join regional or global supply chains as second- or third-tier suppliers. They are typically more closely tied to a small number of business buyers, who are often large enterprises, including TNCs. SMEs are able to gain access to new knowledge on design, processes and control mechanisms, together with market intelligence from large enterprises in these chains. BDS can assist SMEs in joining supply chains by specifically focusing on SMEs' role as providers of goods and services for large enterprises. These services should target SMEs (to assist their capacity upgrading directly) and large firms (incentives and promotional activities for SMEs) in order to create mutually positive relationships. In particular, these would focus selectively on activities that can enhance the demand for SMEs' products and services by large enterprises, and can initiate interactions between these potential buyers and SMEs. These BDS could include contract negotiation, adaptation of production facilities and equipment, technical training and supplier networking (ADB, 2006). After successful linkage into supply chains has been established, additional BDS services can be provided commercially, including technical support and production supervision.

Shared services and experiences for business plan development, marketing, access to financing and international business also drive down the cost of starting and running a business, at both the initial and the growth stages.

Incubators typically operate with combined incomes of rents, service fees and public grants or subsidies (NBIA, 2009). The key success factors of a business and technology incubator includes:

(a) Attracting an adequate number of capable clients (e.g., growth-oriented or innovation-led entrepreneurs) through screening processes;

(b) Networking with input providers (e.g., research institutions, investors, consultants, accountants and local governments);

(c) Providing comprehensive services with discount rates (public sector support is needed);

(d) Providing clear policies and procedures for programme milestones and graduation;

(e) Developing and implementing a specific and clear business plan for the incubator itself under professional management; and

(f) Securing financial support from the public sector.

Although the concept of incubators is currently only operational in selected locations in the Asia-Pacific countries (e.g., East Asia and South-East Asia), its potential could be further realized by setting up additional incubators in universities to nurture knowledge-based enterprises. As BDS is still weak in the developing countries in the Asia-Pacific region, incubator programmes have a larger role to play in developing complementary channels to provide necessary services to entrepreneurs (NBIA, 2009). Although situating incubators at universities is a common practice in developed nations through triangular cooperation among governments, business and academia, such cooperation is nascent in the developing countries of the region. Nurturing technological start-ups through incubation programmes also enhances global competitiveness of SMEs. International development agencies are playing an important role in providing vital inputs towards this purpose. In the Asia-Pacific region, ESCAP is facilitating the establishment of incubators in conjunction with national governments (ESCAP, 2007a).

Business and technology incubation programmes could be a more expensive option for the public sector than other SME development instruments. Despite the small coverage of potential clients, such programmes require the public sector's financial support in order to increase success rates. Some governments may find other policy options (e.g., market-oriented development of BDS providers, or a triangular alliance between government, industry and university) to be more cost-effective. A specific business model that ensures the long-term sustainability of the programme can make business and technology incubation more appealing.

---

[96] For additional information, visit the website of the National Business Incubator Association at www.nbia.org/.

F. Summary

This chapter began by describing the design and objectives of BDS: (a) the provision of non-financial services to SMEs; (b) support of SME promotion activities; and (c) facilitation of SMEs' acquisition of competitive advantages. The discussion differentiated between the operational, advisory and advocacy segments of BDS as well as between the traditional and market-oriented BDS approaches. The traditional approach features much more direct government intervention, while the latter relegates government to the role of facilitator and gives more scope to markets in allocating BDS.

Next, the principal BDS actors and the roles they play in supporting the SME sector were discussed. In addition to SMEs and BDS providers, there are also facilitators, donors and governments. Governments enable the legal and regulatory framework, provide physical and IT infrastructure, and link the other actors in myriad ways. BDS policy should focus upon improving these linkages. Boxes VI.1 and VI.2 explained the roles of SME development agencies, and provided specific examples in various countries of the region.

BDS occurs at the micro-, meso- and macro-levels. At the micro-level, the focus is on improvements within SMEs. Training, consultancy, technology development, access to markets and business linkages are the most common areas of BDS intervention. The meso-level builds the capacity of BDS providers to deliver their services more effectively and efficiently. Box VI.3 highlights how one type of BDS provider, business associations, can enrich their activities. The macro-level involves national and supranational agencies' efforts to upgrade SME skills. A key element of this effort, beyond the institutional factors discussed in the prior chapters, is the provision of business and technology incubation. The Tianjin Women's Business Incubator is an outstanding example of this policy (box VI.4.)

Key policy recommendations

Three recommendations for development support by policymakers to BDS providers are summarized below.

1. Develop public-private partnerships

In addressing the problems that SMEs are facing in developing the required capacities, governments, private institutions and NGOs should conduct benchmarking for the real effectiveness of BDS to assess impact through their PPPs. This would help in devising appropriate mechanisms for maximizing services rendered to SMEs to ensure that they continue to grow, develop and contribute to the national economic and social goals.

2. Create a suitable enabling environment for BDS and raise awareness

Taking into account the present situation of SMEs, service providers should first create awareness among SMEs about the problems they face, with particular focus on professionalism, and product and market diversification. Furthermore, existing institutional infrastructures should be strengthened and new ones created as needed. Necessary resources, such as technical infrastructure, access to information and management training, should also be provided to SMEs. SME-related NGOs, such as chambers of commerce, have a key role to play in resource development.

3. Allow private sector service providers to give a kick-start to BDS

BDS providers should initiate new services, programmes and training sessions as widely as possible in order to provide diversified and comprehensive development services to SMEs. These initiatives should focus on supporting start-ups and facilitate the growth of already running businesses as well as help to avoid prolonged dependency on government subsidies.

CHAPTER VII
Innovation and technology

Innovation is an essential process of change that is necessary in order to maintain the development and growth of an enterprise (Drucker, 2008). Innovation is defined as the ability of an enterprises to "manage knowledge creatively in response to market-articulated demand and/or other social needs" (OECD, 1999). Innovation plays a pivotal role in economic progress by increasing enterprise competitiveness in the global market place.

New scientific and technological advances have created evolutions in innovation processes, and technology is a primary enabler of innovations in enterprises. While market demand orients the market, it requires the integration of research with manufacturing, technology with production, and both research and technology with customers and suppliers.

SMEs are a key driving force of the modern market economy due to their multifaceted approach to innovation.[97] SMEs have amply proved that they can be cradles of major innovations, some of which famously originated in garages. To maintain SMEs' innovation capability requires the promotion of R&D and successful commercialization of technology. However, SMEs are not homogenous in terms of their technological and business attributes. Different SMEs need to have different strategies for enhancing their innovation capability. Policymakers must recognize that in reality very few SMEs go from "garages to riches"; stories like the rise of Apple and Microsoft are true outliers.

provided. These best practices occur in the larger context of national competitiveness, where policymakers can take a holistic approach to human resource development, technology acquisition, science parks and business incubators.

A. Innovation status at the regional level

Three international surveys are examined in this section in order to assess the status of innovation capability in the Asia-Pacific region. The surveys are the Boston Consulting Group (BCG) (2009) International Rankings of Innovation Capability, the INSEAD (2011) Global Innovation Index, and the WEF (2010) Global Competitiveness Report (table VII.1).

The BCG International Rankings of Innovation Capability, produced jointly by BCG, the United States Manufacturing Institute and the United States National Association of Manufacturers, measures the levels of innovation in 110 countries and ranks them with a score calculated from their innovation inputs, including government ability to support innovation through policies and the performance of business innovation. Upper level metrics were calculated by assigning weights to each of the component elements, based on a poll of expert practitioners, scores of innovation inputs and performance (BCG, 2009).

The INSEAD GII (Global Innovation Index), the most recognized global index on innovation capabilities, is computed from an

Table VII.1. Innovation capabilities by region[98]

Region	BCG (2009)		INSEAD (2011)		WEF (2010)	
	Score	Rank (out of 110)	Score (out of 100)	Rank (out of 125)	Score (out of 7)	Rank (out of 139)
East and North-East Asia	1.15	26.20	48.53	27.40	4.08	33.20
South-East Asia	0.59	38.20	36.35	65.43	3.20	60.14
South and South-West Asia	-0.52	71.00	30.76	82.20	2.97	85.00
North and Central Asia	-0.54	70.80	30.64	81.43	3.03	82.86
Developed economies	1.19	19.00	51.32	18.67	4.60	13.33

Sources: BCG, 2009; INSEAD, 2011; and WEF, 2010.

In this chapter, the relationship between innovation, technology and SMEs in the Asia-Pacific region is discussed. It starts with innovation capability at the regional level followed by the advantages of innovation and its attainment at the SME level. Policy priorities to enhance innovation are also discussed. The chapter then moves on to describe several strategies for enhancing innovation by SMEs, including R&D, technology acquisition and transfer, technology commercialization, national innovation system and others. Some of the common obstacles to greater innovation among SMEs are considered, and some examples of best practices in the region are

average of scores across input pillars, which describe the enabling environment for innovation, and output pillars that measure actual achievements in innovation. The normalized score of each country ranges from zero to 100 (INSEAD, 2011).

WEF's Global Competitiveness Report ranks the overall competitiveness of countries through 12 indicators, ranging from infrastructure status to labour market efficiency. The capacity for innovation pillar is calculated from the scores of seven sub-metrics: (a) capacity for innovation; (b) quality of scientific research institutions; (c) company spending on R&D; (d) university-industry collaboration in R&D; (e) government procurement of advanced technology products; (f) availability of scientists and engineers; and (g) utility patents. The final

---
[97] For examples see JSBRI, 2009.
[98] Nations in the Pacific were not included due to the lack of data to give a comprehensive overview.

normalized score ranges from one to seven – a country with companies obtaining technology by conducting formal research, and pioneering their own new products and processes is given the score of seven. A score of one represents a nation with companies obtaining technology exclusively through licensing or imitating foreign companies (WEF, 2010).

Within the Asia-Pacific region, nations with the most innovative capacities are the advanced economies of Singapore; the Republic of Korea; Hong Kong, China; New Zealand; Australia; and Japan. At the regional level, East and North-East Asia is the most innovative (score of 7.1). It is worth noting that the overall level of innovation for these economies is approaching that of developed countries, with the contributions of several outstanding performers, e.g., the Republic of Korea and Hong Kong, China as well as rapidly developing China, as reflected by the INSEAD Index. South-East Asia is the second most innovative region, followed by South and South-West Asia, and North and Central Asia. These rankings also correspond to the relative differences seen in regional socio-economic development levels, particularly criteria such as educational achievement and entrepreneurial development.

B. Why is innovation important for SMEs?

Enterprises innovate either to lower production costs or to create demand for their products or services. At the same time, the pressure to innovate stems from inter-linkages and spillovers from suppliers of inputs or capital goods, competitors, government, customers, consultants and other technology suppliers. The relative importance of these different influences varies by industry and firm size.

Successful companies that are able to foresee changes in the marketplace and shifts in customer preferences are those who lead the advance of technology and new ventures. The ability to innovate is not necessarily coupled with huge investments and advanced technologies, regardless of the size of businesses, but is considered more as a mind-set able to view changes as opportunities. As such, being flexible and open to change (i.e., by incorporating systematic innovations into their daily operations) can be a vital advantage for SMEs in competing against larger enterprises (Drucker, 2008).

As the global marketplace is rapidly changing, marketing of innovative products and services has become of paramount importance for SMEs. Consumers today are brand-aware, technology-ready and quality-conscious. All of these forces pressure SMEs to be innovative, develop better products, improve their processes and speed up their product delivery timeframes (OECD, 2005a).

Within this context, OECD (2005a) has identified four key components of innovations:

(a) Product innovation – the introduction of goods or services that are new or substantially improved;

(b) Process innovation – the introduction of a new or significantly improved production or delivery method;

(c) Marketing innovation – the implementation of a new marketing method involving significant changes in product design or packaging, product promotion or pricing; and

(d) Organizational innovation – the creation or alteration of business practices, workplace organization or external relations.

Product innovation and process innovation are the two most commonly discussed types in economic literature. These two terms have been used to characterize the occurrence of new or improved goods and services, and improvements in the ways to produce goods and services, respectively (Schmookler, 1966). The distinction between the two concepts is fairly obvious at the level of individual firms or industries; however, it can be ambiguous when examined in terms of the overall economy, because the product of one firm (or industry) may end up being used to produce goods or services in another (Fagerberg, 2006).

Another important type is organizational innovation, which involves developing new ways to organize production and distribution (Fagerberg, 2006). This term describes innovation not only within a given firm but also between firms, such as the reorganization of entire industries (Schumpeter, 1934). In addition, marketing innovation has been defined as the implementation of a new marketing method involving significant changes in product design or packaging, product placement, product promotion or pricing (OECD, 2005b).

Components of innovations can be also categorized into two groups: incremental versus radical innovations (Abernathy, 1978; and Porter, 1986).[99] Incremental innovation involves modest changes in existing knowledge and resources or the existing products and services in the market. In contrast, radical innovation involves the development of new businesses or product lines, based on entirely new ideas or technologies (Leifer, 2000). Among different audiences, e.g., engineers, product managers and marketers, the terms "radical" and "incremental" may mean different things (Garcia and Calantone, 2002), but the basic definitions given above should suffice for policymakers. It is notable that incremental innovation may generate great cumulative impact in the long term on the economy and society, even though the radical innovation may have bigger immediate effect (Lundvall, 1992). While policymakers may wish to promote radical innovation due to its high return, incremental innovation dominates the market. An overview of innovation is provided in figure VII.1.

Most SMEs in the developing economies of Asia and the Pacific are struggling to build their innovation capabilities. Compared to larger enterprises SMEs are still more likely to use mature technologies, possess limited technical skills, and lack information about markets and technology (ADB, 2009). Governments have tried to help SMEs move from engagement in traditional, low-productivity activities to more modern and higher productivity ones, through holistic approaches, including education policy and technical and

---

[99] This categorization has been also called incremental versus breakthrough innovations (Tushman and Anderson, 1986) and conservative versus radical innovations (Abernathy and Clark, 1985).

Box VII.1. Opportunities for SMEs through strengthening innovation capabilities: The case of Viet Nam

Viet Nam has undertaken a number of smaller-scale energy generation projects using renewable sources, such as solar water heaters, biomass, and small hydro and wind energy systems. Viet Nam also shows some capacity for manufacturing micro-, hydro- and wind-energy technologies; however, these are underdeveloped and have yet to be applied to large-scale manufacturing.

Renewable energy technologies could provide a significant business opportunity for Vietnamese SMEs by enhancing present research and manufacturing capacities in order to fulfill domestic needs. It also reveals opportunities for Viet Nam to cooperate with neighbouring countries on scaling up the use of renewable energy, especially small-scale technologies, to supply energy to rural areas. For example, Viet Nam can share with Cambodia and the Lao People's Democratic Republic the technologies for the development of rural electrification. This type of cooperation could be supported by international aid agencies, for example, through advanced market commitments to helping to create a new and feasible market for Vietnamese renewable energy technologies in the two neighbouring countries (and others).

Source: Baumuller, 2010.

Figure VII.1. Overview of innovation

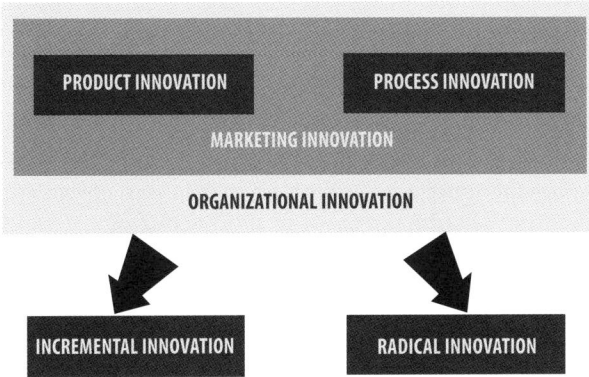

Source: Authors' compilation.

vocational training, formation of science parks, and technology incubation and acquisition (OECD, 2005a).

C. Capacity of SMEs to innovate

Despite popular accounts of high-tech entrepreneurs, the general truth is that most SMEs possess inherent traits that may weaken their innovation capabilities and hinder technological advancement. These include:

(a) Key decisions being taken by individuals, owners or a small group;
(b) Dependence on people rather than processes;
(c) Valuing short-term gains over long-term vision;
(d) Dominant focus on cost cutting and getting more for less; and
(e) Low or no investment in R&D.

Characteristic (e) is not only specific to SMEs. Asia-Pacific businesses, big and small, tend to spend less on R&D than firms in other regions.

Table VII.2 illustrates the proportion of manufacturing enterprises in East and South-East Asia and in South Asia that undertook different innovative activities that are positively related to the size of enterprises. Large enterprises are more active in innovative activities than SMEs in Asia, perhaps due to SMEs' disadvantaged positions in access to financing, volume of outputs, and economies-of-scale, thus leading to less available funds for R&D (ADB, 2009). Also, it is evident that of the three forms of innovative activities (i.e., new product development, upgrading of existing products and new ways of production), enterprises approach innovation mainly through developing a new product line or upgrading an existing product line. Although both Asian subregions show a similar trend, enterprises in South Asia focus more on new product development and upgrading of existing products than their counterparts in East and South-East Asia.

Innovation has to be considered as a central strategy, and must be embedded in the organization and its management. It should be practical enough to be integrated into the existing enterprise systems and implemented as entrepreneurial strategies outside the organization (i.e., in the market place) (Drucker, 2008). There are three key factors involved in successfully achieving innovation: (a) entrepreneurial management; (b) entrepreneurial strategies; and (c) windows of opportunities. Key general recommendations for fostering innovation in SMEs are listed below.

(a) Entrepreneurial management:
 (i) Incorporate entrepreneurship into existing businesses and daily operations (within the organization);

Table VII.2. Asian enterprises that have undertaken innovative activities, by size of firm

(Unit: Per cent)

	East and South-East Asia			South Asia		
	Small	Medium	Large	Small	Medium	Large
Developed a major new product line	32.4	45.6	56.9	36.2	49.3	60.8
Upgraded an existing product line	53.4	63.3	72.2	58.3	70.9	75.4
Introduced new technology that has substantially changed the way that the main product is produced	27.0	41.3	54.3	12.9	25.9	37.3

Source: ADB, 2009.

(ii) Encourage people to be innovative and entrepreneurial by using proper rewards, incentives, and policies;

(iii) Separate entrepreneurship from the existing operations, and create a special location for the new venture. Never make an existing unit the carrier of any entrepreneurial project; and

(iv) Innovations should stem from fields of existing business, since taking innovation out of the organization's own field usually ends up with failures.

In addition, innovation as a "new venture" should be practical and able to be developed into a new business (within the organization) by:

(i) Focusing on the target market;

(ii) Focusing on financial foresight and implementing the right financial policies to support innovation; and

(iii) Building a top management team to manage the process of promoting any new products or services.

(b) Entrepreneurial strategies:

(i) Choosing the right entrepreneurial strategies that fit certain innovations in the market place and maintain the success of the innovation (outside the organization). For example, even though an innovation has the potential to generate high profit from high-end markets, entering the mass market with a low-cost product first would be a better strategy if the company is not mature or if there is more competition in the high-end market. This strategy was widely used by Japanese companies for their entry into the United States market in the 1960s and the 1970s (Drucker, 1985).[100]

(c) Windows of opportunity:

(i) Developing a policy of systematic innovation, analyze changes within and outside organizations at regular intervals and identifying whether there is any opportunity for innovation; and

(ii) Being aware of any unexpected success and unexpected failures within the enterprise – incongruities in daily operation, changes in industry and market structures – and if there is a need for change, there may possibly be opportunities to innovate (within and outside the organization).

---

[100] Most companies in the United States at that time saw high profitability as their greatest strength and focused on the high-end of the market, leaving the mass market undersupplied and underserviced. Japanese companies moved in with low-cost products that had minimum features and which quickly gave them a presence in the United States market. Because the Japanese had taken over the mass market, they soon had the cash flow to move in on the high-end market. As a result, Japanese companies dominated both high-end and mass markets within a short period (Drucker, 1985).

The survival of SMEs in an increasingly competitive environment has led to greater emphasis on improving the innovation process from conception through to design, development and launch. SMEs can learn during the innovation process and hopefully improve the chances of a successful product or service launch. After a new product or service has been launched, lessons learnt during that project can be applied to subsequent projects. Both intra- and inter-project learning activities can occur and will help improve the innovation processes. If this is done on an ongoing basis, then an SME will exhibit continuous improvement in its innovation processes (Terziovski, Sohal and Howell, 2002).

Finally, policymakers have to ensure that innovations are protected so that SMEs can profit from them. Intellectual property rights in the region need to be strengthened, with special attention being given to SMEs' greater access to proper technologies and the ability to use them.

D. Policy priorities to enhance innovation

Technological advancement is the primary basis for the whole innovation process. As technological followers, developing countries should aim to close the "technological gaps" between themselves and developed countries. Governments can positively influence the acquisition of foreign technology through attractive FDI policies, foreign licensing regulations, intellectual property rights regimes and the acquisition of technologies for state enterprises (Feinson, 2003). Governments also have the responsibility to improve the absorptive capacity of local SMEs by fostering human and social capital needs to evaluate, select, implement and modify foreign technologies (Ferretti and Parmentola, 2010).

Policymakers need to analyze why SMEs do not approach technology upgrading as well as commercialization of their innovative ideas with adequate investment. For SMEs, R&D and commercialization of its results are often difficult. SMEs often do not have the knowledge or funds to engage in these innovation activities. To help address this shortcoming, policymakers can invest in improving local and national education and training programmes (OECD, 2000). Since it is generally beyond the reach of small businesses to conduct in-house training, public support for basic education, financial assistance for SME training, and greater co-operation and exchanges between business and universities are valuable strategies for increasing internal innovation abilities (OECD, 2000). With regard to financial challenges, the introduction of supportive tax incentives, can be effective in allowing SMEs to engage in innovative activities with confidence. This issue is considered in greater detail later in this chapter.

It is important to emphasize that financial policy strategies need to involve more than throwing capital at SMEs (OECD, 2004b). The most effective and sustainable financing strategy for SME innovation is to facilitate the fusion of entrepreneurship and finance so that investors are actively involved from the early stages of innovation development. Consequently, traditional policy tools – taxation, subsidies and regulation – are not necessarily always the only appropriate approach (OECD, 2004b).

> **Box VII.2. SME policies for building technological capacity in the Republic of Korea**
>
> In the Republic of Korea, a great deal of effort has been put into improving the technological capacity of SMEs. Four major policy initiatives launched by the Government, including SMBA, for SME technology capacity-building are briefly described below.
>
> **1. Build innovation capacity and promote technology commercialization**
>
> The Inno-Biz programme, a technology innovation certification system, was designed to improve innovation in manufacturing SMEs with proven technology and innovation capabilities (up to ten per cent of all manufacturing SMEs) by providing incentives, e.g., preferential low interest loans, funding and diverse government support programmes. Relevant government ministries and institutions are also required to allot a certain percentage of their R&D budget to support SMEs. In an effort to prevent superior technologies from remaining unused, the Government has also subsidized the cost of facility investment and raw materials required for commercialization of new technologies.
>
> **2. Facilitate the exchange of information and knowledge**
>
> Various policy measures have been taken to reinforce networking among enterprises or between industries, including training with universities and research institutes.
>
> **3. Bridge the financing gap for innovation**
>
> SMBA's direct and indirect SME financing programmes are focused on helping innovative entrepreneurs to set up or expand operations, develop new products and invest in new skilled staff or production facilities. The scope of tax deduction has also expanded to cover the costs of R&D, human resource development and welfare facilities investment of SMEs.
>
> **4. Develop pool of skilled human resources**
>
> SMBA places high priority on human resource development as the engine of SME competitiveness and creativity. It offers a number of measures to improve the quality of labour in SMEs. Its on-site work conditions improvement programme aims to encourage the inflow of skilled workers into SMEs through the development and diffusion of needed equipment aimed at alleviating adverse conditions such as heat, dust, odour and noise at production sites. Additionally, employees who work for SMEs longer than five years are granted the right to purchase public housing ahead of others. In order to change the way that young people perceive SMEs, and to foster friendly ties between college students and SMEs, SMBA has also initiated collegian SMEs experience and the youth employment programmes.
>
> *Sources:* Small and Medium Business Administration, 2011; and ESCAP, 2007a.

Another policy priority is to facilitate the exchange of information and knowledge in order to create positive spillover effects and technology diffusion throughout the country. In this regard, a uniform standard for quality control can help to promote the convergence of technology levels, to counteract the wide disparity of technologies and efficiencies present within the same industry. Governments can also help in the establishment of formal or informal networks to improve technology spillover, for example, through national innovation systems (Feinson, 2003). Research grant programmes that help research institutes and private enterprises forge research arrangements and partnerships are also useful for enhancing the commercialization of research findings.

E. Key strategies for the development of SME innovation

This section elaborates on some of the key strategies and relevant issues that shape the development of SME innovation: R&D; technology acquisition and transfer; technology commercialization; national innovation system; open innovation; reverse engineering; intellectual property rights; and tax incentives. This section concludes with some observations about key obstacles to innovation and determinants of innovation failure and success.

1. Research and development

According to an OECD (2002a) definition, R&D "comprises creative work undertaken on a systemic basis in order to increase the stock of knowledge, including knowledge of man, culture and society, and the use of this stock of knowledge to devise new applications". The term generally refers to three interrelated activities: (a) basic research; (b) applied research; and (c) experimental development. Basic research is theoretical or experimental work that is aimed at acquiring new knowledge of observable facts and phenomena, without explicitly defined applications or uses. Applied research is similar but directed towards a specific practical objective. Experimental development is the use of knowledge gained from research to produce or improve materials, products, processes and services (OECD, 2002a). Basic research can lead to more targeted applied research that feeds into experimental development. Furthermore, experimental development can raise new theories and hypotheses that form new questions for basic or applied research (figure VII.2).

Figure VII.2. Interrelationships among basic research, applied research and experimental development

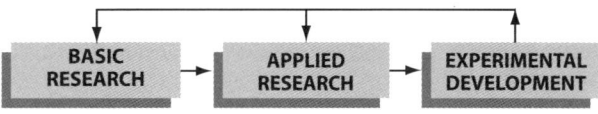

Source: Malaysian Science and Technology Information Centre, 1998.

R&D spending as a percentage of GDP is a good indication of the relative importance of R&D in a national economy. Advanced industrial countries spend between 1 per cent and 3 per cent of their GDP on R&D, 50 to 80 per cent of which is contributed by the industry. Less industrialized countries generally spend between 0.1 per cent and 1 per cent, and the capabilities of the Asia-Pacific developing countries differ widely (World Bank, 2011d). According to the World Bank Development Indicators, Japan (3.4 per cent) and the Republic of Korea (3.2 per cent) top the region, followed by

Singapore (2.5 per cent). Developing countries in Asia and the Pacific, such as Tajikistan, Mongolia, Pakistan and India, spend less than 1 per cent, with the exception of China at 1.4 per cent (World Bank, 2011d). Table VII.3 lists national investment in R&D, as measured by TNC expenditures.[101]

Table VII.3. Trend in R&D spending, by country, 2007[102]

Country	Per cent of GDP
Tajikistan	0.06
Azerbaijan	0.17
Kazakhstan	0.21
Armenia	0.21
Mongolia	0.23
Kyrgyzstan	0.23
Pakistan	0.67
India	0.80
Russian Federation	1.12
China	1.44
Singapore	2.52
Republic of Korea	3.21
Japan	3.44

Source: World Bank, 2011d.

In terms of per capita, Singapore has the highest expenditure, followed by Japan and the Republic of Korea (ESCAP, 2011b) (figure VII.3). Government policies and initiatives in the region have a significant impact on the R&D environment. For example, the Government of Singapore has allocated S$16.1 billion for research, innovation and enterprise for 2011-2016, which is a 20 per cent increase from the previous period (Channel NewsAsia, 2010).

In the Asia-Pacific region, enterprise R&D, both private and state-owned, has shown positive movement in the recent years. Figure VII.4 highlights the fact that enterprise R&D as a percentage of total R&D grew the most significantly in Asian developing economies, between 1996 and 2002. More recently, available data indicates that R&D expenditure has increased in Asia from 27 per cent to 32 per cent of the global share (UNESCO Institute of Statistics, 2011).

In the Asia-Pacific region, government R&D institutes, universities and large firms undertake much of the R&D expenditure in many developing countries. SMEs spend very

---

[101] TNCs, which are responsible for a large share of global R&D, have been relocating their R&D activities in developing countries for a number of reasons, such as access to inexpensive talent and new markets (UNCTAD, 2005b). This trend is particularly evident in the Asia-Pacific region where enterprise R&D, both private and state-owned, has shown positive movement in recent years.

[102] It is clear that developed countries hold a significant advantage in innovation and technology development, although table VII.3 does not tell the whole story. Firms in the Asia-Pacific region are innovating. Even leaving aside the more developed economies of the Republic of Korea, Singapore and Taiwan Province of China, R&D by large enterprises in some lower income Asia-Pacific countries are on the rise especially in sectors such as pharmaceuticals, machinery and transportation equipment (e.g., Bangladesh, China and India) (ADB, 2009). For the most part, however, they do not innovate in the same way as firms in developed countries. Developing country firms are not pushing the frontiers of technology; instead, their innovations consist of introducing modified products and processes nationally, or even subnationally, and are mostly application-oriented (ADB, 2009).

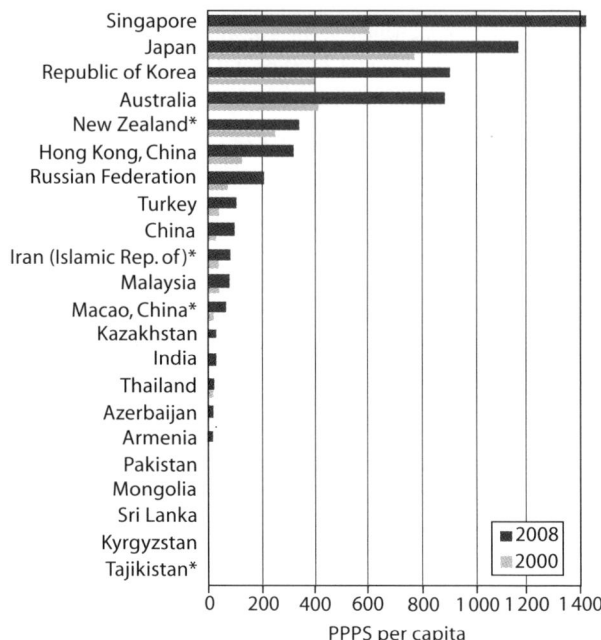

Figure VII.3. Gross domestic expenditure on research and development in Asia and the Pacific (purchasing power parity dollars per capita)[103]

Source: ESCAP, 2011b.
* indicates that the data refer to 2001

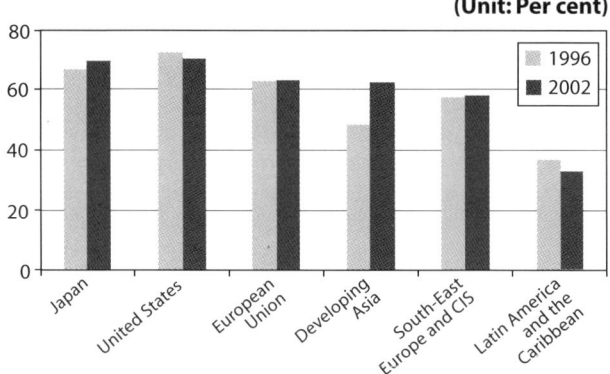

Figure VII.4. Share of enterprise R&D in total R&D by country/region, 1996 and 2002

Source: UNCTAD, 2005c.
Note: Asian developing economies include: China; Hong Kong, China; India; Malaysia; Mongolia; Nepal; Pakistan; Philippines; Republic of Korea; Saudi Arabia; Singapore; Sri Lanka; Taiwan Province of China; Thailand; Turkey; and United Arab Emirates.

little due to lack of skills or lack of funds. R&D policies targeted specifically at SMEs are especially important, as insufficient attention has been paid to the benefits of this strategy to increase innovation and competitiveness. While it is beyond the abilities of SMEs to invest in R&D on a scale comparable to government institutes, universities and larger firms, R&D can be simple, affordable and effective for small businesses.

SMEs generally do not engage in R&D due to funding constraints; however, options exist for overcoming this

---

[103] Purchasing power parities are the rates of currency conversion that equalize the purchasing power of different currencies. They show the ratio of prices in national currencies for the same product or service in different countries for easy comparison (OECD, 2012).

barrier. Funding for R&D can come from internal budgets or government assistance such as grants, subsidies, loan guarantees and tax breaks (Kao and Liang, 2001). If an entrepreneur develops a new product to a stage that entices potential investors, venture capitalists could make funds available for production and marketing. Another important strategy for small businesses is to develop personnel creativity by providing a supportive environment for exchanging ideas and experiments (Kao and Liang, 2001). R&D activities are more challenging for small businesses; however, the benefits justify investing time and funds.

2. Technology acquisition and transfer

Technology acquisition and transfer refers to the process of movement of technology from one entity to another. This process may be considered as successful if the receiving entity (the transferee) can effectively utilize the technology transferred and eventually assimilate it. The strategies for this process involve licensing, R&D contracting, physical assets purchasing, learning know-how and attracting qualified personnel.

There is a negative correlation between R&D intensity – the amount of money spent on R&D and the number of R&D activities – and technology acquisition and transfer (Hall, 1987), possibly because firms are choosing between an internal development strategy with relatively high R&D intensity versus an external development strategy from acquiring technology. However, the success of technology acquisition and transfer is closely related to internal innovation capabilities in two ways. First, the research capability of a firm allows it to make better scans of the environment for relevant external technology sources. Second, its internal research capability increases its absorptive capacity and improves the integration of external knowledge into the production process (Cassiman and Veugelers, 2000).

As table VII.4 shows, technology acquisition and transfer is a major way of technological innovation for both SMEs and large firms in the region. The sources that are perceived as most important for technological innovations include new machinery or equipment, development within the establishment locally and hiring key personnel. In fact, high-performing Asia-Pacific economies have benefited from technology acquisition and transfer over the past few decades. The Republic of Korea, like Japan, initially acquired technology through trade, copying, reverse engineering and technology licensing before domestic R&D was promoted. Singapore and Hong Kong, China relied mostly on foreign trade and FDI for access to knowledge and technology. Indonesia, Malaysia, Thailand and Viet Nam adopted export-focused technology transfer. China has collated all these approaches and applied them at different stages of its development (Dahlman, 2007).

Although technology transfer has enjoyed much visibility and praise in recent decades for its contribution to economic growth in the region, SMEs in some countries have difficulty in taking full advantage of its benefits. As SMEs play a central role in the development and industrialization process in the Asia-Pacific region, there are clear social and economic advantages to promoting technology transfer among them. Advanced manufacturing technologies can provide an SME

Table VII.4. Important sources of technological innovations

Per cent agreeing the factors below are important	East and North-East Asia and South-East Asia				South Asia			
	Small	Medium	Large	All	Small	Medium	Large	All
Embodied in new machinery or equipment	48	49	46	47	26	35	50	36
By hiring key personnel	11	8	8	9	13	15	14	14
Licensing or turnkey operations from international sources	1	2	3	2	2	2	2	2
Licensing or turnkey operations from domestic sources	1	1	1	1	5	3	1	3
Developed or adapted within the establishment locally	13	11	9	11	21	15	7	15
Transferred from the parent company	2	6	12	7	2	2	3	2
Developed in cooperation with clients	11	11	11	11	13	14	11	13
Developed with equipment or machinery suppliers	6	7	7	7	1	3	4	3
From a business or industry association	2	3	2	2	5	1	2	3
Trade fairs and/or study tours	2	1	0	1	8	7	4	7
Consultants	2	1	1	1	3	2	2	3
From universities, public institutions	0	1	0	0	0	0	0	0

Source: Authors' estimates, based on the World Bank Enterprise Survey data (various years).
Notes: East and North-East Asia and South-East Asia include Cambodia, China, Indonesia, the Lao People's Democratic Republic, Malaysia, the Philippines, Republic of Korea, Thailand and Viet Nam. South Asia includes Bangladesh, India, Pakistan and Sri Lanka.

with techniques and tools to simultaneously lower costs, increase quality and speed, and thus make the firm more competitive in the global marketplace (Yusuff, Hashmi and Chek, 2005).

The domestic context of particular countries is important with regard to the level of technology transfer, as weak institutional structures and lack of supportive policies and regulations can seriously hinder the uptake and dissemination of technological knowledge and practices (McCauley, 2009). Additionally, direct government intervention may also be needed to strengthen the capacity of SMEs to plan and implement technology transfer initiatives and to reduce the cost of such initiatives. Table VII.5 lists five main aspects of market failure, its corresponding policy implications and the required governance capabilities, which provides a general framework when developing relevant policies for technology acquisition and transfer.

In recent years, governments have taken an increasingly active role in facilitating technology acquisition by, and transfer to, SMEs in Asia and the Pacific. For example, the Government of Malaysia has committed to helping local businesses obtain foreign technology by allowing them to apply for public funds to buy foreign intellectual properties and technologies (Van Renssen, 2005). Similarly, the Government of the Philippines enacted the Philippine Technology Transfer Act of 2009 to help transfer knowledge out of laboratories to SMEs for commercialization by making R&D institutions and universities the default owner of intellectual property rights resulting from government-funded research (Ilano, 2010).

Table VII.5. Market failures constraining technology acquisition: Implications for government capabilities

Market failure constraining technology acquisition and learning	Policy implications	Required (growth-enhancing) governance capabilities
Trained personnel can easily leave the firm.	Public investment, along with private financing, in the training of new workers or existing workers in new sectors may be required.	Requires subsidies/financing targeted at start-up companies who take on previously unemployed and untrained workers
Innovation companies avoid investing or training in developing countries.	Promote the incentives for TNCs to transfer technologies to create backward and forward linkages with domestic suppliers.	Requires proper identification of potential linkages.
Start-ups discovering new areas of national competence lose rents rapidly.	Subsidize start-up companies with thorough consideration of specific technological effects and market situations.	Develop public-private partnerships to invest in discovery; develop capability to stop subsidies beyond start-up period.
Coordination failure*	Investment subsidies or direct policy investments to push the coordination and tax incentives to encourage technology upgrade.	Significant governance capabilities required to coordinate and oversee investments across associated firms and sectors.
Investment in learning resulted in losses	Public and private financing of learning has to be accompanied with strict selection criteria of learners and the identification of investment aspects.	Policies must ensure high levels of effort in learning.

Source: Modified from Khan, 2009.
* Coordination failure occurs when technology improvements in one sector do not spill over into adjacent, complementary sectors, thus lowering potential profits.

Box VII.3. Strengthening SMEs through technology transfer capacity-building

One of the objectives of the ESCAP Asian and Pacific Centre for Transfer of Technology (APCTT), located in New Delhi, India, is to assist member countries of ESCAP strengthen their capacity to effectively plan and manage the transfer of technologies, particularly for SMEs. As part of this initiative, APCTT has developed a comprehensive web-based tool known as Technology4sme (www.technology4sme.net) that serves as an online technology market for SMEs and provides a free platform for technology buyers and seekers to interact with each other and explore possibilities of cooperation. The website, which has information on 905 technologies in 37 industrial sectors (580 technology offers, 294 technology requests, and 31 joint venture and partnership requests) attracts, on average, more than 1.2 million hits per year. In addition, APCTT has designed the Asia-Pacific Technology Information Tracking and Unified Data Extraction (APTITUDE) Search Engine. APTITUDE searches a list of specified technology databases available in the public domain in addition to technology for SME. Currently, 11 technology databases from a range of countries are linked to APTITUDE and more are scheduled to be added.

In addition to its web-based services, APCTT uses its networks in the region to support and strengthen technology intermediaries in member countries that assist SMEs to build technology partnerships. For example, in 2008, APCTT assisted Mind Branch Asia Pacific, Republic of Korea, to partner with the University of Manchester Intellectual Property Limited, United Kingdom, to gain access to useful technologies for SMEs. Another partnership was facilitated between the Vacuum Equipments Manufacturing Association of Japan and the Engineering Export Promotion Council of India to conduct joint technology exhibitions in Japan and India for the benefit of SMEs.

Box VII.3. *(continued)*

APCTT has also been providing similar support including business-to-business (B2B) meetings with the Nanjing International Technology Transfer Centre, China, the Institute of Information Technology Advancement, Republic of Korea, the Federation of Indian Chambers of Commerce and Industry, and the Foundation for Micro, Small and Medium Enterprises Clusters, India. At the firm level, APCTT has helped SMEs in China, India, Pakistan, Sri Lanka, and other economies to gain access to technologies from Romania, the Iran (Islamic Republic of) and India in areas such as the manufacturing of soda ash, polymers, textiles and animal feed.

APCTT has also developed a manual on *Planning and Implementing Technology Transfer Projects* that can be used to train trainers in member countries so that they can strengthen the capacity of SMEs to effectively implement technology transfer projects (APCTT, 2011).

Source: ESCAP, 2009b.

Box VII.4. APEC SME Innovation Centre

The APEC SME Innovation Centre (SMEIC), an organization facilitating SME innovation in the APEC region, was established in the Republic of Korea in 2006 under the Daegu Initiative. This organization has two major objectives: (a) to help APEC member economies exchange information on SME innovation; and (b) to establish cooperative networks for SME innovation among APEC member countries. In addition to SME innovation model development and innovation policy research, the centre has carried out a variety of activities including seminars, surveys, research and training as well as innovation promotion to facilitate cooperation in SME innovation among APEC member economies. Table VII.6 lists the main mid-term to long-term activities of SMEIC.

One of SMEIC's featured actions is the APEC SME Green Innovation Conference held in 2011. The conference brought together government officials from SME-related and energy ministries, and business representatives from innovative SMEs to (a) develop SME green growth strategies by sharing and discussing success cases and (b) further expand intra-APEC green collaboration.

Source: APEC SMEIC, 2012.

Table VII.6. APEC SME Innovation Centre mid-term to long-term plan

Stages	Foundation building	Diversification	Takeoff
Network building	Host innovation conferences; hold innovation workshops	Promote personnel exchange programmes	Build networks to conduct SMEIC's role as an innovation hub for SMEs
Information exchange	Update the SMEIC website; publish periodicals; publish commissioned studies	Implement Green Initiative projects; facilitate greater exchanges of policy and other information	Establish customized information exchange systems tailored to each member economy
Industrial cooperation	Build a foundation for industrial technology cooperation	Conduct industrial technology cooperation projects involving SMEs of APEC member economies	Expand SMEIC's unique projects designed to build the capabilities of SMEs

---

Box VII.5. Technology transfer through global supply chains

Many manufacturing TNCs disseminate technological and operational knowledge to local suppliers (often SMEs) or subsidiaries through their supply chains. These technology transfers can be achieved through various means – introduction of TNC products, licensing agreements, business process improvement, management methods and training of suppliers/workers – that provide skills and knowledge for local imitations (Dahlman, 2007). For SMEs, establishing links with large enterprises as suppliers and through subcontracting relationships can be an important way to acquire superior technology. SMEs generally fit into supply chains as peripheral suppliers to one or more links in the chain, usually as second- or third-tier (or even lower-tier) suppliers (ESCAP, 2007b). Through their participation in supply chains, SMEs have more chance to receive advanced technology together with technical and management training from upper-tier companies.

3. Technology commercialization

Technology commercialization is the process of bringing a technological discovery, i.e., new products, processes or services, into the commercial market (Jolly, 1997). It involves linking an organization's internal R&D capabilities to a worthwhile market opportunity (Markman, Siegel and Wright, 2008). It is also viewed as the final stage of a national innovation system (see next section) after viable human ideas are converted into a prototype or process and are ready to proceed to the pre-commercialization stage. Studies show that there is a strong linkage between an organization's competitiveness and its ability to commercialize technologies that provide the return on investment in research and development (Markman, Siegel and Wright, 2008; and Nevens, Summe and Uttal, 1990).

Successful technology commercialization requires a dynamic process from the creation of an idea to a successful market launch. As shown in figure VII.5, five sub-processes are involved:

(a) Imagining – commercialization starts at the idea stage. The first step for entrepreneurs is to associate the prospects for technology with potential market opportunity;

(b) Incubating – technology needs to be recognized as being commercially viable. It also requires foreseeing other products' future performance as well as estimating market opportunities and the time frame for a product's realization;

(c) Demonstrating – this involves product development, and requires that the technology fits the demands of customers and works in a marketable way. This may entail product adjustment through either expansion of research scope or making necessary compromises;

(d) Promoting – very few new technologies secure market acceptance, no matter how well conceived and demonstrated. An entrepreneur must tackle the promotional challenge to persuade people to adopt or create the infrastructure to deliver the technology's full benefit; and

(e) Sustaining – realizing the long-term value of the product requires constant marketing efforts.

The four bridges between these five steps are just as important in ensuring stakeholder satisfaction and mobilization of support at each step (Jolly, 1997). These four bridges involve:

(a) Interest and endorsement – this involves mobilizing interest among those whose support is necessary in forging a link between imaging an idea and assembling resources for the R&D phase;

(b) Resources for demonstration – this step is the transition from interest and encouragement to a commitment on the part of sponsors and supporters. It requires the mobilization of substantially larger amount of resources and cooperation of a greater number of actors both internally and outside a company;

(c) Market constituents – this bridge involves the acceptance of the product incorporating a new technology by the first set of customers, together with a host of market constituents. These constituents can include suppliers of complementary products and infrastructure, competitors, "lead users" and other third party players who are essential for any new technology to gain acceptance; and

(e) Complementary assets for delivery – the final bridge is the further spread of the technology in order to establish long-term presence and impact.

The first two bridges are generally connected with the problem of technology transfer while the latter two are more market-related. It is essential to manage these bridges effectively to ensure the success of a new technology in the marketplace.

Within this context, SMEs need to actively interact with academic and research institutions. Meanwhile, science and engineering colleges and research institutions could provide financial assistance for incubating new businesses with new technologies. Such incubation could be supported with technical consultation, workshops, laboratory support and linkages with other agencies for successfully launching new businesses and guiding entrepreneurs during the start-up phase. In developing countries this culture of cooperation needs to be actively fostered as collaboration between SMEs, universities and government R&D institutions is not common practice.

Figure VII.5. Process of technology commercialization

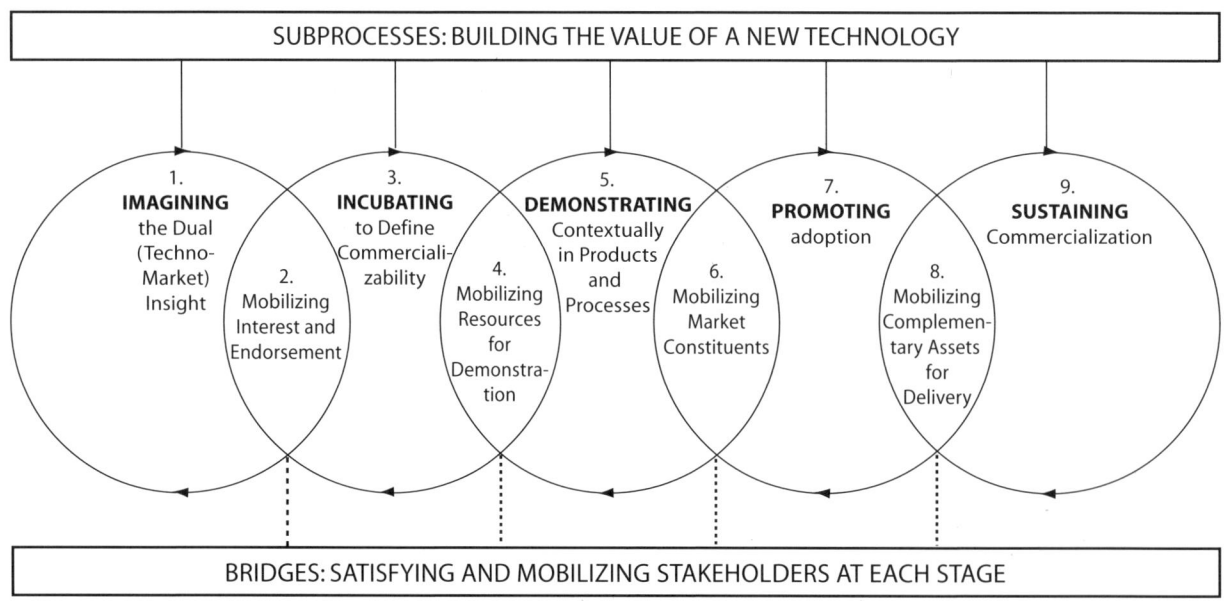

Source: Jolly, 1997.

4. National innovation system

A national innovation system (NIS) can foster cooperation among different stakeholders such as policymakers, research institutions and industry associations (Markman, Siegel and Wright, 2008). The NIS concept became popular in the early 1990s when the importance of science and technology was acknowledged within the context of an innovation system. Although new scientific discoveries and technology do not automatically lead to increased productivity, they remain closely connected with innovation: Without a certain level of technological know-how, the benefits of these technologies may not be fully realized. As such, in order to make new science and technology innovations tangible in the market, more participation and interactions are needed among stakeholders at the national (or subnational) level (ESCAP, 2007a).

Despite the existence of various interpretations and models for an NIS, almost all the definitions highlight the fact that the innovative performance of a country depends, to a large extent, on how different actors relate to each other as elements of a collective system of knowledge, technology creation and utilization (OECD, 1997). For example, Lundvall (1992) defined NIS as "the elements and relationships which interact in the production, diffusion and use of new and economically useful knowledge."

As depicted in figure VII.6, the inner circle shows a "narrow" NIS concept, which includes the institutions and policies directly involved in scientific and technological innovation. The outer circle shows a "broad" NIS perspective, which takes into account the economic, social and political environments of the country examined (see some similarity with the entrepreneurship model illustrated in figures IV.1 and IV.2 of chapter IV). The NIS interactions and linkages, which reflect the absorptive capacity of the system, are determined by the ways in which knowledge and resources flow between the narrow and broad levels, and among the institutions and organizations via both formal and informal routes (Feinson, 2003).[104]

On the other hand, the subnational innovation system (SIS) is a relatively new concept. It is a unit of the innovation system at the subnational level that comprises municipal or local governments, universities and industries – especially SMEs – within a certain public administrative boundary that has formal or informal networks among the actors, and produces innovation results (ESCAP, 2007a). Even though SIS has more locally-specific characteristics due to its geography, local culture and resources, it shares similar characteristics with NIS. Thus, SIS can be viewed as a lower-level innovation system of NIS or a reduced form of NIS. As such, the success of NIS can be determined by the success of SIS.

The importance of making and sustaining connections was demonstrated by a recent survey of manufacturing firms in Indonesia, the Philippines, Thailand and Viet Nam (Machikita, 2009). The survey collected data on the associations among the number and variety of linkages that a firm had and its innovation activity. Linkages, defined as the network with local firms, foreign firms and public organizations, can be broken down into three types:

(a) Production linkages – the connections with customers, suppliers and others through the labour market and the equipment supply chain;

---

[104] However, this comprehensive approach may not always work with less developed countries in the region without developing a well-targeted and manageable plan with reasonable resources in addition to postening trust and cooperation.

Figure VII.6. Actors and linkages in the innovation system

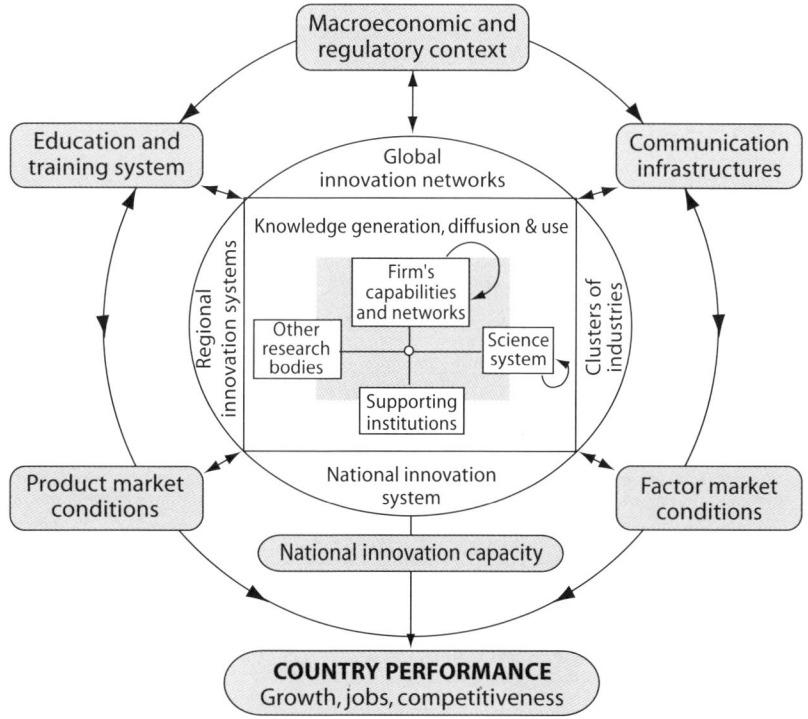

Source: OECD, 1999.

(b) Intellectual linkages – the connections with universities, research institutes, business organizations and public support agencies; and

(c) Firm's internal resources.

The survey results suggested that firms with more types of linkages tended to create more innovations (e.g., new product development, process improvement, organizational changes, and securing new customers and suppliers) than those with fewer types of linkages. Moreover, the number of different types of linkages (e.g., production, intellectual or internal resources) correlated with the variety of innovations. More internal resources also correlated with a higher variety of innovations (Machikita, 2009).

For developing countries in Asia and the Pacific, the role of government is important in the development of innovation systems because governments usually have the most resources and policy tools. Under the system concept of innovation, the primary objective of policy should be facilitating the positive interactions of different stakeholders and enhancing knowledge flows through active participation in the innovation process. With the close linkage between NIS and SIS, it is necessary to design the policy for NIS and SIS in a single framework. Furthermore, cooperation between central and local governments should be reinforced. A "top-down" approach can be adopted, with the central government providing the vision and direction that trickles down to the local government level and related local actors (ESCAP, 2007a).

In NIS, human capital is the key input of innovation and development. The role of human resources is divided into two levels: (a) high quality personnel; and (b) skilled workers (Dahlman and Nelson, 1995). The former level can monitor technological trends, provide capabilities for R&D, and enhance the basis for policymaking, while the latter level is a crucial component for technology diffusion and upgrading. High-quality personnel can be developed through investments in higher education, expansion, setting up of research centres and laboratories, and international exchange and networking. It is also important to create a pool of technically trained workers by investing in, and promoting, secondary education, skills training and life-long learning.

The creation of infrastructure is also essential for an enabling NIS. Apart from physical infrastructure, such as roads and electricity supply, governments also need to invest and build up facilitating infrastructure (such as investment promotion boards, venture capital companies, science and technology information centres, and technology transfer centres) and collaborating infrastructure (such as government research institutes, universities, and design and engineering units) (Ramanathan, 2010).

Innovation culture is an important "soft factor" that determines the success of a NIS. Wieland (2006) defined it as "a group's or society's framework that channels the perception of economic and technological challenges, and provides the strategies to meet them". Although policy effect on innovation culture can be indirect and difficult to measure, government actions remain helpful in fostering an innovation culture by bearing some of the risks to protect those who pursue innovation.

Governments can also allocate more funding for fundamental research that cannot be commercialized directly but will have widespread benefits. Financing and managerial support need to be provided for start-up high-tech companies and SMEs who upgrade technologies. A comprehensive intellectual property framework should be built up to protect innovation, while awards and networks can be used to encourage innovative activities.

5. Open innovation

Traditional research and development models have relied on a heavily funded, internal, centralized approach that sought to hire the best and brightest personnel to develop and commercialize a firms own ideas or innovations (Chesbrough, 2003a). This is known as the closed innovation model and it has been the engine driving innovations for TNCs, such as IBM, for the past 50 years (figure VII.7).

However, four factors coincided to erode the foundations of this model (Chesbrough 2003a and 2003b):

(a) A drastic increase in the number and mobility of knowledge workers;

Box VII.6. National innovation system, Republic of Korea

The Republic of Korea has strengthened its NIS through the constant development of policies and related activities in the fields of R&D, technology acquisition and transfer, and technology commercialization. These are coupled with marketing assistance and financial aid in commercializing innovation (Yim, 2006). Within this context, special funds for SMEs (and individuals) conducting technology commercialization are sourced by the Government, financial institutions and venture capitalists (Kim, 2001). The Government also encourages SMEs to access advanced technologies at local universities and to establish joint ventures with them. In addition, the subnational innovation system has integrated local SMEs into the national technology commercialization process (ESCAP, 2007c) in establishing innovation centres and technology parks (e.g., Daedeok Science Town).[105]

---

[105] Daedeok Science Town, currently known as Daedeok Innopolis, is the research and development district in Daejeon, Republic of Korea. It began to develop in 1973 and is now a key centre for cutting-edge science and technology. It is made up of 232 research and education institutes including the Korea Advanced Institute of Science and Technology, the Electronics and Telecommunications Research Institute and the Korea Aerospace Research Institute. It has become a leader of development in the Republic of Korea's scientific technology (Daejeon Metropolitan City, 2011).

Box VII.7. Review of Lao People's Democratic Republic national innovation system

The Government of the Lao People's Democratic Republic has carried out specific policies to promote innovation and technology development through its national innovation system. For this purpose, the Government has implemented several activities such as training of entrepreneurs, networking with academic, research and technical institutes, promoting technology transfer and enhancing intellectual property rights. However, these activities have achieved limited success due to low technological and innovation capability, lack of motivation to innovate because of the small domestic market, and limited entrepreneurship skills.

To tackle the issues, the Science and Technology Policy Institute of the Republic of Korea conducted a study to review the Lao national innovation system and made the following policy recommendations:

(a) Consider an export-oriented development strategy;
(b) Cultivate an innovation-active culture;
(c) Foster innovation incentives; and
(d) Encourage the private sector to conduct industrial R&D activities.

The study also suggested the following specific programmes for the country:

(a) Establishment of industrial technology centres that can serve as hubs of innovation activities;
(b) Human resource development in science and technology field through international cooperation;
(c) Proper management of technology transfers from overseas; and
(d) Development of science and technology (S&T) parks.

Source: Lee, Kim and Maliphol, 2011.

Box VII.8. Science and technology parks

A science and technology park is a business park where the primary activity of the majority of establishments is research and new product or process development. In addition to the same type of infrastructure and services provided by ordinary industrial parks, science and technology parks emphasize high-level support services and support innovative activities. These activities include consulting through networking with local research and development institutions and universities, advisory services concerning finance and venture capital, marketing and human resources assistance, and searching for joint-venture partners. They are intended for technologically advanced industries involved in, among other areas, electronics, precision engineering, biotechnology, green technology and ICT.

Science and technology parks enable collaboration among key players including the government, firms, financial players, researchers and academics. This leads to knowledge spillovers, reduces the time and expense necessary for launching new businesses, and increases the success rate of new businesses. The numerous benefits can result in a virtuous cycle of new firms creating wealth that funds more commercially viable research, begetting more entrepreneurs. The Hsinchu Science and Industrial Park of Taiwan Province of China is a successful and effective example of this cycle. Hsinchu Park's success has made Taiwan the world leader in semiconductor manufacturing (see the Hsinchu Science and Industrial Park website at www.facebook.com/pages/Hsinchu-Science-Park/138690519488372).

Sources: Falcke, 1999; and European Investment Bank and others, 2010.

(b) The growing availability of venture capital and equity funds;
(c) External options for niche ideas; and
(d) Increased capabilities of external suppliers.

The end result is the rise of a new market for innovation development and commercialization. Companies no longer have strict control and ownership over proprietary ideas due to free movement of their researchers and employees and this creates knowledge flows between firms.

The increased supply of capital from venture/equity funds has also helped firms, especially SMEs, to successfully commercialize innovations, especially those not pursued by large enterprises. Large amounts of information and expertise now exist outside of large enterprises and TNCs. As a result, companies have started to look for ways to take advantage of this new situation in order to increase the efficiency and effectiveness of their innovation processes (Chesbrough, 2003a). This has fostered the growth of both an active search for external sources of innovation, and cooperation between suppliers and competitors.

Figure VII.7. Closed innovation model

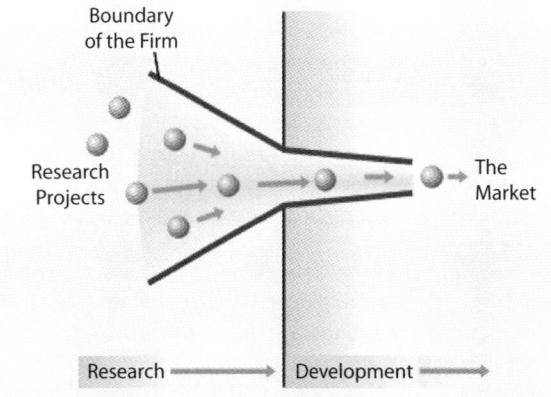

Source: Chesbrough, 2003a.

In the open innovation model (figure VII.8), the commercialization of a firm's innovations is carried out through a variety of means, including both in-house innovation generation and expansion of cooperation

Figure VII.8. Open innovation model

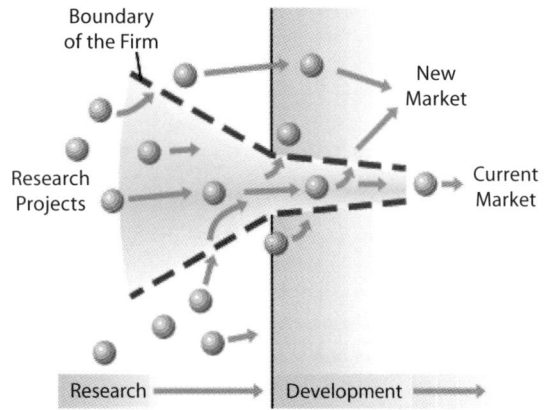

Source: Chesbrough, 2003a.

pathways outside the firm. In particular, firms can generate revenue through channels separate from their current line of business by financing start-up companies (i.e., SMEs), licensing agreements and through the acquisition of outside firms for their technology and know-how.

Open innovation, as defined by its originator Dr. Henry Chesbrough (2003a and 2006), is the designed use of knowledge inflows and outflows to accelerate internal innovation and its commercialization. The key characteristic unique to the open innovation model is the greater exchange of knowledge between firms. This increased openness, in the form of cooperation, has led to more efficient and less costly endeavours to conduct and reap the benefits of their R&D operations. Accordingly, SMEs, both as a source of innovation and as crucial stakeholders in the model, have successfully competed and partnered with TNCs by conducting minimal R&D operations themselves but presenting a potential entry point into new markets (Chesbrough, 2003a).

While individual enterprises pursue open innovation, governments can assist or provide incentives for both SMEs and TNCs to pursue such endeavours. Governments or their agencies can ease legal constraints to allow for quicker developmental processes, and cultivate efficient networking among researchers, firms and entrepreneurs in order to expedite innovation and communication. Some of the best practices can be found in developed countries. For example, in the Netherlands, the Innovation Oriented Research Programme – Leading Technology Institutes scheme offered subsidies for strategic collaboration between private enterprises and publicly-funded research institutes on innovation and technology areas deemed central to the Dutch economy (De Jong, Jeroen and Vanhaverbeke, 2008).

Another example in the Netherlands is Syntens, a publicly-funded intermediary organization that spends substantial time organizing meetings to inform entrepreneurs about specific innovation themes. The organization also aims to increase the innovative ability of SMEs and actively connect SMEs with other innovation actors such as commercial consultants, engineers, public research organizations and higher education institutes (Jong, Jeroen and Vanhaverbeke, 2008). In Belgium, the Vlaams Innovatie Samenwerking programme stimulates the coordination of innovation activities in Flemish companies with financial support from the Government (Jong, Jeroen and Vanhaverbeke, 2008).

6. Reverse engineering

Reverse engineering is a reinvention process that is undertaken mainly when making a competing or alternate product. Reverse engineering can be defined as a process of analysing a subject system to identify the key components and their interrelationships, and to create representations of the system in another form or at a higher level of abstraction (Chikofsky and Cross, 1990). In general, this process chain consists of three main operations: (a) object digitalization to a 3-D model; (b) data analysis and processing; and (c) computer-aided design (CAD) model creation for manufacture (Zhang, 2003). The automotive, electronics and software industries use reverse engineering for a variety of applications. For example, when a new car is launched on the market, competing manufacturers may purchase one and dismantle it to find how it was assembled and how it works. While reverse engineering has advantages, it is important that it be used as a tool for reinvention and not to seek unlawful benefits from the original item (Uhric, 2001). Reverse engineering is a good way to gain insights into a product design and manufacturing, but it is illegal to copy items that are protected by intellectual property rights.

With the globalization of manufacturing activities and the changes in market requirements, a short lead time in product development is essential to satisfy orders. Reverse engineering provides an effective approach to accelerate the product development cycle. It is a cost- and time-efficient means of learning how to produce and improve products by solving the following problems:

(a) Reverse engineering can be applied to understanding the new areas quickly. It is a great tool for coping with the complexity of new products or technologies. It compresses the learning period, and thus enables a company to catch up with the latest trends in its technological field;

(b) Reverse engineering can facilitate production activities. In some situations, designers shape their ideas with simple models made with clay, wood or plaster before the exact CAD models are built for manufacturing. The transformation[106] can be challenging as there is no guarantee that CAD modelling can capture the sculpted model exactly; and

(c) Reverse engineering reduces the risk of product market rejection since for any new product market acceptance has yet to be tested. Market acceptance of reverse-engineered products has already been proven (Wang, 2010). As a result, companies face less uncertainty about market prospects.

In regard to SMEs, reverse engineering is a suitable strategy as it helps to compensate for SMEs' shortage of R&D capabilities. SMEs should be aware that replication is never the final objective of reverse engineering, even though the reverse engineering process can end with the CAD model. Through the application of reverse engineering, SMEs should focus on improving the functionality and quality of the

---

[106] Reverse engineering can facilitate this transformation because the physical models are the source of information for the CAD models (Raja and Fernandes, 2008).

products, and on lowering production costs. The utility of reverse engineering is maximized for the purpose of achieving competitiveness in the market and not for duplication.

7. Intellectual property rights

A crucial aspect of transferring and commercializing technology involves protecting intellectual property (IP) via intellectual property rights (IPRs). IP is the essential element for spawning creativity and innovation, whereas IPRs help to link new ideas to commercialization. Although IPRs allow the owners of intellectual property to limit their availability and accessibility, they also facilitate the transfer of technology by rewarding innovation (International Centre for Trade and Sustainable Development, 2008).

While most of the assets that are internally produced cannot manifest their presence on a balance sheet due to the difficulty of valuing intellectual property assets objectively, those that are purchased can be recognized on a balance sheet at the cost of acquisition[107] (Investorwords, 2012). As the economic importance of intellectual property rights have grown, so too has controversy over their impact on developing countries (RAND, 2010).[108]

Worldwide, the officiating body of member countries for IP/IPRs is the World Intellectual Property Organization (WIPO). According to WIPO (2011), the concept of intellectual property includes rights related to:

(a) Scientific discoveries;
(b) Industrial designs;
(c) Trademarks, service marks, commercial names and designations;
(d) Literary, artistic and scientific works;
(e) Performances of performing artists, phonograms and broadcasts;
(f) Inventions in all fields of human endeavour; and
(g) Protection against unfair competition.

Most people have a general understanding of what is meant by copyright, patents and trademarks, but the other areas covered by WIPO are less well known. Table VII.7 addresses the differences between IP and IPRs.

IPR protection facilitates a number of broad objectives:

(a) Preventing the copying or imitating of an existing product and service;
(b) Developing new innovations through research, development, and commercialization;
(c) Recognizing existing trademarks and brands; and
(d) Recognizing licensing, franchising, and other IP based agreements.

Table VII.7. Differences between intellectual property and intellectual property rights

Intellectual property	Intellectual property rights
Innovations	Patents
Property business information	Trade secrets
Brands and logos	Trademarks
Shapes of items	Industrial designs
Writings, films, photographs	Copyrights

Source: Authors' compilation.

SMEs must understand IP and IPR issues, particularly when commercializing their innovations in global markets, as there are a number of potential benefits. By patenting an invention, SMEs can be granted exclusive rights to enjoy both use and exploitation, and to reduce market competition by preventing others from using their patented invention for commercial gain without permission. Alternatively, it can be a source of income if a firm licences the rights to commercialize to another firm. A patent portfolio, with trademarks, helps SMEs display high levels of expertise and technological capacity in order to increase their market value. Trademarks can also serve as a guarantee of consistent quality to ensure continuous purchase of products and services by those customers who are satisfied and show loyalty to known trademarks (WIPO, 2012).

The most prominent, and widely debated, example of IPR in international policy is the WTO trade-related aspects of intellectual property rights (TRIPS) agreement, which details the regulations for standards, enforcement, and dispute settlement (WTO, 2011a).[109] While this agreement and others are intended to facilitate the transfer of technology, numerous disputes have occurred between developing and developed nations over the protection of IPRs. National governments have an important role to play in educating their business sector about IPRs and in ensuring protection and correct utilization. Within the Asia-Pacific region, Japan has developed a series of specific measures to protect intellectual property by raising awareness of intellectual property systems within SMEs. Measures include providing advice and consulting services for resolving problems related to SMEs' intellectual property (JSBRI, 2010).

SMEs can benefit from the wealth of technological and commercial information available in patent and trademark databases worldwide, provided they can gain access to the information. For example, WIPO GOLD, available on the WIPO website,[110] is a free public resource that provides a one-stop gateway to WIPO's global collections of searchable IP data, facilitating universal access to IP information. The APTITUDE search engine (box VII.3) is another example of information sharing. Policymakers should strive to connect SMEs to these resources wherever feasible. They are valuable to SMEs because they keep SMEs abreast of the latest innovations and patents. They also help SMEs identify potential partners as well as rivals.

In addition to facilitating SMEs' access to IP and IPRs resources, policymakers also need to implement policy

---

[107] In the case of software, slightly different rules apply as it is one of the most readily tradable properties on the Internet (digital) marketplace.
[108] There is a positive correlation between patent activity and economic development. According to the Korea Development Institute, the marginal effect of a 1 per cent increase in patent applications is an 0.11 per cent increase in the rate of economic growth (Goldscheider, 2006)

[109] This issue is reviewed further in chapter VIII.
[110] www.wipo.int/wipogold/en/.

> **Box VII.9. Korean Intellectual Property Office initiatives for IPRs targeted at the SME sector in the Republic of Korea**
>
> The Korean Intellectual Property Office (KIPO) is the major governmental authority responsible for intellectual property matters in the Republic of Korea. It has initiated many policies to assist SMEs in effectively utilizing IPRs.
>
> **A. Free patent management services**
>
> KIPO, in partnership with the Korea Patent Attorneys Association (KPAA), signed a business cooperation agreement to provide SMEs with free patent management services, from pre-filing to registration. The objective is to facilitate first procurement of patents rights by SMEs in a convenient and economical way.
>
> **B. Fee reductions**
>
> KIPO has approved the Fee Regulation to provide additional fee reductions for SMEs until 2005, to encourage IP creation and acquisition activities. According to the scheme, SMEs can obtain a 50 per cent reduction in the application fee for patents, utility models and industrial designs.
>
> **C. Free education**
>
> To further enhance utilization of patent information for the public, including SMEs, KIPO provides applicants with free education on patent information search systems. Also, the KIPO Multimedia Centre offers real-time remote education on patent systems.
>
> **D. SME IPRs Acquisition Campaign**
>
> To raise awareness of IPRs and encourage acquisition by SMEs of IPRs, KIPO has been carrying out the SMEs' IPRs Acquisition Campaign since September 1999. Information workshops on IPRs circulate around 38 cities throughout the country, which help in establishing a relationship between KIPO examiners and SMEs to facilitate the transfer of practical information on IP acquisition and management.
>
> _____
> *Source:* WIPO, undated.

measures to create and enhance awareness about IPs among SMEs, to enable them to use IPRs effectively (box VII.8). A policy scheme can include the following features: (a) awareness raising and sensitization; (b) assistance for capacity-building of SMEs' IP evaluation and negotiations with transferors; (c) seminars, workshops and training; (d) assistance for patent registration; (e) establishment of IP facilitation centres; and (f) partnership development with international agencies such as WIPO. It is important that SMEs gain the capacity, in the form of knowledge or confidence, to value IP and use the correct information to assist during negotiations regarding transfers.

8. Tax incentives

More countries are now using tax incentives than a decade ago and the schemes are more generous than ever (see annex III.2 for a general discussion on SME taxation). More than 20 OECD governments currently provide fiscal incentives to sustain business R&D, up from 12 in 1995 and 18 in 2004. Non-OECD countries, such as Brazil, China, India, Singapore and South Africa, also provide a generous and competitive tax environment for investments in R&D. China provides general tax reductions for R&D firms located in certain industrial zones or for investing in key areas such as biotechnology, ICT and other high-tech fields. India also allows tax deductions at twice the rate of R&D expenditure (OECD, 2010b).

One of the criteria for choosing R&D tax incentives is country-level circumstances, such as overall innovation performance, perceived market failures in R&D, industrial structure, size of firms and the nature of corporate tax systems. Depending on the situation, tax incentives can be provided as one of the elements in a R&D policy package (OECD, 2010b). For the countries trying to maintain neutrality of the tax system as well as stimulate R&D activities, subsidies may be preferred over taxes (e.g., New Zealand). For other economies, high levels of government R&D spending are combined with innovation tax credits to offset the overall shortage of SMEs' innovation capacity, and to steer research to particular goals (e.g., China, Japan and Taiwan Province of China).

Under suitable national circumstances, there is a positive correlation between R&D tax incentives and increases in private research spending (Hall and Van Reenen, 2000). The effectiveness of R&D tax incentives for SMEs largely depends on the design of tax measures. To achieve the desirable results of getting cash into the hands of SMEs to promote R&D activities, regional differences in innovation capabilities and SME-specific needs should be taken into consideration. Based on the experience of its member countries, OECD (2002b) proposed the following design aspects for consideration when making such policies:

(a) Administration: Certainty in R&D tax relief enables enterprises to make long-term corporate planning, while streamlined forms and procedures and information programmes can foster the accessibility of R&D tax provisions;

(b) R&D volume or increment: Although more complex to design and administer, incremental R&D tax schemes may be better for targeting existing or new research and activities by small firms. Volume-based schemes are more straightforward, less subject to fluctuations, but costlier. As a result, the choice of schemes depends not only on policy objectives but also on the tax base, and capacity and resource constraints. Companies in Singapore can – depending on the volume of expenditures on R&D and other factors – claim double tax reductions (UNCTAD, 2000);

(c) Targeted incentives: R&D tax incentives can be provided for small firms and cooperative public-private research to achieve greater spillover effects;

(d) Definition of R&D: Tax incentives can be directed to basic research, applied R&D etc., depending on the research gap being addressed in an economy. A government can also consider extending tax relief to the development aspect of the R&D process, including technology demonstration and engineering improvements, so as not to confine the incentives to laboratory-based processes. In Taiwan Province of China, firms investing in R&D equipment are allowed a depreciation period of two years (UNCTAD, 2000);

(e) Avoidance provisions: Special provisions can prevent firms from avoiding taxes by claiming unwarranted R&D tax relief; and

(f) Foreign firm eligibility: R&D tax rules can increase the attraction of countries as locations for multinational research as well as the benefits accruing to the sponsoring government.

Another example is Singapore, which offers a 150 per cent tax deduction on R&D expenditure in the country. During 2011-2015, this allowance can be increased up to 400 per cent for the first S$ 400,000 of eligible expenditure (Ernst and Young, 2011).

In Japan, legislation introduced in 2009 increased the maximum R&D tax credit available from 30 per cent to 40 per cent of corporate income tax liability (Deloitte, 2009). Japan also offers targeted credits to SMEs, which are central to Japan's economic growth. Similarly, in the Republic of Korea, qualifying companies are able to access a 20 per cent tax credit that can be increased to 30 per cent for SMEs in addition to investment tax credit for R&D equipment (Deloitte, 2011).

F. Obstacles to SMEs' innovation through their development or adaptation of technology

SMEs often come across obstacles throughout the process of developing and adapting the technology for innovation. A field study of SMEs has provided insight into the constraints to acquiring technology for innovation that SMEs face (Chhikara and Sahay, 2008). Some of the issues identified are detailed below.

1. Locating sources of appropriate technology

SMEs sometimes do not plan adequately for locating and choosing appropriate technology for innovation. This can result from simple reasons such as many SMEs just do not know where to search for the technology they need to remain competitive. Smaller firms also tend to rely on a smaller network of individuals or businesses with less access to information. Policymakers can serve as a conduit of information. SMEs fail to use information and communication technology, especially in developing countries where the use of the Internet for e-commerce and information-sharing is not widespread.

2. Financial resources to acquire technology

The next hurdle after locating technology is paying for it. If the necessary technology is too expensive to purchase outright, a leasing arrangement (as described in chapter V) may be an attractive option. In some cases, where the public good is directly at stake, policymakers might consider a subsidy. For example, in Firozabad near Agra, officials of the Government of India supported the local glass industry to adopt gas-based heating. This method creates significantly less pollution, and policymakers needed to provide incentives to help preserve the nearby Taj Mahal.

3. Enhancing product design

SMEs generally find product innovation to be the most profitable in the short-term; however, it is difficult to maintain the continuous effort to enhance product design over the long term. This difficulty is a confluence of financing, human resources and information constraints.

4. Market forces

Following product design, market intelligence is essential for successful technology innovation. SMEs are often constrained by lack of proper research and evaluation about market size, segmentation, customers, suppliers and competitors (Chandra, 2009).

5. Intellectual property and other legal factors

Technology transfer and adaption for innovation involve complicated IP processes, which are expensive. Smaller firms, constrained by limited knowledge and resources, find it difficult to navigate such legal requirements. Education mitigates this challenge (Chandra, 2009);

6. Attitudinal resistance to change

Due to the reliance of SMEs on people rather than processes, as noted above, adoption or development of new technology depends upon the mindset of SME owners. Many owners do not see the need to embrace innovation, particularly if the status quo is profitable.

7. Low human capital investment

Technological innovations make human capital investment central to the start-up and growth of firms. Many Asia-Pacific countries suffer from low levels of technological innovation due to low levels of investment in human capital. The large scale of outward migration of highly-educated professionals exacerbates this problem in the region.[111]

8. Apathy to upgrading skills

Related to the above, many SMEs fail to consider the necessity of constant training for their employees to ensure enhanced innovation capabilities. While some countries in Asia and the Pacific, such as India, the Republic of Korea, Malaysia and Singapore, have conducted skills development training, many countries in the region lag behind in this area due to a lack of funding, trainers or comprehensive policies and programmes. Many employers fear that the employees they train may leave to work for a competitor or may even become a competitor themselves.

---

[111] According to UNDP, "[t]he cumulative brain drain since 1990 has been estimated at 15 per cent for Central America, 6 per cent for Africa, 5 per cent for Asia, and 3 per cent for South America. By some estimates, up to a third of R&D professionals from the developing world reside in OECD countries" (UNDP, 2004b). Visits by the authors to the Greater Mekong Subregion have confirmed this prevailing constraint, which demands urgent attention in Cambodia, the Lao People's Democratic Republic and Myanmar. Conditions are similar in Bhutan, Mongolia and Nepal.

9. Inability to invest for long-term benefits

Many SMEs forfeit the opportunity to upgrade technology because the expenditure is immediate but the benefits may take years to be realized, if at all. Costs are not only in the form of actual cash outlays but also in terms of lost production time. This underscores the centrality of cash flow to SME operations. Another factor in some developing countries is political stability, which influences an SME owner's ability to plan and invest on a long-term basis (APO, 2007).

G. Highlights of national initiatives

Enhancing corporate innovation, particularly in the SME segment, must involve government, universities, R&D institutions and industry associations. In this context, a number of country-specific initiatives have been observed in Asia and the Pacific. It is worthwhile to present some of these initiatives here, as they bolster innovation for SMEs. The following subsections highlight the initiatives taken by some selected countries, and the prevailing innovative and technological environment in the region.

1. Specialized agency (China)

China has a separate Ministry of Science and Technology to build a long-term science and technology base in the SME sector. It formulates national policy for science and technology development, identifies priorities in SMEs' R&D and pursues necessary strategies for enhancing national innovation capabilities (Zhang, 2006).

2. Technology upgrading in rural areas (China)

The Spark programme, launched by the Ministry of Science and Technology, promotes rural industrialization. This programme seeks to upgrade technology in China's rapidly growing rural non-state enterprise sector (e.g., SMEs), which is still suffering from inadequate access to technology, qualified staff and business information. It supports demonstrations of technology and technology adaptation by rural enterprises (World Bank, 2012b). The Spark programme has emerged as one of the most successful outcomes of technology policy reforms in China, particularly for the agricultural sector. The programme has spread to virtually every province in China and has helped develop more than 70,000 projects and many new enterprises, thus contributing to income generation for the rural population (Kuhn, 2011).

3. Comprehensive policy statement (Japan)

The SME Basic Law of Japan promotes business innovation of SMEs by explicitly outlining the fact that the Government "will promote research and development related to technologies for developing new products and services; promote the introduction of plants and equipment to substantially improve the efficiency of production and sale of products; promote the introduction of new methods of business management for integrated control of product development, production, transportation and sale; and take any other necessary measures" (SME Basic Law, 1999).

4. Training for technology management (Japan)

The Institute for Small Business Management and Technology, with nine campuses around Japan, provides training in technology management for SME managers, administrators, those planning start-ups and those assisting SMEs (SME Support, Japan, 2012). The training focuses on the management and leadership aspects of technological development of SMEs, offering small classes and full-time, rigorous courses.

5. Financing research and development (Japan and India)

In Japan, more than 80 per cent of SMEs that carry out R&D source their funds from financial institutions, primarily in the form of term loans (JSBRI, 2009). Such loans require repayment; thus, equity financing is often a more desired source of R&D funding. The Organization for Small and Medium Enterprises and Regional Innovation of Japan has contributed directly to increasing the number of equity funds (JSBRI, 2009). Other financial instruments to encourage R&D include, for example, subsidization of technology transfer and patent registration, collateral-free loans for technology commercialization and various tax breaks.

In India, a revolving fund for technology development was launched in 2010 to assist microenterprises and SMEs with development, demonstration and commercialization of technology innovation. This was done in collaboration with the Technology Information, Forecasting and Assessment Council, a technical organization carrying out technology appraisal of project proposals, and the Small Industries Development Bank of India, a financial institution carrying out financial appraisals of project proposals. The revolving fund covers up to 80 per cent of project costs, which would normally not be more than Rs 100 lakhs, at an interest rate of no more than 5 per cent (Technology Information, Forecasting and Assessment Council, 2009 and 2011).

6. Stakeholder collaboration (Japan)

Survey data from JSBRI (2009) indicates that a large number of SMEs in Japan collaborate with external entities (e.g., customers, universities, financial institutions, other companies, local government bodies and public research institutions) in carrying out R&D.

7. Innovation certification system (Malaysia)

In Malaysia, there is a technology certification system called 1-Innovation Certification for Enterprise Rating and Transformation (1-InnoCERT). The 1-InnoCERT is a certification programme used to recognize and certify innovative SMEs, and to encourage entrepreneurs to venture into high technology and innovation-driven industries. The system guides SMEs, through coaching and business advisory services, in the implementation of innovation systems, processes and business models. Certified companies are eligible to enjoy various privileges, including soft loans, tax exemption and special invitations in government procurement biddings.

Similar to the Republic of Korea's "Inno-Biz," 1-InnoCERT is based on two levels of assessment – a self-assessment portion and an on-site audit. For the first stage, an SME completes an online self-assessment form. If they receive a score of at least 700 out of 1,000, they qualify for an on-site audit by experts.

SMEs will be assessed using four main criteria: (i) innovation ability (R&D activity index, technology innovation system, technology innovation administration, technology accumulation system, and technology analysis ability); (ii) commercialization ability (technology manufacturing ability, ability to develop products using technology and marketing ability); (iii) innovation management ability (management's innovation ability to respond to changes and CEO's sense of value; and (iv) innovation outcome (outcome of technology competitiveness progress, technology management result and forecasting technological achievements). The SME is examined according to the above summarized index and needs to attain an A level in the on-site audit report in order to be awarded a 1-InnoCERT certificate (SME Corp. Malaysia, 2011).

8. Techmarts (India)

Since its inception in 1992, Techmart India has been a one-stop platform held from 14 to 27 November every year for technology providers and technology seekers to assess and negotiate deals related to technology transfer, absorption and assimilation. The main objective of the Techmart is to offer a marketing tool for SMEs to explore new markets and expose themselves to technological developments. Technologies provided in the Techmart are generally low-cost and affordable for SMEs: It also exhibits technologies suitable for employment generation (The Pioneer, 2011; and NSIC, 2011).

9. Technology database (India)

The National Innovation Foundation of India has collected the data of more than 140,000 innovations and traditional knowledge practices from more than 545 districts in India, making it the largest database of its kind in the world. Recently, through student volunteers and without significant external support, the foundation established a portal of 104,000 engineering student projects (websites at www.techpedia.sristi.org or www.techpedia.in) to connect with the needs of informal sector, and small and cottage industries. Through this portal, engineering students can directly provide technical consultations to participating businesses and gain real-life experience in problem solving (for further details see www.nifindia.org).

10. Industrial technology centres (Taiwan Province of China)

A number of industrial technology centres in Taiwan Province of China, including the China Productivity Centre (CPC) and the Industrial Technology Research Institute (ADB, 2009), have provided assistance to SMEs for their technological advancement. CPC is known for its efforts to promote automation production. It sends out teams of engineers to visit clients' plants throughout the country, demonstrate the best means of automation and solve relevant technical problems. CPC has visited more than 1,000 plants and made more than 4,000 suggestions for improvement. It has also carried out more than 500 research projects on improving production efficiency, and has linked enterprises to research centres in order to solve more complex technical problems (ADB, 2009).

The Industrial Technology Research Institute was founded to provide research and development support in applied technologies to advance private sector growth. With six core laboratories, seven technology centres and various business development units, it covers aspects in: (a) information and communication; (b) electronics and optoelectronics; (c) material, chemical and nanotechnologies; (d) biomedical technologies and devices; (e) advanced manufacturing and systems; and (f) green energy and environment. It holds more than 14,571 patents and has assisted in the creation of more than 163 start-ups and spinoffs (Industrial Technology Research Institute, 2011). Other industrial technology centres, such as the Institute for the Information Industry, which develops and introduces software technology, and the Handicraft Promotion Centre, which supports handicraft producers, also contribute to the technological development of SMEs (ADB, 2009).

11. Open Technology Business Incubator (The Philippines)

The Open Technology Business Incubator, launched in 2009 by the Department of Science and Technology in partnership with the Philippine Economic Zone Authority, aims to enhance innovation at SMEs by providing an enabling business environment for the development of technology-led innovation. The Open Technology Business Incubator offers business support services, facilities, and infrastructure to technology companies and potential technology-based start-ups, provides management and consulting services, creates networking opportunities, and cooperates with universities and R&D institutes (Department of Science and Technology, 2009; and Open Technology Business Incubator, undated).

12. Review of national initiatives

The SME sector has limitations in technological capability as well as gaining information about markets and products. In addition to their efforts to facilitate SMEs' access to finance, the selected governments reviewed in this chapter have also carried out a large assortment of programmes and services to help SMEs enhance their knowledge about, and access to, advanced technologies and production methods.

Typical policies in the Asia-Pacific developing countries include: (a) subsidies for technical training via private third parties; (b) establishing government-administered training programmes; and (c) providing a variety of technology extension services (such as testing facilities, tool rooms and technical training centres, and sending missions to international exhibitions) to give enterprises access to new technologies. In some cases, governments have also provided subsidies to develop low-cost production technologies for use by smaller enterprises. One example is a recent public-private partnership-based effort in India to develop a shuttleless loom for smaller enterprises in the textile weaving industry (ADB, 2009). Table VII.8 offers additional examples by country.

Table VII.8. Examples of country programmes for technology development and transfer[112]

Country	Programme	Details
Bangladesh	Government support for technology development and capacity-building	• Expert consultation, technology development and transfer, assistance in meeting quality standard compliances (e.g., ISO certifications), and technical support for issuing "voluntary product certificates"
India	National manufacturing competitiveness programme	• Addressing technology, marketing and skills upgrading needs, mainly in the public-private partnership mode • Lean manufacturing • Eliminating waste throughout the entire business cycle • Promoting new and appropriate technologies for SMEs, assessing current levels of technology and future technological advancement, setting up technology information centres/data banks and an IT portal for information dissemination, and carrying out detailed technology audits
Sri Lanka	Technology improvement programme	• New technical service (Vidata) and common services centres, as well as the science and technology centres, were set up in remote areas of the country. Graduates from science and technology colleges bring their knowledge and skills to the centres for dissemination
Malaysia	Third Industrial Master Plan	• Introduction of technology foresight programmes to be implemented by the Small and Medium Enterprise Corporation Malaysia together with technology-based institutions
Philippines	SME development plan 2003-2004	• Product clinics and advisory services for standards conformity, alternative use of indigenous raw materials, training to sustain quality of raw material inputs and strengthening sharing of facilities
Singapore	Technology innovation programme Local enterprise technical assistance scheme Intellectual property management programme	• One-stop centres offering technology consultancy and practical and downstream technology platforms • Providing up to 50 per cent funding support to hire external experts to improve management and operations • Providing up to 50 per cent funding support to manage intellectual property system more effectively and for the development of new products, processes, ideas, and business modes.
Thailand	Network for promoting innovation to commercialization	• Gathering the research, patent, technology and innovation information related to SMEs interests • Integrating and selecting useful research papers to develop innovative commercial business plans for SMEs • One-stop services for SMEs to commercialize their innovations • Creating alliance and networks with local and international innovation agencies
Korea, Republic of	Various policies on technology	• A total of W 380 billion worth of technology initiatives on innovation and industry-academic research partnerships • Reinforcement of academia and research institute networks, commercialization of developed technology and establishment of digital infrastructure
China	National medium- and long-term plans for science and technology development	• Expediting the establishment of R&D institutes and encouraging enterprises to share the State's R&D tasks in the next 15 years • Adopting preferential banking policies for promoting innovation and start-up of businesses • Increasing investment in science and technology in the next 15 years • Accelerating the implementation of a national strategy on intellectual property right (IPR)
Taiwan Province of China	Heavenly dragons eight-steps project	• Industry-academia links • Information service portals, implementation of information and communications technology, talent cultivation, accumulation of knowledge, online sales and supply chain management

Sources: ADB (2009); Thailand (Innovationsme, 2008); and China (Central People's Government of China, 2006).

---

[112] However, the impact of the examples quoted is often not clear, due to poor implementation and quality of services.

From the above review of the policies and programmes as well as industrial practices prevailing in some Asia-Pacific countries, it has been possible to identify some best practices and successful policy programmes that may be relevant to other countries of the region.

The five most important principles that have emerged from the technology and innovation programmes for SMEs are:

(a) A comprehensive science and technology development policy under a simplified and streamlined institutional framework (both at the national and the subnational levels) offering an enabling environment for SMEs;

(b) Government-subsidized financial assistance to SMEs as well as other key stakeholders for R&D, technology transfer and technology commercialization (e.g., grants, loans and tax break);

(c) The development of national and subnational innovation systems through institutional networking and coordination, capacity-building and infrastructure development (e.g., science and technology parks);

(d) Open-market policy support for technology outsourcing and transfer of technology for SMEs; and

(e) Tools for technology-based SME development such as business and technology incubation and training.

H. Policy recommendations for SME innovation

Some policy recommendations to enhance SMEs' innovation and technology development are presented below.

(a) Human resource development:
- Improve national and local education; invest in secondary and higher education; expand and set up research centres and laboratories.
- Provide technical and vocational training to create a pool of technically trained workers; improve the quality of labour in SMEs.
- Provide opportunities for college students and young entrepreneurs to gain and improve entrepreneurship skills (i.e., a collegian SMEs experience programme and youth employment programme by SMBA).

(b) Infrastructure:
- Provide basic physical infrastructures, such as electricity and information communications.
- Provide research infrastructure, such as public research institutes, universities, and design and engineering houses.
- Develop support infrastructures, such as science and technology parks, and technology transfer centres and markets.

(c) Financial assistance:
- Provide financial assistance (e.g., grants and soft loans) to innovation-driven SMEs for their training or human resource development.
- Subsidize research facility or laboratory investment of SMEs.
- Provide tax incentives, such as tax deductions or tax credits, on SMEs' R&D expenditure.
- Allot a certain percentage of government R&D budget to support SMEs and cover the cost of their R&D indirectly.

(d) Technology acquisition and transfer:
- Promote the association of SMEs with large enterprises to help SMEs gain access to superior technology.
- Create attractive FDI policies and improve foreign licensing regulations.
- Encourage SMEs to buy or licence technologies or foreign intellectual properties by providing financial incentives, such as grants, loans and tax breaks.
- Create an open market policy to support technology outsourcing and transfer for SMEs with various technology providers (e.g., universities, research institutions and large enterprises).
- Stabilize and strengthen legal institutions, particularly with regard to intellectual property rights.
- Actively meet with both entrepreneurs and scientists to craft feasible means for enhancing innovation and technology usage among SMEs.

(e) Technology commercialization:
- Assist in the conversion of an organization's internal R&D capabilities into a market opportunity.
- Facilitate the mobilization of various resources around promising technology for commercialization.
- Encourage cooperation of stakeholders, such as research institutions and industry associations.
- Offer research direction and technology audits to identify opportunities and the best prospects for technology commercialization for SMEs.

(f) Networking:
- Facilitate greater cooperation and exchanges between businesses and universities.
- Establish formal or informal networks to improve technology spill-over.
- Develop national and subnational innovation systems.
- Facilitate the interactions of various stakeholders.
- Enhance knowledge flows through stakeholders' active participation in the national innovation system.
- Establish science and technology parks.
- Reinforce cooperation between central and local governments (a "top-down" approach

can be adopted, with the central government providing the vision and direction to be disseminated down to the local government level and related local actors).

(g) Innovation protection:
- Develop and strengthen the national patent office.
- Protect IP and raise IPR awareness.
- Enable SMEs to use IPR more often.
- Provide advice and consulting services related to SMEs' IPRs.
- Carry out seminars, workshops and training programmes on IP and IPRs.
- Provide assistance for patent registration.
- Train IP and IPR experts at various business associations; develop national IP and IPR professionals, such as patent attorneys.
- Establish IP facilitation centres.
- Develop the partnership and connections with IP and IPR agencies such as WIPO to facilitate SMEs' access to information about IP and IPRs.
- Promote the use of patent and trademark databases, such as WIPO GOLD and APTITUDE created by APCTT.

I. Summary

This chapter covered much ground as innovation and technology affects SMEs in so many ways. It underscored the need for policymakers to function as facilitators and communicators. The pace of technological change is accelerating, and SMEs can use more information and assistance to manage the inevitable shifts in the competitive landscape.

Several examples were provided of "good practices" in policymaking in economies such as China, India, Japan, Malaysia, the Republic of Korea and Taiwan Province of China. Regarding innovation, technology and SMEs, what these countries share is a holistic vision of how to improve the competitiveness of their SMEs, from basic research to technology commercialization. Too often, policy goes awry because it is done in a piecemeal fashion and does not serve a broader national strategy. Countries such as the Republic of Korea excel in their technology policy because they have national and subnational innovation components cooperating in an efficient manner.

There are a number of individual policies that governments can undertake to improve the dissemination of technology and innovation to SMEs. These include the stabilization and strengthening of legal institutions (particularly regarding intellectual property), investment in infrastructure such as broadband Internet funding of science parks and incubators, and favourable tax incentives for R&D. It is the coordination of levels of government – national, provincial, and local – that determines the relative efficacy of such policies. Delegation of authority to local levels wherever possible helps to make policy implementation more time efficient and localized. Above all, policymakers must actively engage both entrepreneurs and scientists in crafting feasible means for improving innovation and technology usage among SMEs. In summation, the major public measures should concentrate on the following areas:

(a) Policy: technology-driven policies and incentives for creating and adopting innovations;
(b) Institutional framework: e.g., industrial technology centres;
(c) Access to finance;
(d) Training and capacity building; and
(e) Strategic partnerships and alliances: e.g., national and subnational innovation systems.

CHAPTER VIII
Market access

One of the most crucial challenges facing SMEs in Asia-Pacific countries is how to create new business (and, therefore, investment) opportunities in regional and global markets. In small economies with a limited domestic market, exports play a crucial role in stimulating economic growth and rapid socioeconomic transformation. SMEs supplying competitive products and services, with greater potential for backward and forward linkages, could contribute substantially to exports and, hence, to higher national income and overall socioeconomic progress. Therefore, development of export-led SMEs should be an important part of any national economic development strategy.

Key success factors for market access, which means freedom to enter a market and sell goods or services,[113] include but are not limited to market intelligence, capacity to learn and adapt, low entry barriers and a solid business network. Within this context, market access can generally be of two types: trade and investment. This chapter is primarily concerned with trade as this is the predominant method of market access for SMEs. However, some of our policy prescriptions are applicable to both trade and investment. These include lowering barriers, communicating regulations and market conditions, holding trade fairs and other forms of promotional events and providing access to finance.

This chapter begins with three theories germane to market access, i.e., market orientation, internationalization and trade. This is followed by trade topics such as the WTO, non-tariff barriers (NTBs), trade finance, quality assurance management and trade promotion tools. Following that, the role of ICT in facilitating market access is considered, concerning aspects like e-commerce, internet marketing and trade facilitation. Strategies are additionally suggested for integrating SMEs regionally and globally through the development of supply chains with the provision of some sectoral cases. The chapter finally concludes with policy implications and recommendations.

A. Market orientation and internationalization of firms

Market orientation is "the organization-wide generation of market intelligence pertaining to current and future customer needs, dissemination of intelligence across departments and the organization-wide responsiveness to it" (Kohli and Jaworski, 1990; excerpted from Amario, Ruiz, and Amario, 2008). The major focus of market orientation is to understand customer needs in both domestic and international markets, so that enterprises can develop products and services to meet these requirements. In short, market orientation means the implementation of a firm's marketing concept and business philosophy to achieve a greater degree of market access. In this regard, a number of researchers have demonstrated that there is a combined effect of market orientation and innovation on firms' positive performance (Verbees and Meulenverg, 2004). The key elements of market orientation include: customer orientation; competitor orientation; inter-functional coordination; long-term focus and profitability; intelligence generation; intelligence dissemination; and responsiveness (Kohli and Jaworski, 1990; and Narver and Slater, 1990).

Traditional studies on market orientation have mainly been limited to large enterprises; however, with the growing importance of SMEs in the world economy, especially in developing economies, it is also expected to be one of the key success factors for SMEs (Spillan and Parnell, 2006). Given the fact that most domestic markets for SMEs in Asia-Pacific countries are limited, there is a need to encourage these SMEs to access international markets to foster their growth. As such, market-orienting efforts such as providing information and incentives to promote their penetration into the international markets would prove beneficial.

The market orientation of SMEs is conceptually related to the phenomenon of internationalization, which, as Singh, Pathak and Naz (2010) noted, is a broad term used by different scholars to connote "exporting, trade, cross-border clustering, cross-border collaboration, alliances/subsidiaries, branches and joint ventures that extend beyond the home country environment". Note also that exporting is at the lower end of the spectrum of internationalization in terms of the time and resources necessary, which reflects the idea that SMEs are subject to greater resource constraints than large firms (Hessels and Terjesen, 2010; and Hollenstein, 2005) and therefore the choice of entry mode is a process of cost-benefit analysis (Sharma and Erramilli, 2004).

There are a number of different theories to explain the process of internationalization and, by extension, the market orientation of firms. One of the first to gain currency is the Uppsala model, which describes internationalization as a series of incremental steps along a risk/reward continuum. From an organizational behaviour perspective, market orientation is a process of continuous learning (Cyert and March, 1963; and Johanson and Vahlne, 1977) that allows a firm to surmount the barriers of scarce resources and information in order to internationalize operations. This cycle typically starts with exporting, and over time the firm moves into more high-risk, high-reward activities such as foreign direct investment (Korhonen, Luostarinen and Welch, 1996; and Erramilli and Rao, 1990).

In addition, firms initially expand where the psychological distance is smallest, i.e., they penetrate foreign markets that are most similar to their own domestic markets (Johanson and Vahlne, 1977 and 2009) before attempting to access overseas markets that are less familiar. An example would be a United States firm expanding internationally to Canada before attempting to enter the Chinese market. In the current version of the Uppsala model, a firm's position within a network of

---

[113] For further details, visit the website at http://lexicon.ft.com/Term?term=market-access.

relationships, its commitment to those relationships and trust-building play a more salient role in the internationalization of firm activities than market similarty (Johanson and Vahlne, 2009).

Another internationalization perspective is the famed "eclectic paradigm" of Dunning (1980). This paradigm is also known as the "OLI Model," because the decision to internationalize and the various possible modes of internationalization rests upon the ownership advantages of firms, the location advantages offered by host nations and the possible internalizing of benefits of firm-owned assets (Dunning, 1980). Firms need to possess assets such as a global brand, technology or managerial know-how to compete in a foreign market with local players. Secondary, they must find that local conditions, such as cheap labour supply or market size, augment their ownership advantages or otherwise enable them to profit. Thirdly, the types of assets owned as well as various competitive and institutional factors compel firms to choose whether to internalize these assets within their boundaries or exploit them through licensing or franchising arrangements.

A contrasting view of internationalization to the incremental approach of the Uppsala model is the idea of "born global" (Armario, Ruiz and Armario, 2008; Knight and Cavusgil, 1996; and Oviatt and McDougall, 1994). This perspective argues that a firm can internationalize from inception; there is no need to proceed in stages. The new firm is able to do business across borders because it already possesses the necessary resources, such as technology (McDougall, Shane and Oviatt, 1994) or a founder with an international orientation (Zahra, Hayton and O'Neill, 2001). These firms are typically in high-tech sectors such as computer software (Armario and others, 2008). However, most SMEs are not high-tech and their internationalization efforts are limited to trade. They are, therefore, not "born global" at best, "instant exporters" (McAuley, 1999).

Figure VIII.1 presents the different degrees of export market penetration based on the size of enterprises in selected countries in Asia and the Pacific. The figure reveals small enterprises account for more than 80 per cent of sales in the domestic market in nine of the 11 Asia-Pacific nations, while in the other two nations they earn between 70 per cent and 80 per cent of their sales from the domestic market. In contrast, large enterprises display a range for domestic sales – from less than 20 per cent in Sri Lanka, to close to 70 per cent in China and India – but their percentage share of domestic sales is much lower than those of SMEs. As a whole, a pattern can be seen from these 11 Asia-Pacific nations – SMEs are oriented towards the domestic market, whereas large enterprises are more directed towards the export market (ADB, 2009). This supports the earlier discussion on the large gap in supply-side capacity between SMEs and large enterprises.

A final theory of high relevance is that of comparative advantage, which is the cornerstone of modern trade theory. This theory was developed by David Ricardo (1772-1823) based on Adam Smith's writings. Put briefly, comparative advantage advocates that a nation should concentrate on producing what it can produce most efficiently, relative to other trading partners, and then trade that item for other goods. This will leave all nations better off than in the case of autarky.

As a simple example, suppose there are two goods (bicycles and cars), two countries (Lao PDR and Thailand) and only one factor of production (labour). Let us further assume Lao PDR has the capacity to make either ten cars or 200 bicycles while Thailand has the capacity to make either 100 cars or 500

Figure VIII.1. Share of total sales sold domestically: Small, medium and large enterprises

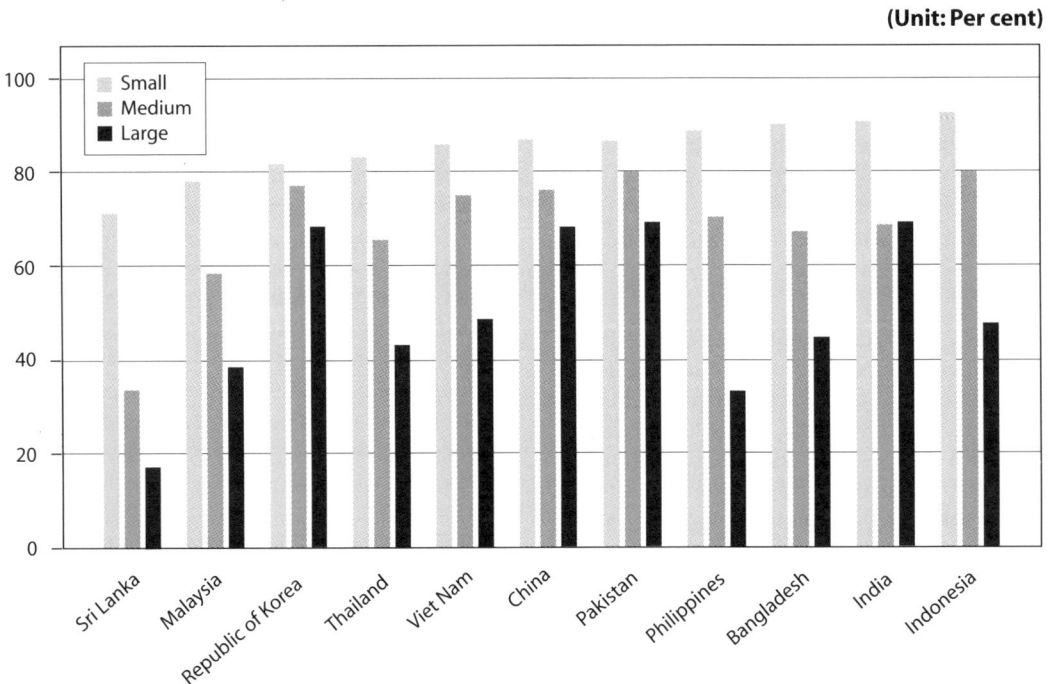

Source: ADB, 2009.
Note: Small-sized firms = 5-49 employees; medium firms = 50-199 employees; and large firms = 200 employees and above.

bicycles. It is immediately clear that Thailand has the absolute advantage in the production of both goods, since it can produce more of each. However, the Ricardian model suggests that mutually beneficial trade could still occur when each country produces the good in which it has a comparative advantage.

To understand this, it is crucial to analyze the marginal opportunity costs of production. The opportunity cost of producing one car in Lao PDR is twenty bicycles foregone. On the other hand, the opportunity cost of producing one car in Thailand is five bicycles foregone. Thailand has a lower opportunity cost and hence a comparative advantage in the production of cars. Conversely. the opportunity cost of producing one bicycle in Lao PDR is 1/20 of a car foregone. The opportunity cost of producing one bicycle in Thailand is 1/5 of a car foregone. The opportunity cost of producing a bicycle in Lao PDR is smaller than in Thailand and hence Lao PDR has a comparative advantage in bicycle production. Thailand should therefore focus on car production and Lao PDR on bicycle production before trading these goods for each other.

The agreed-upon trade price determines the extent to which they would be better off than if they were producing both goods only for their home market; but in general, they would have more of both goods than in the autarky case. Policymakers should keep this concept in mind when developing their SME sector.

B. SMEs' capabilities and challenges for market access

SMEs face more risks on account of fewer resources and limited expertise as compared to larger firms. Effective management of SMEs is crucial for identifying and utilizing knowledge and technology, developing quality products and upgrading production processes in order to meet consumer preferences and demands. SMEs also need to equip themselves with market information on customers, buyers, suppliers, prices, trade regulations and business procedures in the target markets. However, investments in production facilities and collection of data pertaining to marketing research can be a strain on the resources of SMEs.

The major challenges SME face can be categorized broadly in four groups: (a) intensified competition; (b) internationalization; (c) trade liberalization; and (d) management skills. These challenges and their specific capabilities and limitations are summarized in table VIII.1.

As reviewed above, SMEs face impediments to market access, due partially to their inadequate capabilities, and so are often under-represented in the global economy (APEC, 2004). Although barriers to entry into foreign markets differ between firms and countries, the following four factors are critical to market entry capability:

(a) A lack of knowledge of business opportunities, prospective customers, competition status, channels and distribution, local regulations and practices, and taxation is one of the major barriers for SMEs to gaining access to a particular market. Obtaining and gathering information can be time-consuming and costly, and SMEs commonly lack the necessary manpower and financial resources and have restricted information channels to undertake these activities effectively (UNTFN, 2005). Keeping SMEs updated on changing market trends is vital to their survival and success, both in domestic and in international competition;

(b) A well-organized policy and regulatory framework is one of the most fundamental determinants of the success of a country's trade activities (ESCAP, 2004b). Such a framework is crucial to SMEs' growth and expansion into foreign markets, as it can provide the necessary

Table VIII.1. Major challenges, and SMEs' capabilities and limitations

Challenges	Capabilities and limitations

Intensified competition	• Small operational capacity that results in a relatively high cost of production
	• Lack of consumer preferences and inability to create brand loyalty:
	  – Lack of market intelligence
	  – Inability to network
	  – Inability to meet large demands
	  – Uncompetitive price, quality and/or delivery
	• Inadequate institutional support and assistance

Internationalization	• Inability to internationalize operations, due to limited capacity to analyze, penetrate and segment foreign markets • Technical limitations to act as suppliers to foreign buyers/investors
Trade liberalization	• General ignorance of WTO guidelines: – Lack of knowledge and skills to implement the guidelines • Less awareness of opportunities and challenges derived from various trade agreements
Management skills	• Lack of knowledge about new strategies and techniques • Inability to spare time and manpower to acquire new management skills • Lack of knowledge to use e-commerce • Inability to hire appropriately qualified and talented people • Inability to combat anti-competitive practices

Source: Authors' compilation.

export-capable business infrastructure together with other facilitation services. The capability of SMEs to trade internationally will be significantly improved through a modernized and well-established infrastructure (UNTFN, 2005);

(c) Another concern is the trade barriers that exporters face, including tariffs as well as non-tariff barriers such as anti-dumping measures. SMEs are in a very vulnerable position when encountering trade barriers in export markets, due to their size and limited resources. Thus, lower trade barriers will help SMEs participate in international trade activities more readily. With this in mind, regional organizations and forums, such as APEC, ASEAN, ESCAP and OECD, while promoting free trade and economic cooperation in their member countries are efficient tools for lowering trade barriers (UNIDO, 2006a); and

(d) Networking among or between SMEs and larger firms (i.e., participation in international production networks or global supply chains) will allow SMEs to gain access to international markets. It is an important source of information that enhances SMEs' awareness of business opportunities and provides information about engaging in particular markets. These business networks enable SMEs to stay informed of ongoing events and technological advancements within an industry. As such, SMEs' capabilities to access foreign markets can be largely improved through such business networks (UNIDO, 2006a).

Other aspects likely to increase the success rate of SMEs' access to foreign markets, such as greater integration of domestic product standards to international standards and stable global FDI flows, can be also understood in line with the above four factors. SMEs should work with governments to address those issues adequately.

C. Trade environment for facilitating market access by SMEs

The degree of market access for an SME can be affected by the trade environment in which it operates. Relevant factors include, among others, free trade and investment agreements, WTO rules, export products identification, quality standards and certificates and the transportation system including international commercial terms and customs procedures. These pertinent issues are briefly considered below.

1. Impact of trade policy and trade and investment agreements on SMEs

In general, a positive relationship exists between trade liberalization and economic growth (Wacziarg and Welch, 2003). Many countries in the Asia-Pacific region have followed this trend in reforming their trade policies, and an increasing number of liberalized trade/investment agreements have come into force worldwide. The impact of liberalization on SMEs remains uncertain, due to different market situations and development status of SMEs within each country. Trade policy must be designed carefully to minimize any unintended effects on SMEs. Proper policy tools can also be adopted to facilitate SMEs' penetration of international markets.

Lower tariff and non-tariff barriers due to trade agreements can result in increased foreign competition in domestic markets.[114] This increased competition provides incentives to SMEs to improve productivity, as those slow to react may face more pressure and even shut-down. Local firms can benefit from lower costs of cheaper imported inputs, giving them a competitive advantage in both domestic and export markets. The elimination of trade barriers allows large firms to widen their range of suppliers, and indirectly stimulate exports of local SMEs (Tambunan, 2007).

Investment agreements add security, transparency, stability and predictability to the investment framework, which contributes to attracting greater investment inflows (UNCTAD, 2009). As a result, SMEs have more opportunities to integrate into global and regional supply chains through forward or backward linkages with FDI (such as subcontracting). These linkages also trigger positive knowledge spillover when SMEs try to reach the quality standards of TNCs and when trained personnel leave TNCs to start their own SMEs (Dutrénit and Vera-Cruz, 2003).

Currently, free trade areas formulated by trade and investment agreements are not confined to market liberalization and market opening measures alone. They are comprehensive and improve economic cooperation, information sharing and personnel exchange, which creates a positive external environment for SMEs. In addition, some trade/investment agreements may also be specifically designed for SMEs, with the Strategic Action Plan for ASEAN SME Development 2010-2015 serving as an apt example. The plan outlines the framework for SME development that seeks to ensure the advancement of the SMEs within the ASEAN region (ASEAN, 2011). At the same time, regional trade and investment agreements improve regional stability and competitiveness. SMEs inside the region can attract more investments from outside the region, and a virtuous circle is built for future development.

In enhancing SMEs' competitiveness in the liberalization process, government policy plays a crucial role. Governments need to improve long-term capacity and build subcontracting linkages for SMEs by providing technical and financial assistance, skills or vocational training, and market information (Tambunan, 2010). SME agencies can also help SMEs better understand and benefit from trade policy reform by offering relevant information and services. For example,

---

[114] Trade barriers for export products can take various forms such as tariff and non-tariff barriers. Some of them include special import authorization, restrictions on data processing, voluntary export restraints, country quotas, export subsidies, anti-competitive practices and licensing fees (Czinkota and Ronkainen, 2007). Such tariff and non-tariff barriers can cause problems and hinder trade by negatively influencing access to international markets. Due to their size, SMEs are especially exposed to trade barriers as efforts to overcome them are generally time- and resource-intensive (OECD, 2006). SMEs generally are discouraged from internationalizing their businesses, and they might be resistant to paying for consulting services and other measures targeted at entering international markets. Government programmes that support SMEs in overcoming existing trade barriers could help increase their participation. Such measures can include cooperation between governments in reducing barriers and investment in trade consultation services (OECD, 2006).

SPRING Singapore provides two guides about free trade agreements in goods and services with the objective of helping SMEs in Singapore to cope with the new exporting rules as well as take advantage of the lower trade barriers (SPRING Singapore, 2005).

2. World Trade Organization and international trade

In the past few decades, WTO provisions have shaped international trade significantly. In Asia and the Pacific, the SME sector perceives the WTO provisions both as threats and opportunities. Pursuant to the Uruguay Round Agreement and the WTO provisions, the three major issues concerning SMEs are (Kornel, 2006):

(a) Importance of SMEs as exporters;
(b) Growing interest in the environment and sustainable development; and
(c) Scope for increasing trade in services of information and clean technology.

WTO norms have also created the following situations and challenges to SMEs (NSIC, 2008):

(a) The emergence of the "Global Village;"
(b) International trade with fewer barriers;
(c) Erosion of entry restrictions;
(d) Emergence of the service sector in international trade;
(e) Intensified global competition;
(f) Regulations of standards of quality and ownership;
(g) Regulation of investment flows; and
(h) Environmental issues.

In this regard, several key agreements and rules under WTO emerged that directly affect the SME sector (also see annex VIII.1 for a detailed discussion on those agreements and rules):

(a) Sanitary and phytosanitary measures and technical barriers to trade;
(b) Agreement on Trade-Related Aspects of Intellectual Property Rights (TRIPS) and the related issue of transfer of technology;
(c) Trade in services;
(d) Trade-Related Investment Measures (TRIMs); and
(e) Rules of origin.

Countries in Asia and the Pacific have not been able to respond fully to the above-mentioned challenges and agreements. In particular, the SME sector lacks the requisite capacity to deal with them adequately. The key problem in each of these areas is information asymmetry. Policymakers should make sure the SME sector is aware of the new requirements of these international bodies. This is another area where robust public-private dialogue would be beneficial.

Despite these challenges, the new corporate scenario under globalization has provided the scope for SMEs to strengthen their capabilities and go beyond their boundaries. SMEs today have an ample opportunity to modernize their entire business operations with access to all needed inputs, including imported ones. The desired skills of SMEs for their effective integration into regional and global markets include (ESCAP, 2009c):

(a) Exploiting the global export market;
(b) Enhanced scope for partnership and alliances;
(c) Easier communication with customers and suppliers;
(d) Scope of becoming local suppliers to industrial leaders;
(e) Access to state-of-the-art technologies; and
(f) Scope to attract investment.

In this regard, technical assistance programmes for least developed countries (LDCs) has been one of the key functions of the WTO. During the past few years, the WTO has been providing trade-related technical assistance and training to beneficiary countries for adjusting to WTO rules and disciplines, implementing obligations and exercising the rights of membership (WTO, 2001). The products can be grouped broadly under five main categories: (a) general WTO-related technical assistance and training; (b) specialized and advanced technical assistance and training; (c) academic support for training and capacity-building; (d) an integrated approach to trainee programmes and internships; and (e) e-learning (WTO, 2001). These products have been further modified to be more demand-driven, so that the activities add value to the results of those formerly delivered, in both the national and the regional contexts. The WTO secretariat is paying particular attention to the requirements of SMEs that suffer from severe capacity constraints and are unable to face the challenges of globalization (WTO, 2007).

One of the most significant outcomes of the WTO Hong Kong Ministerial Conference in 2005 was the "Aid for Trade" initiative. This initiative was aimed at helping developing countries, particularly LDCs, to build the supply-side capacity and trade-related infrastructure needed to implement, and benefit from WTO provisions, and to expand their trade (WTO, 2005). SMEs are a particular target of this initiative. "Aid for Trade" is an important vehicle for improving the capacities of LDCs in gaining access to regional and global markets.

3. Export product identification, pricing and competition

The identification by policymakers of a potential product for the export market generally requires three steps: (a) analyzing the competitiveness of the home economy; (b) selecting product sectors; and (c) verifying supply-side capacity of the selected product sectors by conducting an export supply survey (ESCAP, 2001b). As shown in figure VIII.2, these stages are followed by a further selection of companies and markets, together with an analysis of possible problems and constraints. After identifying qualified exporters and prospective markets, products need to be defined and their potential for export evaluated. Finally, once the product for export promotion has been selected, a strategy for the following processes has to be developed, which involves developing both pricing and competition strategies.

Figure VIII.2. Stages in the process of export product identification

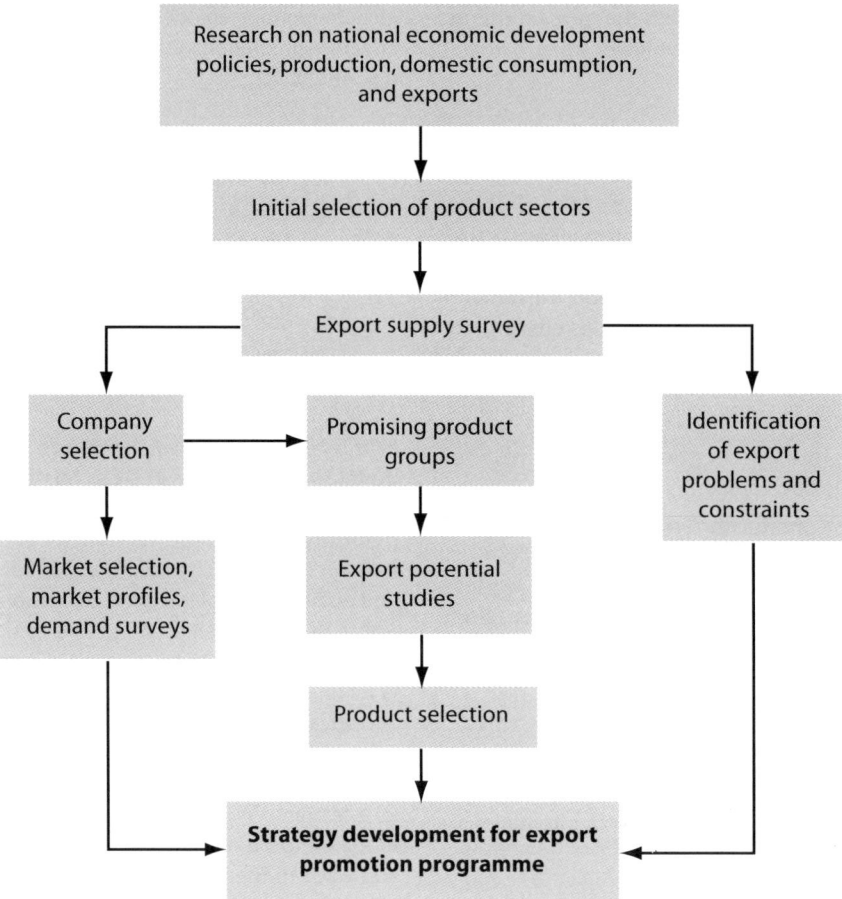

Source: ESCAP, 2001b (Module V, page 5).

Government agencies for trade promotion play a significant role in laying the groundwork for an export promotion programme. They can give invaluable assistance by doing the necessary studies, which SME exporters often cannot afford, to identify what products to promote and to decide which markets offer the greatest opportunity for export growth (ESCAP, 2001b). The relevant agencies can guide this process to increase exports. Training, export promotion centres and the provision of market information to SMEs are the key mechanisms in the process. This issue is revisited later in this chapter.

The price of a product is generally determined by: (a) corporate objectives; (b) costs; (c) customer behaviour and market conditions; (d) market structure; and (e) environmental constraints (Czinkota and Ronkainen, 2007). Depending on these factors, a company can choose between three different strategies for setting a price for their product in national and international markets. While "skimming" is aimed at receiving the highest possible return in a short period, "market pricing" with the following adjustment of production and marketing is the preferred method in large or competitive markets. "Penetration pricing", as a strategy to achieve a maximum volume of sales through low prices, is generally only suitable for mass markets (Czinkota and Ronkainen, 2007).

Even though these factors can be easily understood in theory, in practice many SMEs need support in developing a good pricing strategy, especially when competing in an international market (ESCAP, 2001b). Most importantly, SMEs should be trained in how to determine and control their costs and use their competitive advantage effectively. This includes implementing measures such as cost reductions, cost-effective accounting systems or establishing frameworks for effective pricing (ESCAP, 2001b). The challenge facing policymakers today is to support, facilitate and control the coordination of price-building across different countries. Pricing alignment, which may include centralized pricing authorities and so-called pricing corridors for regions (Czinkota and Ronkainen, 2007), is a primary goal.

4. Quality standards and certificates plus quality assurance management

Another key challenge facing SMEs in developing countries in accessing international markets are the technical barriers they must overcome to meet the requirements of international quality standards. While company-level standardization is often used in large enterprises with specific requirements that differ from company to company, standardization on an industry-level is carried out by professional associations and is far more important (UNIDO, 2006b). A company should first adhere to these industry standards as a requirement for offering products or services within a country; such adherence builds the basis for fulfilling international standards.

Generally speaking, a standard has three attributes – level (company, industry/sector, national, global etc.), subject (automotive, software, food etc.) and aspect (packing, testing, safety, environment etc.) – that defines its applicability (UNIDO, 2006a). Quality certification and total quality management are two prevalent instruments for SME quality standardization. The former refers to the certification by a second or third party to demonstrate that products or services have met specific quality standards while the latter focuses on quality assurance managed by the whole organization (Xydias-Lobo and Jones, 2003).

SMEs must aim to achieve international standardizations in order to participate in global supply chains. ISO comprises of a network of national standardization bodies from 162 countries, and is the world's largest developers of international standards. The ISO 9000 family of standards is an international consensus on good quality management practices and is the primary standard for manufacturers. It is also the main standard used for the purpose of quality conformity assessments. With the latest version, ISO 9001:2008, a supplier can be deemed to have a quality management system that meets international standards. In most instances, it is essential for manufacturers to be certified as ISO 9001 in order to access the market (ISO, 2011).

Another important series of standards is ISO 14000 on environmental management. It is "a framework for the development of an environmental management system and the supporting audit programme" (ISO 14000 Environmental Management Group, 2007). The ISO 14000 standards are important to SMEs as they provide guidance on how to improve environmental performance. Cleaner operations obtain economic benefits, such as reductions in resource use, energy consumption or waste production as well as higher efficiency or the use of recyclable resources (Touchstone, 2010). Applying these standards helps to reduce possible liabilities, improves the public image and attracts new interested stakeholders (IEMA, 2004). Due to their size, SMEs face a number of challenges in the implementation of environmentally beneficial measures. These can include a lack of financial resources, qualified personnel and/or access to technologies. Structural support is needed to foster the implementation of environmental standards among SMEs (Pearson, 2000).

Apart from general standards such as ISO 9000 or ISO 14000 that apply to all companies active in trade, relevant quality assurance and management standards differ from industry to industry. As many SMEs in Asia and the Pacific are suppliers of the automotive industry, the widely accepted ISO/TS 16949 standard plays an important role (ISO, 2011). The ISO/TS 16949 is also issued by national standardization bodies, such as the DQS-Group in Malaysia and the Sri Lanka Standards Institution (UNIDO, 2006c). The Codex Alimentarius Commission, under the Food and Agriculture Organization of the United Nations (FAO), the Hazard Analysis Critical Control Point (HACCP) standards of WTO and the ISO 22000:2005 standards govern food safety (UNIDO, 2006c) Many countries require the latter food management system certification for an enterprise in the food supply chain, ranging from feed producers and primary producers to retail and food service providers (ISO, 2011).

5. Transport system, international commercial terms and customs procedures

The transport system involves trade logistics and facilitation in international and domestic business transactions. Broadly defined, trade logistics covers transport-related physical infrastructure (e.g., roads, ports and warehousing) and associated services (customs, distribution and information management). Trade facilitation includes any related area ranging from institutional and regulatory reform to customs and port efficiency (ESCAP, 2009c). The development of the transport system is aimed at increasing the volume of international (and domestic) trade by reducing the costs and increasing the speed of transporting traded goods without damaging the value of the goods. Insufficient infrastructure, in addition to non-physical issues (e.g., denial of access to foreign vehicles and drivers and other incompatibilities) can be the major reason for delays in the flow of cross-border trade and transport between developing countries (ESCAP, 2009c).

Table VIII.2 presents the quality index of trade and transport-related infrastructure within the Asia-Pacific region. The index is based on a worldwide survey of operators providing feedback on the logistics friendliness of the nations in which they operate and those with which they trade (World Bank, 2011e). In 2009, the developed economies of Australia, Japan and New Zealand had the best quality of transport system in the region. East and North-East Asia are still lagging behind; however, the quality of trade and transport-related infrastructure is not too far off the ones in developed economies in the region, and a trend of further improvement is visible. The development of trade and transport infrastructure in South and South-West Asia, and North and Central Asia were the lowest in the region in 2009, and were also below the world average level of 2.64; however, North and Central Asia made the largest improvements in 2009.

Table VIII.2. Quality of trade and transport-related infrastructure by subregion

Subregion	2006	2009
East and North-East Asia	3.16	3.28
South-East Asia	2.90	2.91
South and South-West Asia	2.27	2.22
North and Central Asia	1.98	2.32
Developed Economies	3.79	3.84

Source: World Bank, 2011e.
Note: 1 = low, 5 = high.

> **Box VIII.1. SPRING, Singapore**
>
> To improve the access of Singaporean SMEs to global markets, the Singaporean enterprise development agency, SPRING, actively promotes the convergence of national standards and relevant international standards in products and services. It also advocates industry involvement and leadership in the development of new international standards. As a result, more than 80 per cent of the Singapore standards are aligned with international standards in order to facilitate greater market access for Singaporean exports. SPRING Singapore has also established the Export Technical Assistance Centre to help SMEs understand and comply with the international standards, technical regulations, green initiatives and compliance requirements for food and electrical/electronics exports.
>
> *Source:* SPRING Singapore, 2008.

The International Chamber of Commerce (ICC) (2011) conceived and maintains internationally accepted commercial terms (Incoterm rules), which are essential to the daily language in international and domestic trade as well as contracts for the sale of goods. The unification and standardization of general phases used in business transactions help traders to avoid costly misunderstandings, and increase the efficiency and transparency of the transaction process (ICC, 2011). The latest version of Incoterms, published in 2010 by ICC, contains 11 rules presented in two distinct transport modes (i.e., general and sea/waterway) (table VIII.3 and figure VIII.3).

Despite being based on commonly accepted commercial terms (e.g., Incoterms) and other international and domestic trade practices, customs procedures vary from country to country. The term "customs procedures" specifically refers to the treatment of goods by national customs authorities. The

Table VIII.3. Incoterms 2010 rules

Rules for any mode or modes of transport	
EXW	EX works
FCA	Free carrier
CPT	Carriage raid to
CIP	Carriage and insurance paid to
DAT	Delivered at terminal
DAP	Delivered at place
DDP	Delivered duty paid
Rules for sea and inland waterway transport	
FAS	Free alongside ship
FOB	Free on board
CFR	Cost and freight
CIF	Cost, insurance and freight

Source: ICC, 2012b.

Figure VIII.3. Incoterms 2010 rules

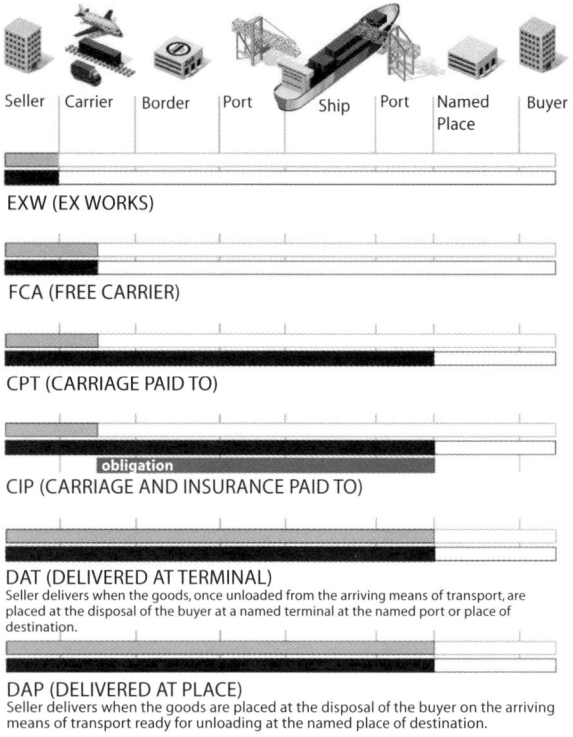
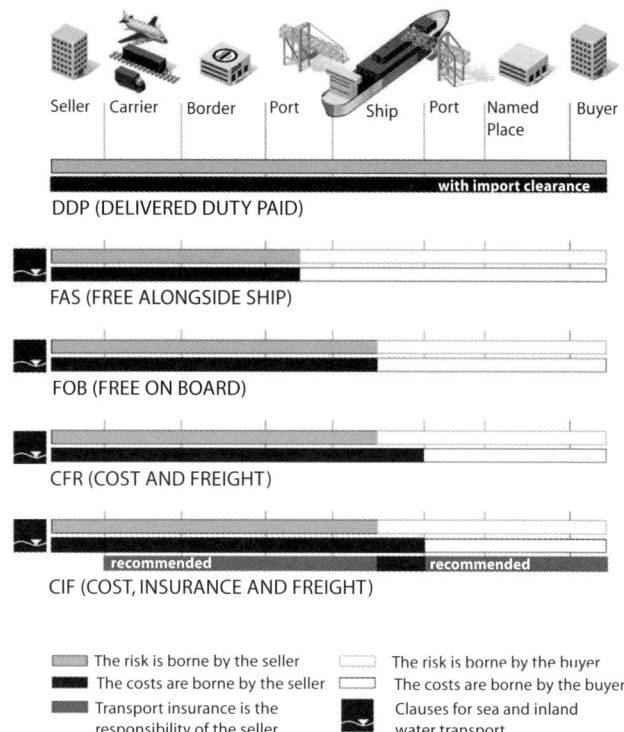

Source: ICC, 2010.

procedures cover the entire range of customs, from import and export of goods, movement of passengers, goods in transit, inspection, duty collection to information management and systems. The general procedures for imports are outlined in figure VIII.4 and include clearance requests, custom declarations, examinations, inspections, paying tax and approval (Kai Ga Shoppers, 2012, based on Japan Customs, 2011).

Table VIII.4 shows the efficiency of customs procedures within the Asia-Pacific region. Apart from the developed economies of the region (i.e., Australia, Japan and New Zealand) which attain the highest efficiency, customs procedures in East and North-East Asia are most efficient on average, with South-East Asia slightly above the world average of 4.2 in 2009. The customs procedures in North and Central Asia are generally have a lower efficiency; however, there has been steady improvement over the years (World Bank, 2011f).

Transport systems, which include commercial terms and customs procedures, facilitate SMEs' access to international markets, providing various logistics services (e.g., shipping, transportation, customs clearance, forwarding and brokerages, warehousing and documentations). Policymakers need to monitor the system, since high costs and unreliable delivery are major obstructions to the export business of SMEs.

Figure VIII.4. Import procedures

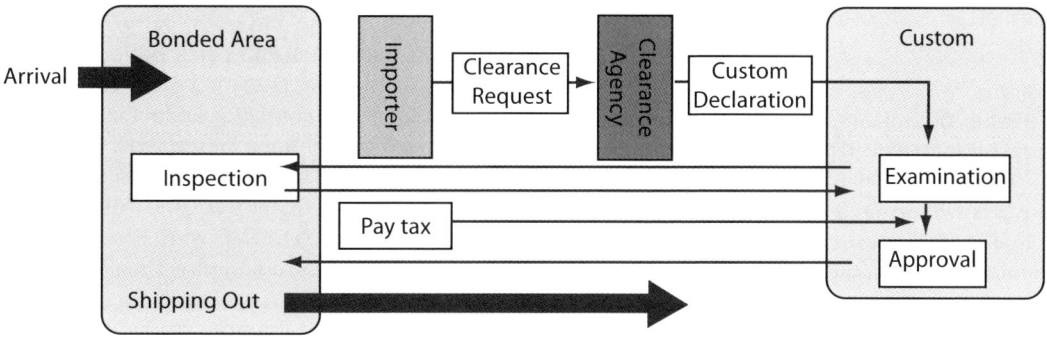

Source: Kai Ga Shoppers, 2012, based on Japan Customs, 2011.

Table VIII.4. Burden of customs procedure by subregion

Subregion	2007	2008	2009	2010
East and North-East Asia	4.70	4.55	4.60	4.70
South-East Asia	3.93	4.02	4.18	4.20
South and South-West Asia	3.29	3.23	3.41	3.70
North and Central Asia	2.99	3.14	3.39	3.48
Developed Economies	4.91	4.97	5.07	5.15

Source: World Bank, 2011f.

D. Trade promotion tools for SMEs

Trade promotion tools, by their very nature, are intended to stimulate interest between foreign buyers and local SME exporters, and specifically to increase the business of SMEs by exposing them to new buyers. Effective trade promotions can result in increased foreign orders for domestic exporters and suppliers.[115] Export-oriented economies in Asia and the Pacific use these tools to garner interest from foreign buyers. Trade promotion tools have been a key driver for continued economic growth in the region. Specific objectives of export promotion initiatives include:

(a) Developing or refining products (and services) for export by communicating with potential customers;

[115] This is achieved by presenting SME export benefits (e.g., low cost, high quality and short and flexible delivery) to foreign buyers.

(b) Gaining new customers/intermediaries in neighbouring, regional and global markets;

(c) Strengthening relationships with existing customers and intermediaries; and

(d) Increasing the amount of exports.

Examples of trade promotion tools include, among others, salespeople, trade fairs/missions, direct mailing/e-mails, homepages and advertising. Figure VIII.5 explains those trade promotion tools, and their targets and costs. For example, a salesperson would be an effective tool for approaching a selected number of prospective customers due to communication effectiveness; however, it involves a higher cost than other methods. On the other hand, traditional direct mailing and e-mail could facilitate contacts by SMEs with a large number of prospective customers at low costs; however, the persuasive power of these methods would be less effective than that of a salesperson. Advertising through mass media could also help SMEs reach a wider range of sales prospects, but it could be too expensive and less effective without specific marketing strategies and appropriate media selection (see chapter 12 of Czinkota and Ronkainen, 2007, for a detailed discussion of this aspect).

The following section considers three major trade promotion tools – trade fairs, buyer-seller meetings and trade missions. Table VIII.5 provides an overviews of the key characteristics of these three tools. The Internet, currently another important

Figure VIII.5. Various trade promotion tools: Cost and target

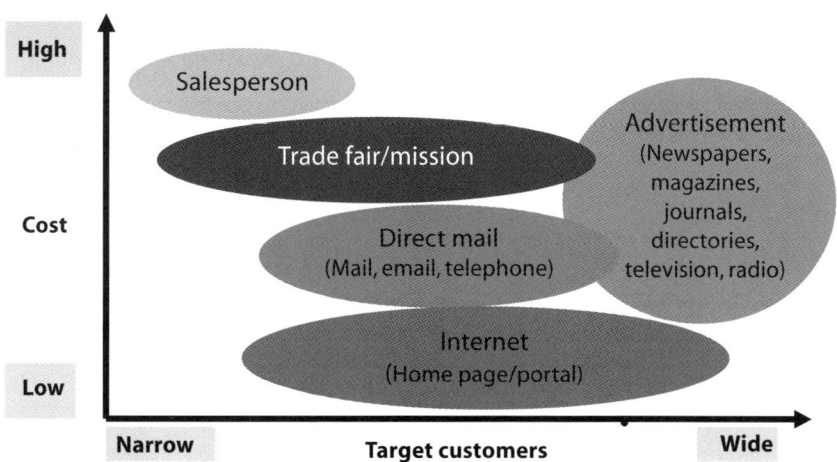

Source: Modified from Japan Finance Corporation, 2008.

trade promotion tool, is covered later in this chapter in the section on ICT applications for SMEs' market access.

1. Trade fairs[116]

Professional events organizers, in collaboration with governments and business associations, organize trade fairs (both domestic and international). They target companies in various industries with exhibits of their latest products and services, information on recent market trends and networking. These fairs can be immensely important for SMEs who cannot afford international advertising to market their products to foreign customers. For example, Vietnamexpo 2011 exhibited products from various Vietnamese companies and sectors (i.e., agriculture, fashion, machinery and equipment) for the international community, thus attracting businesses to the nation (Vinexad, 2008).

Some specific objectives of SME participation in trade fairs include (Czinkota and Ronkainen, 2007):

(a) Providing a chance to examine and see in action those products that are difficult to market indirectly;

(b) "Waving the company flag" against competition to boost the morale of sales personnel and distributors;

(c) Finding an intermediary;

(d) Networking with government officials and decision-makers;

(e) Marketing research and collecting competitive, regulatory and technical intelligence;

(f) Reaching a sizable number of sales prospects at a reasonable cost; and

(g) Strengthening relationships with existing customers, business associations and other stakeholders.

However, trade fairs do have some disadvantages. They can be too costly for firms looking only for one-time or short-term sales. Firms may also have difficulty in choosing the appropriate trade fairs, and participation requires much effort, e.g., registration, preparing materials and setting up displays. SMEs need information about markets, sector, size, reputation and cost of trade fairs in order to choose which trade fairs to attend; but searching for this information is time-consuming. To extract the full benefits from participation in trade fairs, SMEs must conduct the required follow-up activities including direct mailing, visits, trade missions, inviting potential customers for site visits or even opening an office in the target market. These follow-up activities are often difficult for SMEs to execute. According to the Japan External Trade Organization (JETRO) (2011), public support could be sought for successful participation by an SME in a trade fair (e.g., financial support to SME exhibitors

---

Box VIII.2. Trade fairs: Cost and benefit analysis

Although trade fairs provide an effective channel for SMEs to reach prospective customers, they may become expensive diversions without specific marketing strategies (e.g., target customers, selection of right fairs, development of communications materials, training of salespersons, media credentials and follow-up activities). The expenses required for participation in a trade fair typically include: participation fees (e.g., registration, space and furniture, and insurance); booth decoration; staffing; airfare, freight and accommodation; development of promotional materials (in appropriate languages), samples and gifts; and communications. To analyze the costs and benefits of a trade fair properly, the following equation can be used:

$$\frac{\text{Cost of export promotion event}}{\text{Number of inquiries}} = \$ \text{ per inquiry}$$

Source: Authors' compilation.
Note: Inquiries made by potential customers at the fair and after the fair can be included in the total number of inquiries and the number of business cards collected at the fair can also be used as a measure of inquiries.

---

[116] Also referred to as trade shows, exhibitions or expos.

Table VIII.5. Characteristics of three major export promotion events

	Trade fair	Buyer-seller meeting	Trade mission
Size	Large	Middle	Small
Format	Loose gathering, often open to the public, general (e.g., Hanover/Milan); or specialized (e.g., auto show/high-tech)	Structured gathering	Closed door
Target	General public/industry stakeholders	Invited buyers/distributors/partners	Short-listed buyers/distributors/partners/stakeholders
Driver	Often organizer-driven	Often business association-/organizer-driven	Government or business association-driven (crucial support by a local host)
Preparation	Less market research needed and more sales-focused	Proper market research needed, including sales activities	Market-research focused
Scope of sales prospects met	Wide	Medium	Narrow
Quality of sales prospects met	Low	Medium	High
Cost (per sales prospect met)	Low (normally participation fee-based)	Medium	High

Source: Authors' compilation.

at international trade fairs). Organizing buyer-seller meetings and trade missions following trade fairs should also be considered.

2. Buyer-seller meetings

Buyer-seller meetings are a form of initial communication that provides a path for information exchange between key players in demand and supply. In general, buyer-seller meetings are either face-to-face negotiations or conducted through the Internet, telephone, video etc. Many government agencies provide website services where buyers and sellers can post their needs, or goods and services offered. Some agencies act as intermediaries that collect orders from buyers and distribute them to one or several eligible sellers to provide goods and services (Cavusgil and Czinkota, 1990). Although online meeting/matching is most prevalent, due to its convenience and efficiency, face-to-face negotiation is still necessary for two reasons: detailed discussion, explanation and clarification; and necessity to establish lasting business relationships between buyers and sellers (Czinkota and Ronkainen, 2007).

3. Trade missions

A trade mission is an international trip that national agencies organize for government officials and business representatives to explore international business opportunities in target nations. Representatives from the private sector are introduced to important local business contacts and relevant government officials, and thus have crucial contacts for developing business relationships. An example of a recent trade mission to the Asia-Pacific region was the Australian Chamber of Commerce and Industry's trade mission to Sri Lanka in 2010 to discuss business opportunities between the two nations (i.e., diversification of its power industry, port development and potential consultant services for liberalizing its state-owned enterprises) (VECCI, 2010).

E. Key players in trade promotion

Some key players are involved in conducting trade promotion activities. They include trade promotional agencies, foreign branches, commercial attachés and business associations.

1. Trade promotional agencies

Numerous Asia-Pacific nations have established trade promotional agencies that provide a number of export promotion services to facilitate SMEs' market access at the regional and global levels, while also enhancing SME supply-side capacity-building and providing quality business development services. They oversee activities to introduce and promote local products into the international market. Some examples are listed below:

(a) International Enterprise Singapore's collaboration with SPRING Singapore to incorporate Singaporean companies into a capability development programme called BrandPact – which assists them in using distinguishable branding, with unique value propositions, as a business capability in international markets (www.iesingapore.com/wps/portal);

(b) The Philippines' Centre for International Trade Expositions and Missions runs a programme to promote trade and export potentials of selected regions; it introduces homegrown indigenous products to mainstream markets and holds special displays for newly developed products and raw materials (www.citem.gov.ph/main/services.htm);

(c) JETRO (2012a) is a government organization that promotes external trade. JETRO's objective is to ease the access of SMEs to important market information and enable greater export capacity. Activities include surveys of overseas markets, distributing survey data to local parties, and provision of business advice for both Japanese and overseas markets. Its trade tie-up programme is an international business-matching site that allows Japanese companies to display their products and businesses online and connect with other companies around the world. JETRO (2012b) also organizes trade missions and helps SMEs participate in major international trade fairs (www.jetro.go.jp/en/jetro/activities/export/);

(d) The Cambodia Trade Promotion Department promotes Cambodian indigenous products under the name of "Cambodia Quality – Khmer Products", which seeks to present local products with an image of being unique and reliable (www.tpd.gov.kh/khmer_products.php);

(e) The Korea Trade-Investment Promotion Agency (KOTRA) supports SMEs by increasing their knowledge concerning trade and thus reducing the involved market entry costs. KOTRA collects and disseminates market information on business practices, cultures and market conditions, and facilitates the expansion of Korean businesses to international markets (http://english.kotra.or.kr/wps/portal/dken).

(f) The Small and Medium Business Corporation of the Republic of Korea is the main government agency that promotes SMEs' market access. It supports foreign market access for SMEs through export incubators and overseas private consulting centres; the latter offer information about foreign markets and companies, and one-on-one business matching services. It also dispatches trade delegations, holds export conferences and provides SMEs with opportunities to participate in international exhibitions in order to improve their global presence (www.sbc.or.kr/sbc/eng/main.jsp);

(g) SME Corp. Malaysia launched the National Mark of Malaysian Brand programme. Participating Malaysian SMEs are evaluated through stringent standards, with frequent monitoring to ensure quality. The products or services of successful companies are given the right to carry the Malaysian Brand, and are given access to ongoing international trade promotion and advertising of the Malaysia External Trade Development

Corporation (2011b) (www.smecorp.gov.my/v4/node/22); and

(h) The Department of Export Promotion, established under the Ministry of Commerce of Thailand, has five national trade promotion centres within Thailand to provide services to local enterprises and manufacturers. The centres enhance local business potential by matching their needs with foreign buyers and traders through the department's worldwide network (www.thaitradechina.cn/en/about/Default.aspx).

Table VIII.6 summarizes major trade promotion activities in selected Asia-Pacific economies.

Table VIII.6. National programmes for SMEs' market access

Subregion/economy		Programme	Feature
South Asia	India	Government stores programme	• Issue of tender sets free of cost: (a) exemption from payment of earnest money deposit; (b) waiver of security deposit up to the monetary limit for which the unit is registered; and (c) price preference up to 15 per cent over the quotation of large-scale units.
		Export promotion programme	• Products of SME exporters are displayed at international exhibitions, and the expenditure incurred is reimbursed by the government. • Training for SMEs on latest packaging standards for exports and others.
	Sri Lanka	Business development service centre	• Enhance marketing opportunities for SMEs, promote business incubators and sale centres, conduct exhibitions and trade fair programmes, and create links between development service providers, chambers of commerce, advertising organizations, export development boards and SMEs associations.
South-East Asia	Indonesia	Various promotional tools	• Development of promotion tools, including trading boards and exhibitions.
	Malaysia	Various export promotion programmes	• Provide services on exporter development, e.g., exporter training programme, technical and financial assistance. • Export promotion programmes include trade matching, financing international trade events, programmes promoting Malaysian restaurants. • Trade and market information as well as trade advisory and support.
	Philippines	Export assistance network	• Trade facilitation offices serving existing and potential exporters, offering real-time services in export trade information, export procedures and documentation, and buyer linkages.
		Establishment of Philippine trade centres	• Serves as permanent exhibition site for SME export products.
	Thailand	Board of Investment Unit for Industrial Linkage Development (BUILD)	• Organizes meetings and factory tours of registered suppliers and assemblers, organizes subcontracting exhibitions, facilitates local suppliers to display their products and provides financial support to potential suppliers to participate in international exhibitions.
		Programmes of the Office of SME Promotion	• Manages bilateral corporation agreements to promote projects such as franchising, mulberry paper, handcraft, bio-diesel and tourism.
		Department of Export Promotion	• Acting as a one-stop service centre by providing trade information and advisory services, match-making link-ups, business networking and data on Thai products and manufacturers, as well as helping to find suitable trade partners on B2B business portal.
	Singapore	Government Electronic Business (GeBIZ)	• Provides access to procurement opportunities at 120 government agencies.
		Singapore Business Federation Global Sourcing Hub	• Online B2B business portal provides instant access to global opportunities, streamlines and automates sourcing processes and provides access to wider supplier and buyer communities.
		Expert Technical Assistance Centre	• Helps in understanding of and compliance with the standards and technical regulations for food and electrical and electronic exports.
		SPRING	• Develops quality standards and facilitates market access. • Provides marketing toolkit offering comprehensive guides to help SMEs' marketing activities.

Table VIII.6. *(continued)*

Subregion/economy		Programme	Feature
East and North-East Asia	Republic of Korea	Various promotion programmes	• Trade missions to overseas exhibitions. • Dispatches SME employees to overseas markets to become trade professionals.
	China	Various export promotion programmes	• Provides funding for SMEs' international market development and the China International SME Fair.
	Taiwan Province of China	Various promotion and business linkage programmes	• Integrates the resources of local government SME service centres, local chambers of commerce and other relevant agencies, and honourary SME guidance personnel (enterprise service volunteers) to build up comprehensive SME service mechanisms.
	Japan	Various promotion and business linkage programmes	• Facilitates business tie-ups through exhibitions and industrial fairs. • Business Matching Database, which allows Japanese and overseas enterprises to reach out to potential business partners.
		Japan External Trade Organization (JETRO)	• Provides services to Japanese companies through more than 70 offices in more than 50 countries. Also organizes and finances business missions to foreign countries to study local investment environments and market conditions.

Sources: NSIC (2011), SLBDC (2011), Malaysia External Trade Development Corporation (2011a), NAFED (2011), Indonesia Trade Promotion Center (2011), Department of Trade and Industry of the Philippines (2011), BUILD (2011), Agency for SME Development (2011), Department of Export Promotion (2011), GeBIZ (2011), SBF (2011), SPRING (2011c), Small and Medium Business Administration (2011), DFT (2011), Small and Medium Enterprise Administration, (2011b) and JETRO (2011).

2. Foreign branches

To reach potential customers in foreign countries, many trade promotion agencies expand their offices overseas. For example, the Korea Trade-Investment Promotion Agency (KOTRA) established an international network with a number of foreign branches in major (and emerging) export markets to promote Korean products and services, offering a comprehensive support package in every step of the business process to Korean SMEs (KOTRA, 2011). Thailand's Department of Export Promotion also operates Thai trade promotion offices, or Thai trade centres, located in major cities around the world, to foster trade relations between Thai exporters and potential importers (Department of Export Promotion, 2011).

3. Commercial attaché

Commercial attachés are posted to foreign embassies to promote the economic interests of their home country. Generally, they will be based in the economic section of a foreign embassy, which deals with economic relations at a government-to-government level and provides economic information and analysis such as market intelligence on the SME sector to the home country.

4. Business associations[117]

A number of business associations, such as chambers of commerce and federations of industries, provide training for export capacity-building as well as services to promote export focused businesses among their members. The Thai Chamber of Commerce, for example, holds seminars, provides international market information, and organizes meetings between their members and foreign trade representatives. The chamber also coordinates with other business associations within Thailand, such as the Board of Trade of Thailand, which acts as a representative of private trade operators in coordination with the government on issues related to trade promotion. It also provides advice and assistance in solving various trade issues which come from governmental policy and regulations (Thai Chamber of Commerce, 2011).

F. Applications of ICT to facilitate market access

Applications of ICT are widely regarded as an effective strategy for SMEs to gain better access to domestic as well as international markets (Migiro and Ongori, 2010). While the extent and need for ICT applications varies among the different types of SMEs, it can play a powerful role not only by providing new business opportunities but also by increasing their competitiveness (Kotelnikov, 2007). For example, using new technologies and the Internet to their advantage and moving away from traditional forms of business to e-commerce, SMEs can reduce transaction costs by saving on capital, marketing and labour expenses (APEC, 2003).[118] The arrival of broadband, together with the eager adoption of mobile-based technologies, has further empowered small businesses to address competition. ICT can help cut costs by streamlining internal processes, improving services through faster communication with customers and bettering promotion and distribution of products. It has also assisted in broadening market reach through ICT enhanced market intelligence such as online databases of customers, suppliers and competitors (UNDP Asia-Pacific Development Information Programme, 2007).

SMEs can also benefit from online marketplaces, where they can establish direct business ties with customers or other businesses (B2B). The government can assume the role of the

---

[117] See box VI.3 on the comprehensive role that business associations play in SME development.

[118] However, the expectations of the scale of savings from e-commerce need to be balanced, as the empirical evidence is mixed (Santarelli and D'Altri, 2003; and Humphrey and others, 2003).

facilitator, as is the case in the Republic of Korea. The Small and Medium Business Corporation, which is, a Government of the Republic of Korea entity with the mandate to promote SMEs, operates a free online business matching service with the largest database of manufactures and suppliers in the Republic of Korea.[119]

Government involvement is not necessarily required, as there are other successful examples of private web portals for SMEs. Alibaba, a Chinese company, was founded in 1999 and evolved from a simple online bulletin board to the world's largest B2B company. In China, with an estimated 400 million SMEs, one out of 10 SMEs conduct business via Alibaba (Finance Asia, 2010). In India, more than 1 million SMEs are Alibaba members. In total, almost 69 million users from more than 240 countries are registered with Alibaba for conducting global e-business (Alibaba Group, 2011).

ICT can be utilized to facilitate lengthy international trade procedures such as customs clearance. The Government of the Republic of Korea has pursued an e-trade framework since the late 1980s, which has expanded nationwide to cover ICT facilitation in customs clearance. As a result of the project, the use of ICT has enabled SMEs to export through a simplified procedure utilizing an electronic network open to international traders seeking to use ICT for all stages involved in exports, from negotiating between firms to logistic and customs procedures (Yang, 2009).

Given the prospects of ICT applications for the SME community, such as increased access to new markets by reducing transaction costs and an accelerated communication speed, the promotion of ICT policies catering to the needs of SMEs is of unquestionable importance. Acknowledging the significance of SMEs in Asia and the Pacific, the Asian and Pacific Training Centre for Information and Communication Technology for Development (APCICT) has proposed three key recommendations for policymakers:

(a) Raise awareness of the benefits of ICT;
(b) Strengthen ICT literacy and build capacity in the alignment of business and ICT strategies; and
(c) Create enabling environments for the adoption and growth of ICT firms.

One effective policy is that governments themselves use ICT through e-government and e-procurement, as they are often important service providers to SMEs as well as buyers of goods and services of SMEs. This policy can provide an important incentive for SMEs to begin using e-commerce (UNDP Asia-Pacific Development Information Programme, 2007).

---

[119] For more details, see www.gobizkorea.com/.

Box VIII.3. Internet marketing: Republic of Korea

The term "Internet marketing" refers to the use of the Internet for e-mail-based aspects of a marketing campaign. It usually incorporates banner advertisements, e-mail marketing, search engine optimization, e-commerce and other related tools (AMA, 2011). There were nearly 2 billion global Internet users in 2010 – facilitating the growth of Internet marketing with a huge customer base (World Bank, 2010b). Internet marketing has been labelled as highly efficient, with much lower costs, compared with traditional marketing strategies. SMEs are one of the groups that stand to benefit from this booming expansion (Mathews, Healy and Ali, 2006).

One example in the Republic of Korea is Neo Buzz Demolition Tool Co., Ltd. Since its founding in 1989, the company has become one of the country's leading manufacturers of hydraulic breaks, hydraulic attachments and construction equipment (Neo Buzz, undated). Neo Buzz, which originally targeted to the domestic market, now exports to China, Egypt, Iraq, Israel, Italy, Japan, Taiwan Province of China, the United States and Viet Nam – increasing its annual sales revenue by more than 30 per cent in the past three years.

This has largely been the result of the company's online marketing strategy. In 2009, Neo Buzz became a member of one of the leading B2B trade groups, after which inquiries from potential global customers increased tremendously. Buyers visiting Neo Buzz's webpage are able to see the full range of its products with detailed descriptions and features. Customers also have the option to decide whether to meet with company representatives or to negotiate online. This ensures that flexibility, reliability and efficiency of business transactions is cost-effective, making it a great choice for SME exporters.

Box VIII.4. East-West Economic Corridor business database

The Mekong Institute, an intergovernmental organization of the countries of the Greater Mekong Subregion, – which comprises Cambodia, the Lao People's Democratic Republic, Myanmar, Thailand, Viet Nam and the Yunnan Province and Guangzi Autonomous Region of China, with support from the Japan Asean Integration Fund – developed a comprehensive database for business networking and information sharing in the East-West Economic Corridor (EWEC). The objective is to provide a compatible database for SME-related information that is accurate, reliable and timely across the 11 provinces of the EWEC and to promote trade and investment through networking and information sharing.

The database consists of two components: (a) provincial business profiles; and (b) company profiles. The provincial business profiles include provincial-level business information on economic indicators, leading sectors, exports and imports, business-related support infrastructure, incentives and the cost of doing business. The company profiles provide members of the chambers of commerce, industry professionals and business associations along the EWEC with products/services details, production turnover, export and import items, certifications and awards and contact details. Some 1,700 companies were listed in the database at the end of 2011 and can be viewed at www.ewecbiz.com.

Source: EWEC, undated.

G. Trade finance

According to the International Trade Centre (ITC) (2009), trade finance "refers to a wide range of tools that determine how cash, credit, investments and other assets can be used for trade". In this sense, the primary objective of trade finance is no different from SME financing, which is discussed in chapter V.

One of the barriers to exporting that SMEs face is the difficulty of coordinating and receiving payment for their goods and services from their foreign customers. Even if they are capable of identifying overseas customers, they may lack the expertise to transact business smoothly or to ascertain creditworthiness. On the other hand, foreign buyers cannot discern how reliable an SME may be as a supplier. The uncertainty on both sides can discourage international trade from occurring. Another barrier is the additional expense of international trade. Those costs include international marketing, cross-border transportation, customs and duties, transport costs and communications. International trade usually requires a longer business cycle (i.e., marketing, sales, production, delivery and payment) due to the physical distance between sellers and buyers and for processing paperwork and handling exporting and importing procedures. International trade creates extra financing requirements, especially on the exporters' side, for both pre-shipment and post-shipment periods (ESCAP, 2005b). Effective trade finance helps to mitigate the risks inherent in the uncertainty, extra costs and financing needs.[120] Trade finance is also important not just for exports but also for access to raw materials.

---

[120] However, globalization has reduced the risks significantly. For example, the Internet facilitates review of buyers' credit worthiness and international transactions by exporters, while advanced international logistic systems reduce the lead time of exporting and importing.

SMEs generally experience difficulties in accessing adequate trade finance. First, there is commonly a lack of efficient and effective banking and payment systems, particularly in developing countries of the region. In particular, financial constraints such as high costs of finance and a lack of access to finance restrict growth opportunities of SMEs (ITC, 2009). Second, there are challenges in accessing timely, accurate and affordable trade and credit information. SMEs normally operate on tight budgets, and while information may be available it may be unaffordable.

1. Forms of trade finance

Trade finance comprises different financial services. They are broadly aimed at three aspects that, depending on the situation, can be used in different combinations (ITC, 2009):

(a) Raising capital and increasing liquidity;
(b) Facilitating payments, regulating terms and conditions; and
(c) Mitigating risks and uncertainties.

The capital requirements of SMEs largely arise from their need to finance marketing, manufacturing and distribution of their export products. This calls for the use of various forms of trade finance to raise working capital. Trade financial instruments secure buyers' payments, thus influencing the competitiveness of SMEs in domestic and global markets. Mitigating risks such as payment delays or fluctuating exchange rates requires certain financial instruments in order to help avoid or prevent significant losses. Within this context, there are a number of finance methods and instruments available to SMEs, depending on their stage in the trade cycle and the particular financial needs of the firm. Figure VIII.6 illustrates some of these methods and instruments as well as the relevant stage in the trade cycle.

Figure VIII.6. Trade cycle and trade finance methods and instruments for SMEs

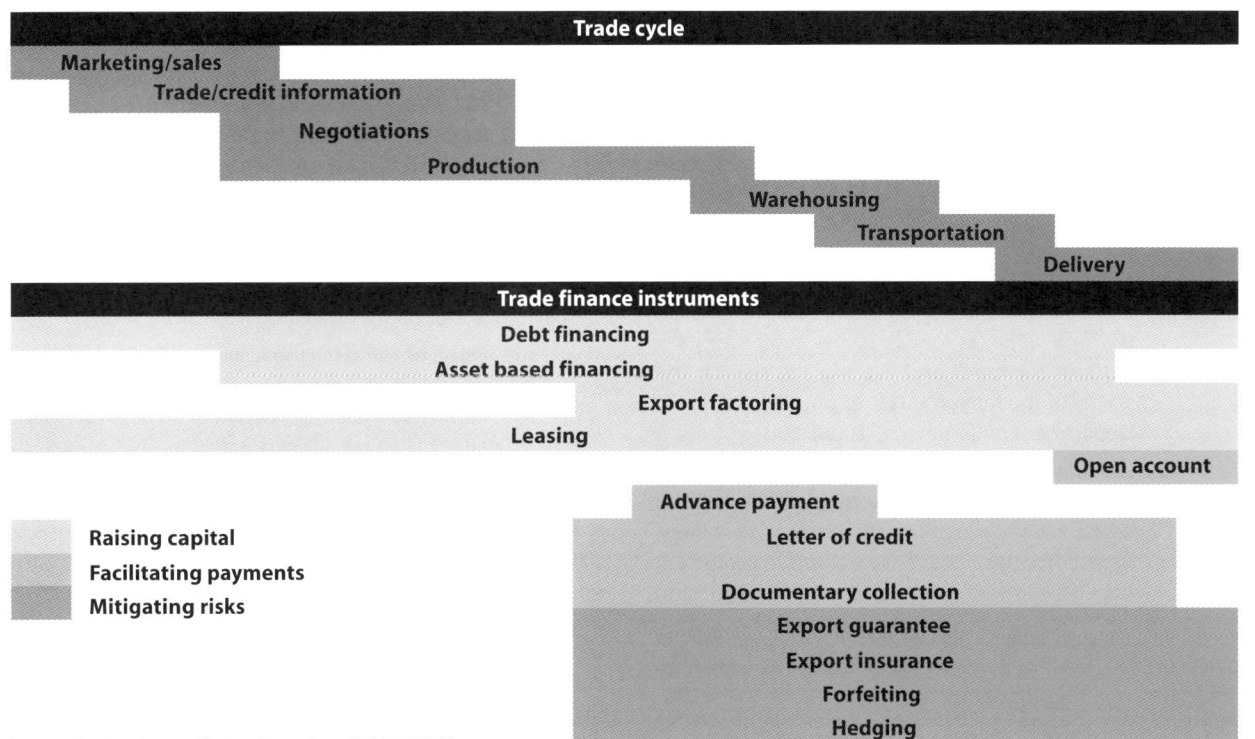

Source: Authors' compilation, based on ESCAP, 2005b.

Some major forms of trade finance instruments are discussed in detail below according to the three categories (i.e., raising capital, facilitating payments and mitigating risks).[121]

(a) Trade finance methods and instruments aimed at raising capital[122]

Raising working capital for SMEs' export operations necessitates short term credits and/or loans in various forms. Such debt financing is required for both the pre-shipment and the post-shipment periods. Pre-shipment finance should support activities before the actual export such as the payment of wages, materials and supplies. SMEs that are active in the export market are especially dependent on this type of trade finance as international trade cycles are generally longer than domestic ones and thus require additional working capital (ESCAP, 2002). Post-shipment finance on the other hand involves financing for working capital after shipment but before the end of the entire export process, i.e., buyers' payments (ESCAP, 2002). It includes short-term credits and/or loans as well as payment terms agreed upon with buyers.

The major financial methods and instruments for raising working capital for export include:

(a) Debt financing – this method of trade finance is typically used to obtain working capital (liquidity) for exporting operations. As reviewed in chapter V, debt financing can be obtained in various forms (e.g., overdrafts, line of credits, term loans etc.). In developing countries, commercial banks and state-supported development banks need more coaching and support to help SMEs access term loans. Such loans could be a stable financial instrument for SMEs' export growth;

(b) Asset-based financing – this is a loan that is often secured through the inventories of goods to be exported. These inventories include raw materials, work-in-process and/or finished products;

(c) Export factoring – a complete financial package that combines working capital financing, credit protection, foreign accounts receivable, bookkeeping and collection services. Export factoring is offered under an agreement between the factor and exporter. The factor is usually a bank or a specialized financial firm. Factors purchase the exporter's short-term foreign accounts receivable (or sometimes mere invoices and trade documents) for cash at a discount from the face value (as low as 50 per cent), normally without recourse, and assume the risk on the ability of the foreign buyer to pay (United States Department of Commerce, 2008); and

(d) Leasing – medium- to long-term financing of payments that need to be made for the use of assets, such as equipment, property or machinery, for export operations. It allows firms to avoid high one-time investments and increase working capital for export operations, by paying the leasing bank or company for the use of assets through monthly rental fees.

(b) Trade finance instruments aimed at facilitating payments

According to ITC (2009), the most important trade finance instruments in this category are cash-in-advance, letters of credit (L/Cs), documentary collection and open accounts, although many SME exporters are conducting export business based on either payment after delivery or open accounts:

(a) Cash in advance – the full payment for products is made up-front, which eliminates the risk for the exporter. This is the most preferred option when the creditworthiness of the importer (buyer) is in doubt;

(b) Letter of credit – an important financial instrument for securing the interests of both parties that is issued by the importer's bank for the exporter's bank. The importer's bank commits to pay as soon as the agreed terms and conditions have been met by the exporter, which is generally verified through the reception of required trade documents (United States Department of Commerce, 2007). This method of payment involves third parties, generally commercial banks, as mediators and thus reduces the risks for both the exporter and the importer. It is preferably used for new trade relations (ITC, 2009). Figure VIII.7 explains the transaction process of an L/C. The primary act is to issue an L/C to the exporter, guaranteeing payment on receipt of documents verifying shipment and transfer of title to the importer. Such documents usually include a draft, also known as a bill of exchange, which is the exporter's formal request for payment, as well as a bill of lading, which specifies the goods shipped and the transfer of title to the importer on payment;

(c) Documentary collections – although similar to L/Cs, documentary collections are, however, specifically shipping and collection documents that are sent from the exporter's bank to the importer's bank in exchange for the payment. Documentary collections can be differentiated between documents against payment – the payment takes place at sight – and documents against acceptance – the payment is made at a later date as specified (ITC, 2009); and

(d) Open accounts – these are the best method of payment for importers, as they usually grant importers a payment period of 30 days to 90 days after the shipment of goods.

One key issue, in addition to the uncertainty of export account receivables, is a divergence in preferred terms of payment that satisfy the interests of the exporter and the importer. As figure VIII.8 shows, a comparison between levels of payment in particular shows the differences in preferred terms of payment. Typically, exporters seek to reduce their risks by letting the importer pay up-front for goods. Importers, in contrast, prefer credits such as open accounts, and they may also require exporters (sellers) to document the shipping process and products (ESCAP, 2005b).

---

[121] For further details, including specialized financial instruments for commodity trade (e.g., warehouse recipt), please see ITC modules on *How to Access Trade Finance*. (www.intracen.org/exporters/obtaining-export-credits) and ESCAP (2005), *Trade Finance Infrastructure Development Handoook for Economies in Transition*.

[122] See also chapter V for a more detailed discussion.

Figure VIII.7. Letter of credit transaction process

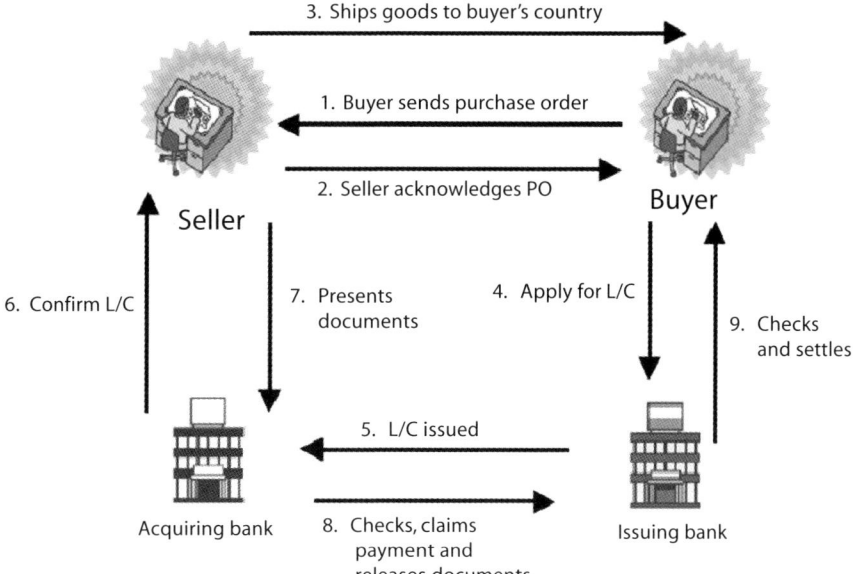

Source: ESCAP, 2005b.

Figure VIII.8. Comparison between terms of payment

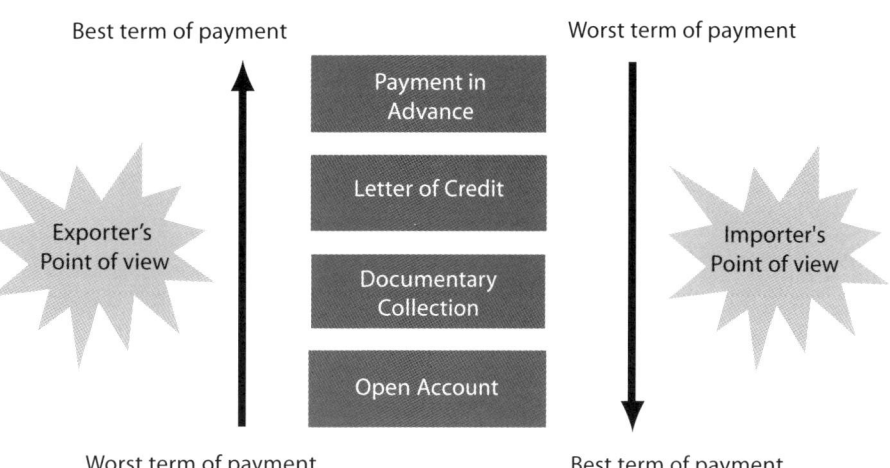

Source: ESCAP, 2005b.

Box VIII.5. Terms of trade payment: Thailand

Importing and exporting enterprises in Thailand use different methods of payment, depending on their size (table VIII.7). SMEs in Thailand are mostly required to make advance payments when importing; larger firms, however, are primarily able to enjoy the benefits of open accounts, and advance payments are seldom required. For both groups, letters of credit are the second-most used payment method, and documentary collections are the least common.

When it comes to exporting, the situation is reversed. A majority of SMEs offer open accounts to buyers, whereas larger enterprises require advance payment or open accounts. Advance payments and documentary collection only play a minor role in payment processes for Thai exporting SMEs.

Thus, SMEs are generally more subject to insecure or unfavourable terms of payment than large companies. Due to their size, higher liquidity requirements as well as increased risks are imposed on them.

Table VIII.7. Methods of payment for importing and exporting enterprises, by size, in Thailand

Method of payment	Importers		Exporters	
	Large enterprises (per cent)	Small and medium-sized traders (per cent)	Large enterprises (per cent)	Small and medium-sized traders (per cent)
Letter of credit	23	29	17	23
Bill of collection	4	5	5	7
Advance payment	10	40	38	10
Open account	63	26	40	60

Source: Duval and Liu, 2009.

(c) Trade finance instruments aimed at mitigating risks and uncertainties

SME exporters face various risks and uncertainties, which can be broadly classified into four groups: (a) commercial risks (e.g., payment default); (b) exchange rate risks (e.g., sudden large floating); (c) transport risks (e.g., damage); and (d) political risks (e.g., restrictions) (ESCAP, 2005b). Some of the major trade finance instruments that reduce the risks are described below:

(a) Export credit guarantee – this is a protection mechanism for banks that are financing exports, which is generally provided by public agencies. It facilitates the access of exporters to finance by offering banks protection from possible losses in the form of financial guarantees. SMEs can profit from an export credit guarantee as it makes acquiring finance from commercial banks easier (ESCAP, 2005b). It is important for public agencies providing an export credit guarantee to weigh the risks involved in supporting firms that are taking up credit under such a scheme;

(b) Export credit insurance – private insurance companies and/or governmental export credit agencies offer this coverage to business entities to insure their export accounts receivable from loss due to the non-payment of valid debt by their debtors (Jones, 2009). Some of the benefits of trade credit insurance are: (i) protection from bankruptcy or insolvency of a customer, and thus a loss on accounts receivable; (ii) favourable financing from an SME's lender, either via favourable eligibility of receivables or the inclusion of accounts in the borrowing formula that are not eligible without credit insurance; (iii) sales expansion; and (iv) reduction of bad-debt reserves and accounts receivable risk concentration (William Gallagher Associates, 2009). In general, the potential risks faced by exporters in international trade are more complex; private insurance companies may not be able to provide enough coverage for the risks. As a consequence, government agencies are commonly established to operate export credit insurance. Specific examples include, among others, Israel's Foreign Trade Risk Insurance Corporation Ltd. and India's Export Credit Guarantee Corporation, both of which provide guarantees to cover trade and export transactions;

(c) Forfeiting – this is a method of trade financing that enables exporters who sell capital goods, commodities or large projects to obtain cash, at a discount, against their longer-term foreign account receivables on a non-recourse basis. In this method, receivables are normally guaranteed by the importer's bank, and exporters typically work with a forfeiter that is either a specialized finance firm or a department in a bank that performs non-recourse export financing to eliminate the risk of non-payment (International Trade Adminstration, 2007); and

(d) Hedging – this is a technique used to reduce the risk of fluctuations in exchange rates and to protect expected profitability in the domestic currency. Hedging involves offsetting one currency position with another (ITC, 2009). The two most common methods are forward and futures contracts. Forward contracts are agreements with a fixed date and exchange rate at the point of delivery of goods. It can be arranged with a bank that agrees to exchange the foreign currency, which will be received from the firm at a previously-fixed exchange rate. Futures contracts are similar to forward contracts but they are generally organized on standardized terms through futures exchanges. The losses and gains are updated every day and the holder must provide enough cash to cover any losses. In developing countries, commodity futures exchanges exist such as the agricultural futures exchange of Thailand (ESCAP, 2005b). In business, forward contracts are used more often than futures because their terms are more flexible and convenient. Although both forward contracts and futures are useful tools to reduce foreign exchange risks, SMEs may need to develop their internal expertise to utilize them or they may seek technical assistance from external financial experts.

(d) Actors facilitating trade finance

Banks play an important role in providing support and security in trade finance. A bank acts as a trusted third party to guarantee delivery from the exporter and payment by the importer. In addition to alleviating credit risk, this arrangement also mitigates foreign exchange risk, as banks are more knowledgeable about foreign currency markets and can help their clients hedge against sudden fluctuations of foreign exchange. Typically, the exporter and importer interact with their local banks, which then coordinate the flow of documents and money (ITC, 2009).

Export credit agencies (ECAs), which are often state-owned (or controlled) development financial institutions, are also major actors in international trade and investment. They generally provide government-backed loans, guarantees and insurance to corporations, including SMEs, seeking to do business in foreign countries with the mandate to promote their own countries' exports and foreign investments (Center for International Environmental Law, 2003). The trade financing instruments most commonly used by ECAs are export credits or loans provided to buyers or suppliers of export goods, and import credits or loans provided to overseas purchasers of domestic goods and services. These are often offered on more favourable terms than those provided by private commercial banks (IPCC, 2000). ECAs consist of bilateral organizations such as export/import banks or investment promotion agencies. Most advanced industrialized countries have national ECAs that are committed to enhancing their economic and business interests overseas (IPCC, 2000). Examples include:

(a) Nippon Export and Investment Insurance (2011) of Japan is an incorporated administrative agency that was created in 2001 as a 100 per cent state-owned agency to manage trade and investment insurance programmes;

(b) The Export-Import Bank of Korea (Korea Eximbank, 2011) is an official export credit agency established in 1976 in the Republic of Korea. It provides comprehensive export credit and guarantee programmes to support Korean enterprises in conducting overseas business. It is also responsible for the operation of some government funds; and

(c) The Export Finance and Insurance Corporation (undated) in Australia is the Government's export credit agency that helps successful businesses to finance and protect export trade or overseas investments when their banks are unable to provide all the support they need.

Unlike commercial banks that aim for a market return on their loans or insurance, ECAs usually only seek to recover their operating and financing costs. They are either official or quasi-official branches of the national government and are a part of a broader government policy framework focused on trade and investment promotion (FERN, undated[123]). Despite this option, SMEs tend to rely more on commercial banks and make only limited use of development banks, or ECAs, for export financing (ITC, 1997). ESCAP and ITC (1997), based on survey data and field experience, found that 33 per cent of the SMEs surveyed turned to commercial banks for support in export activities, whereas only 10 per cent considered development banks to be helpful in this area. Commercial banks were consulted three times more often on export-related issues than development banks.

Box VIII.6. Thai EXIM bank

The Government of Thailand created the Export-Import Bank of Thailand to foster trade as well as support SMEs in expanding into international markets. Established in 1993, it offers a range of financial services. Over the years, these services have been expanded to include not only trade finance instruments such as export credit insurance, but also others such as a credit facility for business expansion, foreign investment advisory services and an SME financial service centre. The Thai EXIM Bank also provides other services to SMEs, such as risk assessment and training for entrepreneurs in trade finance.

With such measures, the bank has reacted effectively to global and regional changes and has continued to emphasize its role as a development bank. It became more proactive in the facilitation and promotion of trade among developing countries in the region. One recent example of its engagement are the measures implemented due to the 2007 financial crisis and the resulting drop in trade finance. The bank increased its export insurance provision by $ 140 million. It also funded an $ 85 million investment in the Small Business Credit Guarantee Corporation to strengthen SMEs and provide capital for loans.

Source: Duval and Liu, 2009.

---

[123] See also the FERN website at www.fern.org/campaign/trade-and-investment/export-credit-agencies.

(e) Consideration for effective trade finance

In order to increase the trade volume of SMEs, it is necessary to help them enter international or export markets more easily. One of the most important factors for SMEs looking to export is the availability and access to trade finance. Some key considerations are explained below:

(a) The costs for SMEs to enter the export market or to increase their trade volume needs to be reduced by providing them with adequate information on trade finance issues. As with other issues that have an impact on SMEs, small businesses are often unaware of the existing options or providers, and do not have the adequate resources or time available to investigate. The public sector has an important role to play in this regard;

(b) There is a need for an adequate policy framework and properly functioning banking systems in the domestic environment. Efficient and effective financial structures are required to ensure optimal SME participation in trade;

(c) Public agencies should provide various trade finance strategies for SMEs that are aimed at providing capital, support services and favourable laws and regulations to increase trade activity. They should also support, directly or indirectly, the establishment of training centres or reformation of curricula in order to increase small business entrepreneur knowledge about trade finance issues; and

(d) Policymakers should also facilitate trade finance by connecting SMEs with local banks, export-import banks and development financial institutions. Government officials need to communicate with both the banking sector and the SME sector to specify expectations and procedures.

H. Special economic zones

Special economic zones (SEZs), also known as free trade zones, are "a part of the territory of a contracting party where any goods introduced are generally regarded, insofar as import duties and taxes are concerned, as being outside the customs territory" (World Customs Organization, 1999). SEZs are a useful tool for SME development through supply-side capacity-building and greater market access; they increase industrial output and attract FDI. They also allow host governments to develop and diversify exports while maintaining protective barriers, creating employment and incorporating new policies. According to the Foreign Investment Advisory Service (FIAS) (2008), the principles incorporated in the basic concept of the special economic zone include: (a) a geographically delimited area (usually physically secured); (b) a single administration; (c) eligibility for benefits based upon physical location within the zone and a separate customs area (duty-free benefits); and (d) streamlined procedures. The phenomenon of SEZs has been successfully utilized to modernize economies in recent years due to the ability to customize of SEZs to fit specific needs. Table VIII.8 summarizes the different variations of SEZs in existence throughout the world.

Table VIII.8. Types of special economic zones

Type of Zone	Development Objective	Physical Configuration	Typical Location	Eligible Activities	Markets	Examples
Free Trade Zone (Commercial Free Zone)	Support trade	Size <50 hectares	Parts of entry	Entrepôt and trade-related activities	Domestic re-export	Colon Free Zone, Panama
Traditional EPZ	Export manufacturing	Size <100 hectares: total area is designated as an EPZ	None	Manufacturing, other processing	Mostly export	Karachi EPZ, Pakistan
Hybrid EPZ	Export manufacturing	Size <100 hectares: only part of the area is designated as an EPZ	None	Manufacturing, other processing	Export and domestic market	Lat Krabang Industrial Estate Thailand
Freeport	Integrated development	Size >100 km^2	None	Multi-use	Domestic internal and export markets	Aqaba Special Economic Zone, Jordan
Enterprise Zone, Empowerment, Urban Free Zones	Urban revitalization	Size <50 hectares	Distressed urban or rural areas	Multi-use	Domestic	Empowerment Zone, Chicago
Single Factory EPZ	Export manufacturing	Designation for individual enterprises	Countrywide	Manufacturing other processing	Export market	Mauritius Mexico Madagascar

Source: FIAS, 2008.

The rationale for the development of an SEZ depends on the home economy's state of development. Developing economies follow infrastructural and policy guidelines for the development of these zones with a typical SEZ policy package including import and export duty exemptions, streamlined customs and administrative controls and procedures, liberal foreign exchange policies and tax incentives.[124] All these policies are aimed at boosting investments and competitiveness as well as at reducing business entry and operating costs (FIAS, 2008). The advantages of SEZ development can be observed both as static and dynamic. Table VIII.9 outlines the generic benefits of developing an SEZ, which can contribute to SME capacity-building as well as allow for greater market access.

Table VIII.9. Advantages of special economic zones

Static advantages	Dynamic advantages
Direct employment creation and income generation	Technology transfer
Export growth and export diversification	Skills upgrading
Increase in foreign direct investment	Local development
Increase in foreign exchange earnings	Empowerment of women
Government revenue	Indirect employment creation

Source: FIAS, 2008.

---

[124] Major tax incentives include tax holidays during the initial years of set up, reduced tax rates after a company starts making a profit and no customs duties on imports and exports (FIAS, 2008).

SEZs offer affordable features that many firms, including SMEs, can exploit. With the facilities provided by SEZs, these zones can act as incubators for SME growth. There are also initial tax incentives, infrastructure support and duty-free trade to help gain a foothold in the competitive export market. Other advantages include:

(a) Market access – SEZs can provide useful networks for SMEs with foreign buyers and investors, providing market access opportunities to SMEs;

(b) Capacity-building – SMEs can gain market intelligence, new knowledge and advance technology from neighbouring companies and investors as well as SEZs;

(c) Avoidance of the informal economy – if an SME is part of an SEZ, there must be a proper registration, dissuading participation in the informal sector; and

(d) Social responsibility compliance – SEZs establish standards regarding waste management, green sustainability, female empowerment, child labour, minimum wages and other worker health and safety issues. Firms operating in the zone must comply.

I. Foreign direct investment and SMEs' increased market access

Since the end of the 1980s, TNCs have invested in the Asia-Pacific region to build value chains, built on national export-oriented development strategies, combined with trade and investment liberalization, low-cost logistics systems and

> **Box VIII.7. Transnational corporations and SMEs**
>
> Collaboration and linkages between TNCs and SMEs can play an important role in providing SMEs with a stable source of capital and technology transfer. This can help to increase SME competitiveness in global markets as the capacity, network and knowledge of TNCs can help SMEs to increase their productivity and profits.
>
> Recently, more complex forms of linkages between TNCs and SMEs, such as outsourcing of side-products, have largely replaced the traditional models of production. This provides SMEs with greater independence and new opportunities while also increasing the pressure for them to compete with many other suppliers.
>
> In the Philippines, the manufacturing group, Metalcast, operates as a supplier to TNCs and produces parts for the automotive, motorcycle and electronics industries. It has link with export markets in Germany, Japan and the United States, and collaborates with TNCs such as Ford, Honda and Sharp. Initially, Metalcast decided to approach TNCs because domestic demand, and thus growth opportunities, were limited. A reorientation towards the export market was necessary in order for the group to expand its business and profit from economies-of-scale.
>
> Together with the support of TNCs, Metalcast improved production processes, adopted new technologies and adjusted its company structure. This enhanced the ability of Metalcast to compete on a global scale and to increase its profits.
>
> *Source:* UNCTAD, 2005c.

> **Box VIII.8. SMEs' foreign market access through trading companies**
>
> SME exporters have, in many cases, been supported by trading houses developed by large manufacturing enterprises. Several large manufacturing groups in Brazil, India and Turkey have established their own trading houses to manage their exporting and importing businesses. The priority of those trading houses is to manage trade for products of the parent firms, but they also act as the marketing channel for a large number of SMEs. In Japan, trading houses have been active in a similar way for more than 100 years (e.g., Mitsubishi and Mitsui). They are generally not involved in production but work as intermediaries between SMEs and international markets. Some governments have encouraged the links between trading houses and SMEs by offering financial incentives such as tax breaks.
>
> *Source:* ITC, 1999.

advanced ICT applications (ESCAP, 2009b). Increased regional FDI flows during the 1990s and 2000s have accelerated the development of global supply chains in Asia and the Pacific.

This upsurge in FDI flows has several explanations. The economic success of the countries in Asia and the Pacific owes much to foreign direct investment and export growth. Most of the countries started their growth through foreign investment in labour-intensive SME sectors, such as garments and apparel manufacturing, where the flexibility of SMEs was fully utilized. Labour-intensive activities were subcontracted to the SMEs, forging links between export growth and the growth of SMEs.[125] Their greater flexibility, low-skilled technology, adaptability to local economic conditions and capacity to serve small communities make SMEs more suited to the conditions of most developing countries than their large, multinational counterparts.

The rapid increase of FDI flows has major implications for two aspects of the SME sector (ESCAP, 2007b and 2009b). First, FDI enables SMEs in domestic markets to act as suppliers of parts and components or basic services, largely on a subcontracting basis, to foreign investors. Second, as SMEs become a part of a global supply chain, they gain skills and knowledge about conducting business across borders. SMEs in Asia and the Pacific have gradually started to become foreign investors themselves or are recipients of foreign investment, usually in the form of joint ventures (e.g., the automotive parts industry in Thailand). These issues are further discussed in the next section.

J. Participation of SMEs in global supply chains

As briefly reviewed in the previous section, one significant development in the Asia-Pacific business community has been the emergence of global and regional supply or value chains.[126] A global supply chain (GSC) refers to the full range of cross-border, value-added business activities that are required to bring a product or service from the conception, design, sourcing raw materials and intermediate inputs stages, to production, marketing, distribution and supplying the final consumer (ESCAP, 2007b). A number of SMEs participate in global supply chains and provide services based on their expertise as suppliers, distributors and business service providers (e.g., third-party logistic providers, financial institutions and market research firms) (see figure VIII.9).

There are two basic types of GSCs (ESCAP, 2007b):

(a) Producer-driven chains or networks, where the lead firm (such as automobile and consumer electric appliance assemblers) plays a central role in exercising control over the network of subsidiaries, affiliates and suppliers;

(b) Buyer-driven chains or networks, where large retailers, marketers and brand manufacturers (such as Levi's in the apparel industry) source from the decentralized network of suppliers.

The basic characteristics of GSCs are:

(a) Policy decisions – the lead firm decides the items/products to be outsourced, the quality/quantity, timing of supplies and pricing;

(b) Capacity-building of suppliers – the lead firm typically demands and helps SMEs to implement improvements in the quality of their products/

---

[125] While these arrangements spurred fantastic development, the rights of workers were often ignored (e.g., the garments/apparel sector in various developing countries in Asia and the Pacific) (Locke, Qin and Brause, 2006).

[126] For further details see ESCAP, 2009a, ESCAP, 2009b, and ESCAP, 2007b, all of which are available at www.unescap.org/tid/publication/publicat.asp.

Figure VIII.9. A simplified global or regional supply chain

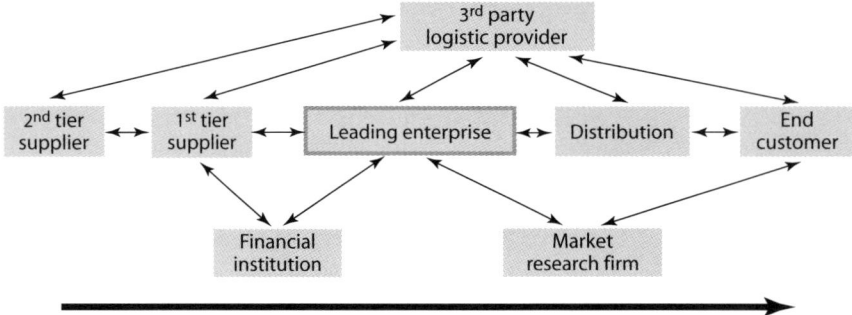

Source: ESCAP, 2007b.

services, their productivity and the upgrading of their human resources;

(c) Product standardization – lead firms ensure consistency and reliability of supplies; and

(d) Global supplier status – an SME can become a global supplier by becoming a vital GSC player.

The development of GSCs in Asia and the Pacific provides business opportunities for export-oriented SMEs and supporting industry SMEs (ESCAP, 2009a). Global supply chains are expected to provide an efficient network by establishing links with large enterprises or even with other efficient SMEs. They help to boost the value-added activities of affiliated SMEs in international trade by providing an established market.

However, SMEs currently play a limited role due to low value-addition and lack of proper networking. SMEs are generally at a disadvantage due to their small scale and lack of knowledge necessary to penetrate regional and global markets (ESCAP, 2007a). SMEs in the Asia-Pacific developing countries typically lack the environment to improve their capacity, including a proper policy and regulatory framework, supporting infrastructure, access to finance, a strong entrepreneurship culture, technology incubation and business development services (ESCAP, 2009b).

In order to participate effectively in GSCs, SMEs must break high entry barriers by meeting a wide range of increasingly stringent global standards with regard to quality, price, timely delivery and flexibility. SMEs that seek to establish partnerships in GSCs should understand the governance of the specific value chain process and structures. As international trade is mostly undertaken by large enterprises of global repute, and since leading firms in GSCs are the key decision makers in managing global production systems and trade, they would be the ones influencing the participation of smaller firms in such chains. It is important that the structure

---

Box VIII.9. Vietnamese SMEs in IBM's global supply chain

The world partner programme of IBM is an example of a TNC's success in investing in local SMEs and incorporating them into GSCs. The programme was designed to help SMEs strengthen their relationship with IBM while, at the same time, gaining competitive advantages in the marketplace. Programme-eligible companies can become a supplier to IBM and receive several forms of assistance – such as having access to IBM's marketing, sales, technical and training programmes. IBM provides skills-building courses and technical assistance to support the development of these SMEs. In addition, being qualified as a partner of IBM also requires SMEs to meet high international product and process standards, which will improve their quality and production – ultimately bringing them more business opportunities.

Source: UNCTAD, 2010c.

Box VIII.10. Subcontracting

SMEs in developing countries can participate in GSCs by entering into subcontracting arrangements with larger enterprises or TNCs. By linking export products through suitable global supply chains with large-scale exporting units, SMEs can build new capabilities. Supplying larger industrial units according to customers' needs/specifications will necessarily lead to improvements in the SMEs' own production efficiency. SMEs with advanced capabilities can become ancillary units to larger units, thus garnering recognition and building their own brand. Outsourcing production to SMEs also increases the profitability of TNCs as they can allocate their resources to their core competencies and higher value-added activities.

Subcontracting may also lead to improvements in technology and proper planning of SMEs' resources. Technology transfer from the lead firm to a subcontractor is determined primarily by the similarity of activity between them, and the degree of technological sophistication involved in the manufacture of the bought-out components and sub-assemblies. These linkages generally comprise the sharing of technical knowhow or the transfer of skills and, sometimes, equipment. The information on production specifications, drawings and designs is the most vital technological linkage, as the supplier must provide goods and services on a made-to-order basis.

Programmes that link SMEs as subcontractors to larger enterprises have been introduced in the Republic of Korea, Singapore and Taiwan Province of China. The programmes help to increase the capacity of SMEs and thus make them more attractive to TNCs as suppliers. Part of the success is that all three economies have strong coordinating agencies to provide support, i.e., the Investment Development Bureau in Taiwan Province of China, the Ministry of International Trade and Industries in the Republic of Korea and the Economic Development Board in Singapore.

Sources: UNCTAD, 2005c; and ITC, 1999.

of a specific value chain and the specific characteristics of the lead firms are fully understood. Policymakers can assist in educating SMEs about these nuances.

The lead firm is supported by numerous smaller enterprises, which are categorized in higher- and lower-tier suppliers of inputs (figure VIII.10). The higher the tier, the greater the value that is added by the supplying enterprises; thus, the supplier in the lower-tier category contributes simple outputs and adds less value (ESCAP, 2007a). Ideally, SMEs would access the GSC in the capacity of a higher-tier supplier, as the lower tiers are generally characterized by unstable conditions and one SME could be easily replaced by another. Alternatively, if direct access to a higher tier is not possible, it would be important for SMEs to have the chance to move up in the GSC and become a provider of higher value (ESCAP, 2007a).

Within this context, the participating SMEs must adhere to stringent operating guidelines, as the price of entry into a global supply chain is high, and these guidelines have the effect of honing the competencies of the SMEs. The lead firm often offers pro bono consulting to its suppliers in order to increase efficiency throughout the chain, but policymakers can also help these efforts by reducing red tape, developing infrastructure and improving both business and general education.

These and other challenges for SMEs can best be understood within the context of specific industry value chains that have particular relevance for regional economies. Three sectoral value chains of actual and potential relevance to SMEs in Asia and the Pacific – agribusiness, garments and apparel and automotive parts – have been selected to illustrate the challenges (box VIII.11).

Figure VIII.10. How SMEs fit into global supply chains

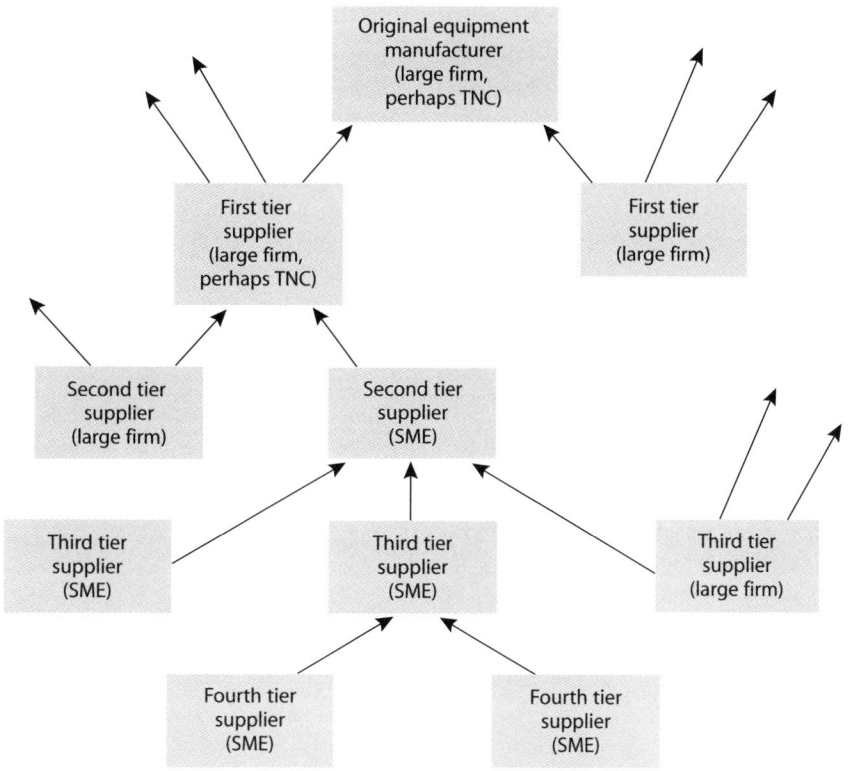

Source: UNIDO, 2001.

Box VIII.11. Challenges in global supply chains: Three case studies

A. Agribusiness[127]

The agribusiness sector has been one of the most vibrant growth sectors internationally, with many of its products sourced from developing economies in Asia and the Pacific. The evolution of agribusiness GSCs, coupled with the dominance of large retailers/supermarkets that control the agro-product brands as well as access to regional and global markets for agro-products imported from developing economies, threatens the exclusion of suppliers unable to meet the new requirements.

However, it also offers significant opportunities for those suppliers who can do so. For example, the trend towards product differentiation such as organic produce, driven both by the tastes of global consumers and the strategies of retailers for higher revenue, is producing significant opportunities for qualified Asia-Pacific SMEs to serve niche markets that are regional or even global in nature. Furthermore, outsourcing by global retailers of technically sophisticated activities, such as bar coding, labelling and the preparation of ready-to-eat food, provide important opportunities for upgrading within the agribusiness GSCs in Asia and the Pacific.

---
[127] Particularly useful sources for this case study include Humphrey, 2005, and Dolan, Humphrey and Harris-Pascal, 2000.

Box VIII.11. *(continued)*

B. Garments and apparel[128]

The garment and apparel industry, which is one of the oldest and largest export sectors, and a classic "starter" industry for export-oriented industrialization, has played a key role in Asia-Pacific's development. It represents a typical buyer-driven value chain/network, with a highly competitive and widely dispersed global industry structure, including regional and local competitors. Entry barriers are relatively lower in the garment manufacturing as opposed to textile manufacturing stage with particular processes like bleaching and dyeing having especially high barriers to entry.

Two key factors shape the structure and dynamics of the apparel global supply chains: (a) pressure to meet stringent international standards (e.g., labour and environmental); and (b) demands from global buyers for cheaper products, higher quality and shorter lead times.

The increasing concentration of production in economies with the capability for "full package production", particularly in China and India, are also expected to have a significant "demand side" effect. It is expected that large retailers will demand further price cuts as well as reductions in the number of their suppliers. This will place significant pressure on those exporting countries without primary textile industries, such as Bangladesh and Cambodia, and on SME producers whose present capabilities to upgrade within GSCs are limited.

C. Automotive parts[129]

The automotive parts industry comprises a complex mixture of firms of very different sizes, types and geographic scope, which produce an enormous variety of products ranging from very simple parts to technologically complex systems. The potential for local sourcing is particularly high because of the large number, size and weight of components and materials required by the sector. For those SMEs able to participate even at the lowest tiers of production, the automotive parts industry can offer significant opportunities to access regional and global markets.

While the benefits are significant, there are also a number of key risks that SMEs face, including:

(a) Fluctuations in the cost of production, especially raw materials like steel, aluminium, and polymers;

(b) Poor negotiation powers due to the fragmented nature of the industry, which in turn limits their pricing power;

(c) Dependence on traders and agents to access overseas markets, which threatens competitiveness; and

(d) Product substitutes due to fast-changing technology.

In Asia and the Pacific, cost competitiveness of the automotive parts industry is often based less on productivity and more on low factor input costs, which are now rising in many countries (e.g., the cost of labour and land). The key challenge for automotive parts suppliers in the region is to improve productivity and lower costs in order to maintain or improve their competitive performance within a GSC. In this context, a coordinated strategy of production relocation and integration within the region could provide opportunities for neighbouring, less-developed, lower-cost economies to become lower-tier suppliers of selected components for the existing automotive parts cluster. Such cross-border production linkages could provide an entry point to the automotive parts GSC as well as exposure to its significant developmental benefits while at the same time strengthening the competitive performance of local SME suppliers.

Several governments (e.g., China, India, Indonesia, Malaysia and Thailand) have initiated cluster-based development in the automotive parts industry, with geographical concentration of SMEs and large enterprises having similar lines of business. Clusters create external economies and favour the emergence of specialized technical, administrative and financial services. This form of networking for SMEs is a means of achieving economies-of-scale. To extend these initiatives further, governments may encourage banks to adopt a cluster-based lending approach to increase availability of funds to SMEs.

Box VIII.12. Four advantages of the global supply chain approach for SMEs

The transformation of regional businesses by the emergence of GSC signals potentially new and important directions for SME development in Asia and the Pacific. The global supply chain approach, in particular, provides the following four advantages for SME development at the national and regional levels:

(a) In recognition of the diversity of developing countries in the region, in terms of economic status and condition as well as natural endowment, the sector-specific value chain-based approach could identify development issues more precisely, while the "one size fits all" tailored approach may not be applicable in all participating countries;

(b) The approach covers a number of essential issues for SME development, as reviewed throughout this publication;

(c) The value chain approach will force policymakers to adopt a programme for regional cooperation that moves the development assistance paradigm beyond national borders; and

(d) The value chain approach is closely linked to the attraction of appropriate FDI, which plays an important role in the development of value chains and therefore helps in promoting intraregional FDI.

Source: ESCAP, 2011a.

---

[128] Particularly useful sources for this case include Gerefi and Memedovic, 2003, ITC, UNCTAD and WTO, 2005, and Nadvi and Thoburn, 2003.

[129] Particularly useful sources for this case study included: Global Production Networks, 2003; Veloso and Kumar, 2002; and Sturgeon and Lester, 2001.

Box VIII.13. Implications of global supply chains for climate change

Despite the apparent impact of climate change and urgent need for adoption and implementation of climate-smart technologies and related initiatives, SMEs do not often consider climate change as an immediate business concern, mainly due to their limited resources. They do not typically have a low-carbon strategy unless they are in an energy-intensive business or have a stake in presenting a clean and green image. Their customers (such as TNCs and other large enterprises) as well as end-consumers (i.e., the public) have become increasingly aware of the impact of products and services on the environment in general and on global warming in particular. As a result, these customers have begun to purchase products and services that are classified and labelled as low-carbon or climate-smart, and/or purchase them from firms actively engaged in clean and green practices. This would ultimately compel SMEs to align themselves with these demands, via the TNCs who are receiving customer feedback directly.

Source: Lee, Kim and Maliphol, 2011.

K. Suggested policies to enhance SME market access

SMEs can maximize their potential through applications of appropriate strategies, the implementation of their knowledge, commercialization of technology and access to regional and global networks. Table VIII.10 presents some policy recommendations for enhancing market access by service type.

In the context of the above recommendations, policymakers should also consider the following issues for designing policy packages to assist SMEs in accessing regional and global markets:.

(a) Transport and logistics infrastructure: These play a vital role in SMEs' integration, as they are the means of coordinating products, people and information around the world. Policymakers should also strive to connect SMEs to other players within GSCs, providing quality logistic infrastructure. ICT is also essential, and policymakers must do what they can to enhance connectivity and computerization;

(b) Strategic alliances: SMEs need the technological and managerial knowhow of the more established players, while the larger firms are looking to save costs by outsourcing some of the lower value-added manufacturing processes. Broadly speaking, linkages between large firms and SMEs have not been developed to the fullest extent in many Asia-Pacific developing countries. Effective policy would further capitalize on the potential for cooperation between SMEs and large firms; and

(c) Integration: Policymakers have three important tasks to fulfill in the area of global integration of SMEs. The first involves information dissemination. SMEs often do not know, or have not heard about the latest developments, e.g., WTO regulations or regional/bilateral free trade agreements. Policymakers must undertake the crucial task of communicating these updates to the SME sector. Second, policymakers must create business-friendly regulations, and pare back regulations that needlessly inhibit business operations. Within this context of global integration, policymakers can offer incentives and infrastructure, such as trade credit guarantees and export-processing zones, with which SMEs can thrive. Third, most of the knowledge about how to exploit global markets resides with companies; however, policymakers serve an essential function in facilitating the connection between large firms and SMEs. While respective players are best positioned to choose their partners, policymakers can provide the forums for matchmaking.

Here are some additional considerations:

(i) Quality/product standards and certificates;
(ii) Trade facilitation/trade finance;
(iii) Specific needs in different corporate life stages;
(iv) Urban versus rural; and
(v) Lack of M&E tools.

L. Summary

This chapter began with a discussion of market orientation and internationalization efforts as well as factors that have an impact on the ability of SMEs to access markets. Some relevant theories were reviewed and some data was provided regarding export trends for SMEs in the Asia-Pacific region. For the most part, SMEs serve foreign markets via exporting as opposed to via investment. The thrust of this chapter hence was concerned with market access via trade.

The influence of trade agreements on SMEs was examined in detail, including SMEs' export capacities, product identification, international quality standards and logistic systems. Of particular importance is the WTO trade regime, with its specific agreements regarding sanitary measures, technical barriers to trade, intellectual property rights, services and trade-related investment measures (see the annex to this chapter). A common issue across these topic areas is the need for policymakers to coach SMEs about what the regulations require and what rights SMEs have in the global trade environment.

The discussion then turned to the major challenges facing SMEs when they globalize, and the various trade promotion tools that policymakers might offer. Trade fairs are among the most popular ways of involving SMEs in international trade, but SMEs must have professional marketing materials, among other things, to be able to derive benefits from them. Other common promotions are buyer-seller meetings and trade missions, while the Internet has steadily gained popularity as a useful tool for market access. Next, examples of effective trade-promotion agencies from selected countries was provided (e.g., Japan, Malaysia, Singapore and Thailand).

Table VIII.10. Recommended policy interventions to enhance SMEs' market access

Type of service	Policy intervention
Business environment	Removal of unnecessary hurdles and obstacles, which are mostly of a legal and/or financial nature.
Export infrastructure	Export industrial estates, export processing zones and bonded production centres.
Training	Entrepreneurship development and managerial skills development, such as marketing, finance, operations, logistics, human resources etc.
Product/service development	Concept development, design, prototype development, modification; dies and moulds development, production, assembly etc.
Technical services	Identification of appropriate technologies, sources and costs, acquisition and information dissemination.
Marketing support	Market intelligence, marketing research, brand promotion, bid intervention, trade fairs and exhibitions, channels and distributions, buyer-seller matching, logistics systems, publicity literature, creditworthiness of importers and marketing outlet and consortia formation.
Information dissemination	A free flow of information on government policies and programmes, training opportunities and facilities, market intelligence and trade fairs and exhibitions.
Trade facilitation	Trade-facilitation processes (such as customs procedures and import and export regulations) as well as competitive support services, such as the transport and communications infrastructure, within the framework of integrated trans-border logistics systems.
Trade finance	Improved access to trade finance (for both exports and imports) and access to finance for small firms without collateral.
Credit guarantees	Public credit guarantee schemes, performance enhancement (default rate) and counter guarantees from credit guarantee companies and institutions.
Networking	Financial and other SME support institutions, R&D institutions, international agencies, foreign SME support organizations, TNCs, government departments, and business/industry associations and chambers of commerce.
FDI promotion	Formulation and implementation of policies and strategies to attract and promote FDI, with a view to strengthening the domestic SME sector.
Consultancy and counselling	Specialized services to address the specific issue(s)/needs (e.g., business development, marketing, finance and accounting, and legal).
Advocacy	Government departments and international organizations for creating policy conducive to SME start-ups, growth and survival

Source: Authors' compilation.

Trade finance is a significant theme in this chapter. Banks functioning as intermediaries between buyers and sellers enable greater international trade by bridging the gap in trust that exists between firms that are unfamiliar with one another. Here again, SMEs often do not know what financing options are available. Policymakers must facilitate the arrangement of trade financing and educate SMEs about it.

Macro-level efforts to involve SMEs in the global economy were then considered. The establishment of special economic zones, free trade zones and industrial parks are typical national policies to spur SMEs towards engaging in global trade. Such zones feature high levels of infrastructure, including ICT, specialized services, expedited regulatory compliance and tax and investment incentives.

Global supply chains are a critical way of exposing SMEs to foreign markets. There are a number of benefits for SMEs joining these chains, but the principal one is that GSCs increase SME competitiveness. The exactitude required in filling orders to the exacting specifications of TNCs prepares SMEs to compete effectively with global rivals. Policymakers need to help SMEs locate relevant global supply chains, assist them in marketing themselves and help to ameliorate the overall business environment, so that TNCs will want to include SMEs in these global supply chains. While these tasks are not easy, the examples of GSCs included in this chapter provide some guidance to government officials about the right steps to take. The chapter concluded with recommended policies for improving SME market access in table VIII.10.

Annex VIII.1
WTO-related agreements and rules

A. Sanitary and phytosanitary measures and technical barriers to trade

WTO has developed sanitary and phytosanitary (SPS) measures to ensure that food quality and safety standards are met, and that these standards are not used as an excuse to protect domestic producers from global competition. It allows countries to set their own SPS standards, but regulations require them to be based on science. Such regulations should be applied to the extent necessary to protect human, animal or plant life/health (WTO, 2011b). The more stringent standards imposed in the food processing sector create a formidable challenge for SMEs. Most Asia-Pacific developing countries view the food processing sector as an industry where they can compete. To meet these SPS standards, SMEs in this sector would have to initiate steps to conform to their requirements and thus incur higher production costs. These higher costs will consequently restrict the export volumes of food products from these developing Asian and Pacific nations; however, by ensuring that agricultural products are marketed only after substantial value addition takes place domestically, the food processing sector in developing countries can provide much needed opportunities for employment to offset the burdens incurred by the SPS measures.

Technical barriers to trade (TBT) refer to a specific international agreement that tries to ensure that regulations, standards, testing and certification procedures in international trade do not create unnecessary obstacles (WTO, 2011b). The agreement also expounds a code of good practice for governmental and non-governmental stakeholders to prepare and apply voluntary trade standards. In addition, the agreement discourages methods that give domestically-produced goods an unfair advantage.

These requirements can increase costs for SMEs as more burdensome certifications and procedures are required to engage in export activities.[130] SMEs must primarily deal with the increasing use of SPS measures and TBT measures on two counts. First, SMEs would have to initiate steps to conform to the requirements of the standards that have a justifiable basis. These standards would include those that are essential for protecting human, animal and plant life/health, or other such compelling reasons. SMEs need to upgrade their production systems to conform to these standards, and policymakers can provide technical and financial assistance.

A second set of initiatives is needed to challenge the SPS/TBT measures that constitute a disguised restriction on international trade. In other words, SMEs would have to improve their level of awareness about the SPS/TBT measures to help them challenge those measures that have been put in place merely for the purpose of restricting trade. Alone,

---

[130] Although these technical standards and regulations vary from country to country, WTO members must conform to "most-favoured-nation" treatment, which is an obligation not to discriminate between "like products" imported from different WTO members (WTO, 2011b).

SMEs may not be able to confront these issues, so governments must create mechanisms that can advocate on their behalf. In this regard, the TBT committee is the major clearinghouse for members to share information, and the major forum for discussing concerns about the regulations and their implementation.

SMEs, especially those in manufacturing and exporting, could prepare themselves by keeping up-to-date on the technical standards and, if need be, seek appropriate advice from government agencies. SMEs can view this challenge as an opportunity to improve the quality of their products, their delivery of safe products to customers and their ability to emit less waste into the environment, all of which will have a positive impact on various stakeholders.

B. Agreement on trade-related aspects of intellectual property rights (TRIPS) and transfer of technology

In today's knowledge-driven global economy, production and protection of intellectual property assets is of immense importance (see chapter VII for an in-depth discussion of this subject). Although SMEs are key players within the innovation processes, they have often lacked the ability to protect what they have created or otherwise to leverage upon it to attain sustained profitability.

To protect intellectual property rights, WTO enacted the Agreement on Trade-related Aspects of Intellectual Property Rights (TRIPS) that sets minimum standards for many forms of intellectual property regulations – including copyright issues, industrial designs, patents, transfer and dissemination of technology etc. (WTO, 2011a). The strengthening of the regime of intellectual property protection has made access to technologies for enterprises in developing countries difficult now that the owners of technologies find themselves in a superior bargaining position. As such, the technology market imposes several constraints on the ability of SMEs to upgrade their production facilities and improve their competitiveness.

Policymakers must recognize this limitation and develop an environment where SMEs can effectively and properly utilize intellectual property rights. Governments of the Asia-Pacific developing economies would have to consider the flexibilities that exist in the WTO agreements, which can be used to develop an enabling environment for SME innovations. For example, while amending the patent law, a government would have to consider the possibility of using an effective compulsory licensing system that can provide SMEs with better access to frontier technologies.

C. Trade in services

The service sector, despite accounting for more than 60 per cent of global production and employment, represents no more than 20 per cent of total trade (WTO, 2011c). This percentage is likely to grow due to the introduction of new transmission technologies (e.g., electronic banking and the Internet), the liberalization of many long-protected monopolies to international competition (e.g., telecommunications and postal services) and regulatory reforms in highly regulated sectors (e.g., transport). When combined with changing consumer preferences, these technical and regulatory innovations have enhanced the "tradability" of services, and have created an opportunity that SMEs can exploit (WTO, 2011c).

Despite the growth and potential of international trade in services, several issues remain that concern SMEs. Foremost is transparency, characterized by the availability of clear, accurate and accessible information, which is a fundamental element in evaluating the opportunities and costs of operating in a given market. In the ongoing negotiations on services, WTO members have highlighted the lack of transparency as a significant barrier to trade in services, particularly for SMEs, since these enterprises have fewer resources to navigate opaque regulatory environments. The lack of transparency results in an inability to challenge trade barriers and other anti-competitive practices.

In this environment, policymakers in the Asia-Pacific region can educate SMEs on the WTO General Agreement on Trade in Services (GATS), which provides a credible and reliable system of international trade in services rules (WTO, 2011c). It ensures fair and equitable treatment of all participants, stimulation of economic activity through guaranteed policy bindings and promotion of trade and development through progressive liberalization. This will ensure that SMEs are aware of the stringent rules and regulations that they will have to navigate in international trade in services.

D. Trade-related investment measures (TRIMs)

While adopting policies that promote export-oriented FDI, many developing countries in Asia and the Pacific have tried to protect their domestic markets from imports and market-seeking investments. Some of these countries impose numerous restrictions on foreign investments in order to protect and foster domestic industries, and to prevent the outflow of foreign exchange reserves. These requirements undoubtedly restrict and/or deter foreign investments in local SMEs or markets, especially those in the export-manufacturing sector. Some of these policies include the adoption of sector-specific negative lists, setting equity limits, local content requirements in manufacturing, restrictions on land ownership and employment of foreign staff and requirements for local staff participation at the management level.

To combat these trade restrictions, WTO enacted TRIMs, which prohibits the use of inappropriate trade-related investment measures (WTO, 2011d).[131] TRIMs is aimed at attracting and regulating foreign investment, and comprises fiscal incentives, tax rebates, and the provision of land and other services on preferential terms. This agreement is aimed at removing trade-restrictive and distorting effects of restrictions and requirements. Although such restrictions and requirements have been relaxed as a result of TRIMs, bilateral investment treaties and liberalization policies, the basic regulatory structure for market-seeking FDI remains in place in the region (ESCAP, 2009a).

As foreign investment contributes to the economic growth of developing countries, many countries tend to establish a multilateral investment framework with mutual benefits for investors and host countries. Such a framework provides transparency and stability while also improving investment conditions, in order to capture opportunities from trade liberalization. With such a transparent environment, foreign investors would not be deterred from investing in export-manufacturing sectors of the Asia-Pacific economies and SMEs could be the recipients of spillover effects.

E. Rules of origin

Rules of origin (RoO) are a set of laws, regulations and administrative procedures that determine a product's country of origin. These rules vary from country to country, and the decision by customs authorities on origins is subject to all kinds of commercial policy measures, such as anti-dumping measures, quota limitations or tariff preferences (WTO, 2011e). Rules of origin are based on the principle of preferential and non-preferential origin – with preferential origin allowing certain goods traded between particular countries to enter at a reduced or zero rate of duty, while non-preferential rules of origin are included in the context of common law tariff regimes (European Commission, 2011).

In order for an importer in an FTA-partner country to enjoy a preferential tariff, exporters must certify that their goods meet the relevant RoO. Because of differences in trade policies of each country, subregional FTAs and the proliferation of bilateral treaties, multiple and overlapping RoO can exist. The required documents pertaining to the origin status, production, shipment and sales of the exported goods (together with the complicated administrative procedures to prove origin) are a real burden on firms, especially SMEs with their limited financial and labour resources (Lim and Kimura, 2010). For example, record-keeping and tracing of input materials arising from different FTA or non-FTA sources could increase costs and result in SMEs failing to claim preferential origin treatment.

As such, additional training and information could be provided to customs authorities and SMEs on RoO-related issues. The adoption of self-certification schemes in some countries may achieve the dual purpose of increasing the knowledge of the private sector on RoO and decreasing the workload of the customs authorities (Erlinda and Balboa, 2009). Thus, joint efforts are required for partner countries to help domestic exporters take advantage of FTAs and enjoy the benefits from international trade activities.

---

[131] TRIMs only prohibit the use of trade related investment measures that are inconsistent with the basic provisions of the GATT 1994 (WTO, 2011d).

CHAPTER IX
Suggested policy framework for the development of SMEs

The SME sector has demonstrated its inherent strength by making significant contributions to national economies in Asia and the Pacific. SMEs help in the development of entrepreneurship, the creation of employment opportunities and social empowerment, particularly for women, the expansion of trade and, above all, income generation. All of these factors raise the standards of living for the nation as a whole. Adaptability, resilience and the ability to manufacture and render services with a high degree of flexibility and cost effectiveness make SMEs a force in today's global economy.

Perhaps the greatest selling point of SMEs is their ability to innovate. SMEs have emerged over the years as a "nursery" for fostering entrepreneurship and innovations, experimenting with various product and process improvements as well as more basic R&D. This openness and flexibility towards new knowledge has been a crucial driver of economic development around the world, including the Asia-Pacific region. One message emphasized in this publication is that the Asia-Pacific countries can and should do more to develop innovations in the SME sector. The region as a whole still lags behind Europe and North America in this critical aspect.

Within this context, it is imperative that government officials recognize the following critical factors:

(a) The need for the reduction of entry barriers (and thus costs) facing new business;

(b) The importance of cash flow to SMEs – the major reason most new and small businesses fail is not lack of profits but lack of cash;

(c) The strengthening of entrepreneurship through training and education; and

(d) The strengthening of networking and information dissemination – a lack of networks and information hinders effective deployment of technology and business development services as well as collaboration with other firms.

Walking in the shoes of the SME owner will go a long way towards crafting effective policies.

This chapter recapitulates some of the major ideas and suggestions for expanding and sustaining SMEs. It begins with a discussion of barriers to SME development as well as issues for associated policy planning in Asia and the Pacific. To facilitate policy prioritization, a supporting tool for policymakers is presented. Then the main points of each chapter are reviewed, and the importance of policymakers empathizing with the small business owner is reiterated. Finally, a comprehensive policy package is proposed, both for the national and the regional levels. A monitoring and evaluation system that creates feedback loops for SME policy is detailed in the annex to this chapter. These feedback loops are necessary for dynamic policymaking.

A. National policy planning: Major constraints and issues

The comprehensive review in this publication of the SME policies and programmes in Asia and the Pacific demonstrates that the nations of the region appreciate the importance of SME development. In many of the countries in the region, the SME sector faces numerous threats and challenges that necessitate a proactive approach by policymakers. National governments and various stakeholders in charge of policy planning would do well to recognize not only the threats and challenges, but also the changing needs of SMEs.

SMEs in the Asia-Pacific region typically face the following constraints:

(a) Absence of a user-friendly enabling environment;

(b) Lack of an adequate and modern infrastructure;

(c) "Shy" entrepreneurship, i.e., lack of confidence and a high level of risk aversion in exploiting opportunities;

(d) Inequality for women entrepreneurs;

(e) Inadequate and/or expensive access to financing;

(f) Obsolete technology;

(g) A lack of R&D and innovation facilities, and commercialization thereof;

(h) Absence of marketing support and information;

(i) Inadequate input of BDS; and

(j) Poor institutional networking, which bars access to GSCs and integration of SMEs into international markets.

Before moving on to the next section, which starts from a broad perspective, and then narrows its focus to specific policy areas, the general points to consider concerning SME policy include:

(a) A comprehensive SME development policy package addressing the problems, needs and prospects of SME development for the domestic, regional and global markets must have feedback mechanisms that reflect the dynamic environment in which SMEs operate, so that policymakers can be proactive in anticipating and tackling SME issues;

(b) Major topics for a comprehensive policy should cover general entrepreneurship development, development of female entrepreneurship, rural enterprises, enhancing competitiveness, providing sound infrastructure and a business enabling environment, financing SMEs, delivering access to technology, R&D and innovations, creating business development services and developing opportunities for global integration;

(c) Policymakers can enhance SME competitiveness by promoting clusters as they produce spillovers of knowledge and agglomeration benefits that all firms can share;

(d) Encouragement of rural industrialization via SMEs, which is a clear priority. In the near term, diversifying agricultural activities can be a viable strategy;

(e) Building a strong base of entrepreneurship and providing support to make the SME sector competitive in the regional and global markets should be the central theme of the SME development agenda. The private sector should be involved as partners in policymaking and the implementation of programmes; thus, public-private partnerships are a crucial mechanism; and

(f) The need to develop SMEs in LDCs, in particular, in the process of globalization in order to remove the economic disparities between LDCs and the developed and developing economies in Asia and the Pacific. Adequate provisions need to be built into the policies in order to encourage them to access the regional and global markets on competitive term.

In addition, two points that deserve repeating are considered here. First, although policymakers naturally want firms to survive, they must provide an easy means of exit for SMEs that fail. Reforming the bankruptcy code is a prime example of a concrete step that governments can take on this issue. Second, as mentioned above, policymakers should concentrate on SME cash flows when considering various policies. Policy options that provide cash today to small business owners are preferable to those that defer cash.

Box IX.1. Prioritizing policies

Resources are scarce and government officials cannot tackle all the issues facing SMEs simultaneously. Policymakers need supporting tools to prioritize the issues and identify effective policy options. Figure IX.1 provides a thought process map for identifying the obstacles to private investment and entrepreneurship.

This map is a simplification, but it helps to prioritize policies, at least in the short term. According to Hausmann, Rodrik and Velasco (2006 and 2005),[132] policymakers need to address the one or two of the most binding constraints on economic growth. They noted that in a low-income country, the problem may be due to low returns on economic activity or to the high cost of finance. Although both conditions may hold, one is likely to be more prevalent than the other.

After considering the root causes shown in the thought process map (figure IX.1), policymakers will need to work from the bottom up. Government officials should first work to provide stability, both legal and financial. Legal stability involves minimizing the threat of expropriation of rents by the government; this is the first action dealing with corruption, taxes and protection of property rights. Note that the focus is not to expunge the threat of expropriation entirely; that would be quixotic and wasteful. The short-term goal should be to perform near the average of a "peer group" of nations while the long-term goal should be to improve performance towards that of an "aspirant group." For example, a middle-income Asia-Pacific country might compare its score on Transparency International's Corruption Perceptions Index (see chapter III) to other middle-income countries. If it is faring worse, it should work to improve its score to that level in the short term. In the long term, it would seek to match the scores of upper-income countries.

The next stage of improvement concerns management of the economy. Officials must ensure that there are sound macroeconomic policies and procedures in place; e.g., ceilings for the overall national debt and for annual budget deficits, an

Figure IX.1. Thought process map for policy prioritization

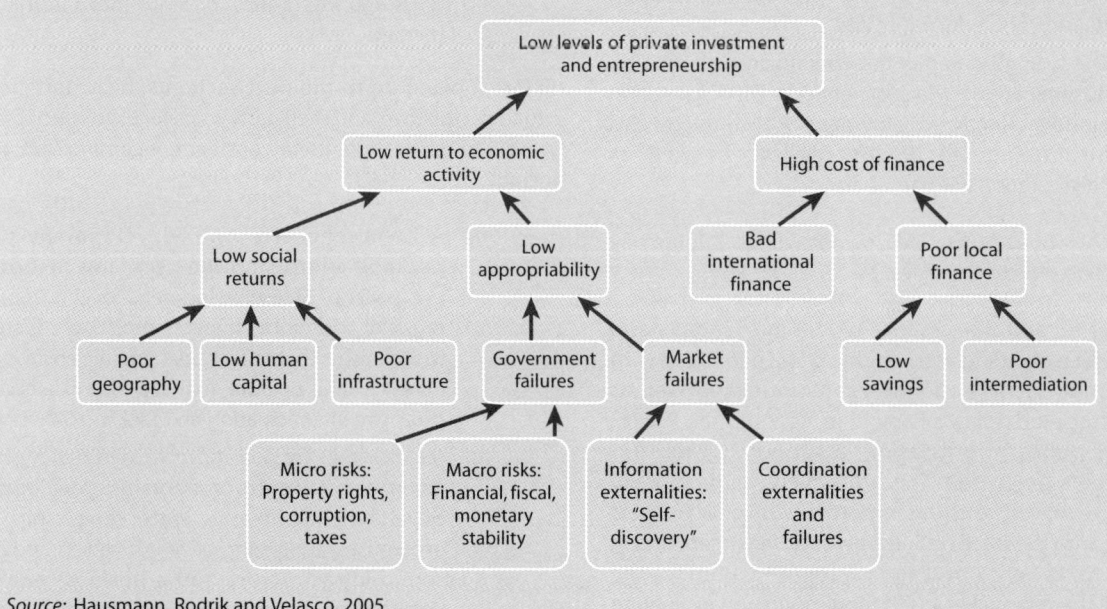

Source: Hausmann, Rodrik and Velasco, 2005.

---

[132] These two papers are particularly relevant to policymakers, as the authors explain the nuances of their model and how piecemeal reform generates suboptimal outcomes.

Box IX.1. *(continued)*

autonomous central bank tasked with fighting inflation, a transparent process for adjusting the national currency if it trades at a fixed rate for other currencies etc. In many cases, both legal and financial stability correlates with one another.

Policymakers have less control over the sources of market failure. Regulations can require transparency among firms in their dealings with suppliers, customers and investors. Such transparency would alleviate the information asymmetry responsible for most market failures.[133] Another means of preventing market failure is simply to avoid intervening. Setting wage and price controls distorts markets because such controls do not allow buyers and sellers to establish their own equilibrium; the new market-clearing price in a controlled market creates inefficiencies that, over time, can lead to failure.

Coordination externalities involve multiple economic actors cooperating to produce mutual benefit; failure occurs when one or more parties refuse to cooperate. Sometimes the issue may be one of standardization. A basic principle for economic development is that a government must establish and enforce a uniform system of weights and measures. At other times, the issue is one of cost and appropriation. It is often necessary for governments to fund basic research because a firm is unwilling to undertake that expense when the entire industry, including its rivals, will benefit.

After tackling the basic causes, government officials then need to move to the next level of causes that are actionable: poor infrastructure, low human capital, a meagre savings rate and underdeveloped financial intermediation. Policymakers would first need to decide which of these constraints is the most pressing before acting. Note that this will likely differ from country to country, depending on the stage of economic development.

B. Summary of recommendations

There are many facets to SME development. It is imperative to design and implement a comprehensive policy package that addresses the development of SMEs' capacity and competitiveness more effectively in order to utilize untapped business opportunities in national, regional and global markets. This chapter proposes some specific activities for immediate action which are designed based on: (a) the centrality of SMEs in adding value; (b) six critical issues in SME development (i.e., business enabling environment, entrepreneurship, access to finance, business development services, innovation and technology and market access); and (c) immediate implementation of the policy options on the basis of stakeholders involved and the need for further feasibility enquiries. Policy recommendations are summarized by issue and presented in turn below.

1. Business enabling environment

The crucial elements of chapter III are the components of the business enabling environment (BEE) and the role of policymakers. There are a number of salient points for government officials but the overarching theme is that appropriate procedures and incentives with reasonable cost implications must be offered to businesspeople if SMEs are to thrive. It goes without saying that modern infrastructure, both physical and ICT, are *sine qua non* for business development. The major policy recommendations are reiterated below:

(a) Design effective public policies based on an understanding of constraints faced by SMEs;

(b) Implement specific programmes enabling SMEs to overcome marketing constraints;

(c) Invite the business sector to interact with policymakers at regular intervals on pressing business issues, including effective infrastructure development;

(d) Place economic and financial safety nets for SMEs to insulate them from the ill-effects of a possible future economic crisis;

(e) Design a fair and transparent legal and regulatory regime for SMEs;

(f) Create a business-friendly environment for SMEs by:
  (i) Providing for relative ease of entry and exit of small firms, particularly for women and young entrepreneurs;
  (ii) Streamlining bureaucratic rules and procedures;
  (iii) Assessing the costs and benefits of specific regulations and eradicating the roadblocks;
  (iv) Simplifying import-export procedures;

(g) Reform the government procurement system, perhaps with the inclusion of e-procurement;

(h) Give adequate attention to trade facilitation measures and address legal and regulatory obstacles;

(i) Identify gender imbalances and make suitable provisions for encouraging female entrepreneurship;

(j) Give priority and incentives to R&D, innovations, high-risk projects and IPR issues in the regulatory framework;

(k) Reduce social stigma for SMEs going bankrupt and provide suitable exit routes; and

(l) Provide incentives for providers of business development services.

2. Entrepreneurship development

The various definitions and concepts surrounding entrepreneurship were discussed in chapter IV, and the importance of innovation and firm expansion was underscored. Various subtopics were then considered, such as female entrepreneurship, rural entrepreneurship and social

---

[133] The classic example of this is the used-car market discussed by Akerlof (1970). In his scenario, only "lemons", i.e., used cars of low quality, will be available in a market characterized by information asymmetry; such a market will eventually collapse. In this scenario, the seller knows the quality of the used car while the buyer does not. The buyer will assume that the used car is of low quality and therefore will offer a low price. The inability of sellers to bridge this information asymmetry drives sellers of high-quality cars from the market as they will not receive a fair price, thereby leaving only "lemons" for sale.

entrepreneurship. Entrepreneurship was considered in relation to various stages of economic development, and data was provided on barriers to entrepreneurship. The chapter concluded with the following general recommendations to policymakers:

(a) Offer a "single window" for permits;
(b) Reform business registration;
(c) Encourage the wide-spread use of the business plan platforms and tools;
(d) Ensure formal property rights;
(e) Provide credit information systems;
(f) Strengthen investor protection;
(g) Simplify tax collection procedures;
(h) Create positive attitudes towards entrepreneurship;
(i) Encourage female entrepreneurs;
(j) Increase resources for entrepreneurship education; and
(k) Create interest in being an entrepreneur as a career.

3. Financing a business

The financing of SMEs was highlighted in chapter V, and the myriad sources of capital that SMEs can tap were discussed, with the focus on the bank-borrower relationship. Emphasis was placed on the need for empathy; banks should recognize the concerns of SMEs with regard to obtaining cash and SMEs must understand the banks' need to mitigate risk. For policymakers, the importance of cash flows to the survival and success of SMEs cannot be overstressed. Therefore, some of the best practices are reiterated below:

(a) Avoid introducing direct credit programmes or the operation by banks of government programmes at subsidized rates;
(b) Do not plan for the government to operate its programmes for financial assistance to the SME sector directly;
(c) Foster SMEs' understanding of the importance of cash flow management as well as useful financial instruments (working capital enhancement, trade credit, cost savings etc.) that improve their cash flows;
(d) Give adequate attention to the provisions of creditors' rights by introducing a suitable set of laws that protect lenders from non-payment;
(e) Promote collateral and a third-party guarantee free lending system that is suitably backed by setting up credit guarantee schemes to encourage lenders to assist SMEs;
(f) Concentrate on policies for promoting availability of risk capital to innovative SMEs mainly at early stages of the financing, possibly through the development of equity and bond markets where feasible to the nations;
(g) Recognize the need for proximity between the lenders and borrowers, particularly for small-scale investment;
(h) Combine entrepreneurship training with commercial loan programmes;
(i) Facilitate international investments in the SME sector; and
(j) Encourage, in association with private sector associations and accounting bodies, small businesses to maintain and report reliable information.

4. Business development services

Beyond the immediate need for cash, SMEs require a plethora of services related to production, supply chain, marketing and overall quality improvements. These business development services (BDS) and the role that policymakers play were discussed in chapter VI. Differentiation was made between traditional and market-oriented modes of BDS, and it was suggested that governments act more as a facilitator rather than as a provider. BDS represents a prime opportunity for public-private partnerships, as the private sector is generally the repository of the expertise that SMEs need. Frequently, however, SMEs do not know where to find the help they require; likewise, consultants do not know which small businesses desire assistance. Policymakers can bridge this gap. Some of the chapter's policy suggestions are highlighted below:

(a) Combine financial services with a BDS package;
(b) Develop public-private partnerships to provide BDS;
(c) Create a suitable enabling environment for BDS and awareness;
(d) Ensure that the capacity of BDS providers and the quality of their services is adequate; and
(e) Allow private sector service providers to give a kick-start to BDS.

5. Innovation and technology

Chapter VII addresses the important issue of innovation and technology. The most crucial message communicated in this chapter is that SME competitiveness and national competitiveness are inexorably linked. Policymakers will boost the innovative edge of firms as they improve their own nation's capacity to innovate. We stress the need for a holistic policy approach that embraces human resource development, science parks, business incubators, technology acquisition and ICT applications. In general, the Asia-Pacific region has lagged behind other parts of the world in terms of R&D spending and technology capacity building; this is a fruitful area for further improvement. The following priorities and policies are provided as guidance:

(a) Priorities:
  (i) Technology-driven policies that encourage and facilitate innovations;
  (ii) Incentives for creating and adopting innovations;
  (iii) Institutional framework, e.g., technology centres;
  (iv) Access to finance;
  (v) Training and capacity-building; and
  (vi) Strategic partnerships and alliances (e.g., national and subnational innovation systems).

(b) Policies:
   (i) Introduce a comprehensive science and technology development policy under a simplified and streamlined institutional framework (at both the national and the subnational levels), offering a friendly enabling environment for SMEs;
   (ii) Government subsidized financial assistance to SMEs as well as other key stakeholders for R&D, technology transfer and technology commercialization (e.g., grants, loans and tax breaks);
   (iii) Development of national and subnational innovation systems through institutional networking and coordination, capacity-building and infrastructure development (e.g., science and technology parks);
   (iv) Open-market policy support for technology outsourcing and transfer of technology for SMEs; and
   (v) Business and technology incubation and training.

6. Market access

In chapter VIII, the significance of global integration for SME development in the region is noted. With regard to this aspect, policymakers can serve as communicators and educators, as SMEs are often unaware of the latest developments in WTO regulations, intellectual property rights, product and service standards and certifications, and requirements for their participation in regional and global supply chains. Over the longer term, efforts to improve BEE should also reap dividends for SMEs trying to tap global markets. With this in mind, key policy issues and integration tactics for SMEs are listed below:

(a) Export infrastructure – export industrial estates; export processing zones; and bonded production centres;

(b) Product-oriented – identification, design, prototype development, modification, dies and moulds, production and assembly;

(c) Marketing support – market information, marketing research, brand promotion, bid intervention, facilitating participation in trade fairs and exhibitions, strengthening of marketing channels and distribution, organizing buyer-seller matching, logistics systems, preparation of publicity literature, assessing creditworthiness of importers, and providing marketing outlet and consortia formation;

(d) Information dissemination – government policies and programmes, training opportunities and facilities, trade fairs and exhibitions etc.

(e) Trade finance – improved access to trade and export finance, and access to finance for small firms without collateral;

(f) Networking – financial and other SME support institutions, interacting with R&D institutions, international agencies as well as SME support organizations in other countries, forging links with TNCs, both between and among SMEs, and connecting with government departments, industry associations and chambers of commerce; and

(g) FDI promotion – FDI policies facilitating the integration of domestic SMEs into global supply chains, consistent with an economy's comparative advantage and development.

Finally, table IX.1 provides a synopsis of major challenges together with policies for addressing them at the national and regional levels, in accordance with the major themes covered in this guidebook.

The above policy options may require further analytical work and technical assistance activities, both at the national and the regional level. This could include, among other activities:

Table IX.1. Recommended actions for challenges of SME development

Challenges	Recommended actions
Business enabling environment	**National** (a) Formulation and implementation of a strategic pro-SME development policy, and placing financial safety nets for SMEs; (b) Establishment of incentives for R&D, innovations, high-risk projects and IPR issues in the regulatory framework; (c) More open and transparent government procurement practices; (d) Fiscal measures – taxation and subsidy measures for the products under consideration, and on import of raw materials and machinery; (e) Productivity improvement through infrastructure development and enhanced logistical efficiency; (f) Lobbying and coordinating with other government ministries and departments for infrastructure development; (g) Improving power and gas supply; (h) Improving rural road links between production, processing and market centres of the products under consideration; and (i) Establishment of special economic zones.

Table IX.1. *(continued)*

Challenges	Recommended actions
	Regional (a) Pro-business regulatory reforms in various functions (e.g., registration, licensing, closure, and bankruptcy) through a regional capacity-building programme which develops best practice manuals and tool kits; (b) Public-private dialogue to develop handbooks and toolkits for business environment reforms; (c) Joint infrastructure development with neighbouring countries at the border areas.
Entrepreneurship development	**National** (a) Improving the framework for entrepreneurship through education, vocational training and incentives; (b) Training of women and youth entrepreneurs; (c) Building the capacity of business associations; (d) Business and entrepreneur incubation; (e) Training of trainers and some other experts (TOTs); (f) Development of training facilities (establishment of courses and training institutes and strengthening such units in the existing agencies); (g) Training of producers, farmers and manufacturers; and (h) Building proper facilities for the training institutes. **Regional** (a) Sharing experiences and best practices for entrepreneurship development through regional programmes; and (b) Building the capacity of regional business associations and networks.

Access to finance	**National**
	(a) Development of a conducive financial services framework and capacity-building of financial institutions; and
	(b) Training on cash flow management and relevant instruments:
	    (ii) Public credit guarantee schemes
	    (iii) Collateral and property rights
	    (iv) SME loans
	    (v) Trade finance
	    (vi) Loans for restructuring and cost saving initiatives
	    (vii) Credit information sharing
	    (viii) Simplified accounting and taxation systems for SMEs
	
	Regional
	(a) South-South cooperation for coordinated regulatory frameworks, including regional monetary and financial systems, to achieve steady and stable fund flows and more stable foreign exchange rates.

Business development services (BDS)	**National** (a) Development of a certification framework for various business development services with quality assurance; (b) Development of public business incubation programmes; (c) Strengthening flow of market information and business counseling services; and (d) Preparation for the establishment of brand image. **Regional** (a) Business matchmaking services between foreign investors, including regional firms and local enterprises, and in particular SMEs, with emphasis on backward linkages in regional and global supply chains; (b) Sharing experiences about the development of commercial and public business advisory services, such as accounting, engineering, legal advice and marketing; and (c) Establishment of laboratory testing facilities, quarantine centres and certification bodies based on cost sharing among participating nations.
Innovation and technology	**National** (a) Develop national and subnational innovation systems; (b) Investment in research and development to build regional brands (e.g., regional products and service development with low costs); (c) Improved capacity for process and product innovation; (d) Foster innovation and a culture of creativity; (e) Increase ICT usage in the SME sector;

Table IX.1. *(continued)*

Challenges	Recommended actions
	(f) Establishment and strengthening of standards and certification, quality testing and accreditation centres; and
	(g) Establishment of product development centres.
	Regional
	(a) Networking and collaboration among research institutes at the regional level.
Market access	**National**
	(a) Encourage capacity-building and export operations of SMEs;
	(b) Enhance SMEs' understanding of international markets, and their practices and rules;
	(c) Identify and implement appropriate trade promotion tools for local products and services while improving their quality and effectiveness;
	(d) Foster global supply chains led by developing-country enterprises, and development of regionally and later globally recognized regional brands;
	(e) Foster strong market orientation in the business sector to penetrate markets and increase market shares;
	(f) Strengthening of enterprises' capacities to meet global supply chain related standards and certificates; and
	(g) Pay adequate attention to trade facilitation measures.
	Regional
	(a) Open markets for trade and investment: avoidance of protectionism (e.g., limited public bailouts of enterprises which are ineffective and inefficient; market mechanisms determine the future of enterprises);
	(b) Regional integration to create a region-wide market (possibly including development of regional regulatory frameworks and infrastructure);
	(c) Strengthening, deepening, consolidation and integration of free trade and investment agreements, possibly on a region-wide basis;
	(d) Promotion of FDI (including intraregional South-South investment) which fosters backward linkages with SMEs;
	(e) Intraregional trade promotion through business networking (e.g., cross-border partnerships among SMEs); and
	(f) Strengthening of region-wide market information dissemination and the use of ICT.

Source: Authors' compilation.

(a) Preparation of feasibility studies on developing country-led supply chains;

(b) Implementing projects to foster and support the development of partnerships between enterprises;

(c) Raising awareness and knowledge among developing countries' SMEs of standards and certification;

(d) Developing national business environments that are more conducive to entrepreneurship and business innovation; and

(e) South-south cooperation of intraregional trade and FDI facilitation and promotion.

Reviewing the national status of SMEs in relation to the issues listed above as well as identifying possible areas of interventions by regional programmes, will lead to greater efficiency. It is again emphasized that local sources of knowledge, especially universities and research institutions, are often overlooked by policymakers who reflexively reach for outside experts. Assessing national sources of expertise should come first.

C. Conclusion

This publication has attempted to develop policy guidelines that will assist policymakers, practitioners, support institutions, chambers and associations in their efforts towards SME development. These guidelines are based on regional (and global) best practices and the vast field experience of the researchers, contributors and authors involved in their preparation. In addition, the United Nations Economic and Social Commission for Asia and the Pacific has played an essential role in guiding and supporting this effort.

This publication is not a substitute for local knowledge; rather, it is aimed at complementing such knowledge. Each sovereign country has developed its own policy frameworks, institutions and linkages with SMEs and entrepreneurs. No one policy guideline can fit all. Thus, individual countries and their institutions must assess the status of their SMEs, level of enterprise, culture, ethos and needs before addressing the emerging issues. Based on this assessment, each nation can develop a plan of action most suited to its particular situation that will enable it to address the requirements of its SMEs and entrepreneurs. Naturally, consultations with experts, SME leaders and other stakeholders are a prerequisite before finalizing any plan that might involve policy changes, reorientation of officials, capacity-building of delivery organizations and encouragement of public-private partnerships. The long-term objectives of all the countries in the Asia-Pacific region are clear – to build the capacity of SMEs, enhance their competitiveness, attain global integration and be partners for progress in economic development, employment generation and the well-being of the population of their countries.

Annex IX.1
Monitoring and evaluation

In the current environment, there is constant pressure and scrutiny to do things correctly and efficiently; in this regard, the monitoring and evaluation (M&E) tool has often been used to ensure proper governance, transparency and accountability of organizations and programmes. OECD (2002a) defines M&E as:

(a) Monitoring – "A continuing function that uses the systematic collection of data on specified indicators, to provide management and the main stakeholders of an ongoing development intervention with indications of the extent of progress and achievement of objectives and progress in the use of allocated funds"; and

(b) Evaluation – "The systematic and objective assessment of an ongoing or completed project, programme, or policy, including its design, implementation, and results. The aim is to determine the relevance and fulfillment of objectives, development efficiency, effectiveness, impact and sustainability. An evaluation should provide information that is credible and useful, enabling the incorporation of lessons learned into the decision-making process of both recipients and donors".

M&E thus comprises two distinct but complementary concepts, with the former based on observation and the latter focused upon analysis of the results. The distinction between monitoring and evaluation can be presented according to a gradation of sophistication, also called the "Six Steps to Heaven" approach (OECD, 2007c). The first three steps are considered to be monitoring and tend to use qualitative indicators, whereas steps 4, 5 and 6 are associated more with quantitative evaluations (see annex table IX.1 for an example).

Annex table XI.1. Six Steps to Heaven: A method for assessing the impact of SME policies

Monitoring	
Step 1	Take-up of schemes
Step 2	Recipients opinions
Step 3	Recipients views of the difference made by the assistance
Evaluation	
Step 4	Comparison of the performance of "assisted" with "typical" firms
Step 5	Comparison with "match" firms
Step 6	Taking account of selection bias

Source: OECD, 2007c.

As the definitions and examples above indicate, M&E is used as a management tool to learn from past experiences and improve future services, to plan and allocate existing resources, and most importantly to understand whether targets have been met. Specific to the development context, M&E is used to (a) determine the worth or significance of a development intervention, (b) contribute to future improvements, (c) consider continuation or discontinuation and (d) account for expenditures to stakeholders (OECD, 2010b).

A. M&E frameworks

In a literature review of more than 100 studies of M&E, Stem and others (2005) noted two points germane to policymakers: (a) it is not necessary to design such systems from scratch since effective approaches already exist; and (b) different M&E needs require different M&E approaches.

When M&E is undertaken for a project, a framework has to be constructed that covers the entire process of the project, from planning to implementation and outcomes, to ensure that the objectives are quantifiably assessed. Three major M&E frameworks – the logical framework approach, result-based impact chain and standard for results measurement – are presented below.

1. Logical framework approach

The logical framework approach is a widely-used project development tool as well as an M&E tool.[134] It involves using causal logic, a baseline study, an impact statement and assessment, client-centred programme design, performance indicators, a learning system and risk assessment to map out how the various components of a project relate to each other in order to meet goals and achieve the desired impact (IFC, 2008).

Annex figure IX.1 illustrates the logical framework and indicates M&E's position. Monitoring focuses on tracking inputs, activities and outputs; evaluation primarily tracks outcomes and impacts in relation to project goals (IFC, 2008).

M&E applies differently at each project level. An overview of programme logics and indicators at various project levels is presented in annex table IX.2.

2. Result-based impact chain

Another popular M&E method is the result-based impact chain, utilized in GTZ's M&E approach. It focuses on analysing the results generated by a project or a programme in order to prove its validity. Annex figure IX.2 outlines the entire result chain and shows how the results are generated.

First, a project or a programme is resourced through inputs (advisers and finance). Using these inputs, an organization launches activities that generate outputs. These outputs are then utilized by target groups or intermediaries, generating medium-term and long-term development results. The results

---

[134] The logical framework approach was developed by USAID at the end of the 1960s and has been used by various bilateral and multilateral development agencies throughout the world.

Annex figure IX.1. Logical framework

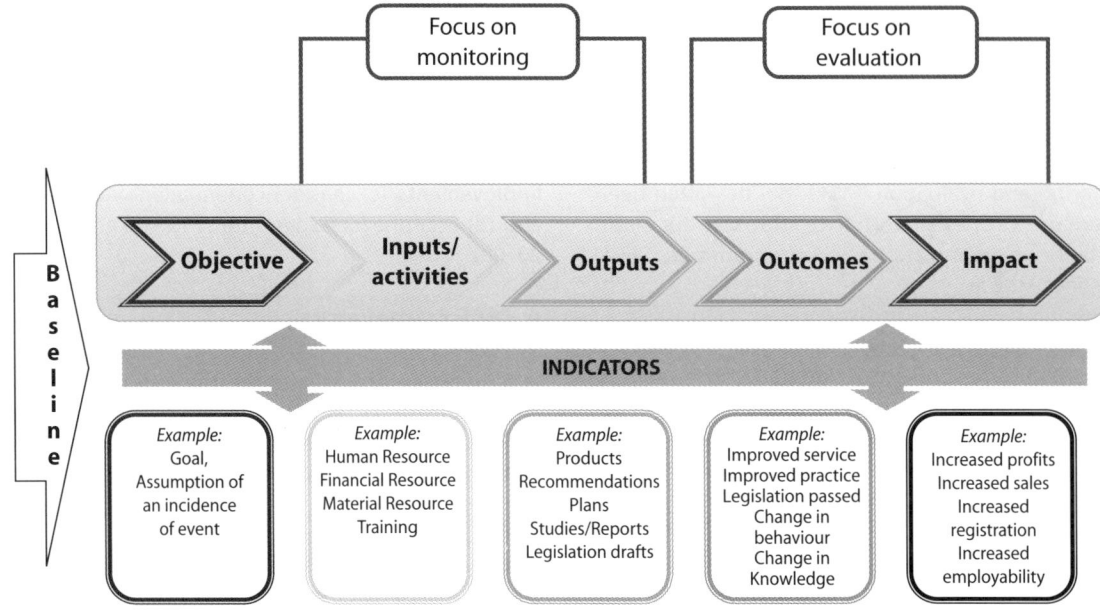

Source: Adapted from IFC, 2008.

Annex table IX.2. Programme logics and indicators at various project levels

Level	Programme/project logic	Indicator
Objectives	What are the problems that the project will address?	The measures for judging whether or not the goal has been achieved.
Inputs	The resources needed to deliver the project activities (funds, people, equipment etc.).	Implementation and work programme targets.
Activities	The activities or tasks that need to be undertaken to accomplish or deliver the identified project outputs.	Implementation and work programme targets.
Outputs	The direct measurable results (goods and services) of the project that are largely under project management's control.	Measures of the quantity and quality of outputs and the timing of their delivery.
Outcomes	What are the expected benefits (or dis-benefits) and to whom will they go? What improvements or changes will the project bring about?	Measures by which achievements at the end of the project can be quantified – indicating that the purpose has been achieved and that these benefits are sustainable.
Impacts	What are the long-term changes that are likely to occur as a result of the project outcomes?	Measures of general quantitative or qualitative changes that can be linked to the project.

Source: Modified from IFC, 2008.

Annex figure IX.2. Results-based impact chain

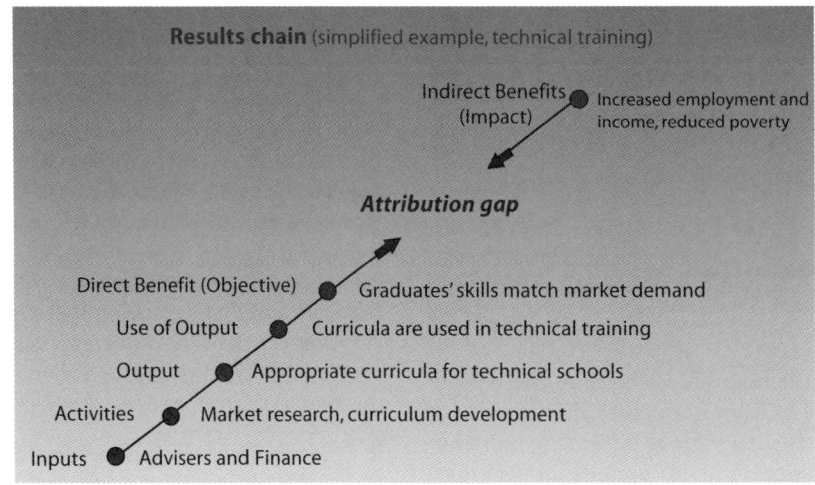

Source: GTZ, 2004.

are defined as changes occurring due to the project and its different facets, which can be direct or indirect. Up to the point where a causal relationship between outputs and observed development changes can be shown, the project is entitled to claim the observed development changes as a "direct benefit", which is also the project objective.

A project or programme also generates impacts beyond the objectives level. This can be difficult to prove as many other factors can also influence the causal relationship between the project and the indirect impacts. This results in an attribution gap in the result chain. Both direct and indirect effects of a project should be considered before implementation, because the results could be insignificant or even negative. Only when the hypotheses on the project's contributions to overarching development results are plausible can the project be valid and successful (GTZ, 2004).

To identify causalities between the project and results, several tasks must be performed. The outcomes attributable to the project or programme, defined as its objectives, must be identified. It is also necessary to identify changes that take place beyond the attribution gap to determine whether they can plausibly be linked to the project. As such a causal relationship may be impossible to prove. It is sufficient to demonstrate plausibly, on the basis of the monitored data on inputs, activities, outputs, use of outputs and outcomes, how the project or programme might have contributed towards the changes in the environment (GTZ, 2004).

This approach is based on a similar logic to the logical framework approach mentioned above and it uses some of the same terminology. However two main differences are observed (IFC, 2008):

(a) The focus is on measuring results throughout a project and analysing the causal impact chain; and

(b) The way the impact is measured and attributed throughout the impact chain differs.

3. DCED standard for results measurement

DCED (2011b) has developed its own M&E process, the standard for results measurement, developed through field experience from various programmes and agencies focusing on private sector development. The DCED method "comprises all of the minimum elements required in any results measurement process". The steps outlined in the standard are:

(a) Articulating the results chain – the first step is to utilize the results chain tool to make each step explicit in the logic of the programme. This allows staff to "think through" the intervention process, clarify assumptions, agree on logic and monitor progress in achieving that logic;

(b) Defining the indicators of change – following clarification of what is expected to happen, it is then possible to define what is expected to change. Indicators should be precise and measurable, either quantitatively or qualitatively, and should include information about the sustainability of changes;

(c) Measuring changes in indicators – at this stage, programmes need to develop a system for measuring changes in the indicators. The first action is to conduct baseline research in order to establish a starting point. It is also strongly recommended that programmes "triangulate", or cross-examine, the information they collect or generate in order to validate and confirm the findings; and

(d) Estimating attributable changes – the standard requires programmes to address the issue of attribution for the key indicators and intermediate steps within the results chain (annex figure IX.3). While rigorous proof is not required, it is important for the programme to build a credible and convincing case;

Annex figure IX.3. Attributable impact

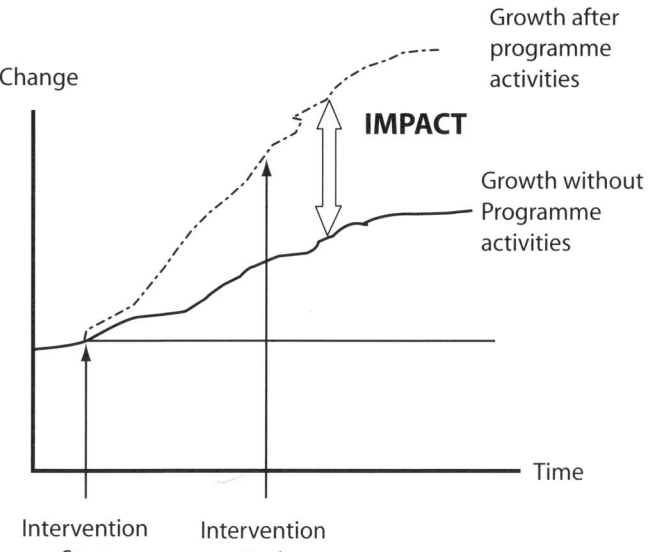

Source: DCED, 2011b.

(e) Capturing wider changes in the system or market – it is important to make an effort to capture wider changes as well. System or market-wide changes can occur as a result of crowding-in and copying, sector growth, backward and forward linkages, and other direct impacts;

(f) Tracking programme costs – there should be a statement of the programme's annual and cumulative costs to put programme achievements into perspective;

(g) Reporting results – the standard calls for programmes to document key changes in indicators. These should be communicated at least annually to internal programme-related persons and the external community; and

(h) Managing the system for results measurement – programmes should develop a system for measuring key indicators at selected intervals. Such a system should include a monitoring plan as well as sufficient financial and human resources, so that it can be sustained and developed.

While the components of the DCED standard are not new, its comprehensiveness is unique. It is the first to combine most of the existing results measurement features together in one complete framework. However, the standard is not entirely complete as it lacks certain elements found in other methodologies. For example, stakeholders participatory techniques are not included, primarily because private sector development generally aims to enable stakeholders to solve their own problems. These stakeholders are often not aware of donor-funded interventions (DCED, 2011b).

4. Data collection

Data forms the basis of all M&E systems. The indicators and research questions in the M&E plan dictate the data required. Generally, the different indicators in an M&E system require three types of data sources – routine, periodic and one-off – as shown in table IX.3 (World Bank, 2009b).

Before selecting a method, consideration must be given to whether a quantitative or qualitative method should be used. Quantitative methods measure directly the status or change of a specific variable, whereas qualitative methods gather information about what people see, feel, believe or do as well as how they behave. It should be noted that the difference between these types of data is not absolute. Qualitative data can be counted and made quantitative; transforming quantitative data the other way is also possible. The appropriate method depends not only on the type of information needed but also on capacities and resources available, how the information will be used and the level of data precision needed (IFAD, 2002). Annex table IX.4 presents some examples of qualitative and quantitative methods.

B. Evaluation

There are different types of evaluations, depending on what is being evaluated and the overall objectives of the M&E process. Formative evaluations are designed to assess programme design before implementation. Process evaluation examines the procedures and tasks related to implementing a programme. Outcome evaluation is used to obtain descriptive data on a project and to document short-term results. Economic evaluations assess costs and funding to determine value for money and efficiency. Impact evaluation systematically identifies the long-term effects (World Bank, 2009b). Annex table IX.5 provides additional details about each type.

Regardless of which evaluation method is applied, there are a number of key principles that should underpin all evaluation practices. According to OECD (2007c), these are:

(a) Evaluation should lead to policy change – e.g., increasing or decreasing the policy budget; whether the policy as a whole is abandoned; creating different objectives; adjusting policy delivery methods etc.;

(b) Evaluation should be part of the policy debate – evaluation should lead to policy learning in order to provide new knowledge and information about future policies;

(c) Evaluators should be "in at the start" – evaluators can assist in crafting clear and tangible policy objectives, planning budgets and highlighting evaluation methods and criteria for policymakers;

(d) Evaluation techniques should always use the most appropriate methodology – e.g., the Six Steps approach as already discussed;

(e) Evaluation should apply to all policies and programmes – it is important to avoid evaluating particular policies and programmes more frequently or rigorously than others; and

(f) International comparisons should be made where necessary – for some policy areas, evaluation can only be undertaken on an international basis, e.g., comparing the impact of tax regimes.

Evaluation can compare the various aspects of a programme with those of other programmes. Policymakers can learn what works in similar regions, countries and policy fields, and for intended beneficiaries. Such comparisons will provide useful benchmarks for assessing the level of success and those areas that require further improvement, as they often reveal gaps in existing programmes.

Annex table IX.3. Types of data sources for different types of indicators

Indicator type	Data collection time frame	Types of data source
Input	Continuously	Routine data sources such as statistics about government services
Output	Quarterly/bi-annually/annually	Routine data sources such as statistics about government services
Outcome	One to three years (short to medium term)	One-off data sources such as special studies (research or evaluation)
Impact	Two to five years (mid term to long term)	Periodic data sources such as surveillance. One-off data sources such as special studies (research or evaluation)

Source: World Bank, 2009b.

Annex table IX.4. Data collection methods, qualitative and quantitative

Qualitative	Quantitative
Semi-structured interviews, case studies, maps, transects, diaries, historical trends/timelines, seasonal calendars, flow diagrams, brainstorming, focus groups, SWOT, drama and role plays, maps, transects, geographic information system (GIS), rich pictures, visioning and well-being ranking	Biophysical measurements, structured questionnaires, maps, transects, geographic information system (GIS), diaries, flow diagrams, nominal group technique, historical trends/timelines, seasonal calendars, matrix scoring and ranking

Source: Authors' compilation.

Annex table IX.5. Types of evaluations

Type of evaluation	When to use	What it shows	Why it is useful
Formative evaluation	During the development of a new programme. When an existing programme is being modified or is being used in a new setting or with a new population.	Whether the proposed programme elements are likely to be needed, understood, and accepted by the target population. The extent to which an evaluation is possible, given the goals and objectives of the evaluation and the programme.	It allows modifications to be made to the plan before full implementation begins. Increases the likelihood that the programme will succeed.
Process evaluation	As soon as programme implementation begins. During the operation of an existing programme.	How well the programme is working. The extent to which the programme is being implemented as designed. Whether the programme is accessible and acceptable to its target population.	Provides early warning of any problems that may occur. Allows programmes to monitor how well their programme plans and activities are working.
Outcome evaluation	After the programme has made contact with at least one person or group in the target population.	The degree to which the programme is having an effect on the target population's behaviour.	Reveals whether the programme is being effective in meeting its objectives.
Economic evaluation	At the planning stage, using cost estimates. During operation of a programme, using actual costs.	The resources that are being used in a programme and their costs (direct and indirect) compared to outcomes.	Provides programme managers and funders with a way to assess effects relative to costs.
Impact evaluation	During the operation of an existing programme at appropriate intervals. At the end of a programme.	The degree to which the programme meets its ultimate goal.	Provides evidence for use in policy, funding and future programming decisions.

Source: World Bank, 2009b.

References

A

AAJ Associates, 2010. Available at www.rsm.aajassociates.com/.

Abernathy, W. and K.B. Clark, 1985. "Innovation: Mapping the winds of creative destruction", *Research Policy,* vol. 14, pp. 3-22.

Acemoglu, D. and S. Johnson, 2005. "Unbundling institutions", *Journal of Political Economy,* vol. 113, No. 5, pp. 949-995.

Adukia, R.S., 2008. *A handbook on Special Economic Zones.* Available at www.allianceindia.co.in/newsite/whitepapers/SEZ.pdf.

Agency for SME Development, 2011. "ASMEDF business portal". Available at www.business.gov.vn/index.aspx.

Agensi Inovasi Malaysia, 2011. *Bumiputera Innovation Policy.* Available at www.innovation.my/innovating-malaysia/formulation-of-the-nis/.

Aggarwal, A., 2005. "Performance of export processing zones: A comparative analysis of India, Sri Lanka and Bangladesh", New Delhi, Indian Council for Research on International Economic Relations.

Akerlof, G., 1970. "The market for 'lemons': Quality uncertainty and the market mechanism", *Quarterly Journal of Economics,* vol. 84, No. 3, pp. 488-500.

Alhabshi, S.M., A.A.A. Khalid and b. Bardai, 2009. *The Development of Corporate Credit Information Database and Credit Guarantee System.* Available at: www.asean.org/documents/ASEAN+3RG/0809/FR/13d.pdf.

Alibaba Group, 2011. "Company overview". Hangzhou, China. Available at news.alibaba.com/specials/aboutalibaba/aligroup/index.html.

Altunbas, Y., A. Kara and D. Marques-Ibanez, 2010. "Large debt financing: Syndicated loans versus corporate bonds", *European Journal of Finance,* vol. 16, No. 5, pp. 437-458.

Amata Corporation, 2006. " 'AMATA' to open Japanese SMEs industrial zone 'OTA Techno Park', ready for rental in June 2006 with expansion plan for phase 2.3". Available at amata.listedcompany.com/news.html/id/120597/group/newsroom_press.

American Marketing Association, 2011. "Dictionary". Available at www.marketingpower.com/_layouts/Dictionary.aspx?dLetter=O.

Anderson, R.D., 2010. "The WTO Agreement on Government Procurement (GPA): An emerging tool of global integration and good governance", *WTO/ESCAP Regional Workshop on Government Procurement for Asian Countries: Basic Documentation.* Bangkok.

Antoncic, B. and R.D. Hisrich, 2000. "Intrapreneurship modeling in transition economies: A comparison of Slovenia and the United States", *Journal of Developmental Entrepreneurship,* vol. 5, No. 1, pp. 21-40.

Armario, J.M., D.M. Ruiz and E.M. Armario, 2008. "Market orientation and internationalization in small and medium-sized enterprises", *Journal of Small Business Management,* vol. 46, No. 4, pp. 485-511.

Asalos, C.F. and G.G. Cherry, 2010. "Filipinnovation forum: Towards an innovation-led development path", *Filipinnovation Magazine,* November 2010.

ASG Tax Corporation, 2009. "Japan tax bulletin". Available at www.gtjapan.com/pdf/newsletter/bulletin/bulletin_200901.pdf.

Asian and Pacific Centre for Transfer of Technology, 2011. New Delhi Available at www.apctt.org/index.html.

_____, 2004. "Technology transfer definitions", *Asia Pacific Tech Monitor,* May-June 2004.

Asian Association of Management Organizations (AAMO), 2007. *SMEs in the Asian Region – Harnessing the Growth Potential.* New Delhi, AAMO.

ADB, 2012a. "Cambodia". Manila, Asian Development Bank. Available at http://beta.adb.org/countries/cambodia/main.

_____, 2012b. "Lao PDR". Manila. Available at http://beta.adb.org/countries/lao-pdr/main.

_____, 2011. *Public-Private Partnership (PPP) Handbook.* Manila. Available at www.adb.org/Documents/Handbooks/Public-Private-Partnership/default.asp.

_____, 2009. *Enterprises in Asia: Fostering Dynamism in SMEs – Key Indicators for Asia and the Pacific 2009; special chapter.* Manila.

_____, 2007, *Special Economic Zones and Competitiveness: A Case Study of Shenzhen, the People's Republic of China,* Pakistan Resident Mission Series No. 2, Pakistan, Pakistan Resident Mission ADB. Manila.

_____, 2006. "Best practice notes on small and medium-sized enterprises support, Manila.

_____, 2002. "Development of SME financing support system". Available at www.adb.org/Documents/Reports/Dev_SME_Fin_System/default.asp.

_____, 2001. "Report and recommendations of the President to the Board of Directors on proposed Loans to the Federated States of Micronesia for the Private Sector Development Program. Manila.

_____, 2000. *Private Sector Development Strategy,* March 2000. Manila.

_____ and International Labour Organization, 2011. *Women and Labour Market in Asia – Rebalancing for Gender Equality.* Bangkok, ILO Regional Office for Asia and the Pacific, and Manila, Asian Development Bank.

APO, 2007. "Entrepreneurship development for competitive small and medium enterprises: Report of the APO survey on entrepreneur development for competitive SMEs". Tokyo, Asian Productivity Organization.

APEC, 2006a. *A Research on the Innovation Promoting Policy for SMEs in APEC: Survey and Case study,* Singapore, Asia-Pacific Economic Cooperation.

_____, 2006b. "The New Guide for SMEs of Korea, the SPi-1357 system to deliver an integrated policy information on/offline in real time", *APEC SME Innovation Briefing,* No. 1, June 2006.

_____, 2004. "Breaking down the barriers for SME exporters". Available at www.apec.org/Press/Features/2004/0301_Breaking_down_the_Barriers_for_SME_Exporters.aspx.

_____, 2003. "Information survey for small and medium enterprises", Singapore, Asia-Pacific Economic Cooperation.

APEC SME Innovation Center (SMEIC), 2012. "Vision of SMEIC". Available at www.apec-smeic.org/about/?menu=vision.

Asset-Based Finance Association, 2011. "FAQs". Available at www.abfa.org.uk/public/faq.asp.

Association for Promotion of International Cooperation, 2011. "A guide to Japan's aid". Available at www.mofa.go.jp/policy/oda/guide/1998/3-4.html.

ASEAN, 2011. "SME Developments in ASEAN". Jakarta. Available at www.aseansec.org/12877.htm.

Atieno, R., 2001. "Formal and informal institutions' lending policies and access to credit by small-scale enterprises in Kenya: An empirical assessment", *African Economic Research Consortium Research Paper 111.* Nairobi.

Australian Tax Office, undated. "GST essentials". Available at www.ato.gov.au/corporate/pathway.aspx?sid=42&pc=001/003/103&mfp=001/001&mnu=44803.

Avantage Ventures, 2011. *Beyond the Margin Redirecting Asia's Capitalism,* Hong Kong, China.

B

Babson College, 2011. "Entrepreneurship". Available at www.babson.edu/Academics/divisions/entrepreneurship/Pages/home.aspx.

Bahl, R. W., 2003. "Reaching the hardest to tax: Consequences and possibilities", paper presented at the "Hard to Tax: An International Perspective" Conference, 15-16 May 2003, Andrew Young School of Policy Studies, Georgia State University.

Baig, A., 2007. "Entrepreneurship development for competitive small and medium enterprises", in *Entrepreneurship Development for Competitive Small and Medium Enterprises.* Tokyo, Asian Productivity Organization.

Baily, P., 2007. "Cambodian small and medium sized enterprises: Constraints, policies and proposals for their development" in H. Lim (ed.), *ASEAN SMEs and Globalization, ERIA Research Project Report 2007, No. 5.* Jakarta Pusat, Indonesia, Economic Research Institute of ASEAN and East Asia.

Bank Indonesia, 2011. "BI Rate". Available at www.bi.go.id/web/en/Moneter/BI+Rate/Data+BI+Rate/.

Bank Negara Malaysia, 2012. "Development Financial Institutions". Kuala Lumpur. Available at www.bnm.gov.my/microsites/financial/0206_dfi.htm#placement.

_____, 2005. *Small and Medium Enterprise (SME) Annual Report,* Kuala Lumpur.

Bank Perusahaan Kecil and Sederhana Malaysia Berhad, 2012. "Corporate Info", Kuala Lumpur. Available at www.smebank.com.my/web/guest/home.

Barseghyan, L. and R. DiCecio, 2009. "Entry costs, industry structure and cross-country income and TFP differences", Working Paper No. 2009-005C, Federal Reserve Bank of St. Louis, United States.

Baumüller, H., 2010. *Aligning Climate and Development Agendas in the Mekong Region: Options for regional collaboration between Vietnam, Cambodia and Laos".* London, Chatham House.

BayanTrade, 2008. "Corporate overview". Makati City, the Philippines, Jakarta, Kuala Lumpur and Singapore. Available at www.bayantrade.com/company.aspx.

BCG, 2009. *The Innovation Imperative in Manufacturing, How the United States Can Restore Its Edge.* Boston, Boston Consulting Group.

Beck, T., A. Demirgüç-Kunt and M.S.M. Peria, 2008. "Banking SMEs around the world: Lending practices, business models, drivers and obstacles", World Bank Policy Research Working Paper No. 4785. Washington, D.C., World Bank Group.

Benston, G.J., 1994. "Universal Banking", in *The Journal of Economic Perspectives,* vol. 8, No. 3, pp. 121-143.

Berger, A.N. and G.F. Udell, 2005. "A more complete conceptual framework for financing of small and medium enterprises", World Bank Policy Research Working Paper No. 3795. Washington, D.C., World Bank Group.

Berry, A., 2007. "The importance of SMEs in the economy", paper presented at the ITD Global Conference on Taxation of Small and Medium Enterprises. 17-19 October 2007. Buenos Aires. Available at www.itdweb.org/smeconference/documents/plenary/PI%20Berry%20ENG.pdf.

Board of Investment Unit for Industrial Linkage Development (BUILD), 2011. Available at http://build.boi.go.th/build/build_content.aspx.

Bodell, R., G. Rabbior and L.W. Smith, 1991. *Entrepreneurship: The Spirit of Adventure,* Toronto, Harcourt Brace Jovanovich.

Bornstein, D., 2004. *How to Change the World: Social Entrepreneurs and the Power of New Ideas.* Oxford, Oxford University Press.

Boschee, J., 2009. "What's the difference: Social enterprise and social entrepreneurship". Available at http://sea-alliance.blogspot.com/2009/06/whats-difference-social-enterprise-and.html.

Brimble, P., 1999. "Business associations and the Asian crisis: An action agenda for the GMS", paper presented at the Subregional Symposium on the Comprehensive

Development of the Greater Mekong Subregion, Bangkok, April 1999.

Brush, C., A. de Bruin and F. Welter, 2009. "A gender-aware framework for women's entrepreneurship", *International Journal of Gender and Entrepreneurship,* vol. 1, No. 1, pp. 8-24.

Burda, M., D. Hamermesh and P. Weil, 2007. "Total work, gender, and social norms", NBER Working Paper, No.13000. Cambridge, MA, United States, National Bureau of Economic Research.

BANSEA, 2012. "Welcome to BANSEA". Singapore, Business Angel Network South East Asia. Available at http://bansea.org/index.php?option=com_content&view=article&id=106.

Business Development Bank of Canada (BDC), undated. "Overview". Available at www.bdc.ca/EN/about/overview/Pages/overview1.aspx.

Business Link, undated. "Advantages and disadvantages of equity finance". Available at www.businesslink.gov.uk/bdotg/action/detail?itemId=1073789573&r.i=1075081703&r.l1=1073858790&r.l2=1084705429&r.l3=1074453334&r.l4=1073864776&r.s=sc&r.t=RESOURCES&type=RESOURCES.

Business New Zealand and KPMG, 2003. "Report of the Business New Zealand – KPMG Compliance Cost Survey". Available at www.businessnz.org.nz/file/598/BusinessNZ-KPMGComplianceCostSurveyReport.pdf.

Business Owner's Toolkit, 2012a. "Asset-based financing". Available at: www.toolkit.com/small_business_guide/sbg.aspx?nid=P10_3000.

_____, 2012b. "Short-term commercial loans". Available at www.toolkit.com/small_business_guide/sbg.aspx?nid=P10_3330.

_____, 2012c. "Working capital lines of credit". Available at www.toolkit.com/small_business_guide/sbg.aspx?nid=P10_3310.

_____, 2012d. "Longer-term commercial loans". Available at www.toolkit.com/small_business_guide/sbg.aspx?nid=P10_3340.

C

Cabinet Office, 2011a. *Growing the Social Investment Market: A vision and strategy.* London. Available at www.cabinetoffice.gov.uk/sites/default/files/resources/404970_SocialInvestmentMarket_acc.pdf.

_____, 2011b. "The big society capital". London. Available at www.cabinetoffice.gov.uk/content/big-society-capital.

Camp, M.S., 2002. "Entrepreneurship and regional economic development: issues and opportunities", paper presented at the annual conference of ACCRA, 2002, Charleston, SC, United States.

Campbell, A., 2009. "Trade credit: What it is and why you should pay attention". Available at http://smallbiztrends.com/2009/05/trade-credit-what-it-is-and-why-you-should-pay-attention.html.

Cassiman, B. and R. Veugelers, 2000. "External technology sources: Embodied or disembodied technology acquisition", Economics and Business Working Paper, No. 444, University Pompeu Fabra, Barcelona, Spain. Available at http://ssrn.com/abstract=224582.

Casson, M., 1995. *Entrepreneurship and Business Culture,* Brookfield, VT, United States, Edward Elgar Publishing.

Cathay Pacific, 2011. *Discovery*, September 2011, p.108.

Cavusgil, T. and M. Czinkota, 1990. *International Perspectives on Trade Promotion and Assistance,* New York, Quorum Books.

Center for International Environmental Law, 2003. "Export credit agencies and the World Trade Organization". Washington, D.C. Available at www.ciel.org/Publications/ECAs_WTO_Nov03.pdf.

Central Bank of Nigeria, 2010. "N200 Billion Small and Medium Enterprises (SME) Credit Guarantee Scheme". Available at www.cenbank.org/Devfin/smefinance.asp.

Central People's Government of China, 2006. "China issues S&T development guidelines". Available at www.gov.cn/english/2006-02/09/content_183426.htm.

Chandler, A., 1962. *Strategy and Structure: Chapters in the History of the American Industrial Enterprise.* Cambridge, MIT Press.

Chandra, N., 2009. "Small and medium enterprises in the national systems of innovation: Exploring the barriers to technology transfer", New Delhi, Jawaharlal Nehru University.

Channel NewsAsia, 2010. "Government Allocates S$16b for R&D over the next 5 years", 17 September 2010. Available at www.channelnewsasia.com/stories/singaporelocalnews/view/1081820/1/.html.

Chesbrough, H. W., 2006. *Open Innovation: Researching a New Paradigm.* Oxford, Oxford University Press.

_____, 2003a. "The era of open innovation", *Massachusetts Institute of Technology Sloan Management Review*, vol. 44, No. 3, pp. 35-41.

_____, 2003b. *Open Innovation: The New Imperative for Creating and Profiting from Technology.* Boston, Harvard Business School Press.

Chhikara, M.S. and A. Sahay, 2008. *Evaluation Study of Medium Enterprises in Manufacturing Sector.* Gurgaon, India, Management Development Institute.

Chidamber, S.R., 2003. "An analysis of Vietnam's ICT and soft services sectors", *The Electronic Journal on Information Systems in Developing Countries,* vol. 13, No. 9, pp. 1-11.

Chikofsky, E.J. and J.H. Cross, 1990. "Reverse engineering and design recovery: A taxonomy", *IEEE Software,* vol. 7, No. 1, pp. 13-17.

China Briefing, 2011. "China Issues Classification Standards for SMEs", 7 July 2011. Available at http://www.china-briefing.com/news/2011/07/07/china-issues-classification-standards-for-smes.html.

CIMC, 2011. "Financing Service", China International Marine Containers. Available at www.cimc.com/res/service_en/finance/201001/t20100106_4211.shtml.

Choudhury, S.D. and J. Rodrigues, 2010. "Bad loans in SME sector rising – SBI Chief", *Reuters*, 11 January 2010. Available at http://in.reuters.com/article/2010/01/11/idINIndia-45296220100111.

CIA World Factbook, 2011. "Overview". Available at https://www.cia.gov/library/publications/the-world-factbook/fields/2116.html.

Coase, R., 1960. "The problem of social cost", *Journal of Law and Economics*, vol. 3, No. 1, pp. 1-44.

Cohoon, J., V.W. McGrath and L. Mitchell, 2010. *The Anatomy of an Entrepreneur: Are Successful Women Entrepreneurs Different from Men*. Kansas City, MO, Ewing Marion Kauffman Foundation.

Comin, D., 2006. "Total factor productivity", *The New Palgrave Dictionary of Economics*. Available at www.people.hbs.edu/dcomin/def.pdf.

Consultative Group to Assist the Poor, 2011. "What is microfinance?" Available at www.cgap.org/p/site/c/template.rc/1.26.1302/.

Covin, J.G., D.P. Slevin and M. B. Heeley, 2000. "Pioneers and followers: Competitive tactics, environments, and firm growth", *Journal of Business Venturing*, vol. 15, No. 2, pp. 175-210.

Colombo Plan Staff College for Technician Education, 2007. "TVET: A tool for promoting entrepreneurship". Available at http://srilanka07.cpsctech.org/?mode=PB.

CGC, 2011. *Credit Guarantee System in Japan 2011*. Tokyo, Credit Guarantee Corporation.

Cyert, R. and J.G. March, 1963. *A Behavioral Theory of the Firm*. Englewood Cliffs, New York, Prentice-Hall.

Czinkota, M. and I. Ronkainen, 2007. *International Marketing*, Eighth Edition. Mason, OH, United States, Thomson South-Western.

D

D'Altri, S. and E. Santarelli, 2003. "The diffusion of e-commerce among SMEs: Theoretical implications and empirical evidence", *Small Business Economics*, vol. 21, pp. 273-283.

Daejeon Metropolitan City, 2011. "Daedeok Science District development in 1970s". Available at www.daejeon.go.kr/language/english//aboutdaejeon/history/daedeok/.

Dahlman, C. and R.R. Nelson, 1995. "Social absorption capability, national innovation systems and economic development in social capability and long-term economic growth", in B. Koo and D. Perkins (eds.), *Social Capability and Long-Term Economic Growth*. New York, St. Martin's Press.

Dahlman, C., 2007. "Technology, globalization, and international competitiveness: Challenges for developing countries", in United Nations Department of Economic and Social Affairs, *Industrial Development for the 21st Century: Sustainable Development Perspectives*. New York.

Daily Times, 2011. "NPLs of SME sector rise to Rs 96 billion by end-December", 16 March 2011. Lahore, Pakistan. Available at www.dailytimes.com.pk/default.asp?page=2011%5C03%5C16%5Cstory_16-3-2011_pg5_2.

Dannreuther, C., 2007. "EU SME policy: On the edge of governance", *CESifo Forum*, vol. 8, No. 2, pp. 7-13.

De Jong, J.P.J., W. Vanhaverbeke, T. Kalvet and H. Chesbrough, 2008. *Policies for Open Innovation: Theory, Framework and Cases*. Helsinki, research project funded by VISION Era-Net.

De la Pena, F.T., 2007. *The Philippine National Innovation Strategy*. Available at www.ibm.com/ibm/governmentalprograms/pdf/filipinnovation.pdf.

De Soto, H., 2000. *The Mystery of Capital: Why Capitalism Triumphs in the West and Fails Everywhere Else*. New York, Basic Books.

De Mel, S., D. McKenzie and C. Woodruff, 2010. "Enterprise recovery following nature disasters", World Bank Policy Research Working Paper No. 5269. Washington, D.C., World Bank.

Deloitte, 2011. "Global survey of R&D tax incentives". Available at www.nam.org/~/media/B649B9CD510242029A8F352E42D4EBB1.ashx?utm_source=nam&utm_medium=alias&utm_campaign=Deloitte_RD_Survey.

_____, 2010. "Japan: Tax focus notes". Available at www.tohmatsu.com/assets/Dcom-Japan/Local%20Assets/Documents/EN/service/tax/jp_s_tax_smes_210610.pdf.

_____, 2009. "Japan: More generous tax credits approved", *World Tax Advisor*, 14 August 2009. Available at http://deloitte.12hna.com/newsletters/2009/WTA/a090814_8.pdf.

Dennis, W.J. Jr., 2005. "Public policy, competition and entrepreneurship in the United States: The wheat, the chafe, and the irrelevant", Senior Scholar's paper in United States Association for Small Business and Entrepreneurship.

Department for Business Innovation and Skills, United Kingdom, 2007. "Survival rates of VAT-registered enterprises, 1995-2004: Key results", *DTI Small Business Service*, URN 07/963, February 2007.

DFID, 2008. *Private Sector Development Strategy – Prosperity for All: Making Markets Work*. London, Department for International Development.

Department of Business Development, undated. Bangkok. Available at www.dbd.go.th/mainsite/index.php?id=1&L=1.

Department of Export Promotion, 2011. "Vision & mission". Bangkok. Available at www.thaitrade.com/page/vision_and_mission.

Department of Science and Technology, 2009. "DOST-PEZA launches open technology business incubator". Manila. Available at http://trc.dost.gov.ph/index.php?option=com_content&view=article&id=296%3Adost-peza-launches-open-technology-business-incubator&Itemid=190.

Department of Statistics Malaysia, 2011. "Census of establishment and enterprises". Available at www.statistics.gov.my/portal/index.php?lang=en.

Department of Trade and Industry of the Philippines, 2011. Manila. Available at www.dti.gov.ph/dti/index.php?p=134.

Didero, M., K. Gareis, P. Marques and M. Ratzke, 2008. "Discussion Paper: Differences in innovation culture across Europe", TRANSFORM Consortium, Bonn. Available at http://www.transform-eu.org/publications/documents/Differences%20in%20Innovation%20Culture.pdf.

Directorate General for National Export Development, 2011. "Profile". Jakarta. Available at http://djpen.kemendag.go.id/app_frontend/links/39-profile.

Dohrmann, J.A., 2008. "Special economic zones in India – an introduction". Available at www.asienkunde.de/articles/a106_asien_aktuell_dohrmann.pdf.

Dolan, C., J. Humphrey and C. Harris-Pascal, 2000. "Horticulture commodity chains: The impact of the UK Market on the African fresh vegetable industry", IDS Working Paper No. 96. Brighton, Institute of Development Studies.

Doner, R. and B. Schneider, 2000. "Business associations and economic development: Why some associations contribute more than others", *Business and Politics*, vol. 2, No. 3, pp. 261-288.

DCED, 2011a. "Promoting private sector development". Donor Committee for Enterprise Development, Cambridge, United Kingdom. Available at www.enterprise-development.org/.

_____, 2011b. *Why have a Standard for Measuring results? Progress and Plans of the Donor Committee for Enterprise Development*. Cambridge, Donor Committee for Enterprise Development.

_____, 2008. *Supporting Business Environment Reforms: Practical Guidance for Development Agencies*. Cambridge, Donor Committee for Enterprise Development.

_____, 2001. *Business Development Services for Small Enterprises: Guiding Principles for Donor Intervention*, Cambridge, Donor Committee for Enterprise Development.

Deutsche Gesellschaft für Technische Zusammenarbeit (GTZ), 2010. "Private sector development in detail". Eschborn, Available at www.gtz.de/en/themen/wirtschaft-beschaeftigung/privatwirtschaft/22416.htm.

_____, 2009. *Microfinance Industry Report: Sri Lanka*. Eschborn.

_____, 2004. *Results-based Monitoring Guidelines for Technical Cooperation Projects and Programmes*. Eschborn.

_____ and Embassy of Japan, 2006. *Private Sector (PSD) Donor Mapping 2006 – Part Two: Consultants' Report on Gaps, Overlaps and Field of Collaboration*, Dhaka.

DP Information Group, 2011. "SME Development Survey 2011". Available at www.dpgroup.com.sg/Attachments/83_SMEDS%202011%20Slides%20Final%20COMMERCIAL%20CONFIDENTIAL.pdf.

Dratch, D., 2011. "10 ways business credit cards are different". Available at www.creditcards.com/credit-card-news/business-credit-cards-10-differences-1269.php.

Drucker, P.F., 2008. *Management: Revised Edition*. New York, Harper Collins.

_____, 1985. *Innovation and Entrepreneurship Practice and Principles*. New York, Harper & Row.

Dunning, J.H., 1980. "Toward an eclectic theory of international production: Some empirical tests", *Journal of International Business Studies,* vol. 11, No. 1, pp. 9-31.

Dutrénit, G. and A.O. Vera-Cruz, 2003. "Clustering SMEs with Maquilas in a local context: Benefiting from knowledge spillover", paper presented at the Conferencia Internacional sobre Sistemas de Inovacao Estrateg-icas de Desenvolvimento para o terceiro Milenio, 2-6 November 2003 , Rio de Janeiro.

Duval, Y. and W. Liu, 2009. "The global crisis: A wake-up call for trade finance capacity building in emerging Asia", in United Nations Economic and Social Commission for Asia and the Pacific, *Challenges and Opportunities for Trade and Financial Integration in Asia and the Pacific.* Bangkok, ESCAP.

E

Ekuiti Nasional Berhad (Ekuinas), undated. Available at www.ekuinas.com.my/index.html.

EMPRETEC, 2008. "Background". Available at www.unctadxi.org/templates/Page____7403.aspx.

Endo, T., 2008. "Broadening the offering choice of corporate bonds in emerging markets: Cost-effective access to debt capital", World Bank Policy Research Working Paper, No. 4655. Washington, D.C., World Bank.

EOS Gallup Europe, 2005. "SME access to finance: Executive summary." Available at http://ec.europa.eu/public_opinion/flash/fl174_en.pdf.

Erlinda, M. and J. Balboa, 2009. "ASEAN Rules of Origin: Lessons and recommendations for best practice", Philippine Institute for Development Studies (PIDS) Discussion Paper Series, No. 2009-36. Makati.

Ernst & Young, 2011. "2011 Asia-Pacific R&D incentives", Available at www.ey.com/Publication/vwLUAssets/2011APAC_RnD/$FILE/2011-Asia-Pacific-R&D-incentives.pdf.

Erramilli, M. and C.P. Rao, 1990. "Choice of foreign market entry by service firms: Role of market knowledge", *Management International Review,* vol. 30, No. 2, 135-185.

ESCAP, 2011a. "Enabling environment for SMEs' productive integration in global value chains: Studies of Bangladesh, Nepal and Sri Lanka, *Studies in Trade and Investment, No. 70.* Bangkok, United Nations.

_____, 2011b. "Research and development", *Statistical Yearbook for Asia and the Pacific, 2011*. Bangkok, United Nations.

_____, 2009a. "Globalization of production and the competitiveness of small and medium-sized enterprises in Asia and the Pacific: Trends and prospects", *Studies in Trade and Investment, No. 65*. Bangkok, United Nations.

_____, 2009b. *Asia-Pacific Trade and Investment Report 2009*. Bangkok, United Nations.

_____, 2009c. *Designing and Implementing Trade Facilitation in Asia and Pacific*. Bangkok, United Nations.

_____, 2007a. *Enhancing the Competitiveness of SMEs: Subnational Innovation Systems and Technological Capacity-Building Policies*. Bangkok, United Nations.

_____, 2007b. *Linking Greater Mekong Subregion Enterprises to International Markets: The Role of Global Value Chains, International Production Networks and Enterprise Clusters, Studies in Trade and Investment No. 59*. Bangkok, United Nations.

_____, 2007c. "Establishment of the sub-national innovation system for strengthening SME's competitiveness", Country Paper – Republic of Korea. Available at www.unescap.org/tid/mtg/sis_kor.pdf.

_____, 2006. *Entrepreneurship and e-Business Development for Women*. Bangkok, United Nations.

_____, 2005a. *Developing Women Entrepreneurs in South Asia: Issues, Initiatives and Experiences*. Bangkok, United Nations.

_____, 2005b. *Trade Finance Infrastructure Development: Handbook for Economies in Transition*. Bangkok, United Nations.

_____, 2004a. *Promoting Business and Technology Incubation for Improved Competitiveness of Small and Medium Industries through Application of Modern and Efficient Technologies*. New York, United Nations.

_____, 2004b. *Addressing Supply-Side Constraints and Capacity-Building*. Bangkok, United Nations.

_____, 2003. *Investment Promotion and Enterprise Development Bulletin for Asia – No. 2*. Bangkok, United Nations.

_____, 2002. *Trade Facilitation Handbook for the Greater Mekong Subregion*. Bangkok, United Nations.

_____, 2001a. *Training Manual on Increasing Capacities in Trade and Investment Promotion*. Bangkok, United Nations.

_____, 2001b. *Export Promotion for Economies in Transition, Central Asia and South Caucasus*. Bangkok, United Nations.

_____, 1997. "Financing of small and medium-sized enterprises: Problems and recommendations", in *Small Industry Bulletin for Asia and the Pacific, No. 30*. New York, United Nations.

EURADA, undated. "RDA and Enterprises". European Association of Regional Development Agencies, Pretoria, South Africa. Available at www.eurada.org/site/index.php?option=com_content&view=article&id=48&Itemid=55&lang=en.

European Central Bank, 2011. "Survey on the access to finance of small and medium-sized enterprises in the euro area: April to September 2011" > Available at: www.ecb.int/pub/pdf/other/accesstofinancesmallmediumsizedenterprises201112en.pdf?af34a23bea99c62d9d41f1a8589121ba.

European Investment Bank, World Bank, Medibtikar, Ville Marseille, 2010. Luxemburg. *Plan and Manage a Science Park in the Mediterranean: Guidebook for Decision Makers*. Available at www.eib.org/attachments/country/plan-and-manage-a-science-park-in-the-mediterranean_en.pdf.

European Commission, 2012. "Introduction to Rules of Origin". Brussels. Available at http://ec.europa.eu/taxation_customs/customs/customs_duties/rules_origin/index_en.htm.

_____, 2009a. *European SMEs under Pressure: Annual Report on EU Small and Medium Enterprises 2009*. Brussels.

_____, 2009b. *Entrepreneurship in Vocational Education and Training: Final report of the Expert Group*. Brussels.

_____, 2007. *Transparency and Dialogue: Final Report*, enterprise and industry publications. Brussels.

_____, 2006. "Risk Capital Action Plan (RCAP)". Brussels. Available at http://europa.eu/legislation_summaries/employment_and_social_policy/job_creation_measures/l24195_en.htm.

_____, 2005. "Eurostat". Brussels. Available at http://epp.eurostat.ec.europa.eu/portal/page/portal/eurostat/home/.

_____, 2003. "Communication from the Commission to the Council and the European Parliament on implementation of the Risk Capital Action Plan (RCAP)". Brussels.

_____, 2000. *Third Round of Bankers and SMEs: Final Report*. Brussels. Available at http://ec.europa.eu/enterprise/policies/finance/files/rt3_en.pdf.

European Foundation for the Improvement of Living and Working Conditions (Eurofound), 2011. "SMEs in the crisis: Employment, industrial relations and local partnership". Dublin, Ireland, and Brussels. Available at www.lex.unict.it/eurolabor/documentazione/altridoc/fe/Eurofound_SME_crisis_June11.pdf.

EURO-Phoenix, 2011. "Factoring: A financing option for small and medium-sized enterprises (SMEs). Available at www.europhoenix.com/node/671.

Evans, C., Ritchie, K., Tran-Nam, B. and M. Walpole, 1997. *A Report into the Taxpayer Costs of Compliance*. Canberra, Australian Government Publishing Service.

Eversole, R., 2004. *Change Makers? Women's Microenterprises in a Bolivian City, Gender, Work and Organization*, vol.11, No. 2, pp. 123-42.

EWEC, undated. "Business Database". Available at www.ewecbiz.com/.

Export Finance and Insurance Corporation, undated. "About EFIC". Sydney, Australia. Available at www.efic.gov.au/about/Pages/aboutefic.aspx.

F

Fagerberg, J., 2006. "Innovation: A guide to the literature", in *The Oxford Handbook of Innovation*, Oxford Handbooks in Business and Management Series. New York, Oxford Handbooks Online.

Falcke, C.O., 1999. "Industrial parks, principles and practice", *Journal of Economic Cooperation Among Islamic Countries,* vol. 20, No. 1, pp. 1-10.

Fang, Y., 2008. "Eco-industrial parks in China". Available at www.eoearth.org/article/Eco-industrial_parks_in_China.

Feinson, S., 2003. "National innovation system overview and country cases", in *Knowledge Flows and Knowledge Collectives: Understanding the Role of Science and Technology Policies in Development.* New York, Rockefeller Foundation.

FERN, undated. "Export credit agencies". Available at www.fern.org/campaign/trade-and-investment/export-credit-agencies.

Fernando, N.A., 2006. *Understanding and Dealing with High Interest Rates on Microcredit.* Manila, Asian Development Bank.

Ferretti, M. and A. Parmentola, 2010. "FDI knowledge spillovers and host government policies: The Iranian experience", *European Business Review,* vol. 22, No. 2, pp.175-194.

Finance Asia, 2011. "Alibaba.com meets the needs of Chinese SME treasuries". Available at www.financeasia.com/News/171865,alibabacom-meets-the-needs-of-chinese-sme-treasuries.aspx?refresh=on.

Fliiby website, 2009. "Banking in Pakistan" Available at www.scribd.com/doc/5131283/banking-in-Pakistan.

Ford, A. and O. Lorenz, 2008. "Tonga: Enforcing contracts quickly, with help from the neighbors" in *Celebrating Reform 2008.* Washington, D.C., World Bank.

FIAS, 2008. "Special economic zones: Performance, lessons learned and implications for zone development". Washington, D.C., World Bank Foreign Investment Advisory Service. Available at www.ifc.org/ifcext/fias.nsf/AttachmentsByTitle/SEZpaperdiscussion/$FILE/SEZs+report_April2008.pdf.

Freear, J., J. Sohl and W.E. Wetzel, 1994. "Angels and non-angels: Are there differences?" *Journal of Businesses Venturing,* vol. 9, pp. 109-123.

G

Ganbold, B., 2008. *Improving Access to Finance for SME: International Good Experiences and Lessons for Mongolia.* Institute of Developing Economies. Available at www.ide.go.jp/English/Publish/Download/Vrf/pdf/438.pdf.

Garcia, R. and R. Calantone, 2002. "A critical look at technological innovation typology and innovativeness terminology: A literature review", *Journal of Product Innovation Management,* vol. 19, No. 2, pp. 110-132.

General Statistics Office of Vietnam, 2011. Hanoi. Available at www.gso.gov.vn/default_en.aspx?tabid=491.

Gereffi, G. and O. Memedovic, 2003. *The Global Apparel Value Chain: What Prospects for Upgrading by Developing Countries.* Vienna, United Nations Industrial Development Organization.

Gibson, T. and H.J. van der Vaart, 2008. *Defining SMEs: A Less Imperfect Way of Defining Small and Medium Enterprises in Developing Countries.* Washington, D.C., The Brookings Institution.

Gill, I. and H. Kharas, 2007. An East Asian Renaissance: Ideas for Growth. Washington, D.C., World Bank.

Glaser, B.G. and A. Strauss, 1967. *Discovery of Grounded Theory: Strategies for Qualitative Research.* Chicago, Aldine Publishing Company.

Global Entrepreneurship Monitor (GEM), 2012. *"2011 Global Report",* Global Entrepreneurship Research Association, London. Available at www.gemconsortium.org/docs/2201/gem-2011-global-report.

_____, 2011. "Special report on social entrepreneurship", Global Entrepreneurship Research Association, London. Available at www.gemconsortium.org/docs/376/gem-report-on-social-entrepreneurship-executive-summary.

_____, 2010. *2010 Global Report,* Global Entrepreneurship Research Association, London. Available at www.gemconsortium.org/docs/download/266.

_____, 2009. 2009 Global Report, Available at www.gemconsortium.org/docs/download/265.

_____, 2007. *2007 Global Report on High-Growth Entrepreneurship,* Global Entrepreneurship Research Association, London. Available at www.gemconsortium.org/docs/269/gem-2007-report-on-high-growth-entrepreneurship.

_____, 2005. *GEM Thailand 2005 Report,* Global Entrepreneurship Research Association, London. Available at www.gemconsortium.org/docs/633/gem-thailand-2005-report.

Global Production Networks, 2003. "Global production networks in Europe and East Asia: The automotive components industry", GPN Working Paper No. 7, Manchester, University of Manchester.

Goldscheider, R., 2006. *Licensing Best Practices: Strategic, Territorial, and Technology Issues, 2006.* New Jersey, Wiley & Sons.

Government Electronic Business (GeBIZ), 2011. "About us". Singapore. Available at www.gebiz.gov.sg/.

Government of Canada, 2003. "SME financing in Canada". Available at www.sme-fdi.gc.ca/eic/site/sme_fdi-prf_pme.nsf/eng/01064.html#note121.

Government Public Relations Department, 2011. "Thailand's National Tourism Development Plan" Bangkok. Available at http://thailand.pr.go.th/view_inside.php?id=5525.

Grameen Bank, 1998. "Credit lending models". Dhaka. Available at www.grameen-info.org/index.php?option=com_content&task=view&id=43&Itemid=93.

Grameen Foundation, 2010. "Debating the merits of for-profit microfinance". Dhaka. Available at www.grameenfoundation.org/debating-merits-profit-microfinance.

Greve, A. and J.W. Salaff, 2003. "Social networks and entrepreneurship", *Entrepreneurship Theory & Practice,* vol. 28, No. 1, pp. 1-22.

Gwartney, J., J. Hall and R. Lawson, 2011. *Economic Freedom of the World: 2011 Annual Report,* Fraser Institute, Calgary, Montreal, Toronto, and Vancouver. Available at www.freetheworld.com/release.html.

H

Hall, B. and J. Van Reenen, 2000. "How effective are fiscal incentives for R&D? A review of the evidence", *Research Policy,* vol. 29, Nos. 4-5, pp. 449-469. Amsterdam, Elsevier.

Hall, B.H., 1987. "The effect of takeover activity on corporate research and development", in A. J. Auerbach (ed.), *Corporate Takeovers: Causes and Consequences.* Chicago, University of Chicago.

Hall, C., 2009. "SMEs financing in the Asia-Pacific region amid the financial crisis: Status, challenges and trends", presentation at the Workshop on SMEs Financing in the Asia-Pacific Region: Crisis and Countermeasures, June 2009, Shanghai, China. Available at www.afdc.org.cn/afdc/event.asp?info_id=31.

_____, 2002. "Profile of SMEs and SME issues in East Asia", in C. Harvie and B.C. Lee (eds.), *The Role of Small and Medium Enterprises in National Economies in East Asia.* Cheltenham, United Kingdom, Edward Elgar.

Hallberg, K., 1999. *Small and Medium Scale Enterprises: A Framework for Intervention.* Washington, D.C., World Bank.

Hang, M. and A. van Weezel, 2007. "Media and entrepreneurship: What do we know and where should we go?" *Journal of Media Business Studies,* vol. 4, No. 1, pp. 51-70.

Harvie, C. and B. Lee, 2008. "Small and medium enterprises in East Asia: Sectoral and regional dimensions", *Studies of Small and Medium Enterprises in East Asia, Volume IV.* Cheltenham, United Kingdom, Edward Edgar Publishing.

_____, 2002. "The role of SMEs in national economies in East Asia", *Studies of Small and Medium Enterprises in East Asia, Volume II.* Cheltenham, United Kingdom, Edward Elgar Publishing.

Hauerstein, K. and F. Niemann, 2002. *SME Constraints in Taxation System,* Jakarta, ADB Technical Assistance.

_____, 2005. *Growth diagnostics.* John F. Kennedy School of Government, Harvard University.

Hausmann, R., D. Rodrik and A. Velasco, 2006. "Getting the diagnosis right", *Finance & Development,* vol. 43, No. 1.

Headd, B., 2003. "Redefining business success: Distinguishing between closure and failure", *Small Business Economics,* vol. 21, pp. 51-61.

Healy Consultants, 2011. "Singapore Company Formation", Singapore. Available at www.healyconsultants.com.

Helms, M.M. (ed.), 2006. *Encyclopaedia of Management.* Farmington Hills, MI, United States, Thomson Gale.

Henrekson, M., 2007. "Entrepreneurship and Institutions", *Comparative Labor Law & Policy Journal,* vol. 28, No. 4, pp. 717-742.

Henrekson, M., D. Johansson and M. Stenkula, 2010. "Labor policy, and high impact entrepreneurship", *Journal of Industry, Competition and Trade,* vol. 10, Nos. 3/4, pp. 275-296.

Hessels, J. and S. Terjesen, 2010. "Resource dependency and institutional theory perspectives on direct and indirect export choices", *Small Business Economics,* vol. 34, No. 2, pp. 203-220.

HM Treasury of the United Kingdom, 2011. "Public private partnerships". Available at www.hm-treasury.gov.uk/ppp_index.htm.

Hofstede, G., 2001. *Culture's Consequences: Comparing Values, Behaviors, Institutions and Organizations across Nations,* second edition. Thousand Oaks CA, Sage Publications.

_____, 1991. *Cultures and Organizations: Software of the Mind.* Berkshire, McGraw-Hill.

_____, 1980. *Culture's Consequences: International Differences in Work-Related Values.* Beverly Hills CA., Sage Publications.

Holdsworth, J.T., 2009. *Collateral Security in Money and Banking.* New York, Cornell University Library.

Holland, R., 1998. "Planning against a business failure", *ADC Info No. 24.* Agricultural Development Centre and Agricultural Extension Service, University of Tennessee.

Hollenstein, H., 2005. "Determinants of international activities: Are SMEs different?" *Small Business Economics,* vol. 24, No. 5, pp. 431-450.

Huifen, C., 2010. *More SMEs Taking the Merger Route.* Singapore, Accounting and Corporate Regulatory Authority.

Humphrey, J., R. Mansell, D. Paré and H. Schmitz, 2003. *"The Reality with E-Commerce in Developing Countries",* London, London School of Economics.

Humphrey, J., 2005. "Shaping value chains for development: Global value chains in agribusiness". Eschborn, Deutsche Gesellschaft für Technische Zusammenarbeit (GTZ).

Hussain, J., C. Millman and H. Matlay, 2006. "SME financing in the UK and in China: A comparative perspective," *Journal of Small Business and Enterprise Development,* vol. 13, No. 4, pp. 584-599.

I

Ibarrarán, P., A. Maffioli and R. Stucchi, 2009. "SME policy and firms' productivity in Latin America", IZA Discussion Paper No. 4486. Bonn, Institute for the Study of Labour.

Ibrahim, A.B. and K. Soufani, 2002. "Entrepreneurship education and training in Canada: A critical assessment," *Education & Training,* vol. 44, Nos. 8/9, pp. 421-430.

Ida, N., 2007. *Environmental issues in 7th ASEM Customs,* DG-Commissioner Meeting, 12-13 November, Yokohama, Japan.

IEMA, 2004. "Taking the First Steps in Environmental Management", Institute of Environmental Management and Assessment, Lincoln, United Kingdom. Available at www.iso.org/iso/ims0404-environment.pdf.

Ilano, M.T.V., 2010. "Philippines launches law to encourage tech transfer", *Science and Development Network*, 20 May 2010. Available at www.scidev.net/en/news/philippines-launches-law-to-encourage-tech-transfer.html.

Indian Institute of Foreign Trade, 2011. "SMEs overseas". Available at www.smeiift.com/sme/SME_Overseas.asp.

Indonesia Trade Promotion Centre, 2011. "DGNED's profile". Available at www.nafed.go.id/office/index/en.

Industrial Credit and Investment Corporation of India Bank, undated. "About us". Available at www.icicibank.com/aboutus/history.html.

Industrial Development Bank of India, undated. "Information on the Constitution of IDBI". Available at www.idbi.com/aboutus_history.asp.

Industrial Finance Corporation of India, 2008. "Genesis of IFCI". Available at www.ifciltd.com/AboutUs/WhatWeAre/tabid/79/Default.aspx.

Industrial Technology Research Institute, 2011. "ITRI Overview". Taiwan, Province of China. Available at www.itri.org.tw/eng/econtent/about/about01.aspx.

Inland Revenue Authority of Singapore, 2011. "GST rates". Available at www.iras.gov.sg/irasHome/page04.aspx?id=1852#gstrates.

Innovationsme, 2008. "NIC & Innovationsme.com". Bangkok. Available at www.innovationsme.com/v17/index.php?option=com_content&view=category&layout=blog&id=39&Itemid=58.

INSEAD, 2011. *The Global Innovation Index 2011*. Available at www.globalinnovationindex.org/gii/main/fullreport/index.html.

Institute for Global Environmental Strategies, 2006. "Improving environmental performance of small and medium-sized enterprises (SMEs)". Kanagawa, Japan. Available at http://enviroscope.iges.or.jp/contents/APEIS/RISPO/spo/pdf/overall/3.5.2_sme.pdf.

Internationaal Ondernemen, 2011. "Venture capital/Investors – providers of private equity", available at www.internationaalondernemen.nl/zoeken/showbouwsteen.asp?bstnum=158119.

International Bank of Reconstruction and Development/World Bank, 2012. *Women, Business and the Law: Removing Barriers to Economic Inclusion*. Washington, D.C.

International Centre for Trade and Sustainable Development, 2008. *Climate Change, Technology Transfer and Intellectual Property Rights*. Winnipeg.

ICC, 2012a. "History of the Incoterms rules", International Chamber of Commerce, Paris. Available at www.iccwbo.org/incoterms_history/.

_____, 2012b. "From the introduction of Incoterms 2010", International Chamber of Commerce, Paris. Available at www.iccwbo.org/Incoterms/index.html?id=40772.

_____, 2010. "Incoterms 2010", International Chamber of Commerce, Paris. Available at www.searates.com/design/images/incoterms/risks_costs_oblagations_transfer.png.

IFC, 2012a. "MIFA promoting micro finance in Asia". Washington, D.C., International Financial Corporation, World Bank Group. Available at www.ifc.org/mifa.

_____, 2012b. "G20 SME finance consultations schedule and documents". Washington, D.C., International Financial Corporation, World Bank Group. Available at www.ifc.org/ifcext/g20ifcsmeconslultation.nsf/Content/Publication13.

_____, 2011a. "BEE Toolkits". Washington, D.C., International Financial Corporation, World Bank Group. Available at www.ifc.org/ifcext/sme.nsf/Content/BEE+Toolkits.

_____, 2011b. *SME Finance Policy Guide SME Finance Policy Guide*. Washington, D.C., International Financial Corporation, World Bank Group.

_____, 2010a. *Scaling-Up SME Access to Financial Services in the Developing World*. International Financial Corporation, World Bank Group, Washington, D.C.

_____, 2010b. "IFC financing to micro, small and medium enterprises in South Asia". Washington, D.C., International Financial Corporation, World Bank Group. Available at www.ifc.org/ifcext/gfm.nsf/AttachmentsByTitle/MSME-Factsheet-SA-10/$FILE/MSME-Factsheet-SA-10.pdf.

_____, 2010c. "IFC financing to micro, small and medium enterprises in East Asia and Pacific". Washington, D.C., International Financial Corporation, World Bank Group. Available at www1.ifc.org/wps/wcm/connect/0f53cc804a430887b7ccbf8969adcc27/2011-MSME-Factsheet-EAP.pdf?MOD=AJPERES.

_____, 2009. *The SME Banking Knowledge Guide*. Washington, D.C., International Financial Corporation, World Bank Group.

_____, 2008. *Monitoring and Evaluation for Business Environment Reform: A Handbook for Practitioners*. Washington, D.C., International Financial Corporation, World Bank Group.

_____, 2007. *Designing a tax system for micro and small business: Guide for practitioners*. Washington, D.C., International Financial Corporation, World Bank Group.

_____ and PricewaterhouseCoopers, 2011. *Paying Taxes 2011 – the Global Picture*. Washington, D.C., International Financial Corporation, World Bank Group.

International Fund for Agricultural Development, 2002. *Managing for Impact in Rural Development: A Guide for Project M&E*. Rome.

ILO, 2009a. *Key Indicators of the Labour Market (KILM), Sixth Edition*. Geneva.

_____, 2009b. *Micro, Small and Medium-sized Enterprises and the Global Economic Crisis: Impacts and Policy Responses*. Geneva.

_____, 2005. *Know About Business: Entrepreneurship Education in School and Technical Vocational Training Institutions*. Turin, International Training Centre of ILO.

_____, 2003a. *Small Enterprise Development: An Introduction to the Policy Challenge*. Geneva.

_____, 2003b. *Developing Commercial Markets for Business Development Services*. Geneva.

_____, 1998. *Labour and Social Issues Relating to Export Processing Zones.* Geneva.

IMF, 2004. *Public-Private Partnerships.* Washington D.C., International Monetary Fund.

_____, 2001. *The Modern VAT.* Washington, D.C., International Monetary Fund.

ISO, 2011. *ISO Standards.* Geneva, International Organization for Standardization. Available at www.iso.org/iso/iso_catalogue.htm.

International Panel on Climate Change (IPCC), 2000. *Methodological and Technological Issues in Technology Transfer,* Cambridge, Cambridge University Press.

International Tax Dialogue, 2007. "Taxation of Small and Medium Enterprises", background paper for International Tax Dialogue Conference, 17-19 October 2007, Buenos Aires. Paris, OECD.

International Trade Administration, 2007. *Trade Finance Guide: A Quick Reference for U.S. Exporters,* Washington, D.C.

ITC, 2009. *How to Access Trade Finance: A Guide for Exporting SMEs.* Geneva, International Trade Centre.

_____, 1999. "Export Strategies for Small Firms", *International Trade Forum Magazine,* No. 1, 1999. Geneva, International Trade Centre.

_____, 1997. *The SME and the Global Market Place: An analysis of competitiveness constraints,* Geneva, International Trade Centre.

_____, United Nations Conference on Trade and Development and World Trade Organization, 2005. *Lao People's Democratic Republic: The Case for a National Export Strategy, Key Issues and Possible Response,* Project LAO/61/89, Support to Trade Promotion and Export Development in the Lao People's Democratic Republic.

Investorwords, 2012. "Intellectual Property". Available at www.investorwords.com/2526/intellectual_property.html.

Irish Tax and Revenue, 2011. "The Business Expansion Scheme (BES) – relief for investment in corporate trades – IT 55", Revenue Commission, Dublin. Available at www.revenue.ie/en/tax/it/leaflets/it55.html.

J

Jaffe, K., S.L. Carciente and W. Zanoni, 2007. "The economic limits of trust: The case of a Latin American informal urban commerce sector", *Journal of Developmental Entrepreneurship,* vol. 12, No. 3, pp. 339-352.

Jalbert, S.E., 2000. *Women Entrepreneurs in the Global Economy.* Washington, D.C., Center for International Private Enterprise. Available at www.cipe.org/programs/women/pdf/jalbert.pdf.

Japan Customs, 2011. "Export/import". Available at www.customs.go.jp/english/exp-imp/index.htm.

Japan Tax Bulletin, 2009. "Quarterly newsletter on important tax and business developments in Japan". Tokyo, ASG Tax Corporation.

Jauch, H., 2002. "Export processing zones and the quest for sustainable development: a Southern African perspective", *Environment and Urbanization,* vol. 14, No. 1, pp. 101-113.

JETRO, 2012a. "About us". Available at www.jetro.go.jp/en/jetro/.

_____, 2012b. "Activities: Supplying Japan with foreign economic information". Available at www.jetro.go.jp/en/jetro/activities/research/.

_____, 2011. "Activities". Available at www.jetro.go.jp/en/jetro/activities/overseas/.

JFC, 2011. *JFC-Micro 2011: Outline and International Cooperation.* Tokyo, Japan Finance Corporation, Micro Business and Individual Unit.

_____, 2009. *2009nenndo Shinnkikaigyou Jittaichousa: Anke-tokekka no Gaiyou,* 21 December, Tokyo, Japan Finance Corporation Research Institute.

_____, 2008. *Sougyou Yell: Sougyou eno Michi Shirube, Sousyuuhen.* Available at www.jfc.go.jp/k/pfcj/pdf/sogyo_yell_06.pdf.

JICA, 2009. "Effective support approaches for small and medium enterprises by development stages, Sri Lanka". Tokyo, Japan International Cooperation Agency Project Discussion Paper.

_____, 2006. *Effective Support Approaches for Small and Medium Enterprises by Development Stages: Final Report.* Tokyo.

JSBRI, 2011. "2011 White Paper on small and medium enterprises in Japan: Rebuilding from the earthquake and surmounting growth constraints". Tokyo, Ministry of Economy, Trade and Industry, and Japan Small Business Research Institute.

_____, 2010. "White Paper on small and medium enterprises in Japan – pulling through the crisis". Tokyo, Japan Small Business Research Institute.

_____, 2009. "White Paper on small and medium enterprises in Japan: Finding vitality through innovation and human resources". Tokyo, Japan Small Business Research Institute.

Johanson, J. and J.E. Vahlne, 2009. "The Uppsala Internationalization Process Model revisited: From liability of foreignness to liability of outsidership", *Journal of International Business Studies,* vol. 40, No. 9, pp. 1411-1431.

_____, 1977. "The internationalization process of the firm: A model of knowledge development and increasing foreign market commitments", *Journal of International Business Studies,* vol. 8, No. 1, pp. 23-32.

Johnsen, P.C. and R.G.P. McMahon, 2005. "Cross-industry difference in SME financing behaviour: An Australian perspective", *Journal of Small Business and Enterprise Development,* vol. 12, No. 2, pp. 160-177.

Johnson, A., 1998. "Functions in innovation system approaches", *DRUID Nelson and Winter Conference Paper No. 106.* Druid's Nelson and Winter Conference, 12-15 June 2001, Aalborg. Available at www.druid.dk/conferences/nw/paper1/a_johnson.pdf.

Jolly, V.K., 1997. *Commercializing the New Technologies: Getting from Mind to Market*. Boston, United States, Harvard Business School Press.

Jones, G.K. and H.J. Davis, 2000. "National culture and innovation: Implications for locating global R&D operations", *Management International Review*, vol. 40, No. 1, pp. 11-39.

Jones, P.M., 2009. "Trade credit insurance", *Primer Series on Insurance, No. 15*, Washington D.C., World Bank.

K

Kai Ga Shoppers, 2012. "Import Procedures". Available at www.kaigaishoppers.com/en/readme.html.

Kao, R. and T.W. Liang, 2001. *Entrepreneurship and Enterprise Development*. Singapore, Pearson Education.

Kappel, V., A. Krauss and L. Lontzek, 2010. *Over-indebtedness and Microfinance: Constructing an Early Warning Index*. Center for Microfinance, University of Zurich.

Katalyst, 2010. Available at www.katalyst.com.bd/.

Kayne, J., 1999. *State Entrepreneurship: Policies and Programs*. Kauffman Center for Entrepreneurial Leadership at the Ewing Marion Kauffman Foundation, Kansas City.

Keppel, U., L.D. Buh and J. Spatz, 2006. *Streamlining Business Regulations and Licensing Procedures: Experiences from the Philippines and Vietnam*. Berlin, Deutsche Gesellschaft für Technische Zusammenarbeit.

Khan, M.H., 2009. "Learning, technology acquisition and governance challenges in developing countries", Research Paper Series on Governance for Growth. London, School of Oriental and African Studies, University of London.

Kim, H.S., 2005. Statement presented at the Joint Event for World SMEs Forum and World Trade Point Federation General Assembly Meeting, 7-9 November 2005 Bangkok, Thailand.

Kim, Y.R., 2001. "Technology commercialization in Republic of Korea", Korea Technology Transfer Center, Seoul. Available at www.wipo.int/export/sites/www/uipc/en/documents/pdf/tmc_korea.pdf.

Klapper, L., 2006. "The role of factoring for SME finance", *Access Finance*, No. 15, December. Washington, D.C., World Bank.

Kleinberg, S. and R. Campbell, 2008. "Business enabling environment and the value chain", Briefing paper for USAID. Washington, D.C.

Knight, G. and S.T. Cavusgil, 1996. "The born global firm: A challenge to traditional internationalization theory", in S.T. Cavusgil and T.K. Madsen (eds.), *Export Internationalizing Research – Enrichment and Challenges: Advances in International Marketing*, vol. 8, pp. 11-26.

Kobayashi, Y., 2011. "Effect of R&D tax credits for small and medium-sized enterprises in Japan: Evidence from firm-level data", Research Institute of Economy, Trade and Industry Discussion Paper Series 11-E-066, September 2011. Tokyo.

Kohli, A.K. and B.J. Jaworski, 1990. "Market orientation: The construct, research propositions, and managerial implications," *Journal of Marketing*, vol. 54, No. 2, pp. 1-18.

Korea Eximbank, 2011. "Overview". Available at www.koreaexim.go.kr/en/exim/glance/manage_01.jsp.

KOTRA, 2011. Seoul, Korea Trade-Investment Promotion Agency. Available at http://english.kotra.or.kr/wps/portal/dken.

KDB, 2010. Available at www.kdb.co.kr/screen/jsp/IHEng/IHEngUMan0 0000001E.jsp.

Korhonen, H., R.Y. Luostarinen and L. Welch, 1996. "Internationalization of SMEs: Inward-outward patterns and government policy", *Management International Review*, vol. 36, No. 4, pp. 315-329.

Kornel, N., 2006. "Trade export a long walk for SMEs", Tanzania Development Gateway. Available at www.tanzaniagateway.org/news/news/article.asp?ID=131.

Kotelnikov, V., 2007. "Small and medium enterprises and ICT", UN-APCICT. Available at www.unapcict.org/ecohub/resources/small-and-medium-enterprises-and-ict/at_download/attachment1.

KPMG, 2012. "Global indirect tax". Available at www.kpmg.com/global/en/whatwedo/tax/globalindirecttax/pages/default.aspx.

Kuhn, R.L., 2011. *How China's Leaders Think: The Inside Story of China's Past, Current and Future Leaders*. New York, Wiley.

Kyoto Chamber of Commerce and Industry, undated. "Wisdom for Future". Kyoto. Available at www.kyo.or.jp/kyoto/e/index.html.

L

Lallana, E.C., Pascual, P. and Andam, Z.R., 2002. *SMEs and e-COMMERCE in Three Philippine Cities*. Prepared by Digital Philippines to the Asia Foundation. Available at http://asiafoundation.org/pdf/SMEsurvey_philippines.pdf.

Larson, D.W. and T.K. Shaw, T.K 2001. "Issues of microenterprise and agricultural growth: do opportunities exist through forward and backward linkages?" *Journal of Development Entrepreneurship*, vol. 6, No. 3, pp. 203-220.

Lazcano, J.M., 2010. "Filipinnovation network hands first award to top three start-up firms", *DOST Digest*, vol. 3, No. 11, November 2010.

Lee, E., 2008. "Do good, get rich", *Black Enterprise*, vol. 38, No. 10, pp. 72-75.

Lee, J.H., J.S. Kim and S. Maliphol, 2011. *Innovation System Diagnosis and STI Strategy Development for Least Developed Countries: Case of Lao PDR*. Seoul, Science and Technology Policy Institute.

Leifer, R., 2000. *Radical Innovation: How Mature Companies can Outsmart Upstarts*. Boston, Harvard Business Press.

Levitsky, J., 1997. "Credit guarantee schemes for SMEs – an international review", *Small Enterprise Development*, vol. 8, No. 2, pp. 4-17.

Levy, F., 2002. "Apex institutions in microfinance", CGAP Occasional Paper No. 6,. Washington, D.C., Consultative Group to Assist the Poor.

Lim, H. and F. Kimura, 2010. "The internationalization of small and medium enterprises in regional and global value chains", Asian Development Bank Institute Working Paper Series No. 231. Tokyo.

Limited Liability Partnership, 2009. "About LLP". Available at www.llp.gov.in/aboutllp.htm.

Locke, K., 2001. *Grounded Theory in Management Research*. London, Sage Publications Ltd.

Locke, R., F. Qin and A. Brause, 2006. "Does monitoring improve labor standards? Lessons from Nike", Corporate Social Responsibility Initiatives Working Paper No. 24. Cambridge, MA, John F. Kennedy School of Government, Harvard University.

Luczak, C. and S. Mohan-Neill, 2009. A theoretical framework for service SMEs based on culture, market orientation and network benefits", *Academy of Marketing Studies*, vol. 14, No. 2, pp.15-19.

Lundvall, B., 1992. *National Innovation Systems: Towards a Theory of Innovation and Interactive Learning*. London, Pinter.

M

Mach, T.L. and J.D. Wolken, 2006. "Financial services used by small businesses: Evidence from the 2003 Survey of Small Business Finances". Available at: www.federalreserve.gov/pubs/bulletin/2006/smallbusiness/smallbusiness.pdf.

Machikita, T., 2009. *Linked Versus Non-linked Firms in Innovation: The Effect of Economics of Network in East Asia*. Bangkok, Bangkok Research Centre.

Malaysia Economic Planning Unit, 2010. "Tenth Malaysia Plan, 2011-2013". Available at http://www.epu.gov.my/html/themes/epu/html/RMKE10/rmke10_english.html.

Malaysia External Trade Development Corporation, 2011a. "For Malaysian exporters". Available at www.matrade.gov.my/en/for-malaysian-exporters.

_____, 2011b. "About MATRADE". Available at http://www.matrade.gov.my/en/about-matrade.

Malaysian Goods and Services Tax, 2012. Available at www.gst.customs.gov.my/portal/page/portal/MYGSET.

Malaysian Science and Technology Information Centre, 1998. "1998 National Survey of Research and Development". Available at www.mastic.gov.my/portals/mastic/publications/R_DSurvey/98/.

Malazgirt, A., 2011. "Case studies of successful commercialization of biotechnology in Daedeok Valley", *Tech Monitor*, March-April, pp. 37-44.

Malik, I., 2008. "DFIs for economic development in Pakistan". Available at www.fcibank.com.pk/Article-DFI-EcnomicDevelopment.html.

Mandl, I. and A. Dorr, 2007. *CSR and Competitiveness – European SMEs' Good Practice*. Vienna, Austrian Institute for SME Research.

Markman, G.D., D.S. Siegel and M. Wright, 2008. "Research and technology commercialization", *Journal of Management Studies*, vol. 45, No. 8, pp., 1401-1423.

MasterCard Worldwide, 2010. Women-owned SMEs in Asia/Pacific, Middle East and Africa: An assessment of the business environment. Available at www.masterintelligence.com/upload/251/178/MC84-WomenSME-S.pdf.

Mathews, S., M. Healy and Y. Ali, 2006. "The Internet and international market growth: A model development", Queensland University of Technology, Australia. Available at http://eprints.qut.edu.au/7210/2/7210.pdf.

Maxi Insurance Broker, 2011. "Our service: Profession & finance". Available at www.maxi-broker.com/our services.php?lang=en&service=6.

McAuley, A., 1999. "Entrepreneurial instant exporters in the Scottish arts and crafts sectors", *Journal of International Marketing*, vol. 7, No. 4, pp. 67-82.

McCauley, D., 2009. "Technology tansfer in the UNFCCC process", presentation at the Asia Clean Energy Forum, 18 June 2009, Manila.

McDougall, P., S. Shane and B.M. Oviatt, 1994. "Explaining the formation of international new ventures: The limits of theories from international business research", *Journal of Business Venturing*, vol. 9, No. 6, pp. 469-487.

McKee, J., 2003. "Capital markets for small and medium enterprises: An evaluation of recent New Zealand experience", presentation at the second Annual Conference of the Pacific Economic Cooperation Council, Finance Forum, 8-9 July 2003, Hua Hin, Thailand.

McVay, M. and A.O. Miehlbradt, 2001. *Developing Commercial Markets for BDS: Can This Give the Scale and Impact We Need?* Geneva, International Labour Organization.

Melchioly, S.R. and Ø. Sœbø, 2010. "ICTs and development: Nature of mobile phones usage for SMEs economic development – an exploratory study in Morogoro, Tanzania", ICT and Development – Research Voices from Africa. International Federation for Information Processing IFIP. Technical Commission 9 – Relationship between Computers and Society Workshop at Makerere, 22-23 March 2010.

Meulenberg, M.T.G. and F.J.H.M. Verbees, 2004. "Market orientation, innovativeness, product innovation, and performance in small firms", *Journal of Small Business Management*, vol. 42, No. 2, p. 134.

Micro, Small and Medium Enterprises Development Institute, 2006. *The Micro, Small and Medium Enterprises Development Act 2006*. New Delhi. Available at www.msmediraipur.gov.in/pdf/msme_act.pdf.

Microfinance Information Exchange, 2010. *Asia 2009 Microfinance Analysis and Benchmarking Report*. Washington, D.C.

Migiro, S. and H. Ongori, 2010. "Information and communication technologies adoption in SMEs: Literature review", *Journal of Chinese Entrepreneurship*, vol. 2, No. 1, pp. 93-104.

Ming, P. and D. Shahnaz, 2009. *Social Enterprise in Asia: Context and Opportunities*. Singapore, Center on Asia and Globalization, Lee Kuan Yew School of Public Policy.

Minister of Community Development, Youth and Sports, 2007. "Report of the Social Enterprise Committee". Singapore. Available at www.mcys.gov.sg/web/SocialEnterpriseCommitteeReport.html.

Ministry of Commerce, 2011. Beijing, Department of Foreign Trade. "Functions", Available at http://wms2.mofcom.gov.cn/.

Ministry of Economic Development, 2009. "Baseline review of angel investment in New Zealand, undertaken as part of the formation of the Seed Co-Investment Fund." New Zealand.

Ministry of Economy and Finance, 2005. "Draft outline of SME development framework: Sub-committee on Small and Medium Enterprises". Phnom Penh, Cambodia. Available at www.mef.gov.kh/documents/PFM/7cg_document/draft_outline_sme.htm.

Ministry of Economy, Trade and Industry, 2011a. Tokyo. "Statistics", Available at www.meti.go.jp/english/.

_____, 2011b. "METI measures and requests in response to the Great East Japan Earthquake". Tokyo. Available at www.meti.go.jp/english/earthquake/index.html.

Ministry of Finance, 1999. "Japanese tax system". Tokyo. Available at www.mof.go.jp/english/tax_policy/tax_system/japanese_tax_system_1999/index.htm#04.

Ministry of Law and Justice, 2005. "The Special Economic Zones Act". New Delhi. Available at http://india.gov.in/allimpfrms/allacts/3111.pdf.

Ministry of Micro, Small and Medium Enterprises, 2011. "Credit Guarantee Fund Scheme for micro and small enterprises". New Delhi. Available at http://dcmsme.gov.in/schemes/sccrguarn.htm.

_____, 2010. *Annual Report, 2009-2010*. New Delhi.

Ministry of National Development Planning, 2010. *Appendices: Regulation of the President of the Republic of Indonesia, Number 5 of 2010, Regarding the National Medium-Term Development Plan 2010-2014*. Jakarta.

Ministry of Science and Technology, 2011. *Small and Medium Enterprises (SMEs) in India*. New Delhi, Department of Scientific and Industrial Research of India.

Ministry of Science and Technology, 2003. "Public awareness of science and technology in Republic of Korea". Seoul. Available at http://unpan1.un.org/intradoc/groups/public/documents/apcity/unpan008046.pdf.

Moffett, M., A. Stonehill and D. Eiteman, 2009. *Fundamentals of Multinational Finance*, third edition. Boston.

Mole, K., 2002. "Augmenting productivity in SMEs: A report for the Small Business Service". Available at www.bis.gov.uk/files/file38303.pdf.

Morduch, J., 2002. "Analysis of the effects of microfinance on poverty reduction", NYU Wagner Working Paper No. 1014. Nerw York. Available at http://pdf.wri.org/ref/morduch_02_analysis_effects.pdf.

Morshed, S.F., 2008. "Current policy regulations: challenges and opportunities for women SMEs", paper presented at the second National SME Women Entrepreneurs Conference – Empowering Women Entrepreneurs toward a Shared Economic Growth, 13 February 2008, SME Foundation, Dhaka.

Mountfield, E. and C. Ozer, 2007. *An East Asian Renaissance: Ideas for Economic Growth*, Washington, D.C., World Bank Group.

Moutray, C., 2008. "Looking ahead: Opportunities and challenges for entrepreneurship and small business owners", SBA Office of Advocacy Working Paper No. 332. Washington, D.C. Available at http://archive.sba.gov/advo/research/rs332tot.pdf.

Munoz, J.M.S. (ed.), 2010. *Contemporary Microenterprise, Concepts and Cases*. Cheltenham, Edward Elgar Publishing.

Muramoto, T., 2009. "SME financing in time of crisis", RIETI report No. 106. Tokyo, Research Institute of Economy, Trade and Industry.

N

Nadvi, K. and J. Thoburn, 2003. "Challenges to Vietnamese firms in the world garment and textile value chain, and the implications for alleviating poverty", paper presented at the European Association of Development Research and Training Institutes Workshop on Clusters and Global Value Chains in the North and the Third World, Novara, Italy, October 2003.

NAFED, 2011. "About NAFED". Jakarta, National Agency for Export Development. Available at www.nafed.go.id/about/index/en.

Nakata, C. and K. Sivakumar, 1996. "National culture and new product development: an integrative review", *The Journal of Marketing*, vol. 60, No. 1, pp. 61-72.

Narver, J.C. and S.F. Slater, 1990. "The effect of a market orientation on business profitability", *Journal of Marketing*, vol. 54. No. 4, pp. 20-35.

National Business Incubation Association, 2012. "Business Incubation FAQ". Athens. Available at www.nbia.org/.

_____, 2009. "Impact of business incubation in the US – lessons for developing countries". Available at www.infodev.org/en/Document.896.pdf.

National Knowledge Commission of India, 2008. "Entrepreneurship". New Delhi.

National Life Finance Corporation, 2008. *Kigyo Sprit: Sougyou ni Yakudatsu Mane Chishiki*. Tokyo.

_____, 2007. *Kokumin Seikatsu Kinyuukouko Report: Chuusyou Kigyou Keiei Joukyou Chousa Kekka*. Tokyo.

NSIC, 2011. "Techmart India 2011". New Delhi, National Small Industries Corporation. Available at www.nsicindia.com/Techmart_India_2011-event-73.html.

_____, 2008. "Building SMEs to win global markets", presentation at the International Tri-Summit at SurajKund Faridabad, India, 18-22 November 2008.

National SME Development Council of Malaysia, 2010. *SME Annual Report 2009/10*. Available at www.smeinfo.com.my/index.php/en/resources/publication/books/sme-annual-report.

Nelson, R.R., 1992. "National innovation systems: A retrospective on a study", *Industrial and Corporate Change,* No. 2, pp. 347-374.

Nemickas, A., B. Senchuk and O. Babanin, 2002. "Ukraine: An assessment of the business enabling environment", International Finance Corporation, World Bank Group, Washington, D.C.

Neo Buzz, undated. Deajeon, Republic of Korea. Available at http://neo-buzz.itrademarket.com/neo-buzz-demolition-tools-co-ltd.htm.

Nevens, T.M., G.L. Summe and B. Uttal, 1990. "Commercializing technology: What the best companies do", *Harvard Business Review,* May-June 1990, pp.154-163.

New Zealand Institute of Chartered Accountants, 2010. "Tax", available at www.nzica.com/tax.aspx.

NZVIF, 2011. "Seed Co-Investment Fund". Auckland, New Zealand Venture Investment Fund Ltd.. Available from www.nzvif.co.nz/seed-co-investment-overview.html.

Niemann, F., 2002. "Development of BDS markets in Indonesia – impact assessment of selected programs". Jakarta, ADB Technical Assistance.

Nippon Export and Investment Insurance, 2011. "Trade and investment insurance business and NEXI". Tokyo. Available at http://nexi.go.jp/en/corporate/trade/.

North, D., 1990. *Institutions, Institutional Change, and Economic Performance.* Cambridge, Harvard University Press.

O

Obamuyi, T.M., 2007. "An exploratory study of loan delinquency among small and medium enterprises (SMEs) in Ondo State, Nigeria", *Labour and Management in Development Journal,* vol. 8.

Office of SME Promotion, 2011. *White Paper of SMEs of Thailand in 2010 and Trends 2011.* Bangkok. Available at http://eng.sme.go.th/Lists/EditorInput/view2.aspx.

Okuda, H., 1993. "Japanese two step loans: The Japanese approach to development finance", *Hitotsubashi Journal of Economics,* vol. 34, pp. 67-85.

Open Technology Business Incubator, undated. "About OTBI". Quezon City, the Philippines. Available at http://otbi.idxtech.net/?page_id=18.

OECD, 2012. "Purchasing power parities – frequently asked questions (FAQs)". Paris, Organisation for Economic Co-operation and Development. Available at www.oecd.org/document/5/0,3746,en_2649_34357_45854149_1_1_1_1,00.html.

_____, 2011a. *Entrepreneurship at a Glance 2011.* Paris, OECD Publishing.

_____, 2011b. *Rural Entrepreneurship.* Paris.

_____, 2010a. *SMEs, Entrepreneurship and Innovation.* Paris.

_____, 2010b. *R&D Tax Incentives: Rationale, design, evaluation.* Paris.

_____, 2009a. "Taxation of SMEs: Key issues and policy considerations", *Tax Policy Study* 18. Paris.

_____, 2009b. *The Impact of the Global Crisis on SME and Entrepreneurship Financing and Policy Responses.* Paris.

_____, 2007a. "SME tax compliance and simplification". Paris. Available at www.oecd.org/dataoecd/22/24/41873897.pdf.

_____, 2007b. "Entrepreneurial attitudes and culture". Paris. Available at www.oecd.org/document/60/0,3746,en_21571361_38013663_38040956_1_1_1_1,00.html.

_____, 2007c. *OECD Framework for the Evaluation of SME and Entrepreneurship Policies and Programmes.* Paris.

_____, 2006. *The SME Financing Gap Theory and Evidence, Volume I.* Paris.

_____, 2005a. *OECD SME and Entrepreneurship Outlook 2005.* Paris.

_____, 2005b. *The Measurement of Scientific and Technological Activities: Guidelines for Collecting and Interpreting Innovation Data: Oslo Manual,* third edition, prepared by the Working Party of National Experts on Scientific and Technology Indicators. Paris.

_____, 2004a. *Women's Entrepreneurship: Issues and Policies.* Paris.

_____, 2004b. "Financing innovative SMEs in a global economy". Paris. Available at www.oecd.org/dataoecd/6/11/31919231.pdf.

_____, 2002a "Glossary of key terms in evaluation and results-based management." Paris.

_____, 2002b. *Frascati Manual: Proposed Standard Practice for Surveys on Research and Experimental Development.* Paris.

_____, 2000. "Enhancing the competitiveness of SMEs through innovation", paper presented at the Bologna 2000 SME Ministerial Conference Business Symposium, 13 June 2000.

_____, 1999. *Managing National Innovation Systems.* Paris, OECD Publishing.

_____, 1997. *National Innovation System.* Paris.

Oviatt, B. and P.P. McDougall, 1994. "Toward a theory of international new ventures", *Journal of International Business Studies,* vol. 25, No. 1, pp. 45-64.

P

Pacific Economic Cooperation Council (PECC), 2003. *Capital Markets for Small and Medium Enterprises: An Evaluation of Recent New Zealand Experience.* Presentation by Juliet Mckee at the 2nd Annual Conference of PECC Finance.

Park, J., B.I. Lim and J. Koo, 2008. "Developing the capital market to widen and diversify SME financing: The Korean experience". Seoul, Korea Institute of Finance.

Partnerships for Public Service, 2011. "Collaboration in times of crisis". Washington, D.C. Available at www.ourpublicservice.org/OPS/publications/download.php?id=127.

Pasadilla, G.O., 2010. "Financial crisis, trade finance, and SMEs: Case of Central Asia", ADBI Working Paper Series, No. 187. Tokyo, Asian development Bank Institute.

Paul, J.V., 2009. "Political economy of special economic zones in India: A conceptual framework". Available at www.articlesbase.com/politics-articles/political-economy-of-indias-special-economic-zones-a-conceptual-frame-work-762527.html.

Pearson, C.S., 2000. *Economics and the Global Environment.* Cambridge, Cambridge University Press.

Peavler, R., 2012. "Short-term business loans". Available at http://bizfinance.about.com/od/businessloans/qt/short-term-small-business-loans.htm.

Persaud, A., 2011. "Our future financial salvation lies in the direction of Basel". London, Centre for Economic Policy Research.

Petkar, A.A., 2010. "Credit ratings: Features and benefits for SMEs", *BCA Journal*, September 2010.

Petrin, T., 1994. "Rural development through entrepreneurship". Keynote paper presented at the Seventh FAO/REU International Rural Development Summer School, Herrsching. 8-14 September 1994. Available at www.fao.org/DOCREP/W6882e/w6882e02.htm.

Pham, T.T.H., 2005. "Private sector perspective on business environment reform – the case of Vietnam", Committee of Donor Agencies for Small Enterprises Development International Conference, Cairo.

Phare, 2000. "An evaluation of Phare-financed programmes in support of SMEs". Programme of Community Aid to Countries of Central and Eastern Europe, Evaluation Unit of the Common Service for External Relations, European Commission, Brussels. Available at http://ec.europa.eu/europeaid/how/evaluation/evaluation_reports/reports/cards/951508_final_en.pdf.

Pope, J., R. Fayle and D.L. Chen, 1991. "The compliance costs of public companies' income taxation in Australia, 1986/87". Sydney, Australian Tax Research Foundation.

Porter, M.E., 2008. "The five competitive forces that shape strategy", *Harvard Business Review,* January 2008, pp. 21-49.

_____, 1990. *The Competitive Advantage of Nations.* New York, Free Press.

_____, 1985. *Competitive Advantage: Creating and Sustaining Superior Performance.* New York, Free Press.

Prahalad, C.K., 2004. *The Fortune at the Bottom of the Pyramid.* Philadelphia, Wharton School Publishing.

President's Commission on Industrial Competitiveness, 1985. *Global Competition: New Reality.* Washington, D.C.

PWCCN, 2012. "Tax services". Beijing, Pricewaterhouse Coopers China. Available at www.pwccn.com/home/eng/tax.html.

R

Raja, V. and K.J. Fernandes, 2008. "Reverse engineering: An industrial perspective", *Springer Series in Advanced Manufacturing.* London, Springer.

RAM Consultancy and Services, 2005. "SME access to financing: Addressing the supply side of SME financing", REPSF Project No. 04/003 Final Main Report. Bangalore, India. Available at www.asean.org/aadcp/repsf/docs/04-003-FinalMainReport.pdf.

Ramanathan, K., 2010. "The concept and role of a national innovation system (NIS) in national development", New Delhi, Asian and Pacific Centre for Transfer of Technology. Available at http://nis.apctt.org/PDF/CSNWorkshop_Report_P2S1_Ramanathan.pdf.

RAND, 2010. *Intellectual Property and Developing Countries: A Review of the Literature.* Santa Monica, CA, United States. Available at www.rand.org/pubs/technical_reports/2010/RAND_TR804.pdf.

Republic of Turkey Small and Medium Enterprises Development Organization, undated. Available at www.kosgeb.gov.tr/Pages/UI/Default.aspx.

Reserve Bank of Australia, 2010. "Main types of financial institutions". Sydney. Available at www.rba.gov.au/fin-stability/fin-inst/index.html#funds.

Revenue Department of Thailand, 2008. "Value added tax". Bangkok. Available at www.rd.go.th/publish/6043.0.html.

Riding, A.L., 1998. "Financing entrepreneurial firms: Legal and regulatory issues", research paper produced for the Task Force on the Future of the Canadian Financial Services Sector.

Rocha, R., S. Farazi, R. Khouri. and D. Pearce, 2011. "The status of bank lending to SMEs in the Middle East and North Africa region: Results of a joint survey by the Union of Arab Bank and the World Bank", Policy Research Working Paper, No. 5607, Washington, D.C., World Bank.

Rocks, S.M., 2010. *Provisions of Standard Commercial Guarantee Agreements,* Washington, D.C., Consultative Group to Assist the Poor.

Ross, S.A., R.W. Westerfield and B.D. Jordan, 2008. *Fundamentals of Corporate Finance*, sixth edition. Boston, McGraw-Hill.

Rozali, M.B., H.M. Taib, F.A. Latif and M. Salim, 2006. "Small firms' demand for finance in Malaysia", Proceedings of the International Conference on Business and Information, 12-14 July 2006, Singapore.

S

Sagamihara City Hall Economy Department, 2008. "Shop Kaigyou Guide". Available at www.city.sagamihara.kanagawa.jp/sangyo/11273/004511.html.

Sandford, C., M. Godwin and P. Hardwick, 1989. *Administrative and Compliance Costs of Taxation.* Bath, United Kingdom, Fiscal Publications.

Santarelli, E. and S. D'Altri, 2003. "The diffusion of E-commerce among SMEs: Theoretical implications and empirical evidence", *Small Business Economics,* vol. 21, pp. 273-283.

Scheela, W. and E.S. Isidro, 2009. "Business angels investing in an emerging Asian economy", *The Journal of Private Equity,* vol. 12, No. 4, pp. 44-56.

Schneider, F. and B. Torgler, 2007. "the impact of tax morale and institutional quality on the shadow economy", *Working Paper No. 0702*, Linz, University of Linz, Department of Economics.

Schumpeter, J.A., 1942. *Capitalism, Socialism, and Democracy*, Reprinted 1975, New York, Harper.

_____, 1934. *The Theory of Economic Development*, Cambridge, United States, Harvard University Press.

Scott, B.R., 1971. *Stages of Corporate Development – Part I*. Boston, Harvard University Intercollegiate Case Clearing House.

Scott, D.L., 1997. *Wall Street Words: An Essential A to Z Guide for Today's Investor*. Boston, Houghton Mifflin Harcourt.

Securities and Exchange Board of India, 2010. "Annual Report 2009-2010". Available at www.sebi.gov.in/annualreport/0910/annualrep0910.pdf.

Self-Counsel Press, 2009. "What are promissory notes?" Vancouver, Canada. available at www.self-counsel.com/news/business/money/244-what-are-promissory-notes.html.

Sen, A., 1999. *Development as Freedom*. New York, Anchor Books.

Shane, S., 2008. *The Illusions of Entrepreneurship: The Costly Myths that Entrepreneurs, Investors and Policy Makers Live By*. New Haven, Yale University Press.

_____, 1995. "Uncertainty avoidance and the preference for innovation championing roles", *Journal of International Business Studies*, vol. 26, pp. 47-68.

_____, 1993. "Cultural influences on national rates of innovation", *Journal of Business Venturing*, vol. 8, No. 1, pp. 59-73.

Sharma, V.M. and M.K. Erramilli, 2004. "Resource-based explanation of entry mode choice", *Journal of Marketing Theory & Practice*, vol. 12, No. 1, pp. 1-18.

ShortTermLoans, 2011. "Benefits of short term loans". New South Wales, Australia. Available at www.shorttermloans.com.au/index.php/short-term-funding/23-benefits-of-short-term-loans.

Sikarwar, D., 2010. "Select LLPs may get 49% FDI", *The Economic Times*, March 11, 2010.

Singapore Business Federation, 2011. "SBF global sourcing hub". Available at crm.sbf.org.sg/cms/index.php?option=com_content&view=article&id=121&Itemid=107.

SingaporeSetup, 2010. "Singapore SMEs embark on mergers and acquisitions". Available at www.singaporesetup.com/singapore-smes-embark-on-mergers-and-acquisitions/.

Singh, G., R.D. Pathak and R. Naz, 2010. "Issues faced by SMEs in the internationalization process: Results from Fiji and Samoa", *International Journal of Emerging Markets*, vol. 5, No. 2, pp. 153-182.

Skatteverket, 2006. "Compliance costs of value-added tax in Sweden". Available at www.skatteverket.se/download/18.906b37c10bd295ff4880002550/rapport200603B.pdf.

SLBDC, 2011. "About SLBDC". Colombo, Sri Lanka Business Development Centre. Available at www.slbdc-lk.org/about.php.

Small and Medium Business Administration, 2011. "SME policies and service". Daejeon, Available at http://eng.smba.go.kr/pub/poli/poli040101.jsp.

_____, 2009. "Certifications". Daejeon, Republic of Korea. Available at http://eng.smba.go.kr/pub/poli/poli04010802.jsp#cer02.

Small and Medium Business Corporation, 2011. "Overview". Seoul. Available at www.sbc.or.kr/sbc/eng/about/overview.jsp.

Small and Medium Enterprise Administration, 2011a. "The definition of SMEs". Taipei, Taiwan Province of China. Available at www.moeasmea.gov.tw/ct.asp?xItem=70&CtNode=261&mp=2.

_____, 2011b. "Taiwan success". Taipei, Taiwan Province of China. Available at www.sme.gov.tw/np.asp?ctNode=277&mp=2.

_____, 2010. "White Paper of small and medium enterprises in Taiwan". Available at www.moeasmea.gov.tw/ct.asp?xItem=9017&ctNode=307&mp=2.

_____, 2009. "Enhancing the function of incubation service". Taipei, Taiwan Province of China. Available at www.moeasmea.gov.tw/ct.asp?xItem=6010&ctNode=469&mp=2.

Small and Medium Enterprises Development Authority, undated. "SMEDA Objectives". Ministry of Industries, Karachi. Available at www.smeda.org/SMEDA-introduction_1.html.

Small Industries Development Bank of India, 2011. "History". Lucknow, India. Available at www.sidbi.in/history.asp.

_____, 2010. *SIDBI Report on Micro, Small and Medium Enterprises Sector*. Lucknow, India.

SME Agency of Japan, undated. "Outline of SME policies". Tokyo. Available at www.chusho.meti.go.jp/sme_english/index.html#top.

SME Bank of Thailand, 2003. "Business performance in 2003". Bangkok. Available at www.smebank.co.th/eng/business-performance-in-2003.html.

SME Bank Pakistan, undated. "FAQs". Available at www.smebank.org/faq.htm.

SME Basic Law, 1999. Available at www.sme.ne.jp/policies/08_kihonhou/.

SME Centre for Asia, 2011. "Programs & services". Makati City, the Philippines. Available at www.smecenterforasia.com/programs-services/.

SME Corp Malaysia, 2011. Available at www.smecorp.gov.my/.

SME Rating Agency of India, undated. Mumbai. Available at www.smera.in/home.aspx.

SME Support Japan, 2012. "The Institute for Small Business Management and Technology". Tokyo. Available at www.smrj.go.jp/utility/english/ovoa/progress/010580.html.

SME World, 2009. "Ras Al Khaimah Free Trade Zone – A haven for Indian SMEs". Available at www.smeworld.org/story/top-stories/ras-ai-khaimah-free-tade-zone.php.

Smilor, R.W. and M.D. Gill, 1986. *The New Business Incubator: Linking Talent, technology, Capital and Know-How.* Lexington, Lexington Books.

Social Enterprise Network Asia, 2010. "PM presided [over] a meeting to promote SE policies in Thailand". Bangkok. Available at http://senetwork.asia/news/se-policy-meeting/.

Song, I., C. Park, J.Y. Lim, D. Oh and Y. Shon, 2005. "Technology transfer in Korea". Korea Technology Transfer Center, Session Report 2813, International Development and Linkages in Technology Transfer. Seoul.

South African LED Network, 2010. "Topic: Business Development Service (BDS)". Available at http://led.co.za/topic/business-development-service-bds.

Spillan, J. and J. Parnell, 2006. "Marketing resources and firm performance among SMEs", *European Management Journal*, vol. 24, Nos. 2-3, pp. 236-245.

SPRING Singapore, 2011a. "Factsheet on new SME definition". Available at www.spring.gov.sg/NewsEvents/PR/Documents/Fact_Sheet_on_New_SME_Definition.pdf.

_____, 2011b. "Treat angel investing like a hobby". Available at www.spring.gov.sg/NewsEvents/ITN/Pages/Treat-angel-investing-like-a-hobby-20110823.aspx.

_____, 2011c. "Quality and standards and enterprise and industry". Available at www.spring.gov.sg/Pages/Homepage.aspx.

_____, 2008. "Gain global market access through GLP". Available at http://apps.spring.gov.sg/QSNEWS/Web/ViewArticle.aspx?id=24.

_____, 2007. *We Improve Market Access by Lowering Trade Barriers and Linking Enterprise to New Business Opportunities.* Available at www.spring.gov.sg/AboutUs/AR/Documents/ar2005_2006/pdf/10-spring_Divider4.pdf.

_____, 2005. *Market Access and Opportunities, Free Trade Agreements (Trade in Goods), Guide for SMEs.* Available at www.spring.gov.sg/Resources/Documents/Guidebook_FTA_Guide_Goods.pdf.

Sridhar, S., 2008. "Innovative financing for small and medium enterprises", ESCAP Conference on Financing for Development, 18-19 June 2008, Bangkok. Available at www.unescap.org/pdd/calendar/FFD2008/papers/SSridhar_paper.pdf.

Startups, undated. "Equity Finance", available at www.startups.co.uk/equity-finance.html.

Stem, C., Margoluis, R., Salafsky, N. and M. Brown, 2005. "Monitoring and evaluation in conservation: A review of trends and approaches", *Conservation Biology*, vol. 19, No. 2, pp. 295-309.

Sturgeon, T.J. and R.K. Lester, 2001. *The New Global Supply-Base: New Challenges for Local Suppliers in East Asia*, paper prepared for the World Bank's Project on East Asia's Economic Future. Washington, D.C., World Bank.

Swiss Agency for Development and Cooperation, 2010. "Private sector development – creating incentives for private sector activities". Bern, Switzerland. Available at www.sdc.admin.ch/en/Home/Themes/Employment_and_income/Private_Sector_Development.

_____, 2006. "Comparative approaches to private sector development – an MMW perspective", Working Paper. Bern.

Szabó, A., 2005. "Microfinance and credit guarantee schemes: Experiences in the economies in transition", paper presented at the BSEC Workshop on Financing SMEs, 13-16 October 2005, Belgrade.

T

Tambunan, T., 2010. "Micro enterprise in a free trade era", in J. Munoz and S. Mark (eds.), *Contemporary Microenterprise: Concepts and Cases*, Cheltenham, United Kingdom, Edward Elgar Publishing Ltd.

_____, 2009. *Impact of Global Economic Crisis on Exports of SMEs in Developing Countries*, Center for Industry, SME and Business Competition Studies, Trisakti University, Indonesia.

_____, 2007. "Trade and investment liberalization effects on SME development: A literature review and a case study of Indonesia", in ESCAP, 2007, *Towards Coherent Policy Frameworks: Understanding Trade and Investment Linkages.* New York, United Nations.

_____, 2006. "Facilitating small and medium enterprises in international trade (export): The case of Indonesia". Bangkok, ESCAP. Available at www.unescap.org/tid/artnet/mtg/Tulus%20Tambunan.pdf.

Tansel, A., 2001. "Economic development and female labor force participation in Turkey: Time-series evidence and cross-province estimates". Available at http://depot.gdnet.org/newkb/fulltext/tansel_female_labour.pdf.

Technology Information, Forecasting and Assessment Council, 2011. "TIFAC-SIDBI Revolving Fund". New Delhi. Available at www.tifac.org.in/index.php?option=com_content&view=article&id=790&Itemid=1384.

_____, 2009. "TIFAC-SIDBI Program". New Delhi. Available at www.tifac.org.in/index.php?option=com_content&view=article&id=790&Itemid=1385.

Technology Resource Center, 2009. "DOST-PEZA launches open technology business incubator". 28 July 2009. Makati City, the Philippines. Available at http://trc.dost.gov.ph/index.php?option=com_content&view=article&id=296%3Adost-peza-launches-open-technology-business-incubator&Itemid=190.

Terjesen, S.A., C.A. Hatcher, T. Wysocki and J. Pham, 2007. "Leading women entrepreneurs of Thailand", in M. Radovic (ed.), *The Perspective of Women's Entrepreneurship in the Age of Globalization*, Florida, University of Florida Press.

Terrell, K. and M. Troilo, 2010. "Values and female entrepreneurship", *International Journal of Gender and Entrepreneurship*, vol. 2, No. 3, pp. 260-286.

Terziovski, M., A. Sohal and A. Howell, 2002. "Best practice in product innovation at varian Australia", *Technovation 22,* pp. 561-569.

Thailand Chamber of Commerce, 2011. "Board of Trade of Thailand roles and duties". Bangkok. Available at www.thaichamber.org/scripts/detail_faq.asp?Tag=2&nFaqID=8.

Thailand Today, 2011. "Thailand's flood situation: The road to recovery". Bangkok. Available at http://thailandtoday.org/situation/545.

The ISO 14000 Environmental Management Guide, 2007. "ISO 14000 Series Environmental Management Systems". Available at www.iso14000-iso14001-environmental-management.com/iso14000.htm.

The Pioneer, 2011. "NSIC Techmart India to explore new markets", 16 November 2011. Available at www.dailypioneer.com/vivacity/20928-nsic-techmart-india-to-explore-new-markets.html.

Thomas, A.S. and S.L. Mueller, 2000. "A case for comparative entrepreneurship: Assessing the relevance of culture", *Journal of International Business Studies,* vol. 31, No. 2, pages 287-301.

Thunderbird Angel Network, 2010. "Difference between venture capitalists and angel investors". Available at www.thunderbirdangelnetwork.org/angel-investor-phoenix-blog/bid/50468/Difference-Between-Venture-Capitalists-and-Angel-Investors/index.html.

Tianjin Women's Business Incubator, undated. Available at www.tjwbi.com/english/.

Tilak, J.B.G., 2002. "Vocational and technical education in Asia: Issues and Cconcerns", in J.P. Keeves and R. Watanabe (eds.), *The Handbook on Educational Research in the Asia Pacific Region.* Denmark, Kluwer Academic Publishers.

Tiwari, D., 2010. "SBI turn venture capitalist, to lend Rs 10 lakh free of interest", *The Economic Times,* 16 February 2010. Available at http://articles.economictimes.indiatimes.com/2010-02-16/news/27631481_1_new-scheme-loan-sme.

TMF Group, 2009. "Russia VAT". Available at www.tmf-vat.com/global-vat/russia-vat.html.

Touchstone, 2010. "Tackling environmental challenges – ISO 14000 family of standards". Available at www.standards.co.nz/touchstone/Issue+15/Environment/Tackling+environmental+challenges.htm?print=true.

Touch Financial, 2000. "Start-up business finance options". Available at www.is4profit.com/business-advice/starting-up/start-up-business-finance-options.html.

Touch Financial Support, 2012. "Invoice discounting – a flexible cash flow finance solution". Available at www.touchfinancial.co.uk/services-solutions/products/invoice-discounting/.

Tradecredit, 2008. "Advantage of trade credit". Available at www.tradecredit.co.uk/advantages-of-trade-credit.html.

Transparency International, 2011. *Corruption Perceptions Index 2010 Results.* Available at www.transparency.org/policy_research/surveys_indices/cpi/2010/results.

_____, 2009. *Global Corruption Report 2009.* Available at www.transparency.org/publications/gcr/gcr_2009.

Troilo, M., 2011. "Legal institutions and high-growth aspiration entrepreneurship", *Economic Systems,* vol. 35, No. 3, pp. 158-175.

Turyakira, P., E. Venter and E.E. Smith, E.E., 2010. "Corporate social responsibility: A competitive strategy for small and medium-sized enterprises in Uganda". Available at www.benafrica.org/downloads/smith.doc.

Tushman, M.L. and P. Anderson, 1986. "Technological discontinuities and organizational environment", *Administrative Science Quarterly,* vol. 31, No. 3, pp. 439-465.

U

Uchikawa, S. and S. Keola, 2009. "Small and medium enterprises in Cambodia, Laos, and Vietnam", BRC Discussion Paper Series No. 10. Bangkok. Bangkok Research Center, IDE-JETRO.

Uhric, C.L., 2001. *The Economic Espionage Act – Reverse Engineering and the Intellectual Property Public Policy.* Available at www.mttlr.org/volseven/Uhrich.pdf.

UNESCO Institute of Statistics, 2011. "Global investments in R&D". Available at www.uis.unesco.org/FactSheets/Documents/fs15_2011-investments-en.pdf.

United Nations, 2011. "Enterprise Africa encourages private sector to support SMEs". Available at http://business.un.org/en/documents/45.

United Nations Conference on Trade and Development, 2010a. *About Enterprise Development.* New York and Geneva, United Nations.

_____, 2010b. *World Investment Report 2011: Promoting Linkages.* New York and Geneva, United Nations.

_____, 2010c. *Integrating Developing Countries' SMEs into Global Value Chains.* New York and Geneva, United Nations.

_____, 2009. *The Role of International Investment Agreements in Attracting Foreign Direct Investment to Developing Countries.* New York and Geneva, United Nations.

_____, 2007. "Science and technology for development: The new paradigm of ICT", *Information Economy Report 2007-2008.* New York and Geneva, United Nations.

_____, 2005a. *Improving the Competitiveness of SMEs through Enhancing Productive Capacity.* New York and Geneva, United Nations.

_____, 2005b. "Globalisation of R&D and developing countries". New York and Geneva, United Nations. Available at www.unctad.org/en/docs/iteiia20056_en.pdf.

_____, 2005c. *World Investment Report 2005: Transnational Corporations and the Internationalisation of R&D.* New York and Geneva, United Nations.

_____, 2002. *World Investment Report 2002.* New York and Geneva, United Nations.

_____, 2001a. *E-finance and Small and Medium-sized Enterprises (SMEs) in Developing and Transition Economies*. New York and Geneva, United Nations.

_____, 2001b. *Improving the Competitiveness of SMEs in Developing Countries – The Role of Finance to Enhance Enterprise Development*. New York and Geneva, United Nations.

_____, 2000. *Tax Incentives and Foreign Direct Investment: A Global Survey*. New York and Geneva, United Nations.

United Nations Development Programme, 2009. *Human Development Report 2009*. New York.

_____, 2007. *UNDP Private Sector Strategy: Promoting Inclusive Market Development – Final Version*. New York.

_____, 2004a. *Business Development Services: How-to Guide*. Bratislava Regional Centre.

_____, 2004b. *Unleashing Entrepreneurship: Making Business Work for the Poor*. New York.

_____, 2003. "One million jobs created by new entrepreneur law in Viet Nam". Available at http://content.undp.org/go/newsroom/choices-one-million-jobs-created-by-new-enterprise-law-in-viet-nam2003-06.en;jsessionid=axbWzt8vXD9?categoryID=349424&lang=en.

UNDP Asia-Pacific Development Information Programme e-Note, 2007. "The role of governments in promoting ICT access and use by SMEs". Available at www.apdip.net.

United Nations Educational, Scientific and Cultural Organization, and International Labour Organization, 2002. *Technical and Vocational Education, and Training for The Twenty-First Century*. Paris.

United Nations Industrial Development Organization, 2010. *UNIDO's Industrial Policy and Private Sector Development Branch*. Vienna.

_____, 2007. "Corporate Social Responsibility and Public Policy: The Role of Governments in Facilitating the Uptake of CSR among SMEs in Developing Countries", Discussion Paper presented at the Expert Group Meeting, 20-21 November 2007, Vienna.

_____, 2006a. *Responsible Trade and Market Access – Opportunities or Obstacles for SMEs in Developing Countries?* Vienna.

_____, 2006b. *Role of standards: A Guide for Small and Medium-sized Enterprises*. Vienna.

_____, 2006c. *Product Quality: A Guide for Small and Medium-sized Enterprises*. Vienna.

_____, 2001. *Integrating SMEs in Global Value Chains: Towards Partnership for Development*. Vienna.

_____, 1999. *SME Cluster and Network Development in Developing Countries: The Experience of UNIDO, 1999-2000*. Vienna.

_____, 1995. *Women, Industry and Entrepreneurship*. Vienna.

_____, undated. "About SPX". Available at www.unido.org/index.php?id=4851.

UNTFN, 2005. *Enabling SMEs to Enter the International Supply Chain*. New York, United Nations Trade Facilitation Network – Global Facilitation Partnership for Transportation and Trade.

USAID, 2010. "USAID and Microenterprise Development". Washington, D.C., United States Agency for International Development. Available at www.usaid.gov/our_work/economic_growth_and_trade/micro/index.html.

_____, 2008. *Final Evaluation of the Enterprise Development Facility Project,* June 2008. Washington, D.C.

_____, 2007. *Booklet of Standardized Small and Medium Enterprises Definition*. Washington, D.C.

_____, 2004. *Analysis of the Role and Place of Small and Medium-Sized Enterprises in Russia*. Washington, D.C.

United States Congress, Office of Technology Assessment, 1995. *Innovation and Commercialization of Emerging Technologies*. Washington, D.C. Available at www.fas.org/ota/reports/9539.pdf.

United States Department of Commerce, 2008. *Trade Finance Guide*, 2008 edition. Washington, D.C. Available at http://trade.gov/publications/pdfs/tfg2008ch9.pdf.

_____, 2007. *Trade Finance Guide: A Quick Reference for US Exporters*. Washington, D.C.

United States International Trade Commission, United States Agency for International Development 2011. "China's consumption of agricultural products increasing substantially as incomes rise, says USITC". Available at www.usitc.gov/press_room/news_release/2011/er0322jj1.htm.

_____, 2010. *Small and Medium-Sized Enterprises: US and EU Export Activities, and Barriers and Opportunities Experienced by US Firms*. Washington, D.C.

UPS, 2007. "Asia Business Monitor". Available at www.upsinasia.com/pdf/AsiaBusiness2007_EN.pdf.

United States Small Business Administration (SBA), 2009. *ABCs of Borrowing Money*. Washington, D.C. Available at http://archive.sba.gov/idc/groups/public/documents/sba_homepage/pub_fm1.pdf.

Utterback, J. and W.J. Abernathy, 1975. "A dynamic model of process and product innovation", *Omega*, vol. 33, No. 4, pp. 639-656.

V

Van Renssen, S., 2005. "Malaysia to aid technology transfer to its businesses", Science and Development Network, 9 August 2005. Available at www.scidev.net/en/news/malaysia-to-aid-technology-transfer-to-its-business.html.

Veloso, F. and R. Kumar, 2002. *The Automotive Supply Chain: Global Trends and Asian Perspectives,* ERD Working Paper No. 3. Manila, Asian Development Bank.

VECCI, 2010. "Australian trade ission to Sri Lanka". Victorian Employers' Chamber of Commerce and Industry. Available at www.vecci.org.au/news/Pages/Australian_trade_mission_to_Sri_Lanka.aspx.

Vietnam Women Entrepreneurs Council, 2007. *Women's Entrepreneurship Development in Vietnam*. Geneva, International Labour Organization.

Vinanchiarachi, J., 2005. "International comparison of national policy instruments and innovation systems for technology development". Available at www.unido.org/fileadmin/import/37949_IAMOT2005_paper741_Vinanchiarachi_reformatted.4.pdf.

Vinexad, 2008. "Vietnam Expo". Available at www.vietnamexpo.com.vn/en/.

Vinh, H.N., 2010. "ICT applications in TVET institutions in Vietnam", *VTET Research and Networking,* vol. 2, No. 1.

Virasa, T. and B. Hunt, 2007. "Global Entrepreneurship Monitor: Thailand 2007 Executive Report". Bangkok, College of Management, Mahidol University.

W

Wacziarg, R. and K.H. Welch, 2003. "Trade liberalization and growth: New evidence", Stanford Graduate School of Business Research Paper No. 1826, Stanford, United States.

Wang, W., 2010. *Reverse Engineering: Technology of Reinvention*. Boca Raton, United States, CRC Press.

Ward, H., 2004. *Public Sector Roles in Strengthening Corporate Social Responsibility: Taking Stock*. Washington, D.C., World Bank.

_____, 2003. "Public policy for corporate social responsibility", report from the WBI Series on Corporate Responsibility, Accountability, and Sustainable Competitiveness, Washington, D.C.

Wattanapruttipaisan, T., 2003. "Four proposals for improved financing of SME development in ASEAN", *Asian Development Review,* vol. 20, No. 2.

Weeke, H., S. Parker and E. Malesky, 2009. "Vietnam's business environment: complying with obligations abroad and competing at home", *Developing Alternatives,* pp. 39-46.

Weeks, J., 2009. "Women business owners in the Middle East and North Africa: A five-country study", *International Journal of Gender and Entrepreneurship,* vol. 1, No. 1, pp. 77-85.

WEF, 2011. *The Global Competitiveness Report 2011-2012*. Geneva, World Economic Forum.

Welford, R., 2005. "Maximizing the benefits of corporate social responsibility for small and medium-sized enterprises participating in regional and global supply chains", paper presented at the Expert Group Meeting on SMEs' Participation in Global and Regional Supply Chains, 9 November 2005, Bangkok, ESCAP.

Western Economic Diversification Canada, 2008. "Overview of free trade zones". Available at www.wd.gc.ca/eng/11140.asp.

Wieland, T., 2006. "Innovation culture, technology policy and the uses of history", International ProACT Conference Paper, 15-17 March 2006, Tampere, Finland.

William Gallagher Associates, 2009. "Trade credit insurance: Coverage for accounts receivable debts". Available at http://wgains.com/Assets/WhitePapers/Credit%20Insurance%20April%202009.pdf.

Williamson, O., 1985. *The Economic Institutions of Capitalism*. New York, Free Press.

Wilson, R.C., 2011. "Internal financing". Available at http://financialanalysttraining.com/internal-financing/.

WIPO 2012. "Small and Medium-Sized Enterprises", available at www.wipo.int/sme/en/.

_____, 2011. Geneva, World Intellectual Property Organization. "What is intellectual property?" Available at www.wipo.int/portal/index.html.en.

_____ undated. "KIPO [Korean Intellectual Property Office] activities targeted at the SMEs sector, Republic of Korea", Geneva, World Intellectual Property Organization. Available at www.wipo.int/sme/en/best_practices/kipo.htm.

Women's World Banking, 2004. "Strategies for Financial Integration: Access to Commercial Debt," *Financial Products and Services: Occasional Paper,* vol. 1, No. 1.

World Bank, 2012a. "Doing business: Economy rankings". Washington, D.C. Available at www.doingbusiness.org/rankings.

_____, 2012b. "Rural Industrial Technology Spark Project". Washington, D.C. Available at www.worldbank.org/projects/P003529/rural-industrial-technology-spark-project?lang=en.

_____, 2011a. *Doing Business: Measuring Business Regulations*. Washington, D.C. Available at www.doingbusiness.org.

_____, 2011b. *Doing Business 2011: Making a Difference for Entrepreneurs*. Washington, D.C.

_____, 2011c. *Doing Business 2011, Latin America: Making a Difference for Entrepreneurs*. Washington, D.C.

_____, 2011d. "Research and development expenditure per cent of GDP", Washington, D.C. Available at http://data.worldbank.org/indicator/GB.XPD.RSDV.GD.ZS.

_____, 2011e. "Logistics Performance Index". Washington, D.C. Available at http://info.worldbank.org/etools/tradesurvey/mode1b.asp.

_____, 2011f. "Burden of customs procedures", Washington, D.C. Available at http://data.worldbank.org/indicator/IQ.WEF.CUST.XQ.

_____, 2010a. *Doing Business 2010: Reforming Through Difficult Times*. Washington, D.C.

_____, 2010b. "Internet users". Washington, D.C. Available at http://data.worldbank.org/indicator/IT.NET.USER/countries?display=graph.

_____, 2009a. *Financial Infrastructure: Building Access through Transparent and Stable Financial Systems*. Washington, D.C.

_____, 2009b. *Making Monitoring and Evaluation Systems Work: A Capacity Development Toolkit*. Washington, D.C.

_____, 2008a. *Monitoring and Evaluation for Business Environment Reform: A Handbook for Practitioners*. Washington, D.C.

_____, 2008b. *Finance for All? Polices and Pitfalls in Expanding Access*. Washington, D.C.

_____, 2006a. "Entrepreneurship: How much does the business environment matter?" *Public Policy Journal No. 313*. Washington, D.C.

_____, 2006b. *Doing Business in 2006: Creating Jobs*. Washington, D.C.

_____, 2005. *Financial Sector Assessment – A Handbook*. Washington, D.C.

_____, 2003. *Private Sector Development Strategy – Directions for the World Bank Group*. Washington, D.C.

_____, 2000. *Anticorruption in Transition: A Contribution to the Policy Debate*. Washington, D.C.

_____, undated. "How we classify countries". Washington, D.C. Available at http://data.worldbank.org/about/country-classifications.

World Business Council for Sustainable Development, 2007. *Promoting Small and Medium Enterprises for Sustainable Development*. Geneva.

World Customs Organisation, 1999. "International Convention on the Simplification and Harmonization of Customs Procedures". Brussels.

_____, 2010. *The Global Competitiveness Report 2010-2011*. Geneva.

WTO, 2011a. "Understanding the WTO: The Agreements – intellectual property protection and enforcement". Geneva, World Trade Organization. Available at www.wto.org/english/thewto_e/whatis_e/tif_e/agrm7_e.htm.

_____, 2011b. "Understanding the WTO: The agreements – standards and safety". Geneva, World Trade Organization. Available at www.wto.org/english/thewto_e/whatis_e/tif_e/agrm4_e.htm.

_____, 2011c. "Services trade". Geneva, World Trade Organization. Available at www.wto.org/english/tratop_e/serv_e/serv_e.htm.

_____, 2011d. "Trade and Investment". Geneva, World Trade Organization. Available at www.wto.org/english/tratop_e/invest_e/invest_e.htm.

_____, 2011e. "Glossary terms". Geneva, World Trade Organization. Available at www.wto.org/english/thewto_e/glossary_e/rules_of_origin_e.htm.

_____, 2007. *2006 Public Forum: What WTO for the XXIst Century?* Geneva, World Trade Organization.

_____, 2005. "Ministerial Declaration: DOHA Work Programme". Geneva, World Trade Organization. Available at www.wto.org/english/thewto_e/minist_e/min05_e/final_text_e.htm.

_____, 2001. "The products". Geneva, World Trade Organization. Available at www.wto.org/english/tratop_e/devel_e/train_e/products_e.htm.

X

Xinhua Economic News, 2008. "Non-performing loan ratio of SMEs hit 22.1 per cent in China", 19 September 2008. Beijing. Available at http://chinareference.eu/cbn/news.php?action=fullnews&id=1924.

Xydias-Lobo, M. and J.T. Jones, 2003. "Quality initiatives and business growth in Australian manufacturing SMEs: An exploratory investigation", School of Commerce Research Paper Series, vol. 03, No. 3.

Y

Yamawaki, H., 2001. *The Evolution and Structure of Industrial Clusters in Japan*. Washington D.C., World Bank.

Yang, J., 2009. "Small and medium enterprises (SMEs) adjustments to information technology (IT) in trade facilitation: The South Korean experience", Asia-Pacific Research and Training Network on Trade Working Paper Series, No. 61. Available at www.unescap.org/tid/artnet/pub/wp6109.pdf.

Yim, D.S., 2006. *Korea's National Innovation System and the Science and Technology Policy*. Seoul, Science and Technology Policy Institute.

Ying, Q., 2009. "SME financing in the Asia-Pacific region: Crisis and countermeasures". Available at www.afdc.org.cn/afdc/UploadFile/200962435516049.ppt.

Yuan, B.J.C. and Huang, Y., 2006. Taiwanese SMEs and Value Creation through Innovative Environment: The Case of Acer Company, IAMOT Conference Archive.

Yunus, M. and Jolis, A., 1998. *Banker to the Poor: The Autobiography of Muhammad Yunus Founder of the Grameen Bank,* London, Aurum Press.

Yussuf, R.M., Hashmi M.S.J. and Chek L.W., 2005. "Advanced manufacturing technologies in SMEs: Strategic requirements for implementation in a developing country, *Asia Pacific Tech Monitor,* May-June.

Z

Zablocki, E.M., 2007. "Formation of a business incubator" in A. Krattiger, R.T. Mahoney, L. Nelsen and others (eds.), *Intellectual Property Management in Health and Agricultural Innovation: A Handbook of Best Practices.* MIHR, Oxford and PIPRA, Davis.

Zahra, S.A., J. Hayton and H. O'Neill, 2001. "Fostering entrepreneurship during international expansion: Managing key challenges", *European Management Journal,* vol. 19, No. 3, pp. 359-369.

Zavatta, R., 2008. *Financing Technology Entrepreneurs and SMEs in Developing Countries: Challenges and Opportunities*. Washington, D.C., World Bank.

Zero2IPO, 2010. *China Venture Capital Annual Report 2010.* Available at www.zero2ipogroup.com/en/research/reportdetails.aspx?r=b68ff1e5-a03a-4aa2-8f9e-93ff5769436d.

Zhang, W., 2006. Regional Consultative Meeting on Sub-national Innovation Systems and Technology Capacity-Building Policies to Enhance Competitiveness of SMEs, 20 January 2006, Seoul.

Zhang, Y., 2003. "Research into the engineering application of reverse engineering technology", *Journal of Materials Processing Technology,* vol. 139, pp. 472-475.

Zou, W., 2003. "The changing face of rural enterprises", *China Perspectives,* vol. 50, November-December 2003.

SUBJECT INDEX

A
Angel Finance 98
Australia
 Corruption 46
 Definition of SMEs 14
 Entrepreneurial activity 67
 Ease of Doing Business 43
 Economic Freedom 45
 Export Credit Agency 171
 Global Competitiveness 45
 Culture 71
 Import procedures 160
 Innovation 132
 R&D 136
 Tax return filing 62
 Trade missions 163
 Transport system 159
 VAT 63

B
Babson College 85
Bangladesh
 Ease of doing business 43
 Economic freedom 45
 Entrepreneurial activity 67
 Entrepreneurship awareness 73
 Global competitiveness 45
 Infrastructure 39
 Investment Climate Fund 11
 SME Foundation 29
 Technology programmes 150
 Women entrepreneurs 32, 75
Bankruptcy 13, 25, 28, 40, 53, 78, 88, 90, 105, 170, 182, 186
Business Development Services (BDS) 2-3, 8, 10, 25, 31, 36-7, 48, 111, 119-129
 Actors 122-3
 Design and objectives 119-120
 Levels of interventions 125, 127
 Market-oriented approach 120-2
 Policy recommendations 129, 184, 186
 Role of SME development agencies 124
 Traditional approach 120-2
Business Enabling Environment (BEE) 1-2, 6, 8-9, 37-53
 Benefits 38
 Components 38-41
 Policy recommendations 53, 183, 185-6
 Reforms 46-50
 Surveys 42-6
 Toolkits 50-3
Business associations 5, 8, 10-2, 47, 56-8, 77, 109, 111, 119, 125-7, 129, 152, 162-3, 165-6, 186
Business plan 2, 11, 17-18, 68-9, 74, 78, 80-6, 91, 98, 103, 113, 119-120, 127-8, 150, 184
Business registration 2, 28, 40, 49, 51, 54, 64, 68, 77, 184
Buyer-seller meetings 4, 10, 124, 161, 163, 177

C
Cambodia
 BEE toolkit 51, 54-8
 Ease of doing business 43
 Enterprise registration reform 49
 Entry barriers to entrepreneurship 69-70
 General Department of Industry 124
 Global competitiveness 45
 Starting a business
 Subnational survey 46
 Trade Promotion Department 163
 VAT 63
Canada
 Business Development Bank 111
 Culture 71
 Tax return filing 62
Cash flow 1, 6, 52, 59, 61-2, 68, 78, 80, 87-8, 91, 91-2, 105-7, 109, 113-5, 134, 148, 181-2, 184, 186
China
 Contribution of SMEs 21
 Credit information systems 78
 Definition of SME 15
 Ease of doing business 43
 Economic freedom 45
 Entrepreneurial activity 67
 Entrepreneurship education 73
 Global competitiveness 45
 Market access programmes 165
 Microfinance 96
 Ministry of Science and Technology 148
 Non-performing loans 102-3
 Personal savings 100
 R&D 136-7
 Rural entrepreneurship 76, 79
 Social entrepreneurial activity 77
 SME clusters 30
 SME financing support system 90
 SMEs Department 124
 Spark Programme 148
 Tax incentives 106, 146
 Technology programmes 150
 VAT 63
 Venture capital 99
 Women entrepreneurs 75, 128
Clusters 1, 7, 30-1, 35, 39, 41, 52, 57, 96, 125, 139, 141, 176, 182
Collateral 2, 6, 9, 20, 40, 50-1, 55, 77, 87-8, 90, 92-4, 96-7, 99, 102, 107-9, 111, 113-5, 117, 178, 184-6
Corporate Bonds 89-90, 97, 116
Corporate Social Responsibility 33, 79
Corruption 38-42, 45-6, 53, 77, 182
Credit guarantee 40, 77, 89-90, 93-6, 102-3, 105-6, 108-9, 112, 114, 116-7, 170-1, 177-8, 184, 186
Credit rating 2, 9, 104-5, 110-1
Culture 69-73
 Entrepreneurial 1, 8-9, 11, 13, 36, 38-9, 78-9, 109, 174
 Dependency 120-1, 123
 National 24, 70, 78
 Women Entrepreneurship 33
Customs procedures
 Procedures 4, 28, 40, 53, 156, 159-161, 166-7, 171-2, 178
 Regulations 10, 19

D

Data collection 192
DCED Standard 191-2
Development financial institutions 8, 102-4, 108, 113, 170-1
Doing business rankings 1, 40, 42-4, 46, 48, 53, 69, 88

E

E-commerce 8, 41, 57, 120, 147, 153, 155, 165-6
Economic
    Development 1, 3-5, 13, 16, 18, 20, 22, 33, 35, 37, 41, 46-7, 53, 65, 67-8, 75, 86, 104, 106, 119, 121, 132, 145, 153, 158, 174, 181, 183-4, 188
    Downturn 2, 6, 105-7, 115
    Freedom 1, 42, 45
Education 1-3, 8-10, 14, 16, 19, 28, 30, 32, 35, 44, 52-3, 56-7, 65, 68-70, 72-6, 78-9, 84-5, 107, 112, 122, 132, 134, 141-2, 144, 146-7, 151, 175, 181, 184, 186
Employment 4-5, 11, 13-6, 20, 22, 30, 32, 38, 40, 46, 51-2, 54, 60-61, 65, 70, 74-5, 96, 101, 105-6, 119, 128, 135, 149, 151, 171-2, 179, 179-181, 188
    Self 33, 65, 70, 73, 74, 78, 85
    Unemployment 68, 73, 106
Entrepreneurs 1-2, 4-5, 8-9, 17, 20, 34-5, 37-8, 40, 42, 45, 48, 53, 62, 65, 67-70, 72-3, 75, 77-81, 84-6, 89, 91, 94, 96-8, 100, 107, 109, 111-2, 114-5, 119, 124, 127-8, 133-5, 140, 143-4, 148, 152, 171, 181, 187-8
    Micro 27, 75
    Women 13, 20, 31-3, 75, 96, 108, 186
    Rural 76
    Youth 13, 20, 36, 96, 127, 151, 186
Entrepreneurship 1-2, 5, 7-9, 13, 20, 24, 36, 38, 51, 59-60, 81, 103, 109, 115, 133-4, 141, 143, 151, 181-4, 186-7
    Awareness creation 72-3
    Culture 39, 69-72, 174
    Definition 65
    Development 2, 6, 12, 65, 178, 186
    Entry barriers 69-70
    Institutional context 66
    Phases of economic development 67-8
    Policy recommendations 77-9
    Rural 75-6, 79
    Social 2, 76-7
    Training 85-6, 112
    Women 33, 35, 48
    Youth 73, 75, 79, 85
European Union 2, 57, 100-1
    Contribution of SMEs 21-2
    Definition of SMEs 16, 25
    Sources of financing for SMEs 101
Export 5, 13, 19, 21, 29, 34-5, 37-8, 42, 44, 46, 53, 61, 65, 75, 79, 96, 103, 105-6, 124, 127, 137, 143, 153, 156, 159-161, 166-170, 172, 174, 176-180, 185, 187
    Credit agencies 170-1
    Credit guarantee 170
    Credit insurance 170
    Markets 10, 28, 30, 33, 57, 154, 156-7, 165, 168, 173
    Procedures 48, 50-1, 183
    Product Identification 4, 156, 157-8
    Promotion 7-8, 10, 29, 31, 96, 162-3, 165
    Contribution of SMEs 21-2

F

Factoring 8, 89-90, 92, 101, 116-7, 167-8
Foreign direct investment (FDI) 4-5, 13, 29, 48, 52, 115, 134, 137, 151, 153, 156, 171-3, 176, 178, 180, 185, 187
Four-Tier National Financial System 2, 112, 114, 116

G

Global supply chains (GSC) 3-4, 8, 10, 34, 36, 48, 52, 57, 128, 139, 156, 159, 173-8, 185-7
Government
    Agencies 10, 97, 102, 105-106, 113, 117, 119-123, 158, 163-164, 170, 179
    Initiatives 32, 72-74, 76, 148-150
    Intervention 2, 38, 53, 90, 93, 108, 129, 138
    Local 30, 47, 64, 76, 86, 90, 95, 128, 141
    Officials 9, 11, 18, 53, 76, 162-3, 171, 178, 181-3
    Policy 5-6, 9, 77-9, 106, 109, 114-6, 165, 135-6, 138, 142, 144, 151-2, 156, 171, 178, 181-5
    Procurement (see public procurement)
    Role in BDS 10, 123-5
    Role in BEE reforms 2, 29, 37, 48-9, 53
    R&D 140, 146
    Tax 59-64

I

Information and communications technology (ICT) 4, 23-4, 26, 41, 147, 149-150
Information asymmetry 110, 114, 116, 157, 183
Incubation 3, 8-9, 25, 27, 30, 70, 119, 119-120, 127, 127-9, 133, 140, 151, 174, 185-6
India
    Contribution of SMEs 21
    Corporate social responsibility 34
    Credit guarantee schemes 96, 116
    Credit rating scheme 105
    Culture 71, 73
    Definition of SME 15-6
    Development finance institutions 104
    Ease of doing business 43
    Economic freedom 45
    Global competitiveness 45
    Limited liability partnership 52
    Market access programmes 164
    Microfinance 96
    National Small Industries Corporation 124
    Non-performing loans 103
    Productivity 27-8
    R&D 136, 146-8
    Seed capital 97
    Starting a business 69
    Techmarts 149
    Technology database 149
    Technology programmes 150
    VAT 63
    Venture capital 99
    Women entrepreneurs 33
Indonesia
    Business development services 120
    Clusters 30

Contribution of SMEs 21
Culture 71
Definition of SME 15
Ease of doing business 43
Economic freedom 45
Education 73
Eximbank 103
Global competitiveness 45
Investor protection 78
Linkages 141
Market access programmes 164
Productivity 27-8
Starting a business 69
Technology acquisition and transfer 137
VAT 63
Industrial parks 8, 41, 143, 178
Informal financing 2, 52, 89, 100-1, 109
Informal sector 9, 13, 16-7, 22, 24-5, 27, 31, 33, 37-8, 40, 52, 59, 64, 77, 109, 149, 172
Infrastructure 1, 4-6, 10, 28, 30-1, 34-9, 41, 44-5, 53, 55, 65, 68-9, 76, 79, 106, 108, 119-120, 122-3, 126-7, 131, 140, 142-3, 149, 151-2, 172, 174-5, 178, 181-3, 185-7
- Business 8-9, 156, 166
- Communications 5, 141, 178
- Digital 96, 129, 150
- Export 178, 185
- Financial 108-9
- Social 104
- Trade 157, 159
- Transport 159, 177

Innovation 1, 3-6, 8-9, 12, 18-20, 27-8, 30-1, 35-6, 44-5, 48-50, 53, 60, 65, 69, 71-3, 107, 109-110, 119-120, 124, 127-8, 131-152, 179-180
- Capabilities 131-3, 137, 146
- Certification system 135, 148-9
- Driven economies 34, 67-8, 77
- Importance of 132-3
- Open 3, 142-4
- National innovation system (NIS) 3, 135, 141-3
- Policy 134-5, 151-2, 181, 183-6
- Technological 137, 147-8

Intellectual Property 78, 84, 142, 147, 150, 152
- Korean Intellectual Property Office 146
- Rights 3, 8, 28, 48, 119, 134-5, 138, 143-6, 151, 157, 177, 179, 185
- World Intellectual Property Office 145

International commercial terms 156, 159-160
Internet 4, 19, 30, 41, 44, 57, 80, 120, 145, 147, 152-3, 161, 163, 165-8, 177, 180
Investor protection 44, 78-9, 116, 184

J

Japan
- BEE Toolkit 51
- Clusters 30
- Contribution of SMEs 21-2
- Competitiveness 29
- Credit guarantee schemes 94-5, 116
- Culture 24, 71
- Definition of SME 15-6
- Disaster 106
- Ease of doing business 43
- Economic freedom 45
- Entrepreneurial activity 67
- Entry and exit 23-4
- External Trade Organization (JETRO) 163
- Female-owned SMEs 32
- Global competitiveness 45
- Global economic crisis 105
- Intellectual property 145
- Market access programmes 165
- Microenterprises 25-6
- Productivity 27
- Public-private partnerships 111
- R&D 135-8, 147-8, 159
- SME Agency 86, 124
- Startups 16-7, 20, 23
- Tax incentives 60
- VAT 63

K

Know About Business 73, 85

L

Lao PDR
- Business regulatory compliance 38
- Ease of doing business 43
- National innovation system 143
- VAT 63

Leasing 2, 8, 51, 55, 89-90, 92, 101, 116, 167-8
Licensing 28, 40, 45-7, 49-50, 54, 106, 132, 134, 137, 139, 144-5, 151, 154, 156, 179, 186
Loans 6, 17, 20, 65, 68, 77-8, 80, 83-4, 87, 94, 96, 100, 102, 105, 109, 113-7, 124-5, 127, 135, 137, 148, 151, 168, 170-1, 185-6
- Bank 2, 90, 92, 97, 99, 101-2, 109, 112-3
- Commercial 8-9, 20, 40, 81, 84, 94, 100, 184
- Long-term 89, 93, 100-2, 104, 107, 111
- Micro 75, 95
- Non-performing 87-8, 103, 106
- Personal 2, 31, 84, 89, 91
- Public 81
- Short-term 89, 93, 99-100, 102-3, 107
- Soft 108, 148, 151
- Two-Step 9, 93, 106

Logical framework 189-191

M

Malaysia
- Contribution of SMEs 21-2
- Culture 71-2
- Definition of SME 15-6
- Ease of doing business 43
- Economic freedom 45
- Entrepreneurial activity 67, 77
- Female-owned SMEs 32
- Financial sources 100
- Global competitiveness 45
- Innovation certification system 148-9
- Market access programmes 164
- Microenterprises 25
- Productivity 27
- R&D 136-8, 147
- SME Bank 103
- SME Corp 34-5, 124, 163
- Technology programmes 150
- VAT 63

Market
    Access 1, 3-8, 10, 12, 20, 28-9, 34, 34-5, 53, 57, 69, 119, 120, 153-178, 178, 183, 185, 187
    Distortion 108, 115
    Efficiency 44-5, 131
    Entry 3, 23, 25, 46, 119, 122, 155, 163
    Failure 48, 108, 114, 122, 138, 146, 182-183
    Information 3, 23, 32, 41, 125-6, 155-6, 158, 163-5, 185-7
    Orientation 1, 18-9, 35, 76, 153, 177, 187
    Research 57, 162, 173-4, 190
Markets
    Capital 18, 78, 97, 99
    Corporate bond 8
    Domestic 3, 5, 10, 18-19, 28, 52, 143, 153-4, 156, 166, 173, 180
    Equity 2, 103, 109-111, 116
    Export 10, 28, 30, 33, 57, 154, 156-7, 165, 168, 171-3
    Global 3, 6, 19, 22, 30, 37-38, 40, 52, 105, 120, 131-2, 138, 145, 153, 157, 159, 161, 167, 173-7, 181-183, 185
    Stock 99-100, 109-110, 113
Marketing 3, 5-6, 8-10, 17, 25, 28, 31, 33, 36-7, 48, 52, 57, 68, 74, 80, 86, 98-9, 103, 105, 119-121, 124-5, 127-8, 132-3, 137, 140, 142-3, 149-150, 153, 155, 158, 161-2, 164-7, 173-4, 177-8, 181, 183-6
Microenterprise 1, 9, 13-4, 21-2, 25-8, 35, 38, 52, 113-4, 124, 148
Microfinance 8-9, 33, 46, 55, 79, 86, 95-7, 102-3, 109, 114, 116, 127
Monitoring and evaluation 4, 50, 121, 127, 181, 189

N

National innovation system (see Innovation)
New Zealand
    Culture 71
    Ease of doing business 43
    Economic freedom 45
    Enterprise survival rates 23
    Female-owned SMEs 32
    Global competitiveness 45
    New Capital Market 110
    R&D 136, 146
    Tax compliance 60
    VAT 63

O

Open innovation (see Innovation)

P

Personal saving 2, 68, 89, 91, 100, 108, 116
Philippines
    Bureau of SME Development 124
    Business permits 49, 53
    Centre for International Trade Expositions and missions 163
    Culture 71
    Ease of doing business 43
    E-commerce 41
    Economic freedom 45
    Education 73
    Female-owned SMEs 32
    Global competitiveness 45
    Information and communications technology 41
    Market access programmes 164
    Metalcast 173
    Microenterprises 25-26
    Open technology business incubator 149
    Productivity 27-28
    SME Centre for Asia 112
    Starting a business 69
    Technology programmes 150
    Technology Transfer Act 138
Policy recommendations 2-3, 51, 90, 129, 143, 151, 177, 181-8
Poverty 5, 13, 119, 190
Private sector development 1, 13, 46-7, 50, 191, 192
Public procurement 34, 50
Productivity 5, 6, 9, 27, 29-31, 34-5, 37, 45-6, 52, 61, 75, 120, 132, 141, 156, 173-4, 176, 185
    Labour 19, 28
    Total factor 27
Property rights 2-3, 6, 8, 28, 37, 40, 45, 48, 77-9, 91, 109, 115, 126, 182, 184, 186

R

Republic of Korea
    Contribution of SMEs 21-2
    Culture 71
    Definition of SME 15
    Ease of Doing Business 43
    Economic freedom 45
    Entrepreneurial activity 67, 77
    E-trade 166
    Export-Import Bank 171
    Female-owned SMEs 32
    Global competitiveness 45
    Internet marketing 166
    Intellectual Property Office 146
    Korean Development Bank 103
    Market access programmes 165
    Microenterprises 25-6
    National innovation system 142
    Productivity 27
    R&D 136-9, 147
    Small and Medium Business Administration 124
    Small and Medium Business Corporation 163, 166
    Technological capacity 135
    VAT 63
Research and Development (R&D) 3, 9, 27, 48, 60-1, 73, 119, 131, 133-140, 142-4, 146-152
Result-based impact chain 189-191
Reverse engineering 3, 20, 135, 137, 144-5
Rules of origin 157, 180
Rural entrepreneurship 75-6, 79, 183

S

Seed capital 17, 39, 77, 89, 97-8, 108, 110, 116
Singapore
    Business environment 44, 53
    Competitiveness 29
    Contribution of SMEs 21
    Culture 71
    Definition of SME 15
    Ease of doing business 43
    Economic freedom 45
    Entrepreneurial activity 67, 77

Female-owned SMEs 32
Global competitiveness 45
International Enterprise 124, 163
Market access programmes 164
R&D 136-7, 146-7
Social enterprise 76
SPRING 124, 157, 159
Technology programmes 150
VAT 61, 63

SME
Common characteristics 1, 20, 25
Competitiveness 1, 8, 28-9, 34-5, 38, 119, 124, 135, 173, 178, 182, 184
Contribution 12, 16, 21-2
Definition 13-6, 61
Entry and exit rates 23-5, 48, 183
Financing 2, 11, 27, 87, 89-100, 102-4, 106, 108-9, 111, 115, 124, 135, 167
Life cycle 18, 88
Typology 5, 16-9, 35

Special Economic Zones 4, 171-2, 178, 185

Sri Lanka
Ease of doing business 43
Economic freedom 45
Global competitiveness 45
Market access programmes 164
R&D 136
SME finance 103
Technology programmes 150
TVET 74, 79

Standards
International 38, 120, 156, 158-9, 176
Safety 59, 179
Quality 4, 8, 29, 57, 126, 150, 156, 158-9, 164, 177

Startups 47, 68, 80, 85, 88, 93, 109

Stock
Exchange 17, 33, 77, 97-9, 110, 115
Market 99-100, 109-110, 113

T

Taiwan Province of China
Contribution of SMEs 21
Culture 71
Definition of SME 15-6
Ease of doing business 43
Economic freedom 45
Entrepreneurial activity 67
Female-owned SMEs 32
Global competitiveness 45
Hsinchu Park 143
Industrial Technology Centres 149
Market access programmes 164
R&D 146-7, 152
Technology programmes 150

Tax
Administration 40, 46, 51, 59, 63-4
Collection 2, 64, 78, 184
Compliance 40, 59-60, 63-4
Credit 6, 27, 60, 62, 105, 146-7, 151
Incentives 3, 34-5, 59-61, 65, 105, 134-5, 138, 146-7, 151-2, 172
Presumptive taxation 62-64

Rate 59-60, 62-3, 105, 172
Reform 61, 91
Revenue 13, 41, 59, 63-4, 77-8
System 56, 59, 62, 64, 109, 146
VAT 54, 59, 61-4

Technical and vocational education and training (TVET) 30, 74, 78-9, 107, 151

Technology
Acquisition 3, 131, 135, 137-8, 142, 184
Centres 30, 143, 149-150, 152, 184
Commercialization 3, 127, 131, 135, 140, 142, 148, 151-2, 185
Database 138
Incubation 3, 30, 127-9, 133, 151, 174, 185
Programmes 150
Transfer 3, 11, 126, 137-140, 142-3, 148-9, 151, 173, 185
Upgrading 31, 134

Thailand
Contribution of SMEs 21
Culture 71
Definition of SME 15-6
Department of Export Promotions 165
Disasters 106
Ease of doing business 43
Economic freedom 45
Entrepreneurial activity 67
Export-Import Bank 171
Global competitiveness 45
Market access programmes 164
Office of Small and Medium Enterprises
Promotion 24, 124
Productivity 27-8
R&D 136-7
Social entrepreneurship 76, 79
Startups 16
Technology programmes 150
Trade payment 169
VAT 63
Women entrepreneurship 32-3

Trade
Barriers 3, 45, 120, 156-157, 180
Credit 89, 91-2, 100-1, 109, 116, 167, 170, 177, 184
Cycle 167-8
Environment 3, 156, 177
Facilitation 40-1, 46-8, 57, 153, 159, 164, 177-8, 183, 187
Fairs 4, 8, 10, 57, 120, 124-6, 137, 153, 161-4, 177-8, 185
Finance 4, 41, 102, 153, 167-171, 177-8, 185-6
Free Trade Agreement 157, 177, 180
In Services 157, 179-180
International 4, 10, 37, 44-5, 156-7, 163-4, 166-8, 170, 174, 178-180
Liberalization 155-6, 180
Logistics 4, 159
Missions 4, 10, 120, 161-3, 165, 177
Policy 3, 57, 156
Promotion 4, 6, 10, 57, 124, 153, 158, 161-5, 177, 187
TRIMS 157, 180
TRIPS 145, 157, 179
WTO 4, 9, 50, 57, 145, 153, 155-7, 159, 176-7, 179-180, 185

Trademarks 124, 145, 152
Transnational corporations (TNCs) 5, 18, 35, 60, 79, 115, 120, 124, 126, 128, 136, 138-9, 142-4, 156, 172-5, 177-8, 185
Transport system 4, 159-160

U

United Kingdom
  Contribution of SMEs 21
  Entry and exit rates 23
  Entrepreneurial activity 77
  Culture 71
  Social entrepreneurship 76
United States of America
  Competitiveness 29
  Contribution of SMEs 21
  Credit Cards 93
  Culture 24, 71
  Definition of SME 16
  Entrepreneurial activity 77
  Entry and exit rates 24
  Financial Sources of SMEs 101
  Innovation 131
  R&D 136
  Small Business Administration 6
  Venture capital 99

V

Venture capital 8-9, 61, 68, 89-90, 98-101, 103, 108, 110-2, 116, 137, 142-3
Viet Nam
  Agency for Enterprise Development 124
  Contribution of SMEs 21
  Definition of SME 16
  Ease of doing business 43
  Economic freedom 45
  Global competitiveness 45
  Innovation 133
  Microenterprise 25-6
  Provincial Competitiveness Index 46
  VAT 63
  Women entrepreneurs 32

W

Women entrepreneurs 1, 31-3, 75, 79, 108, 181
Working capital 2, 6, 55, 87, 89-93, 96, 106-7, 109, 111-112, 115 6, 124, 167-168, 184

Y

Youth 2, 5, 8-9, 13, 20, 36, 65, 70, 73, 75-6, 79, 85, 96, 135, 151, 186